The New Dictionary of Kleinian Thought

The New Dictionary of Kleinian Thought provides a comprehensive and wholly accessible exposition of Kleinian ideas. Offering a thorough update of R. D. Hinshelwood's highly acclaimed original, this book draws on the many developments in the field of Kleinian theory and practice since its publication.

The book first addresses twelve major themes of Kleinian psychoanalytic thinking in scholarly essays organised both historically and thematically. Themes discussed include:

- Unconscious phantasy, Child analysis
- the Paranoid-schizoid and Depressive positions, the Oedipus complex
- Projective identification, Symbol formation.

Following this, entries are listed alphabetically, allowing the reader to find out about a particular theme - from Karl Abraham to Whole Object - and to delve as lightly or as deeply as needed. As such this book will be essential reading for psychoanalysts, psychotherapists as well as all those with an interest in Kleinian thought.

Elizabeth Bott Spillius, whose original background was in anthropology, is a training analyst at the British Institute of Psychoanalysis and a Distinguished Fellow of the British Psychoanalytical Society.

Jane Milton is a Fellow and training analyst at the Institute of Psychoanalysis. She worked as a Consultant Psychiatrist at the Tavistock Clinic before becoming a full time psychoanalytic practitioner.

Penelope Garvey is a Fellow and training analyst at the Institute of Psychoanalysis who works both in private psychoanalytic practice and as a Consultant Clinical Psychologist and Psychotherapist in Plymouth NHS.

Cyril Couve is a Fellow of the British Psychoanalytical Society and is in full time private practice as a psychoanalyst. He was formerly a Consultant Clinical Psychologist at the Tavistock Clinic

Deborah Steiner is a Fellow of the British Psychoanalytical Society. Qualified in both adult and child and adolescent psychoanalysis she has held senior NHS posts.

The New Dictionary of Kleinian Thought

Elizabeth Bott Spillius, Jane Milton, Penelope Garvey, Cyril Couve and Deborah Steiner

Based on *A Dictionary of Kleinian Thought* by R. D. Hinshelwood

Routledge
Taylor & Francis Group

LONDON AND NEW YORK

First published 2011 by Routledge
27 Church Road, Hove, East Sussex BN3 2FA

Simultaneously published in the USA and Canada
by Routledge
711 Third Avenue, New York, NY 10017

Routledge is an imprint of the Taylor & Francis Group, an Informa business

© 2011 The Melanie Klein Trust and Robert Hinshelwood

Typeset in Times by Garfield Morgan, Swansea, West Glamorgan
Printed and bound in Great Britain by
TJ International Ltd, Padstow, Cornwall
Paperback cover design by Andrew Ward

This publication has been produced with paper manufactured to strict
environmental standards and with pulp derived from sustainable forests.

British Library Cataloguing in Publication Data
A catalogue record for this book is available from the British Library

Library of Congress Cataloging-in-Publication Data
The new dictionary of Kleinian thought / edited by Elizabeth Bott Spillius . . .
[et al.].
        p. ; cm.
    Includes bibliographical references.
    ISBN 978-0-415-59258-1 (hbk) – ISBN 978-0-415-59259-8 (pbk) 1. Klein,
Melanie–Dictionaries. 2. Psychoanalysis–Dictionaries. I. Spillius, Elizabeth
Bott, 1924– II. Hinshelwood, R. D. Dictionary of Kleinian thought.
    [DNLM: 1. Klein, Melanie. 2. Psychoanalytic Theory–Terminology–English.
3. Psychoanalysis–Terminology–English. WM 15]
    RC501.4.N49 2010
    616.89'17003–dc22

                                                              2010035937

ISBN: 978-0-415-59258-1 (hbk)
ISBN: 978-0-415-59259-8 (pbk)

Contents

Preface   x
Acknowledgements   xiii

PART I
Main entries   1

1 Unconscious phantasy   3
2 Child analysis   16
3 Internal objects   40
4 Paranoid-schizoid position   63
5 Depressive position   84
6 Oedipus complex   103
7 Projective identification   126
8 Superego   147
9 Envy   166
10 Symbol formation   184
11 Pathological organisations   194
12 Technique   216

PART II
General entries   237

Karl Abraham   239
Acting-out/acting-in   242
Adhesive identification   244
Aggression   245
Alpha-function   247
Ambivalence   248
American psychoanalysis in relation to Klein   249
Annihilation   251

Anxiety   253
Assimilation   255
Autism   256
Babies   258
Baby observation   258
Bad object   258
Basic assumptions   259
Beta-elements   261
Esther Bick   262
Wilfred Bion   263
Bizarre objects   267
Breast   269
Castration   269
Classical psychoanalysis   270
Coitus   270
Combined parent figure   271
Component instincts   273
Concern   277
Confusional states   277
Constitutional factor   278
Contact barrier   279
Container/contained   279
Contempt   285
Controversial Discussions   286
Countertransference   288
Creativity   295
Criminality   296
Death instinct   297
Defence mechanisms   305
Denial   309
Denigration   310
Depersonalisation   310
Depletion   310
Depressive anxiety   310
Development   315
Dreams   315
Economic model   316

Ego	319
Ego psychology	321
Empathy	321
Environment	322
Epistemophilia	323
External object	326
External world/environment	327
Externalisation	334
Faeces	334
Ronald Fairbairn	335
Father	340
Femininity	341
Femininity phase	342
Fragmentation	345
Anna Freud	346
Genetic continuity	347
Good object	348
Gratitude	349
Greed	350
Grid	351
Grievance	351
Guilt	352
Paula Heimann	353
Hysteria	355
Id	357
Ideal object	358
Idealisation	359
Identification	360
Incorporation	364
Infant observation	365
Inhibition	367
Innate knowledge	367
Instincts	369
Integration	373
Internal reality	374
Internalisation	374
Introjection	374

Susan Isaacs	379
Jealousy	380
Betty Joseph	381
Melanie Klein	384
Kleinian Group	386
Libido	388
Life instinct	392
Linking	394
Loss	396
Love	397
Manic defences	398
Manic reparation	400
Masculinity	400
Masturbation phantasies	400
Donald Meltzer	402
Memory and desire	404
Mind–body problem	405
Mother	407
Mourning	408
Nameless dread	408
Narcissism	409
Negative therapeutic reaction	416
Object-Relations School	419
Objects	424
Obsessional defences	426
Omnipotence	432
Paranoia	433
Paranoid defence against depressive anxiety	433
Part-objects	434
Penis and phallus	436
Persecution	438
Personification	439
Perversion	440
Phobia	445
Play	447
Play technique	449
Poisoning	449

Position	449
Preconception	451
Primal scene	451
Projection	453
Ps↔D	456
Psychic change	458
Psychic development	459
Psychic equilibrium	462
Psychic pain	463
Psychic reality	464
Psychosis	466
Realisation	469
Reparation	470
Repression	472
Resistance	474
Restitution/restoration	475
Reverie	475
Herbert Rosenfeld	476
Sadism	479
Hanna Segal	480
Self	482
Skin	483
Social defence systems	488
Society	490
Splitting	491
Structure	497
Symbolic equation	504
Symptom	506
Teeth	507
Thinking and knowledge	508
Transference	515
Treatment alliance	519
The unconscious	520
Unconscious guilt	521
Whole object	523
Bibliography of Kleinian publications 1920–1989	525

Preface

R. D. Hinshelwood's *A Dictionary of Kleinian Thought* (1989, 1991) has proved to be an immensely valuable source of access to Kleinian theory and practice, already translated into at least seven languages and extensively reviewed, quoted and used by students and analysts alike. The great expansion of contemporary Kleinian thinking and writing that has continued since the publication of the 1991 edition made Bob Hinshelwood realize that still another new edition was needed. After the enormous task of creating the two original versions he explained to Elizabeth Spillius and the Melanie Klein Trust that he did not wish to undertake this further work, and the Trust agreed to support the project.

A small group was then formed in 2003, under the chairmanship of and with the participation of Elizabeth Spillius, and consisting also of Penelope Garvey, Jane Milton, Cyril Couve and Deborah Steiner. We had originally conceived of our endeavour as the small to medium task of updating some of the entries. However, we soon found that the 'updatings' could not simply be grafted on to the 'originals'. In many cases the developments appeared to have led to modifications in the original conceptions and these needed to be included in the definitions. Some concepts had become less central; others had been developed and elaborated. This meant more work and far more discussion than we had anticipated. On the whole, we think that our discussions and the ensuing alterations in the entries led to a satisfactorily comprehensive set of definitions, but we are also aware that our definitions lack much of the spontaneity of Bob's original wordings. In addition, the 'style' of the new Dictionary is less consistent that that of the original versions, because each of us writes in his or her own fashion.

In labouring and struggling over this new edition we found ourselves constantly astounded by the creativity involved in producing the Dictionary in the first place. The original inspiration for the project was an idea from Robert Young, Bob Hinshelwood's publisher, which Bob took on and developed with great flair and diligence. As a team of five, we are fully aware of the immense amount of work he did single-handedly.

Kleinian concepts are often about very primitive elements of the human mind. They sometimes seem remote from common sense and rather like those ungraspable particles of subatomic physics, whereas at other times they can feel immediately and intuitively meaningful. However, it is very hard with the written word to pass on a real sense of understanding, and the reader needs to take the concepts further by enquiring into his or her own mind and also other minds. Kleinian concepts are particularly closely linked to the clinical grounding of psychoanalysis – to a major extent Kleinian theory *is* clinical theory, and it takes subjective experience very seriously. Klein's basis was always on the psychological content of her patients' minds as it emerged in the material, and virtually no Kleinian paper appears without a substantial amount of clinical material to back up its argument. Klein, being such an outstanding observer in the consulting room, always fell back on this strength when she felt, during the years of particular contention between 1926 and 1946, that she was pressed to argue her case.

Klein came into professional life and into psychoanalysis relatively late in life, without a background such as medicine or teaching, but with a new clinical technique that allowed her to reach more primitive levels of the minds of adults and children than had hitherto been explored. She was thrilled by the power of her play technique with children and was enthusiastic to demonstrate its usefulness. But the newness and power of her technique failed to give her the secure position she sought, rather the reverse: her exceptional results made her in some ways an awkward and deviant member of the orthodox psychoanalytic community. Kleinian psychoanalysis was at first (and often still is) subject to contentious and often painfully acrimonious debate, tending either to be taken on with passionate enthusiasm or hated and even proscribed. Perhaps this reflects the very material with which it deals – the infantile and psychotic mind, troubled by both loving and destructive passions.

In dealing with the large body of Klein's work and its increasing development in the work of her colleagues and successors, we have followed Bob Hinshelwood's division of entries into 'Main Entries' and 'General Entries'. The Main Entries section is arranged as far as is possible in chronological order, and covers what we now regard as Klein's fundamental concepts, ultimately derived from Freud, further developed by Klein and elaborated by her successors. These are Unconscious Phantasy, Child Analysis, Internal Objects, the Paranoid-Schizoid and Depressive Positions, the Oedipus Complex, Projective Identification, the Superego, Envy, Symbol Formation, Pathological Organisations and finally Technique.

The second part of the dictionary, the General Entries section, arranged in alphabetical order, covers the myriad of concepts that provide the building blocks of psychoanalytic thinking. They are all cross-referenced to the matrix of concepts, and the reader should be able to follow his own path of interest. We have somewhat altered from the original edition what comes under 'main' and what under 'general', partly to avoid repetition as much as possible and partly to highlight topics that we think were of particular importance to Klein ('child analysis') or that have become increasingly important in the last 20 years ('pathological organisations', 'symbol formation').

Klein's very fundamental attention to the concept of anxiety might arguably have deserved a main entry, as might the concept of defence mechanisms, but we decided that the concepts were so large and diverse and came into the definition of so many other concepts that we would avoid repetition by continuing to treat them as Bob had done. 'Anxiety', for example, is central in the definitions of at least seven other entries: 'defence mechanisms', 'depressive anxiety', 'guilt', 'nameless dread', 'paranoid defence against depressive anxiety', 'persecution' and 'phobia'. Similarly the content of the entry on 'defence' is discussed in many other entries, both 'Main' and 'General'.

We decided to keep the comprehensive bibliography of Kleinian publications up to 1989 that Bob had so painstakingly provided in the previous editions. We did not, however, attempt to continue it for the years after 1989, judging that with the burgeoning of post-Kleinian writing since then this would now take up far too much space.

We feel immense indebtedness to Bob Hinshelwood for his imaginative creation of the Dictionary and his generosity in turning over to us, with no strings attached, the task of creating the new edition. We hope that his many grateful and loyal readers will forgive us for inevitably putting our own stamp on the work, and we hope too that they will find that it does justice to and respects his original vision.

Elizabeth Bott Spillius
Jane Milton
Penelope Garvey
Cyril Couve
Deborah Steiner

References

Hinshelwood, R. D. (1989) *A Dictionary of Kleinian Thought*. London: Free Association Books.

Hinshelwood, R. D. (1991) *A Dictionary of Kleinian Thought* (2nd edition, revised and enlarged). London: Free Association Books.

Acknowledgements

Above all we are fundamentally indebted to Bob Hinshelwood for writing the Dictionary in the first place and for his generosity in allowing us to take on this major revision. We are most grateful to the Melanie Klein Trust, who entrusted the work to us and then patiently supported a process that took considerably longer than anticipated.

We have a number of people to thank for support and advice during our task. Elizabeth Spillius was our wise psychoanalytic elder and coordinator. She provided generous hospitality for the many meetings where we helped each other with our individual entries and discussed and debated aspects of Kleinian theory. When we needed further advice we consulted colleagues for help with areas in which they had particular expertise and are very grateful to them. They are: David Bell, Michael Feldman, Alberto Hahn, Chris Mawson, Michael Rustin, Anne Marie Sandler and John Steiner. Hélène Martin and Saven Morris from the Institute of Psychoanalysis library very kindly helped out with reference queries.

Finally we would like to thank the team at Routledge for their helpfulness and efficiency through every stage of publishing the book.

Part I

Main entries

1 Unconscious phantasy

Definition

In Kleinian theory unconscious phantasies underlie every mental process and accompany all mental activity. They are the mental representation of those somatic events in the body that comprise the instincts, and are physical sensations interpreted as relationships with objects that cause those sensations. Phantasy is the mental expression of both libidinal and aggressive impulses and also of defence mechanisms against those impulses. Much of the therapeutic activity of psychoanalysis can be described as an attempt to convert unconscious phantasy into conscious thought.

Freud introduced the concept of unconscious phantasy and phantasising, which he thought of as a phylogenetically inherited capacity of the human mind. Klein adopted his idea of unconscious phantasy but broadened it considerably because her work with children gave her extensive experience of the wide-ranging content of children's phantasies. She and her successors have emphasised that phantasies interact reciprocally with experience to form the developing intellectual and emotional characteristics of the individual; phantasies are considered to be a basic capacity underlying and shaping thought, dreams, symptoms and patterns of defence.

Key papers

Freud, S. (1911, 1916)

1911   'Formulations on the two principles of mental functioning'. Phantasy functions according to the pleasure principle, equating 'reality of thought with external actuality, and wishes with their fulfilment' (p. 225). Phantasies are likely to arise when instinctual wishes are frustrated.

1916–1917 'The paths to the formation of symptoms', Lecture 23 of *Introductory Lectures on Psychoanalysis.*

Sources of 'primal phantasies' (primal scene, seduction by adults, castration) lie in instincts and are part of innate, phylogenetic endowment. Phantasy as *psychical reality.*

Klein, M. (1921, 1923a, 1936, 1952, and indeed most of her papers)

Klein does not define phantasy, but stress on it is evident throughout her work with both children and adults.

1921   'The development of a child'.
            Vivid description of a child's unconscious phantasies accompanying his reality-based activities.

1936   'Weaning'.
            Klein's belief that analysis shows phantasies are in the mind of an infant 'almost from birth'.

1952   'Observations on the behaviour of young infants'.
            Unconscious knowledge of the breast exists at birth and is phylogenetic inheritance (p. 117).

Other

1948   Isaacs, S. 'The nature and function of phantasy'.
            Unconscious phantasy defined as 'the mental corollary, the psychic representative of instinct' and 'the primary content of unconscious mental processes' and described as defence against anxiety.

1962   Bion, W. *Learning from Experience.*
            Assumes that individuals are born capable of 'preconceptions' that, if 'realised' in experience, may give rise to 'conceptions'.

1991   Segal. H. 'Phantasy', in *Dream, Phantasy and Art.*
            Phantasy is a central concept in Kleinian thought, regarded as the core primary activity expressing both impulses and defences. There is continual mutual interaction between phantasies and perception.

1991   Hinshelwood, R. D. *A Dictionary of Kleinian Thought, 2nd edition.*
            Emphasis on Klein's finding that phantasies may accompany 'realistic' activities. Unconscious phantasies tacitly express the belief that bodily sensations are caused by internal mental objects. Detailed discussion of unconscious phantasy in Controversial Discussions, 1941–1945.

Chronology and discussion

The term 'unconscious phantasy': Spellings and meanings

Strachey makes the definitive exposition, as follows:

> 'Phantasy.' The spelling of this word causes a good deal of annoyance.
> The 'ph' form is adopted here on the basis of a discussion in the large
> Oxford Dictionary (under 'Fantasy') which concludes: 'In modern use
> *"fantasy"* and *"phantasy"*, in spite of their identity in sound and ulti-
> mate etymology, tend to be apprehended as separate words, the pre-
> dominant sense of the former being "caprice, whim, fanciful invention",
> while that of the latter is "imagination, visionary notion".' Accordingly
> the 'ph' form is used here for the technical psychological phenomenon.
> But the 'f' form is also used on appropriate occasions (see, for instance,
> *Standard Ed.* 17, 227 and 330).
>
> (Strachey, 1966, p. xxiv)

Susan Isaacs (1948, p. 80) suggests the use of the 'ph' spelling for unconscious phantasy and the 'f' spelling for conscious phantasy. Some analysts
have adopted Isaacs' suggestion, but most British analysts now use the 'ph'
spelling for both unconscious and conscious phantasies, at least in part
because it is often difficult to be sure whether a patient's phantasy is
unconscious, tacitly conscious or fully conscious. Laplanche and Pontalis
(1968) criticise Isaacs' usage because in their view it disagrees with the
profound kinship that Freud wished to emphasise between the conscious
phantasy of perverts, the delusional fears of paranoid patients and the
unconscious phantasy of hysterics. The spelling situation is further complicated by the fact that most American analysts use the 'f' spelling for both
conscious and unconscious phantasies.

The problem of the *meaning* of the term phantasy, however, is as complex
as its spelling. Whatever its spelling and formal definition, the term obsti-
nately continues to imply the contrasting meanings described by the Oxford
Dictionary and Strachey. The first meaning, 'caprice, whim, fanciful inven-
tion', describes something that is trivial, not true or significant according to
accepted beliefs about material reality. The second meaning, 'imagination,
visionary notion', has a connotation of a possibly greater truth that may
transcend accepted beliefs about material reality. Neither the Oxford
Dictionary nor Strachey describes a third possibility, namely, that phantasies might conform to generally accepted beliefs about reality. Thus the
term 'phantasy', and the term 'unconscious phantasy' to an even greater
extent, contain intrinsic contradictions that have allowed and often exacerbated argument and disagreement in psychoanalysis. In general the tendency
in everyday speech and among psychoanalysts is to think of the first meaning

as the dominant one, that is, to expect that phantasies will *not* conform to material reality and that they are likely to be unreal and trivial.

Freud's and Klein's views on unconscious phantasy

Freud introduced the concept of unconscious phantasy, but in his early-published work, especially *The Interpretation of Dreams* (1900), he hardly uses the term; his method of interpreting dreams uses the idea of the 'unconscious wish' but the relation of the unconscious wish to unconscious phantasy is not explicitly discussed. Phantasy appears in the Dora case history (1905), and even more explicitly in 'Hysterical phantasies and their relation to bisexuality' (1908), in which Freud says that some phantasies are 'unconscious all along' but that most exist first as daydreams, that is, as conscious phantasies, which are later repressed.

Freud stresses several aspects of phantasy in different papers. In 'Formulations on the two principles of mental functioning' (1911) he describes the first aspect as follows:

> With the introduction of the reality principle one species of thought-activity was split off; it was kept free from reality testing and remained subordinated to the pleasure principle alone. This activity is *phantasying*, which begins already in children's play, and later, continued as *day-dreaming*, abandons dependence on real objects.
>
> (Freud, 1911, p. 222)

> ... The strangest characteristic of unconscious (repressed) processes ... is due to their entire disregard of reality-testing; they equate reality of thought with external actuality, and wishes with their fulfilment ... Hence also the difficulty of distinguishing unconscious phantasies from memories which have become unconscious.
>
> (Freud, 1911, p. 225)

The second aspect of unconscious phantasy he describes particularly clearly in 1916, saying that there are certain universal 'primal' phantasies that are part of the human phylogenetic inheritance. In his view there are three such phantasies: the primal scene, seduction by an adult and the threat of castration (Freud, 1916–1917). Later in the same paper Freud grapples with questions of the 'unreality' of phantasies and the attitude that analysts should adopt to the phantasies of patients. His thoughts about this matter lead him to a productive new concept, *psychical reality*:

> It remains a fact that the patient has created these phantasies for himself, and this fact is of scarcely less importance for his neurosis than if he had really experienced what the phantasies contain. The

> phantasies possess *psychical* reality as contrasted with *material* reality, and we gradually learn to understand that *in the world of the neuroses it is psychical reality which is the decisive kind.*
>
> 　　　　　　　　　　　　　　　　　　　　(Freud, 1916–1917, p. 368)

Thus it is Freud's clear view that one must analyse what is psychically real to the patient. At the same time, throughout his work Freud's basic idea of phantasy is that it is wish-fulfilling and unrealistic.

Klein adopts Freud's idea of unconscious phantasy, although her idea of phantasy is both broader in scope and more explicitly central in her thinking than Freud's conception of it is in his. She does not make a formal definition of the term but she mentions phantasy in nearly every early paper (e.g. 1921, 1923a, 1923b, 1925, 1933, 1936). She found that the children she analysed were extremely preoccupied with phantasies, both conscious and unconscious, concerning birth, death, the primal scene, bodily processes in themselves and their parents, the external and internal worlds of good and bad objects, the relationships and emotions of the Oedipus complex and the early, cruel superego. She was impressed by the ferocity of small children's conscious and unconscious hateful and destructive phantasies and by their anxiety and guilt about them. Indeed some critics (e.g. Perelberg, 2005) have asserted that Klein thinks that unconscious phantasies are particularly derived from the death instinct, although this emphasis on destructive phantasies is balanced in Klein's later work, by emphasis on loving as well as destructive phantasies together with the idea of conflict between love and hate. Eventually Klein conceptualised the various phantasies she discovered in both children and adults as coalescing into the mental organisations she eventually described as the paranoid-schizoid and depressive positions (Klein, 1935, 1940, 1946) [*see* Paranoid-schizoid position; Depressive position].

Klein's broadened idea of unconscious phantasy comes to include not only the ubiquity of the new contents she discovers in the phantasies of children but also the fact that their phantasies are often concerned with introjection and projection. In other words she observes that children have phantasies of taking things into themselves from outside objects, and putting aspects of themselves and of their internal objects into external objects, so that Klein's conception of phantasy gradually comes to include more interaction between the individual's internal and external worlds than is included in Freud's conception. Thus unconscious phantasy gradually becomes a principal and basic concept for Klein. Hanna Segal thinks that unconscious phantasy became a more central concept for Klein than for Freud. As she puts it:

> I think that the main thrust of Freud's thinking is that phantasy is not a primary activity. It has the same roots as, and is comparable to

dreams, symptoms, parapraxes, and art; it does not underlie dreams, symptoms, thought, and art. For Klein, on the contrary, unconscious phantasy is a core primary activity, an original expression of both impulses and defences, and it is continually interacting with perception, modifying it but also modified by it.

(Segal, 1991, p. 30)

Like Freud, Klein assumes that the activity of phantasising is innate, as are particular phantasies themselves. She goes further, for she thinks that not only are phantasising and phantasies inherited but so also is the ability to make certain sorts of realistic perception. She says:

The fact that at the beginning of post-natal life an unconscious knowledge of the breast exists and that feelings towards the breast are experienced can only be conceived of as a phylogenetic inheritance.

(Klein, 1952, p. 117)

Klein also thinks that the capacity to phantasise begins 'almost at birth', saying:

Analytic work has shown that babies of a few months of age certainly indulge in phantasy-building. I believe that this is the most primitive mental activity and that phantasies are in the mind of the infant almost from birth.

(Klein, 1936, p. 290)

For the most part Klein agrees with the definition of Susan Isaacs, who describes unconscious phantasy as 'the primary content of unconscious mental processes' and '. . . the mental corollary, the psychic representative of instinct' (Isaacs, 1948, p. 81). Isaacs makes a point of including phantasies based on both destructive and libidinal impulses, and she makes it clear that '. . . phantasy soon becomes also a means of defence against anxieties, a means of inhibiting and controlling instinctual urges and an expression of reparative wishes as well' (Isaacs, 1948, p. 62). She also thinks that early phantasies are based on bodily sensations and 'plastic images' – visual, auditory, kinaesthetic, touch, taste, smell – and only later take verbal form (Isaacs, 1948, p. 82). Hanna Segal, similarly, describes the relation between mechanisms of defence and phantasies by saying: 'What an observer can describe as a mechanism is experienced and described by the person himself as a detailed phantasy' (Segal, 1994, p. 6).

The concept of phantasy in the Controversial Discussions

Klein's and Isaacs' views of phantasy became the central conceptual topic of discussion at the Controversial Discussions of the British Psychoanalytical

Society from 1941 to 1945. The main account of these Discussions is provided in the monumental work *The Freud–Klein Controversies, 1941–45* edited by Pearl King and Riccardo Steiner (King and Steiner, 1991).

Not surprisingly, Anna Freud and the Viennese analysts who came to London just before the Second World War followed their view of Freud's usage when discussing the concept of phantasy. When the Viennese defined the term 'phantasy' they tended to follow Freud's 1911 view of phantasy as conforming to the pleasure principle rather than his 1916–1917 description of 'primal' phantasies. All the Viennese and several British analysts disapproved of Klein's early dating of phantasising and object relationships, for they thought that babies were not capable of so complex an activity as phantasising. Anna Freud, Edward Glover, Brierley and others were particularly critical of Klein and Isaacs for broadening the definition of phantasy to include, as Anna Freud put it, 'thinking, reality-thinking, remembering, wishing, longing, in short all mental activities of the infant' (King and Steiner, 1991, p. 424).

Thus the question of unconscious phantasy has had considerable historical importance in the British Psychoanalytical Society. Even though no formal agreement on the definition of phantasy was reached at the Controversial Discussions, the topic is no longer regarded as a contentious issue by the British Psychoanalytical Society. When there is a difference of view there is now an agreement to differ.

The multiple functions of phantasy: Examples

It is generally agreed that phantasy is a complex concept and that many motives, feelings, ideas and experiences may contribute to the formation of particular phantasies. Some phantasies express defensive or destructive motives whereas others are constructive and imaginative; some may suggest hypotheses about internal or external reality for confirmation by experience, whereas others assert unquestioned prior knowledge. Of an infinite potential, three frequently found aspects of phantasy are described here: phantasy and the body, phantasy and the internal world, phantasy as defence.

Unconscious phantasies and the body

In her early work with children Klein found that their phantasies were especially concerned with their own bodies and with their beliefs about the bodies of their parents and the relationship between them. The way phantasies may be used by a child to explain bodily experiences has been well described by Robert Hinshelwood, who notes that an unconscious phantasy involves belief in the activity of concretely felt internal objects (Hinshelwood, 1991, p. 34) [*see* Child analysis].

Phantasy and the internal world

Klein's understanding of children's (and adults') emotional life was greatly enriched by her idea that phantasies about relationships with objects are concerned not only with external but also with internal, introjected objects whose imagined presence inside the individual's body and mind gives rise to an internal world whose events are even more dramatically filled with love and hate than the events of his interactions with his external world. Klein discovered that the children she analysed often had violent and cruel phantasies and, extrapolating backwards, she assumed that small infants were at first preoccupied mainly by feelings of fear and anger and that their phantasies were violent and sadistic, including phantasies of attack directed at the parents, especially the mother. Klein thought that good experiences gradually joined forces with good phantasies so that the infant began to live in a more complex world with phantasies of both good and bad objects. She does not commit herself on the matter of whether experiences cause phantasies or phantasies are primary in shaping the meaning of experience. The general impression she conveys is that influences operate in both directions, but she certainly thinks that the infant is not just a passive recipient of environmental influence. In what amounts to an early description of projective identification Klein says:

> This view of the matter makes it also less puzzling to understand why the child should form such monstrous and phantastic images of his parents. For he perceives his anxiety arising from his aggressive instincts as fear of an external object, both because he has made that object their outward goal, and because he has projected them [the aggressive instincts] on to it [the external object] so that they [the aggressive instincts] seem to be initiated against himself from that quarter.
>
> (Klein, 1933, p. 250)

Phantasy as defence

The idea that defences are expressed through phantasies has been especially emphasised by Hanna Segal, who says that what to the analyst are mechanisms of defence have their content expressed by patients in phantasies (Segal, 1964a, 1964b). In the following example of a phantasy expressing defence, a patient was struggling with the somewhat disagreeable realisation that she was dependent on her analyst. On her return from a holiday break she reported the following dream:

> You were coming to give me a session at my country cottage, but it wasn't a cottage, it was a magnificent house. The doorbell rang. I

thought it would be you but it wasn't, it was my brother's friends, great louts who were going to take our hospitality for granted. I said there wasn't room and they weren't to come in. They left. After they left one of my children said, 'Don't you realise they're desperate for somewhere to stay?' I said, 'Quick, run after them and tell them they can stay in the attic.' I wanted to give each of them £10 but doubted if I'd have enough money (£10 was the patient's fee at the time).

(Spillius, 2007, p. 205)

In this example the underlying phantasy in the dream is expressed through reversal of roles: the patient is in the role of the analyst, the analyst is in the 'brother's friends, great louts' who, as any child would know, were desperate for £10 and a place to stay. And the analyst should pay the patient instead of the patient paying the analyst. The patient saw all this without much difficulty. Equally important, however, was the fact that this session was the start of a slight but gradual development in her attitude about being dependent and her expectations of her analyst. She became more accepting of both her dependency and her dislike of it. The phantasy of role-reversal was no longer so much needed.

Recent uses of the concept of phantasy

Kleinian analysts have continued to use the idea of unconscious phantasy in clinical work and with very little change from the way Klein, Isaacs and other Kleinian analysts used it in the 1940s. Although the concept of phantasy played such a central role in the Controversial Discussions, there have been relatively few British or other European publications specifically concerning theoretical analysis of the concept since that time, and the papers that have been written have been much less confrontational than those of the Controversial Discussions.

Perhaps analysts have become somewhat less concerned about the issues that bothered them during the Discussions, less certain that the analytic method as practised with children and adults can reveal either the exact phylogenetic basis of phantasy or give an exact knowledge of the form that phantasies take in the minds of infants while they are actually infants rather than the form that 'infantile' phantasies may take in the minds of older children and adults when they are in analysis. There have been a comparatively small number of papers on the concept since the 1940s.

Money-Kyrle (1956), like Freud and Klein, thinks that phantasising is an inherited capacity, although he phrases his view in the more scientifically acceptable language of 'mutation' and 'natural selection'. In 1968 Laplanche and Pontalis re-examined Freud's theory of the role of seduction in the development of phantasies, stating that the cause of phantasies of seduction, which Freud had ascribed to phylogenetic inheritance, 'can be understood as a prestructure which is actualised and transmitted by the parental fantasies' (Laplanche and Pontalis, 1968, p. 17).

In his idea of a 'preconception' mating with a 'realisation' to form a 'conception', Bion does not explicitly use the word 'phantasy'; although Segal suggests that his 'preconception' in this formulation can be described as phantasy (Bion, 1962; Segal, 1964b).

Hanna Segal emphasises both the destructive and constructive aspects of phantasy, with special attention to the use of phantasy as a defence but also to phantasy as a possible hypothesis for testing against reality and hence as an important factor in the development of thinking (Segal, 1964a, 1964b, 1991, 1994).

Ronald Britton (1995) in 'Reality and unreality in phantasy and fiction' describes patients' idea of 'the other room' as a phantasied space where the absent object is thought to continue his life with the other member of the oedipal triangle. Robert Hinshelwood (1991) gives a detailed description of the development of the concept of phantasy in the previous edition of the present Dictionary, including a particularly full account of the debate about it in the Controversial Discussions of the British Psychoanalytic Society. John Steiner (1993) has developed the idea that certain patients have a phantasy of a 'psychic retreat' that they believe will protect them from both the persecutions of paranoid-schizoid thinking and the guilt and pain of depressive-position thinking.

The Contemporary Freudian analysts Joseph and Anne-Marie Sandler (1994) and Sandler, Holder, Dare and Dreher (1997) describe the role of phantasy in their model of the mind, which they describe as consisting of the 'past unconscious', the 'present unconscious' and the 'conscious' (Sandler, Holder, Dare and Dreher, 1997). This model is roughly similar to Freud's tripartite, topographical model of the mind as the 'System Unconscious', the 'System Preconscious' and the 'System Conscious' (Freud, 1900). The Sandlers think that the 'past unconscious' cannot be directly experienced, and that the phantasies in it are constructed in the course of analytic work, whereas the phantasies of the 'present unconscious' can be directly experienced and interpreted in the transference. Segal (1994, p. 400) does not agree with the view that the 'past unconscious' cannot be directly analysed. But the difference of view between Segal and the Sandlers arises mainly because Kleinians do not work with Freud's or the Sandlers' topographical model of the mind.

Roger Perron (2001), in the French tradition, discusses Freud's work on phantasy, the problems involved in his concepts of unconscious phantasy, primal phantasy, inheritance of phantasy and the relation between phantasy and reality. He provides a constructive conclusion to Freud's discussions and definitions. But if phantasies are constructed according to the same general schema in all human beings, it is because everyone is subject to the same general conditions: everyone has a mother; each person's psyche is inscribed within the framework of a triangulation in which a second parental figure intervenes (whether – depending on the culture – it is the father, the uncle on the mother's side, etc.); everyone has access to language and to the processes of symbolisation; and so on (Perron, 2001, p. 592). 'Reality is that which resists desire sustained by phantasy' (Perron, 2001, p. 594).

Elizabeth Spillius (2001) compares the role of 'unconscious phantasy' for Freud, especially as he expounds it in his 1911 paper 'Formulations on the two principles of mental functioning', with the role of 'unconscious phantasy' for Klein, who focuses on the pervasive presence and importance of the concept in the thinking and feeling of both children and adults. (Spillius's subsequent view is that her thesis expressed too narrow an interpretation of Freud's ideas on unconscious phantasy because it restricted his definition of it to his 1911 paper.)

Riccardo Steiner (2003) edits several papers on the theme of unconscious phantasy and contributes a detailed Introduction in which he describes the conceptual and practical complexities of the concept of phantasy, including a discussion of the usages of Freud, Klein, Isaacs, Segal and the Contemporary Freudian analysts Mark Solms and Joseph and Anne-Marie Sandler, and also the usage of the concept in France by Laplanche and Pontalis (1968) with their emphasis on the theme of seduction.

Rosine Perelberg (2005, 2006) discusses concepts of phantasy, time and *après-coup*, some of which were expressed at the Controversial Discussions by the Viennese and by future 'Independent' analysts. She holds the view that Kleinian use of the concept of unconscious phantasy at the Controversial Discussions and in later Kleinian thinking does not do full justice to the complexity of Freud's views on the subject.

Although there have been relatively few recent Kleinian papers that make theoretical discussion of the concept of phantasy their central theme, the concept is in daily and continual use in clinical work and is taken for granted as a central aspect of the Kleinian approach.

Key ideas: Summary

- Unconscious phantasies underlie all mental processes and activities. They are a mental expression not only of aggressive and libidinal impulses but also of defence mechanisms against those impulses.
- *Freud's usage*: Unconscious phantasy is an introduced term and its usage is somewhat variable. 1911: Phantasy disregards reality testing and equates reality of thought with external reality. 1916–1917: Phantasying and certain phantasies (primal scene, seduction, castration) are inherited. The concept of *psychical reality*, in contrast to *material reality*, is what the analyst has to deal with.

- *Isaacs*: Unconscious phantasy is defined as 'the primary content of unconscious mental processes' and 'the mental corollary, the psychic representative of instinct'. There are phantasies of defence as well as phantasies of desire.
- *Klein*: Her view of phantasy is based on Freud's and Isaacs' definitions, but is broader than Freud's. Phantasy is more explicitly central in Klein's thought and theory than it was for Freud. Klein discovered the rich expression of a multitude of phantasies in children's play and thought, especially concerning birth, death, primal scene and bodily processes in self and parents. Like Freud, Klein thought that phantasying was an inherited capacity. There was more stress than in Freud on phantasies involving introjection, projection and relation of internal objects to one another and to the external world. Klein's view of unconscious phantasy was important in her eventual development of the concepts of the paranoid-schizoid and depressive positions.

References

Bion, W. (1962) *Learning from Experience*. London: Heinemann.

Britton, R. (1995) 'Reality and unreality in phantasy and fiction', in E. Spector Person, P. Fonagy and S. Figueira (eds) *On Freud's 'Creative Writers and Day-Dreaming'*. London: Yale University Press, pp. 82–106.

Freud, S. (1900) *The Interpretation of Dreams*, *S.E. 5*. London: Hogarth Press, Ch. 7.

—— (1905) 'Fragment of an analysis of a case of hysteria', *S.E. 7*. London: Hogarth Press.

—— (1908) 'Hysterical phantasies and their relation to bisexuality', *S.E. 9*. London: Hogarth Press, pp. 155–166.

—— (1911) 'Formulations on the two principles of mental functioning', *S.E. 12*. London: Hogarth Press, pp. 213–226.

—— (1916–1917) Lecture 23, 'The paths to the formation of symptoms', *Introductory Lectures on Psycho-Analysis*, *S.E. 16*. London: Hogarth Press, pp. 358–372.

Hinshelwood, R. D. (1991) 'Unconscious phantasy', in *A Dictionary of Kleinian Thought*, 2nd edition. London: Free Association Books, pp. 32–46.

Isaacs, S. (1948) 'The nature and function of phantasy', *Int. J. Psycho-Anal.* 29: 73–97.

King, P. and Steiner, R. (1991) *The Freud–Klein Controversies, 1941–45*. London: Tavistock/Routledge.

Klein, M. (1921) 'The development of a child', in *The Writings of Melanie Klein*, Vol. 1. London: Hogarth Press, pp. 1–53.

—— (1923a) 'The role of the school in the libidinal development of the child', in *The Writings of Melanie Klein*, Vol. 1. London: Hogarth Press, pp. 59–76.

—— (1923b) 'Early analysis', in *The Writings of Melanie Klein*, Vol. 1. London: Hogarth Press, pp. 77–105.

—— (1925) 'A contribution to the psychogenesis of tics', in *The Writings of Melanie Klein*, Vol. 1. London: Hogarth Press, pp. 106–127.

—— (1933) 'The early development of conscience in the child', in *The Writings of Melanie Klein*, Vol. 1. London: Hogarth Press, pp. 248–257.

—— (1935) 'A contribution to the psychogenesis of manic-depressive states', in *The Writings of Melanie Klein*, Vol. 1. London: Hogarth Press, pp. 262–289.

—— (1936) 'Weaning', in *The Writings of Melanie Klein*, Vol. 1. London: Hogarth Press, pp. 290–305.

—— (1940) 'Mourning and its relation to manic-depressive states', in *The Writings of Melanie Klein*, Vol. 1. London: Hogarth Press, pp. 344–369.

—— (1946) 'Notes on some schizoid mechanisms', in *The Writings of Melanie Klein*, Vol. 3. London: Hogarth Press, pp. 1–24.

—— (1952) 'On observing the behaviour of young infants', in *The Writings of Melanie Klein*, Vol. 3. London: Hogarth Press, pp. 94–121.

Laplanche, J. and Pontalis, J.-R. (1968) 'Fantasy and the origins of sexuality', *Int. J. Psycho-Anal.* 49: 1–18.

Money-Kyrle, R. (1956) 'The world of the unconscious and the world of common sense', *Br. J. Philos. Sc.* 7. Also in D. Meltzer and E. O'Shaughnessy (eds) *The Collected Papers of Roger Money-Kyrle*. Strath Tay: Clunie Press (1978), pp. 318–329.

Perelberg, R. (2005) 'Unconscious phantasy and après-coup: "From the History of an Infantile Neurosis" (the Wolf Man)', in R. Perelberg (ed.) *Freud: A Modern Reader*. London: Whurr Publishers, pp. 206–223.

—— (2006) 'The Controversial Discussions and après-coup', *Int. J. Psycho-Anal.* 87: 1199–1220.

Perron, R. (2001) 'The unconscious and primal phantasies', *Int. J. Psycho-Anal.* 82: 583–595.

Sandler, J. and Sandler, A.-M. (1994) 'Phantasy and its transformations: a Contemporary Freudian View', *Int. J. Psycho-Anal.* 75: 387–394. Also in R. Steiner (ed.) *Unconscious Phantasy*. London: Karnac (2003), pp. 77–88.

Sandler, J., Holder, A., Dare, C. and Dreher, U. (1997) *Freud's Models of the Mind*. London: Karnac.

Segal, H. (1964a) *Introduction to the Work of Melanie Klein*. London: Heinemann.

—— (1964b) 'Symposium on phantasy – "Fantasy and other mental processes"', *Int. J. Psycho-Anal.* 45: 191–194.

—— (1991) 'Phantasy', in *Dream, Phantasy and Art*. London: Routledge, pp. 16–30.

—— (1994) 'Phantasy and reality', *Int. J. Psycho-Anal.* 75: 395–401.

Spillius, E. (2001) 'Freud and Klein on the concept of phantasy', *Int. J. Psycho-Anal.* 82: 361–373.

—— (2007) 'Freud and Klein on the concept of phantasy', in Elizabeth Spillius, P. Roth and R. Rusbridger (eds) *Encounters with Melanie Klein*. London: Routledge, pp. 163–182.

Steiner, J. (1993) *Psychic Retreats: Organizations in Psychotic, Neurotic and Borderline Patients*. London: Routledge.

Steiner, R. (2003) 'Introduction', in R. Steiner (ed.) *Unconscious Phantasy*. London: Karnac, pp. 1–66.

Strachey, J. (1966) 'Notes on some technical terms whose translation calls for comment', *S.E. 1*. London: Hogarth Press, p. xxiv.

2 Child analysis

Definition

In the 1920s, Melanie Klein began to develop an analytic treatment that enabled her to work with very small children, with limited verbal means of communication. She began to recognise that although children's play seemed very different from communications in adult classical analysis, it was the child patient's way of free associating, and she began to observe and use it to explore their inner conflicts and phantasies. Her abiding interest in the nature of anxiety, and her conviction that children had a capacity to understand themselves, also enabled her to initiate an interpretive approach to her child patients' material in all its forms: play, words, phantasies and behaviour. This brought her into increasing conflict with some colleagues who were using a more educative technique in their work with children.

Key papers

1921   Klein, M. 'The development of a child'.
              The hallmarks of Klein's work are already apparent in her acceptance of speech, play, actions and dreams as expressive of the child's unconscious mind.

1923a   Klein, M. 'The role of the school in the libidinal development of the child'.
              Klein observes the inhibitory effects of aggressive phantasies. The use of a play technique yields more material for analysis [Felix aged 13; Fritz 5; Grete 9].

1923b   Klein, M. 'Early analysis'.
              Klein presents issues such as anxiety, inhibitions, symptoms and symbol formation. She introduces her ideas about the early Oedipus complex and the resolution of Oedipal anxieties as enabling development [Felix; Fritz; Grete].

1925   Klein, M. 'A contribution to the psychogenesis of tics'.
                The tic is traced back to masturbatory anxieties involving
                identification with combined parents in intercourse, as a
                central factor in the formation of the superego.

1926   Klein, M. 'The psychological principles of early analysis'.
                Early sadism and its relation to the early stages of the Oedipus
                complex and the formation of the superego [Trude 3¼; Rita
                2½; Ruth 4¼].

1927a   Klein, M. 'Criminal tendencies in normal children'.
                A cruel superego operates differently from the more normal
                conscience. Increasing interest in the conflict between love and
                hate [Gerald 4; Peter 3¾ and an unnamed boy aged 12].

1927b   Klein, M. 'Symposium on child analysis'.
                Klein argues the need to interpret from the start the positive
                and negative transference.

1928   Klein, M. 'The early stages of Oedipus complex'.
                The early onset of the Oedipus complex at this stage is linked
                to weaning when oral and anal sadistic impulses predominate.
                The pain, hatred and anxiety that such impulses engender are
                stressed.

1929a   Klein, M. 'Personification in the play of children'.
                Children's games originate from internal images, and processes
                of splitting and projection involved in playing serve as a defence
                against anxiety. These processes involve the transference of
                inner figures onto the analyst [Erna 6; George 6; Rita 2½].

1930   Klein, M. 'The importance of symbol formation in the devel-
                opment of the ego'.
                Klein clarifies the underlying causes of childhood psychosis.
                She shows that contact can be made with a psychotic child
                who did not develop a capacity to symbolise and who showed
                no emotion of any kind [Dick 4].

1931   Klein, M. 'A contribution to the theory of intellectual
                inhibition'.
                Further exploration of the child's anxieties about sadistic
                attacks on the mother's body, representing the source of life
                and knowledge, and the consequent inhibition of curiosity and
                learning [John 7].

1932   Klein, M. 'The technique of early analysis'.
                Klein describes her play technique [Peter 3¼; Rita 2½; Trude
                3¼; Ruth 4¼].

1932   Klein, M. 'An obsessional neurosis in a six year old girl'.
              Erna was a very disturbed child who suffered from sleepless-
              ness, obsessional symptoms and severe learning inhibition
              [Erna].

1932   Klein, M. 'The technique of analysis in the latency period'.
              Variations in Klein's technique with different children, for
              example the use of the couch and toys [Grete 9; Inge 7;
              Kenneth 9½; Werner; Egon 9½].

1945   Klein, M. 'The Oedipus complex in the light of early anxieties'.
              Development and modification of her earlier statement on the
              Oedipus complex [Richard 10; Rita 2½].

1955   Klein, M. 'The psychoanalytic play technique, its history and
              significance'.
              An account of the particular discovery that each child case
              enabled her to make.

1961   Klein, M. *Narrative of a Child Analysis.*
              This detailed account of Klein's analysis of Richard, aged 10,
              comprises the whole of Volume 4 of the *The Writings of
              Melanie Klein.*

Chronology and discussion

Freud details his theories about childhood sexuality in 'Three essays on the
theory of sexuality' (1905) and makes his famous observations of a child's
play with a cotton reel in 'Beyond the pleasure principle' (1920). In 1909 he
describes his treatment of a 5-year-old boy, 'Little Hans', conducted
through the child's father. In 1913 Ferenczi describes the sadistic obsessions
with cocks, hens and chickens of a 5-year-old boy whom he calls 'The little
chanticleer', but he talks only of interpretations that might be made if this
had been an adult patient. So there is at this time considerable interest in
children's minds and behaviour, but there is also, as Claudia Frank (2009)
points out, unease about the idea of analysing children, on the grounds that
it might damage the child or take away their innocence. Work with children
was seen predominantly as a means of substantiating what was already
known from the analysis of adults.

Klein in Budapest

Klein's first analysis was in Budapest with Sandor Ferenczi, who also
became her mentor, a situation not unusual at that time. She drew
extensively on his work and paid tribute to his contribution to her later
development in the Preface to the first edition of *The Psychoanalysis of*

Children:

> His strong and direct feeling for the unconscious and for symbolism, and the remarkable *rapport* he had with the minds of children, have had a lasting influence on my understanding of the psychology of the small child.
>
> (Klein, 1932, p. x)

Klein's first paper (1919, published 1921) was given to the Hungarian Psychoanalytical Society and is based on work with her son Erich ('Fritz') as was widely known at the time. She describes this as 'upbringing with analytic features'. Klein maintained much later (Klein, 1955) that this was when she began to use the play technique, but this would not have been in any formalised way. What is innovative is her close observation of a child, based on Freud's theories in relation to childhood, and her serious attention to all aspects of the child's behaviour as expressions of the unconscious mind. The learning difficulties shown by Erich worried Klein and such inhibitions became a particular focus of her work with children.

Klein in Berlin

Klein moved to Berlin in 1921 at the age of 38, fleeing from the rising anti-semitism in Budapest and separated from her husband. Although her personal life was in turmoil, she brought with her a conviction that child analysis would reveal mental phenomena as yet unknown. She gave her second paper 'The child's resistance to enlightenment' to the Berlin Psycho-Analytical Society and this, together with the 1919 paper, comprises Parts 1 and 2 of the 'The development of a child' (1921). In two papers published in 1923 ('Early analysis' and 'The role of the school in the libidinal development of the child') she makes her first statement that it is the resolution of anxiety that enables development. Although aggression as an important factor stunting curiosity was not central at this stage (1931), Klein was already analysing the inhibitory effects of aggressive phantasies. She based her work on a conviction that all activities have a symbolic significance [*see* Symbol formation]. This idea later became part of her concept of projective identification (1946). Although her technique seems at this point to have been broadly explanatory, she was interested analytically in all aspects of the child's behaviour, including resistance, as noted, for example, by Claudia Frank in her research into Klein's detailed clinical notes in the Melanie Klein Archive (Frank, 2009, Ch. 1).

It was to Karl Abraham, who at first supervised her work in Berlin and then took her into analysis at the beginning of 1924, that Klein was most indebted in encouraging her in her new ideas. She writes in the Preface to the first edition of *The Psychoanalysis of Children*:

Abraham clearly understood the great practical and theoretic poten-
tialities of child analysis. At the First Conference of German Psycho-
Analysts at Wurzburg, in connection with a paper I had read upon an
obsessional neurosis in a child (Erna) he said, in words that I shall
never forget; 'The future of psycho-analysis lies in play technique'. . . .
Abraham's confidence in my work encouraged me at that time to
follow the path on which I had started.

(Klein, 1932, p. xi)

Abraham was particularly interested in the difference between melancholia and ordinary mourning and had stressed the importance of an early
sadism so intense that the capacity to love could not develop (1924). Klein's
observations in her child work clearly struck a chord and Abraham wrote
enthusiastically to Freud in 1923:

In my work on Melancholia . . . I have assumed the presence of an
early oral depression in infancy as a prototype for later melancholia. In
the last few months Mrs Klein has skilfully conducted the psycho-
analysis of a three year old with good therapeutic results. This child
presented a true picture of the basic depression that I postulated in
close combination with oral erotism. The case offers amazing insights
into the infantile instinctual life.

(Abraham and Freud, 1965, p. 339)

On her arrival in Berlin, Klein joined the staff at the Berliner Psycho-
analytische Polyklinik, which had been opened by Max Eitingon in 1920.
She also saw some children privately. Although Klein achieved some status
in the Berlin child analysis scene, many of her colleagues at the Polyklinik,
such as the Bornstein sisters Steff and Berta, Ada Muller-Braunschweig and
Ada Schott, did not agree with her developing ideas and were more drawn
to the technique and ideas of Anna Freud, who occasionally came to Berlin
from Vienna and gave guest lectures at the Polyklinik. Hermine Hug-
Hellmuth described the treatment model in Vienna as 'psycho-analytically
based pedagogy' and the belief was that any resistance by the child was to
be overcome, usually by instruction, particularly about sexual matters
(Geissman and Geissman, 1997). To begin with Klein made use of the
existing methods of treating children, which was much as adults were
treated, and she did not start out with the idea of introducing a new
technique. But when she observed the children's resistance to the classical
analytic procedure, fortified by her conviction that children could be
analysed, she began to revise and modify her approach to the treatment of
children.

Grete, aged 9 years, was one of Klein's first patients seen in 1921 at the
Polyklinik and then in 1922 was moved to Klein's own consulting room.

She was a child who stuttered and had marked homosexual phantasies. Klein saw her stutter as an inhibition of her curiosity, particularly on sexual matters, and describes her theory that, for Grete, performances of any kind, such as theatre and concerts, were symbolic of parental coitus and that words and sentences represented the action of the penis. Material from Grete's treatment is not used as extensively in Klein's publications as that of Rita and Felix, for example, but it is notable that Grete was on the couch, so we know that Klein at this point was still using the classical adult technique with children. Also, although she was aware of the negative transference, which at this stage she called resistance, her interpretation of it was patchy (see Frank, 2009).

In 1923 and 1924 Klein began the treatment of Peter, Ruth, Trude and Erna and on these analyses are based many of her ensuing ideas. Klein drew on Abraham's paper ('A short study of the development of the libido viewed in the light of mental disorders', 1924) when she gave a paper in Wurzburg in 1924 based on her clinical work with Erna, which became Chapter 3 ('An obsessional neurosis in a six year old girl') in *The Psychoanalysis of Children* (1932). Klein recognised the signs of severe depression in Erna when she told Klein 'there is something about life I don't like' and was struck, as she watched Erna's play, by the savagery of her inner world. Her observations and the work she did with Erna contributed to Klein's early theories about the role of obsessional symptoms as a defence against psychotic anxiety, the effect of sadistic phantasies on the early Oedipus complex and the subsequent distortion of reality. She also used material from Erna's treatment in her later formulations about envy (1957). Claudia Frank and Heinz Weiss (1996) have traced in detail the beginnings of many of Klein's ideas using material from Erna's treatment and Klein's abundant notes in the Melanie Klein Archive.

In her paper 'The psychological principles of early analysis' (1926) Klein draws on the material from the treatment of four children (Rita, Trude, Ruth and Erna) to develop her ideas. She outlines what she sees as early manifestations of the Oedipus complex:

> At that time she [Trude] had already wished to rob her mother, who was pregnant, of her children, to kill her and to take her place in coitus with her father. These tendencies to hate and aggression were the cause of her fixation to her mother (which at the age of two years was becoming particularly strong), as well as of her feelings of anxiety and guilt.
>
> (Klein, 1926, p. 131)

The sense of guilt exhibited by the children in their games, which she observed in particular in Trude, who, she notes, 'managed to hurt herself almost always just before the analytic hour', struck Klein as weighing very heavily on these small children. This sense of guilt, she believed, came as a result of their unconscious phantasies of making sadistic attacks on the mother's body and its contents. Klein was still feeling her way:

> I cannot determine whether it is neurotic children whom the early working of the Oedipus complex affects so intensely, or if children become neurotic when the complex sets in too soon. It is, however, certain that experiences such as I have mentioned here make the conflict more severe and therefore either increase the neurosis or cause it to break out.
>
> (Klein, 1926, p. 130)

Klein did not think that her ideas conflicted with Freud's chronology:

> Those definite, typical phenomena, the existence of which in the most clearly developed form we can recognize when the Oedipus complex has reached its zenith and which precede its waning, are merely the termination of a development which occupies *years*.
>
> (Klein, 1926, p. 133)

The thorny question of technique and the implications for interpretation and transference in the analysis of children were becoming increasingly an issue between Klein and Anna Freud at this time. Klein stresses the similarities between the analysis of adults and that of children, despite the apparent differences:

> Just as children's means of expression differ from those of adults, so the analytic situation in the analysis of children appears to be entirely different. It is, however, in both cases *essentially* the same. Consistent interpretations, gradual solving of resistances and persistent tracing of the transference to earlier situations –these constitute in children as in adults the correct analytic situation.
>
> (Klein, 1926, p. 137)

Klein's use of transference diverged from that of her contemporaries as she interpreted current transference phenomena and related them to earlier experiences. Seven-year-old Inge had two periods of analysis between 1923 and 1925, and was considered, rather mysteriously, by Klein to be a 'normal' child, in spite of the fact that she suffered from a variety of neurotic symptoms such as dislike of school, difficulties in writing and proneness to bouts of depression. Klein refers to Inge's analysis as 'prophylactic', although she had the longest treatment – 375 sessions in all. A fuller description is given retrospectively in her 1955 paper, although Inge is not actually named (see Frank, 2009, Ch. 5 and Petot, 1991, p. 122). In fact it was the difficulty in making contact with Inge that led Klein to introduce toys as a means of tackling the problem:

> In a session in which I again found the child unresponsive and withdrawn I left her, saying that I would return in a moment. I went into my own children's nursery, collected a few toys, cars, little figures, a few bricks, and a train, put them into a box and returned to the patient. The child, who had not taken to drawing or other activities was interested in the small toys and at once began to play.
>
> (Klein, 1955, p. 125)

Although Klein was faced with what seemed like an almost unanalysable negative transference, she persisted and found a way round the difficulty by introducing the parameter of toys. Alix Strachey, a member of the Bloomsbury group in London, was in Berlin at the same time as Melanie Klein and was also in analysis with Abraham. Both she and her husband James had a keen interest in psychoanalysis and were to play a leading role in Klein's eventual move to London, translating Klein's texts and helping her with her English. Alix Strachey concludes, in a report on one of Klein's presentations:

> . . . the only satisfactory method of reaching valid conclusions on the subject of child analysis – indeed, of forming an understanding of the mentality of the child in general – was by collecting and reviewing direct data as Frau Klein has long been doing, rather than relying on deductions from our existing knowledge of the structure of the adult mind.
>
> (Strachey and Strachey, 1986, p. 329)

This report, written and given to the British Psychoanalytical Society in January 1925, describes Klein's play technique, her belief in direct interpretation to the child, the early Oedipus complex, the importance of the primal scene and the early and continuous development of the superego. It stimulated great interest in London and led to Klein being invited by Ernest Jones to London to give a series of lectures on child analysis to the British Psychoanalytical Society.

Klein in London

In the same year (1926), encouraged and assisted by Ernest Jones, and also in part because of the untimely death of Abraham, Klein moved permanently to London where she continued to treat children and adults. Following the publication of Anna Freud's book *The Psycho-Analytic Treatment of Children* in 1927 in Germany (it was not published in English until 1946),

Ernest Jones organised a Symposium on Child Analysis, which took place in 1927. In her contribution to this Symposium Klein robustly defended her discoveries of the small child's severe superego and, in contrast to Anna Freud, posited that it is the task of analysis to modify the superego rather than strengthen it:

> . . . just because we are able to penetrate further into that critical period before the age of two years. . . . There is then revealed in a far greater degree the severity of the child's superego, a feature Anna Freud herself has on occasion discovered. We find that what is needed is not to reinforce this superego but to tone it down.
>
> (Klein, 1927b, p. 164)

Klein continues to stress the importance of analysing anxiety and guilt and restates her view that the Oedipus complex is set in motion by the trauma of weaning. In her later paper 'Weaning' (1936), however, she modifies this statement to include the loss of the *internal* good object, which leads to the onset of depressive anxieties and conflicts [*see* Depressive position]. She describes how a good relationship to the mother helps to stabilise a 'good object within', which enables the infant to overcome despair and depression.

At this point (1927) disagreements between Klein and Anna Freud concerned the technique of child analysis, in particular whether it was analogous to adult analysis in basic principles and whether a child could form a transference to the analyst. Until this time, Klein had seen anxiety as a spur to creativity, but in 1930 in her seminal paper on her work with 'Dick', she suggests that anxiety and guilt resulting from sadistic attacks on the mother's body can be so crippling as to impede creativity and in children may stifle their capacity to engage in imaginative play, and that it is the working through of such anxieties that enables development to proceed. She expands her idea that early ego defence mechanisms are expulsive (projective) rather than repressive, and that splitting and projection, symbol formation and identification are the foundations of the relation to the external world. Using detailed clinical material she shows how Dick had evacuated his sadistic impulses so totally into external objects that he had no experience of ordinary anxiety, but was so paralysed by terror of retaliatory attacks that he was unable to 'bring into phantasy the sadistic relation to the mother's body' (Klein, 1930, p. 224).

Klein continued to treat children and adults in London, and became a leading figure in the British Psychoanalytical Society. The rise of Nazism in Europe forced the Freud family to leave Vienna and come to Britain in 1938, and subsequently Anna Freud and Melanie Klein became the central protagonists in the discussions of psychoanalytic ideas, which have been recorded by King and Steiner (1991) [*see* Controversial Discussions].

Central ideas emerging from Klein's work with children

The play technique and free association

By 1926 Klein was gaining confidence in the validity of her technique of working with children. She began her 1926 paper ('The psychological principles of early analysis') thus:

> I propose to discuss in detail certain differences between the mental life of young children and that of adults. These differences require us to use a technique adapted to the mind of the young child, and I shall try to show that there is a certain analytical play-technique which fulfils this requirement. This technique is planned in accordance with certain points of view which I shall discuss in some detail in this paper.
>
> (Klein, 1926, p. 128)

However, the play technique as a formal method of analysing children came about very gradually, and evolved from Klein's careful attention to the child in the room and from her recognition that play and action are the child's natural modes of expression. Prior to this, Rita, for example, who was Klein's youngest patient and whose analysis took place between March and October 1923, was treated in Rita's home, where she seems to have made use of her own toys and indeed the whole house and garden (Frank, 2009). Klein began to realise that this environment was interfering with the analysis (Klein, 1955).

It was in the course of her treatment of Inge that Klein, frustrated at not being able to make any headway, provided her own toys for the first time. Thereafter Klein began to adapt her technique systematically, providing a set of toys for each child, which soon became his or her own and represented the continuity of the treatment and the uniqueness of the child's relationship with the analyst. In 'The technique of early analysis' Klein describes the toys thus:

> On a low table in my analytic room there are laid out a number of small and simple toys –little wooden men and women, carts, carriages, motor-cars, trains, animals, bricks and houses, as well as paper, scissors and pencils. Even a child that is usually inhibited in its play will at least glance at the toys or touch them, and will soon give me a first glimpse into its complexes by the way in which it begins to play with them or lays them aside, or by its general attitude towards them.
>
> (Klein, 1932, p. 16)

Klein also advocated having a wash basin and running water available to the child, as games with water:

. . . afford us a deep insight into the fundamental pre-genital impulses of the child, and are also a means of illustrating its sexual theories, giving us a knowledge of the relation between its sadistic phantasies and its reaction-formations. . . . All the ordinary furniture of the room as well, such as chairs, cushions etc., are pressed into the service of its activities.

(Klein, 1932, pp. 33–34)

Klein uses detailed clinical material from three of her patients (Rita 2½, Trude 3¼ and Ruth 4¼) to illustrate her points:

The child expresses its phantasies, its wishes, its actual experiences in a symbolic way through play and games . . . In doing so, it makes use of the same archaic and phylogenetically-acquired mode of expression, the same language as it were, that we are familiar with in dreams; and we can only fully understand this language if we approach it in the way Freud has taught us to approach the language of dreams.

(Klein, 1926, p. 137)

Klein drew criticism for her new approach from Anna Freud on the grounds that the child has a different purpose behind his play from the adult's purpose in free association. Anna Freud believed that the adult could cooperate with the analyst whereas the child could not as its understanding of the analytic process was limited. What was different in Klein's approach to children's play was that she saw it as an externalisation or acting-out within the analytic setting of preoccupations with relationships between objects felt to exist internally. For the analyst, Klein thought that such play provided a means of gaining insight into early unconscious processes; for the child, play afforded a release from and a defence against overwhelming anxiety:

By the division of roles the child succeeds in expelling the father and mother whom, in the elaboration of the Oedipus complex, it has absorbed into itself and who are now tormenting it inwardly by their severity. The result of this expulsion is relief, which contributes in great measure to the pleasure derived from games.

(Klein, 1926, p. 133)

Observing children's activities was drawing Klein's interest in processes and concepts, which had a profound influence on the development of psychoanalytic theory. In 1929 she writes:

I believe these mechanisms (splitting and projection) are a principal factor in the tendency to personification in play. By their means the synthesis of the super-ego, which can be maintained only with more or less effort, can be given up for the time being and further, the tension of maintaining the truce between the super-ego as a whole and the id is diminished. The intrapsychic conflict thus becomes less violent and can be displaced into the external world.

(Klein, 1929a, p. 205)

What Freud (1920, p. 17) had noticed and surmised in his grandson's play was the importance of play in managing internal conflict and turning a passive experience into an active one. Klein took this further (1926, 1927b, 1929a, 1929b) and saw children's urge to play as composed of a number of ingredients: the drive to relate to objects in the external world from a very early age; the need to gain relief through the externalisation of inner conflict; the child's epistemophilic instinct to seek out new objects, toys and playmates as part of a process of symbolisation that enabled the child to develop the means of relating to the external world (Klein, 1930) [*see* Epistemophilia]. That is to say, Klein believed that a child who could not play, and therefore symbolise, was seriously ill. Klein's new approach was drawing considerable interest and admiration. In 1925 Alix Strachey wrote to her husband James: 'She [Klein] really is the only person who's ever regularly analysed children. . . . For it is a fact that she is the only person who possesses a knowledge of the material and *a technique*' (Strachey and Strachey, 1986, pp. 180–181).

Klein (1955) was in no doubt about the significance of her play technique:

> . . . my work with both children and adults, and my contributions to psycho-analytic theory as a whole, derive ultimately from the play technique evolved with young children . . . the insight I gained into early development, into unconscious processes and into the nature of the interpretations by which the unconscious can be approached, has been of far-reaching influence on the work I have done with older children and adults.
>
> (Klein, 1955, p. 122)

It is, as this quotation suggests, artificial to separate Klein's ideas about technique from her other theories such as unconscious phantasy and interpretation, as they are all interrelated and contingent on each other.

The role of interpretation

Klein's technique with children was not just a question of introducing toys. She had taken notice of Anton von Freund's comment, when she presented a paper at the Hungarian Psychoanalytical Association in 1919, that she was addressing only the child's conscious questions and not the unconscious ones. The aggressive phantasies expressed by her child patients in the consulting room, and the fear and guilt they gave rise to, impelled Klein to take a leap of faith and to interpret their anxiety as she saw it. She was astonished by the result. For example, Ruth, aged 4 years and 3 months, was a child who could not be in the room with Klein without her teacher who brought her, and whose only contact with Klein at first was terrified screaming and a refusal to acknowledge her at all: 'I therefore found myself forced to take other measures – measures which once again gave striking proof of the efficacy of interpretation in reducing the patient's anxiety and negative transference' (Klein, 1932, p. 26).

Klein uses material from several sessions to formulate an interpretation of the child's anxiety about her mother's insides and the fear of a baby coming. She writes: 'The effect of my interpretation was astonishing. For the first time Ruth turned her attention to me and began to play in a different and less constrained way' (Klein, 1932, p. 27).

For a more detailed account of Klein's work with Ruth, taken from the Melanie Klein Archive, see Frank (2009, Ch. 1).

The issue of how to talk to the child in the room was a contentious one in the 1920s. Klein was relying to a large extent on her intuitive conviction of the need to address 'the point of maximal anxiety' and on her belief that children could be helped by knowing about themselves and their unconscious mind. She believed that, as with adults, this could only be achieved through interpretation. She also had a flair for being able to understand imaginatively the conflicting feelings of love and hate that children feel towards their parents, their siblings and the primal scene, which gave rise to enormous anxiety and guilt in her child patients. The problems and disagreements at the time regarding what and how to interpret in child analysis were very intertwined with the issue of the transference.

Positive and negative transference

Klein did not use the term 'negative transference' until 1927 in 'Symposium on child analysis' (Klein, 1927b). Prior to that she used the term 'resistance', which was current at the time. When she observed that Felix 'forgets all dreams', she was recognising that children, as well as wanting to be understood, also did not want it, and were showing ambivalence as adults do. There was, in the 1920s, considerable doubt about whether children could form a transference. Anna Freud at this stage (although she revised this view later) believed that children could not form 'new editions' of their original figures because they were still too close to their 'old' or real ones (i.e. the parents). Klein agreed to some extent but she diverged from Anna Freud, particularly because of her experiences in treating Erich (1921) and

Rita (1926), in seeing transference as operating in everyday relationships. Petot (1990) describes Klein's position in this debate thus:

> . . . transference acts not only in the cure, but also in the 'real' relationships of daily life, whether friendly and loving or hostile. Her originality shows itself in the extension of this idea to young children; when the child comes for analysis, its 'real' relationships with real objects are already, in a sense transference relationships. By this we mean that the attitude of the three-year-old to its parents is not determined by the reality of their attitude, but by an internal imago, an imaginary and distorted representation of the parents.
>
> (Petot, 1990, p. 142)

Claudia Frank points out (Frank, 2009, Ch. 1) that Klein's concept of an early severe superego and unconscious guilt enabled her to investigate what might lie behind children's hostility and resistance. Her work with children as young as Rita (2 years 6 months), Peter (3 years 9 months) and Ruth (4 years 3 months) convinced her that children did indeed form a transference, often of a very terrifying kind. She believed that transference processes were in operation from the start, and that all elements of the transference should be interpreted from the start. In describing her work with Peter, she speaks about handling the transference:

> As soon as the child has given me an insight into his complexes, whether through his play, or his drawings or phantasies, or by his general behaviour, interpretation can begin . . . if from the outset the child shows shyness, anxiety or even only lack of trust, this should be regarded as a sign of a negative transference, which makes it necessary to begin interpreting as soon as possible. This leads to a reduction in negative transference by tracing these effects back to the original situation.
>
> (Klein, 1932, p. 21)

Klein disagrees with Anna Freud that the analyst should work by artful means, such as being friendly or reassuring, in a so-called 'introductory phase' in order to establish a positive transference, but she nevertheless seems to perceive the negative transference as a hindrance to arriving at a positive transference, and interpretation as a means of getting round the difficulty. It is also notable that Klein frequently makes what contemporary Kleinians would regard as extra-transference or reconstructive interpretations. She goes on to say in the same paper:

> For interpretation reduces the patient's negative transference by tracing the negative affects involved back to their original objects and

situations. . . . As soon as I had clarified for her [Rita] the cause of her resistance – always carrying it back to its original object and situation – it was resolved, and she would become friendly and trustful again.

(Klein, 1932, p. 21)

For Klein, the understanding of the negative transference becomes crucial to the establishment of the analytic process, and it is a hotly debated matter in the writings of Melanie Klein and Anna Freud. In 'Symposium on child analysis' (1927b) Klein robustly defends various aspects of her approach to her child patients, and with regard to the matter of transference she counters Anna Freud's view that: 'A positive transference is a necessary condition for all analytic work with children. She (AF) regards a negative transference as undesirable' (Klein, 1927b, p. 152).

Klein states that in her view transference, both positive and negative, must be treated within the same analytic framework as with adult patients:

If the analytic situation is not produced by analytic means, if the positive and the negative transference are not handled logically, then neither shall we bring about a transference-neurosis nor can we expect the child's reactions to work themselves out in relation to analysis and the analyst.

(Klein, 1927b, p. 153)

Klein's only paper specifically about transference in 1952 brings together several ideas that she frequently states and clinically illustrates in her writings. In this paper, 'The origins of transference', she describes confidently her view of transference processes beginning in earliest life and involving projection and introjection of powerful feelings of love and hate:

For many years – and this is up to a point still true today – transference was understood in terms of direct references to the analyst in the patient's material. My conception of transference as rooted in the earliest stages of development and in deep layers of the unconscious is much wider and entails a technique by which from the whole material presented the unconscious elements of the transference are deduced.

(Klein, 1952, p. 55)

Unconscious phantasy in children

The idea of phantasy as a continuous accompaniment to children's play was present for Klein from the beginning of her work. Her primary interest in the content of anxiety and her use of the play technique enabled her to experience the extraordinary proclivity in children to produce phantasies in their play, especially their worried construction of the primal scene. It also set her on the path of gradually repudiating the notion of primary narcissism, as evidenced, for example, in her paper on tics (1925) in which she describes her work with Felix, aged 13. Ferenczi had written about tics (1921) as simply a discharge of psychic energy, whereas, in contrast, Klein in 1925 set out to show that even with this prototype of the apparently objectless impulse there were underlying phantasies in the child's unconscious mind. She found that she could interpret phantasy activities that were symbolically represented in the tic, phantasies of a masturbatory kind of doing something to objects, or passively having things done to the self. Klein was also struck, even bewildered, by the liberating effects of her interpretations of unconscious phantasy (Ruth 4¼, in Klein, 1932) (see Chapter 12), but she was also astute enough to realise that a release of phantasy and a relaxing into a more positive attitude to the analyst were crucial therapeutic indicators.

The thorny question of unconscious phantasy in early mental life was at the heart of the Controversial Discussions in 1943–1944. It was Susan Isaacs who formulated the Kleinian thesis of early unconscious phantasy in her seminal paper 'On the nature and function of phantasy' (1948) in which she states that phantasy is the primary content of unconscious mental processes. She puts forward cogently the Kleinian proposition that not only is there an unconscious phantasy life going on in infantile mental life, but these phantasies involve a belief in the activity of concretely felt internal objects, which derive in very early life from the infant's bodily functions [*see* Internal objects]. She writes:

> It has sometimes been suggested that unconscious phantasies such as that of 'tearing to bits' would not arise in the child's mind before he had gained the conscious knowledge that tearing a person to bits would mean killing him or her. Such a view does not meet the case. It overlooks the fact that such knowledge is inherent in bodily impulses as a vehicle of instinct, in the aim of instinct, in the excitation of the organ, i.e. in this case, the mouth.
>
> (Isaacs, 1948, pp. 93–94)

The idea is that there is a mental corollary to every bodily sensation. Hinshelwood describes it vividly:

> A somatic sensation tugs along with it a mental experience that is interpreted as a relationship with an object that wishes to cause that sensation, and is loved or hated by the subject. . . . For instance, a baby that is hungry will, let us say, experience unpleasant feelings of hunger in his stomach. This is mentally represented by the baby feeling a malevolently motivated object actually concretely in his tummy that wants to cause him the discomfort of hunger there. . . . Conversely, when he is fed, the infant's experience is of an object, which *we* can

identify as mother, or her milk, but which *the infant* identifies as an object in his tummy benevolently motivated to cause pleasant sensations there.

(Hinshelwood, 1989, pp. 34–35)

Segal (1964) elaborates the defensive function of phantasy, positing that phantasy is not only the mental representation of an instinct, but also includes defensive processes, such as introjection and projection, mobilised against overwhelming anxiety and conflict. For the infant, in Klein's view, these are closely bound up with bodily activities such as sucking, excretion and crying.

Treating children's play and activities as their natural way of expressing themselves led to a significant shift in the Kleinian view of unconscious phantasy. Play was not merely a repetition of old attitudes, events and traumas from the past, but an externalisation of unconscious phantasy, involving the child's own loving and hateful impulses. The expulsion of inner, unconscious conflicts by means of play and activity led Klein to the realisation of the transference situation as the representation of inner conflicts and anxieties that were being enacted, within the treatment setting, in relation to the analyst.

The nature of early anxieties

Freud's 1926 paper 'Inhibitions, symptoms, and anxiety' had a far-reaching effect on Klein's theoretical development, and she repeatedly returned to it. She took up several ideas, including his discussion of the birth trauma, the loss of the loved object and the operation of the death instinct. Freud argued that anxiety was not related to one particular event, the birth trauma, but that 'anxiety situations' changed at different stages of life. In doing so he was endorsing for Klein the importance of the phantasy or reality *content*, which gives meaning to anxiety.

Klein's approach to child analysis led to specific contributions to the theory of anxiety. She discovered that the cruelty and aggression expressed by children in their play led to a particularly harsh form of remorse and guilt. It was increasingly apparent to her that it was their sadism that frightened little children and made them fearful of an equally sadistic retribution. Although at first she stuck to the view that anxiety and guilt arose from the sexual libido and Oedipal desires, by 1927 (Klein, 1927a) she was increasingly aware of children's struggles to control their aggression. She had discovered in her clinical work the debilitating effect that excessive guilt and anxiety could have on both personal and intellectual development (see Dick in Klein, 1930 and John in Klein, 1931).

Clinically, Klein understood that the anxiety she was dealing with in young children was concerned with a very primitive conflict between sadistic impulses and the remorseful reaction to them. Klein first adopted Freud's term 'anxiety situation' in an unusual paper in 1929 (Klein, 1929b) based on a review of an opera by Ravel and a paper by Karin Michaelis on the artist Ruth Kjar. In this paper, Klein writes:

> Freud assumes that the infantile danger-situation can be reduced ulti-mately to the loss of the beloved (longed-for) person. In girls, he thinks, the loss of the object is the danger-situation which operates most powerfully; in boys it is castration. My work has proved to me that both these danger-situations are a modification of yet earlier ones . . . the attack on the mother's body, which is timed psychologically at the zenith of the sadistic phase, implies also the struggle with the father's penis in the mother.
>
> (Klein, 1929b, p. 213)

In the same paper Klein describes the attacks as not only on the mother's body containing the father's penis, but also on the creative parental inter-course – the primal scene – and the babies felt also to be inside the mother [*see* Combined parent figure]. Intense fears arise of revenge attacks by the parents on the child's own creativity, and if these anxieties are very extreme they lead to the inhibition of imaginative and therefore restorative play. Klein had witnessed manifestations of attacks on the mother's body in several of her child patients (see Rita in Klein, 1923a and Trude and Ruth in Klein, 1923b).

> My observation of the cases of Trude, Ruth and Rita, together with the knowledge I have gained in the last few years, have led me to recognize the existence of an anxiety, or rather anxiety-situation, which is specific for girls and the equivalent of the castration anxiety felt by boys. . . . It is based upon the child's impulses of aggression against her mother and her desires, springing from the early stages of her Oedipus complex, to kill her and steal from her. These impulses lead not only to an anxiety or fear of being attacked by mother, but to a fear that her mother will abandon her or die.
>
> (Klein, 1932, p. 31)

The child's sadistic impulses and the terror of retaliation by mother and father require further attacks against these horrendous figures, resulting in renewed terror of retaliation and further defensive attacks, which Klein recognised as the stuff of nightmares for small children who were still dependent on their parents. The intensity of mounting fear led Klein to see this level of anxiety as psychotic [*see* Paranoia]. For example, she describes a game played by Rita, a child to whose material Klein returns over and over again (1926, 1929, 1932, 1936, 1945, 1955): 'This elephant was supposed to prevent the baby-doll from getting up; otherwise it would steal into the parents' bedroom and do them some harm or take something away from them' (Klein, 1932, p. 132).

In a later expanded version of this paper, Klein modified her understanding of Rita's bedtime ritual with the elephant to include Rita's need for protection from retaliatory attacks from the parental figures:

> As I see it now, the fear of her mother attacking the 'inside' of her body also contributed to her fear of someone coming through the window. The room represented her body and the assailant was her mother retaliating for the child's attacks on her.
>
> (Klein, 1932, p. 17)

Rita's relationship to her mother was very ambivalent, which made her a difficult child to manage. Her frequent expressions of sadness and her constant need to be reassured by her mother that she loved her are developed further in relation to further material from Rita's analysis:

> The piece of paper blackened, torn up and thrown into the water represented her mother destroyed by oral, anal and urethral means, and this picture of a dead mother related not only to the external mother when she was out of sight, but also to the internal mother. Rita had to give up her rivalry with her mother in the Oedipus situation because her unconscious fear of loss of the internal and external object acted as a barrier to every desire which would increase her hatred of her mother and therefore cause her mother's death These anxieties, derived from the oral position underlay the marked depression which Rita developed at her mother's attempt to wean her off the last bottle. . . . Her analysis revealed that the weaning represented a cruel punishment for her aggressive desires and death wishes against her mother.
>
> (Klein, 1945, p. 404)

Freud's remarks on the special nature of defences in relation to the death instinct also gave Klein support for her own observations of her child patients, and led to her departure from the classical theories of the superego and the Oedipus complex (see Chapters 6 and 8).

There is something of a sea change in Klein's thinking (1932) when she describes the propensity for the death instinct, in its projected form as aggression, to come into conflict with the loving instincts [*see* Death instinct]. Klein believed that a good relation to the mother in the earliest months is crucial to the well-being of the infant, and the incorporation of the good object – 'the good breast' – provides the beginnings of a stable core of the personality and a bulwark against overwhelming despair and anxiety. In early infancy the good breast/mother is protected by keeping it very separate from 'the bad breast' – the depriving mother who causes pain and discomfort [*see* Breast; Paranoid-schizoid position]. As the infant matures and the mother is seen more as a whole person the split between good and bad becomes blurred and less total. Awareness of the less than complete goodness of the object leads to fears for it and its survival [*see* Depressive position]. Feelings of guilt begin to emerge and Klein witnessed in her child patients how crushing this guilt could be, giving rise to new and desperate fears that the good, loved object is damaged beyond repair [*see* Reparation].

Thus Klein expands Freud's original idea of the loss of the loved external object to include the loss and possible death of the loved *internal* object and therefore the good aspects of the self (see Klein, 1932, Ch. 8). The anxiety situation becomes an internal one of struggle and tension between loving and hating impulses, with all the consequent implications for development, which Klein saw being played out by the children in her consulting room and which she understood to lie behind their symptoms.

Key ideas

Play technique and free association

The play technique refers to a formalised method of communication with small children in analysis. A box of toys and materials is provided for each child, to use as they wish in each session, and these represent the exclusive relationship of each child to the analyst. Klein believed that close observation of behaviour and play, given that this is a natural mode of expression for small children, would lead to a deeper understanding of the unconscious phantasies and conflicts in the child's mind. Thus she likened play to free association and dreams in adults.

Transference in children, both positive and negative

Klein did not share the view, prevalent in the 1920s and 1930s, that small children could not form a transference to an analyst and therefore could not be analysed in the classical way. Klein's idea was that transference is ubiquitous in children as it is in adults; in Klein's view, from early life, introjected objects, sometimes highly distorted, shape the relation not just with the analyst but with the parents themselves. Klein thought that it was vital in particular actively to interpret the negative transferences of the child, expressed as resistance, hostility and anxiety about the analyst.

Role of interpretation

Klein was always interested in exploring 'the point of maximal anxiety' and she noticed how extremely anxious her child patients became when they expressed aggressive and often violent impulses in their games and play. This sometimes seemed to be so acute as to inhibit the child's ability to carry on and in extreme cases, such as Dick, inhibited development altogether. She came to believe that interpretation of what the child might be frightened of, as for example with Ruth, could bring relief. Some of Klein's interpretations were met with considerable scepticism at the time and still are to this day, but she nevertheless possessed an intuitive flair for understanding imaginatively what the child might be experiencing and the confidence to put her ideas into words to the child.

Unconscious phantasies in children

The idea that unconscious phantasies underlie all mental activity has always been a hallmark of Kleinian thought. Thus Klein rejected the notion of primary narcissism in favour of object-related activity from birth. Observing children's play and games, Klein was struck by the proclivity of children to express vivid and often violently aggressive phantasies of an oral or anal kind. Klein related these to the child's troubled ideas about the primal scene derived from their own bodily functions and distorted by their aggressive impulses towards the mother's body and parental intercourse. Children's phantasies, in Klein's view, involve a belief in the activities and impulses of objects felt to exist concretely within.

The nature of early anxieties

In his 1926 paper 'Inhibitions, symptoms, and anxiety' Freud identified three anxiety situations; the birth trauma, loss of the longed for object and the death instinct. He also made the point that anxiety situations change in the course of development, which encouraged Klein in her belief that it was the *content* of anxiety that should be explored. Freud thought that in girls the basic anxiety was the loss of the object and in boys it was castration. Klein's work with small children led her to understand that there were earlier anxieties in boys and girls that related to their phantasied sadistic attacks on the mother's body and the father's penis and babies inside it. It was, she discovered, their sadism and the sadistic attacks in retribution that frightened small children. These earlier anxieties were about the loss of the loved *internal* object and led to subsequent fears of being abandoned and left to die (see Klein, 1929b).

References

Abraham, H. and Freud, E. (1965) *Letters of Sigmund Freud and Karl Abraham, 1907–1926*. London: Hogarth Press.
Abraham, K. (1924) 'A short study of the development of the libido viewed in the

light of mental disorders', in *Selected Papers of Karl Abraham*. London: Hogarth Press (1927), pp. 418–501.

Ferenczi, S. (1913) 'A little chanticleer', in *First Contributions to Psycho-Analysis*. London: Hogarth Press (1952), pp. 240–252.

—— (1921) 'Psycho-analytical observations on tic', *Int. J. Psycho-Anal.* 2: 1–30.

Frank, C. (2009) *Melanie Klein in Berlin: Her First Psychoanalyses of Children*. London: Routledge.

Frank, C. and Weiss, H. (1996) 'The origins of disquieting discoveries by Melanie Klein: The possible significance of the case of "Erna"', *Int. J. Psycho-Anal.* 77: 1101–1126.

Freud, A. (1946) *The Psycho-Analytic Treatment of Children*. London: Imago.

Freud, S. (1905) 'Three essays on the theory of sexuality', *S.E. 7*. London: Hogarth Press, pp. 123–243.

—— (1909) 'Analysis of a phobia in a five-year-old boy', *S.E. 10*. London: Hogarth Press, pp. 3–149.

—— (1920) 'Beyond the pleasure principle', *S.E. 18*. London: Hogarth Press, pp. 1–64.

—— (1926) 'Inhibitions, symptoms, and anxiety', *S.E. 20*. London: Hogarth Press, pp. 75–176.

Geissmann, C. and Geissman, P. (1997) *A History of Child Psychoanalysis*. London: Routledge.

Hinshelwood, R. D. (1989) *A Dictionary of Kleinian Thought*. London: Free Association Books, pp. 34–50.

Isaacs, S. (1948) 'The nature and function of phantasy', *Int. J. Psycho-Anal.* 29: 73–97.

King, P. and Steiner, R. (1991) *The Freud–Klein Controversies 1941–1945*. London: Tavistock/Routledge.

Klein, M. (1921) 'The development of a child'. in *The Writings of Melanie Klein*, Vol. 1. London: Hogarth Press, pp. 1–53.

—— (1923a) 'The role of the school in the libidinal development of the child'. *Int. J. Psycho-Anal.* 5: 312–331.

—— (1923b) 'Early analysis', in *The Writings of Melanie Klein*, Vol. 1. London: Hogarth Press, pp. 77–105.

—— (1925) 'A contribution to the psychogenesis of tics', in *The Writings of Melanie Klein*, Vol. 1. London: Hogarth Press, pp. 106–127.

—— (1926) 'The psychological principles of early analysis', in *The Writings of Melanie Klein*, Vol. 1. London: Hogarth Press, pp. 128–138.

—— (1927a) 'Criminal tendencies in normal children', in *The Writings of Melanie Klein*, Vol. 1. London: Hogarth Press, pp. 170–185.

—— (1927b) 'Symposium on child analysis', in *The Writings of Melanie Klein*, Vol. 1. London: Hogarth Press, pp. 139–169.

—— (1928) 'The early stages of Oedipus complex', in *The Writings of Melanie Klein*, Vol. 1. London: Hogarth Press, pp. 186–198.

—— (1929a) 'Personification in the play of children', in *The Writings of Melanie Klein*, Vol. 1. London: Hogarth Press, pp. 199–209.

—— (1929b) 'Infantile anxiety-situations reflected in a work of art and in the creative impulse', in *The Writings of Melanie Klein*, Vol. 1. London: Hogarth Press, pp. 210–218.

—— (1930) 'The importance of symbol formation in the development of the ego', in *The Writings of Melanie Klein*, Vol. 1. London: Hogarth Press, pp. 219–232.

—— (1931) 'A contribution to the theory of intellectual inhibition', in *The Writings of Melanie Klein*, Vol. 1. London: Hogarth Press, pp. 236–247.

—— (1932) *The Psychoanalysis of Children. The Writings of Melanie Klein*, Vol. 2. London: Hogarth Press, pp. 16–34.

—— (1936) 'Weaning', in *The Writings of Melanie Klein*, Vol. 1. London: Hogarth Press, pp. 290–305.

—— (1945) 'The Oedipus complex in the light of early anxieties', in *The Writings of Melanie Klein*, Vol. 1. London: Hogarth Press, pp. 370–419.

——(1946) 'Notes on some schizoid mechanisms', *Int. J. Psycho-Anal.* 27: 99–110.

—— (1952) 'The origins of transference', *Int. J. Psycho-Anal.* 33: 433–438. Reprinted in *The Writings of Melanie Klein*, Vol. 3. London: Hogarth Press, pp. 48–56.

—— (1955) 'The psychoanalytic play technique, its history and significance', in *The Writings of Melanie Klein*, Vol. 3. London: Hogarth Press, pp. 122–140.

—— (1957) 'Envy and gratitude', in *The Writings of Melanie Klein*, Vol. 3. London: Hogarth Press, pp. 176–235.

—— (1961) *Narrative of a Child Analysis*. in *The Writings of Melanie Klein*, Vol. 4. London: Hogarth Press.

Petot, J.-M. (1990). *Melanie Klein: Vol. 1: First Discoveries and First System: (1919–1932)* (C. Trollope, Trans.) Madison, CT: International Universities Press.

—— (1991) *Melanie Klein: Vol. 2: The Ego and the Good Object (1932–1960)* (C. Trollope, Trans.) Madison, CT: International Universities Press.

Segal, H. (1964) 'Phantasy and other mental processes', *Int. J. Psycho-Anal.* 45: 191–194. Reprinted in *The Work of Hanna Segal*. London: Free Association Books/Maresfield (1974), pp. 41–48.

Strachey, J. and Strachey, A. (1986) *Bloomsbury/Freud. The Letters of James and Alix Strachey 1924–1925*. London: Chatto & Windus.

Further reading

Aguayo, J. (1997) 'Historicizing the origins of Kleinian psychoanalysis: Klein's analytic and patronal relationships with Ferenczi, Abraham and Jones, 1914–1927', *Int. J. Psycho-Anal.* 78: 1165–1182.

Bick, E. (1968) 'The experience of the skin in early object relations', *Int. J. Psycho-Anal.* 49: 484–486.

Ferenczi, S. (1913) 'Stages in the development of the sense of reality', in *First Contributions to Psychoanalysis*. London: Hogarth Press (1952), pp. 213–239.

Harris, M. (1975) *Thinking about Infants and Young Children*. Strath Tay: Clunie Press.

—— and Bick, E. (1987) *The Collected Papers of Martha Harris and Esther Bick*. Strath Tay: Clunie Press.

Klein, M. (1952) 'Some theoretical conclusions regarding the emotional life of the infant', in *The Writings of Melanie Klein*, Vol. 3. London: Hogarth Press, pp. 61–93.

—— (1952) 'On observing the behaviour of young infants', in *The Writings of Melanie Klein*, Vol. 3. London: Hogarth Press, pp. 94–121.

—— (1959) 'Our adult world and its roots in infancy', in *The Writings of Melanie Klein*, Vol. 3. London: Hogarth Press, pp. 247–263.

Likierman, M. (2002) *Melanie Klein: Her Work in Context*. London: Continuum.

O'Shaughnessy, E. (1964) 'The absent object', *J. Child Psychother*. 1: 134–143.

Segal, H. (1972) 'Melanie Klein's technique of child analysis', in *The Work of Hanna Segal*. London: Jason Aronson (1981), pp. 25–37.

—— (1979) *Klein*. London: Fontana.

Tustin, F. (1972) *Autism and Childhood Psychosis*. London: Hogarth Press.

—— (1981) *Autistic States in Children*. London: Routledge & Kegan Paul.

Winnicott, D. (1971) *Playing and Reality*. London: Tavistock.

3 Internal objects

Definition

In essence the term 'internal object' means a mental and emotional image of an external object that has been taken inside the self. The character of the internal object is coloured by aspects of the self that have been projected into it. A complex interaction continues throughout life between the world of internalised figures and objects in the real world (which are obviously also in the mind) via repeated cycles of projection and introjection. The most important internal objects are those derived from the parents, in particular from the mother or breast into which the infant projects its loving (life instinct) or hating (death instinct) aspects. These objects, when taken into the self, are thought to be experienced by the infant concretely as physically present within the body, causing pleasure (good internal part-object breast) or pain (bad internal part-object breast) The infant's view of the motivation of these objects is based partly on accurate perception by the infant of the external object and partly on the desires and feelings that the infant has projected into the external objects: a malevolent desire to cause pain in the bad object and a benevolent desire to give pleasure in the good object.

Internal objects are experienced as relating to each other within the self. They may be identified with and assimilated, they may be felt as separate from but at the same time as existing within the self and sometimes they are felt to be alien foreign bodies within the self. Within Kleinian theory the state of the internal objects is considered to be of prime importance to the development and mental health of the individual. The introjection of and identification with a stable good object is crucial to the ego's capacity to cohere and integrate experience. Damaged or dead internal objects cause enormous anxiety and can lead to personality disintegration, whereas objects felt to be in a good state promote confidence and well-being.

Internal objects can exist on several levels. They can be more or less unconscious and more or less primitive. Infantile internal objects are experienced initially concretely within the body and mind and constitute a primitive level of the adult psyche, adding emotional influence and force to later perceptions, feelings and thoughts. Internal objects may be represented to the self in dreams, fantasies and in language.

Internal objects are conceptually confusing in that they are described both from metapsychological and phenomenological perspectives. Metapsychologically, the first internal objects are in part a creation of the life and death instincts, can affect the structure of the ego and are the basis of the superego. Phenomenologically they are the content of phantasy but of phantasy that has real effects.

The conceptualisation of internal objects is inextricably linked to Klein's theory of the life and death instincts, her ideas about unconscious phantasy and her theories of the development from the paranoid-schizoid position to the depressive position within which there is a move from part-object to whole-object functioning. This means that no single definition can capture this concept.

Key papers

1910   Freud, S. 'Leonardo da Vinci and a memory of his childhood'.
            Freud writes about Leonardo's identification with his mother.

1914   Freud, S. 'On narcissism: an introduction'.
            The self takes the ego as its love object.

1917   Freud, S. 'Mourning and melancholia'.
            Ego identified with reproached lost object.

1926   Klein, M. 'The psychological principles of early analysis'.
            The introjected mother is distorted by the child's sadistic impulses.

1927   Klein, M. 'Symposium on child analysis'.
            'Imago' differentiated from the original object.

1929   Klein, M. 'Personification in the play of children'.
            Psychosexual stage influences character of imago. Extreme characteristics of imagos described.

1932   Klein, M. *The Psychoanalysis of Children*.
            Life and death instincts influence the character of the introjected (part) object.

1935   Klein, M. 'A contribution to the psychogenesis of manic-depressive states'.
            Move from part- to whole-object relating provokes fear of loss of good objects and concern for its preservation. Increasing

understanding of the complexity of the relationship between the external and internal object.

1940   Klein, M. 'Mourning and its relation to manic-depressive states'.
Mobilisation of defences against the loss of the good object. Mourning involves loss of internal as well as external object.

1942   Heimann, P. 'A contribution to the problem of sublimation and its relation to processes of internalization'.
A clear exposition of the concept with vivid clinical illustration. Process of assimilation discussed.

1946   Klein, M. 'Notes on some schizoid mechanisms'.
Binary splitting of objects necessary for successful establishment of the good object and essential for healthy development. Binary splitting differentiated from fragmentation.

1949   Heimann, P. 'Some notes on the psycho-analytic concept of introjected objects'.
Good exposition of concept; links to bodily sensation emphasised.

1957   Klein, M. 'Envy and gratitude'.
Envy leads to the internalisation of a destructive internal object.

1958   Klein, M. 'On the development of mental functioning'.
Restatement of theory with modification in which extreme primitive internal objects are located in 'deep unconscious' where they remain undisturbed.

1952   Rosenfeld, H. 'Notes on the psycho-analysis of the super-ego conflict of an acute schizophrenic patient'.
Dead or destroyed internal objects function as 'ego-splitting super-ego'.

1959   Bion, W. 'Attacks on linking'.
Internal object as 'ego-destructive superego'.

1964   Rosenfeld, H. 'On the psychopathology of narcissism: A clinical approach'.
Exploration of omnipotent introjection and identification.

1971   Rosenfeld, H. 'A clinical approach to the psychoanalytic theory of the life and death instincts: An investigation into the aggressive aspects of narcissism'.
Exploration of omnipotent introjection and identification.

2004   Sodré, I. 'Who's who? Notes on pathological identifications'.
                Continues the theme of omnipotent introjection of object.

Conceptual difficulties with the term 'internal object'

Lack of distinctiveness of the term

There are a number of conceptual difficulties when thinking about the term
'internal object'. The term is used to refer to a huge variety of phenomena
within the individual, ranging from bodily sensation to parts of the self and
to mental images – phantasies, memories and perceptions. The terms
'internal object' and 'external object' are at times indistinguishable as either
may be used to refer to a mental image. All objects that are perceived or
remembered, whether consciously or unconsciously, are internal in that
they are in the mind, however some differentiation can be made between
those that are experienced as being inside the self and those that are
experienced as being outside the self. The concept of internal object implies
an object that is or has been animate and with whom there is an emotional
connection. By and large the term implies some degree of permanence or
recurrence of experience of the object.

Internal object and instinct

In Klein's early writing the character of the parent that is in the child's
mind is distorted by the prevailing instinct, in particular oral and anal
sadistic drives. In her later theories, internal objects may represent the
instincts; this is particularly true of the split off extreme figures located in
the deep unconscious that Klein writes about in 1958.

Internal object and unconscious phantasy

Klein's view is that instincts are experienced as phantasies, for example the
death instinct manifests itself in the form of a concrete or phantasied
internal attacker.

Self–object differentiation: Experience of me-ness/not-me-ness

Theoretically, self and object are not sharply differentiated. An internal
object combines aspects of the self and the object and can be experienced
as, or thought to be, a part of the self or a foreign body [*see* Projective
identification].

Differentiation of internal object from instincts and reality

Internal objects change and develop with the changes and development of the individual's instincts in relationship to the external world. A developmental process occurs in which instinct, object and realistic perception become increasingly differentiated.

Chronology

Precursors

In *The Interpretation of Dreams* Freud (1900) refers to unconscious memory traces with an implication that they powerfully influence dream and symptom formation. The idea of actually taking objects into the self arises out of elaborations by Ferenczi, Abraham and Freud on the oral stage of development. In 1909 Ferenczi coins the term 'introjection' to describe the (oral) process of taking the outside world into the ego and 'making it the object of unconscious phantasies' (1909, p. 47). He later describes this activity as 'an extension to the external world of the original auto-erotic interests, by including its objects in the ego' (1912, p. 316). In 1910 Freud describes Leonardo da Vinci as preserving his repressed love for his mother in his unconscious, where he remains 'unconsciously fixated to the mnemic image of his mother' and identifies with her (1910, p. 100). Abraham (1911) describes incorporation as the mental counterpart of the oral instinctual impulse.

Freud introduces the idea of narcissistic object-love in 1910, both in a footnote to the *Three Essays on the Theory of Sexuality* (1905) and in his Leonardo da Vinci paper (1910). In 1914 he puts forward a full paper on the idea of the self taking the ego as its love object ('On narcissism: An introduction'). In his important 1917 paper 'Mourning and melancholia' Freud makes use of Abraham's differentiation of normal mourning from severe depression and also his notion of oral cannibalism, to describe how the melancholic ego identifies with the introjected and reproached lost object. Then in 1921 he puts forward the idea that the ego splits, with one part, the conscience, raging against the part of the ego 'which has been altered by the introjection and which contains the lost object' (1921, p. 109). The conscience or critical agency is later named as the superego, which itself is a precipitate of early identifications (1923, p. 34). Freud describes the reason for taking the object into the ego as follows:

> When it happens that a person has to give up a sexual object, there quite often ensues an alteration of his ego which can only be described as a setting up of the object inside the ego, as it occurs in melancholia.

It may be that this identification is the sole condition under which the id can give up its objects. At any rate the process, especially in the early phases of development, is a very frequent one, and it makes it possible to suppose that the character of the ego is a precipitate of abandoned object-cathexis and that it contains the history of those object-choices.

(Freud, 1923, pp. 29–30)

Freud later explains what he means by the term 'identification':

... what is called an 'identification' – that is to say, the assimilation of one ego to another one, as a result of which the first ego behaves like the second in certain respects, imitates it and in a sense takes it up into itself. Identification has been not unsuitably compared with the oral, cannibalistic incorporation of another person. It is a very important form of attachment to someone else, probably the very first, and not the same thing as the choice of an object.

(Freud, 1933, p. 63)

All of this paves the way for Klein's idea of an internal world filled with internal objects.

Klein on internal objects

1925–1932. Early period: Oral and anal attacks on Oedipal objects (character of introjects coloured by psychosexual stage at introjection)

As early as 1925, when writing about 'tics', Klein describes the tic as an activity related to the child's phantasy relationship to his 'internal' objects – his parents in sexual intercourse. Abraham and Ferenczi had described tics as narcissistic activities linked to masturbation, an activity they considered to be an objectless form of discharge. Klein disagrees and argues that the tic is an activity that has regressed from object relations to secondary narcissism.

At this time Klein is beginning to build her theory that the anxiety that she sees in children is caused by their own violent feelings and by their phantasies of having inside themselves a retaliatory mother. In 1926 she describes two highly anxious girls, one of whom, Rita, fears her mother's retaliation for her oedipal wish 'to usurp her mother's place with her father, to steal from her the child with which she was pregnant and to injure and castrate the parents' (1926, p. 132). Klein's view is that the feared mother is not the real (external) mother but an introjected mother:

But here the prohibition of the childish wish no longer emanated from the real mother, but from an introjected mother, whose role she enacted for me in many ways and who exercised a harsher and more cruel influence upon her than her real mother had ever done.

(Klein, 1926, p. 132)

Although at this stage of her writing Klein's focus is on internal objects as bad objects and Rita's father too is a tormenting inner figure, there is also another version of her father as a more helpful figure, who appears in her play represented by an elephant that prevents her from getting up and pursuing her dastardly wishes.

Klein differentiates the child's original real objects from what she calls 'imagos'. 'His relations to them [the original objects] have undergone distortion and transformation so that the present love-objects are now imagos of the original objects' (1927, p. 151). Klein sees the child as preoccupied with the interior of his mother's body and its contents, among which is a hostile penis, which, when introjected with the mother (later to be referred to as the 'combined object'), is felt as particularly hostile and causes extreme anxiety. Klein locates these imagos in the superego which, in an alteration of Freud's theory, she describes as developing prior to the resolution of the Oedipus complex [*see* Oedipus complex; Superego]:

> . . . the super-ego is of a phantastic severity. On account of the well-known formula which prevails in the Ucs this child anticipates, by reason of his own cannibalistic and sadistic impulses, such punishments as castration, being cut to pieces, eaten up, etc., and lives in perpetual dread of them. The contrast between his tender and loving mother and the punishment threatened by the child's super-ego is actually grotesque and is an illustration of the fact that we must on no account identify the real objects with those which children introject.
>
> (Klein, 1927, p. 155)

Klein's frequent assumption, at this stage of her thinking, is that the real object is good (as in the above example) and the imago is bad. This assumption was and is much criticised but it is not one that Klein held for long, and even when she did, 'good' 'real' objects were often fantastic and behaved with extreme violence. This point is illustrated by Petot, who points out that although Klein (1929) considered Gerald's ideal 'fairy mummy' to be nearer reality than the cruel imagos, 'this more realistic imago was nonetheless willing to help the child kill his father, castrate him and eat his penis' (Petot, 1990, p. 260).

For a time Klein has the idea that the character of the internal object is determined by the manner of the prevailing pregenital impulse under which it is introjected. Thus, an object introjected in the oral sadistic stage will be distorted by the process of introjection and will then itself be experienced as full of oral sadism. 'For, when the objects are introjected, the attack launched upon them with all the weapons of sadism rouses the subject's dread of an analogous attack upon himself from the external and internalized objects' (1929, p. 212). Klein has not yet developed her theory of the depressive position and at this early time has the view that the establishment of helpful internal objects depends on the child's successful development towards the genital phase. Klein states that this will occur if there has been a 'sufficiently strong fixation to the oral-sucking phase' (1929, p. 204), in which case the internal object becomes more like the real mother.

Klein's picture of the child's inner phantasy world is one of great complexity in which each of the 'characters', ranging from extreme figures to more realistic figures, exists in a rapidly fluctuating state and from moment to moment may be in alliance with, at war with or taken over by one or more of the others. The anxiety caused by this inner conflict is relieved by 'splitting up and projecting' (1929, p. 205) the imagos into objects in the external world.

1932. Transitional period: The life and death instincts and internal objects

Klein's papers, collected in *The Psychoanalysis of Children* (1932), show her theories in a period of transition from being based on psychosexual stages to an increasing emphasis on the interaction of the life and death instincts; they are at times theoretically inconsistent and difficult to understand. Incorporating Freud's idea of the deflection of the death instinct outwards, the internal dangers (death instinct within) are now experienced as an external bad mother. Klein's theory at this time is that it is the attack on the mother, the turning of the death instinct outwards rather than the process of introjection itself, that turns the mother bad and that the subsequent introjection of the attacked frightening imago triggers in turn the processes of projection:

> When as a small child, he first begins to introject his objects – and these, it must be remembered, are yet only very vaguely demarcated by his various organs – his fear of those introjected objects sets in motion the mechanisms of ejection and projection, as I have tried to show; and there now follows a reciprocal action between projection and introjection, which seems to be of fundamental importance not only for the formation of his super-ego but for the development of his object-relations and his adaptation to reality.
>
> (Klein, 1932, p. 142)

Good objects are established. Klein writes: 'His belief in the existence of kindly and helpful figures – a belief which is founded upon the efficacy of his libido – enables his reality-objects to emerge ever more powerfully and his phantastic imagos to recede into the background' (1932, p. 148). Although this sounds as though Klein is continuing to equate real with good, she makes the point in a footnote that both good and bad imagos can be unrealistic:

> I shall try to show that the child introjects (unrealistic) imagos, both phantasized good imagos and phantasized bad ones, and that gradually, as his adaptation to reality and the formation of his super-ego go forward, these imagos approximate more and more closely to the real objects they represent.
>
> (Klein, 1932, p. 137)

In many of her 1932 chapters, Klein provides detailed descriptions of the various omnipotent methods employed to evade, evacuate, destroy and control threatening internal objects. She also describes the incorporated object as a first form of superego and the 'vehicle of defence against destructive impulses within' (Klein, 1932, p. 127) [*see* Superego].

1935–1945. Theory of the depressive position: Whole objects: Loss, recovery and repair

In 1935 Klein formulates her theory of the depressive position and, from this time, elements of the psychosexual stages become subsumed in her theory under the life and death instincts. From the perspective of individual development, the paranoid-schizoid position comes before the depressive position, but Klein worked out her theory of the depressive position first and she does not clarify her ideas on the earlier paranoid-schizoid position until 1946. She does, however, repeatedly refer to a developmentally earlier stage. She now makes it clear that included in the infant's attack on the mother is his attributing to her own aggression.

Klein's infant is at first incapable of perceiving a whole object and is unable to integrate the good and bad aspects of the object. Klein considers that the early ego only weakly identifies itself with its objects because it is uncoordinated and also because the introjected objects are mainly part-objects. With satisfactory mothering and as the infant's ego becomes more organised, the infant moves from part-object to whole-object relating. The anatomical parts of the objects as well as the good and the bad aspects of itself and its objects (internal and external) are brought together, and enormous changes take place. The relationship to the object becomes more realistic and internal objects are less coloured by instincts; objects are seen as they are, separate from the self and with attributes of their own.

Whole-object relating introduces a very different way of functioning and leads to new anxieties. The infant or individual now fears not only for his own survival but also for that of his object, with whom he now identifies (depressive position functioning). The loved good internal object is no longer thought to be extremely powerful but is felt to be vulnerable to attack and in danger of being destroyed by violent internal objects, by the infant's hatred, by devouring love or by being expelled along with the bad object. Significantly, the absence of the good object is increasingly experienced as a loss, rather than as the presence of a bad persecuting object.

The individual feels the pain of guilt and sadness and at times despair. Klein describes the omnipotent defences that are employed: flight to the idealised internal object (Schmideberg, 1930), obsessional control, denial of the importance of the good object and denial of the bad self and bad objects. Attempts are made to restore the object but reparative activity is fraught with setbacks, not only because they are based on false omnipotence but also because of the breakdown of the differentiation between good and bad objects and the good and bad self. The idealised object may become exacting and persecutory in its demand for restitution and good objects may be eaten up and destroyed in phantasy [see Manic defences; Obsessional defences].

Klein (1935) links her theoretical ideas to observations of patients' behaviour, describing the way in which hypochondriacal symptoms, while sometimes 'paranoiac', may be the result of loving concern for damaged internal objects with whom the individual is identified. She comments on suicidal patients and states that, while the aim of suicide may be to murder the bad objects, its intention is also to preserve the internalised good objects with which the individual is identified and to enable the ego to unite with the loved objects. Klein finds that in the minds of manic patients the parents are killed and then brought back to life, whereas in those of obsessional patients they are separated from each other. She observes that depressed child and adult patients have the dread that they contain dead or dying objects (often parents). Klein returns to this idea later when describing a split between an uninjured live object and an injured dying or dead object as a defence against depressive anxiety (1952).

Klein continues many of the themes of her 1935 paper in 'Mourning and its relation to manic-depressive states' (1940), and goes into greater detail about the omnipotent defences, giving particular attention to obsessional and manic reparation and to the activity of triumphing over the objects. She gives a full description of how she visualises the complex inner world:

> As I have often pointed out, the processes of introjection and projection from the beginning of life lead to the institution inside ourselves of loved and hated objects, who are felt to be 'good' and 'bad', and who are

interrelated with each other and with the self; that is to say, they constitute an inner world. This assembly of internalized objects becomes organized, together with the organization of the ego, and in the higher strata of the mind it becomes discernible as the super-ego. Thus, the phenomenon which was recognized by Freud, broadly speaking, as the voices and the influences of the actual parents established in the ego is, according to my findings, a complex object-world, which is felt by the individual, in deep layers of the unconscious, to be concretely inside himself, and for which I and some of my colleagues therefore use the term 'internalized objects' and an 'inner world'. This inner world consists of innumerable objects taken into the ego [whole self], corresponding partly to the multitude of varying aspects, good and bad, in which the parents (and other people) appeared to the child's unconscious mind throughout the various stages of his development. Further, they also represent all the real people who are continually becoming internalized in a variety of situations provided by the multitude of ever-changing external experiences as well as phantasied ones. In addition, all these objects are in the inner world in an infinitely complex relation both with each other and with the self.

(Klein, 1940, pp. 362–363)

In the same paper Klein explores the relationship between the loss of the internal object and the experience of the actual loss of a loved person, advancing the view that the mourner believes that he has also lost his internal good objects. The real loss reactivates the earlier paranoid anxieties of a retaliating mother bent on punishment and the mourner may feel that 'bad' objects have taken over. Adding to Abraham's idea that the mourner needs to reinstate the lost loved object, Klein explains that the mourner also needs to reinstate the internalised good objects. Other setbacks such as illness may also threaten the individual's feeling of securely containing a good object.

Around this time, in an unpublished piece of writing, possibly written in 1944, Klein explains why she chooses to use the term 'inner object':

My reason for preferring this term to the classic definition, that of 'an object installed in the ego' is that the term 'inner object' is more specific since it exactly expresses what the child's unconscious, and for that matter the adult's in deep layers, feels about it. In these layers it is not felt to be part of the mind in the sense, as we have learnt to understand it, of the super-ego being the parents' voices inside one's mind. This is the concept we find in the higher strata of the unconscious. In the deeper layers, however, it is felt to be a physical being, or rather a multitude of beings, which with all their activities, friendly and hostile, lodge inside one's body, particularly inside the abdomen, a conception to which physiological processes and sensations of all kinds, in the past and in the present, have contributed.

           (Melanie Klein Archive, D16 M2T papers, Wellcome Library)

1930s and 1940s: The 'Internal Objects Group'

There was considerable reaction to the concept of internal object and in the 1930s and 1940s a group of Klein's followers, calling themselves the 'Internal Objects Group', wrote papers in support of the concept and provided clinical examples. These are listed in the next main section but two papers that bring great clarity to the concept are worth mentioning here: 'A contribution to the problem of sublimation and its relation to processes of internalization' Heimann (1942) and 'Some notes on the psycho-analytic concept of intro-jected objects' (Heimann, 1949). In her 1942 paper Heimann describes a patient who is inhabited by devils that roam inside her, causing her pain, making her do things that she does not want to do, eating her from inside, prodding her with forks and making her vomit. Heimann considers the devils to be internal objects and she understands their genesis in the following way:

> The memory-traces of psychical experience, past and present, are not static imprints like photographs, but moving and living dramas, like never-ending scenes on a stage. These inner dramas are composed of the subject and her instinctual impulses towards her original objects (father, mother, brother and their later substitutes, up to and including the analyst), who are seen as they had been felt and are felt to be under the impact of her impulses; in addition, the objects also display her own impulses. Moreover, all the protagonists in the drama, herself and her objects, her own impulses and their responses, derive some features from the actual setting and events of childhood: her own physical and emotional personality during childhood and that of the persons around her, and the things, places and events of that life. Features of the world in which and towards which her instinctual impulses were originally directed, dating from the period of time and the actual occasions in which they were originally felt (and were more or less expressed or denied) become woven into the inner drama played out by her impulses and their objects.
>
>   (Heimann, 1942, p. 11)

In the same paper Heimann also explains how she understands the process of assimilation. She suggests that guilt-inducing attacked objects are inter-nalised and experienced as alien internal objects that demand repair. Reparative activity is tainted by a sense of 'penal servitude' and 'sacrifice'. As the individual becomes able to recognise his own qualities the objects also become more human. The individual 'acquires the right' to absorb aspects of the parents and also the right to exercise his own talents freely (pp. 15–16).

1946. The paranoid-schizoid position: Normal vs. pathological splitting of internal objects

In 1946 Klein formulates the theory of the paranoid-schizoid position [*see* Paranoid-schizoid position]. She introduces the term 'projective identification' to refer to the processes of splitting, projection and re-introjection of parts of the self and objects [*see* Projective identification]. She emphasises the developmental importance to the infant of achieving a division between the good and bad aspects of objects and of the self for the successful installation of a good internal object. She makes a clear statement of the difference between her views and those of Fairbairn (1941, 1944, 1946, 1952), who considers internal objects as a substitute for, and a retreat from, reality and who considers the introjection of the good object as secondary to the introjection of the bad object [*see* Ronald Fairbairn].

Klein makes a distinction between essential binary splitting, in which good and bad are divided, and the fragmentary splitting of the object and the ego. The good object, linked to the life instinct (sucking libido), is felt to be intact, whereas the bad object linked to the death instinct is taken in sadistically and split into pieces; this fragmenting activity of the bad object can, when the infant is full of frustration, greed, envy or hatred, threaten to infect the good breast and interfere with the developmentally important binary split:

> . . . the gratifying breast, taken in under the dominance of the sucking libido is felt to be complete. This first internal good object acts as a focal point in the ego. It counteracts the processes of splitting and dispersal, makes for cohesiveness and integration, and is instrumental in building up the ego. The infant's feeling of having inside a good and complete breast may, however, be shaken by frustration and anxiety. As a result, the division between the good and bad breast may be difficult to maintain, and the infant may feel that the good breast too is in bits.
>
> (Klein, 1946, pp. 5–6)

Importantly in this paper Klein introduces the idea that, when the object is split or fragmented, the ego is split or fragmented along the same lines. Picking up points made earlier by Schmideberg (1934) and Heimann (1942), Klein notes that excessive projective identification depletes and weakens the ego, with the result that it is unable to identify with introjected objects but finds itself overwhelmed by them. These unassimilated objects may be felt as tyrants, and if good aspects of the self have been projected excessively the object may become the ego ideal to which the ego is subservient.

Klein's later papers: 1948 onwards

Klein (1948) suggests that guilt arises not only in relation to whole objects in the depressive position, but also transiently and with increasing frequency in the paranoid-schizoid position towards part-objects. Attempts at integration occur from the beginning and, when good and bad objects and feelings of love and hate come together, guilt about the injured loved object and a desire to make reparation arise, however briefly, at this early stage.

In her paper 'Envy and gratitude' Klein itemises the way in which envy interferes with the introjection of the good object. Envy not only seeks to rob the object, 'but also to put badness, primarily bad excrements and bad parts of the self, into the mother, and first of all into her breast, in order to spoil and destroy her' (Klein, 1957, p. 181). Envy interferes with all good experiences and severely impairs the introjection of good objects. The introjected envious object, referred to by Klein as the 'envious super-ego', interferes with reparation and creativeness. Envy increases the fear of the combined parent figure. Furthermore, envy prevents the infant from being able to make a clear division between good and bad and leads to confusional states. Greed, although less destructive, leads to the internalisation of a destroyed object, an object that is possessed and is therefore felt as an internal persecutor. Klein points out that adverse external circumstances vitally interfere with the process of internalising a good object. In contrast, good experiences and gratitude lead to inner wealth. Klein states that 'early emotional life is characterized by a sense of losing and regaining the good object' (1957, p. 180) [see Envy; External world/environment].

In 1958, returning to the idea of 'planes', which she had mentioned in several earlier papers, Klein restates her theory in which primitive objects are taken into and exist in both the ego and the superego and become modified over time. However, the most terrifying primitive objects that have resulted from intense destructiveness she now describes as being 'split off in a manner different from that by which the superego is formed, and are relegated to the deeper layers of the unconscious' (Klein, 1958, p. 241). Here they remain unmodified by the integrating processes of normal development. These primitive internal objects, terrifyingly bad and ideal, may erupt from within the individual when under stress [see Superego].

In her 1960 paper ('A note on depression in the schizophrenic'), Klein refers to Segal's 1956 paper ('Depression in the schizophrenic') and argues that the schizophrenic has internalised a good object, however impermanent and unstable, and feels despair, guilt and depression at having damaged or destroyed it. She makes a claim for the therapeutic value of

helping the schizophrenic to experience and recover the split-off goodness
of himself and of his object.

Reactions to and preoccupation with the concept

In the 1930s and 1940s, as mentioned above, a group of analysts (Searl,
Schmideberg, Isaacs and Heimann) calling themselves the 'Internal Objects
Group' explore the concept and write papers emphasising the concrete
nature of internal objects and their preverbal basis in the infant's earliest
bodily experiences (Searl, 1932, 1933; Schmideberg, 1934; Isaacs, 1940;
Heimann, 1942, 1949).

In 1934 Strachey makes a significant contribution to the theory of the
therapeutic action of psychoanalysis. Extending and elaborating Klein's
(1929, 1931) views that psychoanalysis can lessen the anxiety caused by the
severe superego and allow the development of more kindly imagos, he
describes the analyst as being introjected as a good object to become an
auxiliary superego (Strachey, 1934).

During this period a number of other analysts also write about the
concept. Glover (1932) puts forward the view that the feeling of having
something separate inside is caused by the lack of integration of the ego
nuclei. Brierley (1939) considers the appearance of the internal object to be
an indication of severe psychopathology. Fuchs (1937) suggests that there
are two forms of identification: the first ('pre-genital') is based on introjections, is a defence against the actual loss of an external object and leads to a
narcissistic identification; the second ('partial') is the identification with an
object as a result of genital impulses in which preservation of the external
object leads to a hysterical identification. Matte-Blanco (1941) makes the
point that objects are normally unobtrusively assimilated into the ego and
that it is only those objects split by aggression that fail to be assimilated.
Alix Strachey (1941) separates out the different meanings of internal into
mental, imaginary and inside. Fairbairn (1944, 1946) proposes a new
structural model in which the ego is divided into three parts, each of which
relates to an internal object of which only one – the bad object – has been
internalised [*see* Ronald Fairbairn]. For a longer discussion of this period,
see Hinshelwood (1991).

Key ideas

Internal versus external world

Klein draws attention to internal psychic activity within the individual
(the interaction that takes place between different parts of the self and
introjected objects and part-objects). The interplay between this internal

activity (the objects and parts of the self within) and objects in the outside world is at the centre of her interest.

Introjection, incorporation, identification, assimilation

Following Freud, Abraham and Ferenczi, Klein thinks that the activity of introjection, incorporation or taking an experience into the self is as fundamental to the mind as the taking in of food or air is fundamental to the body. The individual may or may not identify with that which he has taken in. Assimilation involves a further step in that it involves some recognition that the object or aspect with which the individual identifies has a separate existence.

Concrete bodily experience of active presence in body linked to unconscious phantasy

The first introjects are thought by Klein to be sensations experienced concretely in the body and accompanied by unconscious phantasy. Hunger, for example, might be experienced as the presence of a bad object – a physical pain deliberately caused by an internal pain-inducing presence (bad object). Particularly in the first stages of development, phantasy and internal objects are conceptually difficult to separate.

Part and whole object. Good and bad objects

Klein describes the first objects as part-objects. For example, the infant at first relates to the breast and only later links this part of the mother with other parts such as her eyes, face, hands, and so on. In the paranoid-schizoid position the mother and others are divided also into good and bad aspects, known as 'good' and 'bad' objects. The divisions are therefore both along anatomical and qualitative lines. Over time the infant makes links between the different parts of its objects and, with the advent of the depressive position, other individuals are recognised as whole (whole objects).

Superego

In her early work Klein frequently describes the first internalised part-objects as the early superego. The superego is seen as an internal object and also as an internal structure that contains aspects of the self and objects and has specific functions, such as the task of making moral judgements.

Concrete experience of the object vs. symbolic representation

In Klein's theory of development, internal objects are at first concretely experienced and only gradually represented symbolically. During the working through of the depressive position objects become modified; aspects of the self that have been projected into them are taken back, separation is tolerated, control is relinquished, the loss of omnipotence is mourned and objects become represented in the mind as aspects of the other with which the individual may or may not strive to identify and assimilate in a realistic and non-omnipotent way.

Later developments

All Kleinian writing is concerned with the vicissitudes of the internal objects but the focus is often on mental mechanisms rather than on the object itself. Examples of papers that place the object centre stage are those by Rosenfeld (1983) in which he describes a patient in identification with an intrusive object who does not know whether she is devouring or being devoured, and by Barrows (1999) in which the patient is afraid of being swamped by a damaged object. In 2004 and 2006 The Melanie Klein Trust held two conferences on objects. The first conference entitled *Bad Objects and What We Do With Them* (School of Oriental Studies, London, 2004) contained papers by Bard ('Intimidation by a bad object'), Couve ('Learning to live with a bad object') and Cripwell ('Possession by an enemy'). The second conference entitled *Problems with Good Objects* (Royal College of Physicians, London, 2006) contained papers by Fornari-Spoto ('Addiction to goodness: is the object ever good enough?') and Patrick ('And when I love thee not, chaos is come again'). Bronstein (2001) explores the topic in her chapter, 'What are internal objects?', but very often it is other topics, for example projective identification, narcissism, pathological organisations, perversion and symbol formation, that take centre stage. It is worth noting a few specific points made in these papers in relation to internal objects.

Separation from the internal object and symbolisation

In her 1957 paper 'Notes on symbol formation' Segal makes the point that the ability to think of the internal object and the self as separate from each other is a necessary step in the development of the capacity to symbolise. Steiner (1993) in *Psychic Retreats* separates the move from paranoid-schizoid functioning to depressive position functioning into two phases, 'fear of loss of the object' and 'experience of loss of the object' [*see* Depressive position; Symbol formation].

The role of containment in the move from concrete experience to object representation

Bion (1962) in 'A theory of thinking' describes the infant's experience of the absent mother as the presence of a 'no breast' 'bad' concrete internal object.

If this frustrating experience can be tolerated, the 'no breast' object can develop into a thought. If frustration cannot be tolerated the 'no breast' is treated as a bad internal object to be evacuated. Following Bion, Money-Kyrle (1968) in 'Cognitive development' describes three phases of cognitive development:

1   Concrete belief in a physically present object.
2   The representation of an object in mind and memory.
3   A symbolic representation in words or other symbols.

Bick (1964, 1968, 1986) advances the theory that before the infant can introject or project objects or feelings, he needs to acquire the experience of having an internal space inside him. He does this through the passive experience of being held by an external object. Bick thinks that he experiences this containment largely through skin sensations [*see* Wilfred Bion; Container/contained; Skin; Symbol formation; Thinking and knowledge].

Omnipotent projective identification

Rosenfeld (1964, 1971) explores the idea of omnipotent introjection and projection, in which the desired qualities of the object are appropriated and the self is identified as being the internal object. Sohn (1985) prefers the use of the word 'identificate' when the whole self is taken over by the object with which the self is identified. Sodré (2004) continues this theme of omnipotent introjection of the object and emphasises the importance of distinguishing between omnipotent concrete identification and symbolic identification [*see* Envy; Manic defences; Projective identification].

Motivation for narcissistic identification

Rosenfeld (1971, 1987) and Britton (2003) differentiate between patients whose narcissistic identification with a powerful internal object is in the service of self-protection (libidinal narcissism) and those in whom it is motivated largely by hostility (destructive narcissism). Segal (2007, p. 231) states that she does not agree that a persistent narcissistic identification can be seen as libidinal. Following Klein, Segal differentiates between narcissistic states that are temporary and other more permanent narcissistic structures [*see* Narcissism].

Pathological organisation of internal objects and parts of the self

Rosenfeld (1971) provides a description of the complexity of the internal relationships between the different parts of the self and internal and external objects, in particular the imprisonment or enslavement of the dependent/

libidinal self by the part that is in identification with the powerful 'good' or 'bad' object. He and Meltzer (1968) vividly describe the way in which the different internal objects and parts of the self are personified and represented in the imagination and in dreams. They and others (Joseph, 1971; Segal, 1972; O'Shaughnessy, 1981; Steiner, 1982; Brenman, 1985) show how the object relationships, often involving perverse pleasure, are organised into a system that prevents growth [*see* Pathological organisations].

The superego as a destructive internal object

A number of writers base their understanding of severe mental disorders on the presence inside their patients of a highly destructive superego based on the earliest internalised 'bad' death instinct-containing object. Rosenfeld (1952) writes of patients overwhelmed by the terror of containing dead or destroyed internal objects that function within them as an 'ego-splitting superego', Klein (1957) writes of the 'envious superego' and Bion (1959) describes what he calls the 'ego-destructive' superego; an internal object that refuses to receive projections and thus impedes the capacity for thought. O'Shaughnessy (1999) differentiates a normally severe from an 'abnormal superego' [*see* Envy; Death instinct; Superego].

Internal objects and 'internal representations' in other schools of thought

The Piagetian concept of representation is largely concerned with cognition whereas both Freudian 'mental representations' and Kleinian internal objects are emotionally laden. However, there is a significant difference between the Freudian idea of mental representation, which is a theoretical construct that is not experienced, and the Kleinian concept of internal object. Perlow (1995) excellently reviews the whole topic in *Understanding Mental Objects* and puts forward the following description of a Freudian and post-Freudian mental representation:

> . . . a mental representation of an object refers to a 'schema' which, on the basis of past experience (not necessarily realistic), organizes present experience and provides a context for both present perceptions and for the recall of past memories.
>
> (Perlow, 1995, p. 150)

Perception is an active process and in the Freudian school representations are the 'anticipatory set'. Sandler (1990) considers the internal object to be a theoretical construction made by the analyst, the object itself being evident only in derivatives such as daydreams.

Another school of thought, exemplified by Kernberg (1976) in *Object Relations Theory and Clinical Psychoanalysis*, focuses on the structural changes of representations during development along two axes: 'differentiated-ness' of self and object representations from each other, and 'integrated-ness' of each.

References

Abraham, K. (1911) 'Notes on the psycho-analytic investigation and treatment of manic-depressive insanity and allied conditions', in K. Abraham (ed.) *Selected Papers on Psycho-Analysis*. London: Hogarth Press (1927), pp. 137–156.

Barrows, K. (1999) 'Ghosts in the swamp: Some aspects of splitting and their relationship to parental losses', *Int. J. Psycho-Anal.* 80: 549–561.

Bick, E. (1964) 'Notes on infant observation in psycho-analytic training', *Int. J. Psycho-Anal.* 45: 558–566.

—— (1968) 'The experience of the skin in early object relations', *Int. J. Psycho-Anal.* 49: 484–486.

—— (1986) 'Further considerations on the function of the skin in early object relations: Findings from infant observation integrated into child and adult analysis', *Br. J. Psychother.* 2: 292–299.

Bion, W. (1959) 'Attacks on linking', *Int. J. Psycho-Anal.* 40: 308–315.

—— (1962) 'A theory of thinking', *Int. J. Psycho-Anal.* 43: 306–310.

Brenman, E. (1985) 'Cruelty and narrow-mindedness', *Int. J. Psycho-Anal.* 66: 273–281.

Brierley, M. (1939) 'A prefatory note on "internalized objects" and depression', *Int. J. Psycho-Anal.* 20: 241–245.

Britton, R. (2003) 'Narcissism and narcissistic disorders', Chapter 10 in R. Britton (ed.) *Sex, Death, and the Superego*. London: Karnac, pp. 151–164.

Bronstein, C. (2001) 'What are internal objects?' in C. Bronstein (ed.) *Kleinian Theory: A Contemporary Perspective*. London: Whurr, pp. 108–124.

Fairbairn, R. (1941) 'A revised psychopathology of the psychoses and psycho-neuroses', *Int. J. Psycho-Anal.* 22: 250–279.

—— (1944) 'Endopsychic structure considered in terms of object-relationships', *Int. J. Psycho-Anal.* 25: 70–92.

—— (1946) 'Object-relationships and dynamic structure', *Int. J. Psycho-Anal.* 27: 30–37.

—— (1952) *Psycho-Analytic Studies of the Personality*. London: Routledge & Kegan Paul.

Ferenczi, S. (1909) 'Introjection and transference', in *First Contributions to Psycho-Analysis*. London: Hogarth Press (1952), pp. 35–93.

—— (1912) 'On the definition of introjection', in *Final Contributions to the Problems and Methods of Psychoanalysis*. London: Hogarth Press (1955), pp. 316–318.

Freud, S. (1900) *The Interpretation of Dreams*, *S.E. 4*. London: Hogarth Press.

—— (1905) 'Three essays on the theory of sexuality', *S.E. 7*. London: Hogarth Press, pp. 123–245

—— (1910) 'Leonardo da Vinci and a memory of his childhood', *S.E. 11*. London: Hogarth Press, pp. 57–151

—— (1914) 'On narcissism: An introduction', *S.E. 14*. London: Hogarth Press, pp. 67–102.

—— (1917) 'Mourning and melancholia', *S.E. 14*. London: Hogarth Press, pp. 237–258.

—— (1921) 'Group psychology and the analysis of the ego', *S.E. 18*. London: Hogarth Press, pp. 65–143.

—— (1923) 'The ego and the id', *S.E. 19*. London: Hogarth Press, pp. 3–66.

—— (1933) 'The dissection of the psychical personality', *S.E. 22*. London: Hogarth Press, pp. 57–80.

Fuchs (Foulkes), S. H. (1937) 'On introjection', *Int. J. Psycho-Anal.* 18: 269–290.

Glover, E. (1932) 'A psycho-analytical approach to the classification of mental disorders', *J. Ment. Sci.* 78: 819–842.

Heimann, P. (1942) 'A contribution to the problem of sublimation and its relation to processes of internalization', *Int. J. Psycho-Anal.* 23: 8–17.

—— (1949) 'Some notes on the psycho-analytic concept of introjected objects', *Br. J. Med. Psychol.* 22: 8–15.

Hinshelwood, R. D. (1991) 'Internal objects', in *A Dictionary of Kleinian Thought*, 2nd edition. London: Free Association Books, pp. 68–83.

Isaacs, S. (1940) 'Temper tantrums in early childhood in their relation to internal objects', *Int. J. Psycho-Anal.* 21: 280–293.

Joseph, B. (1971) 'A clinical contribution to the analysis of a perversion', *Int. J. Psycho-Anal.* 52: 441–449.

Kernberg, O. (1976) *Object Relations Theory and Clinical Psychoanalysis*. New York: Aronson.

Klein, M. (1925) 'A contribution to the psychogenesis of tics', in *The Writings of Melanie Klein*, Vol. 1. London: Hogarth Press, pp. 106–127.

—— (1926) 'The psychological principles of early analysis', in *The Writings of Melanie Klein*, Vol. 1. London: Hogarth Press, pp. 128–138.

—— (1927) 'Symposium on child analysis', in *The Writings of Melanie Klein*, Vol. 1. London: Hogarth Press, pp. 139–169.

—— (1929) 'Personification in the play of children', in *The Writings of Melanie Klein*, Vol. 1. London: Hogarth Press, pp. 199–209.

—— (1931) A contribution to the theory of intellectual inhibition', in *The Writings of Melanie Klein*, Vol. 1. London: Hogarth Press, pp. 236–247.

—— (1932) *The Psychoanalysis of Children. The Writings of Melanie Klein*, Vol. 2. London: Hogarth Press.

—— (1935) 'A contribution to the psychogenesis of manic-depressive states', in *The Writings of Melanie Klein*, Vol. 1. London: Hogarth Press, pp. 262–289.

—— (1940) 'Mourning and its relation to manic-depressive states', in *The Writings of Melanie Klein*, Vol. 1. London: Hogarth Press, pp. 344–369.

—— (1946) 'Notes on some schizoid mechanisms', in *The Writings of Melanie Klein*, Vol. 3. London: Hogarth Press, pp. 1–24.

—— (1948) 'On the theory of anxiety and guilt', in *The Writings of Melanie Klein*, Vol. 3. London: Hogarth Press, pp. 25–42.

—— (1952) 'Some theoretical conclusions regarding the emotional life of the infant', in M. Klein, P. Heimann, S. Isaacs and J. Riviere (eds) *Developments in Psycho-Analysis*. London: Hogarth Press, pp. 198–236.

—— (1957) 'Envy and gratitude', in *The Writings of Melanie Klein*, Vol. 3. London: Hogarth Press, pp. 176–235.

—— (1958) 'On the development of mental functioning', in *The Writings of Melanie Klein*, Vol. 3. London: Hogarth Press, pp. 236–246.

—— (1960) 'A note on depression in the schizophrenic', in *The Writings of Melanie Klein*, Vol. 3. London: Hogarth Press, pp. 264–267.

Matte-Blanco, I. (1941) 'On introjection and the processes of psychic metabolism', *Int. J. Psycho-Anal.* 22: 17–36.

Meltzer, D. (1968) 'Terror, persecution, dread – a dissection of paranoid anxieties', *Int. J. Psycho-Anal.* 49: 396–400.

Money-Kyrle, R. (1968) 'Cognitive development', *Int. J. Psycho-Anal.* 49: 691–698.

O'Shaughnessy, E. (1981) 'A clinical study of a defensive organization', *Int. J. Psycho-Anal.* 62: 359–369.

—— (1999) 'Relating to the superego', *Int. J. Psycho-Anal.* 80: 861–870.

Perlow, M. (1995) *Understanding Mental Objects*. London: Routledge.

Petot, J.-M. (1990) *Melanie Klein: Vol. 1: First Discoveries and First System 1919–1932*. Madison, CT: International Universities Press.

Rosenfeld, H. (1952) 'Notes on the psycho-analysis of the superego conflict in an acute schizophrenic patient', *Int. J. Psycho-Anal.* 33: 111–131.

—— (1964) 'On the psychopathology of narcissism: A clinical approach', *Int. J. Psycho-Anal.* 45: 332–337.

—— (1971) 'A clinical approach to the psychoanalytic theory of the life and death instincts: an investigation into the aggressive aspects of narcissism', *Int. J. Psycho-Anal.* 52: 169–178.

—— (1983) 'Primitive object relations and mechanisms', *Int. J. Psycho-Anal.* 64: 261–267.

—— (1987) *Impasse and Interpretation*. London: Tavistock.

Sandler, J. (1990) 'Internal objects and internal object relationships', *Psychoan. Inq.* 10: 163–181.

Schmideberg, M. (1930) 'The role of psychotic mechanisms in cultural development', *Int. J. Psycho-Anal.* 11: 387–418.

—— (1934) 'The play-analysis of a three-year-old girl', *Int. J. Psycho-Anal.* 15: 245–264.

Searl, M. N. (1932) 'A note on depersonalization', *Int. J. Psycho-Anal.* 13: 329–347.

—— (1933) 'Play, reality and aggression', *Int. J. Psycho-Anal.* 14: 310–320.

Segal, H. (1956) 'Depression in the schizophrenic', *Int. J. Psycho-Anal.* 37: 339–343.

—— (1957) 'Notes on symbol formation', *Int. J. Psycho-Anal.* 38: 391–397.

—— (1972) 'A delusional system as a defence against the re-emergence of a catastrophic situation', *Int. J. Psycho-Anal.* 53: 393–401.

—— (2007) *Yesterday, Today and Tomorrow*. London: Routledge (2007), pp. 230–234.

Sodré, I. (2004), 'Who's who? Notes on pathological identifications', in E. Hargreaves and A. Varchevker (eds) *In Pursuit of Psychic Change: The Betty Joseph Workshop*. London: Brunner-Routledge, pp. 53–68.

Sohn, L. (1985) 'Narcissistic organization, projective identification and the formation of the identificate', *Int. J. Psycho-Anal.* 66: 201–213.

Steiner, J. (1982) 'Perverse relationships between parts of the self: A clinical illustration', *Int. J. Psycho-Anal.* 63: 241–251.

—— (1993) *Psychic Retreats: Pathological Organizations in Psychotic, Neurotic and Borderline Patients*. London: Routledge.

Strachey, A. (1941) 'A note on the use of the word "internal"', *Int. J. Psycho-Anal.* 22: 27–43.

Strachey, J. (1934) 'The nature of the therapeutic action of psychoanalysis', *Int. J. Psycho-Anal.* 15: 127–159.

4 Paranoid-schizoid position

Definition

The term 'paranoid-schizoid position' refers to a constellation of anxieties, defences and internal and external object relations that Klein considers to be characteristic of the earliest months of an infant's life and to continue to a greater or lesser extent into childhood and adulthood. Contemporary understanding is that paranoid-schizoid mental states play an important part throughout life. The chief characteristic of the paranoid-schizoid position is the splitting of both self and object into good and bad, with at first little or no integration between them.

Klein has the view that infants suffer a great deal of anxiety and that this is caused by the death instinct within, by the trauma experienced at birth and by experiences of hunger and frustration. She assumes the very young infant to have a rudimentary although unintegrated ego, that attempts to deal with experiences, particularly anxiety, by using phantasies of splitting, projection and introjection.

The infant splits both his ego and his object and projects out separately his loving and hating feelings (life and death instincts) into separate parts of the mother (or breast), with the result that the maternal object is divided into a 'bad' breast (mother that is felt to be frustrating, persecutory and is hated) and a 'good' breast (mother that is loved and is felt to be loving and gratifying). Both the 'good' and the 'bad' objects are then introjected and a cycle of re-projection and re-introjection ensues. Omnipotence and idealisation are important aspects of this activity; bad experiences are omnipotently denied whenever possible and good experiences are idealised and exaggerated as a protection against the fear of the persecuting breast.

This 'binary splitting' is essential for healthy development as it enables the infant to take in and hold on to sufficient good experience to provide a central core around which to begin to integrate the contrasting aspects of the object and the contrasting aspects of the self. The establishment of a good internal object is thought by Klein to be a prerequisite for the later working through of the 'depressive position'.

A different kind of splitting, 'fragmentation', in which the object and/or the self are split into many and smaller pieces is also a feature of the paranoid-schizoid position. Persistent or enduring use of fragmentation and dispersal of the self weakens the fragile unintegrated ego and causes severe disturbance.

Klein considers that both constitutional and environmental factors affect the course of the paranoid-schizoid position. The central constitutional factor is the balance of life and death instincts in the infant. The central environmental factor is the mothering that the infant receives. If development proceeds normally, extreme paranoid anxieties and schizoid defences are largely given up during the early infantile paranoid-schizoid position and during the working through of the depressive position.

Klein holds that schizoid ways of relating are never given up completely and her writing gives the impression that the positions can be conceptualised as transient states of mind. The paranoid-schizoid position can be thought of as the phase of development preceding the depressive position, as a defence against it and also as a regression from it.

Key papers

The early period

1921   Klein, M. 'The development of a child'.
          Suggestion that the child protectively splits off an unwanted
          part of the mother.

1926   Klein, M. 'The psychological principles of early analysis'.

1928   Klein, M. 'Early stages of the Oedipus complex'.
          This paper and the one above describe the child's oral and anal
          sadistic attacks on the mother as resulting in a persecutory
          superego (internal mother imago).

1929   Klein, M. 'Personification in the play of children'.

1930   Klein, M. 'The importance of symbol formation in the devel-
          opment of the ego'.
          This paper and the one above explore the child's use of
          splitting into good and bad and the use of projection as a
          defence and a means of working through internal conflicts and
          anxieties.

1932   Klein, M. *The Psychoanalysis of Children*.
          Klein adopts Freud's concepts of the life and death instincts,
          the deflection of the death instinct and introduces the idea of
          splitting of the id.

1933   'The early development of conscience in the child'.
            The splitting of the id is elaborated (later to become splitting of
            the ego).

The middle period

1935   Klein, M. 'A contribution to the psychogenesis of manic-
            depressive states'.
            The framework of 'positions' is introduced, the depressive
            position is contrasted with the earlier paranoic phase and a
            differentiation made between part- and whole-object relating.

1940   Klein, M. 'Mourning and its relation to manic-depressive
            states'.
            Manic defences of idealisation and denial are elaborated.

The later period

1946   Klein, M. 'Notes on some schizoid mechanisms'.
            The definitive paper in which the 'paranoid-schizoid' position
            is introduced and its anxieties and the defences against them
            are set out.

1952   Klein, M. 'Some theoretical conclusions regarding the emo-
            tional life of the infant'.
            Good summary of both paranoid-schizoid and depressive
            positions. Increasing emphasis on importance of securely
            established good object.

1955   Klein, M. 'On identification'.
            Continued emphasis placed on the importance of a securely
            established good object. Projective identification is illustrated.

1957   Klein, M. 'Envy and gratitude'.
            An expanded description of both the depressive and the
            paranoid-schizoid positions; envy is introduced as the
            expression of the death instinct.

1958   Klein, M. 'On the development of mental functioning'.
            An excellent summary of the 'paranoid-schizoid' position. The
            relationship between splitting and repression is elaborated.

1963   Bion, W. *Elements of Psycho-Analysis*, Ch. 8.
            Fluctuation between paranoid-schizoid and depressive posi-
            tions, symbolised as Ps↔D.

1987   Steiner, J. 'The interplay between pathological organisations
            and the paranoid-schizoid and depressive positions'.
            Movement between the two positions explored.

1998   Britton, R. 'Before and after the depressive position:
            Ps(n)→D(n)→Ps(n+1)'.
            Importance of capacity to fluctuate between the two positions
            is emphasised.

Chronology

Precursors

The early period

In her introduction to the 1948 edition of '*The Psychoanalysis of Children*',
Klein states that her later conclusions about the two positions are derived
'organically' from the hypotheses put forward in that book. In fact she had
been working on the different elements of the two positions since introducing the idea of the child's protective splitting of his object in her first
paper 'The development of a child' (1921). Here she writes about Fritz –
her son, although she does not say so in the paper – and she describes how
he divides his imagined mother (mother imago) into two, one of which is a
'second female imago that he has split off from his beloved mother, in order
to maintain her as she is' (1921, p. 42). This second 'imago' is depicted as a
witch or as a cow. Linking her observations to Freud's theories about
oedipal desires and castration anxiety, Klein explores how children manage
their instincts and the anxieties that they arouse. These early ideas about
protecting the loved mother by dividing off her hated aspects are the
precursors of her later theories about splitting, projection and introjection.

   In a continuation of this theme, Klein repeatedly draws attention to the
extreme characteristics in children and in the imaginary figures in their
minds. Describing Erna in 'Symposium on child analysis' (1927), she writes,
'Erna displayed all the characteristic cleavage of personality, into "devil
and angel", "good and wicked princess"'. In a complex series of papers, in
which she combines Freud's theory of the Oedipus complex with Abraham's
developmental model, Klein argues that the cleavage of personality is due to
the infant's internalisation of different versions of the mother introjected at
different stages: a good mother from the early oral pre-ambivalent stage and
a bad mother from the later stage when sadism is at its height. (Freud, 1924;
Abraham, 1924).

   At this stage of her thinking Klein pictures the infant as full of oral
sadism and as making attempts to penetrate and possess the mother's body.
In consequence, the mother is imagined by the infant to be retaliatory and

equally full of violent feelings. The introjection of this hostile version of the mother is the basis of the early persecutory superego. Here Klein departs from Freud's theory and places the superego at a young age and before the resolution of the Oedipus complex (1926) [*see* Oedipus complex, Superego].

In Klein's view, frustration also plays a part and the frustrated infant wants to 'bite devour and cut' all that the mother contains, which in its imagination also includes the father's penis (1928, p. 187). The introjected mother is now felt by the infant to contain a hostile penis and this 'combined object' – as it was to be called in 1932 (pp. 123–148) – causes extreme anxiety, a level of anxiety that Klein considers to be the basis of psychosis. In 1930 Klein adds the idea that the child's frustration is increased by the frustration of its wish to know about the parents' sexual relationship.

Klein reasons that the experience of having extremely good and extremely bad internal figures causes the child enormous internal conflict, and in 1929 she returns to the idea that the child deals with this by splitting and projection. She illustrates her argument with material from the play of a young boy who, playing the part of a lioness, asks Klein to take the part of a young boy who creeps in at night to the cage of the lioness, steals and kills her cubs but is then killed in retaliation. Klein and her patient change parts, with Klein playing the part of the lioness and subsequently the part of a fairy Mama. Klein concludes that each part represents an aspect of the boy's internalised mother/superego and that the activity of projecting out these different identifications and the different versions of the id enables him to manage and to work through his conflicting feelings and anxieties. The ideas put forward in this paper will develop into the central defences of the paranoid-schizoid position (splitting and projective identification).

> I have come to the conclusion that this splitting of the super-ego into the primal identifications introjected at different stages of development is a mechanism analogous to and closely connected with projection. I believe these mechanisms (splitting-up and projection) are a principal factor in the tendency to personification in play. . . . The intrapsychic conflict thus becomes less violent and can be displaced into the external world.
>
> (Klein, 1929a, p. 205)

Klein continues to develop ideas about the defences of splitting and projection. The following year, drawing on her sessions with a severely disturbed boy called Dick, she proposes that the ego, in fear of the damage that its sadism might do to the object and to the self, violently expels it into the object. The aim is to get rid of the sadism and also to eliminate the retaliatory object (1930). Drawing on Freud (1926), Klein considers this defensive activity to be more violent, to occur earlier and to be fundamentally different from repression. It is important to note that in her theory this kind of splitting, unless excessive, is necessary for the development of a lively phantasy life and the ability to symbolise [*see* Symbol formation]. However, connecting her ideas with those of others, for example Ferenczi, Klein makes the point that a complete denial of reality, if premature and excessive, will interfere with the ability to establish a phantasy life and a relationship to reality and in her view creates a fixation point for schizophrenia (Ferenczi, 1913).

Klein gradually adopts Freud's 1920 ('Beyond the pleasure principle') concepts of the life and death instincts and by 1932 her ideas about infantile sadism are incorporated into the idea that the infant has to manage the anxiety of being attacked from within [*see* Death instinct]:

> We know however, that the destructive instinct is directed against the organism itself and must therefore be regarded by the ego as a danger. I believe it is this danger which is felt by the individual as anxiety.
>
> (Klein, 1932, p. 126)

Klein agrees with Freud's 1923 idea that a part of the death instinct is thrust out by the infant. This projection not only leads to anxiety about a 'bad' object but the infant's oral sadism leads to it fearing a multitude of bad objects (1932, p. 146). Klein attributes this idea to Schmideberg (1930) and is to build on it later when she describes fragmentary splitting in the paranoid-schizoid position. Klein does not overlook the importance of libidinal relationships in infantile development: 'At the same time, his libido is also active and influences the object-relations. His libidinal relations to his objects and the influence exerted by reality counteract his fear of internal and external enemies' (Klein, 1932, p. 147).

She makes a clear statement about the infant's two different sets of feelings and his division of the mother and father into 'good' and 'bad' figures:

> In dividing its mother into a 'good' mother and a 'bad' one and its father into a 'good' father and a 'bad' one, it attaches the hatred it feels for its object to the 'bad' one or turns away from it, while it directs its restorative trends to its 'good' mother and 'good' father and, in phantasy, makes good towards them the damage it has done its parent-imagos in its sadistic phantasies.
>
> (Klein, 1932, p. 222)

The following year Klein writes about the splitting of the id (1933) but in her later papers this split is described as occurring in the self or in the ego. The splitting of the ego will later become central to Klein's theory of the paranoid-schizoid position.

The middle period 1935–1945

Klein's interest moves to a later stage of development, the 'depressive position', and in her groundbreaking paper, 'A contribution to the psychogenesis of manic-depressive states' (1935), she drops the framework of psychosexual stages and places the state of the ego and its relationships, internal and external, within the framework of positions [*see* Depressive position]. She later describes why she had chosen the term 'position' rather than 'phase':

> . . . position was chosen because – though the phenomena involved occur in the first place during the early stages of development – they are not confined to these stages but represent specific groupings of anxieties and defences which appear and re-appear during the first years of childhood.
>
> (Klein, 1948, p. xiii)

While the focus of her 1935 paper is on the depressive position, Klein repeatedly contrasts depressive mental processes with those of 'the earlier paranoiac stage', later to be called the 'paranoid-schizoid position'. Continuing on from Freud's idea of component instincts and the ideas of Abraham, Klein argues that in the mind of the infant introjected objects are represented by their organs. The unintegrated infant in the early stage is aware only of 'parts and portions of the object world' (1935, p. 285).

At this time Klein considers the overall aim of the paranoiac to be the preservation of the ego and that of the melancholic to be the preservation of the 'whole' object. When later Klein develops her ideas about the paranoid-schizoid position, the task of taking in and preserving a good object, albeit a 'part'-object, becomes a, if not the, central task of the paranoid-schizoid position. In her two main papers on the depressive position (1935, 1940) Klein gives vivid descriptions of the use of omnipotence and denial; these defences will play an important part in the paranoid-schizoid constellation.

The 1946 idea of the paranoid-schizoid position

Introduction

At last, in 1946 Klein introduces and sets out her ideas on the paranoid-schizoid position. Her theory of development is now more comprehensive and integrated. The 1946 paper ('Notes on some schizoid mechanisms') is complex and the processes are more clearly described in later papers: 'Some theoretical conclusions regarding the emotional life of the infant' (1952), 'Envy and gratitude' (1957) and 'On the development of mental functioning'

(1958). Many of the ideas that Klein now brings together have featured in her earlier work but in 1946 they are better formulated, more organised and are given a name. Klein makes some additions in 1952 to her 1946 paper (quotations will be referenced as 1946 but will be taken from the 1952 version unless stated otherwise).

It takes time for Klein to settle on a name for this pattern of anxieties and defences. In the 1946 version she uses the terms 'paranoid position', 'schizoid position' and 'persecutory position' interchangeably. It is not until the 1952 version that she combines the two into the term 'paranoid-schizoid position', linking her term 'paranoid position' with Fairbairn's idea of 'schizoid defences'.

Fairbairn

Klein starts her 1946 paper with a long acknowledgement of Fairbairn's contribution. At first Fairbairn had followed Klein and Abraham's oral and anal, schizoid and depressive phases but, whereas Klein's model contains drives expressed in phantasy that seek satisfaction or discharge, Fairbairn's contains a libido that is entirely object seeking: an object-relating energy. Fairbairn considers aggression to be the result of object failure; his focus is not on hate but on frustrated love. Klein, on the other hand, is preoccupied with sadism, the death instinct and the anxiety stirred up by destructive forces that have, at least initially, a constitutional base. Klein's interest starts from the perspective of how the infant manages its (paranoid) anxiety, whereas Fairbairn's starts from how it manages its object relationships. Klein considers that Fairbairn underrates the degree of anxiety about inherent destructiveness in the infant, but in incorporating Fairbairn's term 'schizoid' into her term 'paranoid-schizoid position' she acknowledges the importance of his ideas about the splitting of the ego that accompanies the splitting and repression of the object (Fairbairn, 1944).

The unintegrated ego

Like Winnicott (1945), Klein considers the early infantile ego to be unintegrated and she thinks of it as alternating between a tendency towards integration and, particularly in the absence of the mother or someone to hold it together, a tendency towards disintegration: a falling to bits. This basic lack of integration contributes to the splitting processes of the paranoid-schizoid position.

The death instinct

Klein imagines the infant to be in danger of being flooded by a primordial fear of death, 'the anxiety of being destroyed from within' (1946, p. 5), and she suggests that the ego might be called into being partly in order to project the death instinct outwards, an activity that she describes in the following words:

> I hold that anxiety arises from the operation of the death instinct within the organism, is felt as fear of annihilation (death) and takes the form of fear of persecution. The fear of the destructive impulse seems to attach itself at once to an object – or rather it is experienced as the fear of an uncontrollable overpowering object. . . . The vital need to deal with anxiety forces the early ego to develop fundamental mechanisms and defences. The destructive impulse is partly projected outwards (deflection of the death instinct) and, I think, attaches itself to the first external object, the mother's breast.
>
> (Klein, 1946, p. 4)

Binary splitting, the life instinct, the splitting of the ego

Klein makes the point that the object cannot be split without a corresponding split in the ego (1946, p. 6). She is clear that both good and bad parts of the self are split off and projected:

> It is, however, not only the bad parts of the self which are expelled and projected, but also good parts of the self. . . . The identification based on this type of projection again vitally influences object-relations. The projection of good feelings and good parts of the self into the mother is essential for the infant's ability to develop good object-relations and to integrate his ego.
>
> (Klein, 1946, p. 9)

The central task for the infant in the paranoid-schizoid position is to make and maintain a separation between love and hate and 'good' and 'bad' aspects of itself and its object. This division or binary split protects the ego from being overwhelmed by anxiety and allows it to hold onto a 'good' self and 'good' object that can then provide the base from which the ego starts the process of integrating the 'good' and 'bad' aspects of itself and the 'good' and 'bad' experiences of the object:

> For I hold that the introjected good breast forms a vital part of the ego, exerts from the beginning a fundamental influence on the process of ego development and affects both ego structure and object relations.
>
> (Klein, 1946, p. 3)

Projective identification

The now ubiquitous term 'projective identification' is first used by Klein in 1946 when referring to these splitting and projective processes [*see* Projective identification], and from this time onwards her focus is on the fate of the instincts and the parts of the self in interaction with the object:

> In so far as the mother comes to contain the bad parts of the self, she is not felt to be a separate individual but is felt to be *the* bad self. Much of the hatred against parts of the self is now directed towards the mother. This leads to a particular form of identification which establishes the prototype of an aggressive object-relation. I suggest for these processes the term 'projective identification'.
>
> (Klein, 1946, p. 8)

Omnipotence, idealisation, denial

All of this activity occurs in phantasy and by use of the omnipotent mechanisms of idealisation and denial. Klein has the idea that the infant creates an imaginary powerful idealised breast that is able to defend it against persecuting objects. In a later paper she suggests that greed may contribute to the creation of this fantasy breast and she reasons that an infant might greedily require the image of a breast that provides 'unlimited, immediate and everlasting gratification' (1952).

While the 'good' object is idealised, the 'bad' object and the parts of the self that have experienced the 'bad' feelings are denied, a process that involves the denial of psychic reality. Klein had described denial in the depressive position and now she describes the part it plays in the splitting processes of the paranoid-schizoid position:

> The bad object is not only kept apart from the good one but its very existence is denied, as is the whole situation of frustration and the bad feelings (pain) to which frustration gives rise. This is bound up with denial of psychic reality . . . possible only through strong feelings of omnipotence.
>
> (Klein, 1946 p. 7)

Klein thinks of denial as an extreme form of omnipotent control equal to annihilation and in her 1946 paper she illustrates this point with material from a woman patient who dreams of murdering a young girl. Klein's understanding is that the young girl represents the patient's emotional part that the patient wishes to split off and violently destroy.

Integration

When love or the life instinct is stronger than persecutory or destructive feelings and the death instinct, splitting is less extreme and the ego can begin to integrate itself and, even if only for brief periods, start to synthesise its feelings towards the object. In her 1952 paper Klein suggests that the infant may experience feelings of ambivalence and guilt even towards a part-object and during this early phase of its life.

Fragmentation

In the 1946 paper and more clearly in later papers, Klein makes a distinction between splitting that fragments (and results in the feeling of being in bits and of having an object in bits) and splitting that divides the 'good' from the 'bad':

> The gratifying breast, taken in under the dominance of the sucking libido is felt to be complete. This first internal good object acts as a focal point in the ego. It counteracts the processes of splitting and dispersal, makes for cohesiveness and integration, and is instrumental in building up the ego. The infant's feeling of having inside a good and complete breast may, however, be shaken by frustration and anxiety. As a result, the division between the good and bad breast may be difficult to maintain, and the infant may feel that the good breast too is in bits.
>
> (Klein, 1946, p. 5)

In 1957 Klein returns to Schmideberg's idea that fragmentation has the defensive function of dispersal. Klein had touched on this earlier in 1932 and 1935:

> I have for many years, attributed great importance to one particular process of splitting: the division of the breast into a good and a bad object. I took this to be an expression of the innate conflict between love and hate and of the ensuing anxieties. However, co-existing with this division, there appear to be various processes of splitting . . . concurrently with the greedy and devouring internalization of the object – first of all the breast – the ego in varying degrees fragments itself and its objects, and in this way achieves a dispersal of the destructive impulses and of internal persecutory anxieties.
>
> (Klein, 1957, p. 191)

Confusingly Klein also thought that small fragments could be easier for the ego to assimilate. In normal development, states of disintegration are short-lived and repeated experiences of gratification foster the infant's sense of integration and of being held together. Later Klein writes:

... the feeling of containing an unharmed nipple and breast – although co-existing with phantasies of a breast devoured and therefore in bits – has the effect that splitting and projecting are not predominantly related to fragmented parts of the personality but to more coherent parts of the self. This implies that the ego is not exposed to a fatal weakening by dispersal and for this reason is more capable of repeatedly undoing splitting and achieving integration and synthesis in relation to objects.

(Klein, 1955, p. 144)

Pitfalls and pathological outcomes in the paranoid-schizoid position

Klein considers the level of anxiety and sadism within the infant to be dependent on a combination of constitution and experiences such as birth trauma and the mothering it receives. She thinks in terms of an optimum balance between libidinal and aggressive impulses. An imbalance, due to feelings of persecution being insufficiently counteracted by good feelings, can lead to extreme splitting, thus preventing any contact between the two kinds of experience. Alternatively the result may be fragmentation and confusion.

Patients who split can become cut off from aspects of themselves, for example they may be unaware of their feelings and their thoughts can become disconnected from one another. Klein gives several examples in her 1946 paper; one patient is described as crying but unaware of feeling sad, 'it was not only that parts of her personality did not co-operate with me; they did not seem to co-operate with each other' (1946, p. 17). In 'On identification', Klein (1955) draws on a novel in which parts of the main character, Fabian, leave himself and enter into his victim. In her view Fabian's experience of parts of himself being unavailable, far away or gone altogether, mirrors those of patients who use excessive splitting and projection.

Klein describes excessive projection as leaving the ego too weak to internalise the good object or to assimilate and re-introject parts of itself. Projection of good aspects of the self, if taken to extremes, can result in subservience to the internal or external object that is felt to be the ego ideal. This may lead to a compulsive tie to the object or to the reverse, a compulsive avoidance of the object. Projection of aggression and its associated feelings of strength weakens the ego and leaves the individual feeling powerless. The external object may then be experienced as a persecutor and, if the projection has been of forcefully entering and controlling the object, the individual may be afraid of being controlled and persecuted inside the object and may become claustrophobic. The introjection of the object containing parts of the self may engender the feeling of having a dangerous controlling invader within.

In her 1952 version of 'Notes on some schizoid mechanisms' Klein refers to papers that provide clinical examples of projective identification: Rosenfeld's

'Analysis of a schizophrenic state with depersonalization' (1947) and 'Remarks on the relation of male homosexuality to paranoia, paranoid anxiety and narcissism' (1949). In an appendix to her 1946 paper Klein uses Freud's Schreber case as an example of a patient with an ego and internalised objects in bits who is experiencing an internal and external catastrophe. She concludes that the confusion that results from this kind of fragmented and projective state can be the basis of schizophrenia, and she later describes such patients as being: '. . . unable to distinguish between the good and bad parts of the self, between the good and bad object, and between external and internal reality' (1963, p. 304).

Klein also enumerates a number of factors that can tip the balance between libidinal and aggressive activity. She argues that frustration provokes the infant's oral sadistic phantasies of attacking the breast, the result being that the infant feels the internalised breast to be in bits. Greed, stirred up by aggression, exacerbates this situation by increasing frustration and leads to further sadistic attacks. Without sufficient gratification enabling the infantile ego to cohere, Klein's infant spirals down: the more it feels the breast to be in bits, the more it feels its ego to be in bits. This is well described in a later paper: 'the breast taken in with hatred, and therefore felt to be destructive becomes the prototype of all bad internal objects, drives the ego to further splitting and becomes the representative of the death instinct within' (1955, p. 145).

During this period Klein's colleagues are also exploring these areas of pathology and Rosenfeld in particular is interested in confusional states and their relationship to psychosis (Rosenfeld, 1950). In her 1957 paper 'Envy and gratitude', Klein explains the contribution that envy makes to confusion, stating that good objects and good experiences provoke envy and draw envious attacks. The resulting damage or destruction of the good object and good experiences reduces the likelihood of there being available a good object to introject [*see* Envy].

The relationship between the paranoid-schizoid and depressive positions

In Klein's theory the working through of the paranoid-schizoid phase is essential if the depressive position is to be successfully negotiated. The achievement of a differentiation between the 'good' and the 'bad' self and the 'good' and 'bad' object allows for the establishment of a 'good' internalised object. Some rudimentary integration begins to occur in the paranoid-schizoid position but it is in the depressive position that it is the main task. Integration is achieved by the ego tolerating a gradual reduction in the extreme difference between the two kinds of experience, thus moving from part- to whole-object relating.

When first introducing the idea of the paranoid-schizoid position, Klein draws attention to the considerable overlap between the object relations and the defensive mechanisms employed in both positions and states that the working through of both positions extends over the first few years of childhood:

> Some fluctuations between the paranoid-schizoid and the depressive positions always occur and are part of normal development. No clear division between the two stages of development can therefore be drawn; moreover, modification is a gradual process and the phenomena of the two positions remain for some time to some extent intermingled and interacting.
>
> (1946, p. 16)

The depressive position brings new anxieties and defences but those of the earlier phase are not only retained but are in danger of becoming reinforced. Guilt about a loved injured object can transform into fear of a persecutor and in Klein's view may even lead to psychosis:

> If persecutory fear, and correspondingly schizoid mechanisms are too strong, the ego is not capable of working through the depressive position. This forces the ego to regress to the paranoid-schizoid position and reinforces the earlier persecutory fears and schizoid phenomena. Thus the basis is established for various forms of schizophrenia in later life; for when such a regression occurs, not only are the fixation-points in the schizoid position reinforced, but there is a danger of greater states of disintegration setting in.
>
> (1946, p. 15)

Even those who manage to become well integrated may be driven to strong splitting when under stress later in life: 'Complete and permanent integration is in my view never possible. For under strain from external or internal sources, even well integrated people may be driven to stronger splitting processes, even though this may be a passing phase' (1957, p. 233).

Klein later reflects that she had presented 'perhaps too schematically' the division between the two positions; some of the complexity of the inter-relationship is reflected in her thinking on the connection between splitting and repression [*see* Depressive position; Guilt; Internal objects; Repression].

Key ideas of the paranoid-schizoid position

The early unintegrated ego

Klein considers the early ego to be unintegrated and its first tasks to be to manage overwhelming anxiety and to organise itself sufficiently to allow the stable introjection of a good object around which to integrate.

The life and death instincts in relation to the paranoid-schizoid position

The early unintegrated ego is thought by Klein to be threatened by the anxiety of annihilation within (the death instinct). This threat of internal destructive activity is immediately located outside the self (projected) and perceived as a threat from the object. Good feelings within arising from the life instinct are similarly attributed to the object.

Projection, introjection and projective identification

Klein's view is that both good and bad feelings are projected out right from the beginning of the infant's life and attributed to the primary object. These good and bad aspects of the object are then introjected back into the good and bad parts of the self and a cycle of projection and introjection ensues. Klein attributes the term 'projective identification' to the process in which parts of the object become identified with parts of the self. Klein's followers have significantly developed this idea.

Binary splitting of the object and the ego

Both the ego and the object are split into good and bad aspects, with bad aspects of the self being projected into the 'bad object' and good aspects of the self being projected into the 'good object'. This separation of good and bad or binary splitting protects the fragile ego from the anxiety of annihilation from badness within and bad experience and allows for uncontaminated goodness and good experiences. For Klein, this binary splitting into good and bad is the fundamentally important developmental step that enables the ego to internalise a strong 'good object'. The life instinct, which is thought by Klein as a force for integration in contrast to the death instinct's drive towards disintegration, is at the start of life the driver behind binary splitting.

Omnipotence, idealisation, denial and fragmentation

Binary splitting is achieved through the use of omnipotent mechanisms. Good experiences and the good self and good object are idealised. Bad experiences and bad aspects of the self and object are denied and may be mentally annihilated. An extreme form of splitting, equivalent to annihilation, is fragmentation: a splitting into small pieces. When the infant or individual has fantasies of annihilation of himself or the object or of splitting off and projecting parts of himself, he believes that this has really been achieved. This belief itself affects the way in which the individual's mind works.

Paranoid-schizoid position as a fixation point for psychosis and severe disturbance

The failure to achieve a binary split, with the introjection of a strong enough 'good object' to allow for the gradual integration of good and bad aspects of the self and object, leaves the individual in a precarious mental state in which splitting and fragmentation dominate and in which the individual is unable to separate good from bad or himself from his objects.

Movement between the paranoid-schizoid and depressive positions

Although Klein introduces the paranoid-schizoid position as the first developmental stage, by using the term 'position' she emphasises the idea of a constellation of anxieties and defences to which the individual returns. Klein thought that some fluctuation between the two positions occurs throughout life. This idea has been developed in particular by Bion, and it is common now to think of a moment-to-moment fluctuation between paranoid-schizoid and depressive states of mind.

Later developments

Klein's conceptualisation of a paranoid-schizoid constellation of anxieties and defences is the foundation of a large body of work. However, her ideas were not universally welcomed and were greeted by some with scepticism and anger. The proposition that newborn infants are endowed with sophisticated ego functions, have innate knowledge of the body and are capable of phantasy activity was thought to be far-fetched, and the idea of the death instinct was and is controversial [*see* Controversial Discussions]. While debates about the capacities of the newborn continue and the picture of the newborn alters with each new research finding, Klein's ideas do not stand or fall by such results, a point that is well expressed by Greenberg and Mitchell:

> Klein's depiction of the basic organizations of early object relations does not stand or fall with the premise of constitutionality and the controversial areas within her work which support that premise. Her depiction of early object relations provide powerful tools for understanding the psychodynamics of older children and adults, whether or not they accurately portray the early months of the newborn's experience.
>
> (Greenberg and Mitchell, 1983, p. 148)

Splitting, projective identification and severe disturbance

A vast literature has built up investigating schizoid processes and the mechanism of projective identification, with Bion, Rosenfeld and Segal becoming

interested in the possibility of using the psychoanalytic technique to understand and make emotional contact with psychotic patients. Rosenfeld
explores confusional and persecutory states (1950, 1952). These and other
related papers by Rosenfeld are collected in a volume entitled *Psychotic
States* (1965) [*see* Herbert Rosenfeld].

Bion, following the theme of fragmentation, describes how the psychotic
splits himself up into minute pieces, expels the resulting fragmented parts
of his personality along with his perceptual apparatus and in consequence
finds himself surrounded by 'bizarre objects' (1957, 1959). These and
related papers by Bion are collected in his book *Second Thoughts* (1967) [*see*
Wilfred Bion].

Riesenberg-Malcolm brings a slightly different angle with her idea of
'slicing', in which a static situation is maintained and fragmentation is
avoided by the patient slicing the analyst's interpretations so thinly that
they are denuded of meaning (1990).

Segal gives an example of a schizophrenic patient who splits off and
projects out her depressive feelings into the analyst (1956). This and other
papers on her work with psychotic patients are collected in *The Work of
Hanna Segal* (1981). Segal's later ideas can be found in 'Psychic structure
and psychic change' (1997) and 'September 11', the latter being a description of psychotic mechanisms in society. Both papers are in the collection
Yesterday, Today and Tomorrow (2007) [*see* Hanna Segal].

In his paper 'Unprovoked assaults – making sense of apparently random
violence' (1995), Sohn, working in the area of forensic psychiatry, uses
the idea of projective identification to explain how some violent assaults
made on strangers by patients could be understood as extremely violent
and concrete enactments of the patient's phantasy of swapping places with
his victim.

Klein's ideas about psychotic mechanisms have been and continue to be
actively explored by analysts and psychotherapists working with children.
Bick questions the proposition that the ego's first action is to project out
parts of its death instinct and its libido. She argues that the infant has first
to introject the idea of an object that can contain (1968, 'The experience of
the skin in early object relations'). Her idea is taken further by Tustin
(1981) and Spillius (1989) [*see* Esther Bick; Container/contained; Projective
identification; Skin].

Projective identification and countertransference

A vast literature has built up exploring and expanding the mechanism of
projective identification. Bion distinguishes between pathological projective
identification and normal projective identification in which the projector's motivation is to communicate. His model fleshes out the relationship
between the mother and baby and puts emphasis on the mother's capacity

to take in, contain and transform the feelings that are projected into her (1962b). A major focus of current discussion on technique concerns the examination of the ways in which this kind of transaction takes place between patients and their analysts in the transference and countertransference (Joseph, 1987) [*see* Wilfred Bion; Countertransference; Paula Heimann; Betty Joseph; Projective identification; Technique].

Symbol formation

In her paper 'Notes on symbol formation' (1957), Segal describes the development of a capacity to use symbols rather than symbolic equations as part of the move away from the narcissistic object relationships of the paranoid-schizoid position into more whole-object depressive position ways of relating. Bion and Money Kyrle also explore the move from concrete to symbolic thinking (Bion, 1962a; Money-Kyrle, 1968) [*see* Wilfred Bion; Cognitive development; Hanna Segal; Symbol formation; Thinking and knowledge].

Pathological organisations

From a beginning in Riviere's 1936 paper ('A contribution to the analysis of the negative therapeutic reaction'), a significant body of work, very largely clinical, has built up, detailing the ways in which splitting and projective defences are organised to protect the individual against experiencing the feelings of loss and guilt that emerge at the transition between the paranoid-schizoid and depressive positions. These are now generally referred to by Steiner's term 'pathological organization' (1987). Meltzer (1966) in 'The relation of anal masturbation to projective identification' introduces the idea of the gang. Rosenfeld (1971) in 'A clinical approach to the psycho-analytical theory of the life and death instincts: An investigation into the aggressive aspects of narcissism' outlines both the deadly and the defensive aspects of projective and identificatory processes. The list of papers on this topic is long [*see* Pathological organisations].

The relationship between the paranoid-schizoid and depressive positions

Although developmentally sequential at the beginning of life, the paranoid-schizoid and depressive positions are now thought of as continuously alternating states of mind. Segal in 'Depression in the schizophrenic' (1956) provides vivid examples of fluctuations from one position to the other within sessions from her analysis of a schizophrenic girl. The patient is unable to bear the guilt that she experiences when she begins to link the bad aspects of herself with the good and has to resort immediately to splitting and projection. Steiner explores further the difficulties faced by patients at the intersection between the two positions (1979).

Bion in Chapter 8 of *Elements of Psychoanalysis* (1963) underlines the process of fluctuation from one position to the other. He comes up with the notation Ps↔D, with Ps as disintegration and D as integration. He ascribes positive value to the move from the depressive position to the paranoid-schizoid position and makes a distinction between pathological and non-pathological schizoid processes. In 1970 (*Attention and Interpretation*, p. 124) he emphasises the importance of having the capacity to tolerate states of confusion and disintegration. Then in 'Before and after the depressive position' (1998) Britton develops the idea further and introduces the concept of Dpath, a pathological depressive position state that is a kind of pathological organisation. Britton links his ideas to Steiner's 1987 paper 'The interplay between pathological organisations and the paranoid-schizoid and depressive positions', in which Steiner describes a continuous movement Ps→D→Ps in which regression to a pathological organisation can occur. In an unpublished paper Britton introduces the term 'the uncertainty principle' (2005, unpublished).

References

Abraham, K. (1924) 'A short study of the development of the libido, viewed in the light of the mental disorders', in K. Abraham (ed.) *The Selected Papers of Karl Abraham*. London: Hogarth Press, pp. 418–501.

Bick, E. (1968) 'The experience of the skin in early object relations', *Int. J. Psycho-Anal.* 49: 484–486.

Bion, W. (1957) 'Differentiation of the psychotic from the non-psychotic personalities', *Int. J. Psycho-Anal.* 38: 266–275.

—— (1959) 'Attacks on linking', *Int. J. Psycho-Anal.* 40: 308–315.

—— (1962a) 'A theory of thinking', *Int. J. Psycho-Anal.* 43: 306–310.

—— (1962b) *Learning from Experience*. London: Heinemann.

—— (1963) *Elements of Psycho-Analysis*. London: Heinemann.

—— (1967) *Second Thoughts*. London: Heinemann.

—— (1970) *Attention and Interpretation*. London: Karnac.

Britton, R. (1998) 'Before and after the depressive position: Ps(n)→D(n)→Ps(n+1)', in R. Britton (ed.) *Belief and Imagination*. London: Routledge, pp. 69–81.

Fairbairn, R. (1944) 'Endopsychic structure considered in terms of object-relationships', *Int. J. Psycho-Anal.* 25: 70–92.

Ferenczi, S. (1913) 'Stages in the development of a sense of reality', in *First Contributions to the Theory and Technique of Psycho-Analysis*. London: Hogarth Press (1952), pp. 213–239.

Freud, S. (1920) 'Beyond the pleasure principle', *S.E. 18*. London: Hogarth Press, pp. 3–64.

—— (1923) 'The ego and the id', *S.E. 19*. London: Hogarth Press, pp. 3–66.

—— (1924) 'The dissolution of the Oedipus complex', *S.E. 19*. London: Hogarth Press, pp. 173–179.

—— (1926) 'Inhibitions, symptoms and anxiety', *S.E. 20*. London: Hogarth Press, pp. 75–176.

Greenberg, J. and Mitchell, S. (1983) *Object Relations in Psychoanalytic Theory*. Cambridge, MA: Harvard University Press.

Joseph, B. (1987) 'Projective identification – some clinical aspects', in J. Sandler (ed.) *Projection, Identification, Projective Identification*. Madison, CT: International Universities Press, pp. 65–76.

Klein, M. (1921) 'The development of a child', in *The Writings of Melanie Klein*, Vol. 1. London: Hogarth Press, pp. 1–53.

—— (1926) 'The psychological principles of early analysis', in *The Writings of Melanie Klein*, Vol. 1. London: Hogarth Press, pp. 128–138.

—— (1927) 'Symposium on child analysis', in *The Writings of Melanie Klein*, Vol. 1. London: Hogarth Press, pp. 139–169.

—— (1928) 'Early stages of the Oedipus conflict', in *The Writings of Melanie Klein*, Vol. 1. London: Hogarth Press, pp. 186–198.

—— (1929) 'Personification in the play of children', in *The Writings of Melanie Klein*, Vol. 1. London: Hogarth Press, pp. 199–209.

—— (1930) 'The importance of symbol formation in the development of the ego', in *The Writings of Melanie Klein*, Vol. 1. London: Hogarth Press, pp. 219–232.

—— (1932) *The Psychoanalysis of Children. The Writings of Melanie Klein*, Vol. 2. London: Hogarth Press.

—— (1933) 'The early development of conscience in the child', in *The Writings of Melanie Klein*, Vol. 1. London: Hogarth Press, pp. 248–257.

—— (1935) 'A contribution to the psychogenesis of manic-depressive states', in *The Writings of Melanie Klein*, Vol. 1. London: Hogarth Press, pp. 236–289.

—— (1940) 'Mourning and its relation to manic-depressive states', in *The Writings of Melanie Klein*, Vol. 1. London: Hogarth Press, pp. 344–369.

—— (1946) 'Notes on some schizoid mechanisms', in *The Writings of Melanie Klein*, Vol. 3. London: Hogarth Press, pp. 1–24.

—— (1948) 'Introduction', in *The Psychoanalysis of Children*, 3rd edition. London: Hogarth Press, pp. i–xiv.

—— (1952) 'Some theoretical conclusions regarding the emotional life of the infant', in *The Writings of Melanie Klein*, Vol. 3. London: Hogarth Press, pp. 61–93.

—— (1955) 'On identification', in *The Writings of Melanie Klein*, Vol. 3. London: Hogarth Press, pp. 141–175.

—— (1957) 'Envy and gratitude', in *The Writings of Melanie Klein*, Vol. 3. London: Hogarth Press, pp. 176–235.

—— (1958) 'On the development of mental functioning', in *The Writings of Melanie Klein*, Vol. 3. London: Hogarth Press, pp. 236–246.

—— (1963) 'On the sense of loneliness', in *The Writings of Melanie Klein*, Vol. 3. London: Hogarth Press, pp. 300–313.

Meltzer, D. (1966) 'The relation of anal masturbation to projective identification', *Int. J. Psycho-Anal.* 47: 335–342.

Money-Kyrle, R. (1968) 'Cognitive development', *Int. J. Psycho-Anal.* 49: 691–698.

Riesenberg-Malcolm, R. (1990) 'As if: The phenomenon of not learning', *Int. J. Psycho-Anal.* 71: 385–392.

Riviere, J. (1936) 'A contribution to the analysis of the negative therapeutic reaction', *Int. J. Psycho-Anal.* 17: 304–320.

Rosenfeld, H. (1947) 'Analysis of a schizophrenic state with depersonalization', *Int. J. Psycho-Anal.* 28: 130–139.

—— (1949) 'Remarks on the relation of male homosexuality to paranoia, paranoid anxiety and narcissism', *Int. J. Psycho-Anal.* 30: 36–47.

—— (1950) 'Notes on the psychopathology of confusional states in chronic schizophrenia', *Int. J. Psycho-Anal.* 31: 132–137.

—— (1952) 'Notes on the psycho-analysis of the superego conflict in an acute schizophrenic patient', *Int. J. Psycho-Anal.* 33: 111–131.

—— (1965) *Psychotic States*. London: Hogarth Press.

—— (1971) 'A clinical approach to the psychoanalytic theory of the life and death instincts: An investigation into the aggressive aspects of narcissism', *Int. J. Psycho-Anal.* 52: 169–178.

Schmideberg, M. (1930) 'The role of psychotic mechanisms in cultural development', *Int. J. Psycho-Anal.* 11: 387–418.

Segal, H. (1956) 'Depression in the schizophrenic', *Int. J. Psycho-Anal.* 37: 339–343.

—— (1957) 'Notes on symbol formation', *Int. J. Psycho-Anal.* 38: 391–397.

—— (1981) *The Work of Hanna Segal*. New York: Jason Aronson.

—— (1997) 'Psychic structure and psychic change – changing models of the mind', in N. Abel-Hirsh (ed.) *Hanna Segal: Yesterday, Today and Tomorrow*. London: Routledge (2007), pp. 83–91.

—— (2001) 'September 11', in N. Abel-Hirsh (ed) *Hanna Sega: Yesterday, Today and Tomorrow*. London: Routledge (2007), pp. 37–45.

Sohn, L. (1995) 'Unprovoked assaults – making sense of apparently random violence', *Int. J. Psycho-Anal.* 76: 565–575.

Spillius, E. (1989) 'On Kleinian language', *Free Assoc.* 18: 90–110.

Steiner, J. (1987) 'The interplay between pathological organisations and the paranoid-schizoid and depressive positions', *Int. J. Psycho-Anal.* 68: 69–80.

—— (1979) 'The border between the paranoid-schizoid and the depressive positions in the borderline patient', *Br. J. Med. Psychol.* 52: 385–391.

Tustin, F. (1981) *Autistic States in Children*. London: Routledge & Kegan Paul.

Winnicott, D. W. (1945) 'Primitive emotional development', *Int. J. Psycho-Anal.* 26: 137–142.

5 Depressive position

Definition

'Depressive position' is a mental constellation defined by Klein as central in the child's development, normally first experienced towards the middle of the first year of life. It is repeatedly revisited and refined throughout early childhood, and intermittently throughout life. Central is the realisation of hateful feelings and phantasies about the loved object, prototypically the mother. Earlier there were felt to be two separate part-objects; ideal and loved; persecuting and hated. In this earlier period the main anxiety concerned survival of the self. In the depressive position anxiety is also felt on behalf of the object.

If the confluence of loved and hated figures can be borne, anxiety begins to centre on the welfare and survival of the other as a whole object, eventually giving rise to remorseful guilt and poignant sadness, linked to deepening of love. With pining for what has been lost or damaged by hate comes an urge to repair. Ego capacities enlarge and the world is more richly and realistically perceived. Omnipotent control over the object, now felt as more real and separate, diminishes. Maturation is thus closely linked to loss and mourning. Recognition of the other as separate from oneself encompasses the other's relationships; thus awareness of the oedipal situation inevitably accompanies the depressive position. Emerging depressive anxiety and pain are countered by manic and obsessional defences, and by retreat to the splitting and paranoia of the paranoid-schizoid position. Defences may be transient or become rigidly established, which prevents the depressive position from being faced and worked through.

The term 'depressive position' is used in different but related ways. It can refer to the infantile experience of this developmental integration. More generally it refers to the experience, at any stage of life, of guilt and grief over hateful attacks and over the damaged state of external and internal objects, varying in level of felt catastrophe on a scale from normal mourning for loss to severe depression. The term is also loosely used to refer to 'depressive position functioning', meaning that the individual can take personal responsibility and perceive him-/herself and the other as separate.

Key papers

| 1927 | Klein, M. 'Criminal tendencies in normal children'. First observations of guilt in children after aggressive attacks. |

| 1929 | Klein, M. 'Infantile anxiety-situations reflected in a work of art and in the creative impulse'. Shift observed from dread of attack to fear for the loved object. First mention of reparation. |

| 1932 | Klein, M. *The Psychoanalysis of Children*. Splitting in order to protect the good object; the importance of 'restitution' in sublimation. |

| 1933 | Klein, M. 'The early development of conscience in the child'. Change in nature of superego from vengeful to concerned with guilt and moral sense. |

| 1935 | Klein, M. 'A contribution to the psychogenesis of manic-depressive states'. First explicit exposition of depressive position. |

| 1940 | Klein, M. 'Mourning and its relation to manic-depressive states'. Clearer and more developed exposition. |

| 1945 | Klein, M. 'The Oedipus complex in the light of early anxieties'. Important link made between depressive position and Oedipus complex. |

| 1946 | Klein, M. 'Notes on some schizoid mechanisms'. Introduction of the paranoid-schizoid position, with clearer delineation of the two positions. |

Chronology

Precursors

From as early as Klein (1927) precursors of the depressive position concept are evident in Klein's clinical observations of the aftermath of aggression in child patients:

Little Gerald, for example, possessed a small doll which he nursed most tenderly and often bandaged. It represented his small brother, whom, according to his strict superego, he had mutilated and castrated while the brother was still in his mother's womb.

(Klein, 1927, p. 173)

After her sadism had spent itself in these phantasies, apparently unchecked by any inhibition (all this came about when we had done a good deal of analysis), reaction would set in in the form of deep depression, anxiety and bodily exhaustion.

(Klein, 1929a, p. 200)

Klein (1929b) observes a shift in the quality of anxiety from dread of attack to fear for the safety of the object. It is in this paper also that the concept of reparation is first introduced:

At a later stage of development the content of the dread changes from that of an attacking mother to the dread that the real, loving mother may be lost and that the girl will be left solitary and forsaken.

(Klein, 1929b, p. 217)

Further important precursors appear in 1932 (*The Psychoanalysis of Children*). In the chapter 'The relations between obsessional neurosis and the early stages of the superego' Klein makes reference to the importance of splitting of the mother imago in order to preserve a relationship to a good object, and 'to shield it from his own sadistic impulses' (p. 153). 'Restitutive' (later to be named reparative) impulses are mentioned as fundamental in sublimation (p. 154). From 1932 Klein begins to use Freud's life and death instinct duality [*see* Death instinct; Life instinct] to conceive of conflict between libidinal and destructive impulses.

Then Klein (1933) in 'The early development of conscience in the child' distinguishes between anxiety and guilt, and already almost describes the depressive position in one evocative passage (p. 254). Although in these early years Klein is guided by the strict chronology of phases, which Abraham had elaborated following Freud, the stage is already set for her major shift from phases to dynamic positions.

The depressive position

Following this groundwork, the first explicit description of the depressive position occurs in Klein's 1935 paper 'A contribution to the psychogenesis of manic-depressive states', which constitutes a major theoretical leap. Klein sees the interplay between phantasy and reality as central; the external parent is introjected in more and more realistic form until experienced as a whole rather than a part-object. The ego identifies with this whole object, and remorse and guilt ensue about earlier savage attacks in phantasy on its hated aspects, now realised to be part of an ambivalently needed, loved and hated whole object.

In 1940 in 'Mourning and its relation to manic-depressive states' there is a clearer and more complete exposition of the depressive position, with greater emphasis on its link with loss and mourning. Klein (1945) then makes an important link between the depressive position and the Oedipus complex in 'The Oedipus complex in the light of early anxieties'. The later conceptualisation of the developmentally earlier 'paranoid schizoid position' (Klein, 1946) leads to some reallocation of phenomena and a shifting of emphasis between the two positions [*see* Paranoid-schizoid position].

Segal (1979) and Petot (1982), among others, suggest that although all the basic notions were ready to be assembled in 1932, it was Klein's self-analysis following her loss of a son in 1934 that led her to grasp the essential links between development, depression and mourning, which are stated first in 1935 and further developed in 1940. Key features of the process are represented autobiographically here, in the mourning of the patient Mrs A, and Klein's own creative surge following mourning may be seen as an instance of the very process about which she is theorising.

Key ideas

The processes involved in the depressive position can be considered under a number of headings.

The new emphasis on love and concern for the object

In early work Klein emphasises the vicissitudes of hatred and aggression, with the resultant problems of having to deal with bad, persecuting objects. From 1935 love and the importance of good objects increasingly take centre stage. The central struggle is now to protect, repair and securely establish the good internal object. Fear of reprisal and 'cupboard love' alter and mature into love and true concern for the object, that is, *for the object's own sake* – the ability to put the needs of the object before one's own needs.

Developmentally this ability to love and be concerned is necessary for the integrity and stability of the self; the individual needs a good, stable and helpful figure inside the personality, felt to reside there, felt as loving and so closely loved as to constitute the basic primary identification around which the whole of the individual's identity is formed. Assuming that the parents are reasonably good, the 'good internal object' is initially a very idealised breast or aspect of mother. This is unstable because it is relatively ungrounded in external reality, but as cycles of splitting, projection, introjection and re-integration proceed, the experience of the object becomes more realistic and stable and is ultimately based not just on the breast or the mother but on the father and on the loving and loved oedipal couple.

This development depends on the mutual influence of favourable conditions, both external and internal. Being cared for in a loving way, without too much frustration, is vital. Equally vital, for Klein, are constitutional factors; the infant needs a certain capacity to tolerate frustration and an innate capacity for love that outweighs its inevitable tendencies towards hate and destructiveness:

> . . . [the internal good breast] is therefore an essential source of reassurance against anxiety; it becomes the representative of the life instinct within. The good object can, however, only fulfil these functions if it is felt to be in an undamaged state, which implies that it has been internalized predominantly with feelings of gratification and love. Such feelings presuppose that gratification by sucking has been relatively undisturbed by external or internal factors.
>
> (Klein, 1952, p. 67)

In Klein's final works envy [*see* Envy] emerges as an important constitutional factor influencing the degree to which the good object can be securely integrated in the personality.

The distinction between persecutory anxiety and depressive anxiety (guilt)

Freud describes 'the fatal inevitability of the sense of guilt' (Freud, 1930, p. 132), resulting from ambivalence and conflict caused by the co-existence of life and death instincts. This early passing insight of Freud's presages Klein's idea of the depressive position. As integration of good and bad objects begins the resulting emotions range from raw fear to more differentiated feelings such as loss, guilt and internal reproach. These experiences are sharpened when they coincide with actual losses, such as the loss of the breast in weaning, or with ordinary illnesses or absences of the caretaker.

Klein's early writing refers to 'anxiety and a sense of guilt', but by 1935 she makes a clear-cut distinction between persecutory anxiety and the sort of guilt associated with the depressive position, which she now calls 'depressive anxiety'. Persecutory anxiety is fear for the ego; depressive anxiety is fear for the loved object's survival. Although conceptually distinct, these are often mixed in practice. Fear for the object is often accompanied by fear for the fate of the dependent self, and guilty concern may be accompanied by fear of retaliatory attack. As Klein emphasises, because the good object is the core of the ego, concern for the object must by its very nature have a self-serving element.

Gradations in depressive position experience are also inevitable, with earlier encounters with it more fragmentary and persecuting and harder to sustain than later experiences of it. Descriptions in Klein's writings of the quality and quantity of depressive anxiety differ along a spectrum. At one end is a picture of a terrible, ruined world, with the loved object in pieces and a sense of deep despair:

> . . . only when the ego has introjected the object as a whole . . . is it able fully to realise the disaster created by its sadism and especially through its cannibalism . . . The ego then finds itself confronted with the psychic reality that its loved objects are in a state of dissolution – in bits – and the despair, remorse and anxiety deriving from this recognition are at the bottom of numerous anxiety-situations.
>
> (Klein, 1935, p. 269)

At the other end of the spectrum, following repeated cycles of projection and re-introjection and the progressive establishment of a more and more realistic internal object, depressive pain evolves into a realisation of the other's separateness. Implicit in the work of Klein herself, this has been made explicit and elaborated by later writers. One comes to know that one's mother, for example, has her own separate relationships, indeed her own mind and private thoughts, that exclude oneself. This realisation, essentially a perception of the oedipal situation understood in its broadest sense [*see* Oedipus complex], provokes a keener sense of need, dependency and loss, and a shrinking of omnipotence. It is also likely to provoke envy and jealousy. These elements are difficult to experience and they are likely to give rise to defences against the depressive position.

The move from part- to complete or whole objects, based on the integration of love and hate

Klein's theory of part-objects is a development of Abraham's (1924) theory of 'partial love'. For Abraham, there are stages between Freud's primary narcissism and mature 'object-love' where the object is related to as a separate whole. Between these stages he thinks that the object is in phantasy cannibalistically incorporated, but only partially – often just the breast or the penis. This expresses ambivalence: the object is in one way ruthlessly treated as something there simply to satisfy needs, but in another way spared. Abraham sees love and gratitude as belonging only to the final 'object-love' stage. For Klein, there is no stage of primary narcissism, and part-objects can be loved and hated passionately from the first. However, because they are greatly distorted by projected phantasy, the basis of love is by definition partly narcissistic.

Klein thinks of the early infant as cognitively and perceptually unable to perceive objects as a whole, through simple lack of maturity. The infant at first 'exploits' this immaturity in order to keep widely apart the positive and negative qualities of his object, something Klein sees as an emotional necessity at this early stage. Thus, according to Klein, the mother is perceived in the form of different anatomical parts, such as breasts, and also different aspects, or presences, which are good (gratifying) or bad (frustrating).

As development progresses, Klein's theory is that from around 4 months of age the infant begins to experience people both anatomically and emotionally as whole or 'complete' objects. Objects now become more real rather than overwhelmingly imbued with the infant's projections.

Non-integration due to cognitive immaturity is different from the active ego mechanism of binary splitting into good and bad. Klein suggests that early active splitting is a way of preserving a good experience, a way of protecting love and the good object from the infant's sadism and from the bad object. She comes to think that, as object relationships involve both ego and object, the ego must inevitably be split along with the object. Klein describes how splitting processes become progressively modified:

> It seems that at this stage of development the unification of external and internal, loved and hated, real and imaginary objects is carried out in such a way that each step in the unification leads again to a renewed splitting in the imagos. But, as the adaptation to the external world increases, this splitting is carried out on planes which gradually become increasingly nearer and nearer to reality. This goes on until love for the real and the internalised objects and trust in them are well established.
>
> (Klein, 1935, p. 288)

The whole object is more complex than the part-object. From being either wholly well intentioned or wholly hostile, mother begins to be more realistically perceived as having mixed intentions. This new relation to the mother is central to the depressive position. Formerly a 'good' mother subjected to greedy, damaging demands was thereby changed into a 'bad' mother. Once experienced as a whole object, the mother is seen instead as a good object damaged by the demands, thus ushering in new experiences of pain and responsibility for the infant.

Once she conceives the idea of the depressive position, Klein links the life instinct with the good ego (good object relationship) and the death instinct with the bad ego (bad object relationship). She also comes to distinguish ordinary healthy binary splitting of this sort from pathological splitting or fragmentation, where the good as well as the bad object is attacked and broken up, often through envy or fear of retaliation. Emotional damage of this sort is very hard to repair.

The centrality of loss and mourning in development

Klein's concept of the depressive position follows from the discoveries of Freud (1917) and Abraham (1924) on melancholia, and the importance that the 'fear of the loss of the loved object' has in human experience. Freud contrasts mourning with a melancholic response to loss, in which excessive ambivalence sets up an abnormal and persecuting relationship with an internal object. Although in 'Mourning and melancholia' Freud still lacks a theoretical place for his understanding that mourning, or rather the capacity to mourn, enriches the personality, he briefly touches on this in 'On transience' (Freud, 1916) where, almost anticipating Klein, he describes how *the capacity to mourn*, to bear loss and guilt, can be viewed as an achievement of the ego, bringing aesthetic depth and pleasure. Abraham recognises that mourning and melancholia are part of the same phenomenon, and Klein notes that melancholia tends more to hate than love, and mourning more to love than hate.

In her 1935 paper Klein relates the onset of the depressive position to an actual loss, the loss of the breast in weaning. She sees this as one of the first times that the infant is developmentally able to link a loss (of the external breast and its internal counterpart) to his own greedy or hateful attacks. She can be read as implying that this is the trigger for the depressive position. In later work it is the reverse; only when the object is experienced as a whole can it be truly experienced as lost. Before the object is experienced as whole, absence is not experienced as the loss of something valued but rather as the presence of something bad. The losses experienced in the depressive position are not only concrete losses, such as loss of the breast, but also loss of omnipotence and loss of the phantasy of a blissfully exclusive relation to the ideal breast or mother.

Klein compares the infantile depressive position with adult states of mourning. She makes a radical new suggestion about mourning at any stage of life, namely, that it involves re-experiencing the infantile depressive position, including loss of the internal good objects of childhood, followed by painful work to renew and reinstate them (Klein, 1940).

Freud sees the melancholic as burdened internally with an object that cannot be relinquished, whereas the mourner manages to let the object go and is thus able to form new attachments. Klein's more complex conception of the inner world allows a view of the mourner as able to reinstate the lost loved object internally, in a more real and separate form, strengthening rather than depleting the ego in its task of forming new attachments. Mourning thus becomes necessary and productive in development:

> Thus while grief is experienced to the full and despair is at its height, the love for the object wells up and the mourner feels more strongly that life inside and outside will go on after all, and that the lost loved object can

be preserved within. At this stage in mourning suffering can become productive. We know that painful experiences of all kinds sometimes stimulate sublimations, or even bring out quite new gifts in some people. . . . Others become . . . more capable of appreciating people and things, more tolerant in their relation to others – they become wiser. . . . It seems that every advance in the process of mourning results in a deepening in the individual's relation to his inner objects.

(Klein, 1940, p. 360)

The key concept of reparation

Once Klein relaxes her commitment to classical theory, her early emphasis on sublimation gives way to the new idea of reparation. Sublimation involves constructive re-channelling of libidinal and aggressive impulses into more symbolic activities. In spite of some surface resemblance, reparation is distinct from this, and is even more different from reaction formation, a defence against underlying hostile impulses.

Klein first uses the word reparation in relation to phantasied attacks on the object in 1929b in 'Infantile anxiety-situations reflected in a work of art and in the creative impulse'. She sometimes uses 'restitution' and 'restoration' interchangeably with the word 'reparation'. True reparation is integral to the depressive position. It involves facing loss and damage and making efforts to repair and restore objects internally and usually externally as well. It is often symbolised, for example in dreams, by building and other creative activities. Effective reparation involves a type and degree of guilt that is not so overwhelming as to induce despair but can engender concern and hope. Reparation itself provides a way out of despair, by promoting virtuous rather than vicious cycles in states of depression.

Klein was impressed by the strength of loving and reparative drives in her child patients, alongside the most destructive and sadistic ones:

> Even in the small child one can observe a concern for the loved one which is not, as one might think, merely a sign of dependence upon a friendly and helpful person. Side by side with the destructive impulses in the unconscious mind of both the child and of the adult, there exists a profound urge to make sacrifices, in order to help and to put right loved people who in phantasy have been harmed or destroyed.
>
> (Klein, 1937, p. 311)

Klein is, however, aware that infants and small children (and some adults) do not have the means either in reality or phantasy to repair in wholly non-omnipotent ways. In 1935 she postulates 'manic' and 'obsessional' positions, with their accompanying sorts of reparation, as part of the normal development of the depressive position. She also notes that transient manic phases are an ordinary part of mourning, aiding initial separation from the lost object. Manic and obsessional repair do provide partial solutions, but inevitably involve some degree of triumph and sadism, risking further guilt and/or fears of retaliation. Petot (1982) reads Klein as implying a subdivision in the depressive position, from an early phase that might be termed 'manic depressive' to a later one that is more 'depressive reparative'. We may think in terms of a spectrum of reparative activities, from more omnipotent and less stable at one end to less omnipotent and more stable at the other. As the child becomes more capable and skilful, omnipotent illusion becomes less necessary.

When reparation is performed in defensive (manic or obsessional) ways the repair is to some extent incomplete, self-deceiving and omnipotent. Manic reparation is expansive and omnipotent, avoiding guilt and pain, and involves magically restoring an object that is not separate but remains in phantasy possessed and denigrated. Obsessional acts of reparation are marked by continuing control of the object and ambivalence towards it; they involve magical reversal or undoing, as opposed to the creative and imaginative activity of reparation proper. In both manic and obsessional reparation the internal mother–father couple are in phantasy prevented from coming together, whereas in reparation proper they are released and allowed to come together.

In normal development a virtuous circle ensues once the infant's growing capacities mean that he can experience giving to the other:

> Omnipotence decreases as the infant gradually gains a greater confi-
> dence both in his objects and in his reparative powers. He feels that all
> steps in development, all new achievements are giving pleasure to the
> people around him and that in this way he expresses his love, counter-
> balances or undoes the harm done by his aggressive impulses and
> makes reparation to his injured loved objects.
>
> (Klein, 1952, p. 75)

Reparation in the external world is often wholly or partly impossible; the child has limited control over his environment, and the adult may regret past misdeeds that can no longer be put right. Much reparation must thus take an internal form, including the sad recognition of damage that cannot be repaired.

At the point of making true reparation, one feels loss, guilt and responsibility for one's attacks, while at the same time feeling that all may not be lost – the possibility of retrieving the disaster at least partially remains a hope. Alongside guilt and responsibility other positive forces well up: love, empathy and a desire to make some sacrifice for the object. As the internal good object is repaired and strengthened, so too is the ego with which it is closely identified.

The emergence and development of the moral sense during development

By introducing the concepts of the paranoid-schizoid and depressive positions, Klein brings out a distinction between two different types of innate morality in human beings, with an important evolution in the quality of the superego. A world view structured by the wholesale splitting and projection of the paranoid-schizoid position entails a fight to preserve the good loving self and the good (part-)object from bad persecutors containing the (disowned and projected) aggressive and hating self. The motto is 'kill or be killed'. Although Freud is aware of the importance of love for the parents in the resolution of the Oedipus complex, his primary idea about the formation of the superego at this time, based on fear of castration, has a distinctly paranoid flavour.

Klein's concept of the depressive position entails a morality based no longer on paranoid fears but on depressive guilt at the injuries inflicted in reality and in phantasy on loved objects inside and outside the self. In Klein's words:

> The child's overwhelming fear of losing the people he loves and most needs initiates in his mind not only the impulse to restrain his aggression but also a drive to preserve the very objects whom he attacks in phantasy, to put them right and to make amends for the injuries. . . . Something is now added to the early conception of good and evil: 'Good' becomes the preserving, repairing or re-creating of those objects which are endangered by his hatred or have been injured by it; 'Evil' becomes his own dangerous hatred.
>
> (Klein, 1942, p. 321)

Klein, in contrast to Anna Freud, from the beginning eschews bringing any moral or educative pressure to bear on her child patients. Rather, she observes that analytic work, which simply explores paranoid and depressive states of mind and defences against them as they manifest themselves in analysis, leads naturally to an unfolding of depressive position morality. What then tend increasingly to come to the fore are more integrated capacities for concern, reparation and forgiveness, the predominance of love over hate and an ability to empathise with the other. Money-Kyrle in 1944 ('Towards a common aim: A psychoanalytic contribution to ethics') and 1955 ('Psychoanalysis and ethics') further elaborates the implications of Kleinian theory in terms of the development and functioning of this mature form of 'natural morality'.

Because of its preoccupation with the development of these moral capacities, Kleinian analysis may be seen, mistakenly, to be 'moralising' in both its theory and practice. In fact a moralising attitude on the part of the analyst (a danger indeed intrinsic to all forms of analysis) entails a loss of the analytic stance, with a move on the part of the analyst towards a paranoid-schizoid mode. The analyst becomes identified with an omnipotently ideal object and projects moral inferiority into the patient (Milton, 2000). O'Shaughnessy (1999) shows how easily this may happen when the patient suffers from a highly abnormal, envious superego, where in the transference situation both patient and analyst may relate as one abnormal superego to another.

Defences against experiencing the depressive position

The guilt and loss of the depressive position involve emotional pain, which is hard to bear [*see* Depressive anxiety]. The degree of perceived damage to the object may be too great, and/or the subject's capacities too small; contemplation of the freedom and separateness of the whole object may also give rise to unbearable jealousy and envy. In such cases the depressive experience is likely quickly to be abolished or avoided altogether, at least temporarily, by the operation of psychic defences. This is an ordinary response in infancy and early childhood, where the depressive position is unstable and fluid but one expects increasing capacity to bear and sustain the pain of the depressive position more of the time as development proceeds.

The idea of paranoid defences against the guilt of the depressive position has proved to be clinically very useful. Paranoid defences involve a return to the splitting and denial of the paranoid-schizoid position.

Manic defences are described above in the discussion of reparation. Finally, Klein describes obsessional defences against the depressive position [*see* Obsessional defences]. These involve repetitive acts that aim at repair of the object. They ultimately fail because the object is in phantasy being treated in an omnipotent and very controlling way. Thus the 'repair' involves elements of sadism bound to give rise to further cycles of guilt and persecution. Like manic defences, obsessional defences need to be continually renewed in order to keep depressive experiences at bay, hence the repetitive nature of both.

Working through the depressive position

Klein referred to 'overcoming' the depressive position, although 'working through' is today's common phrase. 'Overcoming' may seem the wrong word if 'depressive position' is being thought of loosely in the sense of 'maturity' or 'capacity to bear loss and separateness'. However, as Likierman (2001) lucidly expresses, 'overcoming' makes sense in relation to the devastating infantile versions of the depressive position that Klein had in mind.

Klein at first adheres to the ideas of Freud and Abraham on sequential developmental stages. Although one of her radical contributions is her conceptual move to a theory of 'positions' rather than 'stages', in her writings this transition is not fully complete. For Klein, the depressive position is more or less 'overcome' by the age of 5 years or so, with the resolution of the infantile neurosis, although it is occasionally revisited later in special circumstances, typically at times of loss and mourning.

Working through the depressive position successfully depends on the interaction of several factors internal and external to the personality. First there is an innate developmental thrust towards integration as the infant's horizons widen and he can take in more of his surroundings, both physical and emotional. Second are factors in the personality, such as the capacity to bear frustration and the relative lack of constitutional envy. Finally the actual nature of the environment, particularly the mother, is crucial in enabling the infant to face the depressive position. Far from ignoring the environment, as Klein is sometimes misunderstood as doing, she tries to show how and why it is so influential [*see* External world/environment]:

> From its inception analysis has always laid stress on the importance of the child's early experiences, but it seems to me that only since we know more about the nature and contents of its early anxieties, and the continuous interplay between its actual experiences and its phantasy-life, can we fully understand *why* the external factor is so important.
>
> (Klein, 1935, p. 285)

> All the enjoyments which the baby lives through in relation to his mother are so many proofs to him that the loved object *inside as well as outside* is not injured, is not turned into a vengeful person. The increasing of love and trust, and the diminishing of fears through happy experiences, help the baby step by step to overcome his depression and feeling of loss (mourning). They enable him to test his inner reality by means of outer reality.
>   . . . Unpleasant experiences and the lack of enjoyable ones . . . increase ambivalence, diminish trust and hope and confirm anxieties about inner annihilation and external persecution.
>
> (Klein, 1940, pp. 346–347)

In addition to differences in actual experiences, individuals, in Klein's view, differ constitutionally as to how much they can make use of experience to modify their ideal and terrifying phantasies. In the 1950s she explores the phenomenon of envy (see Chapter 9) and its role in exacerbating difficulties in working through the depressive position.

The link between the depressive position and the Oedipus complex

Klein observes that the depressive position and the beginnings of the Oedipus complex, as she conceives it, are both closely linked chronologically and also influence one another [*see* Oedipus complex]. For example, making use of a new opportunity for splitting by allocating love to one 'good' parent and hate to the 'bad' other parent can temporarily solve the painful problem of the ambivalence encountered in the depressive position. However, the emerging importance of the other parent is not without problems:

> In both sexes, the fear of the loss of the mother, the primary loved object – that is to say, depressive anxiety – contributes to the need for substitutes; and the infant first turns to the father, who at this stage is also introjected as a complete person, to fulfil this need.
> . . . At the same time, however, new conflicts and anxieties arise, since the Oedipus wishes towards the parents imply that envy, rivalry and jealousy . . . are now experienced towards two people who are both hated and loved
>
> (Klein, 1952, pp. 79–80)

Klein gives her fullest description of the way she sees the relationship between the Oedipus complex and the depressive position in this same paper (Klein, 1952) in which she says that progress towards perceiving the parents as separate individuals, with a relationship to each other, is both a source of reassurance and security and a source of jealousy and feelings of deprivation:

> The infant's capacity to enjoy at the same time the relation to *both* parents, which is an important feature in his mental life and conflicts with his desires, prompted by jealousy and anxiety, to separate them, depends on his feeling that they are separate individuals. This more integrated relation to the parents (which is different from the compulsive need to keep the parents apart from one another and to prevent their sexual intercourse) implies a greater understanding of their relation to one another and is a precondition for the infant's hope that he can bring them together and unite them in a happy way.
>
> (Klein, 1952, p. 79f)

Later developments

The concept of the depressive position is rich and multi-faceted, and from its early days it has stimulated further theoretical innovations:

- Segal (1952) in 'A psychoanalytical approach to aesthetics' traces the roots of creativity to the depressive position, and develops a theory of aesthetics based on this attribution [*see* Symbol formation]. Segal (1957) in 'Notes on symbol formation' goes on to use the idea to distinguish between the symbolic equation (typical of the paranoid-schizoid position) and the true symbol, which can only be formed once self and object are more clearly distinguished in the depressive position [*see* Symbol formation].

- Jaques (1965) in 'Death and the mid-life crisis' links the lifelong struggle with the depressive position to early and late flowerings of creativity in individuals. He highlights a 'mid-life crisis' as a make-or-break phenomenon in an individual's creative life.

- Segal (1956) in 'Depression in the schizophrenic' also studies the incomplete way in which the depressive position may manifest itself in the schizophrenic, with the experience of depression expressed by projection into others. Segal and her contemporaries Rosenfeld and Bion are interested in the way the psychotic patient deals, or rather fails to deal, with the advent of the depressive position in development.

- Bion's (1957, 1959, 1962a) work on the nature of thinking and its vicissitudes in psychotic and non-psychotic patients is organised around the principle of making and breaking the links forged in the depressive position.

- Rosenfeld (1965, 1987) and Steiner (1993) make particular contributions to the study of how borderline and severely narcissistic patients function in relation to the depressive position.

- Bion's (1962b) concept of maternal (and analytic) containment [*see* Container/contained; Thinking and knowledge] allows more detailed conceptualisation of the way primitive phantasy is modified by external reality, a vital process in reaching and working through the depressive position. The concept of containment provides a theoretical basis for understanding the importance of the environment, an importance that Klein states but does not explain in detail. As the main recipient of her infant's projections, the loving and attentive mother experiences their effect and makes sense of them in a way that allows the infant to re-introject previously unbearable mental content in more manageable form. Failures in the mother's capacity to contain the infant's anxieties exacerbate his anxieties and his projection of them.

- Bion (1963) is also mainly responsible for completing the conceptual transition from 'stage' to 'position', showing how, ultimately, depressive and paranoid positions are oscillating states of mind. He establishes the idea of a dynamic equilibrium that he represents as Ps↔D. In spite of an overall thrust, or forward vector, in the depressive direction, disintegration is continually necessary for new integrations and new moves to be made.

- Britton (1998) in 'Before and after the depressive position' has continued this line of thinking, showing how states of apparent permanence of the depressive position really represent stasis, which is likely to be defensive. In the ordinary course of events there are constantly repeated cycles of splitting and re-integration occurring throughout life, in response to its myriad crises, small and large. At the most minute level, analytic sessions allow ordinary moves to be observed from minute to minute between integrated states, states of splitting, of defensive retreat, and sometimes of recovery and reformulation.

- Alvarez's (1992) work in *Live Company* has stressed further Klein's idea of the developmental need for some manic and omnipotent phantasies of repair, particularly in deprived children.
- Steiner (1993). Since Klein, much work has also been done to develop the concept of *pathological organisations of the personality* or, as Steiner (1993) describes them, 'psychic retreats' [*see* Pathological organisations]. These are structured and stable defensive organisations of the personality that develop in order to ward off either or both paranoid and depressive feelings on a long-term basis. Psychic mobility and creativity are partially sacrificed in order to protect the mind from unbearable guilt and persecution.
- Britton (1985, 1989, 1992) takes Klein's formulations linking the depressive position and the Oedipus complex a step further, to show how the depressive position and the Oedipus complex are not just developmentally concurrent, but that working through the one *necessarily entails* working through the other. It is his view that we resolve the depressive position by working through the Oedipus complex, and we resolve the Oedipus complex by working through the depressive position. Just as in the depressive position the idea of sole and permanent possession of the ideal object has to be given up, so in confronting the parental relationship the ideal of one's sole possession of the desired parent has to be relinquished.
- Hobson, Patrick and Valentine (1998). In an interesting and unusual paper these psychoanalytic researchers succeeded in demonstrating empirically that the distinction between the paranoid-schizoid and depressive positions has validity. Showing videos of patients to trained 'blind' observers who were using a specially developed rating scale, they were able to demonstrate highinterrater reliability in terms of distinguishing functioning of the patient in a more depressive or more paranoid mode.

The above examples show the creative thinking stimulated by Klein's concept of the depressive position. Ultimately it underpins much post-Kleinian thinking. Some particularly helpful recent papers on the depressive position, explicating the contemporary use of the concept both clinically and in relation to wider aspects of culture, are those by Roth (2005) and Temperley (2001).

Critiques of the theory of the depressive position

The depressive position has proved its usefulness as a clinical concept in the analysis of children and of adults. Whether small infants actually go through the emotional experiences ascribed to them by Klein is more problematic. Klein drew heavily on her observations of the emotions, expressed through words and play, of the small children she analysed and felt entitled to extrapolate back imaginatively to the world of infants. This is analogous to the way in which Freud had extrapolated back from adults to children.

Petot (1991) shows how some evidence from developmental psychology may usefully be set alongside Klein's theories. He draws attention, for example, to the identification by Piaget and others of a major qualitative shift in cognitive and perceptual capacities at around the age of 4 or 5 months.

Experimental findings concerning cognitive development can of course neither confirm nor disconfirm the sorts of subjective states of mind that Klein describes. They can, however, provide a framework for considering whether or not they are developmentally plausible.

References

Abraham, K. (1924) 'A short study of the development of the libido', in K. Abraham (ed.) *Selected Papers on Psychoanalysis*. London: Hogarth Press (1927), pp. 418–501.

Alvarez, A. (1992) *Live Company*. London: Routledge.

Bion, W. (1957) 'Differentiation of the psychotic from the non-psychotic personalities', *Int. J. Psycho-Anal.* 38: 266–275.

—— (1959) 'Attacks on linking', *Int. J. Psycho-Anal.* 40: 308–315.

—— (1962a) 'A theory of thinking', *Int. J. Psycho-Anal.* 43: 306–310.

—— (1962b) *Learning from Experience*. London: Heinemann.

—— (1963) *Elements of Psychoanalysis*. London: Heinemann.

Britton, R. (1985) 'The Oedipus complex and the depressive position', *Sigmund Freud House Bull.* 9: 9–12.

—— (1989) 'The missing link: Parental sexuality in the Oedipus complex', in J. Steiner (ed.) *The Oedipus Complex Today*. London: Karnac, pp. 83–101.

—— (1992) 'The Oedipus situation and the depressive position', in *Clinical Lectures on Klein and Bion*. London: Routledge, pp. 34–45.

—— (1998) 'Before and after the depressive position', in *Belief and Imagination*. London: Routledge, pp. 69–81.

Freud, S. (1916) 'On transience', *S.E. 14*. London: Hogarth Press, pp. 303–307.

—— (1917) 'Mourning and melancholia', *S.E. 14*. London: Hogarth Press, pp. 237–258.

—— (1930) 'Civilisation and its discontents', *S.E. 21*. London: Hogarth Press, pp. 57–145.

Hobson, R. P., Patrick, M. P. and Valentine, J. D. (1990) 'Objectivity in psychoanalytic judgements', *B. J. Psychiatry* 173: 172–177.

Jaques, E. (1965) 'Death and the mid-life crisis', *Int. J. Psycho-Anal.* 46: 502–514.

Klein, M. (1927) 'Criminal tendencies in normal children', in *The Writings of Melanie Klein*, Vol. 1. London: Hogarth Press, pp. 170–185.

—— (1929a) 'Personification in the play of children', in *The Writings of Melanie Klein*, Vol. 1. London: Hogarth Press, pp. 199–209.

—— (1929b) 'Infantile anxiety-situations reflected in a work of art and in the creative impulse', in *The Writings of Melanie Klein*, Vol. 1. London: Hogarth Press, pp. 210–217.

—— (1932) *The Psychoanalysis of Children. The Writings of Melanie Klein*, Vol. 2. London: Hogarth Press.

—— (1933) 'The early development of conscience in the child', in *The Writings of Melanie Klein*, Vol. 1. London: Hogarth Press, pp. 248–257.

—— (1935) 'A contribution to the psychogenesis of manic-depressive states', in *The Writings of Melanie Klein*, Vol. 1. London: Hogarth Press, pp. 262–289.

—— (1937) 'Love, guilt and reparation', in *The Writings of Melanie Klein*, Vol. 1. London: Hogarth Press, pp. 306–343.

—— (1940) 'Mourning and its relation to manic-depressive states', in *The Writings of Melanie Klein*, Vol. 1. London: Hogarth Press, pp. 344–369.

—— (1942) 'Some psychological considerations: A comment', in *The Writings of Melanie Klein*, Vol. 3. London: Hogarth Press, pp. 320–323.

—— (1945) 'The Oedipus complex in the light of early anxieties', in *The Writings of Melanie Klein*, Vol. 1. London: Hogarth Press, pp. 370–419.

—— (1946) 'Notes on some schizoid mechanisms', in *The Writings of Melanie Klein*, Vol. 3. London: Hogarth Press, pp. 1–24.

—— (1952) 'Some theoretical conclusions regarding the emotional life of the infant', in *The Writings of Melanie Klein*, Vol. 3. London: Hogarth Press, pp. 61–93.

Likierman, M. (2001) *Melanie Klein: Her Work in Context*. London: Continuum.

Milton, J. (2000) 'Psychoanalysis and the moral high ground', *Int. J. Psycho-Anal.* 81: 1101–1115.

Money-Kyrle, R. (1944) 'Towards a common aim: A psychoanalytic contribution to ethics', in *The Collected Papers of Roger Money-Kyrle*. Strath Tay: Clunie Press (1978), pp. 176–197.

—— (1955) 'Psychoanalysis and ethics', in *The Collected Papers of Roger Money-Kyrle*. Strath Tay: Clunie Press (1978), pp. 264–284.

O'Shaughnessy, E. (1999) 'Relating to the superego', *Int. J. Psycho-Anal.* 80: 861–870.

Petot, J.-M. (1991) *Melanie Klein: Vol. 2: The Ego and the Good Object (1932–1960)* (C. Trollope, Trans.). Madison, CT: International Universities Press.

Rosenfeld, H. (1965) *Psychotic States*. London: Hogarth Press.

—— (1987) *Impasse and Interpretation*. London: Tavistock.

Roth, P. (2005) 'The depressive position', in S. Budd and R. Rusbridger (eds) *Introducing Psychoanalysis: Essential Themes and Topics*. London: Routledge, pp. 47–58.

Segal, H. (1952) 'A psychoanalytical approach to aesthetics', *Int. J. Psycho-Anal.* 33: 196–207.

—— (1956) 'Depression in the schizophrenic', *Int. J. Psycho-Anal.* 37: 339–343.

—— (1957) 'Notes on symbol formation', *Int. J. Psycho-Anal.* 38: 391–397.
—— (1979) *Klein.* London: Fontana.
Steiner, J. (1993) *Psychic Retreats: Pathological Organizations in Psychotic, Neurotic and Borderline Patients.* London: Routledge.
Temperley, J. (2001) 'The depressive position', in C. Bronstein (ed.) *Kleinian Theory: A Contemporary Perspective.* London: Whurr, pp. 47–62.

6 Oedipus complex

Definition

Freud's Oedipus complex, to the fore between ages 3 and 5 years, involves wish-fulfilling fantasies of the death of the same-sex parent, with usurpation of their place in the couple. Inverse forms are also central. The boy's fear of castration by the vengeful father and the girl's fear of loss of love lead to abandonment of these wishes and to installation of the superego. Freud describes all this at the phallic level.

Klein, like Freud, sees the Oedipus complex as central, but modifies and extends his ideas in her new conceptions of an earlier Oedipus situation. She postulates infantile preoccupation with an exciting and terrifying parental couple, phantasied first as a 'combined figure': the maternal body containing the father's penis and rival babies. This primitive version of a couple, phantasied as in continuous intercourse, exhibits sadistic oral, urethral and anal features due to projections of infantile sexuality and sadism. Phantasies about the maternal body link to Klein's new understandings of primary femininity and both the male and female Oedipus complexes.

Primitive superego figures develop early, in relation to infantile sadism generally, not simply as a result of the oedipal situation. The splitting characteristic of paranoid-schizoid functioning [*see* Paranoid-schizoid position] facilitates clear and oscillating division of the part-object parents into ideal/loved ones and denigrated/hated ones. Increasing awareness of whole objects, ambivalently regarded, and the onset of depressive guilt for attacks lead increasingly to the need to relinquish oedipal desires and to repair the internal parents, allowing them to come together [*see* Depressive position]. For Klein, the Oedipus complex and the depressive position are closely linked.

Key papers

1897   Freud, S. Letter 71 from 'Extracts from the Fliess Papers'.
            Freud's first mention of the idea of the Oedipus complex in a
            letter to Fliess.

1923b	Klein, M. 'Early analysis'.
	Klein still using classical model. Oedipal material, often pre-genital in nature, observed in children. Centrality of phantasies and fears about the 'primal scene'.
1925	Freud, S. 'Some psychical consequences of the anatomical distinction between the sexes'.
	Freud gives for the first time an account of the Oedipus complex that fully lays out the distinction in his view between male and female oedipal development.
1926	Klein, M. 'The psychological principles of early analysis'.
	'Incipient Oedipus tendencies' described at beginning of second year. Early, severe and cruel superego activity.
1927a	Klein, M. 'Symposium on child analysis'.
	Onset of Oedipus complex dated at weaning.
1927b	Klein, M. 'Criminal tendencies in normal children'.
	Oral and anal sadistic impulses contributing to distorted and frightening versions of sexual intercourse.
1928	Klein, M. 'Early stages of the Oedipus conflict'.
	Klein's first paper devoted to the Oedipus complex. Idea of maternal body phantasied by child as site of sexual activity. New conceptions of female sexuality.
1929b	Klein, M. 'Infantile anxiety-situations reflected in a work of art and in the creative impulse'.
	First explicit mention of combined parent figure.
1932	Klein, M. *The Psychoanalysis of Children*.
	Sexual development of boy and girl further explicated.
1933	Klein, M. 'The early development of conscience in the child'.
	Superego development uncoupled from the Oedipus complex. Begins to emphasise importance of love/hate conflict, using Freud's life and death instinct concepts.
1935	Klein, M. 'A contribution to the psychogenesis of manic-depressive states'.
	Begins to see the Oedipus complex as inextricably linked to the depressive position.

1945	Klein, M. 'The Oedipus complex in the light of early anxieties'. Third and final paper devoted to the Oedipus complex. Now seen as beginning to be worked through when love comes to the fore, at onset of the depressive position.
1952	Klein, M. 'Some theoretical conclusions regarding the emotional life of the infant'. Reciprocal and beneficent relation between Oedipus complex and depressive position.
1957	Klein, M. 'Envy and gratitude'. Deleterious effects of envy on the oedipal situation.

Chronology

Freud and the Oedipus complex

Freud's mention of the idea which would become the Oedipus complex is in a letter to Fliess (Freud, 1897), where he talks about a conclusion he has reached partly through his own self-analysis:

> One single thought of general value has been revealed to me. I have found, in my own case too, falling in love with the mother and jealousy of the father, and I now regard it as a universal event of early childhood . . . we can understand the riveting power of *Oedipus Rex* . . . the Greek legend seizes on a compulsion which everyone recognizes because he feels its existence within himself, Each member of the audience was once, in germ and in phantasy, just such an Oedipus, and each one recoils in horror from the dream-fulfilment here translated into reality, with the whole quota of repression which separates his infantile state from his present one.
>
> (Freud, 1897, p. 265)

The Oedipus complex – the love of one parent and jealous hostility towards the other, with all its complex ramifications for both boy and girl, occurring between the ages of about 3 and 5 – became and remained the 'nuclear complex of development' for Freud throughout his work. Freud's first full account of it is in 1900 in *The Interpretation of Dreams*, although he does not use the actual name 'Oedipus complex' until a later (1905) edition of the work. Here, as in his description of the sexual development of children in Lecture 21 of the 'Introductory lectures' (1905), Freud describes female development simply as parallel and opposite to male development in terms of object of the first desires. Even in 'The ego and the id' (1923b)

Freud refers to dissolution of the Oedipus complex as 'precisely analogous' in boys and girls (p. 32). This is in spite of the fact that he has already expressed some doubt and dissatisfaction with this 'precise analogy' in papers such as 'A child is being beaten' (1919).

In 'The dissolution of the Oedipus complex' (1924) and more particularly in 'Some psychical consequences of the anatomical distinction between the sexes' (1925) Freud states his new thesis about how in his view the Oedipal development of girls is distinct and different from that of boys. The little boy, like Oedipus, in the 'positive' version of the Oedipus complex ('positive' and reversed – 'negative' – versions of the complex occur and oscillate in both sexes) wishes to kill his father and usurp his place in his mother's bed; this wish to possess her arouses fear of retaliatory castration by his all-powerful father. The reality of castration is confirmed by the boy's sexual curiosity, when he discovers that females lack a penis and in his mind therefore must have been castrated. Freud saw the Oedipus complex as 'resolved' for the boy when he internalises his feared father as an authority, with the promise of true potency offered at some time in the future.

For the little girl the problem is more complex, as her lack of a penis confirms for her, in Freud's view, the fact of her castration, her inferiority and her lack of potency, and engenders deep envy of the penis. She must give up her longing for her father and identify with her mother, with the promise that she will eventually be able to attract a man and be given a baby as an equivalent or substitute for the penis. Freud saw the resolution of the Oedipus complex as leading to the installation of the superego. In boys this occurs through internalisation of the feared father. The girl, castrated already, has in a way nothing further to fear, so in Freud's view she does not internalise such a strong superego. Her main fear is not of castration but of 'loss of love' from the parents, and it is this that leads her eventually to give up her oedipal strivings and settle for reality.

Klein and the Oedipus complex

As it did for classical analysis at the time when Klein started her work, the Oedipus complex remained absolutely central for Klein, in both neurosis and normal development – the central cluster of conflicting impulses, phantasies, anxieties and defences. Although at first she attempted to fit her burgeoning new ideas into a strict classical mould, Klein looked at the Oedipus complex from an increasingly divergent point of view.

From her earliest writings Klein gives clinical observations of oedipal material, striking in their richness and complexity, in her child patients: mixtures of pregenital and genital sexual phantasy material that she thinks is often displayed in the child's play. Five-year-old Fritz demonstrates oedipal rivalry with his father through soldier play, and declares that he had a gun 'that can bite like a water animal' (Klein, 1921, p. 39). In her paper 'Early analysis' (1923b, pp. 96–97) in a railway game, Fritz seems to Klein to be phantasising a world inside his mother's body, in which there is a 'pipi train' (representing a penis) and a 'kaki train carrying kaki children' (representing faeces). Trains enter and exit through the 'kaki hole' or sometimes through another hole representing the mouth, which Klein sees as a phantasy of impregnation by eating.

Klein in 'The role of the school in the libidinal development of the child' (1923a) finds inhibitions accompanying violent phantasy versions of the oedipal couple in coitus:

> Felix, aged 13 . . . had never learnt to overcome the difficulty he had from the very first in standing up when he was called upon at school. He associated to this that girls stand up quite differently, and demonstrated the difference in the ways boys stand up by a movement of the hands that indicated the genital region, and showed clearly the shape of the erected penis . . . the inhibition . . . proved to be determined by the fear of castration. . . . The idea that occurred to him once in school that the master, who, standing in front of the pupils, had leant his back against the desk, should fall down, knock over the desk, break it and hurt himself in so doing, demonstrated the significance of teacher as father, and of the desk as mother, and led to his sadistic conception of coitus.
>
> (Klein, 1923a, p. 60)

These phantasies of parental coitus are felt by Klein to be centre stage in a child's mental life. Many inhibitions and neuroses in relation to play and schoolwork, Klein says, are determined by repressed primal scene phantasies (e.g. Klein, 1923a, 1923b) and these assume a more fundamental place in Klein's conception of the Oedipus complex than Freud's.

In 1926 in 'The psychological principles of early analysis' Klein begins explicitly to date the Oedipus complex earlier than Freud, by referring to observations of 'incipient Oedipus tendencies' (Klein, 1926, p. 129) in children at the beginning of the second year. She also observes early, particularly severe and cruel, superego activity. She is still at this stage trying to stick to Freud's idea, which she is later to abandon, that superego formation is intrinsically linked to the Oedipus complex.

Rita, as early as her second year, showed excessive fear and remorse for any small naughtiness, and also hypersensitivity to blame. From the age of 2, she would insist on a bed-time ritual in which she was to be tightly wrapped in bedclothes. When she began analysis at 2 years and 9 months, she revealed her fear that in the absence of this ritual 'a mouse or a butty might come through the window and bite off her butty (genital)' (Klein, 1926, p. 132). In her play, a doll had to be wrapped in the same way, and a toy elephant put beside the bed to prevent the baby doll from getting up:

. . . otherwise it would steal into the parents' bedroom and do them some harm or take something away from them. . . . The reactions of rage and anxiety which followed on the punishment of the 'child' during such games showed, too, that Rita was inwardly playing both parts: that of the authorities who sit in judgement and that of the child who is punished.

(Klein, 1926, p. 132)

The next year in 'Symposium on child analysis' (1927a) Klein dates the beginning of the Oedipus complex even further back, at weaning. In another paper that year, 'Criminal tendencies in normal children' (1927b), to Freud's listing of unconscious incest and parricide as fundamental causes of guilt she adds the child's oral and anal sadistic impulses. It is these sadistic phantasies that also, she believes, contribute to distorted and frightening versions of sexual intercourse (Klein, 1927b).

1928 sees Klein's first paper devoted to the Oedipus complex, 'Early stages of the Oedipus conflict', in which she presents what amounts to a new conception of it. She describes the Oedipus complex setting in with early oral and anal sadistic epistemophilic wishes to enter and possess or destroy the contents of the mother's body, the scene for all sexual activity, and the seat of the fertile organs, babies and the father's penis. This gives rise to an early severe superego leading to persecutory guilt, that is, fear of vengeance based on the talion principle, for sadistic pregenital phantasied attacks on the mother's body and its contents. Klein suggests that these attacks lead to the earliest and deepest oedipal anxieties in both sexes. At this stage Klein is not distinguishing persecutory and what she will later call depressive anxiety. She is still emphasising the vicissitudes of hate and will only later give love its due place.

Unlike Freud, Klein believes in a primary feminine oedipal position. She gives an account of the girl child's early awareness of a vagina and an internal body needing protection. Fascination with, and envy of, the mother's procreativeness is as fundamental for both sexes in Kleinian theory as are castration anxieties and penis envy in Freudian theory. For Klein, the girl's primary desire is to be receptive to a fertile penis. The wish to possess the penis in a phallic manner is part of the girl's inherent bisexuality. It is enhanced by anxieties and frustrations in the feminine position, but is secondary rather than, as Freud believes, a fundamental position for the girl.

In 'Infantile anxiety-situations reflected in a work of art and in the creative impulse' (1929) Klein explicitly introduces the notion of the combined parent figure – father's penis inside mother – first here referred to as the 'united parents', whose menace reflects the sadism with which they are in phantasy attacked. Her 1930 paper 'The importance of symbol formation in the development of the ego' gives a particularly clear summary of Klein's earliest Oedipal situation, at this stage seen as beginning 'at a period when sadism predominates' (Klein, 1930a, p. 219).

In the years 1932–1933 Klein more or less disconnects superego development from the Oedipus complex, first in the second of Klein's three papers on the Oedipus complex (Klein, 1932, Ch. 8), and then in 'The early development of conscience in the child' (1933). Thus guilt is not only the outcome of the Oedipus complex, but is present from the start of it, and guilt affects its whole evolving course. From 1932, Klein begins to use Freud's concept of the life and death instincts as the basis for her idea of a lifelong conflict between loving and hating impulses, although this does not much affect her 1932 chapter on the Oedipus complex. Klein gives a full account of the sexual development of the boy and the girl in 1932 (Chapters 11 and 12). When she discusses this in detail again in 'The Oedipus complex in the light of early anxieties' (1945) Klein brings in important modifications regarding depressive anxieties and reparative wishes, stressing the loving impulses involved in the working through of the Oedipus complex.

Between 1935 and 1952, Klein takes progressive steps in explicating the relation between the Oedipus complex and the depressive position (Klein, 1935, 1940, 1945, 1952). In 'A contribution to the psychogenesis of manic-depressive states' (1935) Klein begins to explore the implications of her new concept of the depressive position for the Oedipus complex. Hostile feelings towards each parent and towards the parental couple lead to sadistic wishes, which in turn lead to depressive anxieties and reparative impulses. She comes to see that the Oedipus complex and the depressive position are fundamentally linked, with the mourning integral to the depressive position involving reinstatement and repair of the good internal parents who have been damaged or lost. Her early idea had been that weaning was the specific event that triggered the turning from mother to father. By now she sees weaning not as a specific trigger, but as an important point at which depressive anxieties are heightened, as the infant might fear that his attacks have damaged and destroyed the breast. She thus comes to see weaning more in the context of other vicissitudes of frustration and loss. Like Freud, Klein stresses the importance of the inverse as well as direct Oedipus complex in both sexes, with the oscillations between the two helping the child to recognise how the same parent is both loved and hated.

1945 sees Klein's third and final paper devoted to the Oedipus complex. Here she revises her earlier view of it emerging through the frustration and hate evoked by weaning. She has in any case already modified her view of a maximal phase of sadism at around 6 months, by now rather seeing sadism as waning over the first 6 months. Now she explains how she sees the Oedipus complex arising when love, guilt and concern come more strongly to the fore, at the onset of the depressive position. Although deprivation may play a part in causing the child to turn away from the breast, Klein thinks that this is secondary to the love that propels him forward, and the libido's inherent search for new objects. Similarly, it is not simply guilt that causes the Oedipus complex to wane, but more positive emotions: the child's love for the parents and his wish to preserve them.

Klein here examines the interweaving of oedipal desires and depressive anxieties as the child struggles to integrate his love and hate, and she shows how sexual impulses gain a new dimension as a means of repairing the effects of aggression. Such reparative sexual phantasies are of great significance for future sexuality.

In 'Some theoretical conclusions regarding the emotional life of the infant' (1952) Klein describes the reciprocal and beneficent relation between the Oedipus complex and the depressive position. Finally, in 'Envy and gratitude' (1957) Klein describes the deleterious effects of envy on the oedipal situation.

Key ideas

The early origin of the Oedipus complex

Although Freud officially dates the Oedipus complex as occurring between 3 and 5 years of age, and taking a purely phallic form, his vivid descriptions of the 18-month-old Wolf Man's shifting identifications with the parents in intercourse show his clinical ideas moving ahead of existing theory (Freud, 1918). Klein often observes such shifting identifications with the primal scene parents in the play of young children, accompanied by a wealth of pregenital material. In the child's ignorance of the facts, phantasies of the primal scene are based on his own needs (oral and anal) and their frustration:

> According to the oral- and anal-sadistic stage which he is going through himself, intercourse comes to mean to the child a performance in which eating, cooking, exchange of faeces and sadistic acts of every kind (beating, cutting, and so on) play the principal part.
>
> (Klein, 1927a, p. 175)

With much evidence of pregenital phantasies, Klein concludes that the Oedipus complex arises before Freud's phallic oedipal phase. She also begins directly to observe oedipal struggles in children during their second year. She sees it beginning in relation to part-objects before evolving into Freud's familiar Oedipus complex, which is about the two parents perceived as whole objects, as persons. So for Klein it begins with phantasies of relations to breast and penis, and phantasies of the relationship between these two part-objects. At first Klein links the onset of the Oedipus complex specifically to weaning, around the end of the first year of life, when frustration causes the infant to turn to the father's penis and become aware of the triangular situation. Finally, she sees the beginnings of the Oedipus complex even earlier, setting in with the onset of the depressive position in the second quarter of the first year, and following its vicissitudes.

The centrality of the primal couple

The relationship between the parents is central to Freud's earlier accounts of the Oedipus complex (Freud 1910, 1918), but in later papers (Freud 1923a, 1924, 1925) this is displaced as a central concern by the castration complex and penis envy. His preoccupation with primal phantasies including the primal scene is once more to the fore in his late works such as 'Moses and monotheism' (1939, pp. 78–79) and 'An outline of psycho-analysis' (1940, pp. 187–189). However, Freud never incorporates the primal scene and its associated phantasies as a principal component of the Oedipus complex in the way Klein does.

Klein finds ample confirmation of Freud's primal phantasies in the analysis of young children, and finds that the younger the child, the more violent, terrifying and bizarre their phantasies tend to be. She finds that the earliest phantasy version of the parental couple is a frightening combined figure – mother's body containing the penis or a number of penises, besides unborn babies and living faecal objects. This figure, first referred to as the 'united parents' in Klein (1929), is well summarised in Klein (1930):

> The child expects to find within the mother a) the father's penis, b) the excrement, and c) the children, and these things it equates with edible substances. According to the child's earliest phantasies (or 'sexual theories') of parental coitus, the father's penis (or his whole body) becomes incorporated in the mother during the act. Thus the child's sadistic attacks have for their object both father and mother, who are in phantasy bitten, torn, cut or stamped to bits. The attacks give rise to anxiety lest the subject should be punished by the united parents, and this anxiety also becomes internalised in consequence of the oral-sadistic introjection of the objects and is thus already directed towards the early super-ego.
>
> (Klein, 1930a, p. 219)

This combined figure is imbued with the sadism of the child, and excites envy as well as fear, as it is seen as enjoying an orgy of continual, mutual gratification at the child's expense. As the child matures towards the depressive position, the parents are seen increasingly as whole and separate persons. Their relationship now evokes pain of a different kind in the child, more to do with exclusion, jealousy and loss of omnipotence. Seen in a loving light, however, it also provides safety for the child, whose developing ego is based around the sense of securely loving parents and a securely loving internal couple.

Uncoupling of the Oedipus complex from the superego

For Klein, the aggression accompanying early pregenital phases of the Oedipus complex creates already complicated relations with the primary figures before genital impulses become dominant. These complex, ambiguous and terrifying figures, when introjected, become internal persecutors. Klein argues that internalised versions of parents who attack the ego are clearly phenomena in the same category as the superego described by Freud. Consequently the superego must also arise at a much earlier age than Freud (1923b) stated when he proposed it as the 'heir to the Oedipus complex' and therefore its main outcome.

Klein believes at first that this sequence of events defined by Freud can be sustained if the process is located at a much earlier age. Early, pregenital phantasies of the oedipal couple could still give rise to superego figures, albeit more primitive than Freud had described. As she pursues her observations, Klein finds herself putting both the Oedipus complex and the superego earlier and earlier. After a while, she can no longer sustain a view of a strict sequence from Oedipus complex to superego. She observes that 'analysis of very young children shows that, as soon as the Oedipus complex arises, they begin to work through it and thereby develop the superego' (Klein, 1926, p. 133). Eventually, both processes seem to her to become so bunched up in the first year or so of life that she finally unhooks one from the other and makes them independent – the superego advancing, in effect, to the earliest moments of life.

For Klein then, unlike Freud, guilt does not emerge when the Oedipus complex comes to an end, but is rather one of the factors that from the beginning mould its course and affect its outcome. Castration fear is an important anxiety in the male, but it is not, as it is for Freud, the main factor leading to repression of the Oedipus complex and the formation of the superego. For Klein, oedipal ambitions and desires in both sexes are ultimately relinquished through feelings of love and guilt, through wishes to preserve the parents and allow them happy and creative intercourse, rather than through more persecutory fears. For example:

> [Freud] has, however, not given enough weight to the crucial role of these feelings of love, both in the development of the Oedipus complex and in its passing. In my experience the Oedipus situation loses its power not only because the boy is afraid of the destruction of his genital by a revengeful father, but also because he is driven by feelings of love and guilt to preserve his father as an internal and external figure.
>
> (Klein, 1945, p. 418)

New understandings of female and male sexual development

Klein's ideas of sexual development in the boy and girl evolve during her writings, and what will be described here is based on the final formulations expressed in her 1945 paper on the Oedipus complex.

Klein thinks that in both sexes the Oedipus complex begins in relation to the mother's breast. The gratifying aspects of the infant–breast relationship are taken in and provide a model for a good relationship. Thus sustained, the infant can turn with oral desire to a new relationship with a phantasied good penis/father. At the same time, frustrating aspects of the mother–breast relationship stimulate the infant's disappointed and hateful turning away to alternative hoped-for sources of oral satisfaction. Inevitable frustrations and disappointments then experienced with the father/penis propel the infant back to the original object, and so on. Thus experiences of a good and bad breast and penis, and direct and inverse oedipal attachments, oscillate in a labile and fluid way. Loving impulses are reinforced by satisfaction, and the infant's innate hateful aggression is reinforced by frustration. The breast and penis in their good (gratifying) and bad (frustrating) aspects are taken in to form the nuclei of both protective/helpful and persecuting superego figures.

Klein observes the co-existence of oral, urethral and anal libido, which are in her view accompanied early on by the first genital desires. In both sexes she thinks there is an inherent unconscious knowledge of the vagina as well as the penis. Genital desires for the father's penis, mingled with oral desires for it based on the experienced model of nipple–mouth, are the root of the early stages of the girl's positive and the boy's inverted Oedipus complex.

Further development of the boy

Klein is ambiguous as to the very earliest chronology (see Petot, 1990, p. 178), but she seems to imply that very early genital awareness in the boy and its accompanying very preliminary and nascent heterosexual position in relation to the mother is mostly at first overlaid by the infant's *feminine position* [*see* Femininity phase], which is part of an important early homosexual or inverted Oedipus complex. This, according to Klein, is arrived at:

> under the dominance of oral, urethral and anal impulses and phantasies and is closely linked to his relation to his mother's breasts. If the boy can turn some of his love and libidinal desires from his mother's breast towards his father's penis, while retaining the breast as a good object, then his father's penis will figure in his mind as a good and creative

organ which will give him libidinal gratification as well as give him children as it does to his mother.

(Klein, 1945, p. 411)

This first homosexual position is the basis for the male child taking in a good internal penis with which he can identify. He can then have loving genital desires towards mother (the direct, heterosexual Oedipus complex), and can face the inevitable fears of retaliatory castration by a vengeful father, sustained by the sense of loving and being loved by a good father. Thus the inverted and positive Oedipus complex develop simultaneously, and interact closely, in boys.

Castration fear is experienced as soon as genital sensations (and thus phantasies) are experienced, which is very early, when oral libido is mostly to the fore, including oral sadistic impulses towards both breast and penis. Thus the feared castration can occur through biting off the penis. Castration is only one of the dangers, as the frustrated boy infant's aggressive phantasies will also involve oral, faecal and urinary attacks on the mother's body, robbing her of the desirable things she keeps to herself inside, namely the father's penis and internal babies. This results in the phantasy of poisoned, dangerous, retaliatory objects that attack him in kind and threaten the precious things he feels he has inside him, the good babies and penis he has taken in during his feminine position, as well as his more visible penis.

If development goes awry, the boy is mostly identified with a bad father/ bad penis, which he feels as a threat to mother. The otherwise productive and reparative qualities of his genitals are in phantasy diminished.

Further development of the girl

Klein thinks the girl infant has early genital sensations, associated with a dawning wish to receive a penis. She also has innate, unconscious knowledge of an important internal space and the potential for children. Father/ father's penis is intuited as a giver of children, and is desired and admired. The relation to the penis as a source of happiness and good gifts is enhanced by a loving and grateful relationship to the breast.

Without a penis, the girl cannot so readily as the boy reassure herself as to her future fertility, and the mother seems particularly magical and powerful. The little girl's phantasies and emotions are predominantly built around her own and her mother's inner world of objects. Her anxieties and doubts about herself intensify her wish to enter and rob the mother's body of its riches, and her persecutory fears about her own body contents are hence all the stronger. The girl's leading anxiety is thus the fear of being attacked and robbed.

The girl's desire to possess a penis and to be a boy is part of her inherent bisexuality, and equivalent to the boy's desire to be a woman. Her wish for her own penis is in Klein's view, however, secondary to her desire to be fertilised by the father's penis, and is enhanced by frustrations in the feminine position. This is thus very different from Freud's idea that the girl has a primary desire to have the penis for herself and eventually has to accept her femininity, and her ability to produce a child, simply as a substitute. In the view of the contemporary Kleinian Ronald Britton (2003) there is evidence that Freud's ideas about the female castration complex and the centrality of penis envy were overvalued and based on the analysis of one case, his daughter Anna.

The Oedipus complex and the depressive position

Klein observes that the depressive position, and the beginnings of the Oedipus complex as she conceives it, are both closely linked chronologically and also influence one another [*see* Depressive position]. For example, in 'Mourning and its relation to manic-depressive states' she writes: 'The sorrow and concern about the feared loss of the "good" objects, that is to say, the depressive position, is, in my experience, the deepest source of the painful conflicts in the Oedipus situation' (Klein, 1940, p. 345).

In the paranoid-schizoid position [*see* Paranoid-schizoid position] there is minimal triangularity because in the infant's experience the good and satisfying mother disappears when he is frustrated, and a different object intrudes in her place, whether it is the bad mother, the father or another object. The infant, in moments of experiencing his good object, is in full possession of it. However, as cognitive and emotional potentials develop, leading to the onset of the depressive position, the infant no longer wholly possesses the good object, but begins to witness a relationship between the parents, in however primitive or partial a form at first.

Turning to father is seen as a result of both the inevitable ambivalence towards mother, and also the inherent, lively drive towards embracing a new object. Klein sees the positive and inverted Oedipus complex as ordinarily oscillating:

> Each object, therefore, is in turn liable to become at times good, at times bad. This movement to and fro between various aspects of the primary imagos implies a close interaction between the early stages of the inverted and positive Oedipus complex.
>
> (Klein, 1945, p. 409)

Making use of a new opportunity for splitting by allocating love to one 'good' parent and hate to the 'bad' other parent will only temporarily solve the painful problem of the ambivalence encountered in the depressive position. It is increasingly realised that the same parent who is the object of oedipal desire in one version is the hated rival in the other. Love and guilt-driven reparative drives then push the individual increasingly towards allowing the couple to come together and relinquishing his desires to over-throw and possess. The emphasis is again different from Freud's: for Klein, the Oedipus complex is eventually resolved primarily through love, rather than through fear of castration and other forms of punishment.

Even before she has worked out the theory of the depressive position, Klein sees the need to tolerate the 'deprivations' of the oedipal situation as central to mental health:

> At a very early age, children become acquainted with reality through the deprivations which it imposes on them. They defend themselves against reality by repudiating it. The fundamental thing, however, and the criterion of all later capacity for adaptation to reality, is the degree in which they are able to tolerate the deprivations that result from the Oedipus situation.
>
> (Klein, 1926, p. 128)

In a similar vein, using a literary source, and presaging her later more profound conceptualisation of the centrality of the loving internal couple, Klein in 'Infantile anxiety-situations reflected in a work of art and in the creative impulse' refers to the child's violent attempts in phantasy to separate the parents in intercourse as leading to 'a rent in the fabric of the world' (Klein, 1929, p. 211).

Klein gives her fullest description of the way she sees the relationship between the Oedipus complex and the depressive position in 'Some theoretical conclusions regarding the emotional life of the infant' (1952), in which she says that progress towards perceiving the parents as separate individuals, with a relationship to each other, is both a source of reassurance and security and a source of jealousy and feelings of deprivation:

> The infant's capacity to enjoy at the same time the relation to *both* parents, which is an important feature in his mental life and conflicts with his desires, prompted by jealousy and anxiety, to separate them, depends on his feeling that they are separate individuals. This more integrated relation to the parents (which is different from the com-pulsive need to keep the parents apart from one another and to prevent their sexual intercourse) implies a greater understanding of their relation to one another and is a precondition for the infant's hope that he can bring them together and unite them in a happy way.
>
> (Klein, 1952, p. 79f)

Effects of envy on the oedipal situation

It is in Klein's 1957 paper 'Envy and gratitude' that her theories surrounding envy are most fully worked out. Here she describes in detail the problems encountered in the Oedipus situation when envy, in Klein's view an oral and anal-sadistic expression of destructive impulses, dominates the personality. Klein believes that the degree of envy in the personality has a constitutional basis, but that it is exacerbated by deprivation [*see* Envy]. The internalisation of the primal good object, the maternal good breast, forms in Klein's view the core of the ego. An envious attitude to the breast will mar its perceived goodness and will lead to confusion between good and bad aspects of the breast/mother. Without a clear initial division between good and bad, love and hate, a core good object cannot be securely established. In turn, the normal progression towards depressive position integration is curtailed, and the individual remains in an abnormally paranoid and grievance-laden state. This gives rise to further vicious cycles and a chronic difficulty in securely internalising a good object.

An insecure early relationship with the mother resulting from envy means that rivalry with the father arises prematurely, with father perceived as a hostile intruder. Primitive phantasies of the combined parental object take on a particularly hateful and anxiety-provoking form. In contrast, when the primal relationship with mother is strong and good, the exclusive relationship can be more easily mourned. Father and siblings can be shared with mother, and love as well as hate can be experienced towards these rivals. Klein feels that excessive envy interferes with adequate oral gratification and tends to trigger premature and insecure genitality, with a compulsive element, for example, leading to obsessive masturbation or promiscuity.

When envy is not excessive, jealousy in the oedipal situation becomes a means of working it through. When jealousy is experienced, hostile feelings are directed not against the primal object but against the rivals, providing an element of distribution. Also, as these new relations develop, they give rise to love and provide new sources of gratification. Bearing in mind that the object of envy is largely oral, the shift from oral to genital desires tends to help by reducing the importance of the mother as a source of oral enjoyment. Jealousy is felt generally as more acceptable, and gives rise to much less guilt than the primary envy of the first good object.

When envy is excessive the girl's premature turn towards the father is based more on hate and envy of the mother and mother's possessions than on love for the father. The envy is carried over into the oedipal situation, so that father or his penis has become an appendage of mother's that the girl wishes to annexe. Klein suggests that in later life every success in relation to men will then be experienced as a victory over another woman, and the conquest and possession of a man may have to be repeated.

In the boy, if envy of the breast is strong, impairing oral gratification, Klein suggests that hatred and anxieties are transferred to the vagina, potentially with severe difficulties in the genital attitude towards women. Klein believes that strong penis envy in women is of oral origin and can be traced back to envy of the breast. In both sexes, she thinks that envy plays a part in the desire to take away the attributes of the other sex, as well as to possess or to spoil those of the parent of the same sex.

Later developments

Klein's developments of Freud's Oedipus complex theory have proved very fruitful in post-Kleinian thinking. The following are some important further developments of her ideas.

Bion: Attacks on linking

Wilfred Bion (1962, 1963) approaches the Oedipus myth from a different vertex to that of the sexual components, without excluding their central importance. He is concerned with the vicissitudes of curiosity and knowledge-seeking (the K link), in Bion's view as fundamental and innate as Love (L) and Hate (H), and leading to knowledge of both external and psychic reality. Bion suggests that in the Oedipus myth, as in the myths of the garden of Eden and the tower of Babel, there is a common theme of an omniscient, god-like superego figure who proscribes as sinful, then punishes, the protagonist's search for truth. Bion sees the oedipal myth as representing a universal preconception that is also a foundation for mental growth. The individual's private oedipal myth leads him or her to investigate the parental couple, discover the procreative link between them and the way in which this differs from the parent–child relationship. Destructive forces in the personality (represented by the omniscient figure in the myths) oppose this search for knowledge.

For Bion, every link at its most fundamental level is equated with the relationships nipple–mouth and/or penis–vagina. His theory of the container, in its broadest form, sees all human contact in terms of container/contained links, some mutually adaptive, others violent or constricting. The coupling of penis and vagina, or mouth and nipple, is taken by Bion (1962) as a prototype of the way mental objects are put together, one inside the other. Thus putting experiences into thoughts, and thoughts into words, entails a repeated chain of linking processes modelled on physical intercourse between two bodily parts. These by their very nature evoke aspects of the oedipal situation – the coupling parents, the dependent child. If knowledge of this cannot be borne, any sort of link in the mind will have to be attacked, resulting in severe disorders of thinking.

Bion sees attacks on linking as resulting from envy and sadism, and stemming from what he calls the psychotic part of the personality (Bion, 1957, 1959). He also suggests that failure of containment in the infantile situation leads to deficits in the individual's own capacity to bear and contain difficult knowledge. Thus both innate and environmental factors influence the problem. In these situations, attacks may be directed not just against pieces of knowledge, but against the knowledge-seeking mental apparatus, or ego function, itself. They result in fragmentation and dispersal of the elements of the Oedipus complex. This is seen in its most extreme form in psychosis. One of the difficulties in the analysis of psychotics is being able to recognise the oedipal fragments scattered in time, and to reveal their interconnections to the patient.

Money-Kyrle: The facts of life

In two key papers on what he calls 'cognitive development' Roger Money-Kyrle (1968, 1971) extends some of Bion's ideas concerning the foundations of mature thinking. Money-Kyrle postulates our need early in life to discover, or recognise, certain basic truths or 'facts of life'. These truths exist first as preconceptions or unconscious templates to which, in Bion's (1962, 1963) terms, 'realisations' have to be 'mated'. The first task is properly to recognise the breast/nipple and its relationship to the mouth. From this basic constellation, in Money-Kyrle's view, concepts of penis and vagina and their relation to each other naturally 'bud off'. The ingredients are thus present for a basic awareness of parental intercourse, and the way babies are made, very early in life.

Money-Kyrle suggests, following Bion, that there is an innate tendency towards discovering the true nature of the mother–baby and mother–father relationships in this way. At the same time, forces such as primal envy will prevent or distort the formation of basic concepts, leaving at least some parts of the mind ignorant or 'cognitively retarded'. Projective identification may then be used to confuse the mother–baby relationship with the parental one. When the creative nature of the parental intercourse is not properly recognised, the Oedipus complex cannot be fully worked through:

> . . . if he 'recognises' his own fantasy of getting totally inside his mother as an example of intercourse, the recognition is really a misconception likely to be used to counteract the true conception, which is beginning to form, of his parents' creative relation to each other.
>
> (Money-Kyrle, 1971, pp. 445–446)

> . . . the more firmly a child's first good object is established inside him . . . the easier it will be for him to conceptualise his parents' intercourse as a

supremely creative act . . . he will have much less incentive to construct a misconception of intercourse as a by-product of fantasies of projective identification.

(Money-Kyrle, 1971, p. 446)

Steiner: Turning a blind eye, and retreat to omnipotence

John Steiner re-examines the Oedipus myth as told by Sophocles, drawing on the work of the classicist Philip Vellacott. He shows how the Oedipus of the plays demonstrates first the phenomenon of 'turning a blind eye' to what he has done, and then later defends against his unbearable guilt by a 'turning to omnipotence'. Steiner demonstrates through clinical illustrations how these mechanisms are common ways of defending against the guilt and mourning associated with working through the Oedipus complex (Steiner, 1985, 1990). He further shows how these mechanisms can form part of pathological organisations of the personality [*see* Pathological organisations] set up to evade psychic reality (Steiner, 1993).

Britton: The notion of triangular space

Ronald Britton (1989, 1998) takes a further step from Klein's link between the Oedipus complex and the depressive position, by showing how the working through of the one is contingent on the working through of the other:

> The depressive position is provoked by, and establishes, that greater knowledge of the object which includes awareness of its continuity of existence in time and space, and also therefore of the other relationships of the object implied by that realisation. The Oedipus situation exemplifies that knowledge. Hence the depressive position cannot be worked through without the Oedipus complex being worked through, and vice versa.
>
> (Britton, 1998, p. 33)

Britton stresses the importance of the internal parental couple in his notion of triangular space and an observing, or third position, in the mind:

> The acknowledgement by the child of the parents' relationship with each other unites his psychic world, limiting it to one world shared with his two parents in which different object relationships can exist. The closure of the oedipal triangle by the recognition of the link joining the parents provides a limiting boundary for the internal world. It creates what I call "triangular space" – i.e., a space bounded by the three persons of the oedipal situation and all their potential relationships. It

includes, therefore, the possibility of being a participant in a relationship and observed by a third person as well as being an observer of
a relationship between two people.

(Britton, 1989, p. 86)

A third position then comes into existence from which object relationships can be observed. Given this, we can also envisage *being* observed.
This provides us with a capacity for seeing ourselves in interaction with
others and for entertaining another point of view whilst retaining our
own, for reflecting on ourselves whilst being ourselves.

(Britton, 1989, p. 87)

Britton shows how this third position cannot develop properly if the
encounter with the parental relationship starts to take place at a time when
the individual has not, for whatever reason, established a secure maternal
object, with serious consequences both for the ability to think and reflect
and, when in analysis, to tolerate the analyst's thinking mind. In less
disturbed patients he also describes the formation of 'oedipal illusions' in
order to deny the reality of the parental relationship.

Britton extends his ideas about triangular space into considering why
some patients cannot tolerate in some cases objectivity and in others
subjectivity. The former demand close empathic understanding, becoming
disturbed by the analyst's objective thinking about them; contact with the
analyst's independent psychic reality seems catastrophically to threaten
their existence. The reverse applies to patients who seek a solely intellectual
understanding, characterised by hypertrophied rationality, and avoid any
emotional experience.

Britton further links these situations to the clinical phenomena of thin-
and thick-skinned narcissism. He theorises the basic problem as a failure of
maternal containment (for reasons in mother, infant or both). Without a
securely based primary object, the third element, father, is either experienced as the incarnation of malignant misunderstanding, to be kept apart
psychically from mother at all costs, or is idealised and clung to. In either
case, the problem is that any sort of coupling, bringing the two elements
together in any way, threatens the patient with a terrifying sense of chaos.
As it is the aim of psychoanalysis to integrate subjective experience and
objective understanding, the very process of analysis is felt to be a threat to
this group of patients.

Sodré: Obsessional mechanisms and the Oedipus complex

Ignês Sodré (1994) links two different sorts of obsessional defence with
difficulties in working through the oedipal situation. She suggests that
obsessional defences that involve rigid adherence to sameness, with the need

for rituals against contamination and disorder, belong to a schizoid way of functioning in which splitting mechanisms are used for the preservation of an exclusively two-person relationship with the object. When, on the other hand, tormenting obsessional doubt predominates, the underlying conflict is due not only to ambivalence and to the difficulty of making a choice between objects, but also to the presence in the patient's mind of the parental couple with whom the patient is, unconsciously, excessively involved. In the first case the triangular situation is eliminated, but in the second it is pervasively present, to the extent that it seems impossible to establish an undisturbed coupling of any sort.

Birksted-Breen: Phallus and penis-as-link

Birksted-Breen (1996) explores the difference between a phantasied phallus and an internalised 'penis-as-link', which provides a structuring function that promotes mental space and thinking. Introjection of the penis-as-link is, for Birksted-Breen, associated with recognition of the full oedipal situation, including the parental relationship and the differences between the sexes. Fantasies of possessing a phallus in Birksted-Breen's sense represent an illusory completeness and a state that is free of desire. While the phallus is the possession of neither sex, the boy or man can more easily believe that his penis gives him possession of it. The girl or woman may adopt a phallic position to deny any lack, and will tend to denigrate men while apparently idealising masculinity.

Phallic sexuality is based on the identification by man or woman with the phallus in order to deny lack and the panoply of feelings associated with it, including need, envy and guilt. It is a narcissistic position that involves denial and attack of the penis-as-link and the parental couple. Birksted-Breen further remarks that Freud's concept of penis envy is frequently phallus envy, which is what gives that envy in some women the intensity of its illusory quality. The phallus is a symbolic equation, whereas the penis-as-link belongs to the area of true symbolisation and is internalised as a function.

Rusbridger: The Oedipus complex structuring the mind; fragments of the Oedipus complex

Richard Rusbridger (2004) in a useful review article about the Oedipus complex points out that the psychoanalytic theory of the Oedipus complex describes a fundamental dynamic of the mind, which in turn structures the mind. The structure turns on the subject's response to witnessing a relationship, believed to be creative as it produced him, of which he is the product and from which he is excluded. This structure and dynamic operate in the mind on all levels of scale, both intrapyschically and interpsychically.

They function on every level of psychosexual development, and determine the form that this development takes. This pattern is present, on different scales, throughout mental life. In this, Rusbridger suggests that it resembles *fractals*, the geometrical curves described by Mandelbrot (1982) that have the property of self-similarity: their basic patterns are repeated at ever-decreasing sizes. (An example of this in nature is a tree: the same pattern of the trunk dividing into branches occurs when each branch subdivides into smaller branches, and when each branch divides further into twigs.)

Many functions of the mind seem to depend on our response to the fact of the separateness and creativity of others, ultimately represented by the sexual pairing of our parents. If we can tolerate and identify with this pairing, these functions include sanity, the ability to think, to symbolise, to be artistically creative, to lead a fulfilling sexual life. If we cannot tolerate it, what will be observed in the mind include narcissistic states, perversion and psychosis. In narcissism, for example, we assert *our* centrality, superiority and creativity and deny the creativity of the parental couple. The centrality of the Oedipus complex in structuring the mind also means that analysing the patient's characteristic reactions to the Oedipus complex is the core task of analysis.

Rusbridger (2004) argues that these reactions can be seen most clearly in the patient's response to the work of analysis. He suggests that *the emergence of meaning* in analysis is a key oedipal moment, for both the analyst and the patient, and as such tends to be attacked. Because of these ubiquitous attacks Rusbridger points out that the oedipal situation in analysis does not consist in only those moments when patterns are evident that one would call 'oedipal'. In fact very often, because of the defences that are deployed against the anxieties aroused by the Oedipus complex, what one sees is not a whole picture but fragments or elements of one. This means that the oedipal situation is seen in this whole process of engendering, disguising, attacking and tolerating meaning.

Rusbridger suggests that we could build up a lexicon of fragmented elements of the Oedipus complex. These might include, for example, themes of exclusion or observation. We may hear about someone who is an excluded or tantalised observer. We may hear about the relationship between power-ful figures and powerless ones – perhaps as reflected in analysis in the relation between the felt-to-be-powerful analyst and the powerless-feeling patient. Other themes may turn on the relationship with boundaries: we may glimpse secret, special, boundaried places, or hear of the wish to breach a boundary of the analytic setting.

Critiques of the Kleinian view of the Oedipus complex

Klein's early dating of the Oedipus complex, and her related set of new ideas, have been both accepted and not accepted in British psychoanalysis. They

have perhaps been accepted in the sense that it is now generally acknowledged that the small child has complex conflicts and fears, genital and
pregenital, about both maternal and paternal figures. However, depending
on theoretical leanings, psychoanalysts either use the term 'Oedipus complex' very specifically to cover only the approximate period designated by
Freud, or use it much more broadly in the sense that Klein and contemporary Kleinians do.

References

Bion, W. (1957) 'Differentiation of the psychotic from the non-psychotic
personalities', *Int. J. Psycho-Anal.* 38: 266–275.
—— (1959) 'Attacks on linking', *Int. J. Psycho-Anal.* 40: 308–315.
—— (1962) *Learning from Experience*. London: Heinemann.
—— (1963) *Elements of Psychoanalysis*. London: Heinemann.
Birksted-Breen, D. (1996) 'Phallus, penis and mental space', *Int. J. Psycho-Anal.* 77:
649–657.
Britton, R. (1989) 'The missing link: Parental sexuality in the Oedipus complex', in
J. Steiner (ed.) *The Oedipus Complex Today*. London: Karnac, pp. 83–101.
—— (1998) *Belief and Imagination*. London: Routledge.
—— (2003) *Sex, Death, and the Superego*. London: Karnac.
Freud, S. (1897) Letter 71. 'Extracts from the Fliess Papers', *S.E. 1*. London:
Hogarth Press, p. 265.
—— (1900) *The Interpretation of Dreams*, *S.E. 4/5*. London: Hogarth Press.
—— (1905) 'Introductory lectures', *S.E. 16*. London: Hogarth Press, pp. 358–372.
—— (1910) 'A special type of object choice made by men', *S.E. 11*. London:
Hogarth Press, pp. 163–175.
—— (1918) 'From the history of an infantile neurosis', *S.E. 17*. London: Hogarth
Press, pp. 3–123.
—— (1919) 'A child is being beaten', *S.E. 17*. London: Hogarth Press, pp. 175–204.
—— (1923a) 'The infantile genital organisation: An interpolation into the theory of
sexuality', *S.E. 19*. London: Hogarth Press, pp. 139–145.
—— (1923b) 'The ego and the id', *S.E. 19*. London: Hogarth Press, pp. 3–66.
—— (1924) 'The dissolution of the Oedipus complex', *S.E. 19*. London: Hogarth
Press, pp. 173–179.
—— (1925) 'Some psychical consequences of the anatomical distinction between the
sexes', *S.E. 19*. London: Hogarth Press, pp. 243–258.
—— (1939) 'Moses and monotheism', *S.E. 23*. London: Hogarth Press, pp. 3–137.
—— (1940) 'An outline of psychoanalysis', *S.E. 23*. London: Hogarth Press, pp.
141–207.
Klein, M. (1921) 'The development of a child', in *The Writings of Melanie Klein*,
Vol. 1. London: Hogarth Press, pp. 1–53.
—— (1923a) 'The role of the school in the libidinal development of the child', in *The
Writings of Melanie Klein*, Vol. 1. London: Hogarth Press, pp. 59–76.
—— (1923b) 'Early analysis', in *The Writings of Melanie Klein*, Vol. 1. London:
Hogarth Press, pp. 77–105.

—— (1926) 'The psychological principles of early analysis', in *The Writings of Melanie Klein*, Vol. 1. London: Hogarth Press, pp. 128–138.

—— (1927a) 'Symposium on child analysis', in *The Writings of Melanie Klein*, Vol. 1. London: Hogarth Press, pp. 139–169.

—— (1927b) 'Criminal tendencies in normal children', in *The Writings of Melanie Klein*, Vol. 1. London: Hogarth Press, pp. 170–185.

—— (1928) 'Early stages of the Oedipus conflict', in *The Writings of Melanie Klein*, Vol. 1. London: Hogarth Press, pp. 186–198.

—— (1929) 'Infantile anxiety-situations reflected in a work of art and in the creative impulse', *Int. J. Psycho-Anal.* 10: 436–443.

—— (1930) 'The importance of symbol formation in the development of the ego', in *The Writings of Melanie Klein*, Vol. 1. London: Hogarth Press, pp. 219–232.

—— (1932) *The Psychoanalysis of Children. The Writings of Melanie Klein*, Vol. 2. London: Hogarth Press.

—— (1933) 'The early development of conscience in the child', in *The Writings of Melanie Klein*, Vol. 1. London: Hogarth Press, pp. 248–257.

—— (1935) 'A contribution to the psychogenesis of manic-depressive states', in *The Writings of Melanie Klein*, Vol. 1. London: Hogarth Press, pp. 262–289.

—— (1940) 'Mourning and its relation to manic-depressive states', in *The Writings of Melanie Klein*, Vol. 1. London: Hogarth Press, pp. 344–369.

—— (1945) 'The Oedipus complex in the light of early anxieties', in *The Writings of Melanie Klein*, Vol. 1. London: Hogarth Press, pp. 370–419.

—— (1952) 'Some theoretical conclusions regarding the emotional life of the infant', in *The Writings of Melanie Klein*, Vol. 3. London: Hogarth Press, pp. 61–93.

—— (1957) 'Envy and gratitude', in *The Writings of Melanie Klein*, Vol. 3. London: Hogarth Press, pp. 176–235.

Money-Kyrle, R. (1968) 'Cognitive development', *Int. J. Psycho-Anal.* 49: 691–698.

—— (1971) 'The aim of psychoanalysis' in *The Collected Papers of Roger Money-Kyrle*. Strath Tay: Clunie Press, pp. 442–449.

Mandelbrot, B. (1982) *The Fractal Geometry of Nature*. New York: W. H. Freeman.

Rusbridger, R. (2004) 'Elements of the Oedipus complex: A Kleinian account', *Int. J. Psycho-Anal.* 85: 731–747.

Sodré, I. (1994) 'Obsessional certainty versus obsessional doubt: from two to three', *Psychoanal. Inq.* 14: 379–392.

Steiner, J. (1985) 'Turning a blind eye: The cover up for Oedipus', *Int. Rev. Psycho-Anal.* 12: 161–172.

—— (1990) 'The retreat from truth to omnipotence in *Oedipus at Colonus*', *Int. Rev. Psycho-Anal.*, 17: 227–237.

—— (1993) *Psychic Retreats: Pathological Organizations in Psychotic, Neurotic and Borderline Patients*. London: Routledge.

7 Projective identification

Definition

Projective identification is an unconscious phantasy in which aspects of the self or of an internal object are split off and attributed to an external object. The projected aspects may be felt by the projector to be either good or bad. Projective phantasies may or may not be accompanied by evocative behaviour unconsciously intended to induce the recipient of the projection to feel and act in accordance with the projective phantasy. Phantasies of projective identification are sometimes felt to have 'acquisitive' as well as 'attributive' properties, meaning that the phantasy involves not only getting rid of aspects of one's own psyche but also of entering the mind of the other in order to acquire desired aspects of his psyche. In this case projective and introjective phantasies operate together. Among British Kleinians there is a tacit assumption that 'projection' and 'projective identification' mean the same thing, and that 'projective identification' is an enrichment or extension of Freud's concept of 'projection'.

Key papers

Klein, M. (1946, 1952)

1946   'Notes on some schizoid mechanisms'.
        Gives a definition but the actual term 'projective identification' is mentioned only in passing two pages after the definition.

1952   'Notes on some schizoid mechanisms'.
        This 1952 version gives the same definition as the 1946 version, but adds a definitive sentence: 'I suggest for these processes the term "projective identification"'.

Rosenfeld, H. (1947, 1964, 1971)

1947   'Analysis of a schizophrenic state with depersonalization'.
              First published description of projective identification in a
              particular clinical case.

1964   'On the psychopathology of narcissism: a clinical approach'.
              In narcissistic states, identification may be formed both by
              introjection and by projection.

1971   'Contribution to the psychopathology of psychotic states: The
              importance of projective identification in the ego structure and
              the object relations of the psychotic patient'.
              Motives for projective identification.

Bion, W. R. (1959, 1962)

1959   'Attacks on linking'.
              Distinguishes normal and pathological projective identifica-
              tion.

1962   *Learning from Experience.*
              Introduces 'container/contained' model of thinking of which
              patient's projective identification is an important aspect.

Other

1987   Joseph, B. 'Projective identification: Clinical aspects'.
              Lucid clinical description of projective identification in three
              patients.

2004   Sodré, I. 'Who's who? Notes on pathological identifications'.
              Normality or pathology depends on whether thinking is con-
              crete or symbolic, not on whether identification is introjective
              or projective.

Chronology and discussion

Antecedents to Klein's use of the concept of projective identification

In a letter to Fliess in 1895, Freud describes the concept of projection for
the first time in the context of discussing paranoia. He says: 'The purpose of

paranoia is thus to fend off an idea that is incompatible with the ego, by projecting its substance into the external world' (p. 209).

Freud (1911) describes projection more completely when discussing Schreber. He says:

> The most striking characteristic of symptom-formation in paranoia is the process which deserves the name of *projection*. An internal perception is suppressed, and, instead, its content, after undergoing a certain kind of distortion, enters consciousness in the form of an external perception.
>
> (Freud, 1911, p. 66)

In the Schreber case history Freud describes the role of projection in delusions of persecution, delusions of jealousy, in erotomania and in megalomania (pp. 63–66). In each case an unwanted perception about oneself or a shameful wish is repressed and perceived in some external person. Complex reversals and denials help to conceal the true source in the self of the forbidden wish or bad quality.

Freud also describes a very different sort of projection, although he does not use the word projection to describe it. In 1910 in 'Leonardo da Vinci and a memory of his childhood' he says:

> . . . the boys whom he [Leonardo] now loves as he grows up are after all only substitutive figures and rivals of himself in childhood – boys whom he loves in the way in which his mother loved *him* when he was a child.
>
> (Freud, 1910, p. 100)

Leonardo thus identified his adult caring self with his mother, and himself as a youth with the beautiful young men whom he cared for as lovingly and as chastely as his mother had cared for him. Freud does not use the concept of projection in describing Leonardo, but in terms of the Kleinian conception of projective identification one could say that Leonardo projected his adult caring self into his idea of his mother, and his youthful self into his young apprentices. His sexuality, Freud thought, was sublimated in his work: first his painting, and later his scientific curiosity and designs for works of engineering.

Thus Freud restricts the word 'projection' to the context of paranoia and repressed, denied bad aspects of the self. What we might nowadays describe as the projection of good aspects of the self and of internal objects he finds other words for – 'substitution', sublimation, even 'cathexis'.

Abraham (1911) in 'Notes on the psycho-analytical investigation and treatment of manic-depressive insanity and allied conditions' discusses a form of projection in the case of psychotically depressed patients in which the patient represses his own hatred of others and instead believes that others hate him. 'This idea is detached from its primary causal connection with his own attitude of hate, and is brought into association with other – psychical and physical – deficiencies' (Abraham, 1911, pp. 144–145). Abraham does not pursue this idea in greater detail as his main interest was in introjection, not projection.

Weiss (1925) explicitly uses the terms 'introjective identification' and 'projective identification' in the context of describing the basis of sexual object choice. He says that in choosing a partner men project the female aspect of themselves into the women whom they choose, and women, similarly, project the masculine aspect of themselves into the men whom they choose. Klein describes this part of the content of Weiss's paper in *The Psychoanalysis of Children* (Klein, 1932, p. 250), although she does not refer to Weiss's use of the terms 'projective identification' and 'introjective identification'. (This matter is further discussed by Massidda (1999) and Steiner (1999).)

Anna Freud (1936). In *The Ego and the Mechanisms of Defence* describes 'identification with the aggressor', in which the individual projects his aggression into an external object with whom he identifies, and 'altruistic surrender' in which, because of fear of 'narcissistic mortification', the individual denies a desire for success or for love and projects such desires into an external object through whom he experiences them vicariously. Both these forms of behaviour, although differing in the content of what is projected, could be described as forms of projective identification.

Development of the concept of projective identification in Klein's own work

Klein's early views

- *1929: 'Personification in the play of children'*. The 'personification' Klein speaks of in this paper is a form of projection in which aspects of the self, most particularly aspects that Klein describes here as the 'id' and the 'superego' in both its threatening and its supportive aspects, are attributed to various external or phantasied figures. Her child patient Erna, for example, was preoccupied by a cruel conflict:

> When Erna played the part of the cruel mother, the naughty child was the enemy; when she herself was the child who was persecuted but soon became powerful, the enemy was represented by the wicked parents. In each case there was a motive, which the ego attempted to render plausible to the super-ego, for indulging in unrestrained sadism.
>
> (Klein, 1929, p. 200)

Later in the paper Klein talks even more explicitly about splitting and projection, saying:

> I have come to the conclusion that this splitting of the super-ego into the primal identifications introjected at different stages of development is a mechanism analogous to and closely connected with projection. I believe these mechanisms (splitting-up and projection) are a principal factor in the tendency to personification in play.
>
> (Klein, 1929a, p. 205)

- *1932: The Psychoanalysis of Children.* In Chapter 8, 'Early stages of the Oedipus conflict and of superego formation', Klein describes the interplay of projection and introjection in building up the child's self, his superego and, as she puts it, 'his object-relations and his adaptation to reality':

> When, as a small child, he first begins to introject his objects – and these, it must be remembered, are yet only very vaguely demarcated by his various organs – his fear of those introjected objects sets in motion the mechanisms of ejection and projection, as I have tried to show; and there now follows a reciprocal action between projection and introjection which seems to be of fundamental importance not only for the formation of his super-ego but for the development of his object-relations and his adaptation to reality. The steady and continual urge he is under to project his terrifying identifications on to his objects results, it would seem, in an increased impulse to repeat the process of introjection again and again, and is thus itself a decisive factor in the evolution of his relationship to objects.
>
> (Klein, 1932, pp. 142–143)

Like Freud, Klein stresses the need to get rid of bad experiences as the basis of projection, but she sees it here not only as a defensive evacuation but also as part of a projection/introjection interplay, which leads to mental development. She does not discuss projective identification conceptually in this book but, as noted earlier, she does mention the concept in a footnote on p. 250 when she briefly mentions the work of Edoardo Weiss on choice of sexual object (Weiss, 1925).

- *1935: 'A contribution to the psychogenesis of manic depressive states'.* In this paper Klein describes the interplay of projection and introjection with increasing confidence and clarity:

> The development of the infant is governed by the mechanisms of introjection and projection. From the beginning the ego introjects

objects 'good' and 'bad', for both of which the mother's breast is the prototype – for good objects when the child obtains it, for bad ones when it fails him. . . . These imagos, which are a phantastically distorted picture of the real objects upon which they are based, become installed not only in the outside world but, by the process of incorporation, also within the ego.

(Klein, 1935, p. 262)

In these various passages Klein describes not only the projection of impulses but also of internal objects and aspects of the self – 'identifications', as she calls them in the quotation above from 1932. This enlarging of the idea of what is projected and introjected meant that the step from thinking about 'projection' to thinking about 'projective identification ' was probably, in her view, not very great.

Emergence of 'projective identification' as a specific, named concept

- *1946*. Even in 1946 Klein did not firmly establish the link between concept and name. In 'Notes on some schizoid mechanisms', first published in the *International Journal of Psycho-Analysis* in 1946, Klein describes the paranoid-schizoid position of which 'projective identification' is a particular aspect. This is her definition of projective identification:

> Together with these harmful excrements, expelled in hatred, split off parts of the ego are also projected on to the mother or, as I would rather call it, into the mother. These excrements and bad parts of the self are meant not only to injure the object but also to control it and take possession of it. Insofar as the mother comes to contain the bad parts of the self, she is not felt to be a separate individual but is felt to be the bad self.
>
> Much of the hatred against parts of the self is now directed towards the mother. This leads to a particular kind of identification which establishes the prototype of an aggressive object relation. Also, since the projection derives from the infant's impulse to harm or to control the mother, he feels her to be a persecutor. In psychotic disorders this identification of an object with the hated parts of the self contributes to the intensity of the hatred directed against other people. So far as the ego is concerned, excessive splitting off of parts of itself and expelling these into the outer world considerably weaken it. For the aggressive component of feelings and of the personality is intimately bound up in the mind with power, potency, strength, knowledge and many other desired qualities.
>
> It is, however, not only the bad parts of the self which are expelled and projected, but also good parts of the self. Excrements

then have the significance of gifts; and parts of the ego which, together with excrements, are expelled and projected into the other person represent the good, i.e. the loving parts of the self. The identification based on this type of projection again vitally influences object relations. The projection of good feelings and good parts of the self into the mother is essential for the infant's ability to develop good object relations and to integrate his ego. However, if this projective process is carried out excessively, good parts of the personality are felt to be lost to the self, and the mother becomes the ego ideal; this process, too, results in weakening and impoverishing the ego. . . .

(Klein, 1946, p. 102)

At this time Klein does not include the term 'projective identification' in these defining paragraphs, although she mentions the term in passing two pages further on in the paper, where she says 'I have referred to the weakening and impoverishment of the ego resulting from excessive splitting and projective identification' (Klein, 1946, p. 104).

- *1952*. Finally, in the 1952 version of her paper on schizoid mechanisms, published in *Developments in Psycho-Analysis* by Klein, Heimann, Isaacs and Riviere, Klein added the crucial defining sentence to the definitional paragraphs quoted above: *'I suggest for these processes the term "projective identification"'*. She also added two new paragraphs, one specifically on projective identification, and 13 new footnotes, mostly to her various colleagues' work on projective identification.

  However Klein apparently wanted 'Notes on some schizoid mechanisms' to be cited as '1946', perhaps to establish some sort of temporal priority. It may be relevant that Rosenfeld had used the term 'projective identification' in his paper 'Analysis of a schizophrenic state with depersonalization' which was published in 1947 in the *International Journal of Psycho-Analysis*. At any rate it is the 1952 version of 'Notes on some schizoid mechanisms' that is cited and reprinted, but it is always described as '1946'.

Klein's references to projective identification after 1952

There are only a few published mentions of the concept of projective identification after 1952, none of them involving conceptual changes.

- *1955: 'On identification'*. In this paper Klein describes projective identification by a character in a novel rather than by a patient, and the paper adds little conceptually to Klein's understandings of 1946 and 1952. It describes the way the central character of the novel projects his whole self into various other people in order to acquire their identity.

(This sort of projection does occur, of course, but it is less common than projection of internal objects and parts of the self.)

- *1957: Envy and Gratitude.* Klein refers briefly to projective identification in this important book of 1957, where she notes the projective character of envy and the difficulty it contributes to making the basic primal split between good and bad that is essential for differentiation and later for integration of the ego and in the perception of objects. Klein thought that envy leads to attacks on the good object that take the form of projection of bad parts of the self into the good object, resulting in confusion between self and object and between the good and the bad self.

Klein's unpublished views on projective identification as expressed in notes in the Melanie Klein Archive (PP/KLE B98, PP/KLE D17)

Klein discusses projective identification in these two sets of unpublished notes. B98 is a file of 106 pages dating from 1946–1947 in which Klein gives many clinical examples of projective identification and emphasises the close relationship between projection and introjection; she stresses the importance of the projection of good as well as bad aspects of the self, a point that she also includes in her published paper of 1946, though with less emphasis. The later file, D17, also contains several unpublished pages of notes on projective identification, which Klein says she was intending to use as the basis of a paper on the topic; these probably date from 1958. There is, however, no trace of the intended paper in the Melanie Klein Archive. In the D17 notes, Klein makes a rather unclear distinction between projection and projective identification as two steps in a single process, a distinction that she does not continue to use. She emphasises yet again that good as well as bad aspects of the self are involved in projective identification, and she says that projective and introjective identification occur in all relationships.

Concluding comments on Klein's use of projective identification

Of course the main point about Klein's work on projective identification is that she introduced the concept, at least in a form that brought it to the attention of other analysts. Edoardo Weiss had used the term in 1925, but only a few analysts have noted this (Massidda, 1999; Steiner, 1999).

Hanna Segal thinks that the name 'projective identification' was suggested to Klein by Roger Money-Kyrle (personal communication). (Segal says nothing about Edoardo Weiss's 1925 paper described above.) Segal thinks that Klein thought of the term in the context of comparing projection with introjection. In the case of introjection, once an object has been taken in several things may happen to it: it may exist inside the subject as an internal object; it may be good or bad; the subject may unconsciously identify with this internal object or with an aspect of it. Klein, according to Segal, thought of projective identification as a parallel process to intro-jective identification, meaning that projective identification was only one of perhaps several possible outcomes of projection, although Klein does not describe what these other outcomes might be.

It is important to note that in both her published and unpublished material Klein did not think of projective identification as an interpersonal concept except in the unconscious phantasy of the subject. She did not discuss the effect of the subject's projections on the object, and indeed we know from other material in the Melanie Klein Archive (PP/KLE C72) that if the 'object' was an analyst, and if the analyst's work was affected by the patient's projection, Klein thought that there was something wrong with the way the analyst was working. She definitely did not think that the analyst's emotional response to the patient was a useful source of infor-mation about the patient.

In the Archive Klein repeats several times that good as well as bad aspects of internal objects and of the self are projected and identified with, and from this repetition it is clear that she thought it was an important point, even though she did not give much emphasis to it in her published statements. She might have been rather surprised to find that her suc-cessors, at least for a time, put more stress on the projective identification of bad aspects of the self.

Further, the overall impression one gets from both Klein's published and unpublished work is that the concept of projective identification was not especially important to her in and of itself. It emerged in the process of her increased clinical and conceptual understanding of processes of splitting, envy, fragmentation and integration, and it was part of her formulation of the paranoid-schizoid position rather than an isolated concept meaningful in its own right. It is perhaps important that in the Archive Klein always refers to her paper 'Notes on some schizoid mechanisms' as 'my splitting paper', never as 'my projective identification paper'. Nevertheless her almost casually mentioned concept has given rise to an enormous literature.

Further developments of the concept of projective identification by British analysts

Specific papers on conceptual aspects of projective identification

Four analysts – Herbert Rosenfeld, Hanna Segal, Wilfred Bion and Ignês Sodré – have made particular conceptual contributions to the concept of projective identification and Joseph Sandler and Ronald Britton have also added useful terminological distinctions. Several other analysts have written papers illustrating the clinical usefulness of the concept.

ROSENFELD ON PROJECTIVE IDENTIFICATION (1947, 1964, 1971, 1983, 1987)

(1947) 'Analysis of a schizophrenic state with depersonalization'. Apart from Klein's own clinical examples, this 1947 paper by Rosenfeld was the first application of Klein's concept of projective identification in a clinical case.

(1964) 'On the psychopathology of narcissism: A clinical approach'. In this paper Rosenfeld states that when an object is omnipotently introjected, or omnipotently projected into, the self becomes so much identified with the incorporated object that all separate identity or boundary between self and object is denied:

> Identification is an important factor in narcissistic object relations. It may take place by introjection or by projection. When the object is omnipotently incorporated, the self becomes so identified with the incorporated object that all separate identity or any boundary between self and object is denied. In projective identification parts of the self omnipotently enter an object, for example the mother, to take over certain qualities which would be experienced as desirable, and therefore claim to be the object or part-object. Identification by introjection and by projection usually occur simultaneously.
>
> (Rosenfeld, 1964, pp. 170–171)

This paper somewhat countered the developing belief among Kleinians that introjective identification was concerned with 'good' aspects of the self and that projective identification was concerned with 'bad' aspects.

(1971) 'Contribution to the psychopathology of psychotic states: The importance of projective identification in the ego structure and the object relations of the psychotic patient'. In this important paper Rosenfeld writes about the *motives* for projective identification. The first motive he describes as a wish, usually an unconscious wish, to communicate something that the subject does not understand about himself to the object, a motive already described by Bion (1959). The second motive is a wish to evacuate something unpleasant from one's own mind by attributing it to someone else – this being the motive so often cited by Freud and also by Klein. The third motive consists of an attempt to control the mind of another – here we see in operation the interpersonal as well as the intrapsychic aspect of projective identification. The fourth motive that Rosenfeld describes is a wish to get rid of an awareness of envy – this I think could be considered as a special case of the evacuation of something unpleasant about oneself. Finally, Rosenfeld thinks that pronounced and repeated projective identification can amount to a form of parasitism in which the subject tries to live parasitically in the mind of the object.

(1983) 'Primitive object relations and mechanisms' and (1987) Impasse and Interpretation. In these works Rosenfeld continues the exploration of motives for projective identification.

HANNA SEGAL (1957)

In her ground-breaking paper 'Notes on symbol formation', Segal says that projective identification is at the heart of the concrete thinking of psychotics:

> Parts of the ego and internal objects are projected into an object and identified with it. The differentiation between the self and the object is obscured. Then, since a part of the ego is confused with the object, the symbol – which is a creation and a function of the ego – becomes, in turn, confused with the object which is symbolized.
>
> (Segal, 1957, p. 393)

WILFRED BION (1959, 1962)

(1959) 'Attacks on linking'. Bion makes explicit an important distinction between 'normal' projective identification used for purposes of emotional communication and 'pathological' projective identification used to excess and in order to attack the object. He also discusses the circumstances – a combination of envious attacks by the subject and emotional imperviousness by the object – that are likely to lead to pathological projective identification. He emphasises the communicative value of 'normal' projective identification, particularly between infant and mother but also between patient and analyst.

(1962) Learning from Experience. Bion used the concept of projective identification in developing his idea of the container/contained model of thinking. [*see* Container/contained.]

IGNÊS SODRÉ (2004)

In 'Who's who? Notes on pathological identifications' Sodré makes another valuable addition to the understanding of processes of identification. She cites Rosenfeld's point, quoted above, about the fact that introjective identification can be just as omnipotent and pathological as projective identification, and she adds: 'Even though "projective identification" is used to describe normal as well as pathological processes, I think that we tend to think of projective processes as more pathological than introjective ones' (Sodré, 2004, p. 57).

The pathological element, Sodré says, is not whether the identification is projective or introjective, but whether the identification is concrete or symbolic. Because we have tended to think of projective identification as 'bad', pathological, we tend to miss the projection of 'good' attributes – something that Klein stressed but her colleagues had for some time tended to ignore.

JOSEPH SANDLER (1976a, 1976b)

In these papers Sandler, a contemporary Freudian analyst, makes a distinction between projective identification as a phantasy and projective identification as behaviourally 'actualised', thus making clear an aspect of the post-Kleinian approach to projective identification that had not been so explicitly stated before. Many Kleinians now use Sandler's term, 'actualisation'.

RONALD BRITTON (1998)

In the Introduction to his book *Belief and Imagination* Britton makes a useful distinction between 'attributive' and 'acquisitive' projective identification, which has been described above in the definition of the concept.

General descriptions and clinical use of the concept of projective identification by British analysts, particularly Kleinians

Betty Joseph (1987) in her paper 'Projective identification: Clinical aspects' is particularly noted for her astute clinical discussion of projective identification in three patients. Among other contributions of particular importance have been the views of Leslie Sohn (1985). In 'Narcissistic organization, projective identification and the formation of the identificate' Sohn describes what he calls the 'identificate', which is developed by patients who project themselves into their object to take possession of the object's desirable qualities. Robert Hinshelwood (1991) in his entry on 'projective identification' in *A Dictionary of Kleinian Thought* (2nd edition) discusses in detail the use of the concept of projective identification in Britain and abroad.

In three papers Michael Feldman (1992, 1994, 1997) gives telling clinical illustrations of projective identification by patients and responses to them by the analyst. In 'Clinical experiences of projective identification' Elizabeth Spillius (1992) describes the clinical expression of projective identification in three patients. David Bell's (2001) paper 'Projective identification' gives a detailed conceptual exposition of projective identification and illustrates it with clinical material. Albert Mason's (in press) 'Vicissitudes of projective identification' discusses the concept conceptually and adds vivid clinical examples. Edna O'Shaughnessy (in press) discusses the concept in 'Contemporary Freudians, Independents and Kleinians: The concept of projective identification and the British Society'. Her enquiries show that while many Independent and Contemporary Freudian analysts think of projective identification as the quintessential Kleinian concept, most are familiar with it and some use it in their work with patients. There is some tendency to think of it as a negative concept, mainly to do with destructiveness.

It is of some interest that Kleinians themselves would not agree that projective identification is the essential Kleinian concept. They would be more likely to think of the paranoid-schizoid and depressive positions as their essential concepts. In Klein's own view, projective identification was probably a relatively minor aspect of the paranoid-schizoid position, and it concerned the projection of 'good' as well as 'bad' aspects of the self. In her view 'splitting', not projective identification, was the essential characteristic of the paranoid-schizoid position. (See Melanie Klein Archive, PP/KLE B98, PP/KLE D17.)

Summary of developments in the concept of projective identification by British analysts

For the most part it is Kleinian analysts in Britain who use the concept of projective identification. Edna O'Shaughnessy's study of the ideas of Independents and Contemporary Freudians about the topic shows that most non-Kleinian British analysts know about the concept, some use it themselves, and Joseph Sandler, as described above, has added to its usefulness by his idea of 'actualisation'. There is a tendency for non-Kleinians to consider projective identification to be largely negative, that is, to concern the projection only of bad aspects of the self.

British Kleinian analysts and the few British non-Kleinian analysts who use the concept of projective identification do not particularly distinguish between 'projection' and 'projective identification'. There is general agreement with Klein's point about excessive projective identification depleting and weakening the ego. Another characteristic of British usage is that there is comparatively little attempt to make formal definitions of the concept. The analysts who use the concept are more interested in its clinical usefulness than in its precise definition.

Unlike Klein, contemporary British analysts have made considerable use of the idea that the analyst's intellectual and emotional responses to the projections of the patient, his countertransference response (though use of that term in this connection depends on how the analyst defines countertransference), may be a useful source of information about the patient. This is the single most important difference between Klein's usage and that of contemporary British Kleinian analysts. The idea about the potential usefulness of the analyst's responses to the patient's behaviour was first described by Paula Heimann (1950) in her paper 'On counter-transference', in which she no longer viewed countertransference solely as a pathological response by the analyst to the patient, but also considered it to be a potentially useful source for understanding the patient. She did not, however, use the idea of the patient's projective identification as the behaviour that the analyst was responding to [*see* Technique, where countertransference is discussed].

Another difference from Klein is that many contemporary British analysts focus on the interpersonal aspects of projective identification much more than she did. The idea of projective identification as an unconscious phantasy is retained, especially by Kleinians, but the effect it is likely to have on the object is also a subject of research.

A further difference from Klein's attitude, which included the projection of good as well as bad aspects of the self, is that at least for a time some British analysts became mainly occupied with the negative, destructive aspects of projective identification. Introjective identification, in contrast, was viewed more positively. This negative view of projective identification has not been true in the case of Herbert Rosenfeld and Ignês Sodré, however, and gradually over time most analysts have come to stress the positive as well as the negative aspects of both types of identification.

Reception of the idea of projective identification by analysts outside Britain

One of the remarkable features of projective identification is the way that the concept has been adopted and/or discussed, not always positively, by other schools of psychoanalytic thought, most especially in the United States. It is not really clear why this should be the case, but the fact that the concept can be used to understand interpersonal interactions is likely to have been a factor, even though this aspect was not important in Klein's own idea of the concept.

Projective identification in Continental Europe

At a conference of the European Psychoanalytic Federation in 2002 three analysts of Continental Europe in a presentation briefly introduced by Elizabeth Spillius discussed the concept of projective identification.

Helmut Hinz (2002) in 'Projective identification: The fate of the concept in Germany' describes the reception of the concept in Germany, stating that the concept was more likely to be understood and accepted if there had been personal contact between German and British Kleinian analysts. Jorge Canestri (2002) in 'Projective identification: The fate of the concept in Italy and Spain' describes the reception of the concept in Italy and Spain and emphasises the difficulty of importing concepts from one psychoanalytic tradition to another. Jean-Michel Quinodoz (in press) in 'Projective identification in contemporary French-language psychoanalysis' gives a detailed, scholarly examination of the use and non-use of projective literature in contemporary French-language psychoanalysis.

Projective identification in Latin America

The impression one gains from Latin American analysts at the present time is that the concept of projective identification was considered more important from the 1940s to the 1960s than it is now, and that the ideas of Lacan and French analysis generally have superseded those of Klein, although there is still considerable interest in Bion's work. Gustavo Jarast (in press) in 'Projective identification: Projections in Latin America' describes the use of the concept of projective identification and countertransference in the work of Racker, with his concept of concordant and complementary identification. He also discusses Grinberg's idea of projective counteridentification, and Willy and Madeleine Baranger's concepts of the 'psychoanalytic bi-personal "field"' and the 'bastion'.

Racker's (1953, 1957, 1958, 1968) central idea is that some identifications involve the same or similar identifications by analyst and patient; other identifications are complementary to one another.

Grinberg's idea of 'projective counteridentification' concerns the response of the analyst to a particularly *intense* use of projective identification by the patient – so intense that Grinberg thinks that all analysts, regardless of their personal conflicts and character, would react to such a projective identification in the same way (Grinberg, 1962, 1979).

Willy and Madeleine Baranger (Baranger, Baranger and Mom, 1983) think that in analysis the analyst and patient through projective and introjective identification jointly create a bi-personal phantasy. The analyst may be able to recognise that he is identified with split-off aspects of the patient's internal world and may be able to interpret this to the patient. In other instances the analyst may become caught up in the patient's projections so that the transference/countertransference neurosis paralyses the analytic process through this construction of what the Barangers call a 'bastion'.

Projective identification in the United States

Although American interest in projective identification developed slowly, by 1997 there were far more American than British papers on the topic. Many of the American papers have been published in *Contemporary Psychoanalysis*, suggesting that the concept is of particular interest to relational analysts. Most traditionally-minded ego psychologists, by contrast, have shown little interest in projective identification.

The process of evaluation of a new and unfamiliar concept by members of another psychoanalytic tradition tends to be accompanied by much attention to definition, and this has certainly been the case in the United States where there is a great deal of discussion about how projective identification should be defined. Part of the difficulty about definition is connected with the fact that many American analysts want to use the idea of projective identification and the analyst's response to it without using the related aspects of the Kleinian conceptual system in which the concept originated. Such attempts to lift the concept out of its conceptual base, so to speak, give the term an arbitrary and rather artificial importance. Further, the emphasis in Britain is on the clinical use of the concept, whereas the emphasis in the United States tends to be on its formal definition and metapsychological status.

A feature that has been much discussed in the American literature is the assumed difference between the terms projection and projective identification. Grotstein is the only American analyst who follows the current but usually tacit British Kleinian usage in stating that it is not useful to make such a distinction (Grotstein and Malin, 1966; Grotstein, 2005). Virtually all other American authors say that in 'projection' the projector loses contact with what he has projected into the other person, whereas in 'projective identification' the link is maintained. (Klein, as Grotstein suggests, would probably have thought that unconsciously the link is always maintained.) Grotstein has written a great many papers (more than ten) on projective identification, with detailed clinical illustrations. In his most recent paper he uses a special term, 'projective *trans*identification' to distinguish instances in which a projector succeeds in evoking a congruent response from the object (Grotstein, 2005).

There is very little emphasis in American analysis on the idea of projective identification as an unconscious phantasy. Many American analysts point out that Klein's use of the term projective identification is 'intrapersonal' whereas Bion's usage is 'interpersonal', and most are interested primarily, or even only, in the interpersonal usage. Most American discussions of projective identification make no mention of the projection of 'good' aspects of the self.

Unlike British analysts, many Americans use Grinberg's 1962 idea of 'projective counteridentification' though not in the sense Grinberg meant, for they usually use it to mean the particular analyst's response to the patient's projection, whereas Grinberg says he uses it to mean the response that *any* analyst would make to a powerful projection (Grinberg, 1962).

In addition to Grotstein, Thomas Ogden (1979, 1982, 1994a, 1994b), Harold Boris (1988, 1990, 1993, 1994a, 1994b), Bryce Boyer (especially 1989, 1990a, 1990b) and Lucy Lafarge (1989) make use of the idea of projective identification clinically in more or less the way it is used in British psychoanalysis, and with a sensitive understanding of Winnicott's general approach as well as awareness of the background of the concept of projective identification in Klein's and Bion's conceptual systems.

Otto Kernberg (1986, 1987) defines projective identification as a more primitive defence than projection. He thinks it consists of three processes: projection of badness into the object (he does not say anything about the projection of goodness); maintaining what he describes as 'empathy' with what has been projected; and inducing the object to experience what has been projected. Projection he regards as a more mature defence in which unacceptable experience is repressed and then projected into the object; empathy is not maintained with what has been projected. He thinks that it is useful to interpret projective identification only to borderline and narcissistic patients, not to psychotic patients, in whom there is too much loss of ego boundaries, and not to neurotic patients who use only projection, not projective identification. One gets the impression that although Kernberg is very familiar with British Kleinian and object-relations theory he focuses on a clear definition of concepts that will be comprehensible to psychiatrists rather than on the intense unconscious emotional and non-verbal communication in the clinical situation that is the focus of interest in all schools of British analysis.

Meissner (1980, 1987), whose work has been carefully examined by Robert Hinshelwood (1991, pp. 201–204), discusses the concept of projective identification and recommends that the term should be abandoned because of its confusion of fantasy and process, of metaphor and mechanism, which results in failures in differentiation of levels and forms of psychic organisation and functioning. Clearly, however, his recommendation has not been followed.

There is a large number of other American papers that describe projective identification more briefly and usually without clinical application. Some of these contributions are described by Spillius (in press) in 'Projective identification in the United States'.

Key ideas: summary

* *Projection and projective identification.* No distinction is made between these terms in Kleinian analysis or by Grotstein in the United States. Otherwise the distinction is based on retaining 'contact' in the case of projective identification and losing it in projection.
* *'Intrapsychic' (Klein) and 'interpersonal' (Bion).* A distinction expressed much more by American than British, European or Latin American analysts. (Projective identification is regarded as both in Britain.)
* *Role of projective identification in symbol formation* – Segal (1957).
* *'Normal' and 'pathological' projective identification* – Bion (1959).
* *Motives for projective identification.* This is explored most notably by Rosenfeld (1964, 1971). Important motives include communication,

evacuation of unwanted internal objects or parts of self, controlling the mind of the other and parasitism (i.e. living inside the mind of the other).

- *'Good' and 'bad' in projective identification*. Development from Klein's equal focus on 'good' and 'bad' elements in projective identification, to Bion's 'normal/pathological distinction, then to greater focus on the pathological aspect, then gradually to equal emphasis once again (Sodré and others). Tends not to be any mention of projection of 'good' aspects in American literature.
- *Projective identification and countertransference*. Countertransference reactions to the projective identifications of the patient.
- *Projective identification in relation to 'container/contained'* – Bion (1959, 1962). Role of projective identification in the ordinary process of containment.
- *Attributive and acquisitive projective identification*. A distinction made by Britton (1998).

References

Abraham, K. (1911) 'Notes on the psycho-analytical investigation and treatment of manic-depressive insanity and allied conditions', in *Selected Papers on Psycho-Analysis*. London: Hogarth Press (1927), pp. 137–156.

Baranger, M., Baranger, W. and Mom, J. (1983) 'Process and non-process in analytic work', *Int. J. Psycho-Anal.* 64: 1–15.

Bell, D. (2001) 'Projective identification', in C. Bronstein (ed.) *Kleinian Theory: A Contemporary Perspective*. London: Whurr, pp. 125–147.

Bion, W. R. (1959) 'Attacks on linking', *Int. J. Psycho-Anal.* 40: 308–315; also in *Second Thoughts*. London: Heinemann (1967), pp. 93–109.

—— (1962) *Learning from Experience*. London: Heinemann.

Boris, H. (1988) 'Torment of the object: A contribution to the study of bulimia', in *Sleights of Mind: One and Multiples of One*. Northvale, NJ: Jason Aronson (1994), pp. 187–205.

—— (1990) 'Identification with a vengeance', *Int. J. Psycho-Anal.* 71: 127–140.

—— (1993) *Passions of the Mind: Unheard Melodies, A Third Principle of Mental Functioning*. New York: New York University Press.

—— (1994a) *Envy*. Northvale, NJ: Jason Aronson.

—— (1994b) *Sleights of Mind: One and Multiples of One*. Northvale, NJ: Jason Aronson.

Boyer, L. B. (1989) 'Countertransference and technique in working with the regressed patient: Further remarks', *Int. J. Psycho-Anal.* 70: 701–714.

—— (1990a) 'Psychoanalytic intervention in treating the regressed patient', in L. B. Boyer and P. L. Giovacchini (eds) *Master Clinicians in Treating the Regressed Patient*. Northvale, NJ: Jason Aronson, pp. 1–32.

—— (1990b) 'Countertransference and technique', in L. B. Boyer and P. Giovacchini (eds) *Master Clinicians in Treating the Regressed Patient*. Northvale, NJ: Jason Aronson, pp. 303–324.

Britton, R. (1998) *Belief and Imagination.* London: Routledge.

Canestri, J. (2002) 'Projective identification: The fate of the concept in Italy and Spain', *Psychoanalysis in Europe*, European Psychoanalytical Federation Bulletin 56, pp. 130–139.

Feldman, M. (1992) 'Splitting and projective identification', in R. Anderson (ed.) *Clinical Lectures on Klein and Bion.* London: Routledge, pp. 74–88.

—— (1994) 'Projective identification in phantasy and enactment', *Psychoanal. Inq.* 14: 423–440.

—— (1997) 'Projective identification: The analyst's involvement', *Int. J. Psycho-Anal.* 78: 227–241.

Freud, A. (1936) *The Ego and the Mechanisms of Defence.* London: Hogarth Press.

Freud, S. (1895) 'Letter to Fliess', *S.E. 1.* London: Hogarth Press, p. 209.

—— (1910) 'Leonardo da Vinci and a memory of his childhood', *S.E. 11.* London: Hogarth Press, pp. 57–151.

—— (1911) 'Psycho-analytic notes on an autobiographical account of a case of paranoia (dementia paranoides)', *S.E. 12.* London: Hogarth Press, pp. 3–82.

Grinberg, L. (1962) 'On a specific aspect of countertransference due to the patient's projective identification', *Int. J. Psycho-Anal.* 43: 436–440.

—— (1979) 'Countertransference and projective counteridentification', *Contemp. Psychoanal.* 15: 226–247.

Grotstein, J. (2005) 'Projective identification: An extension of the concept of projective identification', *Int. J. Psycho-Anal.* 86: 1051–1069.

—— and Malin, A. (1966) 'Projective identification in the therapeutic process', *Int. J. Psycho-Anal.* 47: 26–31.

Heimann, P. (1950) 'On counter-transference', *Int. J. Psycho-Anal.* 33: 84–92.

Hinshelwood, R. D. (1991) Entry on 'projective identification' in *A Dictionary of Kleinian Thought*, 2nd edition. London: Free Association Books.

Hinz, H. (2002) 'Projective identification: The fate of the concept in Germany', *Psychoanalysis in Europe*, European Psychoanalytical Federation, Bulletin 56, pp. 118–129.

Jarast, G. (in press) 'Projective identification: Projections in Latin America', in E. Spillius and E. O'Shaughnessy (eds) *Projective Identification: The Fate of a Concept.* London: Routledge.

Joseph, B. (1987) 'Projective identification: Clinical aspects', in J. Sandler (ed.) *Projection, Identification, Projective Identification*, Madison, CT: International Universities Press, pp. 65–76; also in M. Feldman and E. Spillius (eds) *Psychic Equilibrium and Psychic Change.* London: Routledge (1989), pp. 166–180.

Kernberg, O. (1986) 'Identification and its vicissitudes as observed in psychosis', *Int. J. Psycho-Anal.* 57: 147–158.

—— (1987) 'Projective identification: Developmental and clinical aspects', in J. Sandler (ed.) *Projection, Identification, Projective Identification.* Madison, CT: International Universities Press, pp. 93–115. Also in *J. Am. Psychoanal. Assoc.* 35: 795–819.

Klein, M. (1929) 'Personification in the play of children', *Int. J. Psycho-Anal.* 10: 193–204.

—— (1932) *The Psychoanalysis of Children.* London: Hogarth Press.

—— (1935) 'A contribution to the psychogenesis of manic-depressive states', *Int. J.*

Psycho-Anal. 16: 145–174; also in *The Writings of Melanie Klein*, Vol. 1. London: Hogarth Press, pp. 262–289.

—— (1946) 'Notes on some schizoid mechanisms', *Int. J. Psycho-Anal.* 27: 99–110.

—— (1952) 'Notes on some schizoid mechanisms', in M. Klein, P. Heimann, S. Isaacs and J. Riviere (eds) *Developments in Psycho-Analysis.* London: Hogarth Press.

—— (1955) 'On identification', in M. Klein, P. Heimann and R. Money-Kyrle (eds) *New Directions in Psychoanalysis.* London: Tavistock, pp. 309–345.

—— (1957) *Envy and Gratitude.* London: Tavistock Press; also reprinted in *The Writings of Melanie Klein*, Vol. 3. London: Hogarth Press, pp. 176–235.

Lafarge, L. (1989) 'Emptiness as defense in severe regressed states', *J. Am. Psychoanal. Assoc.* 37: 965–995.

Mason, A. (in press) 'Vicissitudes of projective identification', in E. Spillius and E. O'Shaughnessy (eds) *Projective Identification: The Fate of a Concept.* London: Routledge.

Massidda, G. B. (1999) 'Shall we ever know the whole truth about projective identification?', *Int. J. Psycho-Anal.* 80: 365–367.

Meissner, W. W. (1980) 'A note on projective identification', *J. Am. Psychoanal. Assoc.* 28: 43–86.

—— (1987) 'Projection and projective identification', in J. Sandler (ed.) *Projection, Identification, Projective Identification.* Madison, CT: International Universities Press, pp. 27–49.

Ogden, T. (1979) 'On projective identification', *Int. J. Psycho-Anal.* 60: 357–373.

—— (1982) *Projective Identification and Psychotherapeutic Technique.* New York: Jason Aronson.

—— (1994a) 'The analytic mind: Working with intersubjective clinical facts', *Int. J. Psycho-Anal.* 75: 3–20; also Chapter 5 in *Subjects of Analysis.* London: Karnac Books.

—— (1994b) 'The concept of interpretive action', *Psychoanal. Q.* 63: 2310–2245; also Chapter 7 in *Subjects of Analysis.* London: Karnac Books.

O'Shaughnessy, E. (in press) 'Contemporary Freudians, Independents and Kleinians: The concept of projective identification and the British Society', in E. Spillius and E. O'Shaughnessy (eds) *Projective Identification: The Fate of a Concept.* London: Routledge.

Quinodoz, J.-M. (in press) Projective identification in contemporary French-language psychoanalysis', in E. Spillius and E. O'Shaughnessy (eds) *Projective Identification: The Fate of a Concept.* London: Routledge.

Racker, H. (1953) 'A contribution to the problem of counter-transference', *Int. J. Psycho-Anal.* 34: 313–324.

—— (1957) 'The meaning and uses of countertransference', *Int. J. Psycho-Anal.* 26: 303–357.

—— (1958) 'Counterresistance and interpretation', *J. Am. Psychoanal. Assoc.* 6: 215–221.

—— (1968) *Transference and Countertransference.* London: Hogarth Press.

Rosenfeld, H. (1947) 'Analysis of a schizophrenic state with depersonalization', *Int. J. Psycho-Anal.* 28: 130–139; also in *Psychotic States.* London: Hogarth Press (1965), pp. 13–33.

—— (1964) 'On the psychopathology of narcissism: A clinical approach', *Int. J.*

Psycho-Anal. 45: 332–337; also in *Psychotic States.* London: Hogarth Press (1965), pp. 169–179.

—— (1971) 'Contribution to the psychopathology of psychotic states: The importance of projective identification in the ego structure and the object relations of the psychotic patient', in P. Doucet and C. Laurin (eds) *Problems of Psychosis.* The Hague: Excerpta Medica, pp. 115–128; also in E. Spillius (ed.) *Melanie Klein Today*, Vol. 1. London: Routledge, pp. 117–137.

—— (1983) 'Primitive object relations and mechanisms', *Int. J. Psycho-Anal.* 64: 261–267.

—— (1987) *Impasse and Interpretation.* London: Routledge.

Sandler, J. (1976a) 'Dreams, unconscious phantasies and "identity of perception"', *Int. Rev. Psycho-Anal.* 3: 33–42.

—— (1976b) 'Countertransference and role-responsiveness', *Int. Rev. Psycho-Anal.* 3: 43–47.

Segal, H. (1957) 'Notes on symbol formation', *Int. J. Psycho-Anal.* 38: 391–397; also in *The Work of Hanna Segal.* New York: Jason Aronson (1981), pp. 49–65.

Sodré, I. (2004) 'Who's who? Notes on pathological identifications', in E. Hargreaves and S. Varchevker (eds) *In Pursuit of Psychic Change: The Betty Joseph Workshop.* London: Brunner-Routledge, pp. 53–68.

Sohn, L. (1985) 'Narcissistic organization, projective identification and the formation of the identificate', *Int. J. Psycho-Anal.* 66: 201–213.

Spillius, E. (1992) 'Clinical experiences of projective identification', in R. Anderson (ed.) *Clinical Lectures on Klein and Bion.* London: Routledge, pp. 81–86.

—— (in press) 'Projective identification in the United States', in E. Spillius and E. O'Shaughnessy (eds) *Projective Identification: The Fate of a Concept.* London: Routledge.

Steiner, R. (1999) 'Who influenced whom? And how?', *Int. J. Psycho-Anal.* 80: 367–375.

Weiss, E. (1925) 'Über eine noch unbeschriebene Phase der Entwicklung zur heterosexuellen Liebe', *Int. Z. Psychoanal.* 11: 429–443.

8 Superego

Definition

An internal structure or part of the self that, as the internal authority, reflects on the self, makes judgements, exerts moral pressure and is the seat of conscience, guilt and self-esteem. In Kleinian thinking the superego is composed of a split-off part of the ego into which is projected death instinct fused with life instinct and good and bad aspects of the primary and also later objects. It acquires both protective and threatening qualities. The superego and the ego share different aspects of the same objects; they develop in parallel through the process of introjection and projection. If all goes well the internal objects in both ego and superego, which are initially extreme, become less so and the two structures become increasingly reconciled.

In Klein's view the superego starts to form at the beginning of life, rather than with the resolution of the Oedipus complex, as Freud theorised. The early superego is very severe and in the process of development becomes less severe and more realistic. In pathological development, the early severe superego does not become modified and in extreme cases the terrifying and idealised defused aspects of the primary objects are split off by the ego and banished into an area of deep unconscious. Klein came to think of these defused part-objects as separate from the superego, whereas others consider them as forming an abnormally destructive superego. Whether or not considered as superego, these extreme internal objects are thought by Klein and others to be associated with extreme disturbance and even psychosis. They are considered to be different from the ordinary early severe superego that is based on predominantly fused instincts capable of modification.

Debate continues about the degree to which change can occur in the superego, about the exact nature of its constituent parts and on the question of whether it is best conceptualised as a structure or as a function.

Key papers

1923   Freud, S. 'The ego and the id'.
            Introduction of term 'super-ego'.

1924	Freud, S. 'The economic problem of masochism'. Relationship between death instinct and sadistic superego explored.
1926	Klein, M. 'The psychological principles of early analysis'. Introjected hostile mother described as the basis of early persecutory superego.
1927a	Klein, M. 'Symposium on child analysis'. Superego thought to be a 'highly resistant product, at heart unalterable'.
1927b	Klein, M. 'Criminal tendencies in normal children'. Unconscious guilt linked to the idea of a harsh superego.
1928	Klein, M. 'Early stages of the Oedipus complex'. Pregenital stages of superego described.
1929	Klein, M. 'Personification in the play of children'. Normal superego thought to consist of multiple internal (part-) objects.
1932	Klein, M. 'Early stages of the Oedipus conflict and of superego formation'. Idea of the superego originating in the death instinct is introduced.
1933	Freud, S. 'The dissection of the psychical personality'. Summary of Freud's views on the super-ego.
1933	Klein, M. 'The early development of conscience in the child'. The superego is described as being formed by a division in the instinctual impulse (death instinct fused with libido) in which one part is directed against the other.
1934	Strachey, J. 'The nature of the therapeutic action of psycho-analysis'. Analyst becomes an auxiliary superego.
1935	Klein, M. 'A contribution to the psychogenesis of manic-depressive states'. A description is given of the defences employed at the threshold of the depressive position to meet the demand for repair from a persecutory perfectionist and sadistic superego.
1948	Klein, M. 'On the theory of anxiety and guilt'. Dual aspect of the superego clearly stated.

1952	Klein, M. 'Some theoretical conclusions regarding the emotional life of the infant'. Depressive position thought to modify the extreme severity of the superego
1952	Rosenfeld, H. 'Notes on the psychoanalysis of the superego conflict in an acute schizophrenic patient'. Terror and guilt provoked by destroyed internal object.
1957	Klein, M. 'Envy and gratitude'. Idea of an envious superego introduced.
1958	Klein, M. 'On the development of mental functioning'. Klein removes the terrifying internal figures from the superego and places them in the deep unconscious.
1959	Bion, W. 'Attacks on linking'. Idea of 'ego-destructive superego'.
1962	Bion, W. 'Learning from experience'. Idea of '–K', a kind of 'super' ego activity.
1963	Klein, M. 'On the sense of loneliness'. Loneliness is increased by a harsh superego.
1968	Money-Kyrle, R. 'Cognitive development'. Harsh superego is a misconception.
1985	Brenman, E. 'Cruelty and narrow mindedness'. Idealised cruel superego narrows perception.
1999	O'Shaughnessy, E. 'Relating to the superego'. Differentiation of normal from abnormal superego.
2003	Britton, R. *Sex, Death, and the Superego.* Importance of development of judging functions in ego.

Chronology

Precursors

Freud and the superego

In his early papers, Freud introduces and explores the idea of a *censor* in the ego that deals with unacceptable ideas by 'a splitting of consciousness' (1895, 'The psychotherapy of hysteria'; 1894, 'The neuro-psychoses of defense'). Freud then replaces the loose concept of the censor with the *ego ideal*, an internal representation of parental standards and expectations, and the *conscience*, a separate but related self-critical organisation in the ego that is the embodiment of parental criticism. The conscience motivates the child to conform to the standards of the ego ideal and impulses that come into conflict with the values of the ego ideal are repressed (1914, 'On narcissism').

In a number of papers Freud explores the powerful effect of *unconscious guilt* (or the need for punishment): for example, 'Some character-types met with in psychoanalytic work' (1916). In 1917 in 'Mourning and melancholia', Freud describes the self-destructive way in which one part of the personality can set itself up as a harsh and critical judge over the other. In 1920 in 'Beyond the pleasure principle' he goes on to suggest that 'punishment dreams', illness and a variety of psychological symptoms can be driven by unconscious guilt. In this same paper he introduces the controversial concept of the *death instinct*, an idea that he later includes in his thinking about the harshness of the superego. This idea is significantly built on by Melanie Klein.

Freud introduces the term 'super-ego' itself in 1923, when outlining his structural theory. The superego includes the ego ideal but also has the function of criticising and punishing the ego. Freud considers the superego to be 'the heir to the Oedipus complex' (1923, p. 48). His understanding is that the child gives up his oedipal object cathexes (erotic or libidinal relationship to the introjected parents) and replaces them with identifications with elements of both parents. These identifications are given a special and important place. The resulting internal agency (superego) is made up of the parents' prohibitions as well as their ideals, and is both watchful and critical; guilt results from the internal conflict between the superego and the instincts.

Freud's theory now includes an internal agency, the superego, that monitors, makes judgements, censors and causes guilt. The superego is at times enormously harsh and self-tormenting and Freud goes so far as to describe it as 'a kind of gathering-place for the death instincts' (1923, p. 54). He suggests that the harshness is in part caused by the defusion of instincts that follows the Oedipus complex, which leaves the erotic relationship sublimated but leaves the part of the death instinct that remains within no longer modified or bound by libido. In addition various other authority figures are introjected into the superego.

In a paper that heralds later work by Klein and her followers, Freud explores the role of the death instinct in the unconscious need for punishment. He describes *primary masochism* (death instinct within combined with libido), *secondary masochism* (the result of re-introjection of the death instinct that has been projected out) and finally the relationship between both primary and secondary masochism and the sadistic superego (1924). Freud continues to be concerned with the origin of the severity of the superego and in a footnote in the chapter quoted below he acknowledges Klein's contribution to his thinking:

But the essential difference is that the original severity of the super-ego does not – or does not so much – represent the severity which one has experienced from it (the object) – or which one attributes to it; it represents rather one's own aggressiveness towards it. If this is correct, we may assert truly that in the beginning conscience arises through the suppression of an aggressive impulse, and that it is subsequently reinforced by fresh suppressions of the same kind.

(Freud, 1930, pp. 129–130)

Freud summarizes his views on the superego in 1933 ('The dissection of the psychical personality'), adding that its harshness is due to the child identifying with his parents' superegos rather than with the parents themselves.

Klein and the superego

Early Klein

Klein's conceptualisation of the superego develops and changes in parallel with her developing theories. Struck early on in her work by the violence of the children's phantasies and by their remorse and guilt, she concludes that it is guilt that leads children to inhibit their behaviour and even, at times, to inhibit their phantasies and their thoughts.

Klein dates her realisation of the importance of guilt in young children to 1923 when she analysed Rita, a child whose games were full of rage and punishment and who had been stricken with remorse from the age of 15 months. She describes this realisation in 'The psycho-analytic play technique: Its history and significance' (1955). Klein writes about Rita and another small girl Trude in 'The psychological principles of early analysis' (1926). Here she says that, even by the age of 2 years when her sister was born, Trude had felt enormous anxiety and guilt at wanting to kill her mother and take her place. Linked to this, Klein argues that Trude's anxiety stems not from fear of her actual mother, but from fear of her introjected internal mother who she imagines wants to punish her. These first ideas about a harsh and anxiety-inducing early superego precede Klein's formulation of the concept of projective identification. It is possible that Klein may have thought of the internal mother as containing the child's projected aggression, but she does not spell this out in 1926; her emphasis is on the mother as retaliatory.

Some of these early papers are quite confusing as Klein tries to fit her ideas into Freud's and Abraham's theories of psychosexual stages and insists that she is not altering Freud's theory but is writing about an early version of the superego and about pre-oedipal activity. Her view is that the child begins to work through the Oedipus complex in what traditionally had been called the pre-oedipal stage and that both parents are absorbed into the child's self in a way that corresponds to Freud's ideas about the development of the adult superego [*see* Oedipus complex].

> In the cases which I have analysed the inhibitory effect of feelings of guilt was clear at a very early age. What we here encounter corresponds to that which we know as the super-ego in adults. The fact that we assume the Oedipus complex to reach its zenith round about the fourth year of life and that we recognize the development of the superego as the end-result of the complex, seems to me in no way to contradict these observations.
>
> (Klein, 1926, p. 133)

Like Freud, Klein is struck by the *harshness* of the superego and the particular manner in which this is expressed. She draws on Abraham's theory of pregenital sadism (Abraham, 1924) to explain that the harshness is caused by the child's anal sadism (1927a) and the following year she includes oral sadism:

> The child then dreads a punishment corresponding to the offence: the super-ego becomes something that bites, devours and cuts.
>   The connection between the formation of the super-ego and the pregenital phases of development is very important from two points of view. On the one hand, the sense of guilt attaches itself to the oral- and anal-sadistic phases, which as yet predominate; and, on the other, the super-ego comes into being while these phases are in the ascendant, which accounts for its sadistic severity.
>
> (Klein, 1928, p. 187)

Klein does not explain exactly what she means but her view of the effect of oral sadism is more clearly described later in 1948: '. . . since devouring implies from the beginning the internalization of the devoured object, the ego is felt to contain devoured and devouring objects' (1948, p. 30).

Klein repeatedly remarks on the extreme and contrasting characteristics of the figures in children's play. In 1929 in 'Personification in the play of children' she explains these figures as representing the child's id and different aspects of its superego (different because they were introjected at different periods). Remaining faithful to the psychosexual stages, Klein suggests that development, with its move towards genital impulses, gives access to more positive feelings and the possibility of more helpful figures to mitigate the harshness. She also states but does not explain that the strength of the genital phase depends on the earlier oral sucking stage. She seems to be working at ideas about the division between the good and bad aspects of the self and others, and the subsequent gradual development of a less extreme, more integrated superego and more realistic versions of the objects. In this 1929 paper the 'terrible menacing super-ego' is differentiated from the 'phantastically good' and the 'phantastically bad' and is described as 'wholly divorced from reality' (a theme that Klein returns to in 1958, which will be discussed later):

> I have come to realize that the operation of such imagos, with phantastically good and phantastically bad characteristics, is a general mechanism in adults as well as children. These figures represent intermediate stages between the terrible menacing super-ego, which is wholly divorced from reality and the identifications which approximate more closely to reality. These intermediate figures, whose gradual evolution into the maternal and paternal helpers (who are nearer again to reality) may constantly be observed in play-analyses, and seem to me very instructive for our knowledge of the formation of the super-ego. My experience is that at the onset of the Oedipus conflict and the start of its formation the super-ego is of a tyrannical character, formed on the pattern of the pregenital stages, which are then in the ascendant. The influence of the genital has already begun to make itself felt. . . . *The primacy of the genital phase in relation both to sexuality and to the super-ego requires a sufficiently strong fixation to the oral-sucking stage.*
> (Klein, 1929, pp. 203–204)

Klein concludes that having a superego made up of such opposites causes the ego great difficulty but also provides the impetus for its striving for synthesis (p. 205). This idea of an ego driven towards unifying the internal objects reappears in a very different and very powerful form in 1935, as part of the development that Klein calls the depressive position [see Depressive position].

It is not until 1932 that Klein adopts Freud's 1920 idea of the duality of the life and death instincts. In Chapter 8 of *The Psychoanalysis of Children*, 'Early stages of the Oedipus conflict and of super-ego formation', she links the death instinct to the superego. This is the beginning of an entirely new development for Klein in which she thinks of the superego as containing the death instinct. At the same time she retains the idea of psychosexual stages in superego development. It can be confusing to follow Klein's thinking as she works out her theory of superego development over the next few years. Freud's idea is that the organism, threatened by destructiveness within, deflects most of the destructiveness outwards but that some remains within and has to be managed. Klein proposes that, with the assistance of the object, which has been incorporated during the cannibalistic phase of development, the id (id and ego are used interchangeably by Klein at this time) splits and mobilises one part of the destructive impulses (death instinct) against another part. Klein describes the incorporated object as the 'vehicle of defence against destructive impulses within' and suggests that this first form of the superego activity may be connected to 'primal repression' (1932, p. 127). The part played by the ego is not spelt out.

The following year, in 'The early development of conscience in the child' (1933), Klein suggests that the ego mobilises libido against the death instinct but that, due to the fusion of the life and death instincts, the ego is unable to achieve a complete division between the two. The result is a more mixed division of the id:

> A division takes place in the id or on instinctual levels of the psyche, by which one part of the instinctual impulses is directed against the other.
>
> This . . . earliest defence on the part of the ego constitutes, I think, the foundation-stone of the development of the super-ego, whose excessive violence in this early stage would thus be accounted for by the fact that it is an offshoot of very intense destructive instincts and contains, along with a certain proportion of libidinal impulses, very large quantities of aggressive ones.
>
> (Klein, 1933, p. 250)

The superego seems to be formed from a fusion of the death and life instincts and the introjected object(s), which are gradually modified:

> As far as can be seen, there exists in the quite small child, side by side with its relations to real objects, a relationship to unreal imagos which are experienced both as excessively good and as excessively bad, but on a different plane. Ordinarily, these two kinds of object relations inter-mingle and colour each other to an ever increasing extent. (This is the process which I have described as an interaction between super-ego formation and object-relations.)
>
> (Klein, 1932, p. 151)

Klein's middle period

Following this thinking, Strachey outlines a theory of the therapeutic action of psychoanalysis specifically linked to the superego. His reasoning is that the external object to whom libidinal impulses are directed, the analyst, is introjected to become an auxiliary superego. He argues that by interpreting the transference, the analyst (new internal object) avoids being distorted by primitive unconscious phantasy and is not then identified with either the primitively good or the primitively bad internal objects. If this introjection of a benign superego is successful, the patient is able to sustain an internal object-relationship that is neither based on horrific self-condemnation nor on extreme idealisation (Strachey, 1934, pp. 127–159) [*see* Technique].

In 1935, returning to the theme of the ego's need for unification, Klein makes a great theoretical leap and introduces the concept of 'positions'.

The activity of bringing together the good and bad parts of the self and the object becomes centre stage and guilt, remorse and concern are now conceptualised as developmental achievements resulting from this integration. The 'supportive' functions of the superego are now thought of in the context of the *depressive position*, in which the realisation, that the mother you hate is also the mother who cares for you and whom you love, motivates control over hatred and reparative behaviour for injuries inflicted in the past. An inability to bear the guilt about damage inflicted on the mother may lead to renewed splitting and manic and obsessional attempts to repair the object. (Klein, 1935) [*see* Depressive position; Manic defences; Oedipus complex; Obsessional defences].

Later Klein

Klein had made it clear in 'Mourning and its relation to manic-depressive states' (1940) that objects are introjected into both the ego and the superego. In 1948 she writes more about the superego and her description is different from that of 1932. The unreal excessively good and bad figures, from which the superego was composed, were then described as being on a different plane from the relationship to real objects. While Klein may still be thinking in terms of 'different planes' and 'real objects', neither of these aspects is mentioned in 1948. Instead the superego at this time seems to consist of both the extremely bad and dangerous internal figures (unreal objects). Furthermore, helpful good objects that represent the life instinct are not described as 'excessively good' and sound more like the 'real objects' of 1932. All these figures are described as being introjected simultaneously at the start of life:

> . . . since devouring implies from the beginning the internalization of the devoured object, the ego is felt to contain devoured and devouring objects. Thus the super-ego is built up from the devouring breast (mother) to which is added the devouring penis (father). These cruel and dangerous internal figures become the representatives of the death instinct. Simultaneously the other aspect of the early super-ego is formed first by the internalized good breast (to which is added the good penis of the father), which is felt as a feeding and helpful internal object, and as the representative of the life instinct. The fear of being annihilated includes the anxiety lest the internal good breast be destroyed, for this object is felt to be indispensable for the preservation of life . . .
>
> According to this view the fear of death enters from the beginning into the fear of the super-ego and is not, as Freud remarked, a 'final transformation' of the fear of the super-ego.
>
> (Klein, 1948, p. 30)

In 1952 Klein describes a process by which aspects of the superego, the ego and the objects are 'exchanged' by means of continuous projection and introjection. The superego is *assimilated* by the ego and Klein describes how 'the increased capacity of the ego to accept the standards of the external objects . . . is linked with the greater synthesis within the super-ego and the growing assimilation of the super-ego by the ego'. (1952, p. 87) The ego then responds to demands from the superego to repress aggressive and libidinal impulses. This repression separates the conscious from the unconscious but does not lead to the kind of disintegration that occurs in earlier forms of splitting.

The picture is still unclear as Klein tends to use the word 'ego' to mean two different things: the whole self; and a part of the self, the other parts being the superego and the id. Nor is her use of the word 'assimilate' entirely clear; she may be referring to Heimann's 1942 paper, 'A contribution to the problem of sublimation and its relation to processes of internalization', in which Heimann explains how the withdrawal of projections from the internal objects renders them less monstrous and more human, a process that then allows the individual to absorb the object's good qualities. Heimann explores further these and other issues concerning the establishment of objects within the self in 'Certain functions of introjection and projection in early infancy' (1952) and 'A combination of defences in paranoid states' (1955) [*see* Assimilation; Internal objects; Introjection; Projection].

In 1952 Klein also describes how during latency the organised part of the superego, even though very harsh, is very cut off from its unconscious part. The child projects the organised superego onto his environment and engages in coming to terms with those in authority. This leads to the modification of anxieties and to the strengthening of defences, but in Klein's view the dangerous and persecutory figures still co-exist with idealised ones in the deeper layers.

Klein had in 1946 provided one reason to explain why some objects are introjected and identified with while others are introjected, not assimilated and felt as foreign bodies. In 'Notes on some schizoid mechanisms' (1946, p. 9) she made the suggestion that excessive use of projective identification weakens the ego and leaves it insufficiently strong to assimilate the object without being overwhelmed and dominated by it [*see* Paranoid-schizoid position]. This independent alien internal object is similar to the superego originally described by Freud.

In her important paper 'Envy and gratitude' Klein introduces the idea of the *envious super-ego*, a superego based on 'the earliest internalized persecutory object-the retaliating, devouring and poisonous breast' (1957, p. 231). The 'envious super-ego' is described as containing projected envy and does not allow the child the satisfaction of repair. It increases guilt and persecution. This concept was to be built on by Bion and others (see 'Later developments' below].

Klein's final words on superego and late alteration of theory

Klein's final word on the theory of the superego is in 1958. Although it may appear to be a radical revision, the view that she puts forward is a logical resolution of some of the difficulties and contradictions within her earlier formulations. Klein removes the terrifying figures from the early superego and places them in the deep unconscious. Her theory now accommodates both the extreme and unmodifiable terrifying figures (on a different plane), and also the severe but modifiable superego capable of development:

> The ego, supported by the internalized good object and strengthened by the identification with it, projects a portion of the death instinct into that part of itself which it has split off – a part which thus comes to be in opposition to the rest of the ego and forms the basis of the super-ego. Accompanying this deflection of a portion of the death instinct is a deflection of that portion of the life instinct which is fused with it. Along with these deflections, parts of the good and bad objects are split off from the ego into the super-ego. The super-ego thus acquires both protective and threatening qualities. As the process of integration – present from the beginning in both the ego and the superego – goes on, the death instinct is bound, up to a point, by the super-ego.
>
> (Klein, 1958, p. 240)

Klein goes on to introduce the idea of the terrifying figures being split off into an area of deep unconscious and to note the contrast between the defused nature of these figures and the predominantly fused state of the instincts that are split off into the superego:

> These extremely dangerous objects give rise, in early infancy, to conflict and anxiety within the ego; but under stress of acute anxiety they, and other terrifying figures, are split off in a manner different from that by which the super-ego is formed, and are relegated to the deeper layers of the unconscious. The difference in these two ways of splitting – and this may perhaps throw light on the many as yet obscure ways in which splitting processes take place – is that in the splitting-off of frightening figures defusion seems to be in the ascendant; whereas super-ego formation is carried out with a predominance of fusion of the two instincts. Therefore the super-ego is normally established in close relation with the ego and shares different aspects of the same good object. This makes it possible for the ego to integrate and accept the super-ego to a greater or less extent. In contrast the extremely bad figures are not accepted by the ego in this way and are constantly rejected by it.
>
> (Klein, 1958, p. 241)

Klein is clear that idealised figures are also split off along with the persecutory ones. If development proceeds well, these terrifying and idealised figures remain in the deep unconscious and only intrude into the ego under extreme pressure, and even then the intrusion can be overcome and stability regained. But in neurotic and more particularly psychotic patients the struggle against these threats from the deep unconscious are part of their instability. Klein refers in this paper to Rosenfeld's 1952 paper on the superego of a schizophrenic (see below). He and others explore the theme of the abnormal superego (see 'Later developments' below) [*see* Death instinct; Envy].

In 1963 Klein writes about the lonely feelings described by patients who are beginning to integrate destructive impulses and she suggests that they feel themselves to be completely alone with the bad part of themselves. She describes the situation as being even more painful when the patient has a harsh superego that is strongly repressive of destructive impulses and that does not forgive: 'The harsher the superego, the greater will be loneliness, because its severe demands increase depressive and paranoid anxieties' (1963, p. 313).

Key ideas

- *Timing and relationship between superego and Oedipus complex*: Klein differs from Freud in that for her the introjection of the parents as the foundation of the superego starts at the beginning of life and continues as part of a developmental process. This is far earlier than in Freud's theory, in which the superego arises out of the loss of the loved oedipal objects [*see* Oedipus complex].
- *Harshness of the superego*: Klein's early superego is severe. Her idea of it being based on the earliest death-instinct-containing introjected objects provides an explanation for its early harshness and her developmental theory provides an understanding of how it might become more benign.
- *Transference and the superego*: Klein's ideas lead to a way of understanding the transference and of using transference interpretations to ameliorate the harsh superego; for Klein, this applied to work with children as well as adults. In this she was in clear disagreement with Anna Freud.
- *Superego: Modifiable or unmodifiable?* Both Klein and Freud had the thought that the superego might be unmodifiable and Klein repeatedly turns this idea over in her papers. In 1927 she states, 'I am led to believe from the analysis of children that their super-ego is a highly resistant product, at heart unalterable' (1927a, p. 155). However, in 1929 she is clear that the early severe superego, though normal, can modify; its persistence or ascendancy is abnormal and results in severe disturbance.

By 1933 she states that 'analysis can never entirely do away with the sadistic nucleus of the super-ego' (1933, p. 256) but she believes that it can be mitigated by a strengthening of the ego at the genital level. With the development of her theory of the depressive position, comes the 'progressive assimilation of the super-ego by the ego' (1952, p. 74). In 1958 Klein describes the superego as developing with the life and death instincts predominantly in a state of fusion, but the terrifying internal figures that have resulted from intense destructiveness are no longer part of the superego and now exist in a separate area of the mind in a deep unconscious where they remain unintegrated and unmodified by the normal processes of growth. Klein thinks that this split-off part threatens mental stability when situations of stress lead to an inability to maintain the split. This kind of psychosis-inducing unmodified death instinct is explored by later Kleinians who, unlike Klein, continue to think of it as a type of superego (see 'Later developments' below).

- *Persecutory versus depressive guilt*: Once Klein has introduced the idea of the depressive position, guilt, concern and a desire to protect and repair the object are seen as the result of the realisation that the bad mother who has been attacked and hated is also the good mother. These 'depressive anxieties' can be hard to bear and become persecutory. 'Depressive guilt' may thus deteriorate into 'persecutory guilt' and lead to renewed splitting, thus increasing the persecution. The individual in the depressive position controls his hatred and destructive urges out of a wish to protect and preserve the mother rather than out of fear, as in Freud's theory of the superego or as in Klein's paranoid-schizoid position. This is an important difference between the theories of Klein and Freud on the superego [*see* Depressive position; Guilt; Manic defences; Obsessionality].

- *The superego and psychosis*: Klein's view is that unmodified persecutory guilt leads to severe disturbance. Referring to Rosenfeld's work (see below) she describes that in schizophrenics the superego is almost indistinguishable from their destructive impulses and internal persecutors. She also considers persecutory anxieties to be the root of hypochondria (Klein, 1958).

Later developments

Persecutory and depressive guilt

Searl (1936), originally a supporter of Klein and partly basing her ideas on Strachey (1934), describes the superego as a structure of two ideals. She suggests that the term superego be used to refer to the 'negative ideal' (the 'thou-shalt-not' imperative) and the term 'ego ideal' to refer to the positive ('thou-shalt'). This idea is resurrected much later by Meltzer to distinguish the helpful internal figures of the depressive position from the envious persecutory internal figures of the paranoid-schizoid position, envy being the reason for being stuck with a persecutory superego (Meltzer, 1967; Mancia and Meltzer, 1981).

In an attempt to predict, in the aftermath of the Second World War, German Nazis capable of rehabilitation into responsible jobs, Money-Kyrle (1951) uses the distinction between the depressive position and the paranoid-schizoid position to separate out two broad categories of superego. On the one hand there is the life-enhancing 'depressive position' type of superego capable of personal responsibility, and on the other the sadistic and authoritarian 'paranoid-schizoid position' type of superego, based on obedience and persecution, that had flourished best under the Nazi regime.

In his paper 'Cognitive development', Money-Kyrle (1968) outlines different stages of his thinking about mental illness. In the second stage he had assumed mental illness to be the result of unconscious moral conflict but in the third he considers that the problem is to do with unconscious misconceptions and delusions. His view is that the harsh superego is itself a misconception caused by aggression that has been projected intrapsychically from the ego into the superego, resulting in what he calls 'intrapsychic paranoia' (1968, p. 429). Using Bion's ideas, his papers contribute to the thinking about the 'ego-destructive superego' and its modification.

Grinberg (1978) links the different kinds of guilt (persecutory and harshly punitive on the one hand and depressive on the other) with possibilities of reparation. Brenman (1985) describes the domination of an idealised omnipotent cruel superego that, in order to justify cruelty and evade guilt, narrows perception and prevents the dependence on good objects. In this and other papers compiled in *Recovery of the Lost Good Object* (2006), he draws attention to the patient's need for a good relationship with the analyst to support him in the recognition of his destructive attacks.

Robin Anderson (1997), following a similar theme but not using the term superego, describes the use of violence as a defence against guilt. Exaggeration and violence are used to destroy the subject's capacity to see things as they are and also to destroy the damaged object. Like Brenman, Anderson points out that if guilt is to be borne, the analyst needs to build on positive aspects of the patient's relationship to objects.

A large body of psychoanalytic literature, although not directly mentioning the term 'superego', covers in one way or another the variety of pathological defences against the persecutory guilt of the severe or the pathological superego and the difficulties encountered by the analyst when attempting to help the patient to modify this internal persecutory situation. An important aspect of the move from paranoid-schizoid to depressive functioning are the capacities to face reality and to see clearly, both of which involve the ability to symbolise and to think. Some of these themes are covered below. [*See* Depressive anxiety; Depressive position; Pathological organisations; Technique; Thinking and knowledge; Symbol formation.]

The 'ego-splitting', 'ego-destructive' or 'abnormal' superego

A number of Kleinian analysts take up Klein's thinking about abnormal superego development. Rosenfeld (1952) finds that Klein's ideas illuminate the difficulties of psychotic patients. He describes a patient whose inability to stand the terror and guilt caused by the dead or destroyed internal object (early persecuting superego) leads to a cycle in which the patient projects out the parts of himself containing the object and thereby increases his anxiety of persecution from without as well as from within. Rosenfeld focuses particularly on the patient's management of guilt by splitting or by seeking punishment, and holds the superego responsible for '*ego-splitting*' (1952, p. 72).

In his 1962 paper 'The superego and the ego ideal' Rosenfeld differentiates between the early and later superego and puts forward the idea that an extremely persecutory early superego can drive the latency child to completely split off the persecutory and idealised aspects of the early superego and make defensive, unmodified, uncritical identifications with external objects. The split-off aspects then have to be dealt with when they resurface at adolescence. These ideas were never specifically followed up, but Rosenfeld (1971) was extremely interested in the idea of narcissistic omnipotent identification with either the idealised good object or the idealised bad object (which he thought of as pure defused death instinct) [*see* Pathological organisations].

Bion (1959) introduces the term 'ego-destructive superego' for a particular kind of psychosis-inducing superego and describes its development as being due to the failure of the link between the infant and its mother. Bion extends Klein's idea of projective identification to include what he calls 'normal projective identification', in which the infant communicates its distress to the mother who takes in the distress, experiences it, is not overwhelmed and is able to provide the infant with an experience of being contained and understood. Bion's ego-destructive superego is the result of the infant's introjection of an object that by contrast fails to introject him or his distress, or is felt to introject him only to destroy him. Bion suggests that the failure is due to a combination of the constitution of the infant and the mother's incapacity to introject.

In 1962 Bion introduces the concept of 'minus K' or '−K'. The infant is described as needing an object who can take in its fear of death and manage the feelings of guilt that these feelings arouse. In −K the infant projects not only fear of death, but also envy and hate of the 'undisturbed breast'. The breast is then thought to enviously force 'worthless residue' back into the infant who ends up with a 'nameless dread', an attacking and guilt-inducing accuser that it then re-projects. Bion refers to this accuser as a 'super' ego and describes it as follows:

> . . . an envious assertion of moral superiority without any morals. In so far as its resemblance to the super-ego is concerned . . . shows itself as a superior object asserting its superiority by finding fault with everything. The most important characteristic is its hatred of any new development in the personality as if the new development were a rival to be destroyed. The emergence therefore of any tendency to search for the truth to establish contact with reality and in short to be scientific in no matter how rudimentary a fashion is met by destructive attacks.
>
> (Bion, 1962, p. 97)

O'Shaughnessy (1999), describes an 'abnormal' superego, which she identifies as similar to Rosenfeld's 'ego-splitting' superego, Bion's ego-destructive superego and Klein's terrifying split-off figures. While Klein has removed these figures from the superego, O'Shaughnessy, like Rosenfeld and Bion, sees them as forming an 'abnormal superego'. O'Shaughnessy's essential point is that, to quote, 'It can be seen that Freud, Abraham, Klein and Bion converge on the same dissociative area in regard to the abnormal superego' (1999, pp. 862–863). She contrasts this pathological superego with a harsh but normal superego that can be modified and points out that both kinds of superego exist, that patients move between the two and that both need to be recognised, differentiated, engaged with and worked with in analysis.

Superego: Structure or function; constituent parts

While the question of the structure and function of the superego runs throughout the literature, two writers have specifically addressed this issue. Riesenberg-Malcolm (1999) argues that the terms superego and internal object are interchangeable. For her the qualities of the objects make up the ego and the objects themselves form the superego: 'Most Kleinians think of the superego as a particular function of those internal objects. I personally believe that all internal objects operate as the superego' (1999, p. 60). She also disagrees with Klein's removal of the terrifying objects from the superego. For Riesenberg-Malcolm the deep unconscious is the core of a specific kind of superego; the Bion –K kind of superego, the ego-destructive superego.

Ronald Britton (2003) qualifies Riesenberg-Malcolm's statement that all internal objects operate as the superego; in his view all internal objects might operate as the superego. Approaching the concept from a different angle from that of Klein and his contemporaries, he describes the superego as a structure, 'a place in the psyche to be occupied' (2003, p. 74) and he draws attention to the fact that he now locates the third position of triangular space in the ego, whereas in 1998 he had placed it in the superego. He differentiates the judging functions of the ego and the superego, the ego's function being to make realistic judgements based on experience and the superego's being to make moral ones based on the authority of its position. Britton thinks that problems occur if the observing and judging functions of the ego are usurped by the superego: 'we must not simply be judged by our conscience we must submit our conscience to judgement' (2003, p. 101). He reasons that depressive guilt, which is based on a realistic assessment of damage and repair, occurs in the ego whereas persecutory guilt occurs in the superego. He describes humour as the opposite to morality and sees it as being the result of the self-reflective ego joining with the observing superego, amused at the discrepancy between the self and the ego ideal.

Britton proposes that, as well as ameliorating the superego, psychoanalysis seeks to change the relationship between the ego and the superego and in some cases to depose the envious superego from the position of moral arbitrator. Britton differentiates between the superego and an alien internal object and describes the way that both operate in narcissistic and pathological organisations. He also argues that the character of the actual parents plays a crucial part in the formation of the superego.

References

Anderson, R. (1997) 'Putting the boot in: Violent defences against depressive anxiety', in D. Bell (ed.) *Reason and Passion*. London: Duckworth, pp. 75–87.

Bion, W. R. (1959) 'Attacks on linking', *Int. J. Psycho-Anal.* 40: 308–315.

—— (1962) '–K', in *Learning from Experience*. London: Heinemann, pp. 95–105.

Brenman, E. (1985) 'Cruelty and narrow-mindedness', *Int. J. Psycho-Anal.* 66: 273–281; republished in G. Fornari Spoto (ed.) *Recovery of the Lost Good Object*. London: Routledge (2006).

Britton, R. (1998) *Belief and Imagination*. London: Routledge.

—— (2003) *Sex, Death, and the Superego*. London: Karnac.

Freud, S. (1894) 'The neuro-psychoses of defense', *S.E. 3*. London: Hogarth Press, pp. 45–61.

—— (1895) 'The psychotherapy of hysteria', *S.E. 2*. London: Hogarth Press, pp. 253–305.

—— (1914) 'On narcissism', *S.E. 14*. London: Hogarth Press, pp. 67–102.

—— (1916) 'Some character-types met with in psycho-analytic work', *S.E. 14*. London: Hogarth Press, pp. 309–333.

—— (1917) 'Mourning and melancholia', *S.E. 14*. London: Hogarth Press, pp. 237–258.

—— (1920) 'Beyond the pleasure principle', *S.E. 18*. London: Hogarth Press, pp. 3–64.

—— (1923) 'The ego and the id', *S.E. 19*. London: Hogarth Press, pp. 3–66.

—— (1924) 'The economic problem of masochism', *S.E. 19*. London: Hogarth Press, pp. 155–170.

—— (1930) 'Civilization and its discontents', *S.E. 21*. London: Hogarth Press, pp. 57–145.

—— (1933) 'The dissection of the psychical personality', *S.E. 22*. London: Hogarth Press, pp. 57–80.

Grinberg, L. (1978) 'The "razor's edge" in depression and mourning', *Int. J. Psycho-Anal.* 59: 245–254.

Heimann, P. (1942) 'A contribution to the problem of sublimation and its relation to processes of internalization', *Int. J. Psycho-Anal.* 23: 8–17.

—— (1952) 'Certain functions of introjection and projection in early infancy', in M. Klein, P. Heimann, S. Iaacs and J. Riviere (eds) *Developments in Psycho-Analysis*. London: Hogarth Press, pp. 122–168.

—— (1955) 'A combination of defences in paranoid states', in M. Klein, P. Heimann and R. Money-Kyrle (eds) *New Directions in Psycho-Analysis*. London: Tavistock, pp. 240–265.

Klein, M. (1926) 'The psychological principles of early analysis', in *The Writings of Melanie Klein*, Vol. 1. London: Hogarth Press, pp. 128–138.

—— (1927a) 'Symposium on child analysis', in *The Writings of Melanie Klein*, Vol. 1. London: Hogarth Press, pp. 139–169.

—— (1927b) 'Criminal tendencies in normal children', in *The Writings of Melanie Klein*, Vol. 1. London: Hogarth Press, pp. 170–185.

—— (1928) 'Early stages of the Oedipus conflict', in *The Writings of Melanie Klein*, Vol. 1. London: Hogarth Press, pp. 186–198.

—— (1929) 'Personification in the play of children', in *The Writings of Melanie Klein*, Vol. 1. London: Hogarth Press, pp. 199–209.

—— (1932) 'Early stages of the Oedipus conflict and of super-ego formation', in *The Psychoanalysis of Children, The Writings of Melanie Klein*, Vol. 2. London: Hogarth Press, pp. 123–148.

—— (1933) 'The early development of conscience in the child', in *The Writings of Melanie Klein*, Vol. 1. London: Hogarth Press, pp. 248–257.

—— (1935) 'A contribution to the psychogenesis of manic-depressive states', in *The Writings of Melanie Klein*, Vol. 1. London: Hogarth Press, pp. 262–289.

—— (1940) 'Mourning and its relation to manic-depressive states', in *The Writings of Melanie Klein*, Vol. 1. London: Hogarth Press, pp. 344–369.

—— (1946) 'Notes on some schizoid mechanisms', in *The Writings of Melanie Klein*, Vol. 3. London: Hogarth Press, pp. 1–24.

—— (1948) 'On the theory of anxiety and guilt', in *The Writings of Melanie Klein*, Vol. 3. London: Hogarth Press, pp. 25–42.

—— (1952) 'Some theoretical conclusions regarding the emotional life of the infant', in *The Writings of Melanie Klein*, Vol. 3. London: Hogarth Press, pp. 61–93.

—— (1955) 'The psycho-analytic play technique: Its history and significance', in M. Klein, P. Heimann and R. Money-Kyrle (eds) *New Directions in Psycho-Analysis*. London: Tavistock, pp. 3–22.

—— (1957) 'Envy and gratitude', in *The Writings of Melanie Klein*, Vol. 3. London: Hogarth Press, pp. 176–235.

—— (1958) 'On the development of mental functioning', in *The Writings of Melanie Klein*, Vol. 3. London: Hogarth Press, pp. 236–246.

—— (1963) 'On the sense of loneliness', in *The Writings of Melanie Klein*, Vol. 3. London: Hogarth Press, pp. 300–313.

Mancia, M. and Meltzer, D. (1981) 'Ego ideal functions and the psychoanalytical process', *Int. J. Psycho-Anal.* 62: 243–249.

Meltzer, D. (1967) *The Psycho-Analytical Process.* London: Heinemann.

Money-Kyrle, R. (1951) 'Some aspects of state and character in Germany', in G. Wilbur and W. Munsterberger (eds) *Psychoanalysis and Culture.* New York: International Universities Press, pp. 280–292; republished in *The Collected Papers of Roger Money-Kyrle.* Strath Tay: Clunie Press (1978), pp. 229–244.

—— (1968) 'Cognitive development', *Int. J. Psycho-Anal.* 49: 691–698; republished in *The Collected Papers of Roger Money-Kyrle.* Strath Tay: Clunie Press (1978), pp. 416–433.

O'Shaughnessy, E. (1999) 'Relating to the superego', *Int. J. Psycho-Anal.* 80: 861–870.

Riesenberg-Malcolm, R. (1999) 'The constitution and operation of the superego', in *On Bearing Unbearable States of Mind.* London: Routledge, pp. 53–70.

Rosenfeld, H. (1952) 'Notes on the psychoanalysis of the superego conflict in an acute schizophrenic patient', *Int. J. Psycho-Anal.* 33: 11–31; republished in *Psychotic States.* London: Hogarth Press (1965), pp. 63–103.

—— (1962) 'The superego and the ego ideal', *Int. J. Psycho-Anal.* 43: 258–263.

—— (1971) 'A clinical approach to the psychoanalytic theory of the life and death instincts: An investigation into the aggressive aspects of narcissism', *Int. J. Psycho-Anal.* 52: 169–178.

Searl, M. N. (1936) 'Infantile ideals', *Int. J. Psycho-Anal.* 17: 17–39.

Strachey, J. (1934) 'The nature of the therapeutic action of psychoanalysis', *Int. J. Psycho-Anal.* 15: 127–159.

9 Envy

Definition

The definition of envy used by Klein is the angry feeling that another person possesses and enjoys something desirable, often accompanied by an impulse to take it away or spoil it. Contemporary writing also recognises envy as a painful affliction. Klein thinks that envious impulses, oral and anal sadistic in nature, operate from the beginning of life, initially directed against the feeding breast and then against parental coitus. She sees envy as a manifestation of primary destructiveness, to some extent constitutionally based, and worsened by adversity. The attack on the good object leads to confusion between good and bad, and hence difficulties with depressive position integration. Envy heightens persecution and guilt. Klein came to see gratitude as an expression of love and thus of the life instinct, and as the antithesis of envy.

Key papers

1928   Klein, M. 'Early stages of the Oedipus conflict'.
Envy during the early Oedipus complex, manifest as desire to spoil the mother's possessions.

1932   Klein, M. *The Psychoanalysis of Children*.
A small child's envious attacks on phantasied parental coitus.

1945   Klein, M. 'The Oedipus complex in the light of early anxieties'.
Envy of the mother in the Oedipus complex of both sexes.

1952   Klein, M. 'The origins of transference'.
The prototypical envy-provoking phantasy of the parents combined in everlasting mutual gratification.

1955   Klein, M. 'On identification'.
A literary example showing envy as an important factor in projective identification.

1957   Klein, M. 'Envy and gratitude'.
            Klein's seminal paper on envy and gratitude, where the two are
            first explicitly paired.

1959   Klein, M. 'Our adult world and its roots in infancy'.
            A straightforward and comprehensive outline of the paired
            concepts of envy and gratitude.

Chronology

The term 'envy' has a long history in psychoanalysis, but the meaning has
varied. In psychoanalytic theory it is usually meant in the narrower and less
benign way in which Klein defines it above. Freud (1908) in 'On the sexual
theories of children' introduces the concept with 'envy of the penis' as a
key problem in the psychological development of women. Many psychoanalysts, including Klein, have subsequently challenged the centrality of
this notion to female development. Freud (1921) in 'Group psychology and
the analysis of the ego' also suggests that members of a group can forgo
their envious rivalry with one another in a common idealisation of the
group leader.

In everyday usage the terms envy and jealousy overlap, and 'envy' may
sometimes be used to mean something like 'admiration'. Klein's definition
of envy is well within the dominant traditional usage, although it emphasises the malignant aspects. As Elizabeth Spillius (1993, 2007) points out,
there are difficulties in treating much used words like envy and jealousy as
technical terms, as Klein does, for people are sure to add their version of
the various associations and overlapping meanings. Barrows (2002) points
out that envy was recognised as one of humanity's greatest problems long
before the days of psychoanalysis; that it is after all one of the 'seven deadly
sins', and according to Chaucer the worst one. Barrows points out that the
unique feature of envy is its lack of any positive aim:

> All other 'sins' have an aim which, though it may be misguided or self-
> seeking, seeks to obtain an object of desire. Greed, avarice, lust, pride,
> all in their own ways may be driven by the wish for something desir-
> able, albeit at someone else's expense. Only envy can lead to no gain,
> for the object of admiration is spoilt by envy and thereby rendered
> undesirable.
>
> (Barrows, 2002, p. 4)

Klein's contemporaries

Karl Abraham in 'A particular form of neurotic resistance against the psychoanalytic method' (1919) writes about patients who begrudge the efforts

and skill of the analyst, depreciate him, stubbornly refuse to cooperate with him and try to usurp his place. He describes envy as an unmistakable feature in this and sees it as an oral trait. Joan Riviere (1932) in 'Jealousy as a mechanism of defence' suggests that in some primitive states of mind a jealousy apparently linked to 'triangular situations' may be nearer to envy. Here, the deepest wish is to rob the mother of her possessions. Karen Horney in 'The problem of the negative therapeutic reaction' (1936) argues that the negative therapeutic reaction results from envy of the analyst, that is, a wish to spoil the analyst's work.

Herbert Rosenfeld and Hanna Segal, colleagues of Klein who began to analyse adult schizophrenics in the 1940s, describe how such patients typically mount wholesale attacks on the good object for its very goodness. Working as contemporaries of, and collaborators with, Klein their analysis of these extreme cases of envy helped to delineate the phenomenon (Rosenfeld, 1947, 1952; Segal, 1950).

Klein herself

Klein first refers to envy in 1928 in 'Early stages of the Oedipus conflict'. She sees it as emerging at the earliest stage of the Oedipus complex, as a desire in both sexes to spoil the mother's possessions, particularly the father's penis, which in phantasy the mother contains. Penis envy in Freud's sense occurs for Klein, but succeeds the girl's receptive attitude towards the father, and her wish for a child in the early feminine phase [*see* Oedipus complex]. The receptive attitude will again eclipse penis envy in normal later development.

Klein (1932) in *The Psychoanalysis of Children* gives a detailed clinical account of a small child's envious attacks on phantasied parental coitus. Klein considers envy to be one of the motive forces for the phantasy of pushing into the mother's body to discover and scoop out its contents. Although it was not an idea she developed, Klein in this paper describes such destructive phantasies as linked to the early epistemophilic instinct, implying the interesting paradox that the destructive phantasies have intrinsically positive value. However, such phantasies are in Klein's view also the deepest sources of guilt and lead to fears of harbouring hostile objects engaged in deadly intercourse, and/or threatening the self. Klein considers actual harmonious parents to be deeply reassuring in this respect.

Klein (1945) in 'The Oedipus complex in the light of early anxieties' discusses envy of the mother as an ordinary part of the Oedipus complex in both genders. For the girl, penis envy and the castration complex are exacerbated by frustration of the more basic positive oedipal desires. Klein thinks that children may at one time believe that mother has a penis as a male attribute, but unlike Freud she sees this as far less important than the idea that mother contains the father's penis.

In 1952 in 'The origins of transference' Klein spells out the 'prototype of situations of both envy and jealousy'. Powerful envy associated with frustrated oral desires, combined with the phantasy that some other person (typically father) receives the coveted gratification, leads to a phantasy of the parents combined in everlasting mutual gratification of an oral, anal and genital nature. Klein (1955) in 'On identification' then uses a literary example to illustrate how envy could be a factor driving a person to use extreme projective identification.

Klein's (1957) seminal paper entitled 'Envy and gratitude' first explicitly pairs the two concepts. Here she refers for the first time to envy of the breast, earlier discussed by Riviere (1932). Finally, Klein (1959) in 'Our adult world and its roots in infancy' provides a brief but comprehensive outline of the paired concepts of envy and gratitude.

Key ideas

Innate (primary) envy linked to the death instinct

For Klein, the tendency towards envy differs greatly in people, as does the capacity for love and accompanying gratitude for goodness received. The environment modifies these tendencies, in Klein's view, but does not initially determine their existence. The adaptation of Freud's death instinct concept occurred early in Klein's work [*see* Death instinct] but it was only in her 1957 paper that she linked innate destructive impulses explicitly with envy: 'I consider that envy is an oral-sadistic and anal sadistic expression of destructive impulses, operative from the beginning of life, and that it has a constitutional basis' (Klein, 1957, p. 176). Later in the same paper Klein says:

> In speaking of an innate conflict between love and hate, I am implying that the capacity both for love and for destructive impulses is, to some extent, constitutional, though varying individually in strength and interacting from the beginning with external conditions.
>
> (Klein, 1957, p. 180)

Again in this paper Klein quotes various literary sources (such as Milton, Chaucer and Spenser) to support her thesis of the universally recognised basic destructiveness of envy, and its opposition to love. She refers to Saint Augustine's description of Life as a creative force opposed to Envy, a destructive force, and quotes from the Bible's First Letter to the Corinthians: 'Love envieth not.'

Comparing envy, greed and jealousy

Klein distinguishes between envy, jealousy and greed, which may be confused in everyday usage. Envy, rooted in a two-person relationship, stimulates the impulse to take away and spoil the possession of another. Jealousy involves a three-person relationship:

> Jealousy is based on envy, but involves a relation to at least two people; it is mainly concerned with love that the subject feels is his due and has been taken away, or is in danger of being taken away, from him by his rival.
>
> (Klein, 1957, p. 181)

Greed is compared with envy:

> An impetuous and insatiable craving, exceeding what the subject needs and what the object is able and willing to give. At the unconscious level greed aims primarily at completely scooping out, sucking dry, and devouring the breast: that is to say, its aim is destructive introjection; whereas envy not only seeks to rob in this way, but also to put badness, primarily bad excrements and bad parts of the self into the mother, and first of all into her breast, to spoil and destroy her . . . one essential difference between greed and envy, although no rigid dividing line can be drawn since they are so closely associated, would accordingly be that greed is mainly bound up with introjection and envy with projection.
>
> (Klein, 1957, p. 181)

Envy, jealousy and greed are frequently found in close association. Greedy acquisition, for example, can be a defence against being aware of envy of those who have, or are, what one wishes for oneself. Where envy is strong, jealousy is bound to become stronger and more difficult to overcome.

Psychic consequences of envy

- *Interference with primal splitting*. Klein thinks that the immediate result of an envious spoiling of the good breast is that the essential primal splitting into good and bad is interfered with. The spoiled good object cannot be introjected in a proper, sustaining way. The damage caused to the breast by envy is also an unconscious source of premature guilt, which is felt in a paranoid way as an internal and external threat.
- *Confusional states*. Envious attacks mean that good and bad objects can no longer clearly be distinguished. Mild manifestations of the confusion caused by envy may be indecision and muddled thinking. Severe states of confusion caused by envy are characteristic of psychotic states, as Rosenfeld was later to show. Confusion in a different sense, between internal and external world and between self and other,

occurs as the result of strong projective identifications in an envious individual.

- *Problems with learning.* Confusion between the object's goodness and badness impairs processes of differentiation and introjection. Curiosity is suffused with hostility and thus felt to be dangerous. All this impairs the capacity for thinking and learning.
- *Retaliation for forced introjection.* As a result of the envious forcing (projection) of the self into the object to occupy and spoil it, there may be equally fearful phantasies of a retaliatory entry into the individual for spoiling.
- *Vicious cycles of greed and destructiveness.* The anxieties aroused may lead the individual to turn away from the source of goodness, or to become greedy and/or more destructive and hateful. Both the interference with primal splitting and the increased paranoia generated by excessive envy interfere with the move towards the depressive position. Opportunities are thus lessened for the good, satisfying experiences, which can mitigate envy.
- *Weakening of the ego.* Excessive envy in Klein's view weakens the ego, and puts the individual at risk of character deterioration rather than character strengthening in future adversity.
- *Interference with oedipal development.* Strong envy is associated with an abnormal Oedipus complex in a number of ways [*see* Oedipus complex]. The ordinary jealousies of the Oedipus complex are suffused with more problematic envy. Envy of the mother's possessions, including the phantasied penis of the father, make the phantasies of the combined parent figure more persecuting and persistent. An insecure, enviously based relationship with the primal object can mean that rivalry with the father arises prematurely, with his being seen as a very hostile intruder. Conversely, the libidinal turn from mother to father can be premature and insecure, based as it is on flight from the hated, disappointing mother. To escape from problematic (because envy-ridden) orality, the move to genitality may be premature, insecure and compulsive.

Envy and its link to gratitude

Klein came to see the antithesis of envy as gratitude, an expression of love and thus by implication the life instinct [*see* Instincts]. Klein does not develop the concept of gratitude nearly as fully as she does envy. Envy and gratitude are not explicitly paired until 1957, but the importance of gratitude as a concept arises earlier in Klein's work. Klein (1928) first describes the woman's gratitude to her husband for fulfilling long-thwarted sexual desires. Gratitude then emerges as a feature in Klein's theory of the depressive position (Klein, 1935). Klein (1937) describes the infant's spontaneous gratitude to the mother for her love and care, and also the mother's gratitude to the infant for affording her the enjoyment of loving him. These are seen as part of love, a manifestation of innate 'forces that tend to preserve life' (p. 311), as opposed to the innate destructive impulses [*see* Instincts].

Klein in her much fuller exposition of gratitude (1957) sees it as part of the relation to the good object, which is taken in to form the core of the ego:

> In contrast with the infant who, owing to his envy, has been unable to build up securely a good internal object, a child with a strong capacity for love and gratitude has a deep-rooted relation with a good object and can, without being fundamentally damaged, withstand temporary states of envy, hated and grievance, which arise even in children who are loved and well mothered.
>
> (Klein, 1957, p. 187)

Gratitude is closely bound up with true generosity and gives a sense of inner wealth. Klein sees the capacity for gratitude, like the tendency towards envy, as partly innately determined but, again, influenced by the environment.

Envy: Interaction of constitution and environment

Envy, in Klein's view, is affected by the environment in complex ways [*see* External world/environment]: '. . . in every individual, frustration and unhappy circumstances rouse some envy and hate throughout life, but the strength of these emotions and the way in which the individual copes with them varies considerably' (Klein, 1957, p. 190).

Klein sees the infant as having a phantasy of an inexhaustible breast. When the infant is deprived, the breast is hated and envied for apparently meanly keeping these riches to itself. However, the satisfying breast is also envied: 'The very ease with which the milk comes – though the infant feels gratified by it – also gives rise to envy because this gift seems something so unattainable' (Klein, 1957, p. 183).

Klein links this infantile situation with the analytic observation that patients may become destructively critical of helpful work:

> The envious patient grudges the analyst the success of his work; and if he feels that the analyst and the help he is giving have become spoilt and devalued by his envious criticism, he cannot introject him sufficiently as a good object.
>
> (Klein, 1957, p. 184)

Envy in relation to the depressive position

Klein shows through clinical examples how, when a patient becomes conscious of his envy, he may be able to experience guilt and make reparation. She is impressed by the intense pain and depression that many patients experience when attempting to integrate their increasing awareness of making envious attacks on the analyst's goodness with their conscious positive feelings towards the analyst. This guilty pain can easily prompt a defensive withdrawal back to paranoid-schizoid functioning, as can the pain of consciously recognised envy itself.

When paranoia is strong, for example in psychotic patients, envy is hard to counteract in analysis. Similarly, when envy is strong, paranoia is hard to counteract. When more depressive features predominate in the personality envy will be mitigated more readily, as such patients tend to be more able to experience gratitude and to take in what people have to offer.

Defences against envy

Envious feelings are generally recognised as a painful part of the human condition that can mobilise various defences. Defences against envy are often more problematic than envy itself. A list, which Klein acknowledges is non-exhaustive, is given in her 1957 paper, and others have added to it (see Segal, 1964; Rosenfeld, 1964a; Joseph, 1982, 1986; Sohn, 1985; Spillius, 1993). Sometimes, as Joseph (1986) points out, it is hard to tease out the element of envy itself and the defences against it.

- *Devaluation of the object.* Spoiling, devaluation and ingratitude are inherent in envy and also defend against experiencing it, as the devalued object need not be envied any more. Klein describes how this can become characteristic of object relations for some people.
- *Idealisation.* Klein describes how the typical early defences – omnipotence, denial and splitting – are reinforced by envy. If the object is sufficiently idealised, comparisons with oneself become irrelevant, and the object is omnipotently 'owned' – the self is aggrandised by association. Idealisation may take the form of denigration of the envied object and idealisation of some other object; or some aspect of the envied object may be denigrated and others idealised. An idealised object is unstable, and liable to collapse into its opposite. Strong envy will in any case eventually threaten the ideal object too.
- *Identification with the idealised object.* Linked to the above through projection and introjection, the individual feels that he is the possessor of the coveted attributes of the envied object.
- *Confusion.* Confusion (see above) is a result of envy, where the good object is so attacked that it can no longer be clearly distinguished

from the bad object. Klein also suggests that confused thinking may also be adopted as a defence against the persecution and guilt stirred up by envy.

• *Flight from the mother.* The flight from the mother to other people (starting with father), who are idealised in order to avoid hostile feelings towards the primary object, becomes a means of protecting the breast/mother. This mechanism fails when envy is too strong, and eventually imbues the new relationships too.

• *Devaluation/inhibition of the self.* Klein suggests that this tends to replace object devaluation in more depressive types. By devaluing his own gifts, a person simultaneously denies envy and punishes himself for it. Avoidance of competition and success is also an attempt to protect a precariously established good object, lest it be spoilt by situations liable to cause competitive and envious feelings in the self. Joseph (1982, 1986) also points out that masochistic self-attack indirectly spoils the good given to him by his object, and proves the object impotent to help.

• *Greedy internalisation of the breast.* By this mechanism the breast becomes possessed and controlled in phantasy by the infant, who thus avoids feeling separate and envious. All the good attributed to the breast can now be owned for the self. However:

> It is the very greed with which this internalization is carried out that contains the germ of failure . . . a good object which is well established . . . not only loves the subject but is loved by it. This . . . does not apply, or only in a minor degree, to an idealized one. By powerful and violent possessiveness, the good object is felt to turn into a destroyed persecutor.
>
> (Klein, 1957, p. 218)

• *Projection of envy.* One's own envy may be attributed to others by projection. The individual sees himself as non-envious but surrounded by envious others. This also contributes to a paranoid sense of the world.

• *Stirring up envy in others.* There may be a further step in the projection of envy, in that the projection may be actualised. Stirring up envy in others by one's own success and possessions by projection is a frequent method of defence in envy. The ultimate ineffectiveness of this method derives from the persecutory and depressive anxieties to which it gives rise.

• *Stifling of love and intensification of hate.* Klein thought that this was less painful to bear than the guilt arising from the combination of love, hate and envy. It may not express itself as hate, but take the form of indifference. The individual tends to withdraw from people, but this apparent independence is illusory.

- *Acting-out.* Rosenfeld (1955) describes how various forms of acting-out are used to perpetuate the split in the personality when integration of the enviously destructive parts of the personality threatens to dawn.

Envy and its contribution to psychosis

Klein herself did not analyse psychotic adults, but close contemporaries did during her lifetime, in particular Rosenfeld, Segal and Bion, and their findings are likely to have informed her thinking on the topic of envy. Rosenfeld's (1947) analysis of 'Mildred' shows the unbearable quality of envy associated with psychotic breakdown and manifesting itself in the analytic transference. Mostly Mildred's envious destructiveness was split off, and thus experienced as persecution from outside. In a slightly later paper on confusional states in schizophrenia, Rosenfeld (1950) talks about attacks on the good object contributing to confusional states, but does not mention envy specifically. In later papers, however (e.g. Rosenfeld 1964a), he acknowledges how Klein's 'Envy and gratitude' paper has clarified the phenomenon of confusional states.

Bion (1957) in 'On arrogance' describes how the analyst's capacity to contain the projections of the patient is an important source of envy, particularly for psychotic and borderline patients. Bion sees envy as primarily in opposition to creativity, rather than to gratitude. In Bion's (1959) view envy is manifest fundamentally as attacks on any sort of creative link in the mind. Any perceived link between the parental couple must be obliterated, as must anything that symbolises this. Ultimately, and particularly in the psychotic personality, links between ideas and hence the process of thought itself are attacked and fragmented.

Envy and the negative therapeutic reaction

Klein (1957) mentions how split-off envy may manifest itself as a negative therapeutic reaction in an apparently cooperative patient. She describes how a negative therapeutic reaction may set in secondarily, retrospectively attacking a piece of analytic work that has initially clearly been helpful. This had also been addressed earlier by Riviere (1932) and Horney (1936).

Later developments

The envious superego

Bion (1962) in *Learning from Experience* conceptualises some cases of problematic envy in the personality in terms of an abnormal, envious superego that he calls an 'ego-destructive superego' [*see* Superego]. His hypothesis is that this pathological superego arises during failures of communication between mother and infant. The deficit may be more 'environmental' in that the mother cannot allow her infant's communications to enter her. Bion also hypothesises that an infant with a large endowment of primary envy may withhold communication hatefully and enviously. The impermeable mother (whatever the origin of this figure) is now split off but exists as a hostile force forming the basis of an ego-destructive superego, of which Bion writes:

> It is a super-ego that has hardly any of the characteristics of the super-ego as understood in psychoanalysis: it is 'super' ego. It is an envious assertion of moral superiority without any morals. In short it is the resultant of an envious stripping or denudation of all good and is itself destined to continue the process of stripping . . . till [there is] . . . hardly more than an empty superiority-inferiority that in turn degenerates to nullity.
>
> (Bion, 1962, p. 97)

O'Shaughnessy (1999) in 'Relating to the superego' develops this theme further, with clinical illustrations showing how this abnormal superego usurps the status and authority of a normal superego. In the transference situation, the patient and analyst relate as one abnormal superego to another.

Britton (1989) in 'The missing link' suggests that where maternal containment fails seriously, the individual may be forced into a precarious idealisation of the mother whereupon the oedipal third object becomes imbued by projection with the hostile destructive qualities of an abnormal superego. The primal scene in such patients will assume horrendous qualities and triangular relationships will be experienced as extremely destructive and dangerous.

Envy and narcissistic object relations

Klein (1957) speaks in terms of the paranoid-schizoid position, rather than in terms of narcissistic structures, in her study of envy. Her followers, however, have shown how closely linked envy is to narcissistic organisations of the personality. Rosenfeld (1964b) in 'On the psychopathology of narcissism' shows how narcissistic object relations defend against the recognition of separateness between self and other. The object is either omnipotently incorporated or taken over by projection. The strength and persistence of omnipotent narcissistic object relations, in Rosenfeld's view, are closely related to the strength of the individual's envy. They obviate both the aggressive feelings caused by frustration and any awareness of envy. However, the resulting lack of emotional contact means lack of real pleasure and hence ultimately more potential envy of those who seem to have richer lives.

Rosenfeld (1971, 1987) goes on to describe the complex, rigidified narcissistic structures that could develop in the envious personality. The omnipotently destructive superego figures are often manifest as a phantasied 'gang' or 'mafia' that holds more loving and dependent parts of the personality in thrall [*see* Pathological organisations]. Destructive impulses, bad parts of the self and bad objects are all idealised. Sidney Klein (1980) addresses a similar problem when he describes autistic phenomena even in neurotic patients and traces them to internal objects that are felt to survive in a walled-off state, as if surrounded by a carapace.

Steiner in 'Perverse relationships between parts of the self' (1982) and later in *Psychic Retreats* (1993) also describes such internal psychotic organisations. He points out the perverse quality of internal relationships in these narcissistic structures. Joseph in a number of her papers (1971, 1975, 1986) collected in *Psychic Equilibrium and Psychic Change* (1989) describes clinical manifestations of the death instinct and of envy in the form of character perversions. Destructive aspects are concealed, but a perverse quality suffuses the transference.

'Impenitent' envy

Elizabeth Spillius (1993, 2007) points out that much Kleinian writing about envy addresses unconscious or split-off envy, where the patient may gain relief once the envy is brought into consciousness. Spillius addresses what she calls 'impenitent envy', which is conscious and ego-syntonic. The analyst feels he is observing envious, destructive attacks on good objects. The patient, however, feels that he has legitimate grievances about objects who deserve to be hated. He uses his defences to maintain and enhance what he regards as legitimate grievances. Spillius thinks that such patients also have to evade acknowledging the acute pain, even fear of collapse, that would come from having to mourn the loss or absence of good relationships.

Envy and the motive of the giver

Spillius goes on to put envy in the context of the complex relationship between giver and receiver in early object relationships. A provider may give willingly and lovingly, and allow the recipient to give pleasure in return:

> The receiver's capacity to be given to is a return gift to the original giver. Goodness in the other becomes bearable, even enjoyable. The

receiver introjects and identifies with an object who enjoys giving and receiving, and an internal basis for admiration can develop, and hence emulation of the generous giver becomes possible.

(Spillius, 1993, p. 1209)

On the other hand the giver may take little pleasure in giving and may be narcissistic, and uninterested in, or even hostile to the receiver. Or he may give eagerly and with pleasure, but only in order to demonstrate his superiority over the receiver. Further complexities arise when one imagines the receiver perceiving the state and motives of the giver accurately, or misinterpreting them, and so on. Spillius does not contest the idea of 'constitutional' variations in tendencies to envy, but adds a dimension of environmental complexity to be taken into account.

John Steiner, in an unpublished discussion of Spillius' paper in 1992, stresses that in Kleinian terms the essential element of envy is a hatred of difference between subject and object. Its aim is to reduce this difference by destroying what the object has, whether it is goodness or whether it is difference in gender, generation, and so on. Ultimately envy aims to reduce the subject and the object to a sameness where there is nothing to envy. In this way envy expresses the death instinct [*see* Death instinct], whose aim is to create an undifferentiated, homogeneous, structureless substance.

Envy as a compound state: Britton

Britton (2003) in the chapter of his book *Sex Death and the Superego* 'The ego-destructive superego' does not think that envy itself is 'primary'. He argues that envy is a 'molecule' not an 'atom' – a compound state. He sees one element of it as innate destructiveness, which he further conceptualises as anti-object relational – the need to obliterate 'not self'. Britton also describes this as 'psychic atopia', a sort of 'allergic' tendency towards other minds. This destructive tendency exists along a spectrum in people, as he describes, from misanthropic to xenocidal. The other element of envy he sees as pronounced or excessive covetousness. Thus the envious object relationship Britton sees as: 'a compound of *covetousness* and *xenocide*. The desire to possess the attributes of the object is combined with the urge to destroy the object as the source of such disturbing feelings' (Britton, 2003, p. 127).

A number of useful contemporary papers on the topic of envy are collected in *Envy and Gratitude Revisited*, edited by Roth and Lemma (2008). Kate Barrows (2002) has published a useful and wide-ranging monograph on envy in the *Ideas in Psychoanalysis* series. This includes a discussion of problems of envy at different times of life and manifestations of envy in society.

Controversies around the Kleinian envy concept

Spillius (1993) points out that envy has the special distinction of being one of the 'seven deadly sins', but at the same time it is not frequently the subject of philosophical or social debate: 'It is as if it were recognised on the one hand, while rapidly dismissed on the other' (p. 1199). Spillius summarises the 'storm of disagreement' in the British Psychoanalytical Society provoked by Klein's publication of her 1957 book on envy. Criticisms of Klein's ideas were voiced in a symposium on envy and jealousy held in London in 1969. The chief ground for argument with Klein was that it seemed preposterous to regard such pernicious attacks on goodness as inherent in human nature. There was debate as to what actually constituted envy and how early it could arise in the individual. The theory was criticised as one of despair. There was also concern as to how, if at all, it should be interpreted to the patient. The main critical paper of the symposium was published the same year (Joffe, 1969).

Disagreements over the nature of envy

Joffe (1969) sees envy as 'common currency' in psychoanalysis since its beginning. He considers it complex and secondary, one of many affects and traits that should not be specially privileged, disputing Klein's view of it as an inborn motivating force in human functioning. Joffe's view is that there is no proper distinction between self and object in early life, and hence an idea of the object possessing and withholding something desired by the infant makes no real sense. Joffe's conception of envy, however, seems entirely based on the idea of reactions to deprivation and frustration of various kinds, and he does not thus address Klein's key idea about envious reactions to experiences that might be expected to fulfil and satisfy. As Etchegoyen, Lopez and Rabih (1987) point out, 'the relation between envy and frustration is a two way thoroughfare' (p. 50) since 'envy may generate frustration in so far as it impedes receiving what is available' (p. 50). Having argued against Klein's idea of inborn envy, Joffe interestingly ends his paper by considering a constitutional factor of low inborn threshold of affect tolerance and discharge: 'This plays a big part in deciding whether the individual will have a high toleration of his envious characteristics and of his feelings of envy which may be mobilised from time to time' (Joffe, 1969, p. 543).

Zetzel (1958) in 'Review of Klein's *Envy and Gratitude*' seems to grasp better Klein's idea that excessive envy may cause the infant to sabotage its own pleasure in receiving and thus impair growth and development. However she, like Joffe, disputes Klein's idea of envy as a basic, essentially innate emotional attitude that varies in degree between one individual and another. Again, she disputes the degree of complexity implied in terms of self–object differentiation and in terms of affect, seeing Klein as moving significantly away from mainstream psychoanalytic theory.

Guntrip's (1961) objection to Klein's envy concept is that it seems to him despairing, and he contrasts it with Fairbairn's more hopeful view:

> The infant from the start, she holds, feels envious of the good breast of the mother and wishes to destroy it because he does not possess it himself. In that case there seems little hope of love-relationships of a really durable kind coming into being, and it would appear rather that all love must function as a defence against repressed envy and hate. Fairbairn, on the contrary, holds that it is most important to help the patient to recognise that hate is not the ultimate thing and that always love underlies hate if one penetrates deep enough.
>
> (Guntrip, 1961, p. 344)

This seems in fact to be a misunderstanding of Klein, in that she holds (unlike Freud (1915) in 'Instincts and their vicissitudes' who suggests that 'hate is older than love') that both love and hate operate together and in opposition from the beginning. In Klein's view love is neither 'a defence' nor the 'ultimate thing'; as human beings, our love and hate are in eternal conflict.

Technique of interpretation of envy

Zetzel (1958) wonders how good analysis could help a patient suffering from the sort of excessive envy described by Klein, since accurate interpretation would surely elicit 'unanalyzable negative responses'. At the same time, she fears that an embrace of the innate envy hypothesis might induce the analyst to attribute therapeutic failure defects in the patient: 'One cannot help envisaging the possibility that a premise like Mrs Klein's might, in certain circumstances or in inexperienced hands, lead to an unjustified attitude of analytic omnipotence which could adversely influence the progress of treatment' (Zetzel, 1958, p. 411).

John Steiner (unpublished, 1992) feels that the most important of the criticisms of the Kleinian envy concept is indeed that envy could be prematurely interpreted in a persecuting way, and that analysts may not always have sufficiently acknowledged the extent to which the very idea of envy had been defended against and was thus not available. He feels that our increasing understanding of countertransference has helped analysts to recognise their own difficulties with envy and hence to interpret the patient's conflict with it in a more understanding way.

Etchegoyen et al. (1987) refer to the Scylla of 'supportive psychotherapy' that fails to address the patient's envy and the Charybdis of overinterpreting envy from the superego-ish position of a 'spotless' analyst, both mistakes that they say will lead to vicious circles. In the one, the patient will be reinforced in his paranoia or mania, but will feel subtly uncontained and fail to respect the analyst's work; envy will not arise in the transference and thus it will be unavailable for analysis. In the other case, the patient may submit and idealise the analyst but again the 'treatment' is no such thing.

Spillius (1993) considers that current Kleinian analysts, especially in Britain, speculate less than Klein did about the development of envy in infancy and focus more on the expression of envy in the clinical situation:

> One of the hard-won clinical understandings arising from the insight of Klein is that in some patients envy can be extremely destructive, both to the individual himself and to his objects, including the analyst. In severe cases it is as if envy held the patient in thrall; the patient feels that his convictions and his defensive system are infinitely preferable to his tentative relationship with the analyst as a good object, and he attacks the relationship remorselessly, especially when he feels the analyst has been helpful.
>
> (Spillius, 1993, pp. 1201–1202)

Spillius considers, however, that there has been a gradual assimilation of some of the criticisms of Kleinian usage, such that there is now a greater acceptance of the inevitable ubiquity of envy, more understanding of the need for defences against it and a somewhat less confrontational interpretation of it: 'It is now generally accepted that it is not usually helpful to interpret envy directly to patients who are locked into the psychopathology of the paranoid-schizoid position and have very little insight or interest in understanding their motives' (Spillius, 1993, p. 1202).

References

Abraham, K. (1919) 'A particular form of neurotic resistance against the psycho-analytic method', in *Selected Papers on Psychoanalysis*. London: Maresfield (1927), pp. 303–311.

Barrows, K. (2002) *Ideas in Psychoanalysis: Envy*. Cambridge: Icon Books.

Bion, W. (1957) 'On arrogance', *Int. J. Psycho-Anal*. 39: 144–146.

——— (1959) 'Attacks on linking', *Int. J. Psycho-Anal*. 40: 308–315.

——— (1962) *Learning from Experience*. London: Heinemann.

Britton, R. (1989) 'The missing link: Parental sexuality in the Oedipus complex', in J. Steiner (ed.) *The Oedipus Complex Today*. London: Karnac, pp. 83–101.

——— (2003) 'The ego-destructive superego', in *Sex, Death, and the Superego*. London: Karnac, pp. 117–128.

Etchegoyen, O. R. H., Lopez, B. M. and Rabih, M. (1987) 'On envy and how to interpret it', *Int. J. Psycho-Anal*. 68: 49–61.

Freud, S. (1908) 'On the sexual theories of children', *S.E. 9*. London: Hogarth Press, pp. 207–226.

—— (1915) 'Instincts and their vicissitudes', *S.E. 14*. London: Hogarth Press, pp. 111–140.

—— (1921) 'Group psychology and the analysis of the ego', *S.E. 18*. London: Hogarth Press, pp. 65–143.

Guntrip, H. (1961) *Personality Structure and Human Interaction*. London: Hogarth Press.

Horney, K. (1936) 'The problem of the negative therapeutic reaction', *Psychoanal. Q.* 2: 29–44.

Joffe, W. (1969) 'A critical survey of the status of the envy concept', *Int. J. Psycho-Anal.* 50: 533–545.

Joseph, B. (1971) 'A clinical contribution to the analysis of a perversion', *Int. J. Psycho-Anal.* 52: 441–449.

—— (1975) 'The patient who is difficult to reach', in P. L. Giovacchini (ed.) *Tactics and Techniques in Psychoanalytic Therapy, Vol. 2, Countertransference*. New York: Jason Aronson, pp. 205–216.

—— (1982) 'Addiction to near-death', *Int. J. Psycho-Anal.* 63: 449–456.

—— (1986) 'Envy in everyday life', *Psychoanal. Psychother.* 2: 13–22.

Klein, M. (1928) 'Early stages of the Oedipus conflict', in *The Writings of Melanie Klein*, Vol. 1. London: Hogarth Press, pp. 186–198.

—— (1932) *The Psychoanalysis of Children. The Writings of Melanie Klein*, Vol. 2. London: Hogarth Press.

—— (1935) 'A contribution to the psychogenesis of manic-depressive states', in *The Writings of Melanie Klein*, Vol. 1. London: Hogarth Press, pp. 262–289.

—— (1937) *Love, Guilt and Reparation*, in *The Writings of Melanie Klein*, Vol. 1. London: Hogarth Press, pp. 306–343.

—— (1945) 'The Oedipus complex in the light of early anxieties', in *The Writings of Melanie Klein*, Vol. 1. London: Hogarth Press, pp. 370–419.

—— (1952) 'The origins of transference', in *The Writings of Melanie Klein*, Vol. 3. London: Hogarth Press, pp. 48–56.

—— (1955) 'On identification', in *The Writings of Melanie Klein*, Vol. 3. London: Hogarth Press, pp. 141–175.

—— (1957) 'Envy and gratitude', in *The Writings of Melanie Klein*, Vol. 3. London: Hogarth Press, pp. 176–235.

—— (1959) 'Our adult world and its roots in infancy', in *The Writings of Melanie Klein*, Vol. 3. London: Hogarth Press, pp. 247–263.

Klein, S. (1980) 'Autistic phenomena in neurotic patients', *Int. J. Psycho-Anal.* 61: 395–401.

O'Shaughnessy, E. (1999) 'Relating to the superego', *Int. J. Psycho-Anal.* 80: 861.

Riviere, J. (1932) 'Jealousy as a mechanism of defence', *Int. J. Psycho-Anal.* 13: 414–424.

Rosenfeld, H. (1947) 'Analysis of a schizophrenic state with depersonalization', in *Psychotic States*. London: Hogarth Press, pp. 13–33.

—— (1950) 'Notes on the psychopathology of confusional states in chronic schizophrenias', in *Psychotic States*. London: Hogarth Press, pp. 52–62.

—— (1952) 'Notes on the psychoanalysis of the superego conflict in an acute schizophrenic', in *Psychotic States*. London: Hogarth Press, pp. 63–103.

—— (1964a) 'An investigation into the need of neurotic and psychotic patients to act out during analysis', in *Psychotic States*. London: Hogarth Press, pp. 200–216.

—— (1964b) 'On the psychopathology of narcissism, a clinical approach', in *Psychotic States*. London: Hogarth Press, pp. 169–179.

—— (1971) 'A clinical approach to the psychoanalytical theory of the life and death instinct: An investigation into the aggressive aspects of narcissism', *Int. J. Psycho-Anal.* 52: 169–178.

—— (1987) *Impasse and Interpretation*. London: Tavistock.

Roth, P. and Lemma, A. (eds) (2008) *Envy and Gratitude Revisited*. London: International Psychoanalytic Association.

Segal, H. (1950) 'Some aspects of the analysis of a schizophrenic', *Int. J. Psycho-Anal.* 31: 268–278.

—— (1964) *Introduction to the Work of Melanie Klein*. London: Hogarth Press.

Sohn, L. (1985) 'Narcissistic organization, projective identification, and the formation of the identificate', *Int. J. Psycho-Anal.* 66: 201–213.

Spillius, E. (1993) 'Varieties of envious experience', *Int. J. Psycho-Anal.* 74: 1199–1212.

—— (2007) *Encounters with Melanie Klein: Selected Papers of Elizabeth Spillius*. London: Routledge.

Steiner, J. (1982) 'Perverse relationships between parts of the self', *Int. J. Psycho-Anal.* 63: 241–252.

—— (1993) *Psychic Retreats: Pathological Organizations in Psychotic, Neurotic and Borderline Patients*. London: Routledge.

Zetzel, E. (1958) 'Review of Klein's *Envy and Gratitude*', *Psychoanal. Q.* 27: 409–412.

10 Symbol formation

Definition

The term 'symbol formation' is used in psychoanalysis to denote a mode of indirect or figurative representation of a significant idea, conflict or wish. The ability to move on from relating concretely to archaic objects to relating symbolically to substitute objects (symbols) is both a developmental achievement and a move made because of the anxieties involved in relating to primal objects. Klein extended the ideas of both Freud and Jones on symbols, showing in particular the symbolic significance of play and how sublimation depends on the capacity to symbolise. Segal further developed Klein's theory of symbols, distinguishing between the symbol proper formed in the depressive position and a more primitive version, the symbolic equation, belonging to paranoid-schizoid functioning. In the symbolic equation, the symbol is equated with the thing symbolised.

Key papers

1895   Freud, S. and Breuer, J. *Studies in Hysteria*.
                 Symptom formation through symbolisation.

1900   Freud, S. *The Interpretation of Dreams*.
                 The importance of symbolism in dreams.

1916   Jones, E. 'The theory of symbolism'.
                 Early influential but limited theory of symbolism, for example distinguishing symbolism from sublimation.

1923a   Klein, M. 'The role of the school in the libidinal development of the child'.
                 Learning is inhibited when words and numbers are imbued with frightening, concrete symbolic significance.

1923b   Klein, M. 'Early analysis'.
             Contrary to Jones, Klein concludes that symbolism is the
             foundation of all sublimation.

1929a   Klein, M. 'Personification in the play of children'.
             Symbolisation in play.

1929b   Klein, M. 'Infantile anxiety-situations in a work of art and in
             the creative impulse'.
             Symbolisation in play.

1930   Klein, M. 'The importance of symbol formation in the
             development of the ego'.
             Klein's definitive statement on symbol formation.

1952   Segal, H. 'A psychoanalytic approach to aesthetics'.
             The link between the aesthetics and the depressive position.

1957   Segal, H. 'Notes on symbol formation'.
             Landmark paper on symbolisation.

1974   Segal, H. 'Delusion and artistic creativity'.
             Golding's novel *The Spire* is used to explore some aspects of
             creativity.

1979   Segal, H. Postcript to 'Notes on symbol formation'.
             Segal refines her 1957 symbol theory in terms of Bion's con-
             tainer and contained.

Chronology and discussion

Precursors

Freud on symbolism

Freud mentions symbolism briefly in 'Project for a scientific psychology',
referring to the way a soldier may be prepared to die for a flag, or a knight
may fight for his lady's glove (Freud, 1895, p. 349). Both soldier and knight
are aware that the symbolic object represents the true object of love. Freud
contrasts this 'normal' symbol formation to hysterical symbol formation
where the 'absurd' idea that causes distress to the neurotic is linked to and
symbolically represents the patient's hidden and truly upsetting unconscious idea. Then in *Studies in Hysteria* (1895) Freud and Breuer distinguish
in several passages between an associative determination of symptoms (such
as when Fraulein Elisabeth von R's hysterical leg pain was traced back to
the place where her father used to lay *his* leg for dressings to be done) and a
symbolic one. He gives as an example of the latter the 'violent facial

neuralgia' of Frau Cacilie, which was eventually relieved by abreacting the memories of bitter arguments with her husband where various insults of his had felt 'like a slap in the face'.

The Editor's introduction to Volume 4 of the Standard Edition (*The Interpretation of Dreams*, Part 1) outlines Freud's increasing realisation of the importance of symbolism in dreams over the four editions of this work. In the fourth edition (written in 1914), following an accumulation of material in the second and third editions, an entirely new section on symbolism is introduced, called 'Representation by symbols in dreams' (Freud, 1900, pp. 350–404). For Freud there is a relatively fixed vocabulary of symbols across individuals and cultures. They appear in very diverse forms of expression, not just in dreams but also in symptoms and other products of the unconscious: myths, folklore, religion, etc. In 'Introductory lectures on psychoanalysis' Freud (1916) summarises the range of phenomena represented symbolically in dreams as: 'the human body as a whole, parents, children, brothers and sisters, birth, death, nakedness and . . . sexual life – the genitals, sexual processes, sexual intercourse' (p. 153). The meaning of dream symbols eludes consciousness, yet their unconscious nature cannot be explained by the mechanisms of the dream-work. Thus Freud holds that there are two types of dream interpretation: one based on the dreamer's associations and the other on the interpretation of the symbols, which are not the dreamer's personal creation in the same way.

Jones on symbolism

In his 1916 paper 'The theory of symbolism' (enlarged and republished in 1948) Ernest Jones makes further additions to the psychoanalytic theory of symbolism and also narrows the definition. All symbols (as for Freud) represent ideas of 'the self and of immediate blood relations and of the phenomena of birth, life and death' (Jones, 1948, p. 102). Jones defines symbolisation in a narrow way, seeing desires and desired objects as symbolised only when they are subject to conflict and repression. He distinguishes between symbolisation and sublimation, which for him is implicitly a more mature process. In fact, in contrast to later thinkers, Jones thinks of symbolisation as a primitive mode of expression, wholly defensive rather than creative:

> Symbolism thus appears as the unconscious precipitate of primitive means of adaptation to reality that have become superfluous or useless, a sort of lumber room of civilisation to which the adult readily feels in states of reduced or deficient capacity for adaptation to reality, in order to regain his old, long-forgotten playthings of childhood.
>
> (Jones, 1948, p. 109)

Klein on symbolism

Jones' adoption of a very narrow definition of symbolisation, and his distinction between sublimation and symbolisation, have not proved useful in psychoanalysis. Klein in 'Early analysis' (1923b) considers that, far from being distinct from it, symbol formation is the *basis* of sublimation. When a wider concept of symbolism is admitted we can establish a connection between the early primitive desires and processes in the mind and the later development of the individual. Thus we have a way of conceptualising the way the child's interest in the external world is determined by a series of displacements of affect and interests to ever new objects.

Because in Klein's work bodily sensations are represented in phantasy as relationships with objects, we can in fact see the beginnings of symbolisation as part of the very nature of mental life. When the individual eventually perceives the external world objectively, the meaningfulness of those external objects comes from their investment with the mentally conceived relationships.

Klein at an early stage realised the symbolic value of children's play, something Freud had observed (for example in the cotton reel game) but not yet explicitly theorised. In 'the psychological principles of early analysis' she says: 'In their play children represent symbolically phantasies, wishes and their experiences. Here they are employing the same language, the same archaic, phylogenetically acquired mode of expression as that which we are familiar with in dreams' (Klein, 1926, p. 134).

Some clinical extracts show that even at an early stage of her work, as in 'The role of the school in the libidinal development of the child' (1923a), Klein is aware of how symbolism, often of a rather primitive kind, imbues the phantasies and activities of the child, and may inhibit learning:

> Fritz had a marked inhibition in doing division sums, all explanations proving unavailing, for he understood them quite well, but always did these sums wrong. He told me once that in doing division he had first of all to bring down the figure that was required and he climbed up, seized it by the arm and pulled it down . . . quite certainly it was not pleasant for the number – it was as if his mother stood on a stone 13 yards high and someone came and caught her by the arm so that they tore it out and divided her.
>
> (Klein, 1923a, pp. 69–70)

Abraham (1923) pointed out that the symbolic meaning of the figure '3' from the Oedipus complex – determined namely by the relationship, father, mother and child – is more significant than the very frequent employment of '3' for the male genitals. I shall adduce only one example of this.

> Lisa [aged 17] considered the number '3' insupportable because 'a third person is of course always superfluous' and 'two can run races with one another' . . . but the third has no business there. Lisa, who had a taste for mathematics, but was very inhibited where it was concerned, told me that actually she only thoroughly understood the idea of *addition*; she could grasp 'that one joins with another when both are the same', but how were they added up when they were different?
>
> (Klein, 1923a, p. 67)

And later in the same paper:

> In Lisa's analysis I learnt that in studying history one had to transplant oneself into 'what people did in earlier times'. For her it was the study of the relations of the parents to one another and to the child, wherein of course the infantile phantasies of battles, slaughters, etc., also played an important part, according to the sadistic conception of coitus.
>
> (Klein, 1923a, pp. 71–72)

Klein continues to chart the vicissitudes of symbol formation and the causes and effects of defective symbolisation and its importance in managing anxiety in 'Personification in the play of children' (1929a), 'Infantile anxiety-situations in a work of art and in the creative impulse' (1929b), 'The importance of symbol formation in the development of the ego' (1930) and 'A contribution to the theory of intellectual inhibition' (1931). Important in this early work of Klein's is the idea of the *epistemophilic instinct*, the 'wish to know'. This is for Freud a part-instinct, a part of the libido concerned with voyeurism and exhibitionism, but becomes in Klein's early work a central instinct in its own right. In 'Early stages of the Oedipus conflict' (1928) and 'The importance of symbol formation in the development of the ego' (1930) Klein sees the epistemophilic instinct as exploratory and necessary but also inevitably aggressive, involving phantasies of getting inside the mother to find and often to take over or destroy the riches within, notably mother's babies and father's penis. The inevitable fear of retaliation can then seriously inhibit curiosity and the capacity to learn.

The conflicts and persecution in the phantasies about primal objects (prototypically the mother's body) promote a search for new, conflict-free relationships with substitute (symbolic) objects, for example, importantly, through the child's play. Nevertheless, these attempts sometimes fail: the conflicts tend to follow and can affect the relationship with the substitute object, which eventually promotes further search for yet another substitute. The process of symbolisation is thus both a creative act and a process of defence.

Klein's 1930 paper provides her final theoretical statement on symbol formation. It can be seen that her ideas are considerably different from Jones's:

> Some years ago . . . I drew the conclusion that symbolism is the foundation of all sublimation and of every talent, since it is by way of symbolic equation that things, activities and interests become the subject of libidinal phantasies. I can now add to what I said then (1923b) and state that, side by side with the libidinal interest, it is the anxiety arising in the phase that I have described [of maximal sadism] which sets going the mechanism of identification. Since the child desires to destroy the organs (penis, vagina, breasts), which stand for the objects, he conceives a dread of the latter. This anxiety contributes to make him equate the organs in question with other things; owing to this equation these in their turn become objects of anxiety, and so he is impelled constantly to make other and new equations, which form the basis of his interests in the new objects and of symbolism. Thus not only does symbolism come to be the foundation of all phantasy and sublimation, but, more than that, it is the basis of the subject's relation to the outside world and to reality in general.
>
> (Klein, 1930, pp. 220–221)

(Note: The phrase 'symbolic equation' is used by Klein here in an ordinary sense, not the special sense in which it was to be used by Segal below.)

Klein's insights in this paper are based in particular on her work with Dick, a 4-year-old boy with childhood psychosis. (Nowadays he would probably be diagnosed as autistic.) Klein became convinced that his inability to play, his indifference to everyone and his failure to seek or produce meaning in speech were due to a failure to develop a symbolic relation to things. However, Britton (2008) points out that Klein is able to discern the rudiments of symbolic meaning in Dick's acts. For example, when Dick ran into the space between the double doors Klein was able to interpret his wish to be inside the dark Mummy. Gradually her interpretation of such activities enabled Dick to function more freely.

Further developments after Klein

Hanna Segal: True symbol and symbolic equation

Building further on Klein's work, and making use of Klein's (1946) concept of projective identification in 'Notes on some schizoid mechanisms' [see Projective identification], Hanna Segal in her classic paper 'Notes on symbol formation' (1957) makes an important step in understanding symbol formation through her distinction between the symbol proper and what she calls the 'symbolic equation'. This work makes sense of how some of the symbols that Klein's child patients formed still attracted the anxiety concerning the archaic objects while others did not. As soon as repression breaks down, the defensive function of a symbolic equation is threatened.

The true symbol is recognised as having its own characteristics separate from that which it symbolises, but in the symbolic equation the degree of projection into the new symbolic object means that it remains too close to the original, attracting the same conflicts and inhibitions.

With progress towards the depressive position [*see* Depressive position] whole objects are recognised, internal and external worlds are better distinguished and objects are experienced as separate from the self, having their own qualities rather than being largely coloured by the subject's projections. Symbolic objects can thus be used freely and creatively, without the anxiety associated with their archaic precursors. Omnipotent phantasy possession of the external object is given up and mourned:

> In the symbolic equation the symbol-substitute is felt to *be* the original object. . . . is used to deny the absence of the ideal object. . . . The . . . symbol proper . . . is felt to *represent* the object; its own characteristics are recognised, respected and used. It arises . . . when separation from the object, ambivalence, guilt and loss can be experienced and tolerated. The symbol is used not to deny but to overcome loss.
>
> (Segal, 1957, p. 395)

Segal in her 1979 'Postcript' to her symbol paper indicates that Bion's work on the relationship between container and contained enables further refinement to her theory (Bion, 1962a, 1962b). We can now see that the extent to which a true symbol can or cannot be formed depends not on the existence of projective identification per se but on the nature and degree of projective identification and the degree of disturbances on either or both sides of the container/contained relationship.

Symbolisation and aesthetics

Closely related to symbol formation is the field of aesthetics. Why do writers and artists create, and what psychologically are they doing in the process? What differentiates good art from bad? Klein first addresses some of this in 'Infantile anxiety-situations reflected in a work of art and in the creative impulse' (1929b), where she links the urge to create with the impulse to restore and repair the injured object after a destructive attack. Then in 'Love, guilt and reparation' she says, 'The desire to re-discover the mother of the early days, whom one has lost actually or in one's feelings, is also of the greatest importance in creative art and in the way people enjoy and appreciate it' (Klein, 1937, p. 334).

Ella Sharpe (1930) in 'Certain aspects of sublimation and delusion' says that any artist, from a dancer to a painter, strives to produce a 'perfect' work of art, which will omnipotently both incorporate and restore the parents who have been attacked in phantasy. In 1935 ('Similar and divergent unconscious determinants underlying the sublimations of pure art and pure science') Sharpe goes on to link 'pure' art with order, rhythm and harmony. John Rickman (1940) in 'On the nature of ugliness and the creative impulse' shows how it is important not to confine aesthetics to a study of beauty alone artists struggle to restore damaged internal objects and to represent for us the interplay of creative and destructive instincts.

In her 1952 paper 'A psychoanalytic contribution to aesthetics' Segal takes as a paradigm of creativity the classical tragedy. Here she points out that the ugly content (e.g. hubris, treachery, parricide, matricide) is depicted in a way that is beautiful and satisfying in its inner consistency and psychological truth. The violence of the content is balanced by the rhythm and harmony of the poetic form.

Segal, following Rickman, describes how for the artist the work of art is his way of allaying the guilt and despair arising out of the depressive position and of restoring his destroyed objects. Segal thinks that the creative artist is often neurotic but is able to be acutely aware of his own internal reality rather than evading it, and to express it truthfully through his particular medium, be it words, sounds, paint or clay. To put it another way, the existence of and the conflict between both the life and death instincts must be faced. Artistic expression becomes blocked when depressive anxieties and phantasies cannot be tolerated. One reward, however, is that of all human activities art comes nearest to achieving immortality; a great work of art is likely to escape destruction and oblivion.

Segal contrasts this truly reparative process with manic reparation [*see* Manic reparation; Reparation], which gives rise to a slick quality of prettiness in which the artist demonstrates an easy triumph over the state of his internal world and thus his evasion of pining and guilt. Segal's 1974 paper 'Delusion and artistic creativity' about William Golding's novel *The Spire* explores from a psychoanalytic viewpoint Golding's theme of the differentiation of creativity and delusion.

Later (1991), in 'Imagination, play and art', Segal distinguishes between what she terms 'what if' and 'as if' science fiction. The writer of 'as if' escapist fiction indulges our easy, omnipotent daydreams. 'What if' science fiction writing, on the other hand, is truly imaginative and does not evade psychic reality. Britton (1998) also explores the difference between serious literature and escapist romance, or 'truth seeking and truth evading fiction', in a related way. Serious literature is based on unconscious phantasy and a true representation of psychic reality, whereas escapist literature is based on wish-fulfilling daydream and psychic illusion.

Key ideas: Summary

- Symbolisation as both creative and defensive.
- The capacity for symbol formation as essential for mental development; the need to symbolise primitive bodily processes and relationships.
- The symbolic equation gives way to the symbol proper with the move into the depressive position.
- Aesthetic experience and the struggles of the depressive position.

References

Bion, W. (1962a) 'A theory of thinking', *Int. J. Psycho-Anal.* 43: 306–310.

—— (1962b) *Learning from Experience*. London: Heinemann.

Britton, R. (1998) 'Daydream, phantasy and fiction', in *Belief and Imagination*. London: Routledge, pp. 109–119.

—— (2008) 'Reflections on some contributions of Hanna Segal to psychoanalytic theory'. Unpublished paper given at a conference on the work of Hanna Segal. London, June 2008.

Freud, S. (1895) 'Project for a scientific psychology', *S.E. 1*. London: Hogarth Press, pp. 283–397.

—— (1900) *The Interpretation of Dreams*. *S.E. 5*. London: Hogarth Press.

—— (1916) 'Introductory lectures on psychoanalysis', *S.E. 15*. London: Hogarth Press, p. 153.

Freud, S. and Breuer, J. (1895) *Studies in Hysteria*. *S.E. 2*. London: Hogarth Press.

Jones, E. (1916) 'The theory of symbolism', *Br. J. Psychol.* 9: 181–229.

—— (1948) 'The theory of symbolism', in *Papers on Psychoanalysis*. London: Maresfield Reprints, pp. 87–144.

Klein, M. (1923a) 'The role of the school in the libidinal development of the child', in *The Writings of Melanie Klein*, Vol. 1. London: Hogarth Press, pp. 59–76.

—— (1923b) 'Early analysis', in *The Writings of Melanie Klein*, Vol. 1. London: Hogarth Press, pp. 77–105.

—— (1926) 'The psychological principles of early analysis', in *The Writings of Melanie Klein*, Vol. 1. London: Hogarth Press, pp. 128–138.

—— (1928) 'Early stages of the Oedipus conflict', in *The Writings of Melanie Klein*, Vol. 1. London: Hogarth Press, pp. 186–198.

—— (1929a) 'Personification in the play of children', in *The Writings of Melanie Klein*, Vol. 1. London: Hogarth Press, pp. 199–209.

—— (1929b) 'Infantile anxiety-situations in a work of art and in the creative impulse', in *The Writings of Melanie Klein*, Vol. 1. London: Hogarth Press, pp. 210–218.

—— (1930) 'The importance of symbol formation in the development of the ego', in *The Writings of Melanie Klein*, Vol. 1. London: Hogarth Press, pp. 219–232.

—— (1931) 'A contribution to the theory of intellectual inhibition', in *The Writings of Melanie Klein*, Vol. 1. London: Hogarth Press, pp. 236–247.

—— (1937) 'Love, guilt and reparation', in *The Writings of Melanie Klein*, Vol. 1. London: Hogarth Press, pp. 306–343.

—— (1946) 'Notes on some schizoid mechanisms', in *The Writings of Melanie Klein*, Vol. 3. London: Hogarth Press, pp. 1–24.

Rickman, J. (1940) 'On the nature of ugliness and the creative process', *Int. J. Psycho-Anal.* 21: 294–313.

Segal, H. (1952) 'A psychoanalytic approach to aesthetics', *Int. J. Psycho-Anal.* 33: 196–207.

—— (1957) 'Notes on symbol formation', *Int. J. Psycho-Anal.* 38: 391–397.

—— (1974) 'Delusion and artistic creativity: Some reflections on reading *The Spire* by William Golding', *Int. Rev. Psycho-Anal.* 1: 135–141.

—— (1979) Postcript to 'Notes on symbol formation', in *The Work of Hanna Segal*, New York: Jason Aronson (1981), pp. 60–65.

—— (1991) 'Imagination, play and art', in *Dream, Phantasy and Art*. London: Routledge, pp. 101–109.

Sharpe, E. (1930) 'Certain aspects of sublimation and delusion', *Int. J. Psycho-Anal.* 11: 12–23.

—— (1935) 'Similar and divergent unconscious determinants underlying the sublimations of pure art and pure science', *Int. J. Psycho-Anal.* 16: 186–202.

11 Pathological organisations

Definition

The term 'pathological organisations of the personality' refers to a family of extremely unyielding and tightly knit defences. Their function is to enable patients to avoid overwhelming persecutory and depressive anxieties by avoiding emotional contact with others and with internal and external reality.

There are two main and complementary strands in the concept of pathological organisation. The first strand refers to the dominance of narcissistic and omnipotent 'mad' and 'bad' parts of the self over the rest of the personality. Many authors stress that this tyranny has a tenacious hold because of its perverse, addictive and sado-masochistic character. The second strand concerns 'psychic equilibrium'. Pathological organisations provide patients with a precarious psychic equilibrium that is achieved through the pathological impairment of a potentially more responsive emotional self. Such organisations attempt to provide the patient with a new position, which is conceptualised as lying at a remove from the normal activities and anxieties of both the paranoid-schizoid position (Ps) and those of the depressive position (D). As a result, the more normal fluctuations and equilibrium between Ps and D are drastically curtailed. Their origins are thought to lie in the early emergence of unmanageable destructive tendencies, linked to envy and environmental failure, which undermine the structuring activities of normal schizoid functioning and occasion extreme and overwhelming paranoid anxieties.

Pathological organisations are highly resistant to change and pose considerable technical challenges in analysis. Contributors on pathological organisations provide a specifically Kleinian perspective on major questions raised by Freud, such as those of the negative therapeutic reaction and interminability.

Key papers

1936   Riviere, J. 'A contribution to the analysis of the negative therapeutic reaction'.
First Kleinian formulation of a defensive organisation of the personality.

1964   Rosenfeld, H. 'On the psychopathology of narcissism: a clinical approach'.
Fundamental definition of 'libidinal' narcissistic organisation or omnipotent 'mad' self.

1968   Meltzer, D. 'Terror, persecution and dread'.
Formulates the notion of destructive narcissistic organisation and its tyranny over personality.

1971   Rosenfeld, H. 'A clinical approach to the psychoanalytic theory of the life and death instincts: An investigation into the aggressive aspects of narcissism'.
Definitive formulation of a 'destructive' narcissistic organisation.

1972   Segal, H. 'A delusional system as a defence against the re-emergence of a catastrophic situation'.
Description of a psychotic patient's delusional, omnipotent world providing an unstable equilibrium against an early catastrophic situation.

1975   Joseph, B. 'The patient who is difficult to reach'.
Close scrutiny of how pathological organisations function in the analytic relationship.

1981   O'Shaughnessy, E. 'A clinical study of a defensive organisation'.
Detailed clinical description of a defensive organisation as a pathological formation on the border between Ps and D.

1981   Riesenberg-Malcolm, R. 'Expiation as a defence'.
Illustration of perverse, pathological use of masochistic expiation to avoid persecutory guilt.

1981   Steiner, J. 'Perverse relationships between parts of self: A clinical illustration'.
First use of the term 'pathological organisation'. Beginning of comprehensive theory incorporating both pathological narcissism and equilibrium between the pathological organisation and the paranoid-schizoid and depressive positions.

1982   Joseph, B. 'Addiction to near-death'.
            A malignant self-destructive organisation is erotised and mani-
            fests as an addiction to near-death.

1985   Brenman, E. 'Cruelty and narrow-mindedness'.
            Narrow-mindedness in the service of narcissistic omnipotence
            and cruelty as a defence against helplessness.

1985   Steiner, J. 'Turning a blind eye: the cover-up for Oedipus'.
            Defines perverse use of turning a blind eye to maintain patho-
            logical relation between split parts of the ego.

1987   Rosenfeld, H. *Impasse and Interpretation* (Chapters 5, 6
            and 13).
            Reiterates distinction between libidinal and destructive nar-
            cissism and implications for analytic treatment. Introduces
            a distinction between 'thin-skinned' and 'thick-skinned'
            narcissist.

1987   Steiner, J. 'The interplay between pathological organisations
            and the paranoid-schizoid and depressive positions'.
            More elaborate definition of points of threatening transi-
            tions in Ps and D likely to promote reliance on pathological
            organisations.

1988   Spillius, E. 'Pathological organisations: Introduction'.
            Summary of major contributors and trends in concept of
            pathological organisations.

1990a   Steiner, J. 'Pathological organisations as obstacles to mourn-
            ing: The role of unbearable guilt'.
            The role of unbearable guilt in entrenching a patient's reliance
            on a pathological organisation.

1991   Hinshelwood, R. D. *A Dictionary of Kleinian Thought*, 2nd
            edition.
            General entry on pathological organisations complementing
            Spillius's summary.

1992   O'Shaughnessy, E. 'Enclaves and excursions'.
            Description of how patients induce analysts to enter into
            idealised enclaves with them or into excursions away from
            areas of great anxiety. Both are forms of psychic retreat.

1992   Steiner, J. 'The equilibrium between the paranoid-schizoid and
            depressive positions'.
            Concise statement of subdivisions in PS and D and equilibrium
            between them.

1993   Steiner, J. *Psychic Retreats: Pathological organisations in psychotic, neurotic and borderline patients.*
            New term 'Retreat' describes out of reach or stuck states of mind in spatial terms. They arise from the operation of pathological organisations.

Chronology and discussion

Pathological organisations: A new development after Klein

Work with children provided a major impetus for Klein's own theoretical development, and work with psychotics was seminal for the major contribution of her direct heirs: Bion, Segal and Rosenfeld. It can be said that work with patients with character pathology – borderline, schizoid, narcissistic and perverse – has provided a major impetus for the development of the concept of pathological organisations, which has been and continues to be a central preoccupation of contemporary Kleinians.

The actual term 'pathological organisation' was first used by John Steiner in 1981 and has since gained general acceptance amongst contemporary Kleinians. However, the notion of such an organisation had previously appeared under various names such as 'highly organised system of defence' (Riviere, 1936), 'pathological narcissism' (Rosenfeld, 1964, 1971; Meltzer, 1968) and 'defensive organisation' (Segal, 1972; O'Shaughnessy, 1981). In the 1960s and 1970s Rosenfeld's seminal contribution on pathological narcissism provided the leading theoretical conceptualisation. A variety of Kleinian clinical contributions (Brenman, Joseph, Riesenberg-Malcolm) and others with an added theoretical bent (Meltzer, Segal, Rey, Steiner, O'Shaughnessy, Sohn) show the breadth of preoccupation with the topic. In the 1980s and 1990s John Steiner emerges as the leading contemporary Kleinian theoretician of pathological organisations. He coins the term and offers a more comprehensive theory. Steiner's work relies centrally on Rosenfeld's contribution but also differs in some respects. Pathological organisations is a broader term than narcissistic organisations and Steiner significantly deepens our understanding of the type of equilibrium between these organisations and both the paranoid-schizoid position (Ps) and the depressive position (D). His work culminates in 1993 with his concept of of psychic retreats.

Narcissism and narcissistic object relations

Precursors

Freud begins the study of narcissism and of narcissistic object relations in his study of Leonardo da Vinci (1910) and in his paper 'On narcissism'

(1914). Abraham (1919) further develops the notion in his description of the narcissistic character, as does Reich (1933) with his notion of 'character armour' based on narcissistic relationships as a source of resistance in analysis.

First Kleinian formulation

Joan Riviere's bold and original 1936 paper relies on Klein's freshly formulated notion of manic defences (Klein, 1935) to subsume both Freud's and Abraham's explanations of the negative therapeutic reaction in analysis, namely, Freud's notion of the unconscious sense of guilt (Freud, 1923) and Abraham's notion of a narcissistic character-resistance (Abraham, 1919).

Riviere formulates a 'highly organised system of defence' (p. 307) comprising: the omnipotent denial of depressive despair; the denial of dependence and the contemptuous devaluation of the object; the mastery over objects and control of the analytic situation. This well-knit defensive organisation gives the patient a rigid equilibrium that tenaciously guards against disturbances occasioned either by getting better or by ending the analysis.

Riviere's reliance on Klein's new concept of the manic defences and the depressive position limits this first formulation, but her early contribution has features that prefigure more contemporary conceptions of pathological organisations: the tightly knit defences that yield a *narcissistic* personality organisation resistant to emotional contact; the control exerted over the analyst and the invitation to collude; the rigid, closely guarded equilibrium at the cost of development in analysis and in life in general; and the need for the analyst's imaginative understanding of the patient's underlying primitive anxieties to avoid impatient reactions in the face of the stranglehold on analytic progress.

By contrast, Rosenfeld's work on pathological narcissism and contemporary formulations of pathological organisations rely centrally on Klein's formulation of the paranoid-schizoid position (1946) and of severe disturbances in the paranoid-schizoid position to explain the basic narcissistic fabric of such organisations and their unyielding character.

The paranoid-schizoid position and narcissism

Klein rejects the version of Freud's equivocal notion of primary narcissism – an objectless stage that precedes object relations. Her view is that from birth onwards a relationship to the breast/mother is present. Klein refers to narcissistic states not as objectless but rather as a withdrawal to an 'internalised object, which in phantasy forms part of the loved body and self' (1952, p. 51). Her concept of the paranoid-schizoid position (1946) illustrates her view of narcissism as involving narcissistic object relating from the beginning [see Narcissism]. The schizoid defences of splitting, denial, idealisation and projective identification yield part-object relations, which are by definition narcissistic in character. In spite of their narcissistic character the binary split between idealised and persecutory object relations is crucial for the introjection of a 'good' breast and for later development of relations between self and objects. In 1946 Klein begins to distinguish between normal and abnormal schizoid functioning in the paranoid-schizoid position.

Pathology in the paranoid-schizoid position

In the 1950s the concept of primal envy gains the status of being the prime representative of the death instinct in that it attacks the source of gratification and of life itself: the breast/mother recognised as separate (Klein, 1957). Klein, Rosenfeld and Bion in particular begin to spell out how excessive envy, owing to internal and also to external factors, leads to abnormal formations in the infantile paranoid-schizoid position with grave consequences for all later development. Four themes in particular are pertinent and act as a backdrop for the emergence of the later concept of pathological organisations:

1   Envious attacks on the goodness of the breast/mother experienced as separate lead to a failure in dichotomous splitting (Rosenfeld, 1950, 1952; Klein, 1957). This failure leads to confusion between 'good' and 'bad' objects and 'good' and 'bad' parts of self, and to a lack of differentiation between self and object. Failure in healthy binary splitting promotes the emergence of pathological splits in the development of self and object relations.
2   Envy is linked to excessively omnipotent and destructive forms of projective identification used to either rob or to spoil the object (Klein, 1957, p. 181).
3   The psychotic part of the personality, driven by excessive envy, develops a hatred of both internal and external reality and of all that makes for an awareness of it (Bion, 1957). Excessive fragmentary splitting and violent projective identification mutilate infantile mental functions of thinking and imprison the individual's capacity for contact with reality. Such disturbances in the infantile paranoid-schizoid position can lead to a hatred of emotional life and make progress through both Ps and D extremely difficult.
4   Envy is linked to the dread of having destroyed the source of life itself. Klein (1957) spells out in detail the various defences deployed to avoid the unbearable experience of envy. These defences underlie the

recurrent negative therapeutic reactions that usually follow moments of greater integration and of progress in analytic treatment.

Pathological narcissism: Herbert Rosenfeld's contribution

In his two fundamental papers Rosenfeld (1964, 1971) deepens enormously the Kleinian understanding of pathological narcissism, which is one of the two major strands of thought in the concept of pathological organisations (Spillius, 1988). It is only in his second paper that Rosenfeld (1971) introduces a distinction between libidinal and destructive narcissism. The term libidinal narcissism from then on subsumes much of the contents of his first paper (1964).

Libidinal narcissism

Libidinal narcissism refers to the formation of an omnipotent, delusional 'mad' self. Early awareness of the separateness of the object, experienced as the source of good experience, leads to feelings of dependence on the object. Dependence engenders inevitable frustrations that lead to aggression, paranoid anxiety and pain. Dependence also stimulates envy, which is particularly unbearable to the infant because envy increases the difficulty in admitting dependence and frustrations (Rosenfeld, 1964, p. 171). The self deals with the awareness of both situations by omnipotent introjective and projective identification simultaneously. The self becomes identified with the object, or part-object, by appropriating its desired qualities either by omnipotent incorporation or by forceful projective identification (Rosenfeld, 1964, p. 171). Both aspects of narcissistic object relating contribute to the creation of the omnipotent 'mad' self whereby the awareness of separateness itself and the awareness of envy, frustration and pain are denied. The stimulation of envy plays a key role in the development of narcissistic object relating: 'It seems that the strength and persistence of omnipotent narcissistic object-relations are closely related to the strength of the infant's envy' (Rosenfeld, 1964, p. 171).

Narcissistic object relations also entail the projection of undesirable qualities and feelings into the object. Rosenfeld points out that the analyst is often pictured and related to as a 'lavatory' or 'lap' mother (1964, p. 171). In analysis, narcissistic states are experienced by the patient as ideal: everything unpleasant is evacuated into the analyst and, conversely, every satisfactory or valuable experience, such as the analyst's capacity to bring relief, is omnipotently appropriated by the patient who feels he possesses all the goodness. As a result, awareness of psychic reality is dramatically stunted.

Libidinal narcissism is imbued with destructiveness since it involves a widespread psychic robbery of the valuable parts of the object and the evacuation of bad qualities into the object, which is radically devalued. When the patient's self-idealisation is interfered with by the perception of the analyst as separate, the patient is humiliated by his awareness that it is the analyst who possesses the qualities he had appropriated for himself. He experiences resentment and revenge at being 'robbed 'of his omnipotent narcissism and attempts tenaciously to restore the illusion of omnipotent control (see Rosenfeld, 1971, p. 247).

Destructive narcissism

Rosenfeld's notion of destructive narcissism (1971) refers to different destructive processes than those inevitably involved in propping up the 'mad' self-idealisation of libidinal narcissism, which is achieved predominantly at the expense of the object. Destructive narcissism is equally based on an omnipotent idealisation, but specifically of the destructive or 'bad' parts of the self that: '. . . are directed both against any positive libidinal object relationship and any libidinal part of the self which experiences need for an object and the desire to depend on it' (Rosenfeld, 1971, p. 246). Destructive narcissism is achieved primarily at the expense of the dependent or libidinal self.

It is important to distinguish the notion of 'libidinal' self from that of 'libidinal' narcissism in order to avoid confusion. The term libidinal self is synonymous and interchangeable with the notion of the needy, dependent, desiring self, or the sane self, which, driven by the life instincts, seeks and values object relations for development. Libidinal narcissism by contrast entails a pathological form of self-love and self-idealisation at the expense of the object. The term libidinal narcissism seems justifiable given that Rosenfeld (1964) is offering a new Kleinian object-relations formulation for Freud's equivocal and abstract notion of primary narcissism: the ego as reservoir of, or as the first object of, the libido (Freud, 1914). Rosenfeld comments that many clinically observable conditions that resemble Freud's description of primary narcissism, are in fact primitive object relations of the type he describes as libidinal narcissism (see Rosenfeld, 1964, p. 170).

Libidinal and destructive narcissism operate side by side. Rosenfeld links the predominance of destructive narcissism to a more violent envy that appears both as an overwhelming wish to destroy the analyst who represents the source of life in the transference and also as extremely violent self-destructive impulses (see Rosenfeld, 1971, p. 247). When faced with the reality of being dependent on the analyst the patient would prefer to die, to destroy his analytic progress and insight. Rosenfeld points out that in some patients destructive narcissism is so dominant that they constantly try to get rid of their concern and their love for their objects by killing their loving dependent self.

These destructive parts of the self can, at the level of representation, take the highly organised form of a 'gang', like the mafia, in which the members, through their loyalty to each other and to the leader, make the destructive work more effective and powerful, keep it in power and in this way maintain the status quo. To change and to receive help is experienced as weakness and failure by this highly idealised destructive organisation, which provides the patient with a sense of superiority and self-admiration. The deadly destructiveness manifests as a determined chronic resistance to analysis and a triumph over the analyst as a symbol of life and creativity. Rosenfeld points out that there is often a *perverse erotisation* of this destructive organisation that increases its seductiveness, power and domination over the rest of the personality (1971, p. 249). The libidinal self feels too weak to oppose the destructive process. Clinically it is essential to find access to the libidinal self and to analyse the infantile nature of the omnipotent processes.

Rosenfeld's seminal paper develops the ideas that Donald Meltzer had begun to formulate in his paper 'Terror, persecution and dread' (1968). Meltzer describes how a split-off destructive narcissistic part of his patient, which paraded as a superior, know-it-all business associate, came to the fore in analysis. Meltzer links the patient's pervasive dread directly to the power of the destructive narcissistic organisation and its seductive tyranny over the trapped dependent self.

Later Rosenfeld

In his later work *Impasse and Interpretation* (see Rosenfeld, 1987, Ch. 13) Rosenfeld introduces a distinction between the 'thin-skinned' and the 'thick-skinned' narcissist. The latter has become insensitive to human feelings and appears to be dominated by destructive narcissism. Rosenfeld argues that the envy of such patients has to be confronted firmly in order to avoid impasse in analytic treatment. The thin-skinned narcissist by contrast is hypersensitive and easily hurt. The structure of his narcissism is such that he is not identified with the destructive parts of his narcissism. Rosenfeld thinks that in such patients their narcissism is more in the nature of a compensation for the repeated traumas to their self-regard in early childhood and also a way of triumphing over the parents and the analyst. However, to treat them as if they are identified with the destructive parts of their narcissism leads to retraumatisation of the patient and to impasse in analytic treatment.

In both his 1964 and 1971 papers Rosenfeld refers to envy as the representative of the death instinct, as the main motivating factor for an increased reliance on omnipotence and the development of both libidinal and destructive narcissism. In his later work Rosenfeld (1987) makes more explicit references also to the contribution of environmental factors such as trauma and failure in the development of pathological narcissism: '. . . separation, overindulgence, or, particularly, the lack of a holding and containing environment increase the development and persistence of narcissistic structures' (Rosenfeld, 1987, p. 87).

Contemporary perspectives on libidinal and destructive narcissism

For Rosenfeld the distinction between libidinal and destructive narcissism is important conceptually and clinically. He comes close to suggesting that in narcissistic patients in which libidinal narcissism predominates it may be less difficult and less intractable to gain access to the destructive part of the patient and to analyse his envy (1971, p. 247; 1987, Ch. 6). By contrast, in narcissistic patients in which destructive narcissism predominates it is more difficult to bring destructiveness into the open because envy is more violent, more difficult to face and the destructive parts remain more disguised, more split off and more silent (1971, p. 246; 1987, p. 112).

There is a controversy amongst contemporary Kleinians about the validity of Rosenfeld's distinction between libidinal and destructive narcissism. His theory of destructive narcissism is widely accepted as a seminal contribution. Hanna Segal, however, questions his notion of libidinal narcissism. In her view narcissism and envy are the two sides of the same coin. This entails that narcissism is always destructive because it is hostile to the object as separate and to any life-giving relationship (Segal, 2007). Ronald Britton by contrast finds Rosenfeld's distinction clinically useful. His own reworking of the concept of narcissistic organisations leads him to posit a dichotomy between the libidinal/defensive and hostile/destructive forms of such organisations (Britton, 2003, p. 156).

Clinical contributions and evidence by other Kleinian analysts

Four clinical contributions by Brenman (1985), Segal (1972), Joseph (1975, 1982) and O'Shaughnessy (1981), all of which were written or presented first in the 1970s, will be reviewed briefly. These papers, even if some do not acknowledge Rosenfeld's writings directly, give excellent illustrations of his outline of the severe split in the ego created by pathological narcissism. They invariably point out the costly impoverishment of the sane self that such defensive organisations engender. They show how such splits function in the analytic relationship, the therapeutic difficulties they give rise to and how the concerns and anxieties of the split-off, dependent self are invariably experienced in the analyst's countertransference.

In his 1970 paper 'Cruelty and narrow-mindedness' Brenman (1985) highlights one feature of a patient's destructive narcissistic organisation: an entrenched narrow-mindedness that facilitated his persistent cruelty and his cruel use of righteous grievances. This organisation could only persist because love, compassion and the patient's needy self were squeezed out. The pathological organisation led to a chronically depriving, destructive superego that condemned the patient to a merciless and loveless exile. Brenman illustrates the analyst's work in the countertransference to contain the patient's relentless attempts to pervert and dehumanise his analyst's compassion and human capacity for understanding.

In 'A delusional system as a defence against the re-emergence of a catastrophic situation' (1972), Hanna Segal offers a dramatic illustration of the damaging split in the ego caused by a narcissistic and delusional defensive organisation. This organisation imprisoned and starved the patient's dependent self. Her very ill patient's psychotic delusion of being God-chosen to convert people to Christianity shielded him from contact with reality, from guilt and from his psychic limitations. His infantile experience was massively split off and projected into his analyst, who carried those parts. When a sane part of him called 'baby-Georgie' began to emerge, his destructive 'bad' self perversely insisted that pain to 'baby-Georgie' was best dealt with by kind-heartedly killing him.

Segal understands her patient's rigid clinging to the equilibrium provided by the narcissistic organisation as an elaborate 'defence against the recurrence of an early catastrophic situation' (Segal, 1972, p. 399). Very early traumatic experiences of his mother's depression and desertion following his father's death gave rise to murderous fantasies and a conviction that he had murdered both his parents. To defend himself against this catastrophe:

> . . . he had to wipe out baby-Georgie and his real object relationship and to develop the megalomaniac delusion in which he was self-sufficient and omnipotent and all objects were objects created in his fantasy, predominantly from his own faeces.
>
> (Segal, 1972, pp. 399–400)

In 'A clinical contribution to the analysis of a perversion' (1971, p. 54) and in 'The patient who is difficult to reach' (1975, p. 76) Betty Joseph states that she is presenting material from patients who manifest a clear split in their ego between an out-of-reach dependent self and a more dominant narcissistic organisation as articulated by Rosenfeld (1964). In 'Addiction to near-death' (Joseph, 1982) she invokes more centrally Rosenfeld's (1971) paper on destructive narcissism.

Joseph focuses in great detail on the way patients with such organisations behave in the analytic relationship and on the technical issues that are raised, not on the theory of such organisations. She draws attention to the subtle and tenacious ways in which the analyst is seductively or coercively pulled to enact a split-off part of the patient with which he has become identified. She stresses the importance of locating 'the splitting in the ego and clarifying the activities of the different parts' (Joseph, 1975, p. 79). She underlines how important it is for the analyst not to rush into hasty interpretations but rather to 'carry the projection long enough' to experience the missing part of the patient. Only then does it become possible to interpret the process without pressure rather than participating in the acting-out [*see* Technique].

Joseph's 1982 paper illustrates how her patient's destructive organisation is perversely erotised to strengthen its domination over the rest of the personality, a theme advanced by Meltzer (1968) and Rosenfeld (1971). She describes a patient's malignant absorption into despair and hopelessness as a self-destructive organisation that manifests as an addiction to near-death. The patient tries to recruit the analyst to collude by feeling desperate and hopeless and to react by punishing the patient, an enactment that feeds a masochistic triumph over the analysis. The drive towards life and sanity is split off and projected into the analyst. Such analyses can drag on for years if the analyst does not interpret this massive projection.

Edna O'Shaughnessy, in 'A clinical study of a defensive organisation', (1981) gives a vivid account of the changes in the defensive organisation of a patient in the course of four distinct phases of a 12-year analysis. O'Shaughnessy defines a defensive organisation as a fixation and a pathological formation when early development arouses unbearable and almost overwhelming anxiety. A defensive organisation is a pathological fixed formation in one or other position or on the borderline between them. Omnipotent control and denial and several forms of splitting and projective identification organise the various relations between self and objects in a rigid and restrictive way and give them a narcissistic character. She also draws attention to the rigid equilibrium between such organisations and the paranoid-schizoid and depressive positions. In so doing she echoes a theme that others had alluded to but that John Steiner had begun to formulate (Steiner, 1979) and later significantly develops (Steiner, 1987).

At the beginning O'Shaughnessy's patient felt overwhelmed by anxieties of confusion and fragmentation, as his defensive organisation had broken down. In the next phase his defensive organisation re-established itself in a static and controlling transference. In a third period the patient, in identification with the Abominable Snow Man, gratified his excessive narcissism by possessing all the valuable attributes and by cruelly devaluing his 'pedestrian' analyst. On the other side of the split he was capable of awareness but often disowned this part of himself. He tried to break down his analysis but realised that his destructiveness could be carried and survived by his resourceful analyst.

In the last period, the patient's defensive organisation having weakened, he began to grapple with the problems that lay on the edge of the depressive position. He was more able to face anxieties and allow for contact with reality and his narcissistic organisation was less rigidly organised and controlling and could be thought about.

Pathological organisations: John Steiner's contribution

In his 1981 paper 'Perverse relationships between parts of self: A clinical illustration' John Steiner coins the term 'pathological organisations'. He is deeply influenced by Rosenfeld's seminal contribution on pathological narcissism, which is a central feature of pathological organisations. But pathological organisation is a broader term than narcissistic organisation because it is a more generally found structure. There can be organisations in which obsessional, hysterical, manic or psychotic features predominate.

The basic situation in the paranoid-schizoid position

Relying on the precursors laid down by Klein and Rosenfeld, and also Bion, Steiner (1981) emphasises the serious disturbance in the paranoid-schizoid position. Excessive destructiveness owing to primal envy, compounded by external factors such as trauma and deprivation (Steiner, 1993), give rise to a breakdown in dichotomous splitting that itself provokes more projective identification, as Rosenfeld (1952) and Klein (1957) spelt out. In addition, Steiner relies on Bion (1957, 1959) to complement his view of the basic situation. He mentions 'pathological splitting with a fragmentation of the self and of the object and their expulsion in a more violent and primitive form of projective identification' as a reaction to the failure in dichotomous splitting (Steiner, 1993, p. 7). These combined processes lead to overwhelming paranoid anxieties of disintegration, fragmentation and confusion. For Steiner, the breakdown in dichotomous splitting and the overwhelming anxieties constitute the basic 'catastrophic' situation that instigates the development of a pathological organisation. The organisation in turn has catastrophic consequences for development (Steiner, 1981, 1985, 1987, 1990a, 1993).

Main functions of pathological organisations

The first function of a pathological organisation is to *recreate a split between protective objects and bad or attacking ones* in the face of the collapse in binary splitting. The second is to attempt *to bind and to neutralise the primitive destructiveness* that engendered the collapse. However, as many authors point out, the organisation itself *expresses the destructiveness* against which it is intended to be a protection (Steiner, 1993).

Steiner (1981) emphasises how fragmentary splitting and projective identification lead to fragmentation and confusion in the paranoid-schizoid position and to multiple objects that become assembled into highly organised structures such as the prototypical gang or mafia as described by Rosenfeld (1971). Such organisations are basically *narcissistic* owing to the preponderance of projective identification, which creates objects that are controlled by parts of self projected into them (Steiner, 1981). But Steiner stresses that organisations can also be held together by obsessional mechanisms, by erotisation with a hysterical flavour, by manic mechanisms in which triumph and excitement dominate or by a psychotic structure that imposes a delusional order (Steiner, 1987, p. 71).

The new split and collusive liaison

Such complexly assembled organisations masquerade as a plausible split between protective good objects and bad ones. The gang, for example, presents itself as a protective object in that it promises shelter from dread, persecution and guilt. This 'protective' object is imbued with highly destructive parts but also some good parts of objects and self, which have been recruited so as to give it a more healthy appearance. Conversely, Steiner argues that it is misleading to view the needy, dependent self as an innocent victim that is kept in bondage by a malevolent organisation. He writes:

> Instead I will try to show that a perverse relationship may exist and that the healthy part of the self may collude and allow itself to be *knowingly* taken over by the narcissistic gang. It is this quality which is externalised in the transference and gives rise to the perverse flavour of the interaction.
>
> (Steiner, 1981, pp. 242–243)

The term perverse here refers to a psychic twisting of the truth. For example the patient behaves as if he has no insight but in fact he has considerable insight that he chooses to ignore. The dependent self is under pressure but may also knowingly allow itself to be seduced. This leads to a collusive liaison and to confusion between what are supposed to be the libidinal and the more malevolent parts of the personality. Conversely, when a 'good' part has been recruited by the malevolent gang it may disguise its destructive character and confuse the picture. Hinshelwood (1991, p. 384) also highlights how Steiner emphasises the collusive liaison between the destructive narcissistic parts of the self and the needy parts, as a result of which the pathological split between the two parts of the self is never a clear-cut one.

In his clinical example Steiner illustrates how the patient's destructive narcissistic identification with 'top-brass people' presents itself as a suitable guardian for the dependent needy part of the self but in fact kept the latter stunted. It undermines emotional nourishment in the analytic relationship. When the patient has gained greater insight into this internal imprisonment he continues to collude with the destructive organisation in a perverse way. Steiner shows how the split in the ego is complexly organised, with each side of the split containing some good and some bad parts of the self: 'This fact disguised the essentially destructive nature of the narcissistic organisation on the one hand and on the other hand enabled perverse elements to be associated with the libidinal self which maintained the corrupt collusion' (Steiner, 1981, p. 245).

Turning a blind eye

In a later paper Steiner (1985) links this perverse element to the process of 'turning a blind eye', which he sees as a pervasive and specific defensive process in pathological organisations of the personality. The process reveals: '. . . a borderline attitude to reality in which truth is neither fully evaded as it may be in psychosis, nor for the most part accepted as it may be in neurosis, but is rather twisted and misrepresented' (Steiner, 1985, p. 170).

To explain this process Steiner has recourse to Freud's hypothesis of a splitting of the ego in fetishism, in which two psychical attitudes towards castration exist side by side and do not cancel each other (Freud, 1927). Steiner emphasises the dishonest and perverse aspect of this process, which is tantamount to gambling with reality, hence its addictive appeal. This perverse process is instrumental in maintaining the equilibrium of the organisation and militates against change in analysis even when the patient has clearly become capable of insight. Steiner likens the perverse element to 'psychic glue', which binds good and bad parts of the self together in a seemingly coherent organisation (Steiner, 1973, p. 113).

Equilibrium between pathological organisations and Ps and D

In his paper 'The interplay between pathological organizations and the paranoid-schizoid and depressive positions' (1987) Steiner develops the theme that pathological organisations have characteristics that distinguish them from both positions and exist in an equilibrium with them. Bion's model Ps↔D depicts a continuous series of fluctuations between the two positions so that neither position dominates with any degree of completeness or permanence over time. Steiner extends Bion's schema to provide his triangular model of equilibrium:

Steiner (1979) had defined borderline patients as existing in a position on the border between the paranoid-schizoid and depressive positions. He now suggests that pathological organisations can be conceptualised as being on the border of both positions and that, from this separate position, they maintain a rigid and static equilibrium in relation to both Ps and D.

Transitions in Ps and D

In Ps it is the transition from normal paranoid-schizoid functioning to the more pathological functioning outlined that creates a basic catastrophic situation that promotes reliance on a pathological organisation as a form of protection. Steiner further highlights two phases in the depressive position. In the early phase the reality of the loss of the dead or damaged object is denied by a concrete internalisation and possession of the object. This denial needs to be relinquished so as to face fully the situation of 'the loss of the loved object' as an essential condition for the mourning process to be accomplished. This very painful process entails facing the internal disaster caused by one's sadism against one's objects and the attendant guilt, desolation and despair (Steiner, 1987, 1990b, 1992). When depressive anxiety is overwhelming, the patient may resort to a pathological organisation for protection: 'It is therefore at the transitions which take place within both the paranoid-schizoid and the depressive positions that the individual seems to be most vulnerable to influence of a pathological organisation' (Steiner, 1987, p. 70).

Steiner (1987) shows how a patient's pathological organisation took the form of a powerful and cold ability on her part to cut herself off with a teasing and active secretive silence and a perverse selectiveness, which created a desert-like aridity between patient and analyst. This state offered the patient a safe haven from paranoid fears of fragmentation, from claustro-agoraphobic panic attacks and from fears of death by contamination. Steiner also shows how it protected her from depressive anxieties and guilt every time she made some significant movement towards caring about the analysis and towards showing more curiosity about her own functioning.

In 'Pathological organizations as obstacles to mourning: The role of unbearable guilt' Steiner (1990a) describes how his patient sought refuge again in his pathological organisation to protect himself from the unbearable intensity of his depressive anxieties:

> . . . he increasingly came to disagree with the aims and methods which his organisation deployed on his behalf. He was not, however, able to dissociate himself from it and each time he began to do so he seemed to come up against unbearable guilt. This led to a negative therapeutic reaction in which he retreated once more to the protection of the organisation.
>
> (Steiner, 1990a, p. 89)

In 'Expiation as a defence' Ruth Riesenberg-Malcolm (1991) outlines how a defensive organisation built on masochistic expiation and self-punishment emerged when her patient's persecutory anxiety and schizoid defences had diminished. This organised expiation prevented any real awareness of guilt but exerted a stranglehold on the analysis because change through analysis spells unbearable pain, desolation and death, as described by Riviere (1936). Thereby an impasse was created, which made it very difficult to progress in the analysis but equally difficult to terminate the analysis with both patient and analyst faced with a sense of irreparability. The work of Malcolm shows the emergence of a pathological organisation at a crucial moment of transition into D.

The separate status of pathological organisations and Ps and D

Pathological organisations have special properties (Steiner, 1987), which makes it helpful to consider them as separate from Ps and D. They provide a kind of pseudo-integration under the dominance of narcissistic structures, which can masquerade as the true integration of the depressive position. Sohn's notion of the identificate (1985) emphasises how narcissistic identifications are hollow, chameleonic and have a bland arrogance that is very different from normal healthy identification: more like concrete 'manoeuvrings' that mimic apparently positive situations.

Pathological organisations create an illusion of structure and stability, of relative freedom from pain and anxiety, but it is pseudo-stability and pseudo-integration, albeit of a very tenacious type. Their hasty way, through excessive projective identification, of assembling the fragmented bits of objects and self create a complex organisation that masquerades as a plausible split between protective good objects and bad ones. It is their rigidity and destructive nature and the way they are clung to that marks their difference from healthier Ps activities, such as reversible projective identification and the more fluid equilibrium between moments of persecution and idealisation. Pathological organisations make the negotiation of Ps extremely difficult and also affect the negotiation of D later. On this basis they warrant their separate status, although they are rooted in the activities of the paranoid-schizoid position.

On the question of whether pathological organisations deployed in Ps are the same or different to those deployed in D, Steiner leaves the question open. It is clear is that the main impetus for their emergence lies in Ps. It is also clear that the same pathological organisation can defend against depressive anxieties: 'It seems likely that in the course of development a pathological organisation was initially deployed against the anxieties of the paranoid-schizoid position and, once established, was later brought into play to defend against depressive anxieties' (Steiner, 1990b, p. 113).

Patients who improve in an analysis may also insist that they need their organisation as a protection against catastrophic anxieties of the paranoid-schizoid position when closer scrutiny suggests that they are seeking protection against depressive anxieties. However, Steiner also asserts that pathological organisations can show a more overt obsessional, manic, perverse or psychotic character (1981, 1993). This suggests that although their core is firmly rooted in pathological Ps activities they can acquire new manic and obsessional features that are defensive activities of the depressive position. As Riviere (1936) showed, the manic defence contributes to pathological narcissism.

Psychic retreats

In 1993 Steiner coined the new term 'psychic retreat'. The terms protective shell, safe haven, refuge or retreat from anxieties often feature in the various papers on pathological organisations. Psychic retreats are states of mind in which the patient is stuck and out of reach. They provide peace and protection from threatening contact with reality and they arise from an underlying pathological organisation.

A pathological organisation is an organisation of *defences*. The gang or mafia (or perhaps business company) represents an *organisation of objects* in a pathological organisation. A psychic retreat is perceived consciously by the patient, or pictorially represented in his dreams, in spatial terms and becomes embedded in the analytic relationship (R. Steiner, 2007, personal communication). The retreat can be a cave, an island, a building, a hiding place. The analyst can observe the snail-like attempts by the patient to emerge from the retreat and the hasty reversal back into it when contact with reality, and the analyst, becomes too threatening. The patient experiences his retreat as an idealised shell free from anxiety and pain, as an oppressive prison or deadly place or as a mixture of these.

With the concept of psychic retreat Steiner incorporates more fully into his work Henri Rey's influential notion of the claustro-agoraphobic dilemma (Rey, 1979). The retreat as mental space offers relief from anxiety but it is a trap, a claustrophobic prison that stultifies emotional development. However, expulsion from the retreat is felt to be disintegrative and tantamount to starvation, cold and death. The retreat is then idealised as a place of safety. The concept of a psychic retreat embodies the claustro-agoraphobic dilemma in its very formulation: 'While trapped in a psychic retreat they feel claustrophobic, but as soon as they manage to escape they once again panic and return to their previous position' (Steiner, 1993, p. 53).

Psychic retreats; enclaves and excursions; oedipal illusions

There is a parallel between Steiner's concept of a psychic retreat and O'Shaughnessy's notion of 'enclaves' and 'excursions' (1992). Her main focus is on the very strong pull that the patient exerts on the analyst to become caught up in an enactment by going along with the enclave or the excursion so as to protect the patient's equilibrium in the face of emotional contact that is felt to be too threatening. A patient who tries to turn his analysis into an *enclave* is usually able to find a way to relate to and make some contact with the analyst. He can do so: '. . . provided he finds an already suitable object or reshapes an object to fit what he requires to keep out aspects which threaten him with too much anxiety' (O'Shaughnessy, 1992, p. 609).

She describes a patient's powerful pressure on her analyst to go along with a denuded relationship. This restricted relationship would have become an enclave had the analyst not become aware and struggled to interpret the enactment she was invited to go along with. An enclave deforms the analytic process by leading to one that precludes openness to possibilities of disturbance and also to one that lacks 'extension in the domain of sense, myth and passion' (O'Shaughnessy, 1992, p. 204).

An *excursion* is more dramatic than an enclave: 'An excursion is different – not to do with limiting what is faced and known, but with totally evading emotional contact because of a terror of knowing' (O'Shaughnessy, 1992, p. 605).

Another patient, closer to a psychotic matrix and panic, kept inviting her analyst into making excursions into pseudo-sense. These excursions into continued flight created a state of confused flux in both analyst and patient. They were a way of avoiding the frightening truth that the patient felt her ego was in fragments and her deeper terror that her lack of an emotional centre was irreparable. O'Shaughnessy gives a vivid account of the work done in the countertransference to find a way of getting hold of this more disturbed part of the patient and to prevent the analysis from becoming a series of sterile excursions into pseudo-normality and pseudo-sense.

Ronald Britton (1989) uses the term *oedipal illusion* to describe an oedipal configuration formed as a defensive organisation to deny the psychic reality of the parental relationship. The psychic reality of the parental relationship is known but defended against by an oedipal illusion that is fixed and rigidly clung to in comparison to the more fluid switch between the positive and negative oedipal positions. This illusion, embedded in the transference, protects the patient against 'what is imagined as a calamitous transference' (Britton, 1989, p. 95). Britton's clinical illustration captures the emergence of the patient's disintegrative anxieties, linked to his own explosive and murderous rage against the parental couple, from which his oedipal illusion as an 'ocean of calm in the transference' sheltered him. It is not clear whether the patient's oedipal illusion is rooted in a pathological organisation of the personality as such but this defensive organisation, and its spatial character, bears a resemblance to the notion of a psychic retreat.

Key ideas

- Pathological organisations are extremely unyielding defensive organisations whose aim is to protect the individual from the primitive anxieties of both the paranoid-schizoid and the depressive positions felt to be unbearable by severely restricting his contact with internal and external reality.

• Pathological organisations originate in the infantile paranoid-schizoid position in response to the collapse of healthy dichotomous splitting between 'good' and 'bad' and to anxieties of confusion, disintegration and fragmentation.

• Pathological organisations attempt to recreate a split between protective and bad objects that masquerades as a plausible split between 'good' and 'bad' objects. Multiple projective identifications play a key role in assembling the fragments of self and objects into a new complex organisation with a pathological narcissistic character.

• Such pathological organisations make movement through Ps and D extremely difficult, with severe consequences for development. They also make analytic progress difficult.

References

Abraham, K. (1919) 'A particular form of neurotic resistance against the psychoanalytic method', in *Selected Papers of Karl Abraham*. London: Hogarth Press, pp. 303–311.

Bion, W. (1957) 'Differentiation of the psychotic from the non-psychotic personalities', *Int. J. Psycho-Anal.* 38: 266–275.

—— (1959) 'Attacks on linking', *Int. J. Psycho-Anal.* 40: 308–315.

Brenman, E. (1985) 'Cruelty and narrow-mindedness', *Int. J. Psycho-Anal.* 66: 273–281.

Britton, R. S. (1989) 'The missing link: Parental sexuality in the Oedipus complex', in J. Steiner (ed.) *The Oedipus Complex Today*. London: Karnac, pp. 83–101.

—— (2003) 'Narcissism and narcissistic disorders', in *Sex, Death, and the Superego*. London, Karnac, pp. 151–164.

Freud, S. (1910) 'Leonardo da Vinci and a memory of his childhood', *S.E. 11*. London: Hogarth Press, pp. 59–137.

—— (1914) 'On narcissism: an introduction', *S.E. 14*. London: Hogarth Press, pp. 67–102.

—— (1923) 'The ego and the id', *S.E. 19*. London: Hogarth Press, pp. 3–66.

—— (1927) 'Fetishism', *S.E. 21*. London: Hogarth Press, pp. 149–157

Hinshelwood, R. D. (1991) 'Pathological organisations', in *A Dictionary of Kleinian Thought*, 2nd edition. London: Free Association Books, pp. 381–387.

Joseph, B. (1971) 'A clinical contribution to the analysis of a perversion', *Int. J. Psycho-Anal.* 52: 441–449.

—— (1975) 'The patient who is difficult to reach', in P. Giovacchini (ed.) *Tactics and Techniques in Psycho-Analytic Therapy*, Vol. 2. New York: Jason Aronson, pp. 205–216.

—— (1982) 'Addiction to near-death', *Int. J. Psycho-Anal.* 63: 449–456.

Klein, M. (1935) 'A contribution to the psychogenesis of manic-depressive states', *Int. J. Psycho-Anal.* 16: 145–174.

—— (1946) 'Notes on some schizoid mechanisms', *Int. J. Psycho-Anal.* 27: 99–110.

—— (1952) 'The origins of the transference', in *The Writings of Melanie Klein*, Vol. 3. London: Hogarth Press, pp. 48–56.

—— (1957) 'Envy and gratitude', in *The Writings of Melanie Klein*, Vol. 3. London: Hogarth Press, pp. 176–235.

Meltzer, D. (1968) 'Terror, persecution and dread', *Int. J. Psycho-Anal.* 49: 396–400.

O'Shaughnessy, E. (1981) 'A clinical study of a defensive organisation', *Int. J. Psycho-Anal.* 62: 359–369.

—— (1992) 'Enclaves and excursions', *Int. J. Psycho-Anal.* 73: 603–611.

Reich, W. (1933) *Character Analysis*. New York: Orgone Institute Press (1949).

Rey, H. (1979) 'Schizoid phenomena in the borderline', in J. Le Boit and A. Capponi (eds) *Advances in the Psychotherapy of the Borderline patient*. New York: Jason Aronson, pp. 449–484.

Riesenberg-Malcolm, R. (1981) 'Expiation as a defence', *Int. J. Psycho-Anal. Psychother.* 8: 549–570.

Riviere, J. (1936) 'A contribution to the analysis of the negative therapeutic reaction', *Int. J. Psycho-Anal.* 17: 304–320.

Rosenfeld, H. (1950) 'Notes on the psychopathology of confusional states in acute schizophrenia', *Int. J. Psycho-Anal.* 31: 132–137.

—— (1952) 'Notes on the psycho-analysis of the super-ego conflict in an acute catatonic patient', *Int. J. Psycho-Anal.* 33: 111–131.

—— (1964) 'On the psychopathology of narcissism: A clinical approach', *Int. J. Psycho-Anal.* 45: 332–337.

—— (1971) 'A clinical approach to the psychoanalytic theory of the life and death instincts: an investigation into the aggressive aspects of narcissism', *Int. J. Psycho-Anal.* 52: 169–178.

—— (1987) *Impasse and Interpretation*. London: Tavistock.

Segal, H. (1972) 'A delusional system as a defence against the re-emergence of a catastrophic situation', *Int. J. Psycho-Anal.* 53: 393–401.

—— (2007) 'Narcissism: Comments on Ronald Britton's paper', in *Yesterday, Today and Tomorrow*. London: Routledge, pp. 230–234.

Sohn, L. (1985) 'Narcissistic organization, projective identification and the formation of the identificate', *Int. J. Psycho-Anal.* 66: 201–214.

Spillius, E. (1988) 'Pathological organizations: Introduction', in *Melanie Klein Today, Vol. 1, Mainly Theory*. London: Routledge, pp. 195–202.

Steiner, J. (1979) 'The border between the paranoid-schizoid and the depressive positions in the borderline patient', *Br. J. Med. Psychol.* 52: 385–391.

—— (1981) 'Perverse relationships between parts of self: A clinical illustration', *Int. J. Psycho-Anal.* 63: 241–251.

—— (1985) 'Turning a blind eye: the cover-up for Oedipus', *Int. J. Psycho-Anal.* 12: 161–172.

—— (1987) 'The interplay between pathological organizations and the paranoid-schizoid and depressive positions', *Int. J. Psycho-Anal.* 68: 69–80.

—— (1990a) 'Pathological organizations as obstacles to mourning: The role of unbearable guilt', *Int. J. Psycho-Anal.* 71: 87–94.

—— (1990b) 'The defensive functions of pathological organisations', in B. L Boyer and P. Giovacchini (eds) *Master Clinicians on Treating the Regressed Patient*. New York: Jason Aronson, pp. 97–116.

—— (1992) 'The equilibrium between the paranoid-schizoid and the depressive positions', in R. Anderson (ed.) *Clinical Lectures on Klein and Bion*. London: Routledge, pp. 46–58.

—— (1993) *Psychic Retreats: Pathological Organizations in Psychotic, Neurotic and Borderline Patients*. London: Routledge, pp. 1–53.

12 Technique

In the first edition of his *Dictionary of Kleinian Thought* Robert Hinshelwood gives a fitting tribute to the importance of technique to Klein:

> The power of Klein's original technique for psychoanalysis with children gave impetus to all the later developments in her theory, and to her technique of psychoanalysis with adults. Kleinian writings continue to reflect the clinical emphasis: very few papers are published without detailed case reports to substantiate their point.
>
> (Hinshelwood, 1991, p. 28)

Definition

Technique is a set of prescribed procedures for analyst and patient designed to facilitate making the unconscious conscious. Consistency and regularity of setting, time boundaries and frequency of sessions are emphasised, together with the importance of the analyst maintaining a receptive but discriminating attitude of mind.

Throughout her writing Klein stresses that her work, including her technique, is based on that of Freud, who describes his essential method with adult patients as involving sessions five or six times a week, use of the couch and asking patients to 'free associate', that is, to say to the analyst as best they can what they think and feel, without censorship. His complementary injunction to the analyst is that he should maintain 'evenly suspended attention' and should avoid looking in the patient's material for what he hopes to find (Freud, 1912).

Klein stresses Freud's concept of *transference*, meaning the conscious but also unconscious expression of past and present experiences, relationships, thoughts, phantasies and feelings, both positive and negative, in relation to the analyst. She particularly emphasises the importance of the *negative transference*, which she thinks can be usefully worked with provided it is recognised and understood by the analyst. She emphasises the role in the transference of the 'total situation' of the patient's past and present experiences. Like Freud she emphasises the importance of the patient's defences against the recognition of psychic reality. She also stresses the patient's anxiety as the starting point for the analyst's understanding of the patient's unconscious phantasies and she regards the analyst's *interpretation* as the main tool of analytic therapy.

Although Klein agrees in general with Freud's idea of the life and death instincts, in her technical approach she is more concerned with the specific *content* of instinctual drives than with their abstract conceptualisation. Clinical observation is her starting point and her special gift. In her work, observation and ideas interact with each other to engender new observations and further theories. Thus for Klein technique and clinical content are closely linked and interactive, and she does not attempt to describe technique in purely abstract terms without accompanying clinical content.

Further developments in technique have been made during and since Klein's work by Strachey, Racker, Rosenfeld, Bion, Segal, Joseph and others. There have been two main types of change. First, there is *increased focus on the analyst–patient relationship* as the main source of information about the patient, in contrast to the former view of the patient as an isolated entity who could be observed from an outside 'objective' perspective. Second, in contrast to Freud and Klein there has been a developing view that the analyst's *countertransference* can in certain circumstances be a useful source of information about the patient. These two main trends of change in technique have been accompanied by other less major changes, including a number of useful terminological distinctions.

Key papers

1932   Klein, M. *The Psychoanalysis of Children*.
The climax of Klein's early theory of child development, including the play technique [*see* Child analysis].

1934   Strachey, J. 'The nature of the therapeutic action of psychoanalysis'.
Very influential paper on the analyst/patient relationship and role of the 'mutative interpretation' in psychic change.

1943   Klein, M. 'Memorandum on technique'. (Not published until 1991.)
Succinct statement about importance of transference; first mention of 'situations'.

1950   Heimann, P. 'On counter-transference'.
A description of the analyst's countertransference as 'the patient's creation'.

1952   Klein, M. 'The origins of transference'.
            Klein's technique with adults; transference based on infantile
            object relations; idea of 'total situation'.

1956   Money-Kyrle, R. 'Normal counter-transference and some of
            its deviations'.
            Further description and ideas about analyst–patient relation-
            ship and role of countertransference in it.

1962   Bion, W. *Learning from Experience.*
            Theory of container/contained.

1964   Rosenfeld, H. 'On the psychopathology of narcissism: A
            clinical approach'.
            Differentiates 'libidinal' from 'destructive' narcissism and
            describes ways of analysing the destructiveness of both.

1967   Bion, W. 'Notes on memory and desire'.
            Focus on memory and desire detracts from attention to
            immediate interaction between patient and analyst in the
            present.

1971   Rosenfeld, H. 'A clinical approach to the psychoanalytic
            theory of the life and death instincts: An investigation into the
            aggressive aspects of narcissism'.
            Differentiates 'libidinal' from 'destructive' narcissism and
            describes ways of analysing the destructiveness of both.

1985   Brenman Pick, I. 'Working through in the countertransfer-
            ence'.
            Work to develop understanding of own countertransference is
            essential for understanding the patient.

1985   Joseph, B. 'Transference: The total situation'.
            Definition of 'total situation' with illustrations.

1987   Rosenfeld, H. *Impasse and Interpretation.*
            'Thin-skinned' and 'thick-skinned' narcissistic patients.

1989   Britton, R. 'The missing link: Parental sexuality in the Oedipus
            complex'.
            Concept of 'triangular space'.

1989   Joseph, B. *Psychic Equilibrium and Psychic Change.*
            Joseph develops strong focus on the immediate relationship
            between patient and analyst in the present.

1992   O'Shaughnessy, E. 'Enclaves and excursions'.
            Need for analysts to analyse relationships with patients that
            create enclaves or excursions, which avoid tackling the psychic
            situations that need to be analytically addressed.

1993   Steiner, J. 'Problems of psychoanalytic technique: Analyst-
            centred and patient-centred interpretations'.

Discussion and chronology

Klein's play technique with children [*see* Child analysis]

In her various writings Klein makes clear that in her view the play of children
in analysis is the equivalent of free association by adults. She also thinks that
adult and child analysis have the same aim, namely, to understand patients'
anxiety and by interpretation to relieve it. Her work in child analysis and her
development of the play technique led her to certain ideas and clinical
procedures that influenced her technique with adults: the importance of
transference; the particular importance of analysing the negative as well as
the positive transference; the internal world and the relationships with and
between internal objects, which are lived out in the transference relationship
with the analyst.

Differences in technique with children between Anna Freud and Melanie Klein

In 1927 Anna Freud published a book (English version 1946) called *The
Psycho-Analytic Treatment of Children*, in which she stated her differences
with Klein concerning the analytic treatment of children. First, she thought
there should be a 'preparatory phase' in which the analyst tried to gain the
confidence of the child because she thought that analysis could only work
productively if there was a positive relationship between child and analyst.
It was her view that there needed to be a positive transference, and that
child analysis should contain a considerable educative element. She did not
think that a true transference was possible in child analysis because the
child was still attached to its parents, and she did not agree with Klein's
view that play for children was the equivalent of free association for adults.

Although they were not the only issue, these differences in technique
between Anna Freud and Klein played an important role in the Controversial Discussions [*see* Controversial Discussions]. The issues were not
resolved in the Discussions, although Anna Freud later changed her views
on the necessity for the preparatory phase and the educational aspects of

child analysis, which Klein duly noted in a later 1948 edition of the 1927 paper in which she had responded to Anna Freud's criticisms.

Klein's technique with adult patients

Klein's clinical work with adults follows Freud's ideas except that the norm in Kleinian analysis and in all groups in the British Psychoanalytical Society has become five rather than six sessions a week. Like Freud, Klein tries to find and interpret the locus of the patient's anxiety, and she regards transference interpretation as the main technique for interpreting it. It is probable also that Klein was influenced by James Strachey's important paper, 'The nature of the therapeutic action of psychoanalysis' (1934), which is an early expression of technical focus on the analyst–patient relationship and on the therapeutic effect of transference interpretations, a focus that has been continued by Klein and by later Kleinian analysts. In her published work Klein cites Strachey's work only twice (1943, 1950) but she mentions his point of view more frequently in her Archive, especially in her 'Lectures on technique' (PP/KLE C52 and C53, Wellcome Library), which probably date from 1935/6.

Strachey's conceptual analysis gives a particular understanding of how analytic insight and interpretation can modify a patient's anxiety and misperceptions in a way that may make psychic change possible. He thinks that the patient attributes to the analyst aspects of his 'archaic superego' – archaic not only in the sense of being derived from infancy but also in the sense of being unrealistically ideal or unrealistically punitive. (Such 'attribution' by the patient will later be described as projection or projective identification by Klein and subsequent Kleinian analysts.) Provided the analyst can take in and interpret this process correctly, the patient may be able to see the difference between his archaic superego and the analyst as an 'auxiliary' superego. In a series of small steps, the patient's archaic superego may be somewhat changed, and it is transference interpretations that are most likely to be mutative, for, as Strachey puts it:

> It even seems likely that the whole possibility of effecting mutative interpretations may depend upon this fact that in the analytic situation the giver of the interpretation and the object of the id-impulse are one and the same person.
>
> (Strachey, 1934, p. 289, footnote 18)

In her unpublished lectures on technique Klein attempts to describe what she calls 'the analytic attitude', which she thinks is essential in analysis:

> . . . our whole interest is focused on one aim, namely, on the exploration of the mind of this one person who for the time being has become

the center of our attention . . . we should be able to note undisturbed what the patient's mind presents to us, irrespective even of the ultimate purpose of our work – namely, the cure of the patient. . . . This rather curious state of mind, eager and at the same time patient, detached from its subject and at the same time fully absorbed in it, is clearly the result of a balance between different and partly conflicting tendencies and psychological drives. . . .
(Melanie Klein Archive, First lecture, PP/KLE C52, Wellcome Library)

She emphasises what she describes as Freud's two great discoveries: the unconscious and the transference. She stresses the role of the past and its importance to the patient, and says that the analyst must be prepared to listen at length to the patient, to give him ample time to express all that he needs to convey. She emphasises interpretation as the analyst's main technical instrument and gives many illustrations.

In 1943 during the Controversial Discussions Klein wrote a short paper called 'Memorandum on technique' for the Training Committee of the British Psychoanalytical Society (which, incidentally, was chaired at that time by James Strachey). Klein's brief paper was published much later in King and Steiner (1991). In this paper Klein describes the way she deduces the patient's conscious and unconscious impulses, internal object relations and defences from his descriptions of his feelings and behaviour in the various situations of his past and present life, including his expression of them in the analytic situation. She particularly emphasises the central importance of transference in her work:

From my work with young children I came to certain conclusions which have to some extent influenced my technique with adults. Take transference first. I found that with children the transference (positive or negative) is active from the beginning of the analysis, since for instance even an attitude of indifference cloaks anxiety and hostility. With adults too (mutatis mutandis) I found that the transference situation is present from the start in one way or another, and I came, therefore, to make use of transference interpretations early in the analysis.

(Klein, 1943, p. 635)

In 1952, with the battles of the Controversial Discussions still alive in analysts' minds, Joan Riviere describes the importance of Klein's emphasis on the unconscious and on transference:

The principle at issue is the quite fundamental one of the significance of the unconscious in conscious life. When we realize this fundamental difference in outlook we understand why some analysts see so little in their patients' material, interpret so little, do not even recognize a transference-situation until the patient himself expresses something of it in conscious and direct reference to the analyst, and so on. In that case only a portion of what the patient says or does will be unravelled by analysis.

(Riviere, 1952, p. 17)

Klein's main published paper on technique with adults is 'The origins of transference' (1952), in which she discusses the idea that what to the conscious mind of an adult would be perceived as one object may appear to the infant (and to the unconscious mind of an adult) to be many objects:

There are in fact very few people in the young infant's life, but he feels them to be a multitude of objects because they appear to him in different aspects. Accordingly, the analyst may at a given moment represent a part of the self, of the superego or any one of a wide range of internalized figures. Similarly it does not carry us far enough if we realize that the analyst stands for the actual father or mother, unless we understand which aspect of the parents has been revived.

(Klein, 1952a, p. 54)

Klein also makes clear the breadth and depth of her use of the concept of transference and the way one aspect of transference may be expressed towards the analyst but other aspects may be split off and attributed to other, outside people. She says:

For many years – and this is up to a point still true today – trans-ference was understood in terms of direct references to the analyst in the patient's material. My conception of transference as rooted in the earliest stages of development and in deep layers of the unconscious is much wider and entails a technique by which from the whole material presented the *unconscious elements* of the transference are deduced. For instance, reports of patients about their everyday life, relations, and activities not only give an insight into the functioning of the ego, but also reveal – if we explore their unconscious content – the defences against the anxieties stirred up in the transference situation. For the patient is bound to deal with conflicts and anxieties re-experienced towards the analyst by the same methods he used in the past.

(Klein, 1952a, p. 55)

Finally, Klein describes her idea of the 'total situation', by which she means the complex totality of a person's experience, past and present, which shapes his inner world and is enacted in the transference:

> We are accustomed to speak of the transference *situation*. But do we always keep in mind the fundamental importance of this concept? It is my experience that in unravelling the details of the transference it is essential to think in terms of *total situations* transferred from the past into the present, as well as of emotions, defences, and object-relations.
>
> (Klein, 1952a, p. 55)

Further research in the Melanie Klein Archive has added a new awareness of Klein's kindliness as an analyst and supervisor, of her varied ways of using her concept of projective identification and her readiness to make direct interpretations linking the transference to particular aspects of the patient's past (see Gammill, 1989; Spillius, 2007).

Thus, through her clinical work with both adults and children, Klein was on the alert for both the negative and the positive transference, for signs of the effects of the early superego and the early Oedipus complex, for the complexities of the 'total situation' and for splitting and projection of transference feelings between the analyst and other objects. As Hanna Segal puts it in her 1967 paper 'Melanie Klein's technique':

> . . . It seems to me that it is legitimate to speak of a technique as developed by Melanie Klein in that the nature of the interpretations given to the patient and the changes of emphasis in the analytical process show, in fact, a departure, or, as Melanie Klein saw it, an evolution from the classical technique. She saw aspects of material not seen before, and interpreting those aspects, she revealed further material which might not have been reached otherwise and which, in turn, dictated new interpretations seldom, if ever, used in the classical technique.
>
> (Segal, 1967, p. 4)

Further contributions to technique with adults by other Kleinian analysts

In various ways, trends of change in Kleinian analysis began to become evident from the 1950s onwards (O'Shaughnessy, 1983; Spillius, 1983, 1994). At first there was increased stress on destructiveness and defences against it. Interpretations in 'part-object' 'bodily' language were also a feature of this period, especially in discussions by somewhat dogmatic enthusiasts. Gradually, though rather unevenly, three trends of change began to develop in the 1960s and 1970s. First, destructiveness began to be interpreted in a more balanced way. Second, the immediate use of interpretations in part-object bodily language began to be replaced by descriptions of 'function' – seeing, hearing, thinking, evacuating, etc. Third, the concept of projective identification began to be used more directly in analysing the transference. Arising from the third trend, there has been more emphasis on acting-out (now also sometimes called 'enactment') in the transference and on pressure being put on the analyst to join in, which has been especially important in the work of Betty Joseph. All these developments have been important in the developing technical focus on the analyst–patient relationship and on the analyst's countertransference (Spillius, 1983, 1994, 2007). Edna O'Shaughnessy gives a particularly apt characterisation of the increasing importance of the analyst–patient relationship, saying:

> Over the past fifty years, psychoanalysts have changed their view of their own method. It is now widely held that, instead of being about the patient's intrapsychic dynamics, interpretations should be about the *interaction* of patient and analyst *at an intrapsychic level.*
>
> (O'Shaughnessy, 1983, p. 281)

The development in technique of focus on the analyst–patient relationship

As described above, James Strachey's paper on the 'mutative interpretation' gives an early focus and theoretical statement about the effect of interpreting the analyst–patient relationship in analysis; this paper has had an important influence on all schools of British psychoanalytic thought. Herbert Rosenfeld, a particular admirer of Strachey's paper, describes the importance of the paper and warns against misuse of Strachey's insight:

> . . . we occasionally find the converse situation . . . where an analyst may relate all the material presented to him by the patient in a vague way to the transference such as 'You feel this about me now' or 'You are doing this to me' or they repeat the words of the patient parrot-like and relate them to the session. I think this stereotyped kind of interpretation, which is supposed to be an interpretation of the here-and-now situation, changes Strachey's valuable contribution of the mutative transference into something absurd.
>
> (Rosenfeld, 1972, p. 457)

Although Bion does not cite Strachey as a particular influence, it is possible that Strachey's idea of the process involved in the 'mutative interpretation' may have had some effect on the development of Bion's idea of 'containment' (Bion, 1962, especially p. 90) in which the analyst typically introjects the patient's projections, leading to further emotional and intellectual work by the analyst and then possibly to new interpretations that the patient may be able to introject.

The works of Strachey and of Bion have been important influences in the thinking of Betty Joseph (1985, 1989), which focuses on the analyst–patient relationship in the present. The patient's statements about his past and present life are given due weight but are mainly understood in relation to the immediate transference situation. Joseph is particularly known for her close attention to the patient's responses to interpretations, in which she carefully notes the patient's frequent tendency to try to maintain his existing emotional equilibrium in spite of his conscious desire for therapeutic change (Joseph, 1989). She stays for the most part with the immediate transference relationship in the present situation of the session. Occasionally, however, she makes a potential reconstruction of a possible type of infantile experience that a particular sort of patient might have had. In 'Addiction to near-death', for example, she says:

> I get the impression from the difficulty these patients experience in waiting and being aware of gaps and aware of even the simplest type of guilt that such potentially depressive experiences have been felt by them in infancy as terrible pain that goes over into torment, and that they have tried to obviate this by taking over the torment, the inflicting of mental pain on to themselves and building it into a world of perverse excitement, and that this necessarily militates against any real progress towards the depressive position.
>
> (Joseph, 1982, p. 138)

Such general formulations help the analyst and the reader to conceptualise what is going on in the patient and between analyst and patient, but Joseph does not make such explanatory interpretations explicitly to a patient unless such ideas are very much alive in the immediate situation and the patient is spontaneously reaching for his own understanding of them.

In her 1985 paper 'Transference: The total situation', Joseph develops Klein's idea of the 'total situation', emphasising its complexity and comprehensiveness not so much in the patient's history, which was Klein's focus in discussing this concept, but more in the way the patient's internal situation is expressed in the transference situation with the analyst. As she puts it:

> Much of our understanding of the transference comes through our understanding of how our patients act on us to feel things for many varied reasons, how they try to draw us into their defensive systems; how they unconsciously act out with us in the transference, trying to get us to act out with them; how they convey aspects of their inner world built up from infancy – elaborated in childhood and adulthood; experiences often beyond the use of words, which we can often only capture through the feelings aroused in us, through our counter-transference, used in the broad sense of the word.
>
> (Joseph, 1985, p. 157)

The work of Strachey, Bion and Joseph has influenced most Kleinian analysts so that there has been an increasing emphasis on the interplay between analyst and patient in the immediacy of the session. Although there is some variation of approach, the most usual expectation is that a Kleinian analyst will first concentrate on the expression of the patient's internal object relations in the analyst–patient relationship, and will only later bring in the similarity or lack of similarity of these relationships to remembered experiences of the past.

The 'present' and the role of reconstruction

Freud and Klein often seem to have taken it for granted that the past virtually 'causes' the 'present'. Thus, in her Archive Melanie Klein says:

> Notes on technique
> It cannot be sufficiently stressed and conveyed to the patient that transference phenomena are linked to the past. In recent years the importance of transference to be gathered from the unconscious, as well as from conscious material has been recognized, but the old concept that transference means a repetition from the past seems to have correspondingly diminished. One hears again and again the expression of the 'here and now' laying the whole emphasis on what the patient experiences towards the analyst and leaves out the links with the past.
> (Melanie Klein Archive, PP/KLE D17, Wellcome Library)

In marked contrast to such statements by Klein, Bion in his paper 'Notes on memory and desire' (1967) focuses on the immediate analyst–patient relationship as the essential basis for gaining analytic understanding, and he does not state or imply that the past 'causes' the present. Bion says that the analyst should avoid 'memory' and 'desire' because activities based on either frame of mind will contaminate the analyst's focus on the immediate interaction between patient and analyst and will spoil his receptivity to the moment with his patient. Such focus on the immediacy of the transference has become an important emphasis in the development of Kleinian technique. It does not exclude what the patient says about his memories of his past or his desires for the future, but it directs the analyst's attention to the expression of the patient's internal object relations in his immediate relation with the analyst, which forms the context within which past and future can be better understood. Bion's avoidance of memory and desire has much in common with Freud's advocacy of 'evenly suspended attention' (Freud, 1912, pp. 111–112), though perhaps with even greater stress on the immediacy of the transference/countertransference experience.

Betty Joseph (1985, 1989), as described above, also stresses the importance of the immediate experiences of analyst and patient in interaction in the session. She does not leave out the past, but tends to start with the relationship between the analyst and patient and then brings in the patient's memories of his past that are concordant with his transference experiences in the present.

Michael Feldman (2007) in his paper 'The illumination of history' states that a patient's history is embodied in his internal object relationships, which are expressed in the analyst–patient relationship. Once these relationships have been analysed and understood in the present analytic relationship, underlying anxieties are likely to be reduced so that psychic change can occur in such a way that the patient can achieve a new sort of connection with his history, which may illuminate both present and past.

Although there is some variation among Kleinian analysts in their attitudes towards time and causality, the usual tendency is for the analyst to start with the relationships expressed in the analyst–patient relationship and to bring in memories of the past as they occur in the analysis and show themselves to be linked to the analyst–patient relationship.

Changes in the meaning and use of the term 'countertransference'

Both Freud and Klein had negative views about the term 'countertransference' (Freud, 1910, pp. 144–145; 1915, pp. 160, 165–166, 169–170; Klein, 1957, p. 226), but from the 1950s onwards the growing interest in Britain about the analyst–patient relationship as a central focus of technique began to involve a new sort of attitude towards countertransference, that is, to the conscious and unconscious response of the analyst to the patient.

Klein mentions countertransference in her published work only once (1957, p. 226) and that mention is negative, but the views she expresses in her unpublished Archive leave no doubt about her negative views of the idea that countertransference might be a useful source of information about the patient. In 1958 a group of young colleagues asked her to comment on countertransference, and part of the transcript of Klein's reply reads as follows:

> . . . at one occasion it has been called counter-countertransference. Now, it isn't so. You know, of course that the patient is bound to stir certain feelings in the analyst and that this varies according to the patient's attitude, according to the patient, though there are of course feelings at work in the analyst which he has to become aware of. I have never found that the countertransference has helped me to understand my patient better. If I may put it like this, I have found that it helped me to understand myself better.
>
> (Melanie Klein Archive, PP/KLE C72, Wellcome Library)

In this negative opinion about the usefulness of countertransference Klein was following Freud's view that countertransference was an expression of the analyst's pathology. In her attitude she was somewhat out of step, not only with her young colleagues but also with Paula Heimann (1950), Heinrich Racker (1968), Rosenfeld (1952), Bion (1955) and several other Kleinian analysts.

It seems evident through the various discussions of countertransference that the differences of view stem partly from the way the term is defined. In spite of her negative views about countertransference being a useful source of information about the patient, it is evident that Klein's attitude towards patients, even very difficult patients, was kindly and understanding. She says, for example:

> But it is essential not to attempt to hurry these steps in integration. For if the realization of the division in his personality were to come suddenly, the patient would have great difficulties in coping with it. The more strongly had the envious and destructive impulses been split off, the more dangerous the patient feels them to be when he becomes conscious of them. In analysis we should make our way slowly and gradually towards the painful insight into the divisions in the patient's self. This means that the destructive sides are again and again split off and regained, until greater integration comes about. As a result, the feeling of responsibility becomes stronger and guilt and depression are more fully experienced.

> (Klein, 1957, pp. 224–225)

Klein evidently did not think of her general kindly but insightful attitude towards patients as her countertransference. Like Freud, she implicitly defined countertransference as attitudes towards the patient that were influenced by the analyst's pathology. She had no explicit definitory term for attributes and attitudes in the analyst that were intellectually and emotionally helpful in understanding the patient.

Paula Heimann's (1950) paper, 'On counter-transference', has had a considerable influence on the views of British analysts, including Kleinians. In it Heimann says:

> My thesis is that the analyst's emotional response to his patient within the analytic situation represents one of the most important tools for his work. The analyst's counter-transference is an instrument of research into the patient's unconscious.

> (Heimann, 1950, p. 74)

> From the point of view I am stressing, the analyst's counter-transference is not only part and parcel of the analytic relationship, but it is the patient's creation, it is part of the patient's personality.

> (Heimann, 1950, p. 77)

Heinrich Racker, in a series of papers in the 1940s and 1950s, published in book form in 1968 as *Transference and Countertransference*, says that '. . . the countertransference is the living response to the transference' (1968, p. 3). He distinguishes the 'countertransference neurosis', which involves the analyst's pathology, from more constructive countertransference based on accurate and sympathetic understanding of the patient, and he uses the general term 'countertransference' to include both the neurotic and the useful forms of countertransference. He also distinguishes 'concordant countertransference', in which the analyst identifies with the patient, from 'complementary countertransference', in which the analyst identifies with the patient's internal objects (1968, p. 134). He defines 'counterresistance' by the analyst as a response based on sexual or negative feelings towards the patient, comparable to 'resistance' in the patient (Racker, 1968, pp. 19 and 137).

Like Racker and Heimann, both Rosenfeld and Bion state the need for the analyst to use his countertransference when working with schizophrenic patients. Rosenfeld (1952) in 'Notes on the psycho-analysis of the super-ego conflict in an acute schizophrenic patient' says:

> In my opinion the unconscious intuitive understanding by the psychoanalyst of what a patient is conveying to him is an essential factor in all analyses, and depends on the analyst's capacity to use his countertransference as a kind of sensitive 'receiving set'. In treating schizophrenics who have such great verbal difficulties, the unconscious intuitive understanding of the analyst through the counter-transference is even more important, for it helps him to determine what it is that really matters at the moment.
>
> (Rosenfeld, 1952, p. 76)

Wilfred Bion makes the same sort of point in 1955 in his paper 'Language and the schizophrenic', saying that in the treatment of schizophrenics '. . . the only evidence on which an interpretation can be based is that which is afforded by the counter-transference' (Bion, 1955, p. 224).

Money-Kyrle (1956) in 'Normal countertransference and some of its deviations' analyses countertransference in the analyst–patient relationship. His formulation is similar to that of Racker, though with fewer distinguishing definitions. He thinks that 'normal' countertransference expresses the analyst's interest in the patient and concern for his welfare. When the analysis is going well there is a fairly rapid oscillation between introjection and projection in which the analyst becomes introjectively identified with his patient and, having understood him, 'reprojects' him and interprets.

Periods of non-understanding arise when something in the patient corresponds to something in himself that the analyst has not yet learned to understand. Money-Kyrle says that there are three factors: the analyst's emotional disturbance; the patient's role in bringing it about; and the effect on the patient of the analyst's disturbance. Sometimes insight into this interactive process is rapidly restored and the difficulty is overcome. At other times the analyst may fall back on reassurance, or may get angry with the patient. Money-Kyrle thinks that these unsatisfactory situations probably occur more often than we like to admit, but that it is through them, by silently analysing his own countertransference reactions, that the analyst can increase his insight and learn more about his patient.

Brenman Pick (1985) in 'Working through in the countertransference', like Money-Kyrle, stresses the necessity for the analyst to use his understanding of his own countertransference feelings and responses to the patient in order to make effective interpretations. She lays particular emphasis on the struggle the analyst goes through in recognising and working through his own countertransference responses to the projections of the patient.

Thus the analyst's countertransference, if conscientiously understood and accepted by the analyst, has come to be considered a helpful technical tool. This is the case with all types of patient to some extent, although it is particularly striking in the case of psychotic, borderline and narcissistic patients. Such patients often project their infantile self into the analyst, and it is through introjection of the patient's tormented infantile feelings that the analyst becomes able to understand and to interpret how the patient's benign self is attacked and dominated by the patient's cruel, destructive self, which the patient is likely to have idealised.

On particular aspects of technique with borderline and 'difficult' patients

Much of the development of Kleinian technique has been shaped by work first with psychotic patients and more recently with difficult narcissistic and borderline patients. Herbert Rosenfeld's work with such patients has been especially important. In both 'On the psychopathology of narcissism: a clinical approach' (1964) and 'A clinical approach to the psychoanalytic theory of the life and death instincts: An investigation into the aggressive aspects of narcissism' (1971) Rosenfeld describes patients' internal conflicts between a dependent part of the patient and a dominating, narcissistic, destructive part. The analyst's aim in technique is to locate the dependent, imprisoned part of the patient and to encourage its alliance with the analyst rather than with the destructive part of the self. Then in 1987 in *Impasse and Interpretation* Rosenfeld, in addition to using the ideas developed in his earlier work, distinguishes between 'thick-skinned' patients who need firm handling in analysis and 'thin-skinned' patients who need careful and tactful handling because they have been traumatised in childhood. He also expresses the view that many analysts have not been sufficiently aware that traumatised patients struggle in analysis because they are likely to feel that their analyst, like certain of their past objects, is dangerous and traumatising.

Hanna Segal (1981) in her paper 'The function of dreams', following Freud, says that the normal function of dreams is to express and to some extent satisfy a wish without arousing the forces of repression. In borderline and disturbed patients, however, the dream serves other functions. The technique of the analyst then needs to be devoted less to analysing the content of dreams and more to uncovering their other functions, such as the evacuation of painful and disturbing states from the mind. In some cases this evacuation is successful, but in others it is only partly successful, giving rise to what Segal calls 'predictive' dreams, which are acted out in the session.

Ronald Britton (1989) in 'The missing link: Parental sexuality in the Oedipus complex' discusses the idea of 'triangular space', meaning a space bounded by the three persons (parents and child) of the triangular situation and all their potential relationships. Each member of the triangle becomes at once a witness of one relationship and a participant in another relationship. This provides each individual with a capacity for seeing himself in interaction with others and for entertaining another point of view while retaining his own.

Britton illustrates the missing link by describing a situation with a patient who had only a very minimal capacity to conceive of the particular qualities of her parents' relationship. She experienced Britton's consulting his own mind as if it were parental intercourse and reacted with physical violence at first and later with words: 'Stop that fucking thinking!' In the analytic situation Britton needed to be able to think about his patient in his own independent fashion while simultaneously communicating to the patient his understanding of her point of view, a procedure that she was gradually able to accept.

Edna O'Shaughnessy (1992) in 'Enclaves and excursions' describes the need for the analyst to be aware of two potential dangers in technique. The first is that of allowing himself to be drawn into an 'enclave', meaning a refuge from disturbance. The second is that of succumbing to pressure to move away from knowing what is psychically urgent, so that the analysis will be turned into a series of flights or 'excursions'. Both comfortable enclaves and exciting excursions avoid the psychic situations that need to be addressed.

John Steiner (1993) in 'Problems of psychoanalytic technique: Patient-centred and analyst-centred interpretations' describes a distinction between two types of interpretation. Analyst-centred interpretations aim to convey to the patient the analyst's understanding of the patient's desire to be understood, usually on the patient's own somewhat limited terms; such interpretations typically describe how the patient sees the analyst. Patient-centred interpretations, on the other hand, are of the classical kind 'in which something the patient is doing, thinking or wishing is interpreted, often with the motive and anxiety associated with it' (Steiner, 1993, p. 133). Patient-centred interpretations thus convey understanding, but it is an understanding of the way the analyst sees the patient. Analysis contains both types of interpretation but ultimately, Steiner says, the analyst must find an appropriate balance of patient-centred and analyst-centred interpretations:

> Interpretations may temporarily have to emphasize containment but ultimately must be concerned with helping the patient gain insight, and an analyst who is perceived as reluctant to pursue this fundamental aim is not experienced as providing containment.
>
> (Steiner, 1993, p. 145)

Donald Meltzer (1968) in 'An interruption technique for the analytic impasse' describes his method of attempting to overcome a particular sort of analytic impasse by cutting down the patient's sessions. The type of impasse for which he advocates interruption of the analysis concerns patients whom he considers to be at the threshold of the depressive position but who are unwilling to face its demand for sincerity and capacity to endure mental pain. (He does not suggest 'interruption' for psychotic patients or in the case of patients where the impasse can be clearly related to a known historical event when the patient was two years old or less, or for patients who suffer from underlying catastrophic anxiety.) He also recommends that the analyst should consult a colleague before undertaking interruption of sessions.

Many of Meltzer's colleagues in the British Psychoanalytical Society, however, have not agreed with his technique of interruption. It is better known among child psychotherapists and among the analysts of the considerable number of other countries in which Meltzer treated patients and taught psychoanalysis, including technique, until his death in 2004.

Key ideas

Klein's technique with adults, basically true to Freud

Klein's analytic technique is basically similar to that of Freud in form although its content is different because of the ideas that Klein's analyses of children had led to, especially the usefulness of the negative transference and the equivalence of play and free association. The content of her discoveries in the analysis of children influenced the content of her analysis of adults.

The 'total situation' in the transference

Klein describes the 'total situation' in the transference as the patient's living out of the relationships of his internal world based on the complexities of his past and present experiences. With both children and adults Klein found that the transference is central in the therapeutic work, and it is active from the beginning of the analysis.

Strachey's idea of the mutative interpretation

This has influenced many analysts, including Klein (Strachey, 1934). Mutative interpretations occur in a series of small steps in which the patient sees that there is a difference between his 'archaic superego' and the actual analyst onto whom the patient has projected his archaic superego. In Strachey's view, transference interpretations are the most likely interpretations to lead to mutative interpretations and psychic change, a view shared by Klein and later Kleinian analysts.

Later developments

The technique of contemporary Kleinian analysts differs from that of Klein in several respects.

The emphasis on enactment

Strachey's emphasis on the mutative interpretation, Bion's concept of container/contained and Joseph's approach to equilibrium and psychic change have become the basis of a general focus in technique on the *enactment of aspects of the patient's internal world in the analyst–patient relationship* in the present 'here and now' of the analytic session (Strachey, 1934; Bion, 1962; Joseph, 1989; O'Shaughnessy, 1983).

Increasing emphasis on the present

This focus in technique on the analyst–patient relationship has involved an increasing emphasis on the 'present' (Bion, 1967; Joseph, 1989; Feldman, 2007) together with an understanding of the importance of the patient's 'past' as viewed in the light of the present analyst–patient relationship. There is considerable variation among Kleinian analysts, however, in the extent to which they make use of the patient's explicit memories of his past.

Change in the meaning of 'countertransference'

The meaning of the term 'countertransference' has gradually changed from being defined as a response by the analyst influenced by his own patho-logical tendencies to meaning *all* the responses of the analyst to the patient, many of which are now thought to be capable of contributing to the analyst's understanding of the patient (Heimann, 1950; Rosenfeld, 1952, 1987; Bion, 1955; Money-Kyrle, 1956; Racker, 1968; Brenman Pick, 1985).

Developments in work with narcissistic and borderline patients

Work with borderline and narcissistic patients has led to a number of particular technical emphases and distinctions: the emphasis of Rosenfeld and later Kleinian analysts on the need to tackle the destructive effects of an alliance in the patient between dependent and destructive parts of the self (Rosenfeld, 1964, 1971); distinction between thick-skinned and thin-skinned patients (Rosenfeld 1987); triangular space (Britton, 1989); watching out in technique for 'enclaves' and 'excursions' (O'Shaughnessy, 1982); analyst-centred and patient-centred interpretations (Steiner, 1993).

References

Bion, W. R. (1955) 'Language and the schizophrenic', in M. Klein, P. Heimann and R. Money-Kyrle (eds) *New Directions in Psychoanalysis*. London: Tavistock, pp. 220–239.

—— (1962) *Learning from Experience*. London: Heinemann.

—— (1967) 'Notes on memory and desire', *Psychoanal. Forum* 2: 272–280; also in E. Spillius (ed.) *Melanie Klein Today*, Vol. 2. London: Routledge (1988), pp. 17–21.

Brenman Pick, I. (1985) 'Working through in the countertransference', *Int. J. Psycho-Anal.* 66: 157–166.

Britton, R. (1989) 'The missing link: Parental sexuality in the Oedipus complex', in J. Steiner (ed.) *The Oedipus Complex Today*. London: Karnac Books, pp. 83–101.

Feldman, M. (2007) 'The illumination of history', *Int. J. Psycho-Anal.* 88: 609–625.

Freud, A. (1927) *The Psycho-Analytic Treatment of Children* (English edition, 1945). London: Imago.

Freud, S. (1910) 'The future prospects of psycho-analytic therapy', *S.E. 11*. London: Hogarth Press, pp. 139–151.

—— (1912) 'Recommendations to physicians practising psychoanalysis', *S.E. 12*. London: Hogarth Press, pp. 111–120.

—— (1915) 'Observations on transference-love', *S.E., 12*. London: Hogarth Press, pp. 159–171.

Gammill, J. (1989) 'Some personal reflections on Melanie Klein', *Melanie Klein and Object Relations* 7: 1–15.

Heimann, P. (1950) 'On counter-transference', *Int. J. Psycho-Anal.* 31: 71–84.

Hinshelwood, R. D. (1991) *A Dictionary of Kleinian Thought*, 2nd edition. London: Free Association Books.

Joseph, B. (1982) 'Addiction to near-death', *Int. J. Psycho-Anal.* 63: 449–456; reprinted in M. Feldman and E. B. Spillius (eds) *Psychic Equilibrium and Psychic Change*. London: Routledge (1989), pp. 127–138.

—— (1985) 'Transference: The total situation', *Int. J. Psycho-Anal.* 66: 447–454; reprinted in M. Feldman and E. B. Spillius (eds) *Psychic Equilibrium and Psychic Change*. London: Routledge (1989), pp. 156–167.

—— (1989) *Psychic Equilibrium and Psychic Change*. London: Routledge.

King, P. and Steiner, R. (1991) *The Freud–Klein Controversies 1941–45*. London: Routledge.

Klein, M. (1927) 'Symposium on child analysis', in *The Writings of Melanie Klein*, Vol. 1. London: Hogarth Press, pp. 139–169.

—— (1932) *The Psychoanalysis of Children*. *The Writings of Melanie Klein*, Vol. 2. London: Hogarth Press.

—— (1943) 'Memorandum on her technique', in P. King and R. Steiner (eds) *The Freud–Klein Controversies 1941–45*. London: Routledge (1991), pp. 611–636.

—— (1950) 'On the criteria for the termination of a psychoanalysis', in *The Writings of Melanie Klein*, Vol. 3. London: Hogarth Press, pp. 43–47.

—— (1952) 'The origins of transference', *Int. J. Psycho-Anal*. 33: 433–438; also in *The Writings of Melanie Klein*, Vol. 3. London: Hogarth Press (1975), pp. 48–56.

—— (1955) 'The psycho-analytic play technique: Its history and significance', in M. Klein, P. Heimann and R. Money-Kyrle (eds) *New Directions in Psychoanalysis*. London: Tavistock, pp. 3–22: also in *The Writings of Melanie Klein*, Vol. 3. London: Hogarth Press (1975), pp. 122–140.

—— (1957) 'Envy and gratitude', in *The Writings of Melanie Klein*, Vol. 3. London: Hogarth Press, pp. 176–235.

Meltzer, D. (1968) 'An interruption technique for the analytic impasse', in A. Hahn (ed.) *Sincerity and Other Works: Collected Papers of Donald Meltzer*. London: Karnac Books (1994), pp. 152–165.

Money-Kyrle, R. (1956) 'Normal counter-transference and some of its deviations', *Int. J. Psycho-Anal*. 37: 360–366.

O'Shaughnessy, E. (1983) 'Words and working through', *Int. J. Psycho-Anal*. 64: 281–289.

—— (1992) 'Enclaves and excursions', *Int. J. Psycho-Anal*. 73: 603–611.

Racker, H. (1968) *Transference and Countertransference*. London: Hogarth Press.

Riviere, J. (1952) 'General introduction', in Melanie Klein, Susan Isaacs, Paula Heimann and Joan Riviere *Developments in Psycho-Analysis*. London: Hogarth Press (1952), pp. 1–36.

Rosenfeld, H. (1952) 'Notes on the psycho-analysis of the super-ego conflict in an acute schizophrenic patient', *Int. J. Psycho-Anal*. 33: 111–131; reprinted in *Psychotic States*. London: Hogarth Press (1965), pp. 63–103.

—— (1964) 'On the psychopathology of narcissism: A clinical approach', *Int. J. Psycho-Anal*. 45: 332–337; reprinted in *Psychotic States*. London: Hogarth Press (1965), pp. 169–179.

—— (1971) 'A clinical approach to the psychoanalytical theory of the life and death instincts: An investigation into the aggressive aspects of narcissism', *Int. J. Psycho-Anal*. 52: 169–178; reprinted in E. B. Spillius (ed.) *Melanie Klein Today*, Vol. 1. London: Routledge (1988), pp. 239–255.

—— (1972) 'A critical appraisal of James Strachey's paper on "The nature of the therapeutic action of psycho-analysis"', *Int. J. Psycho-Anal*. 53: 455–461.

—— (1987) *Impasse and Interpretation*. London: Routledge.

Segal, H. (1967) 'Melanie Klein's technique', in *The Work of Hanna Segal*. New York: Jason Aronson (1981), pp. 3–24.

—— (1981) 'The function of dreams', in *The Work of Hanna Segal*. New York: Jason Aronson, pp. 89–97.

Spillius, E. B. (1983) 'Some developments from the work of Melanie Klein', *Int. J. Psycho-Anal.* 64: 321–332.

—— (1994) 'Developments in Kleinian thought: Overview and personal view', *Psychoanal Inq.* 14: 324–364.

—— (2007) 'In Melanie Klein's archive', in *Encounters with Melanie Klein: Selected Papers of Elizabeth Spillius* P. Roth and R. Rusbridger (eds). London: Routledge, pp. 65–126.

Steiner, J. (1993) 'Problems of psychoanalytic technique: Patient-centred and analyst-centred interpretations', in *Psychic Retreats: Pathological Organizations in Psychotic, Neurotic and Borderline Patients.* London: Routledge, pp. 131–146.

Strachey, J. (1934) 'The nature of the therapeutic action of psychoanalysis', *Int. J. Psycho-Anal.* 50: 275–292.

Part II

General entries

Karl Abraham

Biography: Born in Germany, 1877, Abraham became interested in psycho-analysis while a trainee psychiatrist in Zurich with Jung. In 1907 he began a psychoanalytic practice in Berlin, the first in Germany, and he founded the German Psycho-Analytical Society in 1910. He became President of the International Psycho-Analytical Association in 1924, but then died at the height of his professional abilities and reputation in 1925 (H. Abraham, 1974). Abraham was persuaded by Melanie Klein to analyse her in 1924, although this was interrupted some 15 months later by his ill health. He also analysed a number of English analysts, including James Glover, Edward Glover and Alix Strachey. He had a special position within the psycho-analytic movement, as he was one of the first pioneers of psychoanalysis outside Vienna, together with Jung (in Zurich), Ferenczi (in Budapest) and Jones (in London). But more than that, his importance is as an outstanding clinical observer and classical theoretician. Three of his main scientific contributions are outlined.

Pregenital phases of development: Abraham's masterly essay on the develop-ment of the libido and on the growth of object-love (1924a) introduces important differentiations within the oral, anal and genital phases. Abraham sees Freud's 'narcissistic neuroses' as rooted in the oral and early anal phase. The second oral cannibalistic phase and the first anal sadistic phase in particular are imbued with a high level of sadistic impulses, which cause severe conflicts and regressions. They are respectively dominated by the prominence of introjection (oral taking in) and projection (anal expulsion), which contribute to the narcissistic character of psychotic illnesses. For Abraham a partial form of object-love begins in the second anal phase. The object is preserved but treated as a possession to be controlled. This new capacity contrasts with earlier processes of devouring the object, which is then inside the self and has no separate existence. Early partial love in the second year for Abraham gives way to proper object-love after the oedipal phase and when the later genital phase sets in: the object is loved whilst its separateness is more fully accepted.

Melancholia and obsessional neurosis: Abraham's close collaboration with Freud led him to offer a more complex aetiological understanding of melancholia and also to shed light on the different fixation points that delineate the 'choice' between melancholia and obsessional neurosis (1911, 1924a). Abraham worked with manic-depressive patients during their phase of remission. He was able to formulate the predispositions for the psychotic phases of their illness.

In Abraham's view both the melancholic and the obsessional patient deal with the situation of the *loss of the loved object* by anal-sadistic means: the object is sadistically destroyed by faecal attacks and is also violently expelled as faeces. The *melancholic* patient attempts to deal with the ruinous state of the object by a regression to the oral cannibalistic stage, with the aim of incorporating the object inside the self. However, this incorporation is sadistic and cannibalistic so that the introjected object is further damaged and 'continues to exert its despotic power from within' (1924a, p. 490). In classical theory this introjection explains the notion of the abandonment of the object-cathexis and also that of the regression to primary narcissism: two features of psychosis. The *obsessional* patient also deals with the situation of the loss of the object with the same anal-sadistic violence. However, the fateful regression to oral cannibalism does not take place because the more advanced anal aims of preserving and retaining the object by controlling it are dominant. Instead the conflicts around the loss of the loved object call forth the 'phenomenon of psychological compulsion' (1924, p. 431).

Narcissism and chronic resistance to analysis: Abraham made several contributions on the topic of character structure, namely his essays on the oral, anal and genital character types (1921, 1924b, 1925). His most notable contribution in this area, however, is his formulation of a narcissistic personality organisation to explain certain patients' chronic resistance to analysis. Such patients show a cluster of attitudes, such as an unusual defiance and a proneness to feeling humiliated accompanied by a very pronounced narcissistic self-love. Abraham links the latter to an *envious grudge* of the analyst as father and of his capacity. The patient's *envy* manifests as a recurrent depreciation of the analyst's contribution to the treatment and also as an identification with his position, which the patient keeps usurping (1919). Abraham links the abnormal narcissism of such patients to anal-sadistic fixations and as expressions of anal character traits.

Abraham and Klein: Abraham's influence is most evident in Klein's early work. In spite of her early divergence from classical theory about the chronology of the Oedipus complex, and her doubts about the phase of primary narcissism, Klein adheres closely to Abraham's views on the pregenital stages. She sees her early notion of maximal sadism as 'only an amplification' of the 'well established view that oral cannibalism is followed by anal sadism' (Klein, 1932, p. 151). Abraham, perhaps more than Freud, observed and formulated the extreme forms that sadism took in the pregenital stages at a time when love for the object is still weak. These observations are confirmed and expanded upon by Klein in her child analyses. Her formulation of obsessional defences is one example of her reliance on Abraham's insightful distinction between the early and later anal phase and its aetiological import for the 'choice' between melancholia and obsessional neurosis [*see* Obsessional defences]. She abandons Abraham's strict chronology of libidinal organisations as she comes more into her own thinking, but her thorough understanding of their meaning and contents is evident throughout her early work.

Abraham (1924a) diverges from Freud's views on mourning and asserts that in mourning too there is evidence of an introjection of the lost object as an important part of the work of mourning. Freud by contrast (1917) leaves us with an economic account of mourning (detachment of the libido at the behest of reality) that cannot account for the pain of mourning. In her paper on mourning Klein (1940) agrees with Abraham that there is an introjection of the lost loved object in the ego in mourning. She also adds that an essential part of the work of normal mourning is the reinstatement of the temporarily lost internalised good parents, and thereby links mourning as a painful process with the conflicts of the early depressive position [*see* Depressive position].

Joan Riviere (1936) adopts the main elements of Abraham's description of a narcissistic organisation (1919) as an explanation for chronic resistance to analysis. She reformulates his conception of such an organisation with the help of Klein's freshly formulated concept of the manic defences (1935) in her attempts to understand the negative therapeutic reaction and interminability [*see* Pathological organisations].

Klein's debt to Abraham is enormous, not just in analysing her but also in giving her a background of soundly based theory from which to develop. Klein was important to Abraham too, since her work with children was bringing confirmatory evidence about his postulates of the sadism of the early pregenital phases and of the importance of introjection and projection [*see* Child analysis]. Although Abraham, like Freud, barely mentions Klein, it is possible that his own observations in 1924 drew from the material Melanie Klein was reporting from 1919 onwards.

Abraham, H. (1974) 'Karl Abraham: An unfinished biography', *Int. Rev. Psycho-Anal.* 1: 17–72.

Abraham, K. (1911) 'Notes on the psycho-analytic investigation and treatment of manic-depressive insanity and allied conditions', in *Selected Papers on Psycho-Analysis*. London: Hogarth Press, pp. 137–156.

—— (1919) 'A particular form of neurotic resistance against the psycho-analytic method', in *Selected Papers on Psycho-Analysis*. London: Hogarth Press, pp. 303–311.

—— (1921) 'Contribution to the theory of the anal character', in *Selected Papers on Psycho-Analysis*. London: Hogarth Press, pp. 370–392.

—— (1924a) 'A short study of the libido, viewed in the light of mental disorders', in *Selected Papers on Psycho-Analysis*. London: Hogarth Press, pp. 418–501.

—— (1924b) 'The influence of oral erotism on character-formation', in *Selected Papers on Psycho-Analysis*. London: Hogarth Press, pp. 393–406.

—— (1925) 'Character-formation on the genital level of the libido', in *Selected Papers on Psycho-Analysis*. London: Hogarth Press, pp. 407–417.

Freud, S. (1917) 'Mourning and melancholia', *S.E. 14*. London: Hogarth Press, pp. 237–258.

Klein, M. (1932) *The Psychoanalysis of Children. The Writings of Melanie Klein*, Vol. 2. London: Hogarth Press.

—— (1935) 'A contribution to the psychogenesis of manic-depressive states', in *The Writings of Melanie Klein*, Vol. 1. London: Hogarth Press, pp. 262–289.

—— (1940) 'Mourning and its relation to manic-depressive states', in *The Writings of Melanie Klein*, Vol. 1. London: Hogarth Press, pp. 344–369.

Riviere, J. (1936) 'A contribution to the analysis of the negative therapeutic reaction', *Int. J. Psycho-Anal.* 17: 304–320.

Acting-out/acting-in

Freud first described what he called 'acting out' in the case of 'Dora' in 1905, where he says:

> . . . because of the unknown qualities in me which reminded Dora of Herr K, she took her revenge on me as she wanted to take her revenge on him, and deserted me as she believed herself to have been deceived and deserted by him. Thus she *acted out* an essential part of her recollections and phantasies instead of reproducing it in the treatment.
>
> (Freud, 1905, p. 119)

Freud repeats this idea in 1914, saying: '. . . we may say that the patient does not *remember* anything of what he has forgotten, and repressed, but *acts* it out' (Freud, 1914, p. 150).

Thus Freud stressed that patients express themselves in analysis not only in words but also in actions. This behaviour has come to be called 'acting-in' rather than Freud's term of 'acting-out', and nowadays the term 'acting-out' is often used for behaviour that the patient expresses outside the analysis instead of bringing it to his sessions with the analyst.

Klein, like Freud, thought that patients express themselves not only in words but also in their actions towards the analyst. Further, she stressed that many of the patient's comments about other people and situations were actually statements about the patient's feelings and thoughts about the analyst (Klein, 1952).

Freud and Klein looked mainly at the patient's thoughts, feelings and actions towards the analyst. Paula Heimann's 1950 paper 'On counter-transference' showed that the analyst's feelings and thoughts about the patient could be a useful source of information about and understanding of the patient, and this has been followed by heightened awareness of the analyst–patient relationship and its usefulness in understanding the patient.

In his suggestion that the analyst should avoid 'memory' and 'desire', Bion (1967) advocates that acute attention should be given to the immediate emotional events between analyst and patient in the present. Betty Joseph describes this process in detail:

> I find that with these rather unreachable patients, it is often more important to focus one's attention on the patient's method of communication, the actual way in which he speaks and the way in which he reacts to the analyst's interpretations rather than to concentrate primarily on the content of what he says. In other words I am going to suggest that we have to recognize that these patients, even when they are quite verbal, *are in fact doing a great deal of acting*, sometimes in speech itself, and our technique has constantly to take account of this.
>
> (Joseph, 1975, pp. 76–76, italics added)

> . . . the notion of our being used and of something constantly going on, if only we can become aware of it, opens up many other aspects of transference, which I shall want to discuss later. For example, that movement and change is an essential aspect of transference – so that no interpretation can be seen as a pure interpretation or explanation but must resonate in the patient in a way which is specific to him and his way of functioning; that the level at which a patient is functioning at any given moment and the nature of his anxieties can best be gauged by trying to be aware of *how the transference is actively being used.*
>
> (Joseph, 1985, p. 157, italics added)

Segal (1982), putting it succinctly, writes:

> Early infantile development is reflected in the infantile part of the transference. When it is well integrated it gives rise to underlying non-verbal communication, which gives a depth to other communications. When not integrated it gives rise to acting in as a primitive mode of communication.
>
> (Segal, 1982, p. 21)

Ruth Riesenberg-Malcolm also stresses the patient's actions as well as his words:

> The patient does not only express himself in words. He also uses actions, and sometimes words and actions. The analyst listens, observes and feels the patient's communications. He scrutinizes his own responses to the patient, trying to understand the effects the patient's behaviour has on himself, and he understands this as a communication from the patient (while being aware of those responses which come from his own personality). It is this, comprehended in its totality, that is presented to the patient as an interpretation.
>
> (Riesenberg-Malcolm, 1986, p. 40)

Thus analysts listen not only to patients' words but also for the feelings and actions that the words imply, and they are increasingly aware of the need to observe the effects of the analyst's own words and actions on the patient.

See Technique

Bion, W. (1967) 'Notes on memory and desire', in E. Spillius (ed.) *Melanie Klein Today*, Vol. 2. London: Routledge (1988), pp. 17–21.

Freud, S. (1905) 'Fragment of an analysis of a case of hysteria', *S.E. 7*. London: Hogarth Press, pp. 3–122.

—— (1914) 'Remembering, repeating and working through (Further recommendations on the technique of psycho-analysis)', *S.E. 12*. London: Hogarth Press, pp. 145–156.

Heimann, P. (1950) 'On counter-transference', *Int. J. Psycho-Anal.* 31: 81–84.

Joseph, B. (1975) 'The patient who is difficult to reach', in *Psychic Equilibrium and Psychic Change*. London: Routledge (1989), pp. 75–87.

—— (1985) 'Transference: The total situation', in *Psychic Equilibrium and Psychic Change*. London: Routledge (1989), pp. 156–167.

Klein, M. (1952) 'The origins of transference', *Int. J. Psycho-Anal.* 33: 433–438.

Riesenberg-Malcolm, R. (1986) 'Interpretation: The past in the present', in P. Roth (ed.) *On Bearing Unbearable States of Mind*. London: Routledge (1999), pp. 38–52.

Segal, H (1982) 'Early infantile development as reflected in the psychoanalytic process: Steps in integration', *Int. J. Psycho-Anal.* 63: 15–21.

Adhesive identification

The concept of 'adhesive identification' was described by Bick in the early 1970s (Bick, 1986) and by Meltzer (1975). Bick's work in developing a rigorous method of infant observation (Bick, 1964, 1968) produced new hypotheses about the very earliest moments of life, the first object and the first introjection [*see* Infant observation; Skin]. In cases where introjection fails, the earliest stages of development go wrong, as projective identification cannot be properly employed because of an absent sense of internal space [*see* Internal reality]. Meltzer (Meltzer et al., 1975) took up these ideas and found them important in research into a child-analytic technique with autistic children. Meltzer described a child who:

> . . . tended to draw pictures of houses, in which there was a house on this side of the paper, and there was a house on the other side of the paper and when you held it up to the light, you saw that the doors were superimposed, you know, a kind of house where you open the front door and step out the back door at the same time.
>
> (Meltzer, 1975, p. 300)

In the course of this collaboration, Bick and Meltzer began to recognise a pattern in these 'second-skin' formations [*see* Skin]. Bick typically called it an 'act of mimicry'. However, what they began to realise was that the mimicry represented the experience, and phantasy, of 'sticking' to an object as opposed to projecting into it [*see* Projective identification]. A lapse in developing a sense of internal space leads to a tendency to relate to objects in a two-dimensional way, without depth [*see* Autism]:

> This baby had to make the most of his mother just touching him so that he could go to sleep again. During the bath when mother took off the clothes he started quivering and shivering . . . perhaps he was cold because the clothes were taken off, but that was made unlikely by the fact that when mother touched him with a piece of wet cotton wool he also stopped shivering. I would suggest that this touching derives its power from its significance as an adhesion, as a re-establishment of feeling stuck on to mother.
>
> (Bick, 1986, p. 297)

See Skin

Bick, E. (1964) 'Notes on infant observation in psycho-analytic training', *Int. J. Psycho-Anal.* 45: 558–566.

—— (1968) 'The experience of the skin in early object relations', *Int. J. Psycho-Anal.* 49: 484–486.

—— (1986) 'Further considerations of the function of the skin in early object relations', *Br. J. Psychother.* 2: 292–299.

Meltzer, D. (1975) 'Adhesive identification', *Contemp. Psycho-Anal.* 11: 289–310.

——, Bremner, J., Hoxter, S., Weddell, D. and Wittenberg, I. (1975) *Explorations in Autism.* Strath Tay: Clunie Press.

Aggression

This is a complex concept in that aggression can be in the service of self-protection, exploration and life, in the service of destruction and death, or be a mixture of the two. It is difficult to tease out the difference between the death instinct, aggression, sadism, destructiveness, self-destructiveness, self-protection, projection and exploration because, confusingly, all these concepts are sometimes used interchangeably. To add to the difficulty, Klein changes her theory from one in which sadism is an aspect of the life instinct to one in which it is an aspect of the death instinct and in conflict with the life instinct. Even so, sadism and aggression are thought by Klein and her followers to be essential for life and for development.

Freud: Freud had already written about sadism as part of the sexual instinct and about the instinct to master as part of the self-preservative instinct but it is only shortly after the First World War, with the evidence of the deep vein of destructiveness in human beings, that Freud gives aggression equal footing with the libido with his concept of the death instinct (Freud, 1920). In Freud's theory, death instinct (internal self-destructiveness) is converted into aggression and deflected out in the form of an attack on the other. Some death instinct remains within, in the form of self-destructiveness. The life and death instincts remain to some degree fused, whether within, in the form of masochism, or directed out as aggression.

Klein: At the start of her career Klein, working with children, is struck by the sadism and aggression in their phantasies and play. At this time Klein is still following Freud and Abraham's theory of psychosexual stages and she thinks of sadism as a component instinct of libido (i.e. that aggression is part of the life instinct) and that the child's wish to use his sadism to get inside and take control of his mother is driven by oedipal jealousy and rage [*see* Component instincts]. Klein uses the terms aggression, sadism and destructiveness interchangeably. Her focus is on the emotional ramifications of aggressive urges. She believes that children are made enormously anxious by their urge to attack their objects, that they fear their own potential for destruction and that they fear retaliation from their objects for damage done in reality or in phantasy. She concludes that inhibited and obsessional behaviours are attempts by the child to restrict his or her damaging behaviour [*see* Child analysis].

In 1932 Klein adopts Freud's idea of the death instinct. This internal self-destructive force now becomes a central feature of her developmental theory [*see* Death instinct]. Klein, following Freud but also altering his theory, thinks that the infant attributes his death instinct to the object (i.e. projects his death instinct into the object) that is now experienced as an aggressor. Not all death instinct is projected and some of that which remains within is – as in Freud's theory – turned into aggression that is directed against the now seen-to-be aggressive object. These are in Klein's view essential self-protective acts by the immature ego. Some death instinct remains within, in the form of self-destructive activity. As in Freud's theory, life and death instincts are fused in varying quantities and are also combined with introjected objects.

The amount of constitutional death instinct, in combination with the way in which the child is nurtured and of course the situation in which he finds himself, will determine the aggressiveness of the individual. A child who is frustrated will become increasingly full of rage, whereas one who is not will be calmed. In Bion's theory of containment the infant initially projects his fear of death and subsequently other 'bad' feelings into the mother (Bion, 1959). This activity is necessary for development. The infant needs an ego more powerful than his to contain his fears and, in a similar way, patients need an analyst who is able to bear their fear and anger. While this activity is aggressive and may even be felt by the recipient as a destructive attack, it is an essential step for both emotional and cognitive development. The capacity of the mother or analyst to bear the impact of the projected feelings is a crucial factor in the moderation or exacerbation of aggressive feelings [*see* Wilfred Bion; Container/contained; Projective identification; Symbol formation; Thinking and knowledge]. Frustration and aggression are necessary spurs to development and exploration; too much frustration may lead to fragmentation of the ego or to a complete inhibition of liveliness. An individual lacking in aggression, who has projected out all his aggression, is weakened and unable to integrate himself, is unable to stand up to aggressive objects, whether experienced internally or externally, and may be dominated by them. Aggression is necessary for self-protection.

Kleinian writings illustrate the myriad of ways in which aggression is managed by being split off and denied or integrated in pathological and non-pathological ways and how, when acknowledged, the inevitable guilt is managed. Clinical writings also explore the technical issues involved in modifying aggression [*see* Depressive position; Paranoid-schizoid position; Pathological organisations; Projective identification; Structure; Superego; Technique].

Bion, W. (1959) 'Attacks on linking', *Int. J. Psycho-Anal.* 30: 308–315.
Freud, S. (1920) 'Beyond the pleasure principle', *S.E. 18*. London: Hogarth Press, pp. 3–64.
Klein, M. (1932) *The Psychoanalysis of Children. The Writings of Melanie Klein*, Vol. 2. London: Hogarth Press.

Alpha-function

Bion's descriptions were influenced by his interest in mathematics, and he was intent on deriving similar general theorems within psychoanalysis. Bion (1962a, 1962b) generated the neutral term 'alpha-function' as a kind of psychoanalytic algebraic notation that was to be defined by practical results but was initially devoid of meaning:

> It seemed convenient to suppose an alpha-function to convert sense data into alpha-elements and thus provide the psyche with the material for dream thoughts and hence the capacity to wake up or go to sleep, to be conscious or unconscious.
>
> (Bion, 1962a, p. 115)

The concept came from Bion's investigations of the schizophrenic's problem of applying meaning to his experiences. When Isaacs called unconscious phantasy the 'mental representative of instinct' she conveyed a conversion process of some kind across the body/mind (dis)continuum. Bion gave the conversion process the name 'alpha-function' and began to fill in the clinical detail – when it works adequately, and when not. The term 'alpha-function' stands for the unknown process involved in taking raw sense data and generating out of it mental contents that have meaning and can be used for thinking. These resulting products of alpha-function are *alpha-elements* (or alpha-particles).

When alpha-function does not work, the sense data remain unassimilated *beta-elements*, which are usually treated by expulsion of a violent kind (a variant of projective identification) [*see* Beta-elements]. As elements of alpha-function Bion postulated (i) a pre-existing 'preconception', a kind of anticipation, possibly even inherent, that he says must meet (ii) a 'realisation', some occurrence in actual reality that fits, hand in glove, with the preconception; this union of the one within the other creates (iii) a 'conception' that is mentally usable for further thought [*see* Linking]. This paradigm of the union of two elements to create a third is the basic building block of mind, of thoughts, of theories [*see* Container/contained]. Integral with this process is an emotional one in which splits join into a whole, a process he denotes 'Ps↔D', from Klein's theory of the two positions [*see* Depressive position; Paranoid-schizoid position]. The accumulation of alpha-elements (proto-thoughts and thoughts) creates an apparatus for thinking (concepts, theoretical structures, etc.), rather than, as in other theories of thinking, it being the apparatus for thinking that creates thoughts. The failure of alpha-function gives rise to the accumulation of beta-elements and the creation of an apparatus for ridding the mind of unwanted contents.

See Container/contained; Reverie; Thinking and knowledge

Bion, W. (1962a) 'A theory of thinking', in W. R. Bion (ed.) *Second Thoughts*. London: Heinemann (1967), pp. 110–119.
—— (1962b) *Learning from Experience*. London: Heinemann.

Ambivalence

Psychoanalysis has always been theoretically based in the notion of mental conflict, and *ambivalence* means the holding of contradictory feeling states in the relationship towards one object. Freud had described the bisexuality (or sexual ambivalence) of human beings, giving rise to both heterosexual and homosexual oedipal complexes, with the result that love and hate can be felt about both parents. This idea was greatly enhanced by Freud's postulate of a duality of instincts (libido and death instinct). Klein elevated this state of ambivalence to a central place in the key concept of the depressive position [*see* Depressive position]. Conflicting feelings may, in contrast, be alternated, in states that are dissociated mentally from each other, or split [*see* Splitting], giving rise to considerable instability as love and hate abruptly give way to each other [*see* Ideal object]; or impulses may be fused: for example the mixture of libido and destructiveness (sadism), giving rise to an excited sexual sadistic perversion.

See Conflict; Instincts

American psychoanalysis in relation to Klein

Klein of course acknowledged her enormous debt to Freud, Abraham and to a lesser extent to Ferenczi, but otherwise made very few references to other analysts or schools of thought – Fairbairn being one of the few exceptions (Klein, 1946). Perhaps reciprocally, other schools of thought have been slow to become aware of Klein's views. This has been particularly true of analysts in the United States, who have generally disapproved of Klein and Kleinian analysis except for small groups in Los Angeles and San Francisco and some individuals in other American institutes, notably Roy Schafer.

In the United States psychoanalysis developed rapidly after the Second World War, the main school of thought being ego psychology (Hartmann, 1939). Hartmann regarded himself and was regarded as fully 'Freudian' in his approach and was especially sympathetic to the work of Anna Freud, although he developed a 'correct' type of technique based on a rigid interpretation of Freud's theory of drives. This is still often referred to as 'classical' psychoanalysis. His theory also stressed the importance of adaptation by the individual to his environment, a theme that has become important in various ways in most schools of American psychoanalysis.

Ego psychology had a medical emphasis, which is not surprising as its practitioners were mainly medical. Psychiatrists had a strong political position because for many years they controlled the educational centres for training in psychoanalysis in the United States. Eventually in 1988 a court ruling made it possible for psychologists to practice psychoanalysis, which gave American psychologists opportunities to develop both their own psychoanalytic training and the ideas they favoured.

Several American analysts had already begun developing approaches that paid a great deal of attention to cultural and environmental factors (Horney, 1937; Fromm, 1941, 1947) and to interpersonal relationships (Sullivan, 1953), hence the name 'interpersonal psychoanalysis', a school of thought that was also influenced by the object-relations school in Britain.

The interpersonal school was followed by Heinz Kohut's 'self-psychology' (Kohut, 1971, 1977), which emphasised the need for the analyst to develop close empathy with the patient in order to develop the patient's fully spontaneous 'self' when social and family situations had led to its inhibition and malformation. From this emphasis later self-psychologists such as Robert Stolorow developed what they have termed 'intersubjective psychoanalysis' (Stolorow and Attwood, 1992).

Meanwhile Stephen Mitchell and colleagues were developing his vision of 'relational psychoanalysis', which was a compound of Sullivan's inter-personal analysis, British object-relations theory and self-psychology (Greenberg and Mitchell, 1983; Mitchell 1988; Mitchell and Black, 1995).

Alongside these developments was the work of Roy Schafer, first on analytic language (1976), then on the importance of narrative (1983) and finally an account of Kleinian analysis (1997) that has done much to increase the understanding of Kleinian analysis in the United States.

Hans Loewald was another idiosyncratic and influential American analyst with a concentrated interest in understanding the nature of mind and Freud's approach to it (Loewald, 1980). Among other ideas it is his view that Freud's thinking underwent a sea change in 1920 with the writing of *Beyond the Pleasure Principle* when he introduced Eros as connection seeking rather than discharge seeking.

Otto Kernberg has been concerned to develop a comprehensive theory that puts together Freud's structural model, the object-relations approaches of Klein and Fairbairn, and Jacobson's ideas on early identifications (Jacobson, 1964; Kernberg, 1975, 1976, 1984).

Perhaps the most notable development in American psychoanalysis has been the rise and increasing stature of Thomas Ogden, who combines interest in the work of Klein, Winnicott and many others into his own distinctive understanding of psychic development and functioning (Ogden, 1986, 1989, 1994, 1997).

One striking feature in American analysis as a whole is the relative lack of stress on aggression in either its constructive or destructive aspects. Another feature, at least in comparison with technique in British Kleinian analysis, is the focus on the patient's personal history and the relatively weaker focus on the interplay of transference and countertransference in the immediate situation of the analytic session.

Fromm, E. (1941) *Escape from Freedom*. New York: Avon Press.

—— (1947) *Man for Himself*. Greenwich, CT: Fawcett.

Greenberg, J. and Mitchell, S. (1983) *Object Relations in Psychoanalytic Theory*. Cambridge, MA: Harvard University Press.

Hartmann, H. (1939) *Ego Psychology and the Problem of Adaptation*. New York: International Universities Press.

Horney, K. (1937) *The Neurotic Personality of Our Time*. New York: Norton.

Jacobson, E. (1964) *The Self and the Object World*. New York: International Universities Press.

Kernberg, O. (1975) *Borderline Conditions and Pathological Narcissism*. New York: Jason Aronson

—— (1976) *Object Relations Theory and Clinical Psychoanalysis*. New York: Jason Aronson.

—— (1984) *Severe Personality Disorders*. New Haven, CT: Yale University Press.

Klein, M. (1946) 'Notes on some schizoid mechanisms', *Int. J. Psycho-Anal*. 27: 99–110.

Kohut, H. (1971) *The Analysis of the Self*. New York: International Universities Press.

—— (1977) *The Restoration of the Self*. New York: International Universities Press.

Loewald, H. (1980) *Papers on Psychoanalysis*. New Haven, CT: Yale University Press.

Mitchell, S. (1988) *Relational Concepts in Psychoanalysis: An Integration*. Cambridge, MA: International Universities Press.

—— and Black, M. (1995) *Freud and Beyond: A History of Modern Psychoanalytic Thought*. New York: Basic Books.

Ogden, T. (1986) *The Matrix of the Mind*. Northvale, NJ: Jason Aronson.

—— (1989) *The Primitive Edge of Experience*. Northvale, NJ: Jason Aronson.

—— (1994) *Subjects of Analysis*. London: Karnac.

—— (1997) *Reverie and Interpretation*. London: Karnac.

Schafer, R. (1976) *A New Language for Psychoanalysis*. New Haven, CT: Yale University Press.

—— (1983) *The Analytic Attitude*. New York: Basic Books.

—— (1997) *The Contemporary Kleinians of London*. Madison, CT: International Universities Press.

Stolorow, R. and Attwood, G. (1992) *Concepts of Being: The Intersubjective Foundation of Psychological Life*. Hillsdale, NJ: Analytic Press.

Sullivan, H. S. (1953) *The Interpersonal Theory of Psychiatry*. New York: Norton.

Annihilation

Fear of annihilation is not on the list of anxieties in Freud's paper 'Inhibitions, symptoms and anxiety' (1926). Jones (1927) postulates *aphanisis*, a fear that extends beyond castration anxiety to the fear of a deprivation of all possible instruments of pleasure and therefore of existence.

Klein uses Freud's 1926 paper to back up her interest in the content of anxieties. Having adopted Freud's idea of the death instinct in 1932, she goes on several years later to outline the infant's experience of the death instinct: 'I hold that anxiety rises from the operation of the death instinct within the organism, is felt as fear of annihilation (death) and takes the form of persecution' (Klein, 1946, p. 4).

Later she states clearly her disagreement with Freud:

Freud stated that no fear of death exists in the unconscious, but this does not seem compatible with his discovery of the dangers arising from the death instinct working within. As I see it, the primordial anxiety which the ego fights is the threat arising from the death instinct.

(Klein, 1958, p. 237)

In Klein's theoretical model of the paranoid-schizoid position, the first act of the ego is to project out into the object both the life and death instincts. This action divides the object into 'good' and 'bad' part-objects, which are then introjected into the ego and superego. The introjected 'bad' object is experienced as an attacking internal presence. If the constitutional balance between the life and death instincts is in favour of the death instinct and if bad experiences outweigh good ones, then the internal 'bad' object causes the ego to fragment or disintegrate as though annihilated. Klein sees this mechanism as operative in the psychoses and in an appendix to her 1946 paper she uses Freud's writings on Schreber to illustrate the idea of a person whose ego is in pieces. Furthermore, in creating and maintaining the binary split between the 'good' and 'bad' self and object, the ego has to deny part of its experience. In her 1946 paper Klein refers to denial as equivalent to annihilation. She illustrates her point with an example of a patient who dreams that she wants to murder a young girl; Klein understands the patient as wanting to kill off a part of herself. Denial is therefore both a defence against and a contributor to the experience of annihilation [*see* Death instinct; Paranoid-schizoid position].

Klein's idea is that the mother's ability to withstand the annihilatory attacks from the infant is crucial. Bion expands this idea and emphasises the importance of a mother who can take in and tolerate (contain) the infant's fear of annihilation. Many clinical papers illustrate patients whose destructive tendencies are in the ascendant, whether due to constitutional endowment or from lack of containment, and who not only attack their objects but attempt to annihilate their own ego functioning, the making of links, thinking and feeling [*see* Envy; Fragmentation; Splitting; Superego]. Others manage their anxiety by a system of organised defences [*see* Pathological organisations]. Segal, for example, provides several examples of patients who harbour phantasies of annihilation, and explains the reason for the phantasies as follows:

Birth confronts us with the experience of needs. In relation to that experience there can be two reactions, and both, I think are invariably present in all of us, though in varying proportions One, to seek satisfaction for the needs: that is life-promoting and leads to object seeking, love, and eventually object concern. The other is the drive to annihilate: the need to annihilate the perceiving experiencing self, as well as anything that is perceived.

(Segal, 1997, p. 18)

There is now general agreement that all development brings in its train the threat of catastrophe to the mind, and development rests upon small oscillations between the paranoid-schizoid fragmentation and depressive position concern, to which Bion gave the notation 'Ps↔D' [*see* Wilfred Bion; Ps↔D].

Other ideas: Winnicott (1960) holds that the impingement of the environment on infantile omnipotence destroys the infant's 'continuity of being' and is experienced as annihilation. Thereafter the developing personality can assume a feeling only as if he or she existed – a *false self* [*see* Skin]. Tustin (1981) follows Winnicott in describing the consequences of an impingement upon the infant that is not yet ready to give up the primary state (her term is 'primary autism') [*see* Autism].

On the basis of the observation of infants from birth [*see* Infant observation], Bick (1964, 1968) describes the observational evidence for a primary experience of annihilation and demonstrates ways in which the infant can survive these experiences, through skin contact with an external object or, in the absence of an adequate container, omnipotent bodily methods that she calls 'second skin' [*see* Skin; Adhesive identification].

Bick, E. (1964) 'Notes on infant observation in psycho-analytic training', *Int. J. Psycho-Anal.* 45: 558–566.

—— (1968) 'The experience of the skin in early object relations', *Int. J. Psycho-Anal.* 49: 484–488.

Freud, S. (1926) 'Inhibitions, symptoms and anxiety', *S.E. 20*. London: Hogarth Press, pp. 77–175.

Jones, E. (1927) 'The early development of female sexuality', *Int. J. Psycho-Anal.* 8: 459–472.

Klein, M. (1946) 'Notes on some schizoid mechanisms', in *The Writings of Melanie Klein*, Vol. 3. London: Hogarth Press, pp. 1–24.

—— (1958) 'On the development of mental functioning', in *The Writings of Melanie Klein*, Vol. 3. London: Hogarth Press, pp. 236–246.

Segal, H. (1997) 'On the clinical usefulness of the concept of the death instinct', in J. Steiner (ed.) *Psychoanalysis, Literature and War*. London: Routledge, pp. 17–26.

Tustin, F. (1981) *Autistic States in Children*. London: Routledge & Kegan Paul.

Winnicott, D. (1960) 'The theory of the infant-parent relationship', *Int. J. Psycho-Anal.* 41: 585–595.

Anxiety

The history of psychoanalysis has been one of trying to understand the core anxiety of the human condition. From the start Freud's theory is that anxiety is transformed libido and this does not change until 1926 when, in his paper 'Inhibitions, symptoms and anxiety', he introduces the idea of 'signal anxiety'. This anxiety is not a conflicted instinctual tension but is a signal occurring in the ego of an anticipated instinctual tension, in which the ego appreciates situations that would give rise to anxiety. Arguing against Rank's theory of birth trauma as the only underlying anxiety, Freud describes 'anxiety situations' that change at different stages in life: birth trauma, the loss of the loved object (which for boys is castration) and the death instinct [*see* Child analysis – The nature of early anxieties].

Klein is clear about her interest in anxiety: 'From the beginning of my psychoanalytic work my interest was focused on anxiety and its causation' (Klein, 1948, p. 41), and she uses Freud's 1926 paper to back up her view that it is the content of anxieties that is significant. In her early work Klein explores the fears that arise in children and concludes that they are caused by the oedipal child's sadistic phantasies of attacking his mother's body and the retaliation that is anticipated [*see* Child analysis; Oedipus complex; Sadism]. In 1932 with Klein's adoption of Freud's idea of the death instinct, fear of annihilation within is the primary anxiety. This anxiety is immediately dealt with by the ego thrusting out the death instinct into the object, a defence that results in fear of the object. Then in 1935 with the introduction of the idea of the 'depressive position', the anxiety that Klein investigates is depressive anxiety caused by the loss of the loved object and in particular the loss of the internal 'good' object that has been damaged by the child's attacks [*see* Depressive anxiety; Depressive position].

From 1946 with the introduction of the 'paranoid-schizoid' position, Klein returns to the persecutory anxiety caused by the death instinct within, the persecutory fears of the external 'bad' object into whom the death instinct is projected and the persecutory fear of the subsequently introjected 'bad' object. Klein describes these anxieties as primitive and of psychotic proportions and in her view they are linked to the development of the psychoses. Klein's theories of the paranoid-schizoid and depressive positions cover the constellation of defences against the two classes of anxiety thrown up during the course of development. If development proceeds well, persecutory anxieties are to a greater or lesser extent modified and non-paranoid depressive anxiety comes more to the fore [*see* Annihilation; Death instinct; Defence; Depressive position; Paranoid-schizoid position; Projective identification; Unconscious phantasy; Superego].

Technique: In her clinical work Klein's interest is in her patients' anxiety: 'I interpreted what I thought to be most urgent in the material the child presented to me and found my interest focusing on his anxieties and the defences against them' (Klein, 1955a, p. 122). Klein takes particular interest in the specific content of the anxieties. These are frequently unconscious and can only be understood indirectly or seen in dreams and in children's play [*see* Child analysis; Unconscious phantasy]. Klein's ideas have resulted in a technique of deep and penetrating interpretation and from the start this provoked and continues to provoke the criticism that the interpretations themselves cause persecutory anxiety (Geleerd, 1963; Greenson, 1974). Klein and her followers are interested in changes in anxiety over the course of a session and, in particular, shifts between paranoid anxiety and depressive anxiety [*see* Technique].

Controversy: Anna Freud (1927) and Glover (1945) argue that Klein's theory, that anxiety is to do with a tension between the instincts, disposes of Freud's theory of the development of the libido and places aggression, with its capacity to inhibit or distort development, as the crucial element in development. Anna Freud puts forward a view in which the natural unfolding of the phases of the libido is inherent and leads the individual towards adaptation [*see* Ego psychology].

Freud, A. (1927) *The Psycho-Analytical Treatment of Children* (English edition, 1946). London: Hogarth Press.

Freud, S. (1926) 'Inhibitions, symptoms and anxiety', *S.E. 20*. London: Hogarth Press, pp. 77–175.

Geleerd, E. (1963) 'Evaluation of Melanie Klein's narrative of a child analysis', *Int. J. Psycho-Anal.* 44: 493–506.

Glover, E. (1945) 'An examination of the Klein system of child psychology', *Psychoanal. Study Child* 1: 3–43.

Greenson, R. (1974) 'Transference: Freud or Klein?', *Int. J. Psycho-Anal.* 55: 37–48.

Klein, M. (1932) *The Psychoanalysis of Children. The Writings of Melanie Klein*, Vol. 2. London: Hogarth Press.

—— (1935) 'A contribution to the psychogenesis of manic-depressive states', *The Writings of Melanie Klein*, Vol. 1. London: Hogarth Press, pp. 262–289.

—— (1946) 'Notes on some schizoid mechanisms', in *The Writings of Melanie Klein*, Vol. 3. London: Hogarth Press, pp. 1–24

—— (1948) 'On the theory of anxiety and guilt', in *The Writings of Melanie Klein*, Vol. 3. London: Hogarth Press, pp. 25–42.

—— (1955) 'The psycho-analytic play technique: Its history and significance', in *The Writings of Melanie Klein*, Vol. 3. London: Hogarth Press, pp. 122–140.

Assimilation

This is a term used by Paula Heimann in describing a situation in which 'the subject acquires and ascribes those qualities of his internal parents which are suitable and adequate to him' (Heimann, 1942, p. 16). Unassimilated internal objects, by contrast, 'are felt as foreign bodies embedded in the self' (Heimann, 1942, p. 16). She also says that:

> . . . when the injured [internal] object has too much the character of revenge and punishment by the objects . . . these phenomena are such as are usually described as due to the super-ego. I have refrained from using this term (as well as the term 'id') as it has not been possible

within the compass of this paper to discuss the relation between the concepts of internalized objects and of the super-ego (or of the id).

(Heimann, 1942, p. 16, footnote 9)

Klein, in her paper 'Notes on some schizoid mechanisms', says that what Heimann says about certain objects being embedded in the self as foreign objects is true not only of bad objects but also of good objects, if the ego is compulsively subordinated to their preservation (Klein, 1946, p. 9, footnote 2). Thus Heimann and Klein made some links between the ideas of assimilation and non-assimilation on the one hand and the concepts of the superego, ego and the id on the other. In spite of these links with the usual concepts of psychoanalytic psychic structure, however, later Kleinian writers have made little direct use of the concepts of assimilation and non-assimilation of internal objects.

Heimann, P. (1942) 'A contribution to the problem of sublimation and its relation to processes of internalization', *Int. J. Psycho-Anal.* 23: 8–17.
Klein, M. (1946) 'Notes on some schizoid mechanisms', *Int. J. Psycho-Anal.* 27: 99–110; in *The Writings of Melanie Klein*, Vol. 3. London: Hogarth Press, pp. 1–24.

Autism

The severe disturbance in children known as autism was studied (Meltzer et al., 1975; Tustin, 1981, 1986) following successful psychoanalytic work with adult psychotic patients [*see* Psychosis]. The theoretical interest is in the very early psychological states of mind when the predisposition for autism is provoked. The condition is held, therefore, to be one means of access to the very earliest stages of development.

Frances Tustin: Tustin describes how Klein '. . . as long ago as 1930, showed that she had anticipated Leo Kanner's differentiation of "Early Infantile Autism" from mental deficiency by thirteen years' (Tustin, 1983, p. 130). She postulates (1981, 1986) a primary state of 'normal autism', which she links with the auto-erotism that Freud described, a non-object-related search for pleasurable body sensations. She also accepts Winnicott's view of primary infantile omnipotence as equivalent to her term. She proceeds then to distinguish two kinds of autism: (i) one in which the 'normal autism' has been interrupted prematurely for the infant who, in a state of hypersensitivity to experiencing separation, reacts by retreating impenetrably into a preoccupation with his bodily sensations, with a permanent, psychotic *fusion* with the environment (mother); and (ii) another form in which the infant, less severely traumatised, resorts to a permanent reliance on pathological projective identification, with a permanent *confusion* with external objects. Both forms result in a lack of development of the internal world and a preoccupation with bodily sensations. The first of these kinds of autistic states is clearly seen in Winnicott's notion of impingement by external objects prior to the developmental stage at which separation can be tolerated [*see* Annihilation]. Tustin's views therefore bridge the divide between Klein's and Winnicott's views of the earliest states of infantile psychology.

Donald Meltzer: In a slightly different direction, Meltzer et al. (1975) follow Bion's understanding of the growth of the mental apparatus, and the aberrant forms into which the mental apparatus can dissolve. The reversal of the normal process of mental integration brings about disintegration into fragments of sense data [*see* Beta-elements; Thinking and knowledge], resulting in a lack of the proper development for thinkable thoughts (Meltzer, 1978). He also links this with Bick's work on adhesive identification deriving from the observation of 'normal' infants from birth [*see* Adhesive identification]. There seems to be a significant correspondence between observations of autistic children and of normal infants from the earliest days (Meltzer, 1975). Bick (1968) shows the way in which the infant first comes to acquire the sense of being held together, through stimulation of the skin. Where this does not adequately happen, the infant is left with a defective sense of integration, pictured as an inability to hold a sense of a containing space. The absence of a containing space, either internal to himself or external, characterises the autistic child [*see* Skin]; as a result the child looks to intense perceptual and other bodily sensations as mechanisms for holding himself together.

As usual with new understandings of the early experiences of infancy, they can be used to understand the later problems in adult disorders. Sidney Klein (1980) demonstrates autistic aspects of patients who presented with neurotic problems. These were encapsulated in rigid structural isolation, and often conceived in dreams as hard insects or animals with carapaces, reminiscent of the hard, muscular secondary defensiveness described by Bick (1968). These split-off parts of the personality may be related to the organisation of deeply narcissistic elements described by Rosenfeld (1971) [*see* Structure].

Bick, E. (1968) 'The experience of the skin in early object relations', *Int. J. Psycho-Anal.* 49: 484–488.

Klein, S. (1980) 'Autistic phenomena in neurotic patients', *Int. J. Psycho-Anal.* 61: 395–402.

Meltzer, D. (1975) 'Adhesive identification', *Contemp. Psychoanal.* 11: 289–301.

—— (1978) 'A note on Bion's concept of reversal of alpha-function', in *The Kleinian Development, Part III.* Strath Tay: Clunie Press, pp. 119–126.

——, Bremner, J., Hoxter, S., Weddell, D. and Wittenberg, I. (1975) *Explorations in Autism.* Strath Tay: Clunie Press.

Rosenfeld, H. (1971) 'A clinical approach to the psycho-analytical theory of the life and death instincts: An investigation into the aggressive aspects of narcissism', *Int. J. Psycho-Anal.* 52: 169–178.

Tustin, F. (1981) *Autistic States in Childhood.* London: Routledge & Kegan Paul.

—— (1983) 'Thoughts on autism with special reference to a paper by Melanie Klein', *J. Child Psychother.* 9: 119–131.

—— (1986) *Autistic Barriers in Neurotic Patients.* London: Karnac.

Babies

Freud suggests that the baby represents the girl's exultant substitute for a penis, and a triumph for her creativity.

Attacks on mother's body: In Klein's early views (Klein, 1932), mother's babies, believed to reside inside her body, are an extreme provocation to jealousy and envy from early infancy. This gives rise to violent attacks, in phantasy, on mother's body and its contents and dreadful fears of retaliation [*see* Child analysis; Oedipus complex]. The little girl's phantasies of her own babies are therefore a reassurance against the paranoid anxiety of mother's retaliation.

It is much the same for the little boy, who is moved to violence (and paranoid fear) by the added phantasy of mother's body containing father's penis [*see* Combined parent figure]. In both sexes the idea of babies (and also father's penis) in mother's body gives rise to aggressive impulses and paranoid fears that increase the castration anxiety and penis envy described by Freud; these greatly affect the sexual development of the child, with possible resultant inhibitions in adulthood, and in turn influence adults' relations with their own babies as mothers or fathers.

Klein, M. (1932) *The Psychoanalysis of Children. The Writings of Melanie Klein*, Vol. 2. London: Hogarth Press.

Baby observation

See Infant observation

Bad object

Following Freud's (1923) idea of the deflection of the death instinct, Klein puts forward the theory that, in order to manage the anxiety of being destroyed from within, the ego's first act is to project its death instinct out into the object. The object is now felt to be the container of the deadly impulses and bad parts of the ego and is experienced as an external persecutor or 'bad object'. This persecutor is subsequently introjected and is felt as an internal persecutor or 'bad' internal object. The 'bad object' is kept apart from its polar opposite 'good object' into which libido and good feelings have been projected. Good experiences and good parts of the self are linked to the 'good object' and bad experiences and bad parts of the self relate to the 'bad object'. Thus both the object and the ego are split into good and bad. The first 'bad object' is referred to as the 'bad breast'. This object is a part-object rather than a whole object, not only because it is solely bad but also because Klein believes the infant capable of perceiving only part of the mother-object. Over time the parts are brought together into a whole [*see* Death instinct; Depressive position; Good object; Ideal object; Internal objects; Paranoid-schizoid position; Splitting].

Klein emphasises the importance of this separation for healthy development. The failure to achieve this binary split into 'good' and 'bad' in the 'paranoid-schizoid position' leaves the individual without a 'good object' to turn to in times of pain and anxiety, and vulnerable to confusion and persecution. If a 'bad object' dominates internal life the individual may resort to extreme splitting in order to manage the persecution and may fragment to disperse the badness and get rid of his own experience [*see* Psychosis].

The early objects are introjected into the ego and the superego and the first 'bad object' forms the basis of the early severe superego. If this 'bad object' is not sufficiently counterbalanced by good experiences and loving feelings it may operate as a very destructive presence within. Much has been written about this destructive internal object or 'ego-destructive superego' (Bion, 1959) [*see* Pathological organisations; Superego].

Klein (1946) thinks of the first internal objects as being experienced concretely by the infant as pleasant or unpleasant bodily sensations and imagined in unconscious phantasy as being caused by a benevolently or malevolently motivated body part. Hunger, for example, may be felt by the infant as the presence within of a frustrating, hunger-inducing 'bad breast'. The sensation of satisfaction may be felt as the presence within of a 'good breast' [*see* Unconscious phantasy].

Bion, W. (1959) 'Attacks on linking', in *Second Thoughts*. London: Heinemann (1967), pp. 93–109.

Freud, S. (1923) 'The ego and the id', *S.E. 19*. London: Hogarth Press, pp. 3–66.

Klein, M. (1946) 'Notes on some schizoid mechanisms', in *The Writings of Melanie Klein*, Vol. 3. London: Hogarth Press, pp. 1–24.

Basic assumptions

Bion's work with groups began before his training as a Kleinian analyst (Bion, 1948a, 1948b, 1949a, 1949b, 1950a, 1950b, 1951; Rioch, 1970; Trist,

1987). He later gave this earlier work a stronger Kleinian emphasis (Bion, 1955, and later, 1970).

Analysis of the group: Bion (1961) dealt with groups as an analyst working with a patient. The 'group-as-a-whole' exhibits a transference to the group leader in the form of a group culture that, he showed, was suffused with unspoken and unconscious assumptions shared by all the group members. The set of assumptions about the nature of the group, of its leader, of the task of the group and of the role expected of the members has three variants. Bion outlines three such *basic assumptions*, which can be detected in the feeling tone and in the atmosphere of the group:

1   The *dependent basic assumption (BaD)* gives rise to a group of members who rely, often disappointedly, on the words of wisdom of the group leader, as if they assumed that all knowledge, health and life is located in him and is to be derived by each member from the leader.

2   In the *fight/flight basic assumption (BaF)*, the members gather around the excited and violent idea that there is an enemy to be identified, and that the members will be led as part of a conformist phalanx by the leader against this enemy, or alternatively in flight from it. Such an enemy may be 'neurosis' itself in the therapy group, or one of the members of the group, or some suitable object outside the group (an external enemy).

3   Finally, the *pairing basic assumption (BaP)* suffuses the group with a mysterious kind of hope, often with behavioural pairing between two members, or a member and the leader, as if all share the belief that some great new idea (or individual) will emerge from the intercourse of the pair (a messianic belief).

The work group: Bion contrasted the basic-assumption state of a group with what he called the work group, in which the members address the consciously defined and accepted task of the group. In this state the group functions with secondary-process sophistication and attends to an examination of the reality inside and outside the group. Bion's understanding of group functioning bears a similarity with the two levels of psychic functioning outlined by Freud in his topographical distinction of the mind (Wilson, 1983). The work-group state usually shows signs of active basic-assumption states and Bion thought of the basic assumptions as 'valencies', which drew people inevitably together and established group belonging.

Bion attempted to relate basic-assumption characteristics to the working of social institutions: the army, for instance, clearly represented the fight/flight assumption, and the Church, he believed, represented the dependency assumption. The pairing assumption he saw in the aristocracy, an institution concerned with breeding.

This view of the triadic nature of group assumptions has become widespread outside psychoanalysis (de Board, 1978; Pines, 1985). Although Bion made an initial attempt to relate his findings to Klein's concept of projective identification (Bion, 1955), he subsequently dropped these ideas and his work on groups. Later he remoulded the idea of the pairing assumption (Bion, 1970; Menzies-Lyth, 1981) to make it more or less basic to group life in general, seeing it as the principal method for examining the *containing function* of groups and an appropriate way of understanding the relationship between the individual and society – the mystic and the establishment [*see* Container/contained].

Bion, W. (1948a) 'Experiences in groups I', *Hum. Relat.* 1: 314–320.

—— (1948b) 'Experiences in groups II', *Hum. Relat.* 1: 487–496.

—— (1949a) 'Experiences in groups III', *Hum. Relat.* 2: 13–22.

—— (1949b) 'Experiences in groups IV', *Hum. Relat.* 2: 95–104.

—— (1950a) 'Experiences in groups V', *Hum. Relat.* 3: 3–14.

—— (1950b) 'Experiences in groups VI', *Hum. Relat.* 3: 395–402.

—— (1951) 'Experiences in groups VII', *Hum. Relat.* 4: 221–228.

—— (1955) 'Group-dynamics: A review', in M. Klein, P. Heimann and R. Money-Kyrle (eds) *New Directions in Psycho-Analysis.* London: Tavistock (1955), pp. 440–447.

—— (1961) *Experiences in Groups.* London: Tavistock.

—— (1970) *Attention and Interpretation.* London: Tavistock.

de Board, R. (1978) *The Psycho-Analysis of Organizations.* London: Tavistock.

Menzies-Lyth, I. (1981) 'Bion's contribution to thinking about groups', in J. Grotstein (ed.) *Do I Dare Disturb the Universe?* Beverly Hills, CA: Caesura (1981), pp. 661–666.

Pines, M. (1985) *Bion and Group Psychotherapy.* London: Routledge & Kegan Paul.

Rioch, M. (1970) 'The work of Wilfred Bion on groups', *Psychiatry* 33: 56–66.

Trist, E. (1987) 'Working with Bion in the 1940s', *Group Anal.* 20: 263–270.

Wilson, S. (1983) '"Experiences in Groups": Bion's debt to Freud', *Group Anal.* 16: 152–157.

Beta-elements

In generating a theory by which a biological organism becomes an experiencing psyche, Bion (1962) describes a process that he calls *alpha-function*, the essential feature of which is the process of generating meaning out of sensations. The end results of alpha-function are *alpha-elements*, which are the raw material for dreams and for thinking [*see* Alpha-function]. When alpha-function goes wrong or fails, another (abnormal) kind of mental content is generated, which Bion calls *beta-elements*. 'Beta-element' is one of Bion's 'meaning-free' terms intended to be filled up from the experience of using the concept in practice [*see* Wilfred Bion]; there are several features of the term:

1   *Raw sense data*: Experience is generated from raw sense data (a realisation) by meeting with some pre-existing expectation (a preconception), which results in a 'meaning-full' conception [*see* Preconception; Thinking and knowledge]. On occasion, however, such a meeting may fail (failure of alpha-function), with the result that particles of 'undigested' sense data accumulate. These are *beta-elements*.

2   *Evacuation*: Beta-elements may agglomerate into collections (a large-scale visible manifestation might be a schizophrenic's 'word salad' type of speech). These accumulations are processed by evacuation, not by thinking thoughts into dreams and theories. The process of evacuation is that described by Klein as projective identification in its pathological form [*see* Projective identification].

3   *The mental apparatus*: Under the pressure of the accumulation of beta-elements, the mind develops not as an apparatus for thinking, but as an apparatus for '. . . ridding the psyche of accumulations of bad internal objects' (Bion, 1962, p. 112).

See Thinking and knowledge

Bion, W. (1962) 'A theory of thinking', in *Second Thoughts*. London: Heinemann (1967), pp. 110–119.

Esther Bick

Biography: Born 1901 in Poland, Esther Bick studied psychology in Vienna with Charlotte Buhler, but came as a refugee to England, eventually embarking on a psychoanalytic career after the Second World War. She then worked at the Tavistock Clinic and developed a method of infant observation as a training tool for child psychotherapists. However, her interest was in testing Klein's conclusions about the first year of life by direct observation. In the course of this she made her own original discoveries. In spite of her loyalty to Klein, the main Kleinian stream of development has left behind Bick's views, since her death in 1983.

Scientific contributions: Bick contributed a method out of which came four main results concerning the very early stages of development in the first days and weeks of life (Harris, 1984).

Infant observation: Bick started a rigorous method of weekly observations of mothers with babies in their own homes (Bick, 1964). Originally this was a method of teaching child psychotherapists and trainee psychoanalysts to observe rather than to intervene. However, the observations produced immediate results [*see* Infant observation].

Primary skin sensation: Bick's most significant observation concerned the infant's *passive* experience of being held together by an external object sensed through the skin sensations [*see* Skin], and of passively *falling apart* if this object failed (Bick, 1968). The skin is crucial in its function of giving evidence of such an object. This is in contrast to the experiences described by Bion and others, working with schizophrenics, of an active process of splitting and annihilation of the self. The idea that the experience of internal space has to be acquired implies the possibility of a failure to acquire it and therefore of compensatory measures, the most primitive of all defences, which Bick (1968) called 'second-skin' phenomena [*see* Skin].

The primary object: Bick obtained evidence in much greater detail of the nature of this first object that binds the personality together [*see* Paranoid-schizoid position] and has to be introjected in order to give a sense of space into which introjections can be put. The view that the experience of an internal space is one that is *acquired*, through adequate experience, contrasts with the idea of an innate experience of internal space implied in Bion's theories.

Adhesive identification: The possible failure to develop such an integrating primary object (space) appears to be confirmed in work with autistic children (Meltzer et al., 1975) [*see* Autism]. Bick and Meltzer (Meltzer, 1975, 1986) collaborated in describing the ways in which autistic children develop *without* a sense of internal or external space. Their relationship with objects appears to be a 'sticking on to' the object, a mechanism called adhesive identification [*see* Adhesive identification].

Bick, E. (1964) 'Notes on infant observation in psycho-analytic training', *Int. J. Psycho-Anal.* 45: 558–566.
—— (1968) 'The experience of the skin in early object relations', *Int. J. Psycho-Anal.* 49: 484–486.
Harris, M. (1984) 'Esther Bick', *J. Child Psychother.* 10: 2–14.
Meltzer, D. (1975) 'Adhesive identification', *Contemp. Psycho-Anal.* 11: 289–310.
—— (1986) 'Discussion of Esther Bick's paper "Further considerations of the function of the skin in early object relations"', *Br. J. Psychother.* 2: 300–301.
Meltzer, D., Bremner, J., Hoxter, S., Weddell, D. and Wittenberg, I. (1975) *Explorations in Autism*. Strath Tay: Clunie Press.

Wilfred Bion

Biography: Wilfred Bion was a potent and original contributor to psycho-analysis. Like Melanie Klein, his clinical thinking was rooted firmly in that of Freud. He was one of the first to analyse patients in psychotic states using an unmodified analytic technique; he extended existing theories of projective processes and developed new conceptual tools. The degree of collaboration between Hanna Segal, Wilfred Bion and Herbert Rosenfeld in their work with psychotic patients during the 1950s and 1960s, and their discussions with Melanie Klein at the time, means that it is not always possible to distinguish their exact individual contributions to the developing theories of splitting, projective identification, unconscious phantasy and the use of countertransference. As Feldman (2007) has pointed out, these three pioneering analysts not only sustained Klein's clinical and theoretical approach, but deepened and expanded it.

Much of what Bion wrote was not written down with the intention of publishing it. He wrote to pursue his own thoughts. Often he was dissatisfied with them and was reluctant to look at them again. We are indebted to his wife, Francesca Bion, that so much valuable thinking has not been lost.

Wilfred Bion was born in 1897 in Muttra in the United Provinces of Northwest India, where his father worked as an irrigation engineer. He was sent to school in England, where he boarded, from the age of 8 years old. He loved India and had wanted to return there, but in 1979, after having come back to England from California, he died of acute myeloid leukaemia before he could. Unlike Freud, who destroyed so much autobiographical information, Bion (1985) has left a wealth of material about his life and his relationships with his wife Francesca and his children, Parthenope, Julian and Nicola.

He was physically powerful and athletic and even as a boy was excellent at both rugby and swimming. In 1915 he left school, just before he was 18 years old, and joined the Royal Tank Regiment in 1916 in France, where he was on active service until the end of the war. A courageous man, though he would not have claimed this himself, and a natural leader, he was awarded the DSO (Distinguished Service Order), the Legion d'Honneur and, as a young Lieutenant, was put forward for a Victoria Cross for action in an advanced outpost that he had created in a German trench with his tank crew after it had been destroyed.

At the end of the war Bion read History at Oxford University, after which he worked as a school master at his old school in Bishop's Stortford, before leaving to study medicine at University College Hospital in London. He had already become seriously interested in the behaviour of groups (he was very taken with Wilfred Trotter's ideas) and in psychoanalysis, so after qualifying as a doctor Bion studied psychoanalytic psychotherapy at the Tavistock Clinic. In 1938 he began a training analysis with John Rickman. Eric Trist has described this period of Bion's life, in which he worked to develop new group methods, as his 'Group Decade'. In fact Bion never lost his deep interest in group mentality after becoming a psychoanalyst and he regarded the psychoanalytic approach, through the individual and the group relations model, as addressing different facets of the same mental phenomena. He wrote that the two methods provide the practitioner with a 'rudimentary binocular vision'.

In 1940 Bion worked in psychiatric settings in military hospitals, and also worked as Senior Psychiatrist to the War Office Selection Boards. As Francesca Bion has noted, these and his wartime experiences formed the core of his group work at the Tavistock Institute in the years immediately after the war, culminating in his papers published between 1948 and 1951.

In 1950 Bion gave his membership paper to the British Psychoanalytical Society, 'The imaginary twin' (published in 1967 in *Second Thoughts*). His wife had to press him to publish his group papers and he did so when he found a way to incorporate his later psychoanalytic understanding. *Experiences in Groups*, his most successful book in terms of sales, was not published until 1961. In the early 1950s Bion began a second analysis with Melanie Klein, whose work with him was deeply helpful. Although he did not want to be identified narrowly as belonging to a sectarian group or school of thought, he wrote that he was convinced of the:

> . . . central importance of the Kleinian themes of projective identification and the interplay between the paranoid-schizoid positions. Without the aid of these two sets of theories I doubt the possibility of any advance in the study of group phenomena.
>
> (Bion, 1961, p. 8)

As early as 1959 Bion had used Klein's concept of projective identification to unify group and individual processes involved in evoking countertransference enactments in the group or individual analyst:

> . . . in group treatment many interpretations, and amongst them the most important, have to be made on the strength of the analyst's own emotional reactions. It is my belief that these reactions are dependent on the fact that the analyst in the group is at the receiving end of what Melanie Klein (1946) has called projective identification, and that this mechanism plays a very important role in groups. Now the experience of counter-transference appears to me to have quite a distinct quality that should enable the analyst to differentiate the occasion when he is the object of a projective identification from the occasion when he is not. The analyst feels he is being manipulated so as to be playing a part, no matter how difficult to recognize, in somebody else's phantasy – or he would do if it were not for what in recollection *I can only call a temporary loss of insight, a sense of experiencing strong feelings and at the same time a belief that their existence is quite adequately justified by the objective situation without recourse to recondite explanation of their causation.* . . . I believe ability to shake oneself out of the numbing feeling of reality that is a concomitant of this state is the prime requisite

of the analyst in the group: if he can do this he is in a position to give what I believe is the correct interpretation, and thereby to see its connection with the previous interpretation, the validity of which he has been caused to doubt.

(Bion, 1961, p. 149, italics added)

Bion refers to the capacity of the analyst to recognise the 'numbing sense of reality' that accompanies this operation of projective identification, and the ability to shake himself out of it in order to think about what is going on, as 'the prime requisite' of the analyst in the situation, which in the passage quoted is the group. In his later work he applied this finding to another kind of group, the individual human being in analysis.

Bion wrote *Second Thoughts*, published in 1967, to recast his ideas from the 1950s in the context of his work as a psychoanalyst, including ground-breaking work with patients in psychotic states. He did this alongside two other gifted students of Melanie Klein: Hanna Segal and Herbert Rosenfeld. The analysis of psychotic patients formed the basis of his books of the 1960s, work that has been influential in the British Psychoanalytical Society in particular. These are: *Learning from Experience* (1962), *Elements of Psycho-Analysis* (1963), *Transformations* (1965) and *Attention and Inter-pretation* (1970).

Amongst the most clinically useful of the ideas from this period are the interrelated concepts of *containment*, or more precisely *container/contained* ($\female\male$), [*see* Container/contained], the oscillation within this 'structure' of *Klein's two positions* (Ps↔D) [*see* Ps↔D] and the complex ways in which the mental products of such relationships can furnish models or '*precon-ceptions*' for the individual, which, when 'mated' with emotional experi-ences felt to be realisations of them, can promote psychically real concepts capable of growth. This is what Bion meant by '*alpha-function*'. The idea is based upon the necessity for the infant in distress to find a real person willing and able to take in and to suffer the emotional impact and dis-turbance of the projection of it, including the sense of concreteness and indigestibility, without refusing or running away. His wartime experiences had contributed to this understanding in the most convincing way possible. When he read that Klein had stated that the first projective identification of the infant is his fear of imminent destruction, Bion had no trouble believing the truth of it.

Bion kept notes of his thoughts at the time and these were published in 1991 by Francesca Bion as *Cogitations*, the name that Bion used for them. Bion's *Cogitations* clarify many of the obscurities in the highly condensed books of the 1960s, which tend to present the products but not the pro-cesses leading up to them, leaving out the network of preparatory work that went into his thinking. André Green wrote in a detailed review of *Cogitations*:

Compared with Bion's published works, the Cogitations are thrilling to read and often less difficult to assimilate, because the author's formulations are less condensed and because he makes us witnesses to the process of the unfolding of his thought. We literally *follow* him

(Green, 1992, p. 585)

Although his *Memoir of the Future* (1991) is not so easy to follow, the loose and allusive structure of the work contains many clinically relevant transformations of Bion's earlier ideas, reworked into an imaginative but rambling novel. Mid-way between the earlier group papers of the 1950s, together with the clinical psychoanalytic works of the 1960s, and the *Memoir of the Future*, is Bion's concept of 'O', which, although seemingly suited to mystical thinking, is a concept that evolves from and belongs naturally to Bion's explorations in the domain of epistemology and representation, to which he gave the sign 'K', which he established as being of equal significance to those of Love and Hate [*see* Thinking and knowledge].

Bion, W. R. (1948–51) 'Experiences in groups', *Hum. Relat.* 1–4.
—— (1961) *Experiences in Groups*. London: Tavistock.
—— (1962) *Learning from Experience*. London: Karnac.
—— (1963) *Elements of Psycho-Analysis*. London: Karnac.
—— (1965) *Transformations*. London: Heinemann.
—— (1967) *Second Thoughts: Selected Papers on Psychoanalysis*. London: Karnac.
—— (1970) *Attention and Interpretation*. London: Karnac.
—— (1985) *All My Sins Remembered: Another Part of a Life* and *The Other Side of Genius: Family Letters*. (F. Bion, ed.). Abingdon: Fleetwood Press.
—— (1991) *A Memoir of the Future* [revised and corrected]. London: Karnac.
—— (1991) *Cogitations*. (F. Bion ed.). London: Karnac.
Feldman, M. (2007) *Doubt, Conviction and the Analytic Process. Selected Papers of Michael Feldman*. New Library of Psychoanalysis Series. London: Brunner-Routledge.
Green, A. (1992) 'A Review of *Cogitations* by Wilfred R. Bion, edited with a foreword by Francesca Bion', *Int. J. Psycho-Anal.* 73: 585–589.

Bizarre objects

During the 1950s Bion elaborates a comprehensive theory of schizophrenic thought disorder based on the consequences of a fragmentary splitting of the ego, in particular the splitting of the perceptual apparatus:

. . . attacks are directed against the apparatus of perception from the beginning of life. This part of his personality is cut up, split into minute fragments, and then, using projective identification, expelled from the personality. Having thus rid himself of the apparatus of conscious awareness of internal and external reality, the patient achieves a state which is felt to be neither alive nor dead.

(Bion, 1956, p. 39)

The personality is thus depleted, but the ejected fragments of the perceptual apparatus continue an alienated existence as bizarre objects. They intrude omnipotently into an external object to form a particularly persecutory object:

> Each particle is felt to consist of a real external object which is encapsulated in a piece of personality that has engulfed it. The character of this complete particle will depend partly on the character of the real object, say a gramophone, and partly on the character of the particle of the personality that engulfs it. If the piece of the personality is concerned with sight, the gramophone when playing is felt to be watching the patient. The object, angered at being engulfed, swells up, so to speak, and suffuses and controls the piece of personality that engulfs it: to that extent the particle is felt to have become a thing.
>
> (Bion, 1956, pp. 39–40)

In 1957 in his paper 'Differentiation of the psychotic from the non-psychotic personalities' Bion expands his theory to include the consequences of the schizophrenic making fragmenting attacks on all his ego functions:

> . . . consciousness of sense impressions, attention, memory, judgement, thought, have brought against them, in such inchoate forms as they may possess at the outset of life, the sadistic splitting and eviscerating attacks that lead to their being minutely fragmented and then expelled from the personality to penetrate, or encyst, the objects. In the patient's phantasy the expelled particles of ego lead an independent and uncontrolled existence, either contained by or containing the external objects . . . the patient feels himself to be surrounded by bizarre objects.
>
> (Bion, 1957, p. 47)

Through the repeated evacuation of these parts of his or her mind, the schizophrenic's thought and capacity to attend to reality are progressively whittled away. The accumulation of bizarre objects builds up a persecutory egocentric world in which the schizophrenic is destined to remain trapped.

See Wilfred Bion; Psychosis; Thinking and knowledge

Bion, W. (1956) 'Development of schizophrenic thought', *Int. J. Psycho-Anal.* 37: 344–346; republished in *Second Thoughts*. London: Heinemann (1967), pp. 36–42.

—— (1957) 'Differentiation of the psychotic from the non-psychotic personalities', *Int. J. Psycho-Anal.* 38: 266–275; republished in *Second Thoughts*. London: Heinemann (1967), pp. 43–64.

Breast

Klein uses the term 'breast' interchangeably with mother when writing about infants [*see* Mother]. She considers that the infant with his immature and unintegrated ego has only partial perceptions of himself and the objects in his world, all of which are perceived in terms of bodily parts, albeit ones that are imagined as being filled with feelings and motives. The breast is the provider of food and physical closeness and in Klein's view it is the part that represents the mother and the comfort that is derived from being fed and held by her – it is the first part-object. The first act of the ego is to split the breast into a 'good' and a 'bad' part, an activity that increases the partial and unintegrated nature of the object. Over time the 'good' and 'bad' parts of the breast will become integrated into a whole breast and the parts of the mother will become integrated into a whole mother.

See Part-objects

Castration

In Freud's theory the castration complex modifies the Oedipus complex. For the little boy the anxiety of being castrated by his father leads him to relinquish his oedipal object-choices. For the little girl there is no castration anxiety as such but rather a fall from her phallic position, a painful acknowledgement of castration, felt as loss of love. The little girl turns away from mother to father under the aegis of 'penis envy'. Freud's views on femininity as based on 'lack' or 'absence' have been criticised in many quarters in and outside psychoanalysis. Klein herself did not reject Freud's notion of the girl's phallic position, of her rivalrous possession of her father's penis in fantasy and the anxiety of castration this leads to. However, unlike Freud she saw the girl's phallic position or her inverted Oedipus complex as secondary, not as primary, and as a defence against the more primitive anxieties that stem from her early feminine oedipal position Klein described (1932) a more primitive anxiety in girls that drives infantile development and in this sense can be seen as a counterpart to castration anxiety in classical theory. She outlines the fears aroused by the girl's phantasy attacks on her mother's insides, and on the objects that she believes reside there: mother's babies and also father's penis, which, she believes, forms a permanent coitus inside mother. The combined object of mother-with-penis or penis inside breast is extremely violent and frightening [*see* Combined parent figure]. The little girl fears retaliation in kind for her invading, spoiling and robbing attacks on her mother's body and its contents [*see* Child analysis; Oedipus complex].

> Erna's reaction against this intention of robbing and completely destroying her mother's body was expressed in the fear she had . . . that a robber woman would take out everything inside her. it is this fear that I have described as belonging to the earliest danger-situation of the girl and which I consider as an equivalent to the castration anxiety of boys.
>
> (Klein, 1932, p. 56)

Klein thinks that for the boy castration fear is experienced as soon as genital sensations (and thus phantasies) are experienced, which is very early, when oral libido is mostly to the fore, including oral sadistic impulses towards both breast and penis. Thus the feared castration can occur through biting off the penis. Castration is only one of the dangers because, as for the girl, the frustrated boy infant's aggressive phantasies will also involve oral, faecal and urinary attacks on the mother's body, robbing her of the desirable things she keeps to herself inside, namely the father's penis and internal babies. This results in the phantasy of poisoned, dangerous, retaliatory objects that attack him in kind and threaten the precious things he feels he has inside him, the good babies and penis he has taken in during his feminine position, as well as his more visible penis.

Klein believed she had discovered a forerunner of Freud's classical castration anxiety, which, based in the very sadistic pregenital phases, gives it a particularly terrifying quality.

Klein, M. (1932) *The Psychoanalysis of Children. The Writings of Melanie Klein*, Vol. 2. London: Hogarth Press.

Classical psychoanalysis

See American psychoanalysis in relation to Klein

Coitus

A child's play frequently shows the sexual theories about the parents that he or she is trying to explore. Klein observed (in the 1920s) that many of these theories seemed to derive from pregenital phantasies – mutual sucking, biting, feeding with milk, with faeces, beating, etc.

The implications, for Klein, are that phantasies of the primal scene commence very early in life, and that there must be some genital stirrings (premonitions of a parental couple) even in the oral and anal stages. This contrasts with the orthodox theory at the time in which it was thought that ideas of parental intercourse were normally delayed until the genital phase and formed part of the Oedipus complex. The result was that Klein found herself describing pregenital forms of the Oedipus complex and dating earlier and earlier the timing of its origins [*see* Oedipus complex].

Klein also describes an object that she terms the 'combined parent figure', which is the infant's phantasy of the parents in part-object form locked in a primitive, often terrifying version of intercourse.

See Combined parent figure; Linking

Combined parent figure

Klein sees the infant as intensely curious [*see* Epistemophilia] about the inside of the mother's body, which in his phantasy contains many valuable objects, withheld from the infant, including the incorporated penis of the father. In Klein's view this curiosity is closely linked to aggression, and leads to phantasies of forcefully entering the mother's insides and stealing and/or destroying through jealousy and envy, by oral and anal means, these riches that are denied him, including the relationship with father/father's penis. The resulting terror is that mother and the objects inside her will retaliate against the infant. The infant ends up in the midst of a phantasy that all these retaliatory wounded objects are now marauding – as internal persecutors in his own insides after being introjected there, and as the persecuting external figure.

A central part of this complex – mother with father's penis inside her – is an example of what Klein refers to in various ways as a combined parent figure. She refers, for example, to the figure in 1929 (p. 211) and 1930 (p. 219) as the 'united parents', in 1932 as 'combined parents' (p. 133) and 'hostile combined parents' (p. 254) and in 1952a as the 'combined parent figure' (p. 55). Klein refers in 1952b to various versions of this figure:

> . . . combined parent figures such as: the mother containing the father's penis or the whole father; the father containing the mother's breast or the whole mother; the parents fused inseparably in sexual intercourse.
> (Klein, 1952b, p. 79)

The phantasy of the combined parent figure is a very primitive version of a couple; the parents in part-object form are locked excitingly and terrifyingly together in an orgy of continual, mutual gratification at the child's expense. It is the earliest and most primitive phantasy that structures the oedipal situation [*see* Oedipus complex]. This orgy is felt not only to be gratifying but can also in phantasy be dangerous to the parents. This is because the infant's fury and rage lead him or her to imbue this intercourse with as much violence between the parents as he or she is feeling towards them:

> . . . these sadistic masturbation phantasies . . . fall into two distinct, though interconnected, categories. In those of the first category the child employs various sadistic means to make a direct onslaught upon the parents either combined in coitus or separately; in those of the second . . . its belief in its sadistic omnipotence over its parents finds expression in a more indirect fashion. It endows them with instruments of mutual destruction, transforming their teeth, nails, genitals, excrements and so on, into dangerous weapons and animals, etc., and pictures them, according to its own desires, as tormenting and destroying each other in the act of copulation.
>
> (Klein, 1932, p. 200)

Once the idea of envy becomes central in Klein's thinking she identifies envy of the parental intercourse as an important source of the violence and sadism associated with the phantasy of the combined parents (Klein, 1957) [*see* Envy]. Klein thinks that where envy is particularly strong the combined parent figure also becomes particularly strong and impedes working through of the Oedipus complex and the depressive position.

With progress towards the depressive position [*see* Depressive position] in normal development the combined parent figure gives way gradually to the idea of whole-object, separate parents who come together independently. Meltzer (1973), for example, has described the development of sexuality and creativity in the personality in terms of the struggle to move beyond the part-object combined parent figure to reconstruct it in whole objects with more realistic versions of the mother and father, a process inherent in the depressive position. Internally such a realistic parental intercourse forms an internal object that is the basis (or felt to be the fount) of personal creativity: sexual, intellectual and aesthetic.

See Coitus

Klein, M. (1929) 'Infantile anxiety-situations reflected in a work of art and in the creative impulse', in *The Writings of Melanie Klein*, Vol. 1. London: Hogarth Press, pp. 210–218.
—— (1930) 'The importance of symbol formation in the development of the ego', in *The Writings of Melanie Klein*, Vol. 1. London: Hogarth Press, pp. 219–232.

—— (1932) *The Pychoanalysis of Children. The Writings of Melanie Klein*, Vol. 2. London: Hogarth Press.

—— (1952a) 'The origins of transference', in *The Writings of Melanie Klein*, Vol. 3. London: Hogarth Press, pp. 48–56.

—— (1952b) 'Some theoretical conclusions regarding the emotional life of the infant', in *The Writings of Melanie Klein*, Vol. 3. London: Hogarth Press, pp. 61–93.

—— (1957) 'Envy and gratitude', in *The Writings of Melanie Klein*, Vol. 3. London: Hogarth Press, pp. 176–235.

Meltzer, D. (1973) *Sexual States of Mind*. Strath Tay: Clunie Press.

Component instincts

Freud and Abraham: In Freud's theory the sexual instinct can be broken down into a number of basic component or partial instincts that function independently at first. They become fused in the various libidinal stages or organisations, culminating in the oedipal stage, whose outcome shapes the variety of forms that adult sexuality takes after puberty (Freud, 1905). Component instincts are defined with reference to a *bodily source* or *erotogenic zone* (oral, anal, genital) or by reference to an *aim* such as the instinct to master and its offshoot, sadism, the pleasure in seeing and being seen (scopophilia/exhibitionism) and the desire for knowledge. The instinct to master is not sexual to begin with but is recruited in its various forms and becomes part of sexuality secondarily.

Freud then moves away from the narrow definition of *sadism* as a sexual perversion and gives it different meanings (Laplanche and Pontalis, 1973). As a component instinct of the sexual drive, Freud links it with the primal cruelty of children, whose aim is not to make the person suffer but they simply fail to take the other person into account. In 'Instincts and their visciissitudes' (1915) he defines sadism as having the aim of degrading and subjugating the object by violence, not in order to enjoy suffering as such, but rather in the service of gaining mastery. At this time Freud thinks that sadism is primary and masochism is secondary. It is the reversal of sadism onto the subject's own self that leads to masochism with sexual gratification now accompanying it.

The ubiquity of extremely sadistic violent impulses against the object, and extreme masochism in the relation that the ego has with the harshness and severity of conscience (later superego), was evident in Freud's obsessional and melancholic patients. Both Freud (1909, 1917a, 1917b) and Karl Abraham (1916) use the term sadism in mapping out the pregenital oral and anal component instincts. The term sadism in these contexts refers to various oral and anal aims in phantasy of destroying and degrading the object. The ubiquity of sadism is one factor that contributes to Freud postulating his concept of the death instinct as having a separate status.

Aggression and sadism can no longer be seen as mere *component instincts* of the sexual drive. Freud (1920) conceptualises the death instinct as a primary masochism aimed at the destruction of the subject, which, under the influence of narcissistic libido, is directed or deflected outwards towards an object and takes the form of sadism.

Abraham in particular highlights the virulence of the sadistic components of the pregenital stages of libidinal development. In his masterful 1924 essay he does so without reference to Freud's second dualism as such. He carries on writing from within the logic of sadism being a component instinct of sexuality. This marked presence of sadism in the pregenital stages is made more problematic because object-love proper only appears with the genital phase of development. Abraham (1924) contributes more precise delineations of the pregenital stages in particular, alongside which he maps his views on the development of object-love [*see* Karl Abraham].

According to Abraham the early oral (sucking) stage is *pre-ambivalent*, and dominated by appreciative, incorporative aims/phantasies of taking in goodness. The oral (cannibalistic) stage begins with teething at 6 months, and ushers in emotional ambivalence with sadistic aims of cannibalising and forcefully incorporating the object. The very damaged object exerts its tyranny within, as evident in melancholia. In the second year the early anal-sadistic (expulsive) stage is dominated by sadistic phantasies of attacking and destroying the object with bad faeces or destroying the object identified with the part-object faeces, as evident in paranoia. In the later anal (retentive) stage, sadism aims to preserve the object rather than to destroy it. Feelings of pity and concern for the object are evident in obsessive–compulsive neurosis. This stage demarcates neurosis from psychosis (no withdrawal of cathexis) and initiates the first form of partial love for the object treated as a possession. This also marks the movement out of primary narcissism. Love for the object as separate grows through Abraham's genital and oedipal phase.

Klein's position: In her early work (1919–1932) Melanie Klein is very influenced by Freud and by Abraham, who provide her with a clinically based conceptual background to develop her own ideas. Freud's second instinctual dualism only impacts directly on her work in 1932. Prior to 1932 Klein's work with children leads to three departures from Freud and Abraham. First, she questions the neat chronological delineation of the stages, especially from 6 months of age. She asserts that genital, oral and anal trends are all present from that age but she also retains the notion of *phase dominance* as mapped out by Abraham. Thus the oral plays the leading organising role in the first year, the anal in the second year and the genital from the third year. Second, although Klein does not yet assign to aggression and sadism a separate status from the sexual instinct, she begins to see combined sadism rather than infantile sexual impulses as being the prime mover in psychopathology and in development. Klein's view that the component instincts of aggression/sadism play a more decisive role than the sexual instinct itself does is tied to Abraham's view that object-love only emerges as a force in the genital stage. Thirdly, when Klein asserts the beginning of the Oedipus complex at around 6 months, this effectively means that the classical distinction between the genital and the pregenital stages, in which the not-yet-united component instincts dominate, is undermined. But Klein herself does not emphasise such a contradiction between her work and classical theory. Instead she develops her notion of maximal sadism, which is contemporaneous with the beginning of the Oedipus complex and shifts the focus on the problems that aggression, still then a component instinct, poses for development in general.

Maximal sadism and its components: Klein sees her early notion of sadism at its height as 'only an amplification of the accepted and well established view that oral cannibalism is followed by anal sadism' (Klein, 1932b, p. 151). The phase of sadism at its height (1928, 1929, 1930) is unleashed by weaning, which frustrates the early oral incorporative relation with the breast-mother. It begins with oral cannibalism, whose aims are brutally destructive and are soon joined by the equally brutal anal and urethral aims of annihilating the object. Klein has in mind Abraham's crucial distinction that the early anal stage is unmitigated by any desire to conserve the object, a trend that only emerges in the later anal stage.

Maximal sadism and the Oedipus complex are, according to (early) Klein, contemporaneous. The object encountered by the child is the first oedipal object that takes the form of the combined parents: a phantasy of the inside of the 'mother's body which is assumed to be the scene of all sexual processes and development' (1928, p. 188) [*see* Combined parent figure]. These include milk, faeces, babies and the father's penis. This primitive phantasy of an undifferentiated object is experienced as an excluding tantalising coitus, which is exacerbated by the fact that all the objects are imagined to be inside the mother's body. Because the objects are combined, an attack on one object is an attack on all the objects, and against them the child stands alone. Sadism is at its height when the child is compelled by oral-sadistic, urethral-sadistic, anal-sadistic and by the epistemophilic component instincts, to annihilate the combined parents with all the weapons of sadism.

Klein underlines the important role that the epistemophilic instincts play in this stage of development. She writes: 'The early connection between the epistemophilic impulse and sadism is very important for the whole mental development' (1928, p. 188). She refers tentatively to the onrush of problems and questions stimulated by the child's incipient sexual curiosity and the bitter grievances that the many unformulated and unanswered questions leave behind in the unconscious. 'These grievances give rise to an extraordinary amount of hate' (Klein, 1928, p. 188) and generate an early feeling of not knowing.

It seems that the genuine desire to know, linked to the early oedipal situation, becomes subverted and controlled by the aims of sadism so that knowing becomes tantamount to taking possession of and to master by brutal force or to destroy. The combined force of these attacks creates terrifying anxieties capable of causing psychosis and also severe learning inhibitions [*see* Epistemophilia].

Klein details the various aims and phantasies of maximal sadism. Oral cannibalistic phantasies take the shape of scooping out, of biting to pieces and of sucking out. Urethral sadism is particularly emphasised by Klein herself: urine in phantasy becomes a destructive substance that floods and drowns, or a corrosive substance that dissolves and burns (1930). In anal sadistic phantasies the faeces become dangerous weapons or weapons loaded with dangerous substances that explode and destroy or poison and contaminate. Or the object can become equated with excrement and got rid of as such. Klein herself refers to the inexhaustible variety and richness of these sadistic phantasies (1928, p. 132).

Klein finally abandons the classical notion of sadism as being a component instinct of the libido despite its domination of the former. She switches explicitly to Freud's second instinctual dualism [*see* Death instinct]. In 1932 she accepts that she was observing the clinical manifestations of a conflict between the life and death instincts: '. . . in the early stages of development, the life instinct has to exert its power to the utmost in order to maintain itself against the death instinct' (Klein, 1932, p. 150). Thereafter the 'phase of maximal sadism' becomes obsolete, as both love and hate are seen to have been present from birth. The main *contents* of the phase of maximal sadism survive for a while in the form of the 'paranoid position', which Klein first mentions in 1935. Klein later gives Freud's second instinctual dualism her own definite stamp when she formulates the 'paranoid-schizoid position' (1946).

See Sadism

Abraham, K. (1916) 'The first pre-genital stage of the libido', in *Selected Papers on Psycho-Analysis*. London: Maresfield Reprints, pp. 248–279.

—— (1924) 'A short study of the libido, viewed in the light of mental disorders', in *Selected Papers on Psycho-Analysis*. London: Maresfield Reprints, pp. 418–501.

Freud, S. (1905) 'Three essays on the theory of sexuality', *S.E. 7*. London: Hogarth Press, pp. 125–245.

—— (1909) 'Note upon a case of obsessional neurosis', *S.E. 10*. London: Hogarth Press, pp. 155–318.

—— (1915) 'Instincts and their vicissitudes', *S.E. 14*. London: Hogarth Press, pp. 117–140.

—— (1917a) 'Mourning and melancholia', *S.E. 14*. London: Hogarth Press, pp. 237–260.

—— (1917b) 'On transformations of instinct as exemplified in anal-erotism', *S.E. 17*. London: Hogarth Press, pp. 125–133.

—— (1920) 'Beyond the pleasure principle', *S.E. 18*. London: Hogarth Press, pp. 7–64.

Klein, M. (1928) 'Early stages of the Oedipus complex', in *The Writings of Melanie Klein*, Vol. 1. London: Hogarth Press, pp. 186–198.

—— (1929) 'Personification in the play of children', in *The Writings of Melanie Klein*, Vol. 1. London: Hogarth Press, pp. 199–209.

—— (1930) 'The importance of symbol formation in the development of the ego', in *The Writings of Melanie Klein*, Vol. 1. London: Hogarth Press, pp. 219–232.

—— (1932) 'Obsessional neurosis and the early stages of the super-ego', in *The Writings of Melanie Klein*, Vol. 2. London: Hogarth Press, pp. 149–175.

—— (1935) 'A contribution to the psychogenesis of manic-depressive states', in *The Writings of Melanie Klein*, Vol. 1. London: Hogarth Press, pp. 262–289.

—— (1946) 'Notes on some schizoid mechanisms', in *The Writings of Melanie Klein*, Vol. 3. London: Hogarth Press, pp. 1–24.

Laplanche, J. and Pontalis, J.-B. (1973) *The Language of Psycho-Analysis*. London: Hogarth Press.

Concern

See Depressive position; Love

Confusional states

Confusional states are common in schizophrenic patients. Their origins have been described by Rosenfeld (1965). In his 1950 paper 'Notes on the psychopathology of confusional states in chronic schizophrenia' Rosenfeld explains how the extreme anxiety in severe confusional states results from a failure in dichotomous splitting. He links this failure to states in which the destructive impulses threaten to destroy the libidinal impulses, leading to *failure in the basic differentiation between 'good' and 'bad'* as the good object is hated and destroyed by mistake. This leads to intense insecurity and inability to sort out internal states and impulses and the whole self feels in danger of being destroyed.

In 1952 in 'Notes on the psycho-analysis of the superego conflict in an acute schizophrenic patient' Rosenfeld goes further and links primary destructiveness to *envious attacks* on the goodness of the object felt as separate. This leads to a failure in primal splitting and the confusion that ensues. He also links envy to an increase in forceful projective identification, which entrenches *the lack of differentiation between self and object* [*see* Envy]. The ego is confused with the objects as a result of omnipotent forms of projection and introjection that are aimed at denying separation and dependency [*see* Narcissism]. In particular, huge parts of the self are put into the object through the massive and violent operation of the mechanism of projective identification. The central themes of these two papers are assimilated and developed by Klein in 'Envy and gratitude' (1957) [*see* Envy].

A form of fusion of the self with the external world may be achieved in some autistic states of retreat into a sole occupation with bodily sensations [*see* Autism].

This kind of confusion between self and object is secondary and for the purpose of defence. It contrasts with a primary state of fusion and regressive confusion described by ego psychologists (typically Mahler et al., 1975), who follow the classical theory of primary narcissism [*see* Narcissism]. Classical theorists posit a stage of *primary narcissism* in which there is no primary experience of 'me' and 'not-me', no boundary to the ego at birth and therefore no ego at the outset of life. Kleinians (and many others) by contrast posit a rudimentary ego, ego functions and an ego boundary present and active from birth. Confusion of ego and object is thus secondary and the result of omnipotent primitive defence mechanisms, which yield narcissistic object relations [*see* Narcissism].

Klein, M. (1957) 'Envy and gratitude', in *The Writings of Melanie Klein*, Vol. 3. London: Hogarth Press, pp. 176–235.

Mahler, M., Pine, F. and Bergman, A. (1975) *The Psychological Birth of the Human Infant*. London: Hutchinson.

Rosenfeld, H. (1950) 'Notes on the psychopathology of confusional states in chronic schizophrenia', *Int. J. Psycho-Anal.* 31: 132–137.

—— (1952) 'Notes on the psycho-analysis of the superego conflict in an acute schizophrenic patient', *Int. J. Psycho-Anal.* 33: 111–131.

—— (1965) *Psychotic States*. London: Hogarth Press.

Constitutional factor

Klein emphasises the biological basis of loving and destructive impulses, especially envy, and of the biological basis of the balance between the two types of impulse. However, she also stresses the effect of environmental factors. As she puts it:

> In speaking of an innate conflict between love and hate, I am implying that the capacity for both love and for destructive impulses is, to some extent, constitutional, though varying individually in strength and interacting from the beginning with external conditions.
>
> (Klein, 1957, p. 180)

Her statement about the interaction of innate capacities with external conditions contradicts the beliefs of several of her critics who thought that her attribution of personal characteristics to constitutional factors meant that she thought such characteristics were basically unalterable. Klein also thought that the capacity to form relations with objects and to develop unconscious phantasies exists at birth and develops rapidly thereafter.

Bion takes Klein's views about inheritance and environment further, stating his view that infants have 'preconceptions' at birth that soon 'mate' with sense impressions to form 'conceptions' (Bion, 1962, 1963, 1967).

Bion, W. (1962) *Learning from Experience*. London: Heinemann, p. 91.
—— (1963) *Elements of Psycho-Analysis*. London: Heinemann, p. 23.
—— (1967) *Second Thoughts: Selected Papers on Psycho-Analysis*. London: Heinemann, p. 111
Klein, M. (1957) 'Envy and gratitude', in *The Writings of Melanie Klein*, Vol. 3. London: Hogarth Press, pp. 176–235.

Contact barrier

Freud developed this term in the course of describing neurones and the processes of their excitation or resistance to excitation at the point of contact with other neurones (Freud, 1895). (The term 'synapse' had not yet been created for this purpose.) Later Bion used the term 'contact-barrier' to describe the boundary of and point of contact between conscious and unconscious sense impressions. He uses the term 'alpha-function', intentionally devoid of meaning (Bion, 1962, p. 3), to describe the creation of the 'alpha-elements', which form the contact-barrier:

> The man's alpha-function whether in sleeping or waking transforms the sense-impressions related to an emotional experience, into alpha-elements, which cohere as they proliferate to form the contact-barrier. This contact-barrier, thus continuously in process of formation, marks the point of contact and separation between conscious and unconscious elements and originates the distinction between them.
>
> (Bion, 1962, p. 17)

Bion, W. R. (1962) *Learning from Experience*. London: Heinemann.
Freud, S. (1895) 'Project for a scientific psychology', *S.E. 1*. London: Hogarth Press, pp. 292–293, 298–307, 316–319, 323.

Container/contained

The notion of 'containing' has become a decisive concept for most British forms of psychoanalytic psychotherapy inside and outside the Kleinian Group of psychoanalysts, although this now often means that it is used imprecisely. It derives from Klein's original description of projective identification [*see* Projective identification] in which one person in some sense contains a part of another. This has given rise to a theory of development based on the emotional contact of infant with mother and, by extension, a theory of the psychoanalytic contact. The concept gradually formed in the literature as Kleinian analysts moved forward in exploring the implications of the new concept of projective identification:

> The patient . . . showed that he had projected his damaged self containing the destroyed world, not only into all the other patients, but into me, and had changed me in this way. But instead of becoming relieved by this projection he became more anxious, because he was afraid of what I was then putting back into him, whereupon his introjective processes became severely disturbed.
>
> (Rosenfeld, 1952, pp. 80–81)

Here Rosenfeld is using the theory that Klein established of the development of the ego through repeated cycles of introjection and projection, but he is taking it further by recognising that it is not just projection of the object but also projection of parts of the self-projective identification in cycle with introjective identification. Jaques (1953) was similarly experimenting with these kinds of ideas at the same time [*see* Social defence systems].

Bion (1959) is normally credited with the mature form of this model:

> Throughout the analysis the patient resorted to projective identification with a persistence suggesting it was a mechanism of which he had never been able sufficiently to avail himself; the analysis afforded him the opportunity for the exercise of a mechanism of which he had been cheated . . . there were sessions which led me to suppose that the patient felt there was some object that denied him the use of projective identification . . . there are elements which indicate that the patient felt that parts of his personality that he wished to repose in me were refused entry by me . . . When the patient strove to rid himself of fears of death which were felt to be too powerful for his personality to contain he split off his fears and put them into me, the idea apparently being that if they were allowed to repose there long enough they would undergo modification by my psyche and could then be safely reintrojected. On the occasion I have in mind the patient had felt . . . that I evacuated them so quickly that the feelings were not modified but had become more painful . . . he strove to force them into me with increased desperation and violence. His behaviour, isolated from the context of analysis, might have appeared to be an expression of primary aggression. The more violent his phantasies of projective identification, the

more frightened he became of me. There were sessions in which such behaviour expressed unprovoked aggression, but I quote this series because it shows the patient in a different light, his violence a reaction to what he felt was my hostile defensiveness. The analytic situation built up in my mind a sense of witnessing an extremely early scene. I felt that the patient had witnessed in infancy a mother who dutifully responded to the infant's emotional displays. The dutiful response had in it an element of impatient 'I don't know what's the matter with the child.' My deduction was that in order to understand what the child wanted the mother should have treated the infant's cry as more than a demand for her presence. From the infant's point of view she should have taken into her, and thus experienced, the fear that the child was dying. It was this fear that the child could not contain. He strove to split it off together with the part of the personality in which it lay and project it into mother. An understanding mother is able to experience the feeling of dread that this baby was striving to deal with by projective identification, and yet retain a balanced outlook. This patient had had to deal with a mother who could not tolerate experiencing such feelings and reacted either by denying them ingress, or alternatively by becoming a prey to the anxiety which resulted from introjection of the baby's bad feelings.

(Bion, 1959, pp. 103–104)

If the analyst is closed or unresponsive, 'The result is excessive projective identification by the patient and a deterioration of his developmental processes' (p. 105). Although he says that the schizophrenic's disturbance '. . . finds its main source in the inborn disposition' (p. 105), Bion believes that both genetic and environmental influences disturb normal projective identification.

Maternal reverie: Bion (1962a, 1962b) describes the mother's state of mind when she can take in the infant's projected terror as *reverie*. Bion first describes the mother's reverie in 'A theory of thinking' and the same year in *Learning from Experience* he adds, almost in passing, an important detail that is often, as Caper (1999) points out, omitted in explications of reverie and containment. That is, that the mother's link to the father is important in enabling her reverie:

If the feeding mother cannot allow reverie or if the reverie is allowed but is not associated with love for the child or its father this fact will be communicated to the infant even though incomprehensible to the infant.

(Bion, 1962b, p. 36)

Segal describes the process of containment in a paper on technique with schizophrenics. Segal indicates the way in which a patient's ego may be built up through introjection of an object that can contain and *understand* his experiences:

> . . . the nearest I can come to it is to explain it by a model, based on Melanie Klein's concept of the paranoid-schizoid position and Bion's concept of the 'mother capable of containing projective identification'. In this model, the infant's relation to his first object can be described as follows: When an infant has an intolerable anxiety, he deals with it by projecting it into the mother. The mother's response is to acknowledge the anxiety and do whatever is necessary to relieve the infant's distress. The infant's perception is that he has projected something intolerable into his object, but the object was capable of containing it and dealing with it. He can then reintroject not only his original anxiety but an anxiety modified by having been contained. He also introjects an object capable of containing and dealing with anxiety. The containment of anxiety by an external object capable of understanding is a beginning of mental stability. This mental stability may be disrupted from two sources. The mother may be unable to bear the infant's projected anxiety and he may introject an experience of even greater terror than the one he had projected. It may also be disrupted by excessive destructive omnipotence of the infant's phantasy. In this model the analytic situation provides a container.
>
> (Segal, 1975, pp. 134–135)

The analyst is certainly one container, and mother is another, but the theory does not stop there. As is clear, anyone with a maternal aspect to his or her character who can listen (see Langs, 1978) could function in this way [*see* Reverie]. Indeed, society itself may function as an emotional container of one kind or another, more or less defensive. Jaques (1953) explored social institutions in this respect.

Although this development of the concept of projective identification was partly an effort of the whole Kleinian Group in the 1950s, Bion became its major exponent, harvesting the biggest fruits [*see* Projective identification]. The maternal mind in this state of 'reverie' performs a function to which Bion gives a neutral term – 'alpha-function' [*see* Alpha-function; Reverie].

Other non-Kleinians have introduced concepts that are related but distinct to container/contained ideas. In this category could perhaps be included Winnicott's (1967) idea of the mother 'mirroring' the infant's state. He describes the way in which the mother's face is an emotional 'mirror' for infant and child. He describes this as a method of the child's learning about his own internal states. It clearly has some sort of relationship to the kind of projective/introjective cycles that the Kleinians had been developing, although it is not the same. Another term 'holding' that should not be confused with containment is used by Winnicott 'to denote not only the actual physical holding of the infant, but also the total environmental provision prior to the concept of *living with*' (Winnicott, 1960, p. 43). It can thus be seen as a broad umbrella term, within which a specific process such as containment might be seen as being subsumed.

Bion's *theory of thinking* consists of the mating of a preconception and a realisation, the result being a conception and a step in the building of thought and theories [*see* Preconception; Thinking and knowledge]. The relation between the terms in this process is that of the container to the contained.

The mystic and the establishment: Bion (1970) applies his theory of containment to social systems in a radically different way to Jaques [*see* Social defence systems]. He regards the social group as containing the individual. This was an idea considered a long time before by Pichon-Riviere (1931) but without the theoretical back-up that Bion (1970) later possessed. A social group functions to establish a fixed social order of things (the *establishment*). This conflicts with the inspiration and originality of the individual (referred to as the *mystic*, or the genius). He has to be *contained* by the establishment of the group. Often the individual's creativity is crushed by the rigidity of the system 'by compression or denudation'; alternatively certain special individuals erupt in the group, which goes to pieces under their influence (Bion cites Jesus within the constraints of Israel). A final possibility is the mutual adaptation of one to the other, with a development of both the individual and the group. These ideas expand upon and develop one element of his previous theory of groups [*see* Basic assumptions] – the pairing group, in which the pair is the container and the contained.

Thus the outcome is detrimental to the contained, or to the container, or mutually developing to both. Bion saw this social application of the theory of containers as only one level, with similar patterns of containing recurring at the level of the individual containing himself. As an example of an individual struggling to contain himself, he cited the stammerer attempting to contain his emotions in words. Ultimately Bion was working with the idea of the sexual union of the penis contained in the vagina, experienced in all forms of joining and linking. The problems that such a relationship throws up in terms of Klein's early stages of the Oedipus complex affect the linking of all mental problems [*see* Combined parent figure; Linking; Oedipus complex].

When contact between patient and analyst is stultified, the lack of spontaneous moments – which are replete with catastrophe – is an important cause of failure of a psychoanalytic treatment:

The patient will be at a loss to convey his meaning, or the meaning he wishes to convey will be too intense for him to express properly, or the formulation will be so rigid that he feels that the meaning conveyed is devoid of any interest or vitality. Similarly the interpretations given by the analyst, 'the contained', will meet with the apparently co-operative response of being repeated for confirmation, which deprives 'the contained' of meaning either by compression or denudation. Failure to observe or demonstrate the point may produce an outwardly progressive but factually sterile analysis. The clue lies in the observation of the fluctuations which make the analyst at one moment 'the container' and the analysand 'the contained', and at the next reverse the roles . . . The more familiar the analyst becomes with the configuration 'container' and 'contained', and with events in the session that approximate to these two representations, the better.

(Bion, 1970, p. 108)

Without a recognition of the reciprocity, the damaging aspects of the container/contained relationship are likely to crop up unheeded.

Psychic change: Bion had been interested for a long time in the nature of psychic change. His work on the nature of thinking had established the way in which projective-identification-like linking between mental elements gradually built up a thinking apparatus that effected the transmutation of emotional experience into cognitive activity [*see* Thinking and knowledge]. This apparatus for thinking is equally a container of emotional states. It entails the generation of theories with which to think. Development entails the development of this containing, thinking apparatus. However, he was struck by the need in analysis to understand change, and to recognise that it involved unsettling the container of emotional states. He began to look outside psychoanalysis, to other sciences, to examine the conditions for change to take place in theories. He called theories – and all other entities contained in the mind – conjunctions of events: theories are regular conjunctions. Changing the structure of the thinking apparatus therefore demands a destructuring of the theories and a re-establishing of new conjunctions.

This is an activity closely in line with Stokes's (1955) description of the artistic process and might be taken as a general psychic process. Bion did indeed turn this into a general psychic process, and related it to the essentials of Kleinian theory. The restructuring is a process of fragmentation, and Bion designated it as a manifestation of paranoid-schizoid processes. In line with Segal (1952) he placed the restructuring as a part of the depressive position. Change therefore involves oscillations between the paranoid-schizoid and depressive positions – he represented this as Ps↔D [*see* Ps↔D]. These oscillations, however, make severe emotional demands. To sustain the restructuring means sustaining anxieties about disintegration of the mind and gives rise to Bion's view that change involves a potential catastrophe. On the other hand, the restructuring entails all the emotions of the depressive position in relation to a damaged object demanding repair. The capacity to develop entails a process of *catastrophic change* and the capacity to withstand and contain the elements of the process that represent annihilation and death.

Bion, W. (1959) 'Attacks on linking', *Int. J. Psycho-Anal.* 30: 308–315; republished in *Second Thoughts*. London: Heinemann (1967), pp. 93–109.

—— (1962a) 'A theory of thinking', *Int. J. Psycho-Anal.* 33: 306–310.

—— (1962b) *Learning from Experience*. London: Heinemann.

—— (1970) *Attention and Interpretation*. London: Tavistock.

Caper, R. (1999) *A Mind of One's Own*. London: Routledge.

Jaques, E. (1953) 'On the dynamics of social structure', *Hum. Relat.* 6: 3–23.

Langs, R. (1978) *The Listening Process*. New York: Jason Aronson.

Pichon-Riviere, E. (1931) 'Position du problème de l'adaptation réciproque entre la société et les psychismes exceptionnels', *Rev. Fr. Psychanal.* 2: 135–170.

Rosenfeld, H. (1952) 'Notes on the analysis of the superego conflict in an acute catatonic schizophrenic', *Int. J. Psycho-Anal.* 33: 111–131; republished in *Psychotic States*. London: Hogarth Press (1965), pp. 63–103.

Segal, H. (1952) 'A psycho-analytic approach to aesthetics', *Int. J. Psycho-Anal.* 33: 196–207.

—— (1975) 'A psycho-analytic approach to the treatment of schizophrenia', in *The Work of Hanna Segal*. New York: Jason Aronson (1981), pp. 131–136.

Stokes, A. (1955) 'Form in art', in Klein et al. (eds) *New Directions in Psychoanalysis*. London: Tavistock, pp. 406–420.

Winnicott, D. (1960) 'The theory of the parent–infant relationship', in *The Maturational Processes and the Facilitating Environment*. London: Hogarth Press, pp. 37–55.

—— (1967) 'Mirror-role of mother and family in child development', in *Playing and Reality*. London: Tavistock (1971), pp. 111–118.

Contempt

Contempt is one of the triad of key features in the manic defences; the other two are control and triumph (Segal, 1964). Contempt is linked to the defensive (manic) denial of the importance of the object whose value is denigrated (Klein, 1935, 1940). As such it is specifically aimed against one's grateful reliance on one's object, which, if felt and acknowledged, gives rise to feelings of dependence and smallness and undermines one's feeling of control and omnipotence.

See Depressive position; Gratitude; Manic defences

Klein, M. (1935) 'A contribution to the psychogenesis of manic-depressive states', in *The Writings of Melanie Klein*, Vol. 1. London: Hogarth Press, pp. 262–289.
—— (1940) 'Mourning and its relation to manic-depressive states', in *The Writings of Melanie Klein*, Vol. 1. London: Hogarth Press, pp. 344–369.
Segal, H. (1964) *Introduction to the Work of Melanie Klein*. London: Heinemann.

Controversial Discussions (1941–1945)

During the 1920s and 1930s the British Psychoanalytical Society had developed a characteristic style of psychoanalytic theory and practice. This came into conflict with Viennese psychoanalysis. The differences broke out in bitterness in 1926–1927 over Klein's practice of child psychoanalysis using play therapy [*see* Child analysis] but died down with a tendency for the two societies to ignore each other's diverging viewpoints. This was temporarily addressed when Ernest Jones in London and Paul Federn in Vienna began to arrange what were intended to become regular Exchange Lectures between the two Societies. Jones gave the first lecture in 1935 in Vienna (Jones, 1936) and Joan Riviere gave the second in 1936, also in Vienna (Riviere, 1936); Waelder's lecture in 1936 in London was followed by Waelder's response to Riviere, published in 1937 (Waelder, 1937). But by this time the political situation in Europe was deteriorating and the psychoanalytic conflict arrived literally on the doorstep of the British Psychoanalytical Society in 1938 when the Viennese psychoanalysts were forced to emigrate. Freud and Anna Freud came to London and formed the focus of a Viennese group of analysts in London who were opposed to Klein's views. They formed an opposition group together with certain British analysts, notably Edward Glover and Melitta Schmideberg (Klein's daughter), who had become disaffected with Klein's theories after Klein's introduction of the concept of the depressive position in 1935 (Steiner, 1985).

The events that occurred between the Viennese, the small group of Kleinians and the much larger group of British analysts have been comprehensively described by Pearl King and Riccardo Steiner in *The Freud–Klein Controversies 1941–45* (King and Steiner, 1989), which describes in meticulous and scholarly detail the discussions that took place in the British Psychoanalytical Society over the question of whether the ideas introduced by Melanie Klein deviated from Freud's basic propositions so much that they could no longer be considered to be psychoanalysis. The differences at this stage were not specifically about child analysis but centred more around Klein's ideas about the early Oedipus complex, early object relations and unconscious phantasy. A truce was eventually arranged, with an agreement to a series of monthly scientific meetings to discuss the controversial aspects of Klein's theories.

The main Kleinian paper, 'The nature and function of phantasy', was given by Susan Isaacs, whose sophistication and power of argument appear to have surprised the Viennese. Anna Freud and several other Viennese analysts played a vigorous role in the discussion, as did Edward Glover and Melitta Schmideberg. (Edward Glover's view of Klein's approach is described in Glover, 1945.) Eminent 'non-aligned' analysts (meaning neither Kleinian nor Viennese Freudian) also made notable contributions to the discussion. Somewhat later, other papers were given by Paula Heimann ('Certain functions of projection and introjection in early infancy'), by Heimann and Isaacs ('Regression') and by Klein herself ('The emotional life of the infant with special reference to the depressive position'), although by this time Glover had resigned and the Viennese had left the discussions (temporarily) so that the discussions were no longer controversial. These Kleinian papers were eventually published in *Developments in Psycho-Analysis* (Klein, Heimann, Isaacs and Riviere, 1952).

In addition to the papers on Klein's ideas, the membership discussed questions of training, technique and the future structure of the British Psychoanalytical Society. In 1942 Klein's main opponent, Edward Glover, had resigned from the Society when he realised that he would not be acceptable to the general membership as a future President. Melitta Schmideberg went to the United States.

Sylvia Payne, a longstanding 'non-aligned' British analyst, became President of the British Psychoanalytical Society in 1944. Under her skilful guidance a structure was devised that contained what developed into the Society's three 'Groups': a small group of Kleinians, a relatively small group of Anna Freud and the Viennese (whom Sylvia Payne had persuaded to return to the Society) and a comparatively large group of non-aligned analysts who were for some time called the 'Middle' Group and eventually the 'Independent' Group.

From 1945 onwards, an informal 'Gentleman's Agreement', originally arrived at by three women (Sylvia Payne, Melanie Klein and Anna Freud), made an attempt to achieve equality of membership on committees and in the scientific life of the Society. By 2005 the Society decided that it no longer needed to govern itself in this manner. By this time the Kleinian Group had grown considerably in size and was approximately the same size as the Independent Group. The Contemporary Freudian group is about half the size of the other two. Individual members of each group continue to develop their ideas in their own way.

See Oedipus complex; Unconscious phantasy

Glover, E. (1945) 'Examination of the Klein system of child psychology', *Psychoanal. Study Child* 1: 1–43.

Jones, E. (1936) 'Early female sexuality', *Int. J. Psycho-Anal.* 16: 262–273.

King, P. and Steiner, R. (1989) *The Freud–Klein Controversies 1941–5*. London: Routledge.

Klein, M., Heimann, P., Isaacs, S. and Riviere, J. (1952) *Developments in Psycho-Analysis*. London: Hogarth Press.

Riviere, J. (1936) 'On the genesis of psychical conflict in earliest infancy', *Int. J. Psycho-Anal.* 17: 395–422.

Steiner, R. (1985) 'Some thoughts about tradition and change arising from an examination of the British Psycho-Analytical Society's Controversial Discussions', *Int. Rev. Psycho-Anal.* 12: 27–71.

Waelder, R. (1937) 'The problem of the genesis of psychical conflict in earliest infancy', *Int. J. Psycho-Anal.* 18: 456–473.

Countertransference

Countertransference was thought by both Freud and Klein to be a misperception of the patient caused by the analyst's psychopathology (Freud, 1910, 1914–1915; Klein, 1957; Melanie Klein Archive, C72, Wellcome Library).

Countertransference then underwent a redefinition in the 1950s to mean all the analyst's perceptions of the patient, accurate as well as distorted. Paula Heimann's groundbreaking paper of 1950, 'On counter-transference', defines countertransference as 'an instrument of research into the patient's unconscious' and says that '. . . the analyst's countertransference is not only part and parcel of the analytic relationship, but it is the patient's *creation*, it is a part of the patient's personality'. She does not, however, think of the patient's projective identification as the stimulus for the analyst's countertransference, as projective identification is a concept that she never uses. At this same time, Heinrich Racker was also asserting that countertransference had 'specific characteristics . . . from which we may draw conclusions about the specific character of the psychological happenings in the patient' (Racker, 1953b, p. 129).

Heimann and Racker were not alone. Ferenczi (1919) had described the offputting quality of the analyst who defends himself against any countertransference, and Fenichel (1941) also criticised the 'blank screen' view of the analyst's role. There was a gradual and developing tendency for countertransference to be thought of as a possible source of information about the patient (Winnicott, 1947; Berman, 1949; Little, 1951; Gitelson, 1952; Reich, 1952; Weigert, 1952).

Heimann (1950, 1960) and Racker (1953a), however, draw attention to the aspect of countertransference that is a *specific* response to the patient, and distinguish it clearly from the intrusion of the analyst's own neurosis and neurotic transference into the psychoanalytic work. This significant idea, though rejected by Klein herself, was specifically acknowledged by Rosenfeld (1952) and by Bion (1955).

Normal projective identification and the analyst as container: Subsequently Money-Kyrle (1956) and later Bion (1959) formulate clear pictures of the analyst as a container for the patient's difficult experiences, which, through the analytic process of putting experience into words, are thereby *contained*. In Bion's conception of the interaction between infant as projector and mother as container, the infant cries and thus performs a form of projective communication in which his distress is actually felt (introjected) by the mother. If she is a capable mother and in reasonably good form at the moment she can do mental work inside herself to define the problem and to find what is needed to deal with it. This is an important ego function involved in mothering [*see* Reverie]. The process of defining the distress and dealing with it is communicated in the act of caring for the infant – say by soothing and feeding him. This is a form of projecting back (reprojecting) the distress in the form of an action that shows that the distress has been understood and alleviated.

The child, once the mother has begun to provide and minister to his distress, can then take back his experience of distress – reintroject it – but now in a modified form. It is now an understood experience and in the interaction between the intrapsychic worlds of these two people, mother and baby, meaning has been generated. By introjecting this understood experience the infant can come to acquire the understanding that the mother has: for example, if mother is accurate, he can realise through her ministrations that a certain experience means hunger. The accumulated occasions on which experiences have been understood begin to amount to an acquisition, inside the baby himself, of an internal object that has the capacity to understand his experiences. This, as Segal puts it, 'is a beginning of mental stability' (Segal, 1975, p. 135). Segal described this mother–child interaction as a model for the therapeutic endeavour of the analyst [*see* Container/contained].

Normal and defensive countertransference: One of the problems in using countertransference in this way is the status of the analyst's feelings: whether they lead him to understand the patient or whether they result in his defensive evasion of his own feelings, with subsequent harm to the progress of the analysis. Money-Kyrle expresses this problem well when he describes 'normal countertransference'. When the process of analysis is going well, he says:

> . . . there is a fairly rapid oscillation between introjection and projection. As the patient speaks, the analyst will, as it were, become introjectively identified with him, and having understood him inside, will reproject him and interpret. But what I think the analyst is most aware of is the projective phase – that is to say, the phase in which the patient is the representative of a former immature or ill part of himself, including his damaged objects, which he can now understand and therefore treat by interpretation, in the external world.
>
> (Money-Kyrle, 1956, pp. 331–332)

However, Money-Kyrle goes on to say, this is '. . . normal only in the sense of being an ideal. . . . his [the analyst's] understanding fails whenever the patient corresponds too closely with some aspect of himself which he has not yet learned to understand' (p. 332). In this case the analyst fails, by reason of his own neurosis, to comprehend the patient. This becomes apparent to the analyst as the feeling '. . . that the material has become obscure'. This causes strain for the analyst, and is an event to which the patient also responds. The strain and anxiety tend, Money-Kyrle says, to diminish further the capacity to understand, and a vicious circle sets in. It is at these points that the traditional concept of countertransference comes in – the interference by the analyst's own personal difficulties in the course of his understanding of the patient's difficulties. The analyst:

> . . . may become conscious of a sense of failure as the expression of an unconscious persecutory or depressive guilt . . . when that interplay between introjection and projection breaks down, the analyst may tend to get stuck in one or other of these two positions; and what he does with his guilt may determine the position he gets stuck in. In accepting the guilt, he is likely to get stuck with an introjected patient. If he projects it, the patient remains an incomprehensible figure in the external world.
>
> (Money-Kyrle, 1956, p. 334)

This framework provides a clear view of what can go wrong with countertransference. Little (1951), Gitelson (1952) and many others have speculated on a particular method of getting out of this entrapment with one's own unconscious: by confiding one's mistake to the patient. But this method is condemned by Heimann (1960) as burdening the patient with the analyst's own personal matters. Money-Kyrle also argued, with clinical illustration, that the confession may amount to a collusion with the patient's projections. If the analyst has failed to understand, the patient is in a position to project into the analyst an impotent part of himself, so a subsequent attitude of contrition and humility on the analyst's part is not necessarily taken by the patient in the way it is intended by the analyst. The patient may instead take the analyst's attitude as confirmation of the projected impotence. Money-Kyrle describes a patient who responded to the analyst's loss of understanding by:

> . . . behaving as if he had taken from me what he felt he had lost, his father's clear, but aggressive, intellect, with which he attacked his impotent self in me. By this time, of course, it was useless to try to pick up the thread where I had first dropped it. A new situation had arisen which had affected us both. And before my patient's part in bringing it about could be interpreted, I had to do a silent piece of self-analysis

involving the discrimination of two things which can be felt as very similar: my own sense of impotence at having lost the thread, and my patient's contempt for his impotent self, which he felt to be in me. Having made this interpretation to myself, I was eventually able to pass the second half of it on to my patient, and, by so doing, restored the normal analytic situation.

(Money-Kyrle, 1956, pp. 336–337)

The process described here by Money-Kyrle involves a cycle of projective identification into the analyst followed by the analyst's modification (silent piece of self-analysis) and the re-projection to the patient in the form of the analyst's interpretation, for possible re-introjection by the patient.

The interplay of transference and countertransference: Money-Kyrle's view of countertransference developed the Kleinian idea of transference [*see* Transference]. With the idea of projective identification the analyst is more than just misperceived by the patient:

> We see the patient not only as perceiving the analyst in a distorted way, reacting to this distorted view, and communicating these reactions to the analyst, but as also doing things to the analyst's mind, projecting *into* the analyst in a way which affects the analyst.
>
> (Segal, 1977, p. 82)

Joseph (1975) has considerably refined the idea of the analyst's sensitivity to the patient's enactments in the transference [*see* Acting-out/acting-in]. She describes the analyst's own experience as very important in sensing how the patient is 'drawing the analyst in':

> . . . how our patients act on us for many varied reasons; how they try to draw us into their defensive systems; how they unconsciously act out with us in the transference, trying to get us to act out with them; how they convey aspects of their inner world built up from infancy – elaborated in childhood and adulthood, experiences often beyond the use of words, which we can only capture through the feelings aroused in us, through our counter-transference.
>
> (Joseph, 1985, p. 62)

This increased sensitivity has enabled analysts to make headway with difficult 'unreachable' borderline patients who 'seem stuck' [*see* Pathological organisations; Psychic equilibrium].

Projective counter-identification: Grinberg (1962), endorsed by Segal (1977), uses the term 'projective counter-identification' to describe a process in which the analyst becomes identified with what the patient has projected into him. He says:

> In previous papers I have dealt with some changes in the analytic technique resulting from the analysand's massive use of projective identification. The excessive use of this mechanism, in certain situations, gives rise to a specific reaction in the analyst, who is unconsciously and passively 'led' to play the sort of role the patient hands over to him. For this particular reaction, I suggested the term 'projective counter-identification'.
>
> (Grinberg, 1962, p. 436)

Grinberg believes that this analytic response is caused by the violence of the patient's projection, not by the analyst's own susceptibilities. He believes that *any* analyst would react in the same way to such massive projective identification, although other authors have doubted this assertion on the grounds that there is no evidence to assume that Grinberg is right in assuming that *all* analysts would react in the way Grinberg describes (Finell, 1986). Grinberg thinks that the violence of the patient's projection is caused by 'an exaggerated intensity of its emotional charges or to the violence with which this same mechanism was imposed on him [the patient] during childhood' (Grinberg, 1962, p. 436).

The analyst's mind as the patient's object: In recent years it has steadily emerged how sensitive patients are to the analyst's feelings and the analyst's methods of coping with those feelings, defensive or otherwise. Because one of the implications of the cycle of projective and introjective identifications is that the process of modification is in the analyst, who is required to have the stability of mind to cope with extremely difficult anxieties without becoming overly disturbed himself, it is in fact the patient's perceptions of the analyst's ability to modify anxiety that is really the important component. Rosenfeld (1987) and many others have drawn attention to this. For example, in discussing timing of interpretations, Rosenfeld writes:

> In some situations one can interpret *too* quickly what one has recognized, with the result that the patient experiences what is said as a rejection of him . . . the analyst has been experienced concretely as expelling the projected feelings and so expelling the patient as well.
>
> (Rosenfeld, 1987, p. 16)

Brenman Pick, in a detailed examination of this issue, stated: 'The patient receiving an interpretation will "hear" not only words or their consciously intended meaning. Some patients indeed only listen to the "mood" and do not seem to hear the words at all' (Brenman Pick, 1985, p. 158). In discussing a very disturbed patient, Brenman Pick emphasised that this problem '. . . involves a massive effort in managing one's feelings, and that even in so ill a patient, enquiry was, I believe, being made into the question of how I coped with my feelings' (p. 163). The significant external object for the patient is a mental one, not a physical one; it is the analyst's mind and the way it works [*see* Container/contained; Reverie].

Working through in the countertransference: The countertransference is now considered to be an important instrument for understanding the transference; the idea of the analyst as having experiences that he has to work through for himself in his own mind has continued to develop, and it is now understood that the mind of the analyst, with its fallibilities as well as its capacity to make accurate interpretations, is an extremely important aspect of the *total situation* (Joseph, 1985). Previously (in the 1940s and 1950s) the patient's objects in analysis were mainly thought of as parts of the analyst's body (especially the breast and penis). More recently it has been thought that the part-objects to which the patient relates and into which he or she projects are parts of the analyst's mind. As Brenman Pick puts it:

> I have been trying to show that the issue is not a simple one; the patient does not just project into an analyst, but instead patients are quite skilled at projecting into particular aspects of the analyst . . . into the analyst's wish to be a mother, the wish to be all-knowing or to deny unpleasant knowledge, into his instinctual sadism, or into his defences against it. And above all he or she projects into the analyst's guilt, or into the analyst's internal objects.
>
> (Brenman Pick, 1985, p. 161)

The patient's acute awareness of the analyst's mind and its contents and functioning led Brenman Pick to describe the psychoanalytic encounter thus: 'If there is a mouth that seeks a breast as an inborn potential, there is, I believe, a psychological equivalent, i.e. a state of mind which seeks another state of mind' (p. 157) [*see* Technique].

Berman, L. (1949) 'Counter-transferences and attitudes of the analyst in the therapeutic process', *Psychiatry* 12: 159–166.

Bion, W. (1955) 'Language and the schizophrenic', in M. Klein, P. Heimann and R. Money-Kyrle (eds) *New Directions in Psycho-Analysis*. London: Tavistock, pp. 1220–1239.

—— (1959) 'Attacks on linking', *Int. J. Psycho-Anal.* 40: 308–315; republished in *Second Thoughts*. London: Heinemann (1967), pp. 93–109.

Brenman Pick, I. (1985) 'Working through in the counter-transference', *Int. J. Psycho-Anal.* 66: 157–166.

Fenichel, O. (1941) *Problems of Psycho-Analytic Technique*. New York: Psycho-Analytic Quarterly Inc.

Ferenczi, S. (1919) 'On the technique of psychoanalysis', in *Further Contributions to Psychoanalysis*. London: Hogarth Press, pp. 177–188.

Finell, J. S. (1986) 'The merits and problems with the concept of projective identification', *Psychoanal Rev*. 73: 103–128.

Freud, S. (1910) 'The future prospects of psycho-analysis', *S.E. 11*. London: Hogarth Press, pp. 144–145.

—— (1914–1915) 'Papers on technique', *S.E. 12*. London: Hogarth Press, pp. 83–173.

Gitelson, M. (1952) 'The emotional position of the analyst in the psychoanalytic situation', *Int. J. Psycho-Anal*. 33: 1–10.

Grinberg, L. (1962) 'On a specific aspect of countertransference due to the patient's projective identification', *Int. J. Psycho-Anal*. 43: 436–440.

Heimann, P. (1950) 'On counter-transference', *Int. J. Psycho-Anal*. 31: 81–84.

—— (1960) 'Counter-transference', *Br. J. Med. Psychol*. 33: 9–15.

Joseph, B. (1975) 'The patient who is difficult to reach', in P. Giovacchini (ed.) *Tactics and Techniques in Psycho Analytic Therapy*, Vol. 2. New York: Jason Aronson, pp. 205–216.

—— (1985) 'Transference: The total situation', *Int. J. Psycho-Anal*. 66: 447–454; reprinted in E. B. Spillius (ed.) *Melanie Klein Today*, Vol. 2. London: Routledge (1988), pp. 61–72.

Klein, M. (1957) 'Envy and gratitude', in *The Writings of Melanie Klein*, Vol. 3. London: Hogarth Press, pp. 176–235.

Little, M. (1951) 'Counter-transference and the patient's response to it', *Int. J. Psycho-Anal*. 32: 32–40.

Money-Kyrle, R. (1956) 'Normal counter-transference and some of its deviations', in *The Collected Papers of Roger Money-Kyrie*. Strath Tay: Clunie Press (1978), pp. 330–342.

Racker, H. (1953a) 'A contribution to the problem of countertransference', *Int. J. Psycho-Anal*. 34: 313–324.

—— (1953b) 'The meaning and uses of countertransference', read at a meeting of the Argentine Psychoanalytic Association in May 1953. Reprinted in *Transference and Countertransference*. London: Karnac (1982), pp. 127–173.

Reich, A. (1952) 'On counter-transference', *Int. J. Psycho-Anal*. 32: 25–31.

Rosenfeld, H. (1952) 'Notes on the psycho-analysis of the superego conflict in an acute catatonic schizophrenic', *Int. J. Psycho-Anal*. 33: 111–131.

—— (1987) *Impasse and Interpretation*. London: Tavistock-Routledge.

Segal, H. (1975) 'A psycho-analytic approach to the treatment of schizophrenia', in *The Work of Hanna Segal*. New York: Jason Aronson (1981), pp. 131–136.

—— (1977) 'Counter-transference', *Int. J. Psycho-Anal. Psychother*. 6: 31–37; republished in *The Work of Hanna Segal*. New York: Jason Aronson (1981), pp. 81–87.

Weigert, E. (1952) 'Contribution to the problem of terminating psychoanalysis', *Psychoanal. Q*. 21: 465–480.

Winnicott, D. W. (1947) 'Hate in the counter-transference', in *Collected Papers: Through Paediatrics to Psycho-Analysis*. London: Hogarth Press, pp. 194–203.

Creativity

The creative achievements of human beings, who are endowed, at the outset of life, with base instincts, were always of interest to Freud. He coined the term 'sublimation' to denote the transforming of a basic instinct for bio-logical satisfaction into a form of conduct and civilised achievement in the 'sublime' and non-physical world of symbols. Klein's work introduces further subtleties and complexities into the issue of creativity, to which there are several strands.

Reparation: Klein writes a note about the creative process in 1929, describing it in relation to a destructive attack in phantasy, on or by persecutors. The creative effort was a subsequent attempt to restore the damage to objects felt to be external or internal. In that paper Klein uses the term 'reparation' for the first time, and thereafter creativity in Kleinian writings has tended to be seen as a manifestation of reparation. The concept of reparation gained considerably in its significance when Klein introduced the idea of the depressive position [*see* Depressive position; Reparation]. Much of subsequent Kleinian interest in aesthetics (Segal, 1952, 1974; Stokes, 1955) has focused on the key role of reparation [*see* Symbol formation].

In creativity the libidinal drives outweigh the destructive ones. In the process of investigating the nature of thought and of theory creation, Bion (1962) described, in his own terminology, the kind of unconscious activity that he discerned in Poincaré's account of scientific creativity, which entailed a loosening of all the links that bind the elements into a theory, with a subsequent re-patterning around a new focal point, for which Bion took from Poincaré the term 'the selected fact'. In this Bion saw a process that he described as a movement towards the paranoid-schizoid position (loosening of integration) followed by the reorganising around a new point, a nipple, that brings the parts together again in a movement back towards the depressive position. He represented this by the symbol Ps↔D [*see* Ps↔D].

Play: In her early work Klein dwells a great deal on the nature of play as an *externalisation of phantasy activity*, particularly unconscious phantasy. Unconscious phantasy is the basic building block of the mind itself [*see* Unconscious phantasy] and represents not only the unfolding of instinctual impulses within the mental field, but also the attempts to overcome the conflicts and pain to which the instinctual drives give rise. The process of externalisation is part of this activity to create a more congenial psychical world. In the act of play, therefore, the child – and, indeed, the playful adult – is rehearsing, in a public and symbolic way, much of the basic pain of the human situation and exploring new solutions for it. The act of play itself is thus a creative process. Part of this process is the search for new objects towards which some of the impulses can be turned, thereby diminishing the internal tensions and conflicts.

Winnicott (1971) emphasises the importance of play in his particular way, in order to distinguish his views from the Kleinian stress on destructiveness. Referring to Klein's stress on reparation, Winnicott writes: 'In my opinion Klein's important work does not reach to the subject of creativity itself' (Winnicott, 1971, p. 70). Play, in his view, is included within the category of transitional phenomena, a concept Klein herself did not use.

Linking: In addition, in Freud's recasting of his instinct theory, the libido (life instincts) acquired characteristics beyond just the sexual, and these included a synthetic function of bringing things together – the paradigm, of course, being the coming together of partners in intercourse. This aspect of creativity has been stressed more by Meltzer (1973) in describing the structure of the personality as given by the internal parents in a creative relationship inside the individual. He describes this as a god-like presence inside each person from which derives a sense of creativeness, which can inspire the individual to his own constructive and creative efforts, and the important aspect of the personality is the relationship the individual has with his internal copulating parental couple [*see* Combined parent figure; Linking].

Bion, W. (1962) Learning *from Experience*. London: Heinemann.
Klein, M. (1929) 'Infantile anxiety-situations reflected in a work of art and in the creative impulse', in *The Writings of Melanie Klein*, Vol. 1. London: Hogarth Press, pp. 210–218.
Meltzer, D. (1973) *Sexual States of Mind*. Strath Tay: Clunie Press.
Segal, H. (1952) 'A psycho-analytic approach to aesthetics', *Int. J. Psycho-Anal.* 33: 196–207.
—— (1974) 'Delusion and artistic creativity', *Int. Rev. Psycho-Anal.* 1: 135–141.
Stokes, A. (1955) 'Form in art', in M. Klein, P. Heimann and R. Money-Kyrle (eds) *New Directions in Psycho-analysis*. London: Tavistock (1955), pp. 406–420.
Winnicott, D. W. (1971) *Playing and Reality*. London: Tavistock.

Criminality

Freud (1916) described certain kinds of characters who persistently behave in self-defeating ways. Typically he pointed out how *criminality* is an externalisation of guilt from unconscious sources [*see* Unconscious guilt]. Between 1916 and 1924 Freud drew particular attention to the importance of unconscious guilt. Klein was occupied with the exceptional degrees of violence she found in the play of quite ordinary children, with their responses to it and with their struggles to curb these impulses in themselves.

During her dispute with Anna Freud about child analysis (Freud, 1927) [*see* Child analysis] she reported the case of a child who showed strong violent tendencies in his phantasies, together with a harshly inhibiting superego (Klein, 1927) [*see* Unconscious guilt]. Klein was interested in the fact that the worst violent crimes committed by adults often resemble the phantasy wishes that children enact in their play. In both cases she realised that a process of externalisation (into play or into actual crime) often corresponded with Freud's view of criminals from an unconscious sense of guilt, and that this externalisation was a way of mitigating the internal violent conflict between these destructive, sadistic wishes and the equally harsh superego prohibitions. The external action allows the real world to reassure the ego that the harsh and violent retaliatory threats are not as fearful as the internal ones, that the external superego is not so omnipotent and can be fooled and that, in the case of play, new phantasies can be generated that will ameliorate the violence [*see* Superego].

In this way Klein also confirmed Freud's view that criminal tendencies did result from an internal situation of guilt arising from a superego of extraordinary harshness; and she remarked on the closeness of these unconscious levels of guilt to the paranoia of psychotic patients [*see* Aggression; Psychosis; Superego].

Freud, A. (1927) *The Psychoanalytic Treatment of Children*. London: Imago (1946).
Freud, S. (1916) 'Some character-types met with in psycho-analytic work: III Criminals from a sense of guilt', *S.E. 14*. London: Hogarth Press, pp. 332–333.
—— (1920) 'Beyond the pleasure principle', *S.E. 18*. London: Hogarth Press, pp. 1–64.
Klein, M. (1927) 'Criminal tendencies in normal children', in *The Writings of Melanie Klein*, Vol. 1. London: Hogarth Press, pp. 170–185.

Death instinct

This concept has been and remains the focus of controversy. From the start Jones (1935) places views about the death instinct on his list of the important differences between the British and Viennese Societies. One aspect of this debate concerns Freud's view of its significance and many of the papers written on the subject contain references to Freud, as if thereby proving or disproving the concept's validity. Isaacs in a reply in 1943 during the Controversial Discussions states:

> Freud opened up many possible lines of research, not all of which have been taken up and explored by every psychoanalyst. Notably his views on the death instinct and his concept of incorporated objects have been left on one side or rejected by many workers.

> . . . again, I do most definitely claim that Melanie Klein's views are derived from Freud's own theories and observations. They are in large part identical with his. Where they differ they are a necessary development of his work.
>
> (King and Steiner, 1991, p. 377)

The concept is beset by confusion, which is in part due to the way in which the death and life instincts are fused and defused (see below) with the result that the presence of the death instinct is inferred from the observation of a number of different mental states and activities. All of the following, for example, can be suggestive of the presence of the death instinct: a fear of falling apart and disintegrating, self destructiveness, destructiveness, innate hostility to the outside world, envy, sadism, and strong and aggressive libidinal desires.

Freud: Freud's theories are concerned with conflict. Initially he reasons that the child's sexual impulses are in conflict with society, he then considers the conflict to be between the sexual instincts or libido and the ego instincts but, finally, having come to the view that the ego instincts and libidinal instincts are different versions of the same instinct, he argues that the conflict is between the life instinct that strives for survival and the death instinct that seeks for dissolution [*see* Instincts].

Freud introduces the idea of the death instinct in 1920 in 'Beyond the pleasure principle' as a biological drive and expands on its psychological significance in 1923 in 'The ego and the id'. His view is that under the influence of the life instinct some of the death instinct is deflected out in the form of an attack on the object. A statement of his ideas is contained in the passage below:

> Besides the instinct to preserve living substance and to join it into ever larger units, there must exist another, contrary instinct seeking to dissolve those units and to bring them back to their primaeval inorganic state. That is to say, as well as Eros there was an instinct of death. The phenomena of life could be explained from the concurrent or mutually opposing action of these two instincts . . . a portion of the [death] instinct is diverted towards the external world and comes to light as an instinct of aggressiveness and destructiveness. In this way the instinct itself could be pressed into the service of Eros, in that the organism was destroying some other thing, animate or inanimate instead of destroying its own self. Conversely, any restriction of this aggressiveness directed outwards would be bound to increase the self-destruction, which is in any case proceeding. At the same time one can suspect from this example that the two kinds of instinct seldom – perhaps never – appear in isolation from each other, but are alloyed with each other in

varying and very different proportions and so become unrecognizable to our judgment. In sadism, long since known to us as a component of sexuality, we should have before us a particularly strong alloy of this kind between trends of love and the destructive instinct; while its counterpart, masochism, would be a union between destructiveness directed inwards and sexuality – a union which makes what is otherwise an imperceptible trend into a conspicuous and tangible one.

(Freud, 1930, p. 119)

As can be seen from the above, some death instinct is thought to remain within and some of this remaining death instinct is fused with libido to form sexual masochism. Other fusions occur, resulting for example in 'moral masochism'. Not all the death instinct is fused; some remains unfused as primal sadism (Freud, 1924, p. 164). Furthermore, sometimes instincts become defused:

So far as the psycho-analytic field of ideas is concerned, we can only assume that a very extensive fusion and amalgamation, in varying proportions, of the two classes of instincts takes place, so that we never have to deal with pure life instinct or pure death instincts but only with mixtures of them in different amounts.

Corresponding to a fusion of instincts of this kind, there may, as a result of certain influences, be a *de*fusion of them. How large the portions of the death instincts are which refuse to be tamed in this way by being bound to admixtures of libido we cannot at present guess.

(Freud, 1924, p. 164)

Freud writes about the superego of the melancholic as follows 'What is now holding sway in the super-ego is, as it were, a pure culture of the death instinct' (1923, p. 53) and describes it as 'a kind of gathering-place for the death instincts' (1923, p. 54). Freud argues that this is in part the result of defusion of the instincts following the desexualisation of the relationship with the father in the resolution of the Oedipus complex.

Klein

Precursors to Klein's adoption of the theory of the death instinct; sadism: Klein's interest begins in her work with children and in her observation of the presence of extremely harsh and punitive attitudes in the children themselves and in the figures in their imagination. Klein considers the harsh internal figure to be the introjected hostile mother whose hostility towards the child stems from the sadistic phantasised attacks that the child has made on her. Klein views this hostile internal mother as an early version of the superego, a superego that precedes the resolution of the Oedipus complex (here Klein begins to depart from Freud's theory and comes into direct conflict with Anna Freud) [*see* Superego].

Klein's adoption of the idea of the death instinct: In 1932 in *The Psychoanalysis of Children*, Klein adopts Freud's ideas about the life and death instincts but she disagrees with the idea that no fear of death exists in the unconscious; for her the fear of death is the primordial fear and she believes the newborn infant to be in danger of being flooded by this terrible anxiety: 'We know however, that the destructive instinct is directed against the organism itself and must therefore be regarded by the ego as a danger. I believe it is this danger which is felt by the individual as anxiety' (Klein, 1932, p. 126). Furthermore: 'I hold that anxiety arises from the operation of the death instinct within the organism, is felt as fear of annihilation (death) and takes the form of fear of persecution' (Klein, 1946, p. 4).

Klein provides vivid descriptions of children's phantasies to illustrate how she understands their experience of this internal danger. One child, for example, feels that he has fierce animals inside him who help him against his enemies but who could turn against him and attack him from within, and another child imagines his excreta to be offensive weapons but fears that they will destroy his body. Klein also draws attention to the expression 'to burst with rage' (1932, p. 127).

Death instinct and the paranoid-schizoid position: Klein agrees with Freud's idea that a part of the death instinct is thrust out by the infant and she too thinks that some remains within. Klein's theory of development starts with an unintegrated ego with a tendency towards integration and also a tendency towards disintegration. The ego's first act is the projection of the life and death instincts into the object. Klein uses the term projection whereas Freud uses the term deflection. In a late paper she spells out with clarity how she sees the difference; for her, projection involves both the attribution of death instinct to the object and also a conversion of the remaining death instinct into aggression that is directed towards the now persecutory object:

> Here I differ from Freud in so far as it seems that Freud understood by deflection only the process whereby the death instinct directed against the self is turned into aggression against the object. In my view, two processes are involved in that particular mechanism of deflection. Part of the death instinct is projected into the object, the object thereby becoming a persecutor; while that part of the death instinct which is retained in the ego causes aggression to be turned against that persecutory object.
>
> (Klein, 1958, p. 238)

The projection of the two instincts results in the object being split into a 'good' and a 'bad' part. These 'part-objects' now containing 'good' and 'bad' parts of the self are introjected into the ego, which, if not already split, now splits in relation to the object – the object cannot be split without a corresponding split in the ego (1946, p. 6). Klein believes this 'binary' splitting of the ego and object to be an essential step in bringing order into the situation and a vital developmental step [*see* Paranoid-schizoid position].

The relative strength of the integrating life instinct against the disintegrating death instinct, as well as the capacity of the mother or caretaker to help the infant manage his persecutory anxieties and destructive feelings, will determine whether life instincts and integration or death instincts and splitting dominate [*see* Depressive position]. When the death instinct is in the ascendant the ego is weakened by the 'bad' object relationship, is increasingly unable to integrate and may split into small pieces or fragment: 'The breast taken in with hatred, and therefore felt to be destructive becomes the prototype of all bad internal objects, drives the ego to further splitting and becomes the representative of the death instinct inside' (Klein, 1955, p. 145).

The death instinct and envy; frustration, greed and envy: Klein considers that frustration and greed increase the tendency of the infant to attack the object, thereby reducing the chance of the presence of a 'good' object available for introjection. In her later work she draws particular attention to constitutional envy. Envy has the aim of destroying the good object by both destructive introjection and destructive projection, and in Klein's view envy is a manifestation of the death instinct [*see* Envy]: 'I consider that envy is an oral-sadistic and anal-sadistic expression of destructive impulses, operative from the beginning of life, and that it has a constitutional basis' (Klein, 1957, p. 176).

The destructive internal object (superego): In Klein's theory the early extremely 'good' and 'bad' objects are introjected into both the ego and the superego. The resulting early superego, which contains unfused life and death instincts as well as the early extreme introjects, is very severe. Over time, via the processes of introjection and projection, the internal objects mingle not only with each other but also with subsequently introjected objects, and if all goes well they gradually modify. However, Klein repeatedly finds that the superego of her patients is extremely resistant to change, it remains harsh and does not modify, and in 1957 she refers to an 'envious' superego (p. 231).

Later developments: Despite uncertainties – for example Money-Kyrle (1955) in his paper 'An inconclusive contribution to the theory of the death instinct' finds the different characteristics attributed to the death instinct hard to reconcile with one another – and despite criticisms such as those of Kernberg (1969, 1980), Kleinian analysts make use of the concept of the death instinct in their clinical writings.

Death instinct, envy and the fragmenting superego: Many writers highlight the presence of a destructive fragmenting internal agent based on the death instinct, often referring to it as a manifestation of envy and as a kind of superego. Klein herself changes her theory in 1958, removing the extreme early introjects from the superego and placing them in the deep unconscious where they remain out of reach and unmodified. Whatever the location of this destructive presence, and whatever it is called, there is considerable agreement of there being a destructive anti-life or life-hating force that has the upper hand in some patients and in some cases can induce psychosis. Rosenfeld (1952) refers to a superego that is responsible for ego-splitting and psychosis, and Bion (1957) describes the psychotic individual's use of fragmentation to destroy the apparatus of awareness and thus avoid painful emotion. In 'Attacks on linking' (1959) Bion refers to what he calls an 'ego-destructive superego' that attacks the ego function of linking. O'Shaughnessy (1999) outlines the difference between a normally severe and an abnormal superego [*see* Superego]. In her paper 'On the clinical usefulness of the concept of the death instinct' written in 1987 and published in 1997, Segal outlines her view of this fragmenting activity:

> Birth confronts us with the experience of needs. In relation to that experience there can be two reactions, and both, I think, are invariably present in all of us, though in varying proportions. One, to seek satisfaction for the needs: that is life-promoting and leads to object seeking, love, and eventually object concern. The other is the drive to annihilate: the need to annihilate the perceiving experiencing self, as well as anything that is perceived.
>
> (Segal, 1997, p. 18)

Segal makes the link with envy:

> There is an intimate link between the death instinct and envy. If the death instinct is a reaction to a disturbance produced by needs, the object is perceived both as disturbance, the creator of the need, and as the unique object, capable of disturbance removal. As such, the breast is hated and envied. And one of the pains that has to be avoided by self-annihilation and object annihilation is the pain caused by the awareness of the existence of such an object.
>
> (Segal, 1997, p. 24)

Bion (1959, p. 106) and Segal (1997) make the point that both constitutional and environmental factors contribute to the formation of this
deadly internal force:

> An objection to the concept of the death instinct which is often put
> forward is that it ignores the environment. This is certainly incorrect,
> since the fusion and the modulations of the life and death drives, which
> will determine the eventual development are part of developing rela-
> tionships to the early objects and, therefore, the real nature of the
> environment will deeply affect the process.
>
> (Segal, 1997, p. 25)

The structural organisation of the death instinct and perversion: Many papers
draw attention to a personality structure in which an internal organisation
derives perverse satisfaction from attacking the good parts of the ego.
Rosenfeld (1971) uses the term 'negative narcissism', by analogy with
Freud's (1914) theory of the turning of the libido towards the self in his
descriptions of narcissism:

> When he is faced with the reality of being dependent on the analyst,
> standing for the parents, particularly the mother, he would prefer to die,
> to be non-existent, to deny the fact of his birth, and also to destroy his
> analytic progress and insight representing the child in himself, which he
> feels the analyst, representing the parents, has created . . . As the
> individual seems determined to satisfy a desire to die and to disappear
> into nothing, which resembles Freud's description of 'pure' death
> instinct, one might consider that we are dealing in these states with the
> death instinct in complete defusion. However, analytically one can
> observe that the state is caused by the activity of destructive envious
> parts of the self which become severely split off and defused from the
> libidinal caring self which seems to have disappeared. The whole self
> becomes identified with the destructive self . . . It appears that these
> patients have dealt with the struggle between their destructive and
> libidinal impulses by trying to get rid of their concern and love for their
> objects by killing their loving dependent self and identifying themselves
> almost entirely with the destructive narcissistic part of the self which
> provides them with a sense of superiority and self-admiration.
>
> (Rosenfeld, 1971, pp. 173–174)

[*See* Envy; Narcissism; Pathological organisations; Perversion; Structure;
Superego.]

Differences in conceptualization of the death instinct: A degree of uncertainty
and a lack of uniformity remain in regard to the death instinct. Britton

(2003, pp. 3–4) prefers to think in terms of an original destructiveness that is turned outwards from the start, an anti-object relational force that may also turn inwards to attack object attachments in the mind, including the mental and perceptual capacities. He refers to a 'destructive instinct' rather than to a death instinct and he separates this from the fear of annihilation that he considers to be more a fear of falling apart than a fear of death (R. Britton, 2005, unpublished). Rosenfeld, Bion and Segal, like Britton, suggest an anti-object relational force involving destructive attacks on both the self and on the object. Rosenfeld and Britton differentiate situations in which the primary motivation is defensive and to do with an obliteration of painful awareness – an activity to do with getting rid of an experience – from those in which the motivation is to gain the pleasure of triumphing over the object – an activity to do with having an experience. Rosenfeld suggests that some patients prefer death to being helped by the analyst. Segal thinks that pleasure in triumphing over life and the object is always present but she and Rosenfeld think in terms of fusion of life and death instincts:

> Libidinalization is always present as part of fusion of the life and death instincts. But fusion can take many different forms. In healthy development the fusion of the life and death instinct is under the aegis of the life instinct, and the deflected death instinct, aggression, is at the service of life. Where the death instinct predominates the libido is at the service of the death instinct. This is particularly evident in perversions.
>
> (Segal, 1997, p. 23)

In contrast, Feldman in his paper 'Some views on the manifestation of the death instinct in clinical work' (2000) rejects the idea that this kind of perverse excitement is to do with a fusion between the instincts. He has the view that the death instinct does not drive towards death but actually requires that the victim be kept alive to gain satisfaction from the repeated triumph over developmental forces by 'attacking spoiling and undermining' (2000, p. 64).

See Perversions

Bion, W. (1957) 'Differentiation of the psychotic from the non-psychotic personalities', *Int. J. Psycho-Anal.* 38: 266–275.
—— (1959) 'Attacks on linking', *Int. J. Pscho-Anal.* 40: 308–315; also in *Second Thoughts.* London: Karnac (1984), pp. 93–109.
Britton, R. (2003) *Sex, Death, and the Superego.* London: Karnac.
Feldman, M. (2000) 'Some views on the manifestation of the death instinct in clinical work', *Int. J. Psycho-Anal.* 81: 53–65.
Freud, S. (1914) 'On narcissism'. *S.E. 14.* London: Hogarth Press, pp. 67–104.

—— (1920) 'Beyond the pleasure principle', *S.E. 18*. London: Hogarth Press, pp. 7–64.

—— (1923) 'The ego and the id', *S.E. 19*. London: Hogarth Press, pp. 12–96.

—— (1924) 'The economic problem of masochism', *S.E. 19*. London: Hogarth Press, pp. 157–170.

—— (1930) 'Civilization and its discontents', *S.E. 21*. London: Hogarth Press, pp. 57–175.

Jones, E. (1935) 'Early female sexuality', *Int. J. Psycho-Anal.* 16: 263–273.

King, P. and Steiner, R. (1991) *The Freud–Klein Controversies 1941–45*. London: Routledge.

Klein, M. (1932) *The Psychoanalysis of Children. The Writings of Melanie Klein*, Vol. 2. London: Hogarth Press.

—— (1946) 'Notes on some schizoid mechanisms', in *The Writings of Melanie Klein*, Vol. 3. London: Hogarth Press, pp. 1–24.

—— (1955) 'On identification, in *The Writings of Melanie Klein*, Vol. 3. London: Hogarth Press, pp. 141–175.

—— (1957) 'Envy and gratitude', in *The Writings of Melanie Klein*, Vol. 3. London: Hogarth Press, pp. 176–235.

—— (1958) 'On the development of mental functioning', in *The Writings of Melanie Klein*, Vol. 3. London: Hogarth Press, pp. 236–246.

Money-Kyrle, R. (1955) 'An inconclusive contribution to the theory of the death instinct', in D. Meltzer (ed.) *The Collected Papers of Roger Money-Kyrle*. Strath Tay: Clunie Press (1978), pp. 285–296.

O'Shaughnessy, E. (1999) 'Relating to the superego', *Int. J. Psycho-Anal.* 80: 861–870.

Rosenfeld, H. (1952) 'Notes on the psycho-analysis of the superego conflict of an acute schizophrenic patient', *Int. J. Psycho-Anal.* 33: 111–131.

—— (1971) 'A clinical approach to the psycho-analytical theory of the life and death instincts: an investigation into the aggressive aspects of narcissism', *Int. J. Psycho-Anal.* 52: 169–178.

Segal, H. (1997) 'On the clinical usefulness of the concept of the death instinct', in J. Steiner (ed.) *Psychoanalysis, Literature and War*. London: Routledge, pp. 17–26.

Defence mechanisms

Developmental and anti-developmental defences: Defences are paradoxical in that they are an essential aspect of human psychological activity; they can foster development or they can hinder it. Defences may start off by providing protection for the ego but if never given up they can interfere with healthy development. For example, in Klein's theory of the 'paranoid-schizoid position', the achievement of binary splitting of the self and object into 'good' and 'bad' protects the fragile immature ego and is a prerequisite for ego organisation and healthy development. However, if splitting is rigidly retained and knowledge of reality defended against, splitting is destructive of development.

Instinctual impulse, basic mental function and defence: Some of the mental activities used for defence are fundamental to mental functioning. Ferenczi, Freud and Abraham describe defences involving the activity of instinctual impulses: 'projection', depending on anal expelling; 'introjection', depending on oral incorporating. Klein too thinks of projection and introjection as the way in which the individual relates to his objects and to the world; they are the mechanisms involved in building up the internal world and are the basis of all cognitive and emotional activity, exploration, knowledge and symbol formation [*see* Internal objects; Projective identification; Symbol formation; Unconscious phantasy].

Freud: Freud initially describes defence as 'fending off', particularly in the case of hysteria – the fending off of sexual impulses by 'repressing' all knowledge of them. For some time Freud virtually equates the terms defence and repression, although he also writes about 'conversion' in hysteria (1905), speaks of 'isolation' and 'regression' and of symbolic doing and undoing and isolation in the Rat Man's obsessional neurosis (1909b), of projection when discussing paranoia and projection and 'displacement' in little Hans' phobia (1909a). In the case of Schreber, Freud (1911) maps out the different strategies of projection and identification and he also mentions the projection of an internal catastrophe into a delusion of the end of the world. Eventually, in 1926, Freud defines 'defence' as the general term and 'repression' as a particular instance of it (Freud, 1926, p. 163). He also suggests the possibility of an earlier defence than repression (p. 164) and in his later papers (1927, 1940) he writes about 'disavowal' – a splitting of the ego; the idea of splitting is one that had occurred earlier in Freud's writing [*see* Splitting]. Freud also implies that defences are directed against aggressive as well as against libidinal impulses, as in the case of Little Hans (1909a). However, Little Hans' expression of defence against his aggressive impulses was somewhat indirect; he was not directly anxious about his own aggression, he was anxious about being punished for it by his father. And one could argue that his fear about his aggressive impulses only arose because of his libidinal impulses towards his mother.

Klein: In her first paper (1921) Klein suggests a protective splitting of the object. This is something that she returns to later. Between 1924 and 1926 in the analysis of the 6-year-old girl Erna, Klein finds that the presenting obsessional neurosis covers underlying paranoia. She goes on to conclude that the degree of oedipal sadism that she observes in many children causes them extreme anxiety, necessitating defensive activity aimed at getting rid of the sadism and destroying the persecuting parental object.

Developmental stage and defence: By 1932 Klein takes the view that the 'early' defence mentioned by Freud is specifically against the death instinct.

In 1946 with the introduction of her theory of the paranoid-schizoid position, splitting and projection (projective identification) and introjection are the first 'defensive' acts of the ego. The death instinct, which threatens to overwhelm the ego, is split off and projected out into the object, the life instinct is similarly projected out into the object and a 'good' and a 'bad' object are introjected. Klein brings in these object-relating defences at a stage in infant development that had been thought by Freud to be objectless. These defences are contrasted with repression and referred to as 'early', 'psychotic' or 'primitive'.

Klein divides these primitive defences into two constellations that she calls 'positions':

- *Defences of the paranoid-schizoid position.* These defences are omnipotent and are against the death instinct and the anxiety of annihilation; they include splitting (both binary splitting and fragmentation), denial, idealisation, projective identification and introjection. Klein often describes these defences as extreme and severe, although it is not clear whether she means extreme in amount or in degree [*see* Denial; Idealisation; Introjection; Paranoid-schizoid position; Projective identification; Splitting].
- *Defences of the depressive position.* These defences are against feelings of loss of, and guilt about damage to, the 'whole' object; they include manic defences involving triumph over and contempt for the object and obsessional defences involving control of the object. Included also is the return to earlier defences, for example the paranoid defence against depressive guilt that involves splitting and denial. Omnipotence is a feature in these defences but omnipotence is gradually given up in the depressive position [*see* Denial; Depressive position; Idealisation; Introjection; Obsessional defences; Projective identification; Splitting].

Although initially chronological in terms of development, there is a to-and-fro between the positions and there is an increasing interest in the oscillation between them. Both Bion (1970) and Britton (1998) take the view that a 'retreat' to paranoid-schizoid functioning is necessary for development and could therefore be considered more as an advance than a retreat. Klein has little to say about the 'neurotic' defence of repression but she is clear that it is a part of whole-object relating when greater integration of the self and object has been achieved and splitting has lessened [*see* Repression].

Defence and the structure of the ego: Freud had suggested that the only way in which the ego might be able to give up its objects is by taking them in and identifying with them. Introjection and identification can alter the structure of the ego, as in Freud and Klein's theories of superego formation and in Klein's theory of the splitting and fragmentation of the ego in the paranoid-schizoid position. Significantly for Klein, the introjected 'good' object becomes the core around which the ego coheres [*see* Death instinct; Depressive position; Fragmentation; Internal objects; Superego].

Unconscious phantasy and defence: Phantasies are involved in both the processes of defence against anxiety and in the content of the anxiety defended against. For example, an individual may have the phantasy of having a persecutor within (and may experience this concretely) and may defend himself with an unconscious phantasy of splitting off and ejecting this persecutor by a particular means, for example through the anus or through the eyes. This will leave the individual feeling depleted and weak. Thus phantasies are developed, unconsciously, to defend against other phantasies – a confusion pointed to and elucidated by Segal (1964). In the early stages of life, phantasies are omnipotent; the individual believes in the material reality of the phantasy and phantasies may be experienced as somatic sensations and also somatic sensations may be stimulated or simulated [*see* Masturbation phantasies; Unconscious phantasy].

Defensive systems and pathological organisations: A considerable amount of attention has been given to the way in which defences are often organised, making them highly resistant to treatment [*see* Pathological organisations]. Many writers, in particular Joseph (1981), have shown how the analyst can be drawn into acting a part in the patient's defensive system [*see* Betty Joseph; Projective identification].

Bion, W. (1970) *Attention and Interpretation*. London: Tavistock.
Britton, R. (1998) 'Before and after the depressive position: Ps(n)→D(n)→Ps(n+1)', in *Belief and Imagination*. London: Routledge, pp. 69–81.
Freud, S. (1905) 'Fragment of an analysis of a case of hysteria', *S.E. 7*. London: Hogarth Press, pp. 7–112.
—— (1909a) 'Analysis of a phobia in a five year old boy', *S.E. 10*. London: Hogarth Press, pp. 3–149.
—— (1909b) 'Notes upon a case of obsessional neurosis', *S.E. 10*. London: Hogarth Press, pp. 151–318.
—— (1911) 'Psychoanalytic notes on an autobiographical account of a case of paranoia', *S.E. 12*. London: Hogarth Press, pp. 3–82.
—— (1926) 'Inhibitions, symptoms and anxiety', *S.E. 20*. London: Hogarth Press, pp. 75–174.
—— (1927) 'Fetishism', *S.E. 21*. London: Hogarth Press, pp. 149–157.
—— (1940) 'Splitting of the ego in the process of defence', *S.E. 23*. London: Hogarth Press, pp. 271–278.
Joseph, B. (1981) 'Defence mechanisms and phantasy in the psychoanalytic process', *Bull. Eur. Psycho-Anal. Fed.* 17: 11–24.

Klein, M. (1921) 'The development of a child', in *The Writings of Melanie Klein*, Vol. 1. London: Hogarth Press, pp. 1–53.

—— (1926) 'The psychological principles of early analysis', in *The Writings of Melanie Klein*, Vol. 1. London: Hogarth Press, pp. 128–138.

—— (1932) *The Psychoanalysis of Children*. The Writings of Melanie Klein, Vol. 2. London: Hogarth Press.

—— (1946) 'Notes on some schizoid mechanisms', in *The Writings of Melanie Klein*, Vol. 3. London: Hogarth Press, pp. 1–24.

Segal, H. (1964) *Introduction to the Work of Melanie Klein*. London: Heinemann.

Denial

Like other primitive defence mechanisms, denial refers to a defensive activity of an early, primitive and violent kind. Freud (1927) describes the term 'scotomization' as referring to the obliteration of something that has been perceived and he differentiates this from repression and disavowal. For Klein, denial seems to contain elements of 'scotomization' and 'disavowal'. Denial is involved in the process of binary splitting when the 'bad' aspects of the object are disposed of and denied, leaving an unblemished 'good' or idealised object (Rosenfeld, 1983). She thinks denial is connected with phantasies of' annihilation of the unwanted part of the object and also of the ego that perceives it (Klein, 1946) [*see* Annihilation; Splitting]. In this sense denial is omnipotent and violent and differs from repression, which tends to be thought of as a removal from consciousness of the reality or memory of an internal or external event or experience in which both the subject and object remain intact. However, the way the terms are used often lacks precision, with a tendency for Kleinians to use the terms 'splitting' and 'denial' and for classical Freudians to refer to 'repression' [*see* Paranoid-schizoid position; Primitive defence mechanisms; Repression; Splitting].

Denial is specifically involved in the manic defences (Klein, 1935), in which denying the limitations of the self and the importance of the objects on which the subject actually depends are key elements.

See Depressive position; Manic defences; Narcissism; Pathological organisations

Freud, S. (1927) 'Fetishism', *S.E. 21*. London: Hogarth Press, pp. 149–157

Klein, M. (1935) 'A contribution to the psychogenesis of manic-depressive states', in *The Writings of Melanie Klein*, Vol. 1. London: Hogarth Press, pp. 262–289.

—— (1946) 'Notes on some schizoid mechanisms', in *The Writings of Melanie Klein*, Vol. 3. London: Hogarth Press, pp. 1–24.

Rosenfeld, H. (1983) 'Primitive object relations and mechanisms', *Int. J. Psycho-Anal.* 64: 261–267.

Denigration

See Contempt; Manic defences

Depersonalisation

A schizoid state of ego disintegration that features being cut off from one's sense of self or one's sense of being connected to the outside world. Klein (1946) makes a link between excessive projective identification and splitting and states of ego disintegration. Rosenfeld (1947) shows how splitting mechanisms and projective identification underlie his patient's states of depersonalisation. Klein elaborates further the effects of intrusive projective identification on the ego, which may lead to the sense that parts of self are felt to reside outside the newly appropriated identity. She does so by reference to a novel by Julian Green, called *If I Were You* (Klein, 1955).

See Paranoid-schizoid position; Projective identification

Klein, M. (1946) 'Notes on some schizoid mechanisms', in *The Writings of Melanie Klein*, Vol. 3. London: Hogarth Press, pp. 1–24.
—— (1955) 'On identification', in *The Writings of Melanie Klein*, Vol. 3. London: Hogarth Press, pp. 141–175.
Rosenfeld, H. (1947) 'Analysis of a schizophrenic state with depersonalisation', *Int. J. Psycho-Anal.* 28, 130–139.

Depletion

Projection depletes the ego (in phantasy) of that which is projected and affects the way in which the individual interacts with his or her objects. For example, in cases of excessive (pathological) projective identification, the self, depleted of aggression, feels weak. The phantasy of the ego spread around in other objects leaves a sense of emptiness and the individual feels unable to withstand anxiety. This leads to further projective defences, which impair the introjection and assimilation of good and supporting objects, and the individual instead feels overwhelmed by them. 'Depletion' is a term that is descriptive of the patient's experience of the process that results in depersonalisation.

See Projective identification; Depersonalisation

Depressive anxiety

Both Segal (1979) and Grosskurth (1986) suggest that the development of Klein's understanding of depressive anxiety – the characteristic pain of the depressive position – was stimulated by her own bereavement at her son's death in 1933.

The loved good object and its loss: In two papers (1935, 1940) Klein concerns herself with manic-depressive states and with mourning. Starting with the views of Freud and Abraham that these states result from the experience of losing a loved object, Klein's contribution is:

- To show that the loss is felt, in phantasy, to be related to the individual's sadistic impulses, which are felt to have successfully injured or damaged the loved object. Experiences of loss and mourning in Klein's view echo the sense of damage and loss during the infantile depressive position [*see* Depressive position].
- To elaborate Freud's (1926) description of 'the loss of the loved object' by showing how the experience of loss importantly includes, in phantasy, the loss of the loved good *internal* object:

> The poignancy of the actual loss of a loved person is, in my view, greatly increased by the mourner's unconscious phantasies of having lost his *internal* 'good' objects as well. He then feels that his internal 'bad' objects predominate and his internal world is in danger of disruption.
>
> (Klein, 1940, p. 353)

The loved good internal object that is so threatened in states of mourning arises during development from the introjection of an external object with which the ego gradually identifies:

> As the ego becomes more fully organized, the internal imagos (the introjected parents and the basis for the superego) will approximate more closely to reality and the ego will identify itself more fully with 'good' objects. The dread of persecution, which was at first felt on the ego's account, now relates to the good object as well and from now on preservation of the good object is regarded as synonymous with the survival of the ego.
>
> (Klein, 1935, p. 264)

The ego begins to relate to the whole object, which alters the experience of loss:

> Hand in hand with this development goes a change of the highest importance; namely, from a partial object-relation to the relation to a complete object . . . the ego arrives at a new position, which forms the

foundation of the situation called the loss of the loved object. Not until the object is loved as *a whole* can its loss be felt as a whole.

(Klein, 1935, p. 264)

The nature of depressive anxiety: In 'Mourning and its relation to manic-depressive states' Klein writes:

> . . . there are two sets of fears, feelings and defences [which] can, for purposes of theoretical clearness, be isolated from each other. The first set of feelings and phantasies are the persecutory ones . . . The second set of feelings which go to make up the depressive position I formerly described without suggesting a term for them. I now propose to use for these feelings of sorrow and concern for the loved objects, the fear of losing them and the longing to regain them, a simple word derived from everyday language – namely 'pining' for the loved object. In short – persecution (by 'bad' objects) and the characteristic defences against it, on the one hand, and pining for the loved ('good') object, on the other, constitute the depressive position.

> (Klein, 1940, p. 348)

The term 'pining' has come to be used less in the literature than the terms 'guilt' or 'depressive anxiety'. It is not in fact clear if these two terms are synonymous:

> The question now arises: is guilt an element of depressive anxiety? Are they both aspects of the same process, or is one a result or a manifestation of the other? . . . I cannot at present give a definite answer.

> (Klein, 1948, p. 36)

Klein's contemporary Joan Riviere gives an especially poignant description of depressive anxiety in her paper 'A contribution to the analysis of the negative therapeutic reaction':

> . . . all one's loved ones *within* are dead and destroyed, all goodness is dispersed, lost, in fragments, wasted and scattered to the winds; nothing is left *within* but utter desolation. Love brings sorrow, and sorrow brings guilt; the intolerable tension mounts, there is no escape, one is utterly alone, there is no one to share or help.

> (Riviere, 1936, p. 313)

Another moving, more contemporary account of the anxieties, bearable and unbearable, of the depressive position is given by Priscilla Roth (2005).

Persecutory and depressive anxieties: The distinction between persecutory and depressive anxieties is clearer in theory than in practice. Depressive anxiety depends on whether the:

> anxiety is mainly related to the preservation of the ego – in which case it is paranoiac – or to the preservation of the good internalized objects with which the ego is identified as a whole . . . The anxiety lest the good objects and with them the ego should be destroyed, or that they are in a state of disintegration, is interwoven with continuous and desperate efforts to save the good objects.
>
> (Klein, 1935, p. 269)

Klein finds that the simple equation of persecutory anxiety with part-objects and depressive anxiety with whole objects cannot be sustained:

> My further work . . . has led me to the conclusion that though in the first stage destructive impulses and persecutory anxiety predominate, depressive anxiety and guilt already play some part in the infant's earliest object-relation, i.e. in his relation to his mother's breast . . . That is to say I now link the onset of depressive anxiety with the relation to part-objects. The modification is the result of . . . a fuller recognition of the gradual nature of the infant's emotional development.
>
> (Klein, 1948, pp. 35–36)

Psychosis, envy and depressive anxiety: Klein describes a particularly persecutory form of guilt when envy is abnormally high:

> It appears that one of the consequences of excessive envy is an early onset of guilt. If premature guilt is experienced by an ego not yet capable of bearing it, guilt is felt as persecution and the object that arouses guilt is turned into a persecutor. The infant then cannot work through either depressive or persecutory anxiety because they become confused with each other.
>
> (Klein, 1957, p. 194)

Segal (1956), analysing schizophrenics, shows clearly that schizophrenics have a capacity to experience depression in spite of their fixation in the paranoid-schizoid position. Their recourse is immediate fragmentation and projection of the fragments of themselves when they are endangered by depressive feelings. The consequent deterioration of their own mental state is linked with the analyst experiencing the projected despair and depression for the patients.

Defences against guilt and depressive anxiety: There are various defences that are specific against guilt and depressive anxiety. One of the more frequent forms of defence is the angry _turning away from the object_, a mechanism that may accelerate the oedipal turning away from the breast or from mother and lead to problems with the new object. Another common mechanism referred to in Klein's earlier papers is the _externalisation_ of the superego, as a relief from internal persecution and guilt.

Perhaps the major defence against depressive anxiety is the _reversion to a paranoid relation_ to the object [_see_ Paranoid defence against depressive anxiety]. In the earliest stages of the depressive position, guilt is so painful that it is experienced as a deliberate persecution, and this is the basis of this reversion.

Important defences against depressive anxiety are gathered together in a group and referred to as the _manic defences_ [_see_ Manic defences]. In 1935 Klein described these comprehensively for the first time. The ego's:

> . . . torturing and perilous dependence on its loved objects drives the ego to find freedom. But its identification with these objects is too profound to be renounced . . . The sense of omnipotence, in my opinion, is what first and foremost characterizes mania.
>
> (Klein, 1935, p. 277)

The manic defences comprise: omnipotence, which tinges all the others; denial of psychic reality, with a consequent tendency to denial of external reality; denial of the importance of the good objects; and a phantasy of control and mastery of objects upon which the ego is dependent.

Reparation: It is through true reparation, as opposed to manic or obsessional reparation, that the individual is able to work through depressive anxiety [_see_ Manic reparation; Reparation].

Freud, S. (1926) 'Inhibitions, symptoms and anxiety', _S.E. 20_. London: Hogarth Press, pp. 77–175.

Grosskurth, P. (1986) _Melanie Klein_. London: Hodder & Stoughton.

Klein, M. (1935) 'A contribution to the psychogenesis of manic-depressive states', in _The Writings of Melanie Klein_, Vol. 1. London: Hogarth Press, pp. 262–289.

—— (1940) 'Mourning and its relation to manic-depressive states', in _The Writings of Melanie Klein_, Vol. 1. London: Hogarth Press, pp. 344–389.

—— (1948) 'On the theory of anxiety and guilt', in _The Writings of Melanie Klein_, Vol. 3. London: Hogarth Press, pp. 25–42.

—— (1957) 'Envy and gratitude', in _The Writings of Melanie Klein_, Vol. 3. London: Hogarth Press, pp. 176–235.

Riviere, J. (1936) 'A contribution to the analysis of a negative therapeutic reaction', _Int. J. Psycho-Anal._ 17: 304–320, in A. Hughes (ed.) _The Inner World and Joan Riviere_. London: Karnac (1991), pp. 134–153.

Roth, P. (2005) 'The depressive position', in S. Budd and R. Rusbridger (eds) *Introducing Psychoanalysis: Essential Themes and Topics*. London: Routledge, pp. 47–58.

Segal, H. (1956) 'Depression in the schizophrenic', *Int. J. Psycho-Anal.* 37: 339–343.

—— (1979) *Klein*. London: Fontana.

Development

See Psychic development

Dreams

With the development of the idea of unconscious phantasy, the nature of dreams implicitly became moulded anew. Freud's classical theory regards dreams as the activity of a disturbed mind. In order to preserve sleep the sleeper constructs, in disguised form, a fanciful solution to the disturbing conflict. Dreams thus represent wish-fulfilment. Anxiety dreams, however, which wake the dreamer, seem to be a failure of the process as a result of the intensity of the disturbance.

Anxiety dreams are not such a problem for Kleinian theory. The Kleinian idea of unconscious phantasy as the ubiquitous bedrock of all mental processes gives a new view of the nature of dreams. The dream is an expression (in disguised form) of unconscious phantasy as well as of defences against their conscious appreciation. It therefore represents the unconscious phantasy of object relation as stimulated by the active impulses (good or bad) of the moment.

Bion (1962) introduces the idea of 'beta-elements' and 'alpha-function' in which raw sense data (beta-elements) are converted into 'alpha-elements', which are mental contents with meaning that can be used for thinking or dreaming [*see* Alpha-function; Wilfred Bion; Container/contained]. Meltzer (1983) following Bion regards dreams and unconscious phantasy as synonymous and considers that conscious waking life is the manifest content of a dream. In this sense dreams are the internal space '. . . where meaning is generated' (Meltzer, 1981, p. 178).

Segal (1981), also using Bion's ideas and drawing heavily on her own writing on symbolisation, differentiates dreams that are symbolic (as in Freud's theory) from those that are experienced as concrete happenings. She focuses on the function of dreams and describes patients who use their dreams for evacuation. Segal draws attention to evacuative dreams that are predictive, in that the dream is enacted in the session. Later Segal (2007) illustrates how both psychotic and non-psychotic functioning can be present in the way that dreams are brought to sessions and in the dreams themselves. She notes that it is important to distinguish between a communication and an evacuation [*see* Hanna Segal; Symbol formation].

Quinodoz (1999), in a paper that emphasises technique ('Dreams that turn over a page'), considers dreams that appear regressive but actually indicate progress in the patient's capacity to integrate hitherto expelled fragments.

Bion, W. (1962) *Learning from Experience*. London: Heinemann.
Meltzer, D. (1981) 'The Kleinian expansion of Freudian metapsychology', *Int. J. Psycho-Anal.* 62: 177–185.
—— (1983) *Dream-Life*. Strath Tay: Clunie Press.
Quinodoz, J.-M. (1999) 'Dreams that turn over a page', *Int. J. Psycho-Anal.* 80: 225–238.
Segal, H. (1981) 'The function of dreams', in *The Work of Hannah Segal*. New York: Jason Aronson, pp. 89–97.
—— (2007) 'Interpretation of dreams – 100 years on', in N. Abel-Hirsch (ed.) *Yesterday, Today and Tomorrow*. London: Routledge, pp. 14–24.

Economic model

Freud's metapsychology, the most abstract level of his theory of the mind, comprises four conceptual models: the topographical, the dynamic, the economic and the developmental. In her early work in particular Klein relies on and fully absorbs Freud's views on the centrality of unconscious phantasy in infantile mental life and in shaping the infantile sexual drive (Isaacs, 1952). She relies both on Freud's and more particularly on Abraham's developmental map of the libidinal stages. She accepts Freud's transition from the topographical to the structural theory and the accompanying change in his theory of anxiety. Klein's early work with young children leads her to enlarge considerably on the content of infantile phantasies around the maternal body and the primal scene and also on their chronology. Her developmental model becomes increasingly different from classical theory, and openly so in her views on the early Oedipus complex, and on the little girl's Oedipus complex in particular. She also elaborates the complexity of internal structure in the structural model by treating introjection and projection as basic processes of the unconscious mind and describing the central role they play in the development of the internal world and the structures of the self. Her tendency is to assert the complementarity between her emerging viewpoint and Freud's theories, even when their ideas differ considerably.

It is clear, however, although not generally emphasised, that Klein's theories, even in her early work when she was more reliant on classical theory, never make use of Freud's model of the mind as an energy system operating on closed economic lines. It is noticeable that in her entire work Klein does not make use of the economic concepts of cathexis and de-cathexis or anti-cathexis, which are central to Freud's quantitative formulation of mental processes. Freud's ideas developed in the wake of nineteenth-century physical science based on the conservation of energy. He introduced this principle into psychoanalytic psychology as *a law of the conservation of mental energy,* and his earliest work concerned the fate of the hypothetical mental energy and its quantitative distribution (Freud, 1895) [*see* Instincts]. Klein's views developed during the period when the solidity of nineteenth-century science was breaking down. It is also probable that Klein, without the influence of a scientific background, was free from the rigorous scientific baggage Freud carried with him into psychology. She did not adhere to the conservation principle of (emotional) energy. Loving and aggressive impulses can spread and multiply, as it were. Thus impulses towards external objects always 'spread' to internal objects, and vice versa. As Greenberg and Mitchell perceptively comment about Klein: '. . . love for one object does not limit, but increases love for others. In adult love, for example, the beloved is loved not instead of the original oedipal objects but in addition to them' (Greenberg and Mitchell, 1983, p. 144). In other words there is no 'law of conservation of love'.

Clifford Yorke (1971) suggests that Klein exchanged for the quantitative distribution of the libido an interest in the quantitative balance between the life and death instincts. This is not strictly true and is probably encouraged by the equally mistaken view that Klein sees all development as a pre-determined (innate) unfolding. In fact, she refers to the way in which aggressive impulses can bring out a struggle to develop loving impulses, or can be a spur to advance perhaps prematurely into the genital position. The fluidity of impulses, their multiplication and the apparently defensive manipulation of them to enhance love over aggression are outside the Freudian economic model of quantitative conservation. Her theory relies dominantly on a dynamic formulation of the mind, of its conflicts, anxieties and group of defences, and eschews the economic conceptual model.

These views were allowed to develop as a consequence of Klein's version of the nature of instincts and unconscious phantasy. As Isaacs eventually explicitly states it: 'Phantasy is (in the first instance) the mental corollary, the psychic representative, of instinct. There is no impulse, no instinctual urge or response which is not experienced as unconscious phantasy' (Isaacs, 1952, p. 83) [*see* Unconscious phantasy]. Thus what is in the mind is a 'representation', not a physical quantity or quality. This seems to fore-shadow the current interest in communication theory concerned with the distribution of information. Like information, phantasies of relationships with objects are not subject to a law of conservation.

This difference is best highlighted in Klein's seminal paper on mourning (1940). She makes a determined attempt to go beyond Freud's economic formulation of the work of mourning as a battleground between the pleasure ego, which retains its cathexes of the lost object, and the reality ego, which is able to withdraw its cathexes by submitting to the reality

judgement that the object is no more (Freud, 1917). This economic formulation left Freud unable to explain why mourning is so painful. Klein by
contrast brings mourning under the umbrella of the infantile conflicts of the
depressive position, which are evoked by loss. She links the pain of the
work of mourning directly to her dynamic understanding of what bereavement mobilises: the unconscious loss of the loved parental couple, the
depressive anxieties that ensue, the deployment of manic and obsessional
defences and the gradual reinstatement of the loved internal parents, all of
which pave the way for sadness proper. This dynamic understanding has
more bite and also more depth than Freud's economic formulations of
mourning and incidentally shows the limitations of the economic model.

Klein's implicit abandonment of the economic model seems linked with
her ability to marry drive theory with her object-relations theory and also
with her tendency throughout her work to foreground a dynamic model of
mind instead. The pleasure principle of mental functioning, which regulates
processes in the unconscious mind, stipulates that the build-up of undis-
charged excitations causes unpleasure and puts pressure on the mental
apparatus to perform a work that will discharge this mental energy in a way
that does not threaten the ego. Freud's prototype for this work remains the
dream-work. O'Shaughnessy points out that:

> Melanie Klein described something similar to the pleasure principle but
> from another perspective – an early mechanism of defence which she
> named projective identification. In her view the young infant defends his
> ego from intolerable anxiety by splitting off and projecting unwanted
> impulses and feelings, etc., into his object. This is an object-relations
> perspective on the discharge of unpleasurable tensions and stimuli.
>
> (O'Shaughnessy, 1981, p. 182)

In his theory of thinking Bion (1967) returns to the question of how we
acquire a capacity to deal with absence and frustration and to think about
experience in the face of the infant's poor ability to tolerate frustration [*see*
Container/contained; Thinking and knowledge]. He also makes use of the
concept of voiding the mind by projective identification and of the crucial
role of the mother's containing function to deal with such projections and
help the development of thoughts and thinking. Failure in containment
leads to excessive projective identification and to omnipotence, which
seriously undermines the capacity to think about experience. His theory,
however, is thoroughly dynamic and relational and eschews any economic
concept.

Bion, W. (1967) *Second Thoughts*. London: Heinemann.
Freud, S. (1895) 'Project for a scientific psychology', *S.E. 1*. London: Hogarth Press,
    pp. 283–397.

—— (1917) 'Mourning and melancholia', *S.E. 14*. London: Hogarth Press, pp. 237–258.

Greenberg, J. and Mitchell, S. (1983) *Object Relations in Psycho-Analytic Theory*. Cambridge, MA: Harvard University Press.

Isaacs, S. (1952) 'The nature and function of phantasy', in M. Klein, P. Heimann, S. Isaacs and J. Riviere (eds) *Developments in Psychoanalysis*. London: Hogarth Press (1952), pp. 67–121.

Klein, M. (1940) 'Mourning and its relation to manic-depressive states', in *The Writings of Melanie Klein*, Vol. 1. London: Hogarth Press, pp. 344–369.

O'Shaughnessy, E. (1981) 'A commemorative essay on W. R. Bion's theory of thinking', *J. Child Psychother.* 7: 181–192.

Yorke, C. (1971) 'Some suggestions for a critique of Kleinian psychology', *Psychoanal. Study Child* 26: 129–155.

Ego

There is considerable debate about the use of the term 'ego', which is a Latinisation introduced in the course of translation of Freud's work into English. From the description of the structural model of 'id', 'ego' and 'superego' onwards, there has been a tendency in classical analytic theory and in ego psychology to describe the ego in terms of mechanisms. Such a mechanistic stance appears to be in line with the original intentions that Freud set himself in his early 'Project' (Freud, 1895) but antagonistic to the more humanistic style of his literary and classical interests, of his language and of the general impulsion during the course of his career towards human experience (Freud, 1925). He came to drop the attempt to devise a neurological determinism (Schafer, 1976; Bettleheim, 1983; Steiner, 1987).

Klein does not use the term 'ego' in as precise a way as Freud came to do with his structural model of the ego, the id and the superego. She often uses 'ego' interchangeably with 'self', although in a late paper she does give her definition of both terms:

> The ego, according to Freud, is the organized part of the self, constantly influenced by instinctual impulses but keeping them under control by repression; furthermore it directs all activities and establishes and maintains the relation to the external world. The self is used to cover the whole of the personality, which includes not only the ego but the instinctual life which Freud called the *id*.
>
> (Klein, 1959, p. 249)

For Klein the ego exists at birth and it has considerable capacities. (This is in contrast to the ego psychology and self-psychology schools of thought, in which the origin of the ego is thought to occur some months after birth.) For Klein the ego at birth has a pre-existing knowledge of the breast and of the mother (Klein, 1952b, 1959). Because of the trauma of birth and the loss of the intra-uterine situation, the ego at birth suffers from persecutory anxiety (Klein, 1948, 1950, 1952a). The primal phantasies of projection and introjection begin at birth, which Klein describes as follows:

> The young infant would be in danger of being flooded by his self-destructive impulses if the mechanism of projection could not operate. It is partly in order to perform this function that the ego is called into action at birth by the life instinct. The primal process of projection is the means of deflecting the death instinct outwards. Projection also imbues the first object with libido. The other primal process is introjection, again largely in the service of the life instinct; it combats the death instinct because it leads to the ego taking in something life-giving (first of all food) and thus binding the death instinct working within.
>
> (Klein, 1958, p. 238)

It is thus apparent that Klein thinks that the newborn is capable of object relations at birth, and of recognising in phantasy and to some extent in reality the separate existence of himself and his external object. In the development of the ego, its relationship with the good object is crucial: 'For I assume', Klein says, 'that the ego develops largely round this good object, and the identification with the good characteristics of the mother becomes the basis for further helpful identifications' (Klein, 1959, p. 251).

The early ego: The ego, at first, alternates between states of integration and disintegration: '. . . the early ego largely lacks cohesion, and a tendency towards integration alternates with a tendency towards disintegration, a falling to bits' (Klein, 1946, p. 4). This was described later by Bick (1968) in infants in their first week of life [*see* Esther Bick]. Whereas classical analysis is concerned with the ego as an organ that seeks discharge of the instinctual tensions in some form of satisfaction, and can be described objectively in terms of its structure and function, Klein sees the ego in a different way: as the experience it has of itself. She describes this in terms of the phantasies it has of struggling with anxieties experienced in the course of its relations with objects, which, although they are perceived in the colours of the instincts, create a world of experiences, anxieties, loves, hates and fears rather than states of discharge. The ego's struggle is to maintain its own integrity in the face of its experiences of objects that appear to threaten its annihilation but are also necessary for its survival [*see* Psychic development].

In 'Envy and gratitude' (1957) Klein describes the early functions of the ego. It deals with what Klein regards as the primordial anxiety – the death instinct within – by projection, which deflects the threat outwards. In the normal course of the paranoid-schizoid position the ego also splits the primal object, the breast, into a good breast and a bad breast and keeps the good breast apart from the bad breast, thus protecting it and enhancing the security of the ego. This 'normal' splitting makes it possible somewhat later, in the process of development of the normal depressive position, for these relatively clearly defined, separate and antagonistic objects to be recognised as different aspects of the same object (Klein, 1957, pp. 192–194) [see Splitting]. Thus, paradoxically, the early splitting of the object 'is essential for integration; for it preserves the good object and later on enables the ego to synthesize the two aspects of it' (Klein, 1957, p. 192).

Bettelheim, B. (1983) *Freud and Man's Soul*. London: Hogarth Press.
Bick, E. (1968) 'The experience of the skin in early object relations', *Int. J. Psycho-Anal.* 49: 484–486.
Freud, S. (1895) 'Project for a scientific psychology', *S.E. 1*. London: Hogarth Press, pp. 283–397.
—— (1925) 'Negation', *S.E. 19*. London: Hogarth Press, pp. 235–239.
Klein, M. (1946) 'Notes on some schizoid mechanisms', in *The Writings of Melanie Klein*, Vol. 3. London: Hogarth Press, pp. 1–24.
—— (1948) 'On the theory of anxiety and guilt', in *The Writings of Melanie Klein*, Vol. 3. London: Hogarth Press, pp. 25–42.
—— (1950) 'On the criteria for the termination of a psycho-analysis', in *The Writings of Melanie Klein*, Vol. 3. London: Hogarth Press, pp. 43–47.
—— (1952a) 'The origins of transference', in *The Writings of Melanie Klein*, Vol. 3. London: Hogarth Press, pp. 48–56.
—— (1952b) 'On observing the behaviour of young infants', in *The Writings of Melanie Klein*, Vol. 3. London: Hogarth Press, pp. 94–121.
—— (1957) 'Envy and gratitude', in *The Writings of Melanie Klein*, Vol. 3. London: Hogarth Press, pp. 176–235.
—— (1958) 'The development of mental functioning', in *The Writings of Melanie Klein*, Vol. 3. London: Hogarth Press, pp. 236–246.
—— (1959) 'Our adult world and its roots in infancy', in *The Writings of Melanie Klein*, Vol. 3. London: Hogarth Press, pp. 247–263.
Schafer, R. (1976) *A New Language for Psychoanalysis*. New Haven, CT: Yale University Press.
Steiner, R. (1987) 'A world wide international trade mark of genuineness?', *Int. Rev. Psycho-Anal.* 14: 33–102.

Ego psychology

See American psychoanalysis in relation to Klein

Empathy

Empathy is a benign form of projective identification that can be included under 'normal projective identification' [see Projective identification]. When one talks of 'putting oneself in someone else's shoes' this is a description of empathy, but it is also a description of a process of putting a part of oneself, some capacity for self-perception, into someone else's position – in particular it is an experiencing part of oneself that is inserted in order to gain an understanding, in phantasy, of their experience. There is an imaginative component to this specialised sort of projective identification, and for it to succeed there needs to be a resonance with the individual's own experience. This is a normal enough activity on the part of sensitive people, and can be loosely included within the group of phantasies of projective identification (Klein, 1959). Money-Kyrle includes empathy as part of the 'normal counter-transference' of the analyst, which helps him to gain insight about the patient (Money-Kyrle, 1956). Feldman similarly categorises empathy under projective identification of good parts of the self, projected in love. He points out, however, that even such positive projections, if carried out to excess, will impoverish the ego, which becomes too dependent on the other who contains in phantasy the good parts of the self (Feldman, 1992).

One important aspect of this empathic identificatory process is that there is no loss of reality, no confusion of identity. It should also be noted that it has a larger conscious component than many forms of projective identification. It is characteristic of the omnipotence of pathological projective identification [*see* Projective identification] that the boundaries between the self and the object are destroyed. This differs from empathy, in which a proper, realistic awareness of who and where one is at the time of projecting remains intact.

Meissner (1980), however, has argued that it is false to include empathy and other non-psychotic phenomena within the term 'projective identification'. He dismissed as confusing the broadening of the concept of 'projective identification' beyond its reference to the disturbed ego boundaries of schizophrenics.

See Concern; Projective identification

Feldman, M. (1992) 'Splitting and projective identification', in R. Anderson (ed.) *Clinical Lectures on Klein and Bion*. London: Routledge, pp. 74–88.

Klein, M. (1959) 'Our adult world and its roots in infancy', in *The Writings of Melanie Klein*, Vol. 3. London: Hogarth Press, pp. 247–263.

Meissner, W. W. (1980) 'A note on projective identification', *J. Am. Psychoanal. Assoc.* 28: 43–67.

Money-Kyrle, R. (1956) 'Normal counter-transference and some of its deviations', *Int. J. Psycho-Anal.* 37: 360–366.

Environment

See External world/environment

Epistemophilia

Freud (1916–1917) sees epistemophilia as a component instinct of the libido, related to scopophilia (voyeurism/exhibitionism). For Klein this 'part-instinct' of Freud's becomes a central instinct in its own right. The question of intellectual inhibition interested Klein from the start. In her earliest papers (1921, 1923) following Freud's model, Klein is concerned with the way sexual curiosity is inhibited by castration anxiety. However, even in 1923 her clinical approach indicates that she is aware of the inhibiting effect of aggressive phantasies. Then in 'Early stages of the Oedipus conflict' (1928), 'The importance of symbol formation in the development of the ego' (1930) and 'A contribution to the theory of intellectual inhibition' (1931) Klein shows how she sees the epistemophilic instinct as exploratory and necessary but also aggressive, involving phantasies of getting inside the mother to find, and often to take over or destroy, the riches within – notably mother's babies and father's penis. The inevitable fear of retaliation can then seriously inhibit curiosity and the capacity to learn:

> The early connection between the epistemophilic impulse and sadism is very important for the whole mental development. This instinct, activated by the rise of the Oedipus tendencies, at first mainly concerns itself with the mother's body, which is assumed to be the scene of all sexual processes and developments. The child is still dominated by the anal-sadistic libido position which impels him to wish to *appropriate* the contents of the body. He thus begins to be curious about what it contains, what it is like etc. So the epistemophilic instinct and the desire to take possession come quite early to be most intimately connected with one another and at the same time with the sense of guilt aroused by the incipient Oedipus conflict.
>
> (Klein, 1928 p. 188)

In her early work Klein relies on Abraham to formulate her phase of maximal sadism. This means that the highly sadistic phantasies she uncovers are unmitigated by love, which for Abraham comes to the fore only in the genital stage. But from 1932, when she accepts Freud's theory of the life and death instincts as a fundamental principle, she studies love and hate in interaction. In Klein's pre-1932 discussions of epistemophilia the anxieties investigated are (according to her later two categories of persecutory and depressive) essentially persecutory. Then in 'A contribution to the psychogenesis of manic-depressive states' (1935) she discusses how the capacity to learn and to work may be hampered by depression and despair about damaged objects.

Thinking and knowledge – the work of Bion: Bion (1956, 1957, 1962a) tackles the problem of the intellectual deficit in schizophrenics in a series of papers, and goes on to elaborate a theory of thinking [*see* Thinking and knowledge]. Bion's theory of thinking is intimately linked with his theory of container/contained. A mother through her reverie tries to understand her infant's experiences and feelings [*see* Container/contained; Reverie]. The infant introjects an external object (mother) who can understand and process his experiences for him and who can gradually introduce him to himself. Gradually introjected is not simply the object but the containing function itself. Thus the capacity for thought and rationality is dependent upon – in fact, emergent from – emotional life of the most early and primitive kind.

In the course of this theorising Bion elevates the epistemophilic desire for knowledge to a status equivalent to that of love and hate. He describes (1962b) emotional links between container and contained as being of three types. Thus we have not simply the usual psychoanalytic concerns of *Love* (*L*) and *Hate* (*H*), but in addition '*K*', representing a desire or a drive to know the other. For Bion, K is as essential for psychic health as is food for physical well-being, and is of paramount importance for growth and development of mind and personality. It can be seen as a more elaborated form of Klein's epistemophilic instinct. It is important to note that Bion sees both mother and infant as growing and developing from their experience together, which he describes as 'commensal'.

'Minus K' (–K): The infant may lack an adequate actual external object able or willing to take in his projective identifications and return them to him in a modified, tolerable form. The result is continued projective identifications of ever-increasing force, leading to a progressive depletion of the ego and the loss of function, with an accumulation of objects in the external world that have been increasingly violently assaulted by omnipotent projective identifications into them. Instead of an apparatus for thinking, the mind then becomes '. . . an apparatus for ridding the psyche of accumulations of bad internal objects' (Bion, 1962a, p. 112).

Bion also describes an evasion of knowing and of truth, which he calls 'minus K'. For Bion (1957) there is a dynamic conflict between two aspects of the mind. On the one hand, to the fore in psychotics but present to some extent in us all, 'the psychotic part of the personality' seeks to evade reality by evacuative projection of any painful or disturbing mental content. The non-psychotic part of the personality can bear, and seeks, truth. Bion sees truth and an accurate perception of internal and external reality as essential nourishment for the mind. An important factor in the psychotic part of the personality in Bion's view is the infant's own envy:

> . . . one wonders . . . why such a phenomenon as that represented by –K should exist. The answer to that question must be sought in psycho-analytic work with individual patients. I shall consider one factor only – Envy . . . using as a model an emotional situation in

which the infant feels fear that it is dying . . . the infant splits off and projects its feelings of fear into the breast together with envy and hate of the undisturbed breast. . . . The breast in K would moderate the fear component in the fear of dying that had been projected into it, and the infant in due course would reintroject a now tolerable and growth-stimulating part of the personality. In –K the breast is felt enviously to remove the good or valuable element in the fear of dying and force the worthless residue back into the infant. The infant who started with a fear of dying ends up by containing a nameless dread.

(Bion, 1962b, p. 96)

Whatever the balance of external and internal factors in the breakdown of the K link, the result is severe depletion of the ego and the internalisation of an object that strips and denudes of meaning; this is one version of the extremely harsh superego: 'It is an envious assertion of moral superiority without any morals' (Bion, 1962b, p. 97). Brenman (1985) gives good clinical examples of this kind of denuding, moralising and denigrating object, as does O'Shaughnessy (1999).

O'Shaughnessy (1981) can also be consulted for a good exposition of Bion's theories of 'K'.

Bion, W. (1956) 'The development of schizophrenic thought', *Int. J. Psycho-Anal.* 37: 344–346.

—— (1957) 'Differentiation of the psychotic from the non-psychotic personalities', *Int. J. Psycho-Anal.* 38: 266–275.

—— (1962a) 'A theory of thinking', *Int. J. Psycho-Anal.* 43: 306–310; republished in *Second Thoughts*. London: Heinemann (1967), pp. 110–119.

—— (1962b) *Learning from Experience*. London: Heinemann.

Brenman, E. (1985) 'Cruelty and narrow-mindedness', *Int. J. Psycho-Anal.* 66: 273–281.

Freud, S. (1916–1917) *Introductory Lectures, S.E. 15/16*. London: Hogarth Press.

Klein, M. (1921) 'The development of a child', in *The Writings of Melanie Klein*, Vol. 1. London: Hogarth Press, pp. 1–53.

—— (1923) 'The role of the school in the libidinal development of the child', in *The Writings of Melanie Klein*, Vol. 1. London: Hogarth Press, pp. 59–76.

—— (1928) 'Early stages of the Oedipus conflict', in *The Writings of Melanie Klein*, Vol. 1. London: Hogarth Press, pp. 186–198.

—— (1930) 'The importance of symbol formation in the development of the ego', in *The Writings of Melanie Klein*, Vol. 1. London: Hogarth Press, pp. 219–232.

—— (1931) 'A contribution to the theory of intellectual development', in *The Writings of Melanie Klein*, Vol. 1. London: Hogarth Press, pp. 236–247.

—— (1935) 'A contribution to the psychogenesis of manic-depressive states', in *The Writings of Melanie Klein*, Vol. 1. London: Hogarth Press, pp. 262–289.

O'Shaughnessy, E. (1981) A commemorative essay on W. R. Bion's theory of thinking', *J. Child Psychother.* 7: 181–192.

—— (1999) Relating to the superego. *International Journal of Psychoanalysis*, 80: 861–870.

External object

In Kleinian theory, as in many other psychoanalytic approaches, there is an objectively 'real' external world and external object 'out there'. However the subject's perception of the external object is coloured to a greater or lesser extent by what is projected [*see* Internal objects; External world/ environment; Projective identification]. The way that the internal colours and distorts the external is of course a central preoccupation of psycho-analysis generally. In Kleinian theory, perception of the 'real' external object will be distorted by the subject's projection onto it of aspects of himself as well as his own expectations, which will be a blend of previous experience and unconscious phantasy expectations arising from the active phantasy of the moment. In addition, depending on the strength of the phantasy, the subject will have a greater or lesser ability to see the external object as it really is or actually change the object by unconscious provocative manoeuvres to accord with his or her perceptions (see Joseph, 1985). The object's actual qualities are important in so far as they match the subject's expectations and in so far as the object has the quality to move in accord with the patient's perceptions or to resist [*see* Projective identification].

In the paranoid-schizoid position the psychic mechanisms are character-ised by omnipotence, so that projective and introjective identifications grossly distort the psychic reality of the external object. This at first is relatively unhindered until the infant begins to move towards the depressive position and, with much emotional struggle, to develop a more realistic perspective on his object [*see* Depressive position; Paranoid-schizoid position].

The external object is of course not merely the physical object but is invariably also its psychological presence: both conscious and unconscious emotional activity. For example Sandford (1952) describes an anxious patient who had introjected her mother's projected anxiety and how this is experienced in the transference relationship. Rosenfeld (1987) in Chapter 13 of *Impasse and Interpretation* discusses projections from mother to child before and after birth.

Of vital importance in Kleinian thinking are the vicissitudes of *loss* of the external object (Klein, 1940). Losses such as that of the breast in weaning, and loss of the object through separation and death, have profound effects on the subject's inner world. In Klein's view the external loss is accom-panied by loss of the internal object, which has to be painfully reinstated through the process of mourning – a process that, if it can be sustained, strengthens the ego and leads to development.

Klein, M. (1940) 'Mourning and its relation to manic-depressive states', in *The Writings of Melanie Klein*, Vol. 1. London: Hogarth Press, pp. 344–369.
Joseph, B. (1985) 'Transference: The total situation', *Int. J. Psycho-Anal.* 66: 447–454.

Rosenfeld, H. (1987) *Impasse and Interpretation*. London: Tavistock.
Sandford, B. (1952) 'An obsessional man's need to be kept', *Int. J. Psycho-Anal.* 33: 144–152.

External world/environment

> From its inception analysis has always laid stress on the importance of the child's early experiences, but it seems to me that only since we know more about the nature and content of its early anxieties, and the continuous interplay between its actual experiences and its phantasy-life, can we fully understand *why* the external factor is so important.
>
> (Klein, 1935, p. 285)

Klein's new contributions to psychoanalysis concern primarily the nature of the inner world and the role of innate factors in the personality. She is sometimes inaccurately portrayed as regarding the environment as irrelevant or unimportant. In fact the environment is as central for Klein as is the inner world; she sees the individual as, from the beginning, intimately involved with his external objects, projecting into them and introjecting them in constant cycles. The actual nature of the external world will modify the extremes of phantasy. A poor environment will be damaging, but an individual's constitution may either help him to make the best of a poor environment or influence him to make the worst of a good one. Klein's emphasis on constitution is also part of a dialectic that counters an opposite tendency in psychoanalysis to concentrate in a concrete way on the external, forgetting the centrality for psychoanalysis of *psychic* reality.

The interaction of phantasy and environment: An individual's current version of psychic reality, for Klein, exists as an internal pattern or template, an approximation to 'external reality'. It is a compound of experience and phantasy, and is constantly subject to modification through the introjection of experience. A way of conceptualising transference different from that of classical analysis follows from this: everyone, including parents, will be perceived through the distortion of transference projections, and development will involve gradual modification of this transference:

> . . . an inner world is being built up in the child's unconscious mind, corresponding to his actual experiences and the impressions he gains from people and the external world, and yet altered by his own phantasies and impulses.
>
> (Klein. 1940, p. 345)

In the process of acquiring knowledge, every new piece of experience has to be fitted into the patterns provided by the psychic reality which prevails at the time; whilst the psychic reality of the child is gradually influenced by every step in his progressive knowledge of external reality.

(Klein, 1940, p. 347)

Role of an adverse environment: A poor environment will, in Klein's view, be seriously damaging:

Unpleasant experiences and the lack of enjoyable ones, in the young child, especially lack of happy and close contact with loved people, increase ambivalence, diminish trust and hope and confirm anxieties about inner annihilation and external persecution; moreover they slow down and perhaps permanently check the beneficial processes through which in the long run inner security is achieved.

(Klein, 1940, p. 347)

In her study of the child 'Dick' (Klein, 1930), Klein suggests that some of this psychotic child's serious disturbance is linked to a rather loveless early environment with an anxious mother. In fact, taking it as a given that the environment is important, Klein's plea is for more understanding of the role of internal phantasy, which has to be addressed alongside alterations to the external world if children are to be properly helped. In a public lecture 'On criminality' in 1934, she points out:

Naturally in cases where children, not only in phantasy, but also in reality, experience some degree of persecution through unkind parents and miserable surroundings, the phantasies will be greatly reinforced. There is a common tendency to over-estimate the importance of unsatisfactory surroundings, in the sense that the internal psychological difficulties, which partly result from the surroundings, are not sufficiently appreciated, It depends, therefore, on the degree of the intra-psychical anxiety, whether or not it will avail much merely to improve the child's environment.

(Klein, 1934, p. 260)

Supporting Klein's emphasis on the internal world, Ernest Jones (1935) in 'Early female sexuality' states:

The Viennese would reproach us with estimating the early phantasy life too highly at the expense of external reality. And we should answer that there is no danger of any analyst's neglecting external reality, whereas it is always possible for them to underestimate Freud's doctrine of the importance of psychical reality.

(Jones, 1935, p. 273)

The importance of constitution: Constitutional factors may, in Klein's view, make it difficult for the individual to benefit from reality testing even when the environment is adequate:

> The extent to which external reality is able to disprove anxieties and sorrow relating to the internal reality varies with each individual, but could be taken as one of the criteria for normality.
>
> (Klein, 1940, p. 346)

> Whether feelings of frustration or gratification predominate in the infant's relation to the breast is no doubt largely influenced by external circumstances but there is little doubt that constitutional factors, influencing from the beginning the strength of the ego, have to be taken into account . . . the ego's capacity to bear tension and anxiety, and therefore in some measure to tolerate frustration, is a constitutional factor. This greater inborn capacity to bear anxiety seems ultimately to depend on the prevalence of libido over aggressive impulses.
>
> (Klein, 1952a, pp. 67–68)

Thus the individual is not simply a passive recipient of environmental influences, but has an active role in shaping his or her own development.

> . . . the impact of the environment is of major importance *at every stage* of the child's development. Even the good effect of the earliest upbringing can be to some extent undone through later harmful experiences, just as difficulties arising in early life may be diminished through subsequent beneficial influences. At the same time we have to remember that some children seem to bear unsatisfactory external conditions without severe harm to their character and mental stability, whereas in others, in spite of favourable surroundings, serious difficulties arise and persist.
>
> (Klein, 1952b, p. 96f)

> My accumulated observations, however, have convinced me that the impact of these external experiences is in proportion to the constitutional strength of the innate destructive impulses and the ensuing paranoid anxieties. Many infants have not had very unfavourable experiences and yet suffer from serious difficulties in feeding and sleeping, and we can see in them every sign of great anxiety for which external circumstances do not account sufficiently.
>
> It is also well known that some infants are exposed to great deprivations and unfavourable circumstances, and yet do not develop excessive anxieties, which would suggest that their paranoid and envious traits are not predominant.
>
> (Klein, 1957, pp. 229–230)

The need for sensitive parenting: Particularly in her public lectures (see Klein 1936, 1937) Klein stresses the need for loving, sensitive parenting of a liberal kind. She does not, however, stress conceptually the actual external parents' personalities and behaviour as part of her theoretical system. Often, particularly in the early papers, parents are implicitly included as reasonably functioning people whose behaviour mitigates the anxieties arising from the child's inherently sadistic phantasies. For example, accompanying the little girl's sadistic, early oedipal desire to rob the mother's body of its valuable contents, including father's penis, giving rise to dread of being robbed by mother in retaliation, Klein tells us that: 'The presence of the real, loving mother diminishes the dread of the terrifying mother, whose introjected image is in the child's mind' (Klein, 1929, p. 217).

However, an early paper of Klein's does refer explicitly to a child, Peter, who is severely traumatised by a cruel and deprived family environment. Already here in 1927 Klein is speculating on how the severe early superego, formed not just through internalised parents but also as a result of the child's own sadistic phantasies, may either be modified or, as in Peter's case, exacerbated by his experiences:

> Compared with the neurotic child he [Peter] had actually had experience of an overwhelming super-ego, which the other child had only evolved from inner causes. Thus it was also with his hatred, which, in consequence of his *real* experience, found expression in his destructive acts.
>
> (Klein, 1927, p. 183)

The mother–infant relationship: In her later work Klein states more specifically the importance of the details of the mother–infant relationship. In 'Notes on some schizoid mechanisms' she writes of one of her cases:

> External experiences are, of course, of great importance in these developments. For instance, in the case of a patient who showed depressive and schizoid features, the analysis brought up with great vividness his early experiences in babyhood, to such an extent that in some sessions physical sensations in the throat or digestive organs occurred. The patient had been weaned suddenly at four months of age because his mother fell ill. In addition, he did not see his mother for four weeks. When she returned she found the child greatly changed. He had been a lively baby, interested in his surroundings, and he seemed to have lost this interest. He had become apathetic . . .
>
> Much light was thrown in the analysis on the influence these experiences had on his whole development. His outlook and attitudes in adult life were based on the patterns established in this early stage.
>
> (Klein, 1946, pp. 15–16)

In 'On observing the behaviour of young infants' Klein observes how varying temperamental factors in infants that affect feeding can be modified or exacerbated by the behaviour and attitude of the mother:

> We have of course to take into full consideration every detail in the way the infant is fed and handled by his mother. It can be observed that an initially promising attitude towards food may be disrupted by adverse feeding conditions; whereas difficulties in sucking can sometimes be mitigated by the mother's love and patience.
>
> (Klein, 1952b, p. 96)

The infant will in turn affect the mother, and benign or vicious cycles can arise:

> . . . the mother's actual relation to her child is in indirect and subtle ways, influenced by the infant's response to her. A contented baby who sucks with enjoyment, allays his mother's anxiety; and her happiness expresses itself in her way of handling and feeding him, thus diminishing his persecutory anxiety and affecting his ability to internalise the good breast. In contrast, a child who has difficulties over feeding may arouse the mother's anxiety and guilt and thus unfavourably influence her relation to him.
>
> (Klein, 1963, p. 312)

> Innate aggressiveness is bound to be increased by unfavourable external circumstances and, conversely, is mitigated by the love and understanding that the young child receives; and these factors continue to operate throughout development. But . . . the importance of internal factors is still underrated. Destructive impulses, varying from individual to individual, are an integral part of mental life, even in favourable circumstances, and therefore we have to consider the development of the child and the attitudes of the adults as resulting from the interaction between internal and external influences. . . . The struggle between love and hate . . . can to some extent be recognized through careful observation. Some babies experience strong resentment about any frustration and show this by being unable to accept gratification when it follows on deprivation.
>
> (Klein, 1959, p. 249)

Bion's theory of containment: Bion (1962b), in his theory of maternal containment, provides an important missing link, namely a specific theory of how maternal care affects the child [*see* Container/contained; Thinking and knowledge]. Bion's theory assumes that one of the most important elements of the early environment is the mother's mind. Through his realistic, or communicative, projective identifications the infant arouses in the mother feelings that he cannot as yet bear or make sense of. The mother, with her more mature mind and her love for her child, through her 'reverie' 'contains' and gives meaning to the unbearable mental content, which can then be returned to the infant in a more manageable form. In time the infant introjects not only processed mental content but also the containing capacity itself.

Intrusive objects and failures of containment: Bion (1962a) theorises that a poorly functioning container, a 'projective-identification-rejecting object', will be taken in and experienced by the infant as a wilfully misunderstanding object with which it will become identified. Bion evocatively describes such an internal object as 'a greedy vagina-like breast that strips of its goodness all that the infant receives or gives leaving only degenerate objects' (1962a, p. 115). A fear of dying, for example, will become stripped of what meaning it has and replaced by 'nameless dread'.

Fraiberg et al. (1975) talk of 'ghosts in the nursery' when undigested trauma of the parental generation is unconsciously passed on to the next generation through projection. Rosenfeld, particularly in his book *Impasse and Interpretation* (1987), discusses patients traumatised by the projections encountered in their early environment, and warns of the danger of re-creation of such trauma in analysis. Gianna Williams (1997) writes about 'no-entry' defences in patients who have not been contained as infants and also have been used as receptacles for the projections of their disturbed mothers.

Projective identification acting on the environment: Bion's theory of containment has also shown us how we often cause alterations in our environment (i.e. the way our objects behave and respond to us) by the way in which we project. This has led to important developments in contemporary Kleinian theory and practice [*see* Countertransference; Projective identification]. Bion shows how projective identification may remain a phantasy on the part of the person projecting, or it may be accompanied by evocative behaviour that leads to responses in a receptive other. (Sandler (1976), from a different theoretical background, refers to this as 'role-responsiveness'.) This can lead in effect to a self-fulfilling prophecy about the nature of that other. Here we see the power of the internal world of one individual to coerce and seduce the other into enactment. In this case re-introjection will simply reinforce the internal status quo, rather than leading to new knowledge of the world. Rosenfeld (1987) in his later work is interested in the way such mechanisms could lead to analysts unwittingly re-traumatising some already traumatised patients.

If, however, the analyst is able to contain his or her countertransference, he or she will be able to disconfirm the phantasies of the patient about the nature of the object. The analyst can then act, in the way Strachey (1934) describes, to modify the patient's archaic projected superego.

The environment and analytic technique: The internal versus external world dialectic comes up again in relation to analytic technique, thinking about how both Klein and contemporary Kleinian psychoanalysts see the balance between detailed attention to the transference situation and attempts at reconstruction of the 'actual' past. There are interesting differences in emphasis here within the Kleinian school [*see* Technique]. Interestingly, study of Klein's original notes shows that she herself privileged reconstruction over transference interpretation in a way that would not be considered typically 'Kleinian' today.

See External object; Internal objects; Social defence systems

Bion, W. (1962a) 'A theory of thinking', *Int. J. Psycho-Anal.* 43: 306–310; reprinted in *Second Thoughts*. London: Maresfield Reprints, pp. 110–119.
—— (1962b) *Learning from Experience*. London: Heinemann.
Fraiberg, S., Adelson, E. and Shapiro, V. (1975) 'Ghosts in the nursery: A psychoanalytic approach to the problems of impaired infant–mother relationships', in *Clinical Studies in Infant Mental Health*. London: Tavistock (1980), pp. 164–196.
Jones, E. (1935) 'Early female sexuality', *Int. J. Psycho-Anal.* 16: 262–273.
Klein, M. (1927) 'Criminal tendencies in normal children', in *The Writings of Melanie Klein*, Vol. 1. London: Hogarth Press, pp. 170–185.
—— (1929) 'Infantile anxiety situations reflected in a work of art and in the creative impulse', in *The Writings of Melanie Klein*, Vol. 4. London: Hogarth Press, pp. 210–218.
—— (1930) 'The importance of symbol formation in the development of the ego', in *The Writings of Melanie Klein*, Vol. 1. London: Hogarth Press, pp. 219–232.
—— (1934) 'On criminality', in *The Writings of Melanie Klein*, Vol. 1. London: Hogarth Press, pp. 258–261.
—— (1935) 'A contribution to the psychogenesis of manic-depressive states', in *The Writings of Melanie Klein*, Vol. 1. London: Hogarth Press, pp. 262–289.
—— (1936) 'Weaning', in *The Writings of Melanie Klein*, Vol. 1. London: Hogarth Press, pp. 290–305.
—— (1937) 'Love, guilt and reparation', in *The Writings of Melanie Klein*, Vol. 1. London: Hogarth Press, pp. 306–343.
—— (1940) 'Mourning and its relation to manic-depressive states', in *The Writings of Melanie Klein*, Vol. 1. London: Hogarth Press, pp. 344–369.
—— (1946) 'Notes on some schizoid mechanisms', in *The Writings of Melanie Klein*, Vol. 3. London: Hogarth Press, pp. 1–24.
—— (1952a) 'Some theoretical conclusions regarding the emotional life of the infant', in *The Writings of Melanie Klein*, Vol. 3. London: Hogarth Press, Press, pp. 61–93.

—— (1952b) 'On observing the behaviour of young infants', in *The Writings of Melanie Klein*, Vol. 3. London: Hogarth Press, pp. 94–121.

—— (1957) 'Envy and gratitude', in *The Writings of Melanie Klein*, Vol. 3. London: Hogarth Press, pp. 176–235.

—— (1959) 'Our adult world and its roots in infancy', in *The Writings of Melanie Klein*, Vol. 3. London: Hogarth Press, pp. 247–263.

—— (1963) 'On the sense of loneliness', in *The Writings of Melanie Klein*, Vol. 3. London: Hogarth Press, pp. 300–313.

Rosenfeld, H. (1987) *Impasse and Interpretation*. London: Tavistock.

Sandler, J. (1976) 'Countertransference and role-responsiveness', *Int. Rev. Psycho-Anal.* 59: 285–296.

Strachey, J. (1934) 'The nature of the therapeutic action of psychoanalysis', *Int. J. Psycho-Anal.* 15: 127–159.

Williams, G. (1997) *Internal Landscapes and Foreign Bodies*. London: Duckworth.

Externalisation

Klein uses the term 'externalization' extensively in her early attempts to understand the mechanisms involved in the formation of play. Later the term would be changed to *projection*, with which it is largely synonymous.

See Creativity; Play; Technique

Faeces

Freud discovered that in the unconscious mind there is a symbolic equation between faeces, money, penis and baby on the basis of their perceptual identity as gifts that can be given or taken away (Freud, 1905, 1917). Abraham (1924) considered faeces to be the prototype of the internal object – concrete, sensual, internal and yet expellable. In Klein's view of internal objects faeces are one possible source of experiences of internal objects – in that they give rise to anal sensations – and they can be expelled (projected) [*see* Internal objects].

Faeces represent a part-object that acquires unconscious significance because of the elaboration in phantasy of the functions of defaecation: expulsion and retention. Contriving the physical expulsion produces anal sensations, which are then represented mentally as an unconscious phantasy of expelling a bad object [*see* Unconscious phantasy]. The passing of faeces occurs in infancy as such a regular conjunction with feeding that it has been endowed with a medical name, the so-called 'gastro-colic reflex'. The experiencing of these regular physiological events leads to the construction in phantasy of equally regular conjunctions of experiencing – taking in a good object and expelling a bad one: one of the infant's earliest defensive manoeuvres.

Meltzer (1965) describes one infantile use of faeces in an anal form of masturbation to elicit unconscious phantasies in the interest of supporting a narcissistic state [*see* Masturbation phantasies; Narcissism].

See Part-objects

Abraham, K. (1924) 'A short study of the development of the libido', in *Selected Papers on Psychoanalysis*. London: Hogarth Press (1927), pp. 418–501.

Freud, S. (1905) 'Three essays on the theory of sexuality', *S.E. 7*. London: Hogarth Press, pp. 125–245.

—— (1917) 'On transformations of instinct as exemplified in anal erotism', *S.E. 17*. London: Hogarth Press, pp. 125–134.

Meltzer, D. (1965) 'The relation of anal masturbation to projective identification', *Int. J. Psycho-Anal.* 47: 335–342.

Ronald Fairbairn

Biography: Fairbairn was somewhat of an outsider amongst British psychoanalysts. He was born in 1889 and worked all his life in Edinburgh. He was originally an academic (in Classics) but after the First World War trained as a doctor and then in psychoanalysis, which he practised in his home city, in isolation from London, until he died in 1964. He was one person outside Klein's own circle whom she allowed to influence her considerably. He did not participate very much in the life of the British Psychoanalytical Society. However, he greatly influenced a number of analysts in Britain (Guntrip, 1961; Sutherland, 1963; Padel, 1987) and in America he was one of the first respected British object-relations analysts, perhaps because he was most fearless in stating *systematically* his objection to Freud's instinct theory while retaining a tripartite structure resembling Freud's structural model.

Scientific contributions: Fairbairn had been greatly influenced by Klein. He adopted her term 'position', but spoke of the *schizoid position* instead of the paranoid position, as she then (in the 1930s) called it [*see* Paranoia]. He investigated deeply the first stages of emotional life through working with schizoid individuals, whilst at that time Klein was occupied with developing her notion of the depressive position in the slightly later periods of infantile development. As a result, he drew attention to the early splits in the self to which Klein later turned her attention. In fact she had herself been interested for a long time in the fragmented states of thinking in psychotic children, but in the early 1940s she became interested in adult schizo-phrenics, severely psychiatrically disturbed patients whom she got to know particularly through supervising the work of some psychiatrists who were now joining the Kleinian Group.

Opposition to the depressive position: Fairbairn criticises Klein for placing too much emphasis on depression and for following Abraham's emphasis on obsessions in the 'psychotic' early phases. Fairbairn claimed that psychoanalysts had relatively neglected hysteria since 1912, when Abraham and Freud began turning their interest to manic-depressive illnesses. Fairbairn links the states of dissociation in hysteria with the fragmentation of the schizoid personality. If Freud had continued to study the superego through hysteria and schizophrenia, Fairbairn claims, he would not have pursued the trajectory that later came to be named the 'depressive position' by Klein. The orally formed superego structure is a defensive organisation, he believes, against what is beneath. What is repressed is inherently structural. He thinks that dreams are dramatisations of: '. . . (i) relationships between ego-structures and internalized objects, and (ii) interrelationships between ego-structures themselves' (Fairbairn, 1951, p. 170). In particular, the internalised 'bad' object is split into an exciting one and a rejecting one. So whereas Klein, in her work on the depressive position, had been focusing on anxiety about the fate of the object – how it is damaged, split, etc. – Fairbairn was drawing attention to structural aspects of the splitting and fragmentation of the ego.

Fairbairn argues that there was some abnormality of development in schizophrenia (as opposed to manic-depressive illness) that Klein had overlooked. In bringing to the fore states of dissociation in hysteria and schizophrenia he postulates a 'schizoid position', which he claims preceded the depressive position and was fundamental to it. It explains and determines the future pathology of the personality, and he goes on to describe a systematic categorisation of conditions on the basis of splits within the ego and the object.

Klein agreed that the onset of the depressive position was on the basis of a prior working-through of another kind of anxiety, not of the depressive type. She had always described the paranoia she found in children and their persecutory anxiety, and had used the term 'paranoid position'. Whereas she had then thought of the paranoid position as secondary in importance to the depressive position, she now agreed with Fairbairn that the prior position was of great significance and also that splitting was a crucial element, as were the forms of paranoid projection (externalisation) that she had described. She acknowledges Fairbairn's important contribution of the term 'schizoid position' by combining it with her own to produce the term 'paranoid-schizoid position'. However, Klein is at pains to point out her differences with Fairbairn in other respects (especially the abandonment of any theory of instincts):

It will be seen that some of the conclusions which I shall present in this paper are in line with Fairbairn's conclusions, while others differ fundamentally. Fairbairn's approach was largely from the angle of ego-development in relation to objects, while mine was predominantly from the angle of anxieties and their vicissitudes . . . the particular emphasis he laid on the inherent relation between hysteria and schizophrenia deserves full attention. His term schizoid would be appropriate if it is understood to cover both persecutory fear and schizoid mechanisms.

(Klein, 1946, p. 3)

Klein had begun to realise that there was a whole class of primitive defence mechanisms that were specifically directed against sadism and the death instinct, and she now acknowledged with Fairbairn that they were different from the obsessional mechanisms that she had originally pinpointed as the candidate for the specific defences against sadism and to which she had later added the manic defences.

Introjected objects: Fairbairn accepted that the initial stage of the ego resulted in an introjected object, but he thought of this as the bad object. There was no need to introject the good object and only the bad had to be defended against by introjecting and then splitting. This is in contrast to Klein, who thinks that from the outset both good and bad objects are introjected; the introjection of a good object is crucial in establishing the stability of the core of the ego and reveals the struggles of the infant to protect himself and his good object from the 'bad' object (Klein, 1946).

There is a significant difference of focus to be appreciated. Fairbairn regards the infantile ego as unified to begin with and as driven by needs for object-relatedness. The encounter with the external object, its vicissitudes and failures leads to the setting up of internal objects established to defend against (he says to repress) the external bad object. This contrasts with Klein's view that the infantile ego is unintegrated to begin with, prone to persecutory anxiety owing to the projection of the death instinct and uses binary splitting and schizoid mechanisms to establish the security of the internal world. The split within the ego is crucial for later integration and leads to the construction of a divided external world based on the internal manoeuvres.

Endopsychic structures: Fairbairn's and Klein's approaches to the phenomena of splitting and fragmentation of the self are radically different. Characteristically, Klein maps a wide panorama of varied and varying phantasies experienced by the person about the state of his 'self'. In contrast, Fairbairn reduces the phenomena to strictly categorisable segments. He describes two basic splits that separate two endopsychic structures from a central ego. Each structure comprises (i) a part of the ego, (ii) an internalised object with which part of the ego is identified and (iii) an internal relationship between the ego-part and the internal object. Each endopsychic structure is composed of such a tripartite 'object-relation system'. One such structure contains a libidinal aspect of the ego (the *libidinal ego*) with its libidinal (*exciting*) object; the second endopsychic structure contains an anti-libidinal ego (the *internal saboteur*, reminiscent of the superego) with an anti-libidinal object (the *rejecting object*). In addition, there remains a *central ego* after these two parts have been split off.

This internal world of three endopsychic structures seems to be fixed and is clearly loosely related to Freud's own tripartite structural model: ego, id (the libidinal ego) and superego (the anti-libidinal ego). However, whereas Freud believes that the various structures of the mind grew directly or indirectly out of the id, Fairbairn contests this and argued that they developed out of the primitive and originally unified ego. The notion that there is an ego at the outset is exactly in line with Klein and against Freud's notion of primary narcissism. However, Fairbairn contests Klein because she adhered '. . . uncritically to Freud's hedonistic libido theory' (Fairbairn, 1949, p. 154), which stipulates that libido is pleasure-seeking. If early Klein adhered to Freud's ideas about infantile sexuality she never espoused his economic model of metapsychology, which grounds the notion of pleasure in the principle of energy conservation [*see* Economic model].

Instinct theory: Fairbairn is opposed to instinct theory. According to Guntrip (1961), Fairbairn's great disciple and proselytiser, Fairbairn thought it was mechanistic and was looking for a more humanistic theory. Consequently, he speaks only of objects. He quarrels with the term 'oral phase', for instance, saying that it might as well be called the 'breast phase' since it is the breast (the object) that is of importance to the child: libido is object-seeking. He regards the mouth as expressing a particular *strategy* for relating to the object. In this case the mouth is merely the inborn instrument for the strategy (nothing to do with an instinct).

In this way Fairbairn believed he had gone beyond instinct theory and the energy model of the mind, which some regard as the cornerstone of classical psychoanalytic theory. Klein, on the other hand, actually went beyond instinct theory in a quite different way. Guntrip and others (e.g. Sutherland, 1963; Kernberg, 1980; Greenberg and Mitchell, 1983) reiterated the view that Klein's theory was only a way-station, halfway to a full object-relations approach, and that Fairbairn completed this journey. This view is questionable: their journeys were in different directions. Klein retains an instinct theory that highlights the role of unconscious phantasy rather than tension reduction, and which is integrated within an object-relations theory and a flexible and fluid view of internal structure. Fairbairn, on the other hand, substitutes a monolithic and seemingly inflexible system of endopsychic structures (object-relations systems) as an ingenious, object-relations version of the orthodox id/ego/superego structure.

One could say that Klein reinterprets the concept of 'instinct' to mean the experience of an object 'given by' the bodily sensations of the instinctual impulse, which give rise to phantasies, whereas Fairbairn recasts instinct as the 'energy' to seek out objects.

Splitting: The discovery of the importance of splits in the system of ego-part/relationship/object is to be credited to both Fairbairn and Klein, stimulating each other's observations. Klein clearly continued to reflect on the problem, and although she did not acknowledge the similarity with Fairbairn's view she toyed with a similar idea: a special kind of splitting that left an unmodified primitive object-relations system in a 'deeply unconscious' part of the mind (Klein, 1958, p. 241) [*see* Structure].

Love: Fairbairn is most emphatic about the importance of object relations in human experience. He demonstrates, more critically than Klein, that classical theories of instinctual satisfactions (drive reduction) view objects as incidental to the subject, merely for the release of tensions. In contrast he emphasises the genuine feeling *for* objects. It is this quality of trying to link human love and concern with scientific understanding that made him of such interest to the Christian minister Guntrip [*see* Love].

Later developments: Fairbairn's ideas have weathered quite well. He had two important followers – Guntrip (1961) and Sutherland (1963) – and he is widely recognised by many American writers (e.g. Ogden, 1983). However, Fairbairn's intricate theoretical probing has not been significantly developed by later adherents.

Fairbairn, R. (1949) 'Steps in the development of an object-relations theory of the personality', *Br. J. Med. Psychol.* 22: 26–31; republished in *Psycho-Analytic Studies of the Personality*. London: Routledge & Kegan Paul (1952), pp. 152–161.
—— (1951) 'A synopsis of the development of the author's views regarding the structure of the personality', in *Psycho-Analytic Studies of the Personality*. London: Routledge & Kegan Paul (1952), pp. 162–179.
Greenberg, J. and Mitchell, S. (1983) *Object Relations in Psychoanalytic Theory*. Cambridge, MA: Harvard University Press.
Guntrip, H. (1961) *Personality Structure and Human Interaction*. London: Hogarth Press.
Kernberg, O. (1980) *Internal World and External Reality*. New York: Jason Aronson.
Klein, M. (1946) 'Notes on some schizoid mechanisms', in *The Writings of Melanie Klein*, Vol. 3. London: Hogarth Press, pp. 1–24.
—— (1958) 'On the development of mental functioning', in *The Writings of Melanie Klein*, Vol. 3. London: Hogarth Press, pp. 236–246.
Ogden, T. (1983) 'The concept of internal object relations', *Int. J. Psycho-Anal.* 64: 227–241.

Padel, J. (1987) 'Positions, stages, attitudes or modes of being', *Bull. Eur. Psychoanal. Fed.* 12: 26–31.
Sutherland, J. D. (1963) 'Object relations theory and the conceptual model of psycho-analysis', *Br. J. Med. Psychol.* 36: 109–124.

Father

Through her elaboration of the role of mother, Klein modifies Freud's thinking about the father in a number of ways. The child's preoccupation with father, father's penis and fears of castration all remain significant for Klein, but in the context also of early preoccupations with the female genitals, the mother's breast and the inside of her body and the mother's internal babies. The penis thus ceases to be the only object of desire and envy, and the girl child's receptive desire to be given a baby by the father takes precedence over her longing for a penis, rather than being a substitute for it [*see* Oedipus complex]. In Klein's view object relations first occur with 'part-objects', the first being the mother's breast and her internal spaces. Father's first appearance is as a phantasised internal possession of the mother – the penis inside the mother [*see* Combined parent figure]. However, very soon after birth Klein thinks that the father is perceived in his own right as a 'third object', at first in some partial way. If the relationship with mother is problematic in some way then this third object will be experienced as a persecutor, a dangerous penis; but if the relationship is secure, then it will be experienced as a more benign presence. The infant will turn to the father/penis both from frustration with the breast and also out of love, in order to spare the mother/breast from his aggression and greed.

Klein's conception of the Oedipus complex is complex and many-faceted for both sexes. As for Freud, father is both a love object and a hated rival for both sexes at different times. The move from whole to part-objects as the depressive position sets in is intimately connected with the beginnings of the Oedipus situation, early in the first year of life. Importantly for Klein the Oedipus complex is resolved as much or more through love of the father (and the mother) as through fear of castration. Thus the parents are allowed to come together as a couple as the child's growing love and maturity allows him to relinquish his omnipotent possession of them, and allow the father to love and protect the mother. Klein (1937) writes movingly in 'Love, guilt and reparation' about fatherhood and the complementary roles of the parents.

Kleinian authors have frequently referred to the need, in healthy development, to be able to perceive and to accept difference. This includes the difference between mother and father and the difference between the nurturing parent–child relationship and the sexual, creative relationship between mother and father (e.g. Money-Kyrle, 1968, 1971). Rather than focusing on father per se, the emphasis in contemporary Kleinian writing is often on the vicissitudes of tolerating and integrating the parental relationship, so that the internal vantage point of a 'third position' can be achieved (Britton 1989, 1998). Britton (2003) has also written an interesting critique of Freud's female castration complex, which he suggests might have been Freud's generalisation from a female case or cases where the picture was abnormal.

Meltzer (1967) describes the beginning of differentiation of male and female during the very early phase of 'sorting of zonal confusions'. Then, at the threshold of the depressive position:

> The roles of the father's penis and testicles begin to be clearly distinguished from the many roles of the mother's internal penises and the basis to be laid for the proper differentiation of male and female, some of which had already been worked out during the sorting of zonal confusions. But now the full acknowledgement of the creative and reparative role of the father is possible.
>
> (Meltzer, 1967 p. 40)

Trowell and Etchegoyen (2002) have produced a useful and thorough re-evaluation of the significance of fathers in contemporary psychoanalytic thinking, and include the contributions of a number of authors working in the Kleinian tradition.

Britton, R. (1989) 'The missing link: Parental sexuality in the Oedipus complex', in J. Steiner (ed.) *The Oedipus Complex Today*. London: Karnac, pp. 83–109.
—— (1998) *Belief and Imagination*. London: Routledge.
—— (2003) 'The female castration complex: Freud's big mistake?', in *Sex, Death, and the Superego*. London: Karnac, pp. 57–70.
Klein, M. (1937) 'Love, guilt and reparation', in *The Writings of Melanie Klein*, Vol. 1. London: Hogarth Press, pp. 306–343.
Meltzer, D. (1967) *The Psycho-Analytical Process* Strath Tay: Clunie Press.
Money-Kyrle, R. (1968) 'Cognitive development', *Int. J. Psycho-Anal.* 49: 691–698.
—— (1971) 'The aim of psychoanalysis', in D. Meltzer (ed.) *The Collected Papers of Roger Money-Kyrle*. Strath Tay: Clunie Press, pp. 442–449.
Trowell, J. and Etchegoyen, A. (eds) (2002) *The Importance of Fathers: A Psychoanalytic Re-Evaluation*. London: Routledge.

Femininity

During the 1920s and 1930s there was much debate about the psychology of women in psychoanalytic circles, and challenges to Freud's theories about femininity, for example from Karen Horney (1926, 1932). Ernest Jones (1935) and Joan Riviere (1934) were among those who made specific use of Klein's observations in their papers on female sexuality. Klein herself (1932,

1945) wrote extensively about her new ideas on female development and femininity [*see* Oedipus complex].

Klein's descriptions of phantasies about the internal world literally opened up the subject of interiority in women. In Klein's view small children of both sexes have interest not just in the presence or absence of a phallus, but in breasts, the vagina and in particular the mother's internal space, where phantasied babies, the father's penis and other riches are to be found [*see* Combined parent figure]. Wishes to intrude into mother and annexe her riches lead to feelings of persecution, and a particular fear for the little girl that her own internal space will be robbed in retaliation. For Klein, unlike Freud, the little girl has an early awareness of having a vagina and an important space inside her.

In Klein's view the girl's desire to possess a penis and to be a boy is part of her inherent bisexuality, and equivalent to the boy's desire to be a woman. However, she thinks that rather than being primary, this is secondary to the girl's desire to be fertilised by the father's penis, and is exacerbated by frustrations in the feminine position. Ronald Britton (2002, 2003) suggests that there is evidence that Freud's ideas about the female castration complex and the centrality of penis envy were overvalued and based on the analysis of one case, his daughter Anna.

See Oedipus complex

Britton, R. (2002) 'Forever father's daughter: The Athene–Antigone complex', in J. Trowell and A. Etchegoyen (eds) *The Importance of Fathers*. London: Routledge, pp. 197–218.
—— (2003) 'The female castration complex: Freud's big mistake?', in *Sex, Death, and the Superego*. London: Karnac, pp. 57–70.
Horney, K. (1926) 'The flight from womanhood', *Int. J. Psycho-Anal.* 7: 324–329.
—— (1932) 'The dread of women', *Int. J. Psycho-Anal.* 13: 348–360.
Jones, E. (1935) 'Early female sexuality', *Int. J. Psycho-Anal.* 16: 263–273.
Klein, M. (1932) *The Psychoanalysis of Children. The Writings of Melanie Klein*, Vol. 2. London: Hogarth Press.
—— (1945) 'The Oedipus complex in the light of early anxieties', in *The Writings of Melanie Klein*, Vol. 1. London: Hogarth Press, pp. 176–235.
Riviere, J. (1934) 'Review of Freud's *New Introductory Lectures*', *Int. J. Psycho-Anal.* 15: 329–339.

Femininity phase

One of Klein's important contributions to psychoanalytic theories of sexual development is to identify an early phase in both boys and girls of identification with the mother, the 'femininity phase'. This is a phase fraught with fear and conflict, when both sexes imagine the mother to be full of riches:

babies, father's penis (or penises) and dangerous and desirable faeces (also in part equated with babies). The child wishes to be like the mother, to possess such riches too. Thus phantasies arise of robbing mother in order to appropriate the babies, as well as to destroy them as rival babies. Unlike Freud, Klein believes in a primary feminine oedipal position. The girl child, according to Klein, is from early days aware of a vagina and internal space in both herself and mother. Her primary desire is to be receptive to a fertile penis. She also wishes to possess the penis in a phallic manner, exacerbated by anxieties and frustrations in the feminine position, and this is part of her inherent bisexuality. However, this is a secondary rather than, as Freud believes, a fundamental primary position for the girl.

Klein's postulation of a femininity phase in both sexes gives the male child a complex of equivalent importance to the castration complex in girls:

> As in the castration complex of girls, so in the femininity complex of the male, there is at bottom the frustrated desire for a special organ. The tendencies to steal and destroy are concerned with the organs of conception, pregnancy and parturition.
>
> (Klein, 1928, p. 190)

> In women there is universally the wish to be a man, expressed perhaps most clearly in terms of penis envy; similarly one finds in men the feminine position, the longing to possess breasts and to give birth to children. Such wishes are bound up with an identification with both parents and are accompanied by feelings of competitiveness and envy, as well as admiration of the coveted possessions. These identifications vary in strength and also in quality, depending on whether admiration or envy is the more prevalent.
>
> (Klein, 1963, p. 306)

This situation deepens and complicates the fear of castration by the father that Freud has already described:

> The boy fears punishment for his destruction of his mother's body, but, besides them, his fear is of a more general nature, and here we have an analogy to the anxiety associated with the castration wishes of the girl. He fears that his body will be mutilated and dismembered, and this dread also means castration. . . . The dread of the mother is so overwhelming because there is combined with it an intense dread of castration by the father. The destructive tendencies whose object is the womb are also directed with their full oral – and anal – sadistic intensity against the father's penis, which is supposed to be located there . . . this anxiety subjects the boy to the tyranny of a superego

which devours, dismembers and castrates and is formed from the image of mother and father alike.

(Klein, 1928, p. 190)

Of great importance for the boy becomes the relative balance between his sadistic and his loving impulses. This will ultimately determine how much he can achieve a heterosexual position that is stable and loving as opposed to rivalrous and envious:

The greater the preponderance of sadistic fixations, the more does the boy's identification with his mother correspond to an attitude of rivalry towards the woman, with its blending of envy and hatred; for on account of his wish for a child, he feels himself at a disadvantage and inferior to the mother.

(Klein, 1928, p. 190)

. . . it is a condition for a firm establishment of the heterosexual position that the boy should succeed in overcoming this phase . . . the boy often compensates the feelings of hate, anxiety, envy and inferiority that spring from his feminine phase by reinforcing his pride in the possession of a penis and that he displaces that pride onto his intellectual activities. This displacement forms the basis of a very hostile attitude of rivalry towards women and affects his character formation in the same way as envy of the penis affects theirs. The excessive anxiety he feels on account of his sadistic attacks on his mother's body becomes the source of very grave disturbances in his relations to the opposite sex. But if his anxiety and sense of guilt becomes less acute it will be those very feelings which give rise to the various elements of his phantasies of restitution that will enable him to have an intuitive understanding of women.

(Klein, 1932, p. 250)

The boy's belief in his own capacity for love and reparation will help him to move beyond his femininity phase and form an identification with his father's potency, strengthening his own capacity for heterosexuality.

. . . a necessary condition for sexual potency should be that the boy believes in the 'goodness' of his penis – that is, in his capacity to make restitution by means of the sexual act. This belief is bound up with . . . the belief that the inside of his body is in a good state.

(Klein, 1932, p. 251)

See Combined parent figure; Oedipus complex

Klein, M. (1928) 'Early stages of the Oedipus conflict', in *The Writings of Melanie Klein*, Vol. 1. London: Hogarth Press, pp. 186–198.

—— (1932) *The Psychoanalysis of Children*. *The Writings of Melanie Klein*, Vol. 2. London: Hogarth Press.

—— (1963) 'On the sense of loneliness', in *The Writings of Melanie Klein*, Vol. 3. London: Hogarth Press, pp. 300–313.

Fragmentation

Klein considers fragmentation from two viewpoints, unintegration and severe splitting.

Unintegration: At first the early infantile ego is thought by Klein to be unintegrated and, when not held by another mind (the mother), will disintegrate and give rise to a sense of falling apart, of going to pieces. This lack of integration is a normal experience in individuals under stress or exhaustion when the usual 'containers' are weakened or absent. Short-lived experiences of going to pieces are part of normal development.

Severe splitting: Klein thinks of fragmentation as the result of an active and severe splitting of the ego in the paranoid-schizoid position in which the mechanism of denial is accompanied by phantasies of annihilation of, for example, the 'bad' object and annihilation of the self in relation to that object. Following Schmideberg (1930), Klein thinks of fragmentation as a way of dispersing destructive impulses and persecutory anxieties. Fragmentation indicates the presence of extreme persecutory anxiety. If persistent, fragmentation and its accompanying state of disintegration weaken the ego and lead to extreme confusional states. In an appendix to her 1946 paper Klein describes Schreber as someone with an ego in bits [*see* Confusional states; Denial; Paranoid-schizoid position; Splitting].

Bion (1957) describes the psychotic as splitting his ego into minute pieces, expelling the resulting fragments and experiencing himself as being surrounded by 'bizarre objects' [*see* Bizarre objects]. Segal (1997), in her paper on the death instinct, describes patients in whom the presence of the death instinct within causes them to want to annihilate not only the object but also the perceiving self [*see* Death instinct].

Bion, W. (1957) 'Differentiation of the psychotic from the non-psychotic personalities', *Int. J. Psycho-Anal.* 38: 266–275.

Klein, M. (1946) 'Notes on some schizoid mechanisms', in *The Writings of Melanie Klein*, Vol. 3. London: Hogarth Press, pp. 1–24.

Schmideberg, M. (1930) 'The role of psychotic mechanisms in cultural development', *Int J. Psycho-Anal.* 11: 387–418.

Segal, H. (1997) 'On the clinical usefulness of the concept of the death instinct', in *Psychoanalysis, Literature and War*. London: Routledge, pp. 17–26

Anna Freud

Biography: Freud's youngest daughter was born in 1892 in Vienna and remained his companion until his death, accompanying him to London in 1938 where she remained in the family house after Freud's death until her own in 1982. She was not just Freud's daughter but made significant contributions to psychoanalysis in her own right and carried the banner for conservative loyalty to Freud's theoretical position (Solnit, 1983; Yorke, 1983).

Scientific contributions: Anna Freud entered the ring in 1926 as a protagonist of the form of child analysis pioneered by Hug-Hellmuth, and in opposition to Melanie Klein. Although her opposition was later modified (Freud, 1946; Geleerd, 1963), the training in child analysis that she set up and which became The Anna Freud Centre in London remained separate from the British Psychoanalytical Society after she arrived in 1938 [*see* Child analysis; Controversial Discussions].

In 1936, Anna Freud published her most famous book, *The Ego and the Mechanisms of Defence*, and that, together with Hartmann's work in Vienna and the USA (Hartmann, 1939, 1964), created a whole line of development of psychoanalysis arising out of the specific study of the ego and its relations with the other psychic agencies. Ego psychology has remained the dominant school of psychoanalysis in the United States. However, until her death, Anna Freud expressed her unhappiness with American ego psychology, and always underlined the importance of the topographical model, a model rejected by the ego psychologists.

Freud, A. (1936) *The Ego and the Mechanisms of Defence*. London: Hogarth Press.

—— (1946) 'Preface' to *The Psycho-Analytic Treatment of Children*. London: Imago.

Geleerd, E. (1963) 'An evaluation of Melanie Klein's *Narrative of a Child Analysis*', *Int. J. Psycho-Anal.* 44: 493–506.

Hartmann, H. (1939) *Ego Psychology and the Problem of Adaptation*. London: Imago.

—— (1964) *Essays on Ego Psychology*. London: Hogarth Press.

Solnit, A. (1983) 'Anna Freud's contribution to child and applied analysis', *Int. J. Psycho-Anal.* 64: 379–390.

Yorke, C. (1983) 'Anna Freud and the psycho-analytic study and treatment of adults', *Int. J. Psycho-Anal.* 64: 391–400.

Genetic continuity

The term 'genetic continuity' has an important role in psychoanalytic theory and practice. It is the assumption that psychological aspects of the personality in the present have a continuity with preceding stages of development. Thus Freud evolved the view that adult neurosis arose from traumatic occurrences and phantasies in childhood. But more than this, normal features of the personality, such as the superego, are assumed to develop from its precursors, the oedipal parents in the preceding stage of development.

It was on the basis of genetic continuity that Freud made his inferences, from adults, about psychological development in children. The theory of genetic continuity was tested when Freud and Little Hans' father investigated the psychoanalytic theory of child development by direct analysis of material from a 5-year-old child (Little Hans) during the phases of development that had been hypothesised from the analysis of adults (Freud, 1909).

When Klein began to analyse children she found herself also speculating about earlier stages of development than those she was analysing. Although she analysed children as young as 2 years and 9 months, she found that there was a great deal of fundamental development to be described before that age. Her inferences were therefore also based on the principle of genetic continuity, as well as other evidence that eventually included direct infant observation [*see* Esther Bick; Infant observation].

Dishearteningly, Klein found that her contributions to the psychoanalytic theory of development were disputed. Waelder, upholding orthodox psychoanalysis as understood in Vienna, read a headmasterly paper to the British Psychoanalytical Society in 1936 (a different version was published later: Waelder, 1937), admonishing Klein's developments as deviations from true Freudian theory. He delivered a prolonged debate on what is valid psychoanalytic inference. This produced a retort from Isaacs in defence of the scientific validity of Klein's inferences about the first year of life (Isaacs, 1938). Open controversy broke out during the Controversial Discussions in 1943–1944 [*see* Controversial Discussions].

The dispute over what is a valid psychoanalytic inference and what is not has never really been settled, with a tendency for analysts to dispute one another's inferences. Agreement that the present had its precursors in the past has not extended to agreement on what exactly those precursors comprise. For example, Klein attributed, partly on the basis of genetic continuity, an early form of the superego to the early pregenital phases of development [*see* Superego]. On the grounds of genetic continuity, Fenichel (1931) agreed that there might well be 'precursors of the superego' but that they were quite different from the superego itself and should not be referred to by the same term because those precursors had some different characteristics. The problem arose, therefore, in the terminology – if there is a genetic continuity, how should the continuum be divided up? Answers to that question have rested on a mixture of non-scientific motives, including simply allegiance to a particular preceding theory.

Fenichel, O. (1931) 'The pregenital antecedents of the Oedipus complex', *Int. J. Psycho-Anal.* 9: 47–70.

Freud, S. (1909) 'Analysis of a phobia in a five-year-old boy', *S.E. 10*. London: Hogarth Press, pp. 3–149.

Isaacs, S. (1938) 'The nature of the evidence concerning mental life in the earliest years', unpublished, but incorporated into Isaacs (1952) 'The nature and function of phantasy', in M. Klein, P. Heimann, S. Isaacs and J. Riviere (eds) *Developments in Psycho-Analysis*. London: Hogarth Press, pp. 67–121.

Waelder, R. (1937) 'The problem of the genesis of psychical conflict in earliest infancy', *Int. J. Psycho-Anal.* 18: 406–473.

Good object

Even before formulating her theories of the positions, Klein describes the infant as dividing itself and its objects into 'good' and 'bad':

> In dividing its mother into a 'good' mother and a 'bad' one and its father into a 'good' father and a 'bad' one, it attaches the hatred it feels for its object to the 'bad' one or turns away from it, while it directs its restorative trends to its 'good' mother and 'good' father.
>
> (Klein, 1932, p. 222)

By 1946 Klein considers that the first task of the infant is to separate good experiences of the self and object from bad experiences. At this early stage of development the infant feels its experiences concretely as the presence of an object within or without. The experience may be good when a need is satisfied or bad when hunger or anxiety is felt. Good experiences will be felt as the presence of a 'good' object or breast and bad experiences will be felt as the presence of a 'bad' object or breast. The primary task of the paranoid-schizoid position involves this binary splitting into good and bad so that the good self and good object can be protected from bad destructive aspects. Early objects are described as part-objects in that they are conceived in the mind of the infant in terms of bodily parts and in terms of goodness and badness [*see* Bad object; Paranoid-schizoid position; Part-objects; Splitting].

In Klein's theory the secure introjection of the good object is of great importance as it forms the core of the ego around which emotional development takes place. The first introjected 'good' object is an 'ideal' object, as the splitting process involves the denial of all bad experiences in relation to the object and its idealisation. Klein often uses the terms 'ideal object' and 'good object' interchangeably and the 'good' object is on a continuum. The unrealistic nature of the extremely 'good' or 'ideal' object leaves it unstable and constantly under threat from reality with the possibility of disappointment and resultant sudden alteration into an extremely bad object. The loss or threatened loss of the 'good' object can lead to extreme persecutory anxiety or persecutory guilt in the paranoid-schizoid position and to depressive anxiety or depressive guilt in the depressive position. The infant or individual on the threshold of the depressive position may retreat back to defensive splitting and idealisation to protect his 'good' or 'ideal' self and object. However, if things go well, the extreme difference between the 'good' and 'bad' object reduces, the object becomes more realistic and more secure and the infant moves forward to the depressive activities of mourning the loss of the 'good object', of bearing the guilt and of striving to make reparation [see Denial; Depressive anxiety; Depressive position; Guilt; Ideal object; Reparation].

Klein, M. (1932) *The Psychoanalysis of Children. The Writings of Melanie Klein*, Vol. 2. London: Hogarth Press.
—— (1946) 'Notes on some schizoid mechanisms', in *The Writings of Melanie Klein*, Vol. 3. London: Hogarth Press, pp. 1–24.

Gratitude

Gratitude is a specific feeling towards an object and needs to be distinguished from gratification, which is the satisfaction of a bodily need. Klein sees gratitude as one of the important expressions of love, and as the antithesis of envy (Klein, 1957). (Bion has a different angle on this, seeing creativity as the antithesis of envy.) Klein sees the capacity for gratitude, like the tendency towards envy, as having an innate component, influenced in its expression by the environment. The capacity for gratitude in Klein's view strengthens the personality and gives the individual a sense of inner wealth that leads to such things as generosity and the ability to recover from states of hatred and grievance. O'Shaughnessy (2008) gives a useful review and discussion of the topic.

See Love; Envy

Klein, M. (1957) 'Envy and gratitude', in *The Writings of Melanie Klein*, Vol. 3. London: Hogarth Press, pp. 176–235.
O'Shaughnessy, E. (2008) 'On gratitude', in P. Roth and A. Lemma (eds) *Envy and Gratitude Revisited*. London: International Psychoanalytic Association, pp. 79–91.

Greed

Greed is in Klein's words 'an impetuous and insatiable craving, exceeding what the subject needs and what the object is able and willing to give' (Klein, 1957, p. 181). This introjective process is destructive in its effects, since the breast is completely devoured, sucked dry. Although Klein sees greed as aggressive and closely associated with envy, they are however to be distinguished, since envy 'not only seeks to rob in this way, but also to put badness, primarily bad excrements . . . into the mother . . . in order to spoil and destroy her' (Klein, 1957, p. 181) [*see* Envy].

Klein sees the strength of greed as partly determined by innate factors. It can cause difficulties in introjecting a good object. Greed is reinforced by anxiety and can lead to vicious circles of insecurity:

> Some very greedy infants also give early signs of a developing interest in people in which, however, a similarity to their greedy attitude towards food can be detected. For instance, an impetuous craving for the presence of people often seems to relate less to the person than to the attention desired. Such children can hardly bear to be left alone and appear to require constantly either gratification by food or by attention. This would indicate that greed is reinforced by anxiety and that there is a failure . . . in establishing securely the good object in the inner world.
>
> (Klein, 1952, p. 99)

> There is no doubt that greed is increased by anxiety – the anxiety of being deprived, of being robbed and of not being good enough to be loved. The infant who is so greedy for love and attention is also insecure about his own capacity to love; and all these anxieties reinforce greed. This situation remains in fundamentals unchanged in the greed of the older child and adult.
>
> (Klein, 1959, p. 254)

A greedy individual in Klein's view is liable to be ambitious, which has positive aspects but may also be associated with endless hungry dissatisfaction. Greed frequently leads to vicious circles, as the greedily attacked and scooped out object becomes in phantasy a resentful persecutor, greedily attacking in return. Fear of persecution and diminished resources then can lead to further attempts at greedy incorporation, and so on.

The end result of greed may also be an inhibition of oral impulses and a restriction of introjection, intended to spare the objects that are so hungered for; this may lead to an anorexic state and a depleted internal world.

Klein, M. (1952) 'On observing the behaviour of young infants', in *The Writings of Melanie Klein*, Vol. 3. London: Hogarth Press, pp. 94–121.

—— (1957) 'Envy and gratitude', in *The Writings of Melanie Klein*, Vol. 3. London: Hogarth Press, pp. 176–235.

—— (1959) 'Our adult world and its roots in infancy', in *The Writings of Melanie Klein*, Vol. 3. London: Hogarth Press, pp. 247–263.

Grid

See Wilfred Bion; Thinking and knowledge

Grievance

Klein mentions patients' specific grievances in her writings but does not treat the idea of grievance as a conceptual category in her general theory. In everyday usage there is a tendency to think of 'grievance' as more serious, longstanding and perhaps also more pathological than 'complaint', although dictionary definitions do not recognise this difference. (For example, both Chambers Dictionary (1993) and The Shorter Oxford Dictionary (1964) define 'grievance' as 'complaint', and 'complaint' as 'grievance'.)

A growing number of psychoanalysts in both in the United States and Britain have become interested in grievance and its links with entitlement, narcissism, revenge and hatred. In the United States the main writers have been Murray (1964), Rothstein (1977), Galdston (1987), Lansky (2001) and LaFarge (2006).

In Britain the authors most concerned with the analysis of grievance have been Ronald Britton (1989), John Steiner (1993, 1996), Sally Weintrobe (2004) and Michael Feldman (2009). Weintrobe (2004) thinks that individuals who are preoccupied with 'grievance' tend to idealise themselves and to deny their dependence on objects, whereas individuals who make 'complaints' tend to address objects who are not idealised and on whom the complaining individuals know they are dependent.

Britton (1989), Steiner (1993, 1996) and Feldman (2009) stress the narcissistic element in grievance and all three cite Herbert Rosenfeld's paper on 'destructive narcissism' (Rosenfeld, 1971). These three authors also relate grievance specifically to patients' failures in coping adequately with the feelings and thoughts generated by the Oedipus complex [*see* Oedipus complex]. Feldman, in addition, lays particular stress on patients' deriving hostile, perverse gratification from the repetitive 'nursing' of grievances (Feldman, 2009).

Britton, R. (1989) 'The missing link: Parental sexuality in the Oedipus complex', in J. Steiner (ed.) *The Oedipus Complex Today*. London: Karnac, pp. 83–101.

Feldman, M. (2009) 'Grievance: The underlying Oedipal configuration', in *Doubt, Conviction and the Analytic Process*. London: Routledge, pp. 194–215.

Galdston, R. (1987) 'The longest pleasure: A psychoanalytic study of hatred', *Int. J. Psycho-Anal.* 68: 371–378.

LaFarge, L. (2006) 'The wish for revenge', *Psychoanal. Q.* 75: 447–475.

Lansky, M. (2001) 'Hidden shame, working through, and the problem, of forgiveness in The Tempest', *J. Am. Psychoanal. Assoc.* 49: 1005–1033.

Murray, J. M. (1964) 'Narcissism and the ego ideal', *J. Am. Psychoanal. Assoc.* 12: 471–511.

Rosenfeld, H. (1971) 'A clinical approach to the psychoanalytic theory of the life and death instincts: An investigation into the aggressive aspects of narcissism', *Int. J. Psycho-Anal.* 52: 169–178.

Rothstein, A. (1977) 'The ego attitude of entitlement', *Int. Rev. Psycho-Anal.* 4: 409–417.

Steiner, J. (1993) 'Revenge, resentment, remorse and reparation', in *Psychic Retreats: Pathological Organizations in Psychotic, Neurotic and Borderline Patients.* London: Routledge, pp. 74–87.

——— (1996) 'Revenge and resentment in the "Oedipus situation"', *Int. J. Psycho-Anal.* 77: 433–443.

Weintrobe, S. (2004) 'Links between grievance, complaint and different forms of entitlement', *Int. J. Psycho-Anal.* 85: 83–96.

Guilt

Guilt is an anguished state of mind arising when one feels that one has broken a rule, has wrongly done harm or caused distress to another. In psychoanalytic theories the same word is used to cover a considerable range of different emotional experiences, which can be confusing.

Freud emphasised the importance of guilt and realised that unconscious guilt [see Unconscious guilt] was a powerful motive force for self-punishment or for a motivated kind of failure (Freud, 1916, 1924). He made it a central aspect of his final model of the mind, the structural model, in which the ego is in a constant struggle to ward off the attacks of the superego. That conflict between the ego and the superego results in the experience of guilt, as the superego berates the ego for contravening the internal standards embodied in the superego.

Guilt, specifically 'depressive guilt', is a central, inherent feature of Klein's depressive position [see Depressive position]. It comes with the realisation of the attacks that one has made on one's loved objects. Depending on the degree to which the depressive position has been worked through, guilt is experienced along a spectrum between, at one end, a feeling of hopeless damnation or despair and, at the other, a sense of pained remorse for which one feels able to make reparation [see Reparation]. The ability to make reparation contributes to the strength and creativity of the ego.

In the paranoid-schizoid position 'persecutory guilt' is often referred to. This consists not so much of regret *for the other's sake* over the harm done to another, but a fear of dangerous (and talionic) reprisal from the other.

The guilt is thus not a 'moral' guilt, but a fear for the survival of the ego, which feels under threat of death. Guilt, as it develops in the depressive position, has evolved out of the preceding sense of persecution and fear of death and hence the most primitive form of depressive guilt merges into persecutory guilt.

See Depressive anxiety; Reparation

Freud, S. (1916) *Introductory Lectures on Psycho-Analysis*, *S.E. 15/16*. London: Hogarth Press.
—— (1924) 'The economic problem of masochism', *S.E. 19*. London: Hogarth Press, pp. 157–170.

Paula Heimann

Biography: Paula Heimann was born in Danzig in 1899 of Russian parents. She trained in medicine and then psychoanalysis in Berlin. She left following the Reichstag fire, when she was temporarily arrested, and arrived in London, her husband having previously moved to Switzerland. In London, Heimann retrained as a psychoanalyst with Melanie Klein and became her staunchest supporter (with Susan Isaacs) throughout the difficult times in the 1940s when the Kleinian Group came under attack from Edward Glover and the émigré analysts from Vienna. Mysteriously, she and Klein began to disagree, although this never became public, and finally in 1955 Heimann left the 'Klein Group' [*see* Kleinian Group], to the stunned amazement of the rest of the British Psychoanalytical Society. She was subsequently an important member of the 'Independent Group' of analysts in the Society until her death in 1982.

Scientific contributions: Heimann was a crucial protagonist in the Controversial Discussions in 1943–1944, during which she read a paper spelling out the Kleinian view of internal objects, and also a joint one with Susan Isaacs on regression (both published in 1952). Her work at this stage was seen to clarify, both clinically and theoretically, concepts that Klein had initiated, especially the ideas of the depressive position and internal objects. Internal objects had been the subject of Heimann's paper to become a Member of the British Psychoanalytical Society (Heimann, 1942).

Assimilation: Later Heimann followed up one important aspect of that paper, which concerned the fate of the internal object. This was to do with the question of whether the object was introjected into the ego or the superego. Heimann described a process of 'assimilation' of certain objects, which thus became parts of the ego, potentially available for introjective identification, in contrast to the process whereby certain other objects remained unassimilated and became hostile internal persecutors (Heimann, 1942) [*see* Assimilation]. Her work has generated the view of the internal world as an arena of internal object relationships of varying kinds and was, in embryo, the beginnings of a systematic Kleinian view of the structure of the personality. Klein used the idea of assimilation in her later paper on the paranoid-schizoid position (Klein, 1946).

Countertransference: The most well known of Heimann's papers is 'On counter-transference' in 1950, which gives the first detailed exposition of the analyst's countertransference as a possibly useful source of information about the patient. Heimann's view of countertransference contradicted the views of Freud and Klein, both of whom thought that the analyst's countertransference was largely an expression of the analyst's psycho-pathology (Freud, 1912; Klein, 1957, p. 226; Melanie Klein Archive, C72, Wellcome Library). Heinrich Racker (1948) had written an earlier paper with similar views to those of Heimann, but it was not published in English until 1953 and it was probably not known to Heimann at the time she wrote her paper. There was a considerable interest in reviewing the nature and possible use of countertransference at this time [*see* Countertransference].

The problem of distinguishing between the analyst's feelings that are a useful source of information about the patient from those that are defensive against the patient has been a source of continuing interest and debate (Money-Kyrle, 1956; Brenman Pick, 1985; Rosenfeld, 1987).

Heimann's disagreement with Klein: According to Pearl King, Klein asked Heimann to withdraw her paper (on countertransference) in 1950 (King, 1983, p. 6). Heimann refused to retract her paper and has taken the credit for an important innovation that others were at the time considering (see Racker, 1948; Little and Langs, 1981).

In 1955 at the Geneva Congress of the International Psychoanalytical Association Heimann gave another paper, 'The dynamics of transference interpretation' (Heimann, 1956), and Klein gave a first version of her paper 'Envy and gratitude', with which Heimann came to realise that she pro-foundly disagreed. 'In the months that followed', Pearl King says:

> It gradually became clear that Paula Heimann was parting company with Melanie Klein and her group. At Melanie Klein's request she resigned from the Melanie Klein Trust in November 1955, and then she made a statement to the (British) Society that she no longer wished to be considered a member of the Klein Group.
>
> (King, 1983, p. 7)

The exact basis of the disagreement between Heimann and Klein has never been explicitly described.

Heimann became an active and enthusiastic member of the Independent Group in the British Psychoanalytical Society and continued to write many papers until her death in 1982.

Brenman Pick, I. (1985) 'Working through in the counter-transference', *Int. J. Psycho-Anal.* 66: 157–166.

Freud, S. (1912) 'Recommendations to physicians practising psychoanalysis', *S.E. 12*. London: Hogarth Press, pp. 109–120.

Heimann, P. (1942) 'A contribution to the problem of sublimation and its relation to processes of internalization', *Int. J. Psycho-Anal.* 23: 8–17.

—— (1950) 'On counter-transference', *Int. J. Psycho-Anal.* 31: 81–84.

—— (1952) 'Certain functions of introjection and projection in early infancy', in M. Klein, P. Heimann, S. Isaacs and J. Riviere (eds) *Developments in Psycho-Analysis*. London: Hogarth Press, pp. 122–167.

—— (1956) 'The dynamics of transference interpretation', *Int. J. Psycho-Anal.* 37: 303–310.

—— and Isaacs, S. (1952) 'Regression', in M. Klein, P. Heimann, S. Isaacs and J. Riviere (eds) *Developments in Psycho-Analysis*. London: Hogarth Press, pp. 169–197.

King, P. (1983) 'Paula Heimann's quest for her own identity as a psychoanalyst: An introductory memoir', in M. Tonnesmann (ed.) *About Children and Children-No-Longer: Collected Papers 1942–80*. London: Routledge (1989), pp. 1–9.

Klein, M. (1946) 'Notes on some schizoid mechanisms', in *The Writings of Melanie Klein*, Vol. 3. London: Hogarth Press, pp. 1–24.

—— (1957) 'Envy and gratitude', in *The Writings of Melanie Klein*, Vol. 3. London: Hogarth Press, pp. 176–235.

Little, M. and Langs, R. (1981) 'Dialogue: Margaret Little/Robert Langs', in *Transference Neurosis and Transference Psychosis*. New York: Jason Aronson, pp. 269–306.

Money-Kyrle, R. (1956) 'Normal counter-transference and some of its deviations', *Int. J. Psycho-Anal.* 57: 360–366.

Racker, H. (1948) 'A contribution to the problem of countertransference', *Int. J. Psycho-Anal.* 34: 313–324.

Rosenfeld, H. (1987) *Impasse and Interpretation*. London: Tavistock.

Hysteria

Klein: Klein herself writes very little about hysteria. Her main reference to the subject is in her 1923 paper 'Early analysis', in which she is working very much within Freud's theory to elucidate the question: What are the conditions for successful sublimations and symbol formation to become possible rather than symptoms? In this context she interrogates Freud's paper on Leonardo da Vinci (1911) and asks why he did not develop hysteria, given the importance of his early fellatio phantasy (the vulture's tail opening his mouth)? In hysteria, fellatio phantasies often manifest in the form of the conversion symptom 'globus hystericus'. Klein's formal argument leads her to the answer that fixations should not occur too early, so that symbol formation can function and lead to successful sublimations into non-sexual activities. An example of this is da Vinci's later scientific interest in the flight of birds. In her later work Klein does not say more about the subject of hysteria.

Brenman: More recently Eric Brenman in his paper 'Hysteria' (1985) revisits the topic, commenting that analysts no longer encounter the type of hysteric patients that Freud did at the end of the nineteenth century. However, Brenman argues that patients, both male and female, with hysterical personalities are still identifiable. He looks at such personalities in the light of more contemporary theories of pathological narcissism and outlines their serious narcissistic disturbances. They manifest a combination of catastrophic fears, experiences and fantasies but also a radical denial of these in a way not dissimilar to the classical hysteric who, although paralysed, affects a *belle-indifférence* to convince the physician that apart from their symptom they are well. Brenman describes how such patients present as able to make an apparent relation with an external object. However, the object is made to fulfil the function of holding the patient together, whilst the serious possibilities of depressive breakdown and disintegration are denied. In spite of the absence of conversion symptoms the analyst becomes the target of sustained attempts to *convert* him to agree with the patient's 'malformations'. Brenman has in mind more particularly the type of narcissistic identifications such patients make, which are shallow, skin-deep and more with an omnipotent phantasy object than with a real one. It is this shallow version of psychic reality that they turn into a truth, and they try to recruit the analyst to collude in sharing an indifference to their real disturbance.

Britton: Ronald Britton (2003) puts forward a different perspective in agreement with other analysts (Green, Kohon and Bollas). He sees hysteria as a psychoanalytic state that has features in common with the borderline syndrome but is not the same. In hysteria the patient attempts to possess the object in the realm of love whereas in the borderline syndrome the claim is to possess in the realm of knowledge. Britton explains that the hysteric wishes to have exclusive possession of the analyst's love, to the exclusion of any other reality apart from love. The analyst is made to feel very important and invited into 'an unconscious collusive partnership of mutual admiration' (2003, p. 25). In the borderline transference the patient insists on a complete intersubjective understanding so that the analyst's deriving of knowledge from any other third source is systematically annihilated. The analyst often feels constrained and tyrannised. Britton also makes use of this particular insight in the hysteric demand for exclusive love to re-visit Freud's paper on the erotic transference: 'Observation on transference-love'

(1915). He links this paper with Freud's probable preoccupation with the difficulties that Breuer encountered with Anna O. and the actual enactment that took place between Karl Jung and Sabina Spielrein.

Brenman, E. (1985) 'Hysteria', *Int. J. Psycho-Anal.* 66: 423–432.
Britton, R. (2003) *Sex, Death, and the Superego: Experiences in Psychoanalysis.* London: Karnac.
Freud, S. (1911) 'Leonardo da Vinci and a memory of his childhood', *S.E. 11*. London: Hogarth Press, pp. 63–137.
—— (1915) 'Observation on transference-love', *S.E. 12*. London: Hogarth Press, pp. 159–171.
Klein, M. (1923) 'Early analysis', in *The Writings of Melanie Klein*, Vol. 1. London: Hogarth Press, pp. 77–105.

Id

In his structural theory, Freud (1923) describes a tripartite model of the mind that comprises three agencies: the id, the ego and the superego. The id encompasses all the primitive instinctual endowments, and from it grows the ego and the superego. Views divergent from Freud developed particularly in the British Psychoanalytical Society as a result of the greater emphasis on object relations, notably those of Fairbairn and Klein.

Fairbairn: Fairbairn (1952) dismisses the concept of instincts and replaces it with the idea that impulses are 'strategies' of relating to objects, since the human individual is object-seeking rather than pleasure-seeking. This shift of emphasis away from the concept of instinct, in his view, offered psychoanalysis a way out of the model that had led Freud to postulate the death instinct as beyond the pleasure principle [*see* Ronald Fairbairn].

Klein: Klein adopts a clinical approach to the id that not only includes the death instinct [*see* Death instinct] but emphasises instincts in the form of their mental representation rather than their physiological origins. She directs her attention to phantasy, and unconscious phantasy as the representation of instincts [*see* Unconscious phantasy].

In her early work Klein's loyalty is to Freud's 'structural model', but gradually the 'id' acquires new meanings as she develops her own theories. She embraces Freud's theory of the death instinct, giving it clinical reference points, and her model of psychic conflict concerns the clash not between the life instinct and the death instinct *per se* but between their representatives in unconscious phantasy. Because psychic conflict results, in her view, from the impact of the death instinct on object relations, the 'id' tends to become a representative of the death instinct in her writing. The Freudian conflict between the ego and the id (stimulated by the demands of the superego upon the ego) is replaced, in effect, by Klein's notion of the conflict between the life instinct and the death instinct [*see* Anxiety].

See Death instinct; Instincts

Fairbairn, R. (1952) *Psycho-Analytic Studies of the Personality*. London: Routledge & Kegan Paul.
Freud, S. (1923) 'The ego and the id', *S.E. 19*. London: Hogarth Press, pp. 3–66.

Ideal object

Freud (1921) describes a process of idealisation in the act of love and develops it in relation to his concept of narcissism and the ego ideal.

Klein describes idealisation as an early defence mechanism and part of the process of splitting. In Klein's view the first act of the ego is to split off and project out the death instinct, which is causing intense anxiety within. At the same time the ego also projects out libidinal or loving feelings into the object. In this way the ego and the object are split or separated into a 'good' or 'ideal' part on the one hand and an extremely bad part on the other. 'The presence in the mind of the good (ideal) object enables the ego to maintain at times strong feelings of love and gratification' (Klein, 1952, pp. 70–71). Klein often uses the terms 'ideal object' and 'good object' interchangeably. For her, the 'ideal object' is the extremely 'good object'. Her view is that the infant experiences its initial drives and emotional states very powerfully and with enormous intensity. The first 'good object' is therefore felt to be extremely good and, given the extreme nature of the split, is an 'ideal object' in that all its bad aspects and all bad experiences in relation to it are denied. Klein maintains that this kind of binary splitting is essential for the initial protection of the self and object and that it is a prerequisite for the secure introjection and installation of a 'good object' around which the ego can begin to cohere. She describes the infant as creating an imaginary powerful breast that can defend it against all persecutory experience. In 1952 Klein suggests that the infant might greedily require the image of a breast that provides 'unlimited immediate and everlasting gratification' (Klein, 1952, p. 64). The infant falls back on the splitting processes of the 'paranoid-schizoid position' when he faces the anxieties of the 'depressive position' [*see*: Bad object; Death instinct; Depressive position; Good object; Internal objects; Libido; Paranoid-schizoid position; Splitting].

Idealisation and envy: The greater the constitutional endowment of death instinct or envy and the greater the accumulation of bad experience, the greater is the need for extreme splitting. Idealisation of the object can protect the individual from feeling persecuted from without. However, the presence of an ideal object also provokes envy and necessitates a rigidly maintained split. This also risks a situation in which the object is felt to oscillate between ideal and persecutory.

Idealisation and persecution: The 'ideal object' may be felt by the individual as persecutory in as far as it makes demands for a perfection that can never be achieved; the ideal object is introjected into the ego and into the superego and plays a part in the early severe superego [*see* Superego].

Omnipotent introjection of the ideal object: Idealisation of the self protects from persecution within and the individual may omnipotently introject the 'ideal object', identify himself with it and believe himself to be nothing but good and the possessor of magical reparative powers. Britton (2003, p. 107) writes about the ego that is in identification with the ideal object as the 'ideal ego' [*see* Depressive position; Manic defences; Narcissism].

Britton, R. (2003) *Sex, Death, and the Superego*. London: Karnac.
Freud, S. (1921) 'Group psychology and the analysis of the ego', *S.E. 18*. London: Hogarth Press, pp. 67–143.
Klein, M. (1935) 'A contribution to the psychogenesis of manic-depressive states', in *The Writings of Melanie Klein*, Vol. 1. London: Hogarth Press, pp. 262–289.
—— (1952) 'Some theoretical conclusions regarding the emotional life of the infant', in *The Writings of Melanie Klein*, Vol. 3. London: Hogarth Press, pp. 61–73.

Idealisation

Freud (1921) described a process of idealisation in the act of love and developed it in relation to his concept of narcissism and the ego ideal. Klein includes idealisation along with denial and omnipotence in the manic defences and in a footnote in 1940 she describes it in the following way: 'Idealization is an essential process in the young child's mind, since he cannot yet cope in any other way with his fears of persecution (a result of his own hatred)' (Klein, 1940, p. 349).

Idealisation is part of the process of the binary splitting of the paranoid-schizoid position (1946), in which Klein views the first act of the ego as being to split off and project out both the life and the death instincts into the object. The object is in consequence split into a 'good' or ideal part and a 'bad' part. Idealisation is both the process and the result of this extreme splitting in which all bad and inadequate aspects of the self and the object are denied and kept away from the 'good' part, the result being an ideal, adequate, unblemished self and object. Idealisation takes place in phantasy and is omnipotent.

In Klein's theory mental health depends on the secure introjection of a good 'ideal' object around which the ego can cohere: 'The presence in the mind of the good (ideal) object enables the ego to maintain at times strong feelings of love and gratification' (Klein, 1952, pp. 70–71). The greater the strength of the death instinct and the worse the environment, the greater the need for a powerfully good alternative object to which the ego can turn for protection and thus the greater the need for idealisation, a point taken up by Alvarez (1992) in relation to working with children. Klein describes the infant as creating an imaginary powerful breast that can defend it against all persecutory experience [*see* Good object; Ideal object; Internal objects; Paranoid-schizoid position].

In 1952 Klein suggests that the infant might greedily require the image of a breast that provides 'unlimited immediate and everlasting gratification' (Klein, 1952, p. 64).

Pitfalls of idealisation: Idealisation involves denial of both material and psychic reality and needs to be given up if the self and object are to be realistically perceived [*see* Depressive position; Symbol formation]. The ideal object is introjected into the ego and into the superego and plays a part in the early severe superego. The ideal object, whether experienced as being external or internal, is enormously persecuting as its standards can never be met [*see* Superego]. Omnipotent introjection and identification with an ideally good or ideally bad object may offer protection from envy and persecution but it prevents development [*see* Narcissism; Pathological organisations; Projective identification].

Alvarez, A. (1992) *Live Company*. London: Routledge.
Freud, S. (1921) 'Group psychology and the analysis of the ego', *S.E. 18*. London: Hogarth Press, pp. 67–143.
Klein, M. (1940) 'Mourning and its relation to manic-depressive states', in *The Writings of Melanie Klein*, Vol. 1. London: Hogarth Press, pp. 344–369.
—— (1946) 'Notes on some schizoid mechanisms', in *The Writings of Melanie Klein*, Vol. 3. London: Hogarth Press, pp. 1–24.
—— (1952) 'Some theoretical conclusions regarding the emotional life of the infant', in *The Writings of Melanie Klein*, Vol. 3. London: Hogarth Press, pp. 61–93.

Identification

The term identification is often used interchangeably with the terms introjection, internalisation and incorporation. Conceptual distinctions between them can, however, be made. Identification is the result of the psychical process of introjection whereby an object or part-object, or an aspect/attribute of the object, is taken into the self and assimilated, thereby leading to a permanent transformation in the self: hence the term introjective identification. Not all introjections, however, lead to identifications. The process of introjection relies on phantasies of incorporation whereby the object or an aspect of the object is taken into the self. Such incorporative phantasies are best understood as psychical elaborations that mimic and metaphorise the original oral experience of ingestion of milk and also the sensual experience and enjoyment of being at the breast [*see* Incorporation; Introjection]. The term internalisation is synonymous with introjection and is used by Klein more prominently in her two papers on the depressive position (1935, 1940) because of its obvious link with the establishment of internal objects that make up the internal world.

By contrast identification is not used interchangeably with the term projection, or expulsion, although in fact the object has become identified with the part of the self that has been projected. Klein's late concept of projective identification (1946) links the two terms directly [*see* Projective identification]. In Klein's theory projective and introjective identification operate in tandem from the beginning of mental life and their interplay shapes the internal world that is set up first in the paranoid-schizoid position, when projective identification is more dominant, and later in the depressive position when there is an increase in introjective identification. Both are primitive processes occurring very early in development when there is little distinction between phantasy activity and reality [*see* Paranoid-schizoid position]. Phantasy 'is' reality, and phantasy constructs the reality of the internal world on the basis of these primitive forms of introjective and projective identifications, which in turn shape the way the external world is organised and experienced.

In Freud's work the important concept of identification is both a defence mechanism and also a process whereby the ego or self is formed and acquires an identity. Freud (1914) establishes a link between narcissistic object choice (the object chosen on the model of the self) and identification, since the self or one of its agencies are formed by identification with objects. Freud (1910) understands da Vinci's homosexual object choice as the result of an identification with his mother; his love for younger men is then formed on the model of he himself being loved by his mother. Then in 1917 Freud posits the crucial role of identification with the lost and reproached object, due to oral incorporation, in the genesis of melancholia. The notion of identification as a relic of past object relations features centrally in his structural theory: identifications with both parents take the place of pre-ceding oedipal attachments and contribute to the formation of the superego (Freud, 1923).

In 1921 Freud describes primary identification as the original, infantile mode of relating to an object prior to object choice: the self *is* the object, as compared to later identifications when the self is *like* the object. He also proposes that an external object such as the leader can be put in the place of the agency of the ego ideal of each individual and thereby help to constitute group identity through identification. Ferenczi (1909) had contrasted the predominance of the process of introjection in neurotics to that of projec-tion used by paranoiacs. He established a link between oral impulses and introjection and between anal impulses and projection that Karl Abraham

(1924) was to take up extensively later in his work on manic-depressive psychosis and obsessional neurosis. The well-established notion that identifications with objects affect centrally the structure and development of the self was taken up fully and developed further by Klein.

Identification in the paranoid-schizoid position: In Klein's theory it is important to distinguish two, albeit overlapping, things. These are firstly the interplay between, or the repeated cycles of, introjection and projection, as basic processes of the infantile ego operative from birth onwards. Secondly there are those processes of introjective and projective identification, which are more specific defence mechanisms, whose functions are best understood when located within the theory of the two positions. In Klein's view the early ego is active from the beginning but it is unintegrated and incoherent. The group of schizoid mechanisms in which projective identification plays a central role [*see* Paranoid-schizoid position] create the conditions for its integration and unification by instituting a crucial binary split between 'good' and 'bad' part-object relations and by keeping them wholly separate. This division in the ego, paradoxically, allows the early incoherent ego to develop an identification with the 'good' object, the idealised breast.

The idealised breast is formed by the projection of omnipotent, idealising phantasies that create an inexhaustibly gratifying, beneficent and loving breast, devoid of any bad, frustrating and persecutory elements that are all projected into and help create the 'bad' breast. It is crucial that this 'good' breast is experienced as a wholly good, complete and undamaged part-object for it to be able to allow the early incoherent ego to gain more coherence. For Klein the introjection of the 'good' breast is a precondition for normal development: 'it comes to form a focal point in the ego and makes for cohesiveness of the ego' (1946, p. 9). Through introjective identification the internal 'good' breast is set up and

> strengthens the infant's capacity to love and trust his objects, heightens the stimulus for introjection of good objects and situations and is therefore the essential source of reassurance against anxiety; it becomes the representative of the life instinct within and forms the helpful and benign aspect of the early super-ego.
>
> (1952, p. 67)

These ideas suggest that the 'good' part-object that is introjected is a less idealised and split-off part-object. The introjection of a 'good' breast and the resulting identification promote the ego's integration, counteract the process of splitting and dispersal and help the infant's access to the depressive position.

Klein's late concept of projective identification (1946) casts a new light on the concept of projection. The identification element of projection seemed, up to then, secondary to the expulsive and sadistic aspects of projection of bad parts against the breast or the mother's body, or in attempts to annihilate the persecutor. Projective identification into an object means that the object has become identified with that part of the self, but it also means that that part of the self is preserved and not annihilated and so is the object. In addition it is not only bad parts of the self that are projected but also good parts. The projection of good parts is essential for the development of good-object relations and for the integration of the ego (Klein, 1946). The baby can introject the 'good' object insofar as he projects into it his love and good parts. He can project 'good' parts in so far as he has introjected 'good' parts of the object.

Identification and the depressive position: Around the focal point provided to the ego by the internal 'good' breast the ego unifies further to gain access to whole-object relating. There is movement from the breast to a complete mother: the mother's body and its phantasied contents, and the combined parental couple, which includes the father's penis inside her. The mother as a loved object needs to have been introjected or internalised: it is the internal presence of such an object that leads to depressive anxieties, because the ego becomes aware of its own incapacity to protect its good internal objects from the bad objects and from its own sadistic impulses. The identification with the good internalised mother who is felt to be injured reinforces the drive to make reparation and to inhibit destructive impulses (Klein, 1952, p. 73). Paranoid anxiety from the paranoid-schizoid position needs to have decreased sufficiently and the ego needs to be sufficiently integrated for there to be a more successfully established internal object that is both loved and hated – if not, the internalisation can miscarry. The ego cannot develop love for its good objects without having to negotiate a crushing feeling of guilt and despair in relation to them. This central drama in the depressive position is worked through with the help of the manic and obsessional defences and the oedipal positions [*see* Depressive position; Oedipus complex]. It is this continuous process of working through and reworking throughout life, which allows the ego to establish more stable and realistic identifications with the loved parents inside the self and to experience both their separate existence and their own union as sources of security, that mitigates more tolerable forms of rivalry and jealousy.

In recent years some Kleinian analysts (Bick, 1968; Meltzer, 1975) have described a phenomenon that they call adhesive identification [*see* Adhesive identification]. In this state, which can be seen best in the identification processes of the autistic child or patient, there is an imitative identification in which the ego has no ability to introject anything at all and no ability to project parts of itself into an object [*see* Skin]. The failure appears to be in the development of a sense of space [*see* Internal reality], so there can never be phantasies of projecting into, or introjecting, since there is no possibility of phantasising about internal spaces. This results in a world lacking in a third dimension, and the only possibility is a form of imitative clinging onto the outside of an inside-less object.

Abraham, K. (1924) 'A short study of the libido, viewed in the light of mental disorders', in *Selected Papers on Psycho-Analysis*. London: Hogarth Press, pp. 418–501.
Bick, E. (1968) 'The experience of the skin in early object relations', *Int. J. Psycho-Anal*. 49: 484–488.
Ferenczi, S. (1909) 'Introjection and transference', in *First Contributions to Psycho-Analysis*. London: Hogarth Press, pp. 30–79.
Freud, S. (1910) 'Leonardo da Vinci and a memory of his childhood', *S.E. 11*. London: Hogarth Press, pp. 63–137.
—— (1914) 'On narcissism: An introduction', *S.E 14*. London: Hogarth Press, pp. 73–102.
—— (1917) 'Mourning and melancholia', *S.E. 14*. London: Hogarth Press, pp. 237–258.
—— (1921) 'Group psychology and the analysis of the ego', *S.E. 18*. London: Hogarth Press, pp. 69–143.
—— (1923) 'The ego and the id', *S.E. 19*. London: Hogarth Press, pp. 19–66.
Klein, M. (1935) 'A contribution to the psychogenesis of manic-depressive states', in *The Writings of Melanie Klein*, Vol. 1. London: Hogarth Press, pp. 262–289.
—— (1940) 'Mourning and its relation to manic-depressive states', in *The Writings of Melanie Klein*, Vol. 1. London: Hogarth Press, pp. 344–369.
—— (1946) 'Notes on some schizoid mechanisms', in *The Writings of Melanie Klein*, Vol. 3. London: Hogarth Press, pp. 1–24.
—— (1952) 'Some theoretical conclusions regarding the emotional life of the infant', in *The Writings of Melanie Klein*, Vol. 3. London: Hogarth Press, pp. 61–93.
Meltzer, D. (1975) 'Adhesive identification', *Contemp. Psychoanal*. 11: 289–301.

Incorporation

The term 'incorporation' refers to a set of omnipotent phantasies close to the bodily experiences of taking in, whereby an object, or a part of an object, is felt to have been taken inside the self. The early incorporated objects are felt to be physically present inside the body, taking up space and being active there. Later incorporations are less concrete and more symbolic in character. Incorporation is the phantasy activity that underlies the process of introjection and the mechanism of defence objectively described as introjective identification. The register of orality provides the prototype of incorporation, but there can be other modes of incorporation in phantasy, such as through the skin, the eyes, the rectum and the genitals.

See Introjection

Infant observation

The imperative in child analysis after the First World War was to substantiate Freud's views about childhood, which he had formulated by extrapolating back from adulthood. The same imperative began to be felt about the discoveries of the infant's experiences in the first year of life, which had come from Klein's analysis of older children (of about 2½ years onwards). In the early 1950s attempts were made to observe this developmental age.

The problem is one of being an outside observer without a direct method of becoming a listener-in to the internal world of the infant. The stage of development is one at which possibilities of communication are greatly reduced. The method with adults is a mutual verbal communication; with older children it is their play, observed and at times participated in [see Child analysis]. With infants, a new method is necessary. The infant in Klein's view conceptualises everything in terms of objects in relation to his body, its parts and their sensations and direct satisfactions. Without some form of accessible symbolic communication, is any entry into the infant's world possible at all?

This question was vigorously debated in the Controversial Discussions in 1943. When Susan Isaacs' 1943 paper ('The nature and function of phantasy') was later published (1948) she included an exhaustive introduction attempting to validate the process of psychoanalytic inference – if Freud had extrapolated back to childhood from adults, then it was valid for Klein to extrapolate to infancy from her work with children.

Klein herself made direct observations on infants, interpreting, on the basis of her own discoveries, the kinds of experience in their minds. Interestingly, when her paper was eventually published (Klein, 1952) it showed just how much she paid attention to the environment of mother and mother's state of mind as the primary environment of the child. It effectively supported Winnicott's later dictum: 'there is no such thing as an infant' (Winnicott, 1960). Joseph (1948) discussed a brief observation in terms of the problem of making a therapeutic intervention. Apart from these serendipitous observations, the interest in infants made slow progress.

Non-symbolic communication: When it was eventually understood that there are different varieties of projective identification (Bion, 1957) [see Projective identification], a way forward to a method of infant observation became possible. Projective identification is not a symbolic form of communication, but it was realised that the direct impact of one state of mind upon another can have communicative potential outside the world of symbols ('normal projective identification'). Thus analysts who were becoming sensitised to using their own reactions as instruments of understanding [see Countertransference] could come to understand a method that did not require symbolic expressions of the internal world. In the infant-observation method, however, the direct impact of states of mind must primarily be those between the infant and the mother. Thus mother, in a sense, becomes a vehicle for making manifest the infant's interactions with objects – equivalent to the playthings of the child in analysis.

Formal infant observation: Esther Bick began this work in 1948, as a training exercise for student child psychotherapists and psychoanalysts (see di Ceglie, 1987; Glucksman, 1987; Magagna, 1987). Bick began systematic observations of infants with their mothers in the home on a weekly basis throughout the first year of life (Bick, 1964, 1968 and, posthumously, 1986). As may be expected, the results partly confirmed the results of child analysis and partly contributed new facts and theories, some of which remain at present somewhat outside the mainstream of Kleinian thought [*see* Esther Bick], for example the passive quality of being held together by the first object, and the nature of adhesive identification.

Bick described the very earliest attempts at introjecting an object that would hold the personality together [*see* Paranoid-schizoid position]. She saw, in the mother–infant interaction, that this first object was particularly experienced through skin contact, and the sense of the skin as a containing object.

See Adhesive identification; Skin

Bick, E. (1964) 'Notes on infant observation in psycho-analytic training', *Int. J. Psycho-Anal.* 45: 558–566.
—— (1968) 'The experience of the skin in early object relations', *Int. J. Psycho-Anal.* 49: 484–486.
—— (1986) 'Further considerations of the function of the skin in early object relations', *Br. J. Psychother.* 2: 292–299.
Bion, W. (1957) 'Differentiation of the psychotic from the non-psychotic personalities', *Int. J. Psycho-Anal.* 38: 266–275.
di Ceglie, G. (1987) 'Projective identification in mother and baby relationship', *Br. J. Psychother.* 3: 239–245.
Glucksman, M. (1987) 'Clutching at straws: An infant's response to lack of maternal containment', *Br. J. Psychother.* 3: 340–349.
Isaacs, S. (1948) 'The nature and function of phantasy', *Int. J. Psycho-Anal.* 29: 73–97.
Joseph, B. (1948) 'A technical problem in the treatment of the infant patient', *Int. J. Psycho-Anal.* 29: 58–59.
Klein, M. (1952) 'On observing the behaviour of young infants', in *The Writings of Melanie Klein*, Vol. 3. London: Hogarth Press, pp. 94–121.
Magagna, J. (1987) 'Three years of infant observation with Mrs Bick', *J. Child Psychother.* 13: 19–39.

Winnicott, D. W. (1960) 'The theory of the infant–parent relationship', *Int. J. Psycho-Anal.* 41: 585–595.

Inhibition

Inhibition refers to a state or to a process in which an aspect or aspects of mental or physical activity are blocked. Freud (1900) develops the mechanical theory of a blocking-up of mental energy. Klein stresses instead the inhibition of symbolic activity and, particularly in her early work, the inhibition of children's' play, as this was a prevalent symptom in the disturbed children that she saw. Klein considers that inhibition is driven by fear. She describes how the child's fears of his own sadistic impulses, and his anxiety about the retaliation that these impulses might provoke, cause him to inhibit his mental activity. Sometimes, in psychotic children, all mental activity is inhibited (Klein, 1930; Rodrigue, 1955).

Klein (1932) expands this idea to show that sadism has the effect of inhibiting development in general and disturbs the natural unfolding (epigenesis) of the libidinal phases.

See Development; Libido; Paranoid-schizoid position; Sadism

Freud, S. (1900) *The Interpretation of Dreams, S.E. 4/5.* London: Hogarth Press.
Klein, M. (1930) 'The importance of symbol formation in the development of the ego', in *The Writings of Melanie Klein*, Vol. 1. London: Hogarth Press, pp. 219–232.
—— (1932) *The Psychoanalysis of Children. The Writings of Melanie Klein*, Vol. 2. London: Hogarth Press.
Rodrigue, E. (1955) 'The analysis of a three-year-old mute schizophrenic', in M. Klein, P. Heimann and R. Money-Kyrle (eds) *New Directions in Psycho-Analysis*. London: Tavistock (1955), pp. 140–179.

Innate knowledge

Two aspects of this are important in Kleinian thinking: the idea of 'unconscious phantasy' and Bion's ideas about 'innate preconceptions'.

Unconscious phantasy: Instincts are represented in the mind as unconscious phantasies of relationships with objects. The various instincts give rise to phantasies of objects and active relationships with them that are not as yet known in external reality. The primitive conceptions of objects are based on the bodily sensations involved in the instincts [*see* Unconscious phantasy].

As an example, when the newborn feels his cheek against the breast, an inborn reflex causes him to root for the nipple. The theory of unconscious phantasy suggests that the infant will have some *mental representation* of this event – that is, there will be a phantasy of an object to turn to and suckle from. Isaacs (1948) in her key paper goes to some lengths to try to convey the idea of a somatic knowledge actually embedded in the physical sensations. Freud had already concerned himself briefly with this debate in his reflections on Little Hans: '. . . the sensations of his penis had put him on the road to postulating a vagina' (Freud, 1909, p. 135). Klein was more explicit: '. . . the quite small child, which seemingly knows nothing about birth, has a very distinct "knowledge" of the fact that children grow in the womb' (Klein, 1927, p. 173). There was considerable resistance among Klein's critics to accepting the idea of such innate knowledge.

These endowed capabilities are thus inherent in bodily sensations. In the process of mental representation these sensations are experienced as affective relationships with objects. The objects that are then phantasised are not physical, nor in fact concrete in the normal sense; they are endowed with a primitive sense of place, within or without the self, and with affective motivations of benevolence or malevolence. In the first instance, therefore, they are *affective objects* [*see* Part-objects].

Kleinians think of this innate knowledge of objects and of activities performed on them or by them as a form of knowledge very different from the adult's. The infant does not have proper use of the distance receptors of hearing and seeing, and his knowledge is therefore limited to his skin inwards; knowledge is confined to a sense of separate identity from an object. This kind of knowledge, though very different, enters into and forms the basis for the later *experience* (as opposed to the perception) of objects when the eyes, ears, etc. are mastered properly.

Innate preconceptions: Bion (1962) was interested in further study of the process by which sense data are converted to usable mental contents. He terms the elaboration of sense data into the unconscious phantasy of an object *alpha-function* [*see* Alpha-function]. The innate knowledge he calls a *preconception* [*see* Preconception; Thinking and knowledge], and it is available at the outset to 'mate' with a realisation of this object. The result of a mating is, in Bion's terms, a *conception*. He is trying to convey that the reality of objects has to meet a function of the ego that will *give the realisations meaning*. The quality of having meaning is an innate endowment that is progressively elaborated in the world of external objects.

See Constitutional factor; Unconscious phantasy

Bion, W. (1962) *Learning from Experience*. London: Heinemann.
Freud, S. (1909) 'Analysis of a phobia in a five-year-old boy', *S.E. 10*. London: Hogarth Press, pp. 3–149.
Isaacs, S. (1948) 'The nature and function of phantasy', *Int. J. Psycho-Anal.* 29: 73–97.

Klein, M. (1927) 'Criminal tendencies in normal children', in *The Writings of Melanie Klein*, Vol. 1. London: Hogarth Press, pp. 170–185.

Instincts

Freud's concept of the human sexual instinct, more than the other instincts he refers to, is rigorously defined. In German Freud uses two terms: 'Instinkt' and 'Trieb' (Freud, 1905). Both terms have been translated into English as 'instinct' and this lack of differentiation has tended to lead to an overemphasis on the biological meaning of instinct as a genetically pre-given set of sexual responses, as in the case of animal instinct (Laplanche and Pontalis, 1973). Freud uses the term 'Instinkt' precisely to mean animal instinct – typically various sets of biologically prefixed behaviour patterns that show little *variability* in individuals across a species. He also uses the same term to raise the question as to whether primal phantasies, which he claims are universal, are inherited like animal instincts (Freud, 1918, p. 120). 'Trieb' in contrast connotes the irresistible nature of a more general orientation or of a pressure.

Freud defines 'Trieb' as having four components: *pressure, source, aim* and *object* (Freud, 1915a). In the heyday of nineteenth-century science, Freud proposed his 'Project for a scientific psychology' that would conform to laws of psychic determinism analogous to the laws of physics (Freud, 1895). As his theory of the unconscious mind evolved, Freud was clear that he was putting forward a mentalist theory (Freud, 1915b). The economic model in Freud's metapsychology posits that stimuli such as libidinal wishes put an internal pressure on the psychic apparatus to function towards discharge in accordance with the principle of constancy. The term *pressure* refers to a quantitative economic factor: libido [*see* Libido] is the hypothesised quantum of energy that puts a demand on the psychic apparatus to work by wish fulfilment. The *source* of the drive refers to erogeneous bodily zones (mouth, anus and genitals), which are initially linked to vital functions essential for survival. The infantile sexual drive is auto-erotic: it separates itself from the ego instinct, on which it leans, and constitutes itself qua sexual instinct through the activity of phantasy.

The drive according to Freud passes through various organisations: the oral, urethral, anal, phallic-oedipal and ultimately the genital. The *aim* of the drive is satisfaction but in psychoanalysis aims refer mostly to the underlying unconscious phantasies, which shape or inhibit the choice of an object and actual sexual behaviour with this object. Freud emphasises the variability in his broad categories of aims: passive–active, sado-masochistic, phallic-castrated, masculine–feminine. Finally the *object* refers to the person or part of a person whereby the aim is achieved whether in reality or in phantasy. The object in the human sexual drive shows a considerable variability and contingency and is only 'chosen' in its definite form as a result of the vicissitudes of the subject's developmental history (Laplanche and Pontalis, 1973). Such a complex definition of instinct actually marks the significant way in which Freud's notion of a sexual instinct differs from the more narrow biological readings of his theory that have tended to prevail. The sexual instinct is especially plastic, unlike animal instinct. By contrast, Freud's notions of an ego instinct and that of a death instinct are not nearly as clearly and systematically defined as that of the sexual instinct.

Instinctual dualism and conflict: Psychic conflict, central to Freud's theory of the mind, needs to be grounded in an overarching dualism of opposing forces. Conflict in his topographical theory (Freud, 1915b) between the unconscious and the ego is based ultimately on the *first dualism* between the repressed sexual wishes, and their derivatives, and the ego, which is motivated by the ego instincts. The latter, however, are very loosely defined as a driving force towards self-preservation in the human being. It never receives the detailed conceptual attention that Freud gives to the sexual drive. Interest is to the ego instinct what libido is to the sexual instinct (Freud, 1916–1917). It supports the ego's defences engaged in conflict.

Freud's first instinctual dualism became threatened for two reasons. He began to theorise the ego's development with his notion of narcissism (Freud, 1914): the ego as a unity is born in narcissism, it is the first object of the libido and it precedes object choice. Since the ego is itself libidinised, Freud's first dualism became undermined and left Freud with an unacceptable instinctual monism. In addition Freud and his colleagues had realised the crucial role that destructive sadistic and masochistic tendencies play in psychopathology and how the compulsion to repeat such unpleasurable scenarios acts as obstacles in analytic treatment. Pregenital libidinal organisations were imbued with extreme oral and anal sadism linked to the presence of a harsh and deadly superego (Freud, 1917; Abraham, 1924). It became conceptually untenable to understand aggression merely as the component instincts of cruelty and of the drive for mastery, or as mere components of the sexual instinct. The ubiquitous role of destructive aggression in the human mind added to the logical necessity for a separate concept.

Freud announced his *second instinctual dualism* in 1920 ('Beyond the pleasure principle'). Now the death instincts are opposed to the life instincts. The life instincts or Eros now subsume both the sexual instincts and the ego instincts of self-preservation. The death instinct or Thanatos is at first directed inwards. It strives towards a return to zero and tends first towards self-destruction. The life instinct and libido help to divert a large part of this tendency outwards into destructiveness towards external objects; another part becomes linked with the sexual instinct in the form of sadism proper, and some continues its work internally in the form of erotogenic masochism (Freud, 1924).

Freud fully acknowledged the speculative nature of his hypothesis of a primary masochism and was open to its rebuttal by his colleagues. But he also remained convinced of its validity (Freud, 1920) on the basis of the prevalence of the repetition of unpleasure in the 'phenomena of masochism immanent in so many people' (Freud, 1937). Laplanche and Pontalis (1973) point out that Freud (1926) did not make full use of his second instinctual dualism to explain the various modalities of psychic conflict and never gave it a more direct clinical relevance. The death instinct remains an abstract, speculative biological conception in Freud's work – a mythical force, usually concealed, that seeks to conduct life into death in all living matter.

Freud's concept of the death instinct as stemming from a primary masochism has met with numerous objections. Many leading analytic figures (Jones, Fenichel, Anna Freud and Hartmann, amongst others) who accept instinct theory and a primary dualism between love and hate have rejected the notion of a primary masochism on the basis that aggression and sado-masochism can be explained differently. For example, aggression is often understood as primary but as triggered by the object and directed towards the object, which inevitably causes frustration: by either not being there when needed or by virtue of its separateness so that it is ambivalently incorporated with love and hate. In contemporary psychoanalysis it is only the Kleinian and Lacanian analytic groups that have accepted the concept, albeit with very different formulations.

Klein and instinct theory: Klein was the first to develop a theory that combines both an instinct and an object-relations perspective. Fairbairn's (1952) narrow reading of Freud as a mechanistic thinker who used anti-quated neurological notions of mental energy in his economic model led him to reject the notion of instinct altogether. He tried to replace it with his redefinition of libido, not as pleasure-seeking but as object-seeking. In effect this redefinition got rid of Freud's more subtle and complex theory of the human sexual instinct. Klein by contrast quietly eschewed Freud's econ-omic model and used what seemed central and radical in Freud's under-standing of the sexual instinct. Although rooted in bodily experience as its source it gives rise to the primary mental events, which are infantile phan-tasy elaborations of bodily experience in relation to an object. Susan Isaacs (1948) showed how these elaborations, known as *unconscious phantasies*, make up, in effect, the substance of the infantile mind [*see* Unconscious phantasy].

In her early work Klein observed and understood the ubiquity and central importance of the primal scene phantasy in the mental life of young children and its role in psychic conflict. As Klein's came more into her own and, relying on the clinically grounded concepts of Abraham in particular, she highlighed the dominant role of combined sadism as the prime mover in psychical conflict. As sadism came to have more and more emphasis it became a separate entity, a set of impulses that, although linked with oral and anal phases of the libido, gave rise to a separate clinical phenomenology and separate sets of defences [see Sadism]. Klein finally abandoned the classical notion of sadism being a component of libido and switched explicitly to Freud's second instinctual dualism, which other analysts had not really adopted. In 1932 she accepted that she was observing the clinical manifestations of a conflict between the life and death instincts: '. . . in the early stages of development, the life instinct has to exert its power to the utmost in order to maintain itself against the death instinct' (Klein, 1932, p. 150). She embraced the second instinctual dualism and gave it an original Kleinian stamp in her understanding of the structure of the self, of object relations and of psychic conflict in her theory of the two positions.

Abraham, K. (1924) 'A short study of the libido, viewed in the light of mental disorder', in *Selected Papers on Psycho-Analysis*. London: Hogarth Press, pp. 418–501.

Fairbairn, W. R. D. (1952) *Psychoanalytic Studies of the Personality*. London: Tavistock.

Freud, S. (1895) 'Project for a scientific psychology', *S.E 1*. London: Hogarth Press, pp. 283–397.

—— (1905) 'Three essays on the theory of sexuality', *S.E. 7*. London: Hogarth Press, pp. 123–143.

—— (1914) 'On narcissism: An introduction', *S.E. 14*. London: Hogarth Press, pp. 67–102.

—— (1915a) 'Instincts and their vicissitudes', *S.E. 14*. London: Hogarth Press, pp. 109–117.

—— (1915b) 'The unconscious', *S.E. 14*. London: Hogarth Press, pp. 159–209.

—— (1916–1917) *Introductory Lectures on Psycho-Analysis*, *S.E. 16*. London: Hogarth Press, pp. 320–339.

—— (1917) 'Mourning and melancholia', *S.E. 14*. London: Hogarth Press, pp. 237–258.

—— (1918) 'From the history of an infantile neurosis', *S.E. 17*. London: Hogarth Press, pp. 3–122.

—— (1920) 'Beyond the pleasure principle', *S.E. 18*. London: Hogarth Press, pp. 3–64.

—— (1924) 'The economic problem of masochism', *S.E. 19*. London: Hogarth Press, pp. 159–172.

—— (1926) 'Inhibitions, symptoms and anxiety', *S.E. 20*. London: Hogarth Press, pp. 77–175.

—— (1937) 'Analysis terminable and interminable', *S.E. 23*. London: Hogarth Press, pp. 209–216.

Isaacs, S. (1948) 'The nature and function of phantasy', *Int. J. Psycho-Anal.* 29: 73–97.

Klein, M. (1932) *The Psychoanalysis of Children. The Writings of Melanie Klein*, Vol. 2. London: Hogarth Press.

Laplanche, J. and Pontalis, J.-B. (1973) *The Language of Psycho-Analysis*. London: Hogarth Press.

Integration

Like Freud, Klein does not see the ego or self as integrated or unitary to begin with, but that integration is *the developmental task*. This task is conceived differently at various stages in her work: Firstly, up to about 1932 Klein is preoccupied with the struggle to integrate the internal imagos of the parents into a mature superego. Next, between 1935 and 1946 comes the depressive position: With the integration of good and bad objects during development, splitting becomes progressively more realistic [*see* Depressive position].

Finally, from 1946 onwards, Klein is predominantly concerned with the integration of the ego itself [*see* Paranoid-schizoid position]. Integration depends on love impulses predominating over destructive impulses. Hate can only be mitigated by love, and if the two are kept apart this cannot occur:

> However . . . the coming together of destructive and loving impulses, and of the good and bad aspects of the object, arouse the anxiety that destructive feelings may overwhelm the loving feelings and endanger the good object. Thus there is conflict between seeking integration as a safeguard against destructive impulses and fearing integration lest the destructive impulses endanger the good object and the good parts of the self.
>
> (Klein, 1963, pp. 301–302)

The stably internalised good object is 'one of the preconditions for an integrated and stable ego' (Klein, 1955, p. 144). It acts as a focal point in the ego around which integration can occur. Klein emphasises the importance that the good or ideal part-object breast is also complete. Under the influence of oral libido the gratifying breast taken in is felt to be complete whereas the frustrating breast, which is attacked with oral sadism and taken in, is felt to be in fragments. This good and complete object acts as a focal point in the ego (1946, pp. 5–6). Later, loved and hated, good and bad, are synthesised within and the internal world becomes more similar to the external world. Complete and permanent integration is, however, impossible, as under strain from internal or external sources renewed splitting inevitably occurs, leading to the need for a further cycle of working through and integration.

Integration is promoted by the push of anxiety to move on to a new level of maturity, combined with the pull of biological development. In clinical practice Kleinian technique has emphasised more and more the last of these forms of integration – the integration of splits within the ego, with resulting enrichment of the personality, which is experienced as more whole. The transference relationship is viewed as being split into various aspects, many of which are projected outside the analytic consulting room and are experienced in relation to apparently extra-analytic objects. This dispersal of relationships and of experience results from the processes of splitting together with projective identification [*see* Technique].

See Development

Klein, M. (1946) 'Notes on some schizoid mechanisms', in *The Writings of Melanie Klein*, Vol. 3. London: Hogarth Press, pp. 1–24.
—— (1955) 'On identification', in *The Writings of Melanie Klein*, Vol. 3. London: Hogarth Press, pp. 141–175.
—— (1963) 'On the sense of loneliness', in *The Writings of Melanie Klein*, Vol. 3. London: Hogarth Press, pp. 300–313.

Internal reality

See Psychic reality

Internalisation

See Introjection

Introjection

This term was first coined by Ferenczi when psychoanalysts (Freud, Abraham) in their association with Jung began to look at psychotic patients. Ferenczi (1909) contrasts the paranoiac, who uses projection to expel from his ego unpleasant impulses, with the neurotic, who uses introjection to take into his ego a large part of the outside world and make it the object of unconscious phantasies. Ferenczi was one of the first to point out the correlation on the one hand between oral impulses and introjection, and on the other between anal ones and projection, correlations that Abraham was to take up extensively later in his work with manic-depressives.

Freud (1915, 1925) adopts the term introjection in his formulation that the pleasure-ego is formed by an introjection of everything that is a source of pleasure and by the projection of that which brings unpleasure. Freud (1917) also formulates the introjection of a lost, reproached object that brings unpleasure in the form of melancholia. Whereas Freud (1917) does not think that in mourning there is an introjection of the lost loved object, Abraham (1924) thinks that such an introjection is part of the work of mourning. The notion that introjection and identification [*see* Identification] play a central role in the development of both the ego and the superego was well established when Klein began her work.

In Klein's metapsychology the interplay between introjection and projection and the activity of omnipotent phantasy and hallucinatory wish-fulfilment are dominant processes in the infantile mind. Klein from early on maintains that both good and bad objects are introjected and that both good and bad internal objects are projected. Her ideas become firmer after she has postulated the concept of projective identification (Klein, 1946). Introjection of both good and bad objects leads to the presence of these objects in the internal world or inside the ego. Klein describes the nature and function of these introjected, inner objects from a variety of conceptual perspectives.

Introjection as defence mechanism: Some of these introjections are introjective identifications, which function as defence mechanisms deployed to modify anxiety in the same way that projective identification is a schizoid defence against paranoid anxiety. Both introjective and projective identification as defence mechanisms need to be distinguished from the more general cycles of introjection–projection. Thus in the paranoid-schizoid position the setting up of a 'good' breast inside the self by introjective identification is a major source of protection from and reassurance against persecutory anxiety in relation to the 'bad' breast, both internal and external (Klein, 1946). Similarly, Klein points out that, in the depressive position, when the ego becomes aware of its inability to protect its loved internalised objects and experiences depressive anxiety '. . . the ego makes greater use of introjection of the good object as a mechanism of defence' (Klein, 1935, p. 265). Introjective identification is one of the most important mechanisms used to build up a secure personality through the experience of having good objects safely located inside the self, with the ensuing experience of an internal sense of goodness, self-confidence and mental stability (Hinshelwood, 1991).

In her paper on mourning Klein (1940) refers to a more established internal world that is more populated and in which there is cohesion and reciprocal relations between objects. The situation of loss and mourning provides the occasion to carry on the life task of working-through the conflicts of the depressive position. What is threatened and at the centre of the pain of mourning is the loss of cohesion and harmony between the ego and the internal parents. Instead chaos prevails in the internal world. The loved objects are not annihilated or got rid of but the internal relation with them is in peril. Mania and triumph are the means of gaining mastery over the vengeful and damaged internal parents. When mania abates, pining and sorrow for the loved internal objects come back and allow for the re-establishment of a cohesive and harmonious world of internal objects. This continuous working-through strengthens the process of introjective identification with loved objects and the ego's integration and stability [*see* Depressive position].

Introjection and agency: Klein also uses the term introjection to explain the constitution of agencies such as the ego or the superego but there is no consistent rationale as to which of the introjects contribute to the development of the ego or superego. Thus the very early introjection of a 'good' breast is pivotal for ego integration but it also contributes to the formation of 'the helpful and benign aspect of the early super-ego' (Klein, 1952, p. 67); it depends very much on the context in which Klein is writing. Following Freud's later growing emphasis on the unconscious sense of guilt, a consistent feature of Kleinian theory has been to highlight the harsh and archaic features of the superego. In her early work Klein (1926, 1928) formulates a phase of maximal sadism synchronous with the early Oedipus complex. This explains the introjection of both excessively good and sadistic parental imagos that populate the early superego. These severe and distorted introjects were a result of the child's projection of its extremely sadistic impulses into its oedipal objects at a time when loving impulses were too weak to mitigate such destructiveness.

When Klein (1933) fully adopts Freud's second drive dualism as active from birth she understands the sadistic nucleus of the early superego as preceding the early Oedipus complex and as being linked with the projection of the death instinct into early objects. It is only later, after she has formulated both positions, that she writes that the early introjection of the 'good' and 'bad' breasts '. . . is the foundation of the super-ego and influences the development of the early Oedipus Complex' (Klein, 1958, p. 240). The severe superego becames linked more directly with the death instinct. In 1957 Klein introduces the idea of the envious superego, which is based on the early internalisation of a persecutory part-object: the retaliating, devouring and poisonous breast (1957, p. 231).

Introjection, identification and assimilation: Paula Heimann (1942) introduces the useful term *assimilation* to distinguish between internal objects that become part of the ego by identification and, as an internal resource, enhance, support and protect the ego's capacities for integration and development. By contrast, other internal objects are not assimilated and do not lead to identification: they are experienced as foreign bodies, which remain alien in the personality. In ordinary development the superego is severe to begin with and the 'good and 'bad' breast are not fused. The persecutory breast is not assimilated into the ego and is felt as an alien object, whereas the idealised breast is pivotal for early ego development and becomes assimilated. But as Klein points out it is also part of the benign superego and helpful to the ego. As a rule in the course of normal development the superego objects tend to become more fused and integrated. The gap between the ego and superego also diminishes and so does the gap between these internal objects and external ones [*see* Internal objects; Superego]. Objects that are assimilated are no longer available for the cycles of projection and introjection.

In more pathological development the superego introjects can be extremely ego destructive and suffused with unmitigated envy. Such a superego cannot be assimilated and it systematically strips the child of the satisfaction of making reparation. The concept of an envious, ego-destructive superego was taken up by Bion (1959) and more recently by contemporary Kleinians such as Brenman (1985), Riesenberg-Malcolm (1999) and O'Shaughnessy (1999).

Bion's *bizarre objects* (1957) are a result of excessive fragmentary splitting and violent projective identification of the apparatus of perception itself. These lead to an impoverishment of the capacity to think and create psychotic objects that cannot be assimilated [*see* Bizarre objects]. In Henri Rey's description of the schizoid condition, excessive fragmentary splitting and projective identification lead to 'pathological part-objects' (Rey, 1994). These cannot be assimilated and are not available for identity development, hence the unstable identity and proneness to identity diffusion that prevail in schizoid states.

Introjection and phenomenology: Klein also describes internal objects in order to capture the way in which they are experienced – from a phenomenological point of view (Bronstein, 2001). Thus the early 'good and bad' breasts in the paranoid-schizoid position are largely created through omnipotent phantasies that build on early bodily experience, pleasurable or painful. There is little differentiation between the object represented in phantasy and the object as experienced physically and sensually by the infant (Money Kyrle, 1968). Internal objects acquire a phantastic quality, such as having good and bad intentions and a life of their own. Hinshelwood offers an evocative picture of the phenomenology of such objects in the infant's internal world:

> If the infant's internal world is believed, in phantasy, to contain very bad or persecuting objects that seem to endanger the ego, then one phantasy is to internalize or introject the external 'good' object. For example, the hungry child (who believes there is a bad object gnawing at his tummy from the inside) can experience the internalization of mother's milk as an ideal and everlasting object going into him and replacing the bad one and, indeed, saving him.
>
> (Hinshelwood, 1991, p. 333)

The more primitive or more deeply unconscious objects, such as the internal 'good' and 'bad' breasts, the penis and the mother's body and the combined parents, are experienced in a concrete way. In 1940 Klein refers to the baby experiencing his incorporated parents as inner objects felt 'to be live people inside his body' (1940, p. 345). Less unconscious phantasies become more representational. In her 1935 paper Klein gives the example of a patient's hypochondriacal fears of a tapeworm eating its way through his body and giving him cancer. Klein sees the tapeworm as a more accessible representation of the combined parents in a hostile alliance against him. These objects, into whom he has projected his greed and extreme sadism, gnaw at him from inside and cause a fear of losing blood. As a child he imagined a little man inside his stomach who gave him wrong and perverse orders he had to follow (1935, p. 273). This example illustrates a transition: the tapeworm phantasy is representational and symbolic but also very close to bodily experience itself. It helps to explain why Klein maintained that in the deep unconscious the internal object is felt to be a 'physical being or a multitude of beings', hostile and friendly, that lodge 'inside the body, particularly inside the abdomen, a conception to which physiological processes and sensations of all kinds, past and present, have contributed' (D16, Melanie Klein Trust papers, in Hinshelwood, 1997, p. 885).

Abraham, K. (1924) 'A short study of the libido, viewed in the light of mental disorders', in *Selected Papers on Psycho-Analysis*. London: Hogarth Press, pp. 418–501.

Bion, W. (1957) 'Differentiation of the psychotic from the non-psychotic personalities', *Int. J. Psycho-Anal*. 38: 266–275.

—— (1959) 'Attacks on linking', *Int. J. Psycho-Anal*. 40: 308–315.

Brenman, E. (1985) 'Cruelty and narrow-mindedness', *Int. J. Psycho-Anal*. 66: 273–281.

Bronstein, C. (2001) 'What are internal objects?' in *Kleinian Theory: A Contemporary Perspective*. London: Whurr, pp. 108–124.

Ferenczi, S. (1909) 'Introjection and transference', in *First Contributions to Psycho-Analysis*. London: Hogarth Press, pp. 30–79.

Freud, S. (1915) 'Instincts and their vicissitudes', *S.E. 14*. London: Hogarth Press, pp. 117–140.

—— (1917) 'Mourning and melancholia', *S.E. 14*. London: Hogarth Press, pp. 237–258.

—— (1925) 'Negation', *S.E. 19*. London: Hogarth Press, pp. 235–239.

Heimann, P. (1942) 'A contribution to the problem of sublimation and its relation to processes of internalization', *Int. J. Psycho-Anal*. 23: 8–17.

Hinshelwood, R. D. (1991) 'Introjection', in *A Dictionary of Kleinian Thought*, 2nd edition. London: Free Association Books, pp. 331–334.

—— (1997) 'The elusive concept of internal objects (1934–43): Its role in the formation of the Klein Group', *Int. J. Psycho-Anal*. 78: 877–897.

Klein, M. (1926) 'The psychological principles of early analysis', in *The Writings of Melanie Klein*, Vol. 1. London: Hogarth Press, pp. 128–138.

—— (1928) 'Early stages of the Oedipus complex', in *The Writings of Melanie Klein*, Vol. 1. London: Hogarth Press, pp. 186–198.

—— (1933) 'The early development of conscience in the child', in *The Writings of Melanie Klein*, Vol. 1. London: Hogarth Press, pp. 248–257.

—— (1935) 'A contribution to the psychogenesis of manic-depressive states', in *The Writings of Melanie Klein*, Vol. 1. London: Hogarth Press, pp. 262–289.

—— (1940) 'Mourning and its relation to manic-depressive states', in *The Writings of Melanie Klein*, Vol. 1. London: Hogarth Press, pp. 344–369.

—— (1946) 'Notes on some schizoid mechanisms', in *The Writings of Melanie Klein*, Vol. 3. London: Hogarth Press, pp. 1–24.

—— (1952a) 'Some theoretical conclusions regarding the emotional life of the infant', in *The Writings of Melanie Klein*, Vol. 3. London: Hogarth Press, pp. 61–93.

—— (1957) 'Envy and gratitude', in *The Writings of Melanie Klein*, Vol. 3. London: Hogarth Press, pp. 176–235.

—— (1958) 'On the development of mental functioning', in *The Writings of Melanie Klein*, Vol. 3. London: Hogarth Press, pp. 236–246.

Money-Kyrle, R. (1968) 'Cognitive development', *Int. J. Psycho-Anal.* 49: 691–698.

O'Shaughnessy, E. (1999) 'Relating to the superego', *Int. J. Psycho-Anal.* 80: 861–870.

Rey, H. (1994) 'The schizoid mode of being and the space-time continuum', in J. Magagna (ed.) *Universals of Psychoanalysis in the Treatment of Psychotic and Borderline Patients*. London: Free Association Books, pp. 8–30.

Riesenberg-Malcolm, R. (1999) 'The constitution and operation of the super-ego', in *On Bearing Unbearable States of Mind*. London: Routledge, pp. 53–70.

Susan Isaacs

Biography: Susan Isaacs was born (1885) and brought up in Lancashire and retained her regional accent all her life (Gardner, 1969). She was academically outstanding, and remained an eminent educationalist throughout her psychoanalytic career. She taught generations of teachers at the Institute of Education in the University of London, and for a brief period ran an experimental progressive school for very young children (Malting House School in Cambridge). She was an enormous asset to the Kleinian Group in its early days and later during the trials of the Controversial Discussions, because she brought the rigour of academic debate to the clinical intuitions of the practitioners. She died in the prime of her career in 1948.

Scientific contributions: Isaacs's written work is spread between psychoanalysis and education. Like Klein she was anxious to distinguish the two. Her psychoanalytic work is largely a rigorous exposition of Klein's ideas, with much clinical illustration. Isaacs and Heimann were the main protagonists in the Controversial Discussions (Isaacs, 1948; Isaacs and

Heimann, 1952). Isaacs' sharp wit and quick thinking on her feet gave the Kleinian Group the advantage in these debates, winning points but rarely convincing the opposition [*see* Controversial Discussions].

Isaacs' great and lasting contribution has been her thorough exposition of Klein's concept of unconscious phantasy, which she presented at the Controversial Discussions and which has become the classic Kleinian paper on the topic (Isaacs, 1948). It seems likely that the initial idea, coming from the clinician Klein, was taken up by the academic thinker Isaacs in partnership [*see* Unconscious phantasy].

Gardner, D. E. M. (1969) *Susan Isaacs*. London: Methuen.

Isaacs, S. (1948) 'The nature and function of phantasy', *Int. J. Psycho-Anal.* 29: 73–97.

—— and Heimann, P. (1952) 'Regression', in M. Klein, P. Heimann, S. Isaacs and J. Riviere (eds) *Developments in Psycho-Analysis*. London: Hogarth Press (1952), pp. 169–197.

Jealousy

Klein points out that envy belongs to a two-person situation and jealousy to a three- person situation. Like Freud, she sees jealousy as inherent in the Oedipus situation, although her dating of this is much earlier than Freud's. The earliest relationship to mother and her breast is an exclusively two-person one:

> . . . though in that exclusive form it possibly does not last longer than a few months, for the phantasies relating to the father and his penis-phantasies which initiate the early stages of the Oedipus complex-introduce the relation to more than one object. In the analysis of adults and children the patient sometimes comes to experience feelings of blissful happiness through the revival of this early exclusive relation. . . . Such experiences often follow the analysis of jealousy and rivalry situations in which a third object, ultimately the father, is involved.
>
> (Klein, 1952, p. 49n)

The violence and intensity of early jealousy typically becomes mitigated with the compensations of new relationships:

> Jealousy is, as we know, inherent in the Oedipus situation and is accompanied by hate and death wishes. Normally, however, the gain of new objects who can be loved – the father and siblings – and other compensations which the developing ego derives from the external world, mitigate to some extent jealousy and grievance. If paranoid and

schizoid mechanisms are strong, jealousy – and ultimately envy – remain unmitigated.

(Klein, 1957, p. 197)

Klein distinguishes between envy and jealousy, which may be confused in everyday usage. Envy, rooted in a two-person relationship, stimulates the impulse to take away and spoil the possession of another. Jealousy involves a three-person relationship:

Jealousy is based on envy, but involves a relation to at least two people; it is mainly concerned with love that the subject feels is his due and has been taken away, or is in danger of being taken away, from him by his rival.

(Klein, 1957, p. 181)

Because jealousy is based on thwarted love, whereas envy is based on hatred of another's possessions and a wish to spoil them, jealousy is generally an easier affect to accept and tolerate in oneself and others than envy, and provokes less wholesale defences. In practice, the two may sometimes be hard to distinguish, and may occur in mixed form. For example, apparent jealousy of mother's relationship with father may be based more on envy of mother's phantasied possession of father than on jealousy of the love that father receives. Sodré (2008), in her discussion of pathological jealousy using Shakespeare's Othello as an illustration, shows how closely knit envy and jealousy can be.

Klein, M. (1952) 'The origins of transference', in *The Writings of Melanie Klein*, Vol. 3. London: Hogarth Press, pp. 48–56.
—— (1957) 'Envy and gratitude', in *The Writings of Melanie Klein*, Vol. 3. London: Hogarth Press, pp. 176–235.
Sodré, I. (2008) 'Even now, very now', in P. Roth and A. Lemma (eds) *Envy and Gratitude Revisited*. London: International Psychoanalytic Association, pp. 19–34.

Betty Joseph

Early years: Betty Joseph was born in 1917, and grew up in the Midlands near Birmingham. She undertook social work training at Birmingham University, and during a long summer holiday worked in a pioneering child guidance clinic established by Emmanuel Miller in the East End of London. She was introduced to the work of Melanie Klein at this time, and she went on to train as a psychiatric social worker at the London School of Economics. She moved to Salford, near Manchester and helped to set up a child guidance clinic there. She had by this time become more interested in psychoanalysis, and Manchester was at this time (1940) the only place outside London where there were any psychoanalysts. Esther Bick, who was working in Manchester, recommended Michael Balint, who had been her own analyst, and Joseph began analysis with him. A few years later Balint mentioned that some senior colleagues were coming from London to interview potential candidates and, after being interviewed by Susan Isaacs and Marjorie Brierley, Joseph was accepted for the training. Balint decided to move to London and suggested that Joseph move as well, which she did in 1945. She lived in Bloomsbury, and initially worked as a psychiatric social worker in the East End of London.

Joseph was part of an interesting and varied group of students; some were relatively young, such as Lois Monroe, whereas others, such as Bion and Money-Kyrle, who had returned from war service, were considerably older and more experienced. After qualifying she decided to undertake further clinical supervision with Hanna Segal, and subsequently with Melanie Klein and Paula Heimann. Joseph then went into analysis with Heimann for about 4 years, a few years before Heimann broke with Klein and left the Kleinian Group. Joseph also valued her supervision with Ella Sharpe, and her contact with Susan Isaacs and Joan Riviere, both of whom she admired.

Joseph was not only a student of Klein, but she became one of a circle of people who had close contact with her, both professionally and socially. This group included Bion, Segal, Rosenfeld and Jaques, and there was a considerable amount of sharing and discussion of Klein's evolving ideas as well as the work of the various talented members of this group.

Clinical and theoretical development: In Joseph's first publication in 1948 she discussed problems in dealing with infants and young children. She produced several further papers relating to child and adult patients, which followed closely the clinical and theoretical approach of Klein, Segal and others. It was not until the 1970s that she began to find her own distinctive voice, and began the development of her own ideas on technique and on psychic change that have been so influential. It was particularly in the course of her work with an apparently rather 'normal' patient (1971) that she began to focus on the problem of how to reach the patient with her interpretations. The interpretation might seem like a 'correct' and insightful one but it had little or no effect on the patient. She realised that she had to try to find the part of the patient that she *could* engage with and that could respond to her interventions. This approach, also vividly described in her important paper 'The patient who is difficult to reach' (1975), led her more and more to concentrate on what was going on in the consulting room between patient and analyst, trying to follow the moment-to-moment movements taking place. She described the way she would, for example, observe in detail the patient's response to an interpretation, how it was heard and understood, how it was used, whether it relieved or increased anxiety, etc.

Joseph's work is based on the belief that real psychic change is brought about through interpretative work based on what the patient experiences in the session, in his or her interaction with the analyst, rather than explanatory formulations or historical reconstructions. Thus, for example, in the treatment of perverse patients she studied how the perversion could be seen to be enacted in the transference, often in small and subtle ways. Furthermore, by following the moments at which it emerged, one could get an idea about the function that the perverse mechanisms fulfilled in preserving the patient's precarious equilibrium. Her assumption was that any significant problem or aspect of the patient's personality, including the persistent presence and influence of the patient's history, would find expression in the transference – if only the analyst can recognise and tolerate it. Freud stressed that nothing could really be analysed 'in absentia'; Joseph agrees, adding that thanks to our increased technical understanding more can now be recognised as being enacted in the relationship with the analyst, enabling us to discover what is actually present and active in the patient.

Joseph assumes that one of the important ways, of course, in which the analyst is alerted to what is going on in the transference is through the analyst's countertransference. She suggests paying close attention to what is actually being experienced by the analyst, the way he or she is being nudged, unconsciously manipulated, provoked, etc. into some kind of enactment that the patient requires and from which he may also derive gratification.

Joseph's stress on working with what is going on in the present, in the consulting room, has led her to feel that the patient's history is always present and is always part of the work, but, like Bion, she believes the analytic work is most effective when this history is generally somewhere at the back of the analyst's mind rather than when it is being used to organise the material. She argues that it is more helpful in promoting proper understanding and psychic change when the analyst can follow how the patient's history is being lived out, however subtly, in the session; or possibly when fragments of the patient's history are evoked in the analyst's mind, out of what is being experienced or spoken about in the room. She emphasises the difference between starting from the present and rediscovering history, and starting from history and basing one's understanding on the analyst's view of the history.

Joseph's broader influence: The technical understanding and the clinical approach that Joseph has developed over the past 35 years has gradually acquired considerable influence and importance in psychoanalytic thinking and practice. Joseph has been widely valued as a teacher and clinician, not only in the United Kingdom but also in many European centres and in the United States where she regularly visits to conduct clinical seminars and lectures. In 1995 Joseph was awarded the prestigious Sigourney Award in New York in recognition of her contribution. She remains (in 2010) a highly valued clinical teacher, lecturer and supervisor, both in London and abroad.

She has published a large number of important papers, some of which were collected together in *Psychic Equilibrium and Psychic Change* (1989). Since 1962 she has conducted a clinical workshop, which has been an important forum for the development of her ideas, and the exchange of ideas between Joseph and the members of the workshop. A number of the more recent participants in this workshop celebrated this institution by publishing a collection of papers by themselves and some close colleagues under the title *In Pursuit of Psychic Change* (Hargreaves and Varchevker, 2004).

An interview with Betty Joseph is published on the website of the Melanie Klein Trust (http://www.melanie-klein-trust.org.uk/interview%20 with%20joseph.htm).

Hargreaves, E. and Varchevker, A. (2004) *In Pursuit of Psychic Change*. London: Routledge.
Joseph, B. (1948) 'A technical problem in the treatment of the infant patient', *Int. J. Psycho-Anal*. 29: 58–59.
—— (1971) 'A clinical contribution to the analysis of a perversion', *Int. J. Psycho-Anal*. 52: 441–449.
—— (1975) 'The patient who is difficult to reach', in P. Giovacchini (ed.) *Tactics and Techniques in Psycho-Analytic Theory*, Vol. 2. New York: Jason Aronson, pp. 205–216.
—— (1989) *Psychic Equilibrium and Psychic Change*. London: Routledge.

Melanie Klein

Biography: Melanie Klein was born in Vienna in 1882, the youngest of four children. According to Grosskurth (1986) her father was a not very successful doctor, and her mother kept the family together by opening a shop selling flowers, until the family fortunes were suddenly increased by a successful sweepstake ticket. Academic learning and appreciation of cultural pursuits were very important in her family, and Melanie was extremely ambitious; she did well in school, emulating her older siblings, particularly her brother and her favourite sister, both of whom died young.

Klein married Arthur Klein, a chemical engineer, when she was 21 and they had their first child, Melitta, 10 months later. Their son Hans followed 3 years later, and their third child, Erich, was born in 1914. Melanie was frequently depressed during the years of her marriage, especially when she and her husband lived in small towns. She was particularly attached to her mother, and became very depressed after her mother died in 1914. She first heard of Freud at about the same time. Uwe Peters (1985) notes that when living in Budapest shortly before the First World War Klein's husband worked in the same office as Sandor Ferenczi's brother, and it is possible that this was her route to her first psychoanalysis, which was with Ferenczi. Klein presented an account of the development of her 5-year-old son Erich to analysts at the Budapest Society, and Ferenczi encouraged her to continue in this work, telling her that he thought she had a particular aptitude for it. Phyllis Grosskurth (1986, pp. 95–99) is convinced that Klein also analysed Melitta and Hans, but the meticulous research of Claudia Frank in the Melanie Klein Archive shows that this is exceedingly unlikely (see Frank, 2009, pp. 17–20).

In 1921 Klein went to Berlin where she developed further her work with children, analysing 16 children and developing what came to be called the 'play technique' (see Frank, 2009). In 1924 she was able to have analysis with Karl Abraham, sadly brought to an end by his illness and premature death in 1925. In 1924 Klein met Alix Strachey, who wrote enthusiastic letters to her husband James about Klein's work, which led to an invitation to Klein to give lectures on child analysis in England, which in turn eventually led to an invitation from Ernest Jones to come permanently to England in 1926 (see Meisel and Kendrick, 1986). Klein's work developed rapidly with both child and adult patients, and she was delighted by the interest of her English colleagues in her ideas.

In April 1934, however, Klein was devastated by the death of her son Hans in a mountain accident in Austria, which may have contributed something to the ground-breaking new thought of her 1935 paper, 'A contribution to the psychogenesis of manic-depressive states', which is generally recognised as the first and major statement of a new theory of the development of infantile thought and feeling. It was followed in 1940 by 'Mourning and its relation to manic-depressive states', in 1946 by 'Notes on some schizoid mechanisms' and in 1957 by 'Envy and gratitude'. These four papers give the first and basic tenets of Kleinian theory.

Kleinian theory was challenged by Klein's daughter Melitta and Melitta's analyst Edward Glover as early as 1934, and by the views of the Viennese analysts who arrived in London in 1938. During the 'Controversial Discussions' [*see* Controversial Discussions] held in London from 1941 to 1945, Susan Isaacs gave an impressive presentation of Klein's theory of child development. Sylvia Payne gave an equally impressive display of negotiating skill in keeping the Kleinians, the 'original' English analysts and the Viennese Freudians together in one Society. Klein's position gradually became more accepted and the current organisation of the British Psychoanalytical Society was established (King and Steiner, 1991).

Klein's work continued to develop after the Controversial Discussions until her death in 1960. She was not always an easy colleague, although she was sometimes greatly admired, even loved, by her students, such as James Gammill (Gammill, 1989). Her work stimulated many original contributions by a succession of her associates, analysands and students: Joan Riviere, Susan Isaacs, Paula Heimann, Roger Money-Kyrle, Herbert Rosenfeld, Hanna Segal, Wilfred Bion, Donald Meltzer, Betty Joseph – a creative process that is continuing with the current generation.

Frank, C. (2009) *Melanie Klein in Berlin* (Trans. S. Leighton and S. Young). London: Routledge.

Gammill, J. (1989) 'Some personal reflections on Melanie Klein', *Melanie Klein and Object Relations*, Vol. 1: December.

Grosskurth, P. (1986) *Melanie Klein: Her World and Her Work*. New York: Alfred K. Knopf.

King, P. and Steiner, R. (1991) *The Freud–Klein Controversies 1941–45*. London: Routledge.

Klein, M. (1935) 'A contribution to the psychogenesis of manic-depressive states', in *The Writings of Melanie Klein*, Vol. 1. London: Hogarth Press, pp. 262–289.

—— (1940) 'Mourning and its relation to manic-depressive states', in *The Writings of Melanie Klein*, Vol. 1. London: Hogarth Press, pp. 344–369.

—— (1946) 'Notes on some schizoid mechanisms', in *The Writings of Melanie Klein*, Vol. 3. London: Hogarth Press, pp. 1–24.

—— (1957) 'Envy and gratitude', in *The Writings of Melanie Klein*, Vol. 3. London: Hogarth Press, pp. 176–235.

Meisel, P. and Kendrick, W. (1986) *Bloomsbury/Freud. The Letters of James and Alix Strachey 1924–1925*. London: Chatto & Windus.

Peters, U. H. (1985) *Anna Freud: A Life Dedicated to Children*. London: Weidenfeld & Nicolson.

Kleinian Group

Klein's colleagues fall into separate groups from different stages of her career (Grosskurth, 1986). There was no clearly bounded 'Kleinian Group' until the mid-1940s. (The groupings of analysts in the British Psychoanalytical Society are in any case 'informal', in the sense that they are not explicitly recognised in the Constitution of the Society.)

Klein's earliest supporters were eminent members of the British Psychoanalytical Society, such as Ernest Jones, Alix and James Strachey (Meisel and Kendrick, 1986) and Edward Glover, who decided to invite Klein to settle in Britain in 1926 in spite of some unease about her new theories on the Continent. A number of other people supported her views, among them Marjorie Brierley and at first also Klein's own daughter, Melitta Schmideberg.

At first, in London, Edward Glover was enthusiastic. He wrote a highly complimentary review of Klein's book *The Psychoanalysis of Children*

(1932). Ernest Jones continued to be a firm supporter, and Klein attracted a number of other adherents: Joan Riviere, Susan Isaacs, Nina Searl and, a little later, Paula Heimann. This group continued to be loyal to her and supported her through the tragedy of her son Hans' death in a climbing accident in 1934 and her ensuing depression. During this period she wrote the remarkable paper 'A contribution to the psychogenesis of manic-depressive states' (1935), which came to be recognised as her first major statement of her new, distinctively 'Kleinian' theory. By this time Glover and Melitta Schmideberg were becoming antagonistic both towards Klein's ideas and her person, and this increased through the 1930s and finally erupted into open and virulent hostility during the Controversial Discussions in the early 1940s (see King and Steiner, 1991).

Meanwhile Klein and her group of colleagues were discussing the nature of phantasy, internal objects and the theoretical framework of the depressive position. We know too from the Melanie Klein Archive (Wellcome Library) and from the records of the British Psychoanalytical Society that during the early 1930s Klein was teaching courses on technique at the British Institute of Psychoanalysis.

After the end of the Second World War in 1945 the small set of Kleinian analysts began to change. Susan Isaacs died in 1948, Joan Riviere took a waning interest in the work as she grew older, becoming particularly disconcerted by the virulence of the rivalry with the classical analysts from Vienna, and Paula Heimann eventually sought a greater degree of professional independence in 1955 [*see* Paula Heimann].

When Klein's work on manic-depressive disorders and the depressive position came out during the 1930s, an interest developed within adult and child psychiatry (previously most interest in psychoanalysis in the 1920s and 1930s had been amongst educationalists and the literary intelligentsia). Several doctors sought training with Klein – W. Clifford M. Scott, John Bowlby, Donald Winnicott. They were all important people for her cause because they were medically qualified and therefore influential within the institutions that were important, and they all had established reputations of their own It seems likely that these were people from whom Klein gathered some of the important experience for understanding schizoid mechanisms and the mechanism of projection, which she developed into the concept of projective identification. Most of these people broke away from – or never saw themselves as full members of – the Kleinian Group as it was forming under the pressures of the disputes in the 1940s, after Anna Freud's arrival in London.

Shortly after the war a number of young doctors, some émigrés who had not previously been analysts, came for training with Klein. They were perhaps the true second generation, and they stuck with the group: notable were Hanna Segal, Herbert Rosenfeld and Wilfred Bion. It was these people, together with the solid support of the more retiring Roger Money-

Kyrle and the later addition of Donald Meltzer, who pushed forward Kleinian thought; Betty Joseph, although not medically qualified, was also a very valued member of this group.

Finally, from the 1950s onwards there has been a considerable interest in 'training as a Kleinian', not only in Britain but also in other countries, particularly in Latin America and to some extent Italy, which meant that for some time various analysts came to Britain for further training in Kleinian analysis. It is worth stressing however that there is *not* a separate 'Kleinian training', and that although students are free to choose their training analyst and supervisors, all British Institute students study a broad curriculum and are exposed to a range of ways of thinking and working. Since Bion's brief period in the United States, a small group of Klein-orientated analysts has developed in North America.

Grosskurth, P. (1986) *Melanie Klein: Her World and Her Work*. New York: Alfred A. Knopf.

King, P. and Steiner, R. (1991) The *Freud–Klein Controversies 1941–45*. London: Routledge.

Klein, M. (1932) *The Psychoanalysis of Children. The Writings of Melanie Klein*, Vol. 2. London: Hogarth Press.

—— (1935) 'A contribution to the psychogenesis of manic-depressive states', in *The Writings of Melanie Klein*, Vol. 1. London: Hogarth Press, pp. 262–289.

Meisel, P. and Kendrick, W. (1986) *Bloomsbury/Freud: The Letters of James and Alix Strachey*. London: Chatto & Windus.

Libido

The term libido in Freud's work has a variety of definitions (Laplanche and Pontalis, 1973). It has a *qualitative* meaning in that it refers to wishes and desires of a sexual and loving nature; Freud always maintained that libido is specific to the sexual instinct and does not pertain to the ego instincts or to his later concept of the death instincts. For Freud: 'It is the dynamic manifestation of the sexual instinct in mental life' (1923, p. 244). Freud also uses libido as a *quantitative* concept: a hypothetical mental energy that, he postulates, underlies the transformations of the sexual instinct. It serves 'as a measure of processes and transformations occurring in the field of sexual excitation' (Freud, 1905, p. 217).

Thus Freud uses this hypothesis to describe the displacement of libidinal cathexes in three ways: (i) with respect to various objects in phantasy as evident in primary process functioning in the formation of dreams and symptoms, or in reality as evident in the way he traces the transformations in object-love in the course of development, or in the transformations of love from ego to object-libido and vice versa; (ii) with respect to its sublimation into a non-sexual aim (artistic, intellectual) and (iii) with respect to the bodily source of excitation, the various erogeneous zones where it originates.

As a quantitative concept libido is central in Freud's *economic* model [*see* Economic model], in which he describes an economics of the libido subject to the law of quantitative conservation and the quickest route to satisfaction. This economic model is perhaps best grasped in Freud's many descriptions of the primary process at work in the unconscious, where psychical reality dominates. He hypothesises the free mobility of libidinal cathexes, in displacements and in condensations, from one or many 'ideational representatives' to a new one: the work of substitution central to distortion in dream and symptom formation. Unconscious libidinal impulses make a demand on the mind to be satisfied by the quickest route: by hallucinatory wish-fulfilment.

Phases of the libido: According to classical theory the development of infantile sexuality goes through a variety of libidinal organisations or psychosexual stages. The *oral* stage is organised around the primacy of the oral erogenous zone, where the elaborations in phantasy of the function of ingestion give incorporative meanings such as 'eating' and 'being eaten' to the oral object relationship. The *anal-sadistic* stage, dominant in the second year, is organised around the primacy of the anal zone, where elaborations in phantasy of the functions of expulsion and retention and symbolic substitutes for the faeces (copro-symbols) structure the anal object relationship. This organisation is marked by increased sadism and sado-masochistic modes of relating. The *phallic-oedipal* organisation dominates between 3 and 5 years under the primacy of the genital organs: penis and clitoris. According to Freud, the elaboration in phantasy is around one primary symbol, the phallus, that initiates the dichotomy phallic/castrated. The object relation is organised around the two oedipal positions and, although marked by intense rivalry, love is in the ascendant. The genital organisation resumes its completion at puberty when the outcome of the dissolution of the Oedipus complex by the castration complex leads to a change of object (mother to father) and for the girl a change of zone (clitoris to vagina), whilst for the boy the oedipal attachments have been given up. A new dichotomy, masculine/feminine, appears [*see* Oedipus complex].

Karl Abraham: Karl Abraham (1924) contributed more precise delineations of the pregenital stages in particular, alongside which he mapped his views on the development of object-love. Each of Freud's stages was subdivided into two, resulting in six altogether:

1   The early oral (sucking) stage is pre-ambivalent, with archaic urges of appreciative possessiveness based on incorporative phantasies of taking in and retaining goodness.

2   The later oral (cannibalistic) stage, with the advent of teething at 6 months, ushers in emotional ambivalence with sadistic phantasies having the upper hand: the object is cannibalised and forcefully incorporated. This damaged object exerts its tyranny within, as evident in melancholia.

3   In the second year of life the early anal-sadistic (expulsive) stage is dominated by sadistic phantasies to attack and destroy the object with bad faeces or to destroy the object identified with the *part-object* faeces, as evident in paranoia.

4   The later anal-sadistic (retentive) stage is marked by sadism in the form of phantasies of retaining and controlling the object rather than destroying it. The urges to possess and conserve the object gives rise to feelings of pity and concern for the object, evident in obsessive–compulsive neurosis. This stage demarcates neurosis from psychosis (no withdrawal of cathexis) and initiates the first form of object-love – that is, *partial love* for an object treated as possession, which marks the movement out of primary narcissism.

5   From age 3 years the earlier of the two genital stages, the phallic-oedipal, is highly ambivalent, with conflicts around castration.

6   The later genital stage, after puberty, is post-ambivalent, with true object-love; there is a waning of oedipal choices and the object is loved as a separate whole object. For Abraham, libido gains in strength only late, with the advent and strengthening of genitality from age 3 years onwards.

Klein and libido theory: Klein's theories of the libido fall into two phases – before and after the period 1932–1935. She then adopts Freud's second dualism of the life and death instincts, which she develops in her own way with unprecedented clinical relevance.

1920–1932: In her early work Klein shows her indebtedness both to Freud's complex understanding of infantile sexuality and also to Abraham's detailed and clinically grounded conceptualisations of the pregenital stages. She demonstrates the ubiquity of the primal scene phantasy in the child's mental life, and accepts the centrality of the Oedipus complex, whilst altering considerably the timing of its beginning to the first year of life. She does not see the phallic phase as being primary in the development of femininity but rather as secondary and defensive. These confident departures from classical orthodoxy are followed by another: she finds that the libidinal stages are more flexible and not as rigidly marked as Freud and Abraham had described. In her view genital impulses and phantasies – and anal/urethral ones also – appear in the first year, which makes it conceptually possible for her to posit an early Oedipus complex. However, she does not throw out the sequence of stages altogether, and adheres to the notion of phase dominance whereby certain libidinal impulses achieve primacy but not at the exclusion of others. Thus in the first year the oral impulses have primacy over the other drive strivings, which allows Klein to argue that the less vocal early genital impulses are easily eclipsed and can remain unnoticed [*see* Oedipus complex; Superego].

Klein, like Freud and particularly Abraham, was very preoccupied with the roles that sadism and destructive aggression play in the pregenital stages and in the alarming defusion of the drives that affect overall libidinal development. Klein's early notion of *maximal sadism*, whereby the inside of the mother's body and the combined parents are attacked with all the convergent aims of sadism (Klein, 1928), yields a terrifying early psychotic anxiety and terrifying inner imagos made more insuperable for the developing child because of Klein's own adherence to the classical view that love only gains in strength with the advent of genitality in the third year. However, her allegiance to Abraham's seminal distinction between the early and later anal stage, and the appearance of feelings of pity and concern for the object, help her to formulate the notions of restoration and of obsessional repair, which lead to the later concept of reparation [*see* Obsessional defences; Superego].

After 1935: Klein's emphasis changes with the introduction of the depressive position in 1935 [*see* Depressive position]. At this point Klein comes to see the developmental history of the infant in terms of the quality and organisation of object relations, internal and external. From then on her emphasis is on the accumulation of internal objects: of what kind, in what condition and in what relation to each other and to the self. This theory of internal objects is closely linked with the operation of unconscious phantasy operative from the beginning of mental life [*see* Internal objects; Introjection]. Although Klein continues to make use of her thorough understanding of the contents of libidinal organisations, the stage view of development further loses prominence and her views on phase dominance become absorbed in her broader theory of the two positions (Klein, 1952) [*see* Instincts].

Libido and the second dualism: In Freud's second dualism (Freud, 1920) libido is subsumed together with the ego instincts under the larger notion of Eros, a principle of the life instinct whose aim is to maintain cohesion, to establish ever greater unities and to preserve and bind together (Freud, 1938). Freud did not develop the implications of this statement for his libido theory. Two questions are raised, however. This new definition of the life instincts and hence of libido does not seem to fit in the economic model of a tendency towards reduction of tensions and energy conservation by the quickest route to satisfaction. In addition it remains unclear what forms the life instincts take in the early pregenital stages, since in classical stage-theory love only comes to the fore as a significant force in the genital stages whilst sadism dominates the earlier phases.

Klein by contrast elaborates the second drive dualism and gives it specific shape from the beginning of mental life. In the paranoid-schizoid position the breast is sought actively and experienced with intense libidinal gratification but also with strong loving feelings, which are projected to create the idealised 'good' breast, which is in turn introjected to form a focal point for ego integration. Infantile object-love mixed with gratification is *present from the beginning* and strong enough to omnipotently create an idealised part-object that offers protection against the terrors linked to the death instincts represented by the persecutory 'bad' breast [*see* Paranoid-schizoid position].

In the depressive position ambivalence emerges and love for the object is in the service of the various forms that omnipotent repair and, ultimately, proper reparation takes precedence. Love or libido also fuels the two oedipal positions, which are attempts to work through the conflicts engendered by the hatred of the combined parents [*see* Depressive position; Oedipus complex].

Abraham, K. (1924) 'A short study of the development of the libido', in *Selected Paper on Psychoanalysis*. London: Hogarth Press, pp. 418–501.

Freud, S. (1905) 'Three essays on the theory of sexuality', *S.E. 7*. London: Hogarth Press, pp. 125–245.

—— (1920) 'Beyond the pleasure principle', *S.E. 18*. London: Hogarth Press, pp. 3–64.

—— (1923) 'Two encyclopedia articles', *S.E. 18*. London: Hogarth Press, pp. 255–259.

—— (1938) 'An outline of psycho-analysis', *S.E. 23*. London: Hogarth Press, pp. 141–205.

Klein, M. (1928) 'Early stages of the Oedipus conflict', in *The Writings of Melanie Klein*, Vol. 1. London: Hogarth Press, pp. 186–197.

—— (1952) 'Some theoretical conclusions regarding the emotional life of the infant', in *The Writings of Melanie Klein*, Vol. 3. London: Hogarth Press, pp. 61–93.

Laplanche, J. and Pontalis, J.-B. (1973) *The Language of Psycho-Analysis*. London: Hogarth Press.

Life instinct

From *The Psychoanalysis of Children* (1932) onwards Klein expressly uses Freud's theory of the opposed life and death instincts as the foundation of her work. She often uses 'libido' or 'libidinal forces' synonymously with 'life instinct'. She always refers to the life instinct in relation to the death instinct. In her earlier work she sees the life instinct as struggling against the power of the death instinct:

. . . the libido gradually consolidates its position by its struggle with the destructive instinctual drives.

Side by side with the polarity of the life-instinct and the death-instinct, we may, I think, place their interaction as a fundamental factor in the dynamic processes of the mind. There is an indissoluble bond between the libido and destructive tendencies which puts the former to a great extent in the power of the latter. But the vicious circle dominated by the death instinct, in which aggression gives rise to anxiety and anxiety reinforces aggression can be broken by the libidinal forces when these have gained in strength; in the early stages of development, the life-instinct has to exert its power to the utmost in order to maintain itself against the death-instinct. But this very necessity stimulates sexual development.

(Klein, 1932, p. 150)

In later work a sense of balance emerges. The life instinct is described as powering the ego and its defences, and pushing towards integration: 'The ego's urge towards integration and organization clearly reveals its derivation from the life instinct' (Klein, 1952, p. 57). Klein also (1952b) links the life instinct explicitly to love. In her late works (1957, 1958) she refers to the ego being called into action, indeed into very existence, by the life instinct at birth. She refers to the balance between the life and death instincts as being constitutionally determined:

If in the fusion the life instinct predominates, which implies an ascendancy of the capacity for love, the ego is relatively strong, and is more able to bear the anxiety arising from the death instinct and to counteract it.

(Klein, 1958, pp. 238–239)

See Death instinct

Klein, M. (1932) *The Psychoanalysis of Children. The Writings of Melanie Klein*, Vol. 2. London: Hogarth Press.
—— (1952a) 'The mutual influences in the development of the ego and the id', *Psychoanal. Study Child* 7: 51–53.
—— (1952b) 'Some theoretical conclusions regarding the emotional life of the infant', in *The Writings of Melanie Klein*, Vol. 3. London: Hogarth Press, pp. 61–93.
—— (1957) 'Envy and gratitude', in *The Writings of Melanie Klein*, Vol. 3. London: Hogarth Press, pp. 176–235.
—— (1958) 'On the development of mental functioning', in *The Writings of Melanie Klein*, Vol. 3. London: Hogarth Press, pp. 236–246.

Linking

In Kleinian theory linking is a fundamental concept, linked to integration [*see* Integration]. In the depressive position aspects of the object and of the ego, previously divided, are brought together. By the same token, attacks on linking are seen as an important feature of pathology.

Psychosis and attacks on linking: Important discoveries about links and attacks on links were made by colleagues of Klein, particularly Bion, Segal and Rosenfeld, while analysing psychotic patients. In Bion's (1959) theory of schizophrenia he described the attacks on the ego itself, which represented the experiences that Klein (1946) regarded as the effects of the death instinct acting within – the feeling of falling to pieces. Bion described particularly an attack on the awareness of internal reality [*see* Annihilation; Paranoid-schizoid position]. The severance of thoughts within the mind is characteristic of schizophrenics and was described by Rosenfeld (1947) and by Segal (1950):

> The fact that many things are tolerated in consciousness in the schizo-phrenic must not blind one to the necessity of interpreting what is repressed. Schizophrenics, more than others, repress the links between different trends of thought. They often tolerate in their ego thoughts and phantasies which would probably be repressed in the neurotic; but on the other hand they repress the links between the various phantasies and between phantasy and reality.
>
> (Segal, 1950, p. 118)

It is the *links* between mental contents that are attacked by the schizo-phrenic. Freud had also described this process of isolation of thought from affect in severe obsessional neurosis:

> In this disorder, as I have already explained, repression is effected not by means of amnesia but by a severance of causal connections brought about by withdrawal of affect. These repressed connections appear to persist in some kind of shadowy form, and they are thus transferred, by a process of projection, into the external world, where they bear witness to what has been effaced from consciousness.
>
> (Freud, 1909, pp. 231–232)

Although Freud and Segal describe the process in terms of repression, Bion describes its *violent* quality:

> It is to be expected that the deployment of projective identification would be particularly severe against thought, of whatsoever kind, that

turned to the relations between object-impressions, for if this link could be severed, or better still never forged, then at least consciousness of reality would be destroyed even though reality itself could not be.

(Bion, 1957, p. 50)

The end result is that the schizophrenic lives in a fragmented world, with primitive ideas unusable in his mind:

All these are now attacked till finally two objects cannot be brought together in a way which leaves each object with its intrinsic qualities intact and yet able, by their conjunction, to produce a new mental object.

(Bion, 1957, p. 50)

The destruction of these connections and conjunctions leads to the patient feeling 'surrounded by minute links which, being impregnated now with cruelty, link objects together cruelly' (Bion, 1957, p. 50) [*see* Bizarre objects; Psychosis]. Bion calls these particles 'beta-elements' [*see* Beta-elements]. The effect is well on the way to what Freud called a 'world catastrophe' (Freud, 1911, p. 70):

This is a disaster for mental life which is then not established in the normal mode. Instead of thinking based on the reality principle and symbolic communication within the self and with other objects, an anomalous enlargement of the pleasure ego occurs, with excessive use of splitting and projective identification as its concrete mode of relating to hated and hating objects. Omnipotence replaces thinking and omniscience replaces learning from experience in a disastrously confused, undeveloped and fragile ego.

(O'Shaughnessy, 1981, p. 183)

Here, added to the narcissistic withdrawal of the libido from objects in reality, which Freud had described as the world catastrophe, is described the idea of an omnipotent violent splitting up and projection of the ego. The ego is the focus of aggression, not just of libidinal love [*see* Narcissism].

Oedipal linking: Bion (1959) takes these observations on psychotic patients further to establish a more general, formal theory. He regards any coupling activities as based on an innate predisposition to conceive of the link between a container and its contents, typically the nipple in the breast or the penis in the vagina. The attack on the link between two internal mental objects is an attack on the internal parental couple [*see* Primal scene]. Because of the connotation of the oedipal couple, the conjoining of two mental objects is felt not only to arouse envy but to be the basis for internal, mental creativity.

Container and contained: The coupling of penis and vagina, or mouth and nipple, is taken by Bion (1962) as a prototype of the way mental objects are put together, one inside the other. Thus, putting experiences into thoughts, and thoughts into words, entails a repeated chain of linking processes modelled on physical intercourse between two bodily parts [*see* Container/contained]. With this model Bion goes on to investigate the nature of thought itself and described its basis in the linking together of thoughts, in the mating of preconceptions (expectations) with realisations [*see* Thinking and knowledge]. The particular kind of links that go to make up thinking are designated by the notation 'K' and they exist alongside other kinds of links, 'L' and 'H', representing loving and hating the object [*see* Epistemophilia].

Bion, W. (1957) 'Differentiation of the psychotic from the non-psychotic personalities', *Int. J. Psycho-Anal.* 38: 266–275; republished in *Second Thoughts*. London: Heinemann (1967), pp. 43–64.
—— (1959) 'Attacks on linking', *Int. J. Psycho-Anal.* 40: 308–315.
—— (1962) *Learning from Experience*. London: Heinemann.
Freud, S. (1909) 'Notes upon a case of obsessional neurosis', *S.E. 10*. London: Hogarth Press, pp. 153–320.
—— (1911) 'Psycho-analytic notes on an autobiographical account of a case of paranoia', *S.E. 12*. London: Hogarth Press, pp. 3–82.
Klein, M. (1946) 'Notes on some schizoid mechanisms', in *The Writings of Melanie Klein*, Vol. 3. London: Hogarth Press, pp. 1–2
O'Shaughnessy, E. (1981) 'A commemorative essay on W. R. Bion's theory of thinking', *J. Child Psychother.* 7: 181–192.
Rosenfeld, H. (1947) 'Analysis of a schizophrenic state with depersonalization', *Int. J. Psycho-Anal.* 28: 130–139.
Segal, H. (1950) 'Some aspects of an analysis of a schizophrenic', in *The Work of Hanna Segal*. New York: Jason Aronson (1981), pp. 101–120.

Loss

Freud (1917) described the similarity between depressive illnesses and mourning and the central aspect of loss in the nature of the problem. These losses linked up with his preceding views about the special importance of castration in childhood development. In 1926, when he investigated the nature of anxiety, he saw a number of situations of loss: the loss at birth, weaning, castration and so on through the developmental cycle.

Loss of the internal object: Klein adds to this by describing these losses as having a crucial similarity, in that they all arouse anxiety through creating a sense of an insecure *internalised good object* (Klein, 1940) [*see* Depressive position]. In this she adds significantly to Freud's (1917) theory in which he was impressed by the melancholic's aberrant mourning reaction when the external object had not actually been lost. She also develops Abraham's (1924) work in which he describes the manic-depressive's preoccupation with lost objects represented by faeces and their oral incorporation into the ego over which they cast their shadow.

Thus Klein develops the direction in which Abraham and Freud had been pointing and also adds her theory of the depressive position. Thus loss and mourning become, for Klein, not just vicissitudes but centrally important aspects of development.

See Depressive anxiety; Mourning

Abraham, K. (1924) 'A short study of the development of the libido', in *Selected Papers on Psycho-Analysis*. London: Hogarth Press (1927), pp. 418–501.
Freud, S. (1917) 'Mourning and melancholia', *S.E. 14*. London: Hogarth Press, pp. 237–258.
—— (1926) 'Inhibitions, symptoms and anxiety', *S.E. 20*. London: Hogarth Press, pp. 75–176.
Klein, M. (1940) 'Mourning and its relation to manic-depressive states', in *The Writings of Melanie Klein*, Vol. 1. London: Hogarth Press, pp. 344–369.

Love

Klein follows Abraham (1924) in trying to understand the kind of love that *feels for* the object rather than the love described in classical psychoanalysis, in which the object is merely what the subject satisfies himself upon. Freud's 'anaclitic love' is the latter, essentially a form of cupboard love. In contrast, Klein describes, partly from direct observation of infants, how 'gratification is as much related to the object which gives the food as to the food itself' (Klein, 1952, p. 96).

Love, gratitude and envy: In Klein's view there is a generous love from the beginning. Gratification simply helps to bring out gratitude towards the object. However, from the beginning gratification brings not only love and gratitude but also envy. In so far as the infant can sustain an attitude of gratitude to the loved object, and in so far as the actual external object (mother) can help to bring out gratitude, the infant can grow stronger in his belief in love and the good parts of himself. In Klein's view an important part of the security of the infant lies in the balance of envy versus gratitude in the personality, since envy destroys love and gratitude, and gratitude mitigates envy [see Envy].

Love in the paranoid-schizoid position: In the paranoid-schizoid state of mind the object is split into an ideal, loved object and a very bad, hated object. Love is by definition narcissistic, as the object is two-dimensional, imbued with exaggerating projections rather than being seen as its complex and imperfect self. The loving relationship with the ideal object tends to be imbued with moralism; self in relation to ideal object is felt to be righteous and the bad object is condemned and disowned as wicked. Since projective identification is occurring to an extreme degree the self is depleted and dependence on the object is extreme. The situation is also inherently unstable, and when disappointment and frustration occur the ideal phantasy can no longer be maintained and adoration of an ideal object gives way abruptly to hatred and reproach of an irredeemably bad object, which in its turn is felt as extremely persecuting.

Love in the depressive position: When Klein describes the depressive position she enters upon descriptions of quite new affective states – new, that is, to the descriptive pens of psychoanalysts. In fact they are much closer to the affects that are the preoccupation of the novelist and the ordinary person. She seeks to convey the qualities of a particular, poignant kind of love: a pining. Klein is here following up Abraham's notion of 'true object-love', the experience of whole objects. Love in the depressive position is for the non-ideal object, the good object that is also blemished and flawed [*see* Depressive position]. As this becomes established, the love, in spite of the flaws, tends not to switch so violently to hatred and a degree of emotional stability begins to develop. There is here the capacity for tolerance and forgiveness. Love in the depressive position is marked indelibly with concern and forgiveness.

However, the flawed whole object can give rise to the experience that the good object is, or was, perfect and has been injured and damaged by one's attacks, with the arousing of an anguished concern. In turn, this concern gives rise to the wish to restore and repair [*see* Guilt; Reparation].

See Whole object

Abraham, K. (1924) 'A short study of the development of the libido', in *Selected Papers on Psycho-Analysis*. London: Hogarth Press (1927), pp. 418–501.
Klein, M. (1952) 'On observing the behaviour of young infants', in *The Writings of Melanie Klein*, Vol. 3. London: Hogarth Press, pp. 94–121.

Manic defences

The pain of the depressive position occurs throughout life, and is met at times by a defensiveness in most people [*see* Depressive position]. Of paramount importance are the manic defences – states which in minor degree are common in everyone. The manic defences are typically omnipotent: 'The *sense of omnipotence* is what first and foremost characterises mania and, further, mania is based on the mechanism of *denial* . . .' (Klein, 1935, p. 277). Important elements of the manic defence are denial, omni-potent control and disparagement of the object (accompanied by idealisation of the self). In Klein's (1935) words: *'first of all denied is psychic reality* and the ego may then go on to deny a great deal of external reality' (p. 277) She comments that: 'The ego is unwilling and unable to renounce its good internal objects and yet endeavours to escape from the perils of dependence on them' (p. 277).

> 'Surely', argues the ego, 'it is not a matter of such great importance if this particular object is destroyed. There are so many others to be incorporated'. This *disparagement* of the object's importance and the contempt of it is, I think, a specific characteristic of mania.
> (Klein, 1935, p. 278)

Dependency is 'perilous' because the loved and needed object is also the hated one, putting the ego at risk of both persecutory and depressive anxieties. In mania, at the same time, the ego 'endeavours ceaselessly to *master and control* all its objects, and the evidence of this effort is its hyperactivity' (p. 277). This control:

> . . . is necessary for two reasons: (a) in order to deny the dread of them [the objects depended upon] which is being experienced, and (b) so that the mechanism . . . of making reparation to the object may be carried through.
> (Klein, 1935, p. 278)

So important are the mechanisms involved in mania that Klein, for a period in the late 1930s, referred to the *manic position*. These defences protect the subject from experiencing the painful consequences of dependence on good loved objects and the painful consequences of such dependence. Manic defences, however, lead to further problems:

> . . . sadistic gratification of overcoming and humiliating it, of getting the better of it, the *triumph* over it, may enter so strongly into the act of reparation . . . that the 'benign circle' started by this act becomes broken. The objects which were to be restored change again into persecutors . . . As a result of the failure of the act of reparation, the ego has to resort again and again to obsessional and manic defences.
> (Klein, 1940, p. 351)

See Paranoid defence against depressive anxiety; Reparation

Klein, M. (1935) 'A contribution to the psychogenesis of manic-depressive states', in *The Writings of Melanie Klein*, Vol. 1. London: Hogarth Press, pp. 262–289.
—— (1940) 'Mourning and its relation to manic-depressive states', in *The Writings of Melanie Klein*, Vol. 1. London: Hogarth Press, pp. 344–369.

Manic reparation

In the early stages of development, the infant employs omnipotent mechanisms to establish the security of the ego. Consequently, when the depressive position first bears down on him [*see* Depressive position] he may experience the loved objects as irreparably damaged – mirroring the extreme violence of his omnipotent phantasies. The anguish of wanting to repair so totally damaged an object stems from the fact that this is experienced as a vastly demanding task. As a result the whole situation has to be belittled and the task made light of, as if it can be accomplished by magic.

Later in life even normal stresses can provoke the contemptuous phantasy that anyway the object is not worth bothering about. But the contempt and belittling are manic defences against the severity of the anguish, and assist the subject to feel less helpless and dependent on his important good objects that appear to him damaged and bring out such an onerous responsibility [*see* Depressive anxiety]. The end result, however, is that the contempt damages the objects even more, and may therefore lead to a vicious circle.

See Manic defences; Paranoid defence against depressive anxiety; Reparation

Masculinity

See Father; Femininity; Oedipus complex

Masturbation phantasies

Klein was interested from the beginning of her work in the phantasy content of anxiety, and she concentrated at first on the sexual phantasies. She used Freud's idea of masturbation phantasies, which once accompanied physically stimulating activity but had subsequently become unconscious:

> . . . an unconscious phantasy has a very important connection with the subject's sexual life; for it is identical with the phantasy which served to give him sexual satisfaction during a period of masturbation. At that time the masturbatory act was compounded of two parts. One was the evocation of a phantasy and the other some active behaviour for

obtaining self-gratification at the height of the phantasy. Originally the action was a purely auto-erotic procedure for the purpose of obtaining pleasure from some particular part of the body, which could be described as erotogenic. Later, this action became merged with a wishful idea from the sphere of object-love.

(Freud, 1908, p. 161)

Klein elaborated this idea of the concrete and physical nature of these phantasies into an object-relational form. Although Abraham (1921) and Ferenczi (1921) both used the symptom of tic as evidence for an auto-erotic phase, Klein bluntly challenged them (Klein, 1925). Instead she described a case of tic in which phantasies accompanied the various physical movements; each movement, she noted, represented symbolically a part of a sexual act with an object. She used this to mark out her own approach, concentrating upon the *object relations* involved in instinctual impulses [*see* Child analysis; Narcissism; Unconscious phantasy]. It challenged the view of a primary phase of auto-erotism and narcissism and asserted that unconscious masturbation phantasies were embedded in all activity:

Let me give an illustration of the effect of masturbation phantasies on sublimation. Felix, aged thirteen, produced the following phantasy in analysis. He was playing with some beautiful girls who were naked and whose breasts he stroked and caressed. He did not see the lower parts of their bodies. They were playing football with one another. This single sexual phantasy . . . was succeeded during the analysis by many other phantasies, some in the form of daydreams, others coming to him at night as a substitute for onanism and all concerned with games. These phantasies showed how some of his fixations were elaborated into an interest in games. In the first sexual phantasy . . . coitus had already been replaced by football. This game, together with others, had absorbed his interest and ambition entirely.

(Klein, 1923, p. 90)

Klein was demonstrating that embedded in the process of narcissistic gratification there were phantasies of objects associated with the 'masturbation'. Later Heimann, in developing the Kleinian view of narcissism [*see* Narcissism], described masturbation as a phantasy of an erotic relation with an *internal* object:

autoerotism is based on phantasies concerning an inner gratifying 'good' breast (nipple, mother) which is projected on to, and thus represented by, a part of the infant's own body. This process is, as it were, met halfway by the erotogenic quality of the child's organs.

(Heimann, 1952, pp. 147–148)

The erotogenous zones allow the use of the body for generating unconscious phantasies, especially intensely through masturbatory manipulation. Erotic sexuality is therefore a commonly contrived set of unconscious phantasies elaborated defensively against persecutory or depressive anxieties. Meltzer (1966) described a case in which anal masturbation was employed to engender unconscious phantasies. Masturbation phantasy as a clinical phenomenon has gone somewhat out of fashion among contemporary Kleinians, who often use words such as 'excitement' or 'erotised defences' rather than specific reference to the masturbatory phantasies of the patient.

Abraham, K. (1921) 'Contribution to a discussion on tic', in *Selected Papers on Psycho-Analysis*. London: Hogarth Press (1927), pp. 322–325.

Ferenczi, S. (1921) 'Psycho-analytic observations on tic', in *Further Contributions to the Theory and Technique of Psychoanalysis*. London: Hogarth Press, pp. 142–174.

Freud, S. (1908) 'Hysterical phantasies and their relation to bisexuality', *S.E. 9*. London: Hogarth Press, pp. 155–166.

Heimann, P. (1952) 'Certain functions of projection and introjection in early infancy', in M. Klein, P. Heimann, S. Isaacs and J. Riviere (eds) *Developments in Psycho-Analysis*. London: Hogarth Press (1952), pp. 122–168.

Klein, M. (1923) 'Infant analysis', in *The Writings of Melanie Klein*, Vol. 1. London: Hogarth Press, pp. 77–105.

—— (1925) 'A contribution to the psychogenesis of tic', in *The Writings of Melanie Klein*, Vol. 1. London: Hogarth Press, pp. 106–127.

Meltzer, D. (1966) 'The relation of anal masturbation to projective identification', *Int. J. Psycho-Anal.* 47: 335–342.

Donald Meltzer

Biography: Donald Meltzer was born in 1922. He trained in medicine and child psychiatry in the United States and came to London in 1954 specifically for further training with Melanie Klein. He remained in analysis with her until her death in 1960.

Meltzer's skilled evocation of clinical material made him a leading member of the Kleinian Group, and his clinical interest in both child and adult analysis always remained central to his analytical thinking and to his development of psychoanalytic theory. He was influential in developing the training in child psychotherapy that had been started by Esther Bick at the Tavistock Clinic and he worked closely with her and with Martha Harris, his second wife, in developing it further. In the 1970s his views on technique and the training of psychoanalysts brought him into conflict with the Kleinian Group and the Institute of Psychoanalysis in London, from which he eventually withdrew in the 1980s.

Meltzer wrote extensively and was much in demand as a speaker and teacher in many countries, an activity that he enjoyed and continued until his death in 2004. He made many contributions to Kleinian psychoanalysis, in particular his detailed understanding of the development of the psycho-analytic process (Meltzer, 1967), his work on both infantile and perverse sexuality (Meltzer, 1973), his exegesis of the work of Freud, Klein and Bion (Meltzer, 1978, 1986), his work on dreams (1984) and his various studies of projective identification, narcissism and borderline states (Meltzer, 1992; Hahn, 1994). In *The Psychoanalytical Process* (Meltzer, 1967) he was able to open up a new outlook on projective identification by describing pro-jective identification with internal objects, and he observed the growth of the patient's mind (and the analyst's mind as well) in the consulting room through the development of the interaction between transference and countertransference.

Meltzer's interest in teaching led to several major commentaries on Kleinian writings: *The Kleinian Development* (Meltzer, 1978), which presents the relevant strands of Freud's clinical writings; Klein's detailed case history in *Narrative of a Child Analysis* (1961); and finally the work of Bion as a continuous thread of intellectual and clinical development. Meltzer also enriched the Kleinian literature on dreams by developing a revised theory of dreaming as unconscious thinking in which meaning is generated (Meltzer, 1984). In this book on dreams he also discusses the differentiation between signs and symbols and explores in detail the practice of dream investigation and interpretation.

His description of a borderline personality in 1968 ('Terror, persecution and dread') was an early discussion of a narcissistic personality structure organised around destructive impulses – a view further developed by Rosenfeld (1971a) and many others [*see* Pathological organisations]. Meltzer's continuing interest in psychotic children led him to run a research seminar on childhood autism, which culminated in *Explorations in Autism* (Meltzer et al., 1975) [*see* Autism]. In *The Apprehension of Beauty* (Meltzer and Williams, 1988) he introduces the 'aesthetic conflict' as an early developmental phenomenon in the baby's relation to the external world, where the aesthetic experience of the budding relationship to the mother stimulates both the wish to know her and the frustration created by the mystery of the mother's unknowable aspects. He emphasises the reciprocity of the aesthetic experience and the pathological consequences that follow the failure in the aesthetic apprehension of the object.

In *The Claustrum: An Investigation into Claustrophobic Phenomena* (Meltzer, 1992) Meltzer revisits the concept of projective identification, not in terms of quantity or quality of projective mechanisms but in terms of the choice of object that is projected into. In his thorough phenomenological examination of 'intrusive identification' (as he prefers to call it), Meltzer suggests that this object is in unconscious phantasy the mother's body (as stated by Klein) and that the parts of the self that take up residence inside the various compartments of the internal mother's body will determine the identificatory disturbance that accounts for the quality and degree of the patient's pathology. He discusses the various technical aspects of treating these difficult narcissistic patients, with particular emphasis on adolescents.

His view since the 1970s has been that the consolidation of Bion's work on thinking and emotional experience (Meltzer, 1978) is the growing point in Kleinian thought, and this view has allowed him to create an epistemology that is richly documented in *Sincerity and Other Works: Collected Papers of Donald Meltzer* (Hahn, 1992).

Hahn, A. (1994) *Sincerity and Other Works: Collected Papers of Donald Meltzer.* London: Karnac.

Klein, M. (1961) *Narrative of a Child Analysis.* London: Hogarth Press.

Meltzer, D. (1967) The *Psychoanalytical Process.* London: Heinemann.

—— (1968) 'Terror, persecution and dread', *Int. J. Psycho-Anal.* 49: 396–400.

—— (1973) *Sexual States of Mind.* Strath Tay: Clunie Press.

—— (1978) *The Kleinian Development.* Strath Tay: Clunie Press.

—— (1984) *Dream Life: A Re-examination of Psychoanalytic Theory and Technique.* Strath Tay: Clunie Press.

—— (1986) *Studies in Extended Metapsychology A Clinical Application of Bion's Ideas.* Strath Tay: Clunie Press.

—— (1992) *The Claustrum: An Investigation of Claustrophobic Phenomena.* Strath Tay: Clunie Press

Meltzer, D., Bremner, J., Hoxter, S., Weddell, D. and Wittenberg, I. (1975) *Explorations in Autism: A Psychoanalytic Study.* Strath Tay: Clunie Press.

Meltzer, D. and Williams, M. (1988) *The Apprehension of Beauty: The Role of Aesthetic Conflict in Development, Art and Violence.* Strath Tay: Clunie Press.

Rosenfeld, H. (1971) 'A clinical approach to the psychoanalytical theory of the life and death instincts: An investigation into the aggressive aspects of narcissism', *Int. J. Psycho-Anal.* 52: 169–178.

Memory and desire

Freud's advice in his papers on technique to develop an 'evenly-suspended attention' (Freud, 1912) has been augmented by Bion's recommendation to avoid 'memory' and 'desire' (Bion 1967a, 1967b, 1970, 1992). 'Psychoanalytic observation', Bion says, 'is concerned neither with what has happened nor with what is going to happen but with what *is* happening' (Bion 1967a, p. 17). Only in this way can the immediate psychic reality of the session be allowed to develop and become known. Bion designates this psychic reality by the symbol 'O', and describes it thus: 'I shall use the sign O to denote that which is the ultimate reality represented by terms such as ultimate reality, absolute truth, the godhead, the infinite, the thing-in-itself' (Bion, 1970, p. 26).

Bion, W. R. (1967a) 'Notes on memory and desire', *Psychoanal. Forum* 2: 272–280; reprinted in E. B. Spillius (ed.) *Melanie Klein Today*, Vol. 2. London: Routledge (1988), pp. 17–21.

—— (1967b) *Second Thoughts*. London: Heinemann, pp. 143–146.

—— (1970) *Attention and Interpretation*. London: Tavistock, pp. 41–54.

—— (1992) *Cogitations*. (F. Bion, ed.) London: Karnac, pp. 294–296.

Freud, S. (1912) 'Recommendations to physicians practising psycho-analysis', *S.E. 12*. London: Hogarth Press, pp. 111–120.

Mind–body problem

The relation between the mind and the body is a central philosophical question. It is also a problem for psychologists and has profound implications for psychiatric treatments, drug treatment and psychotherapy. The problem has remained stubbornly insoluble for philosophers, and psychology may be in a position to inform philosophy.

On the great Cartesian dichotomy psychologists have both floundered and quarrelled. Freud was no exception. He was influenced by the remarkable results and progress of the nineteenth-century natural sciences, including physiology. On the other hand the Romantic tradition of German 'Naturphilosophie' emphasised a Hegelian metaphysical and introspective approach to philosophical problems. The dichotomy is whether to approach the mind from the objective study of the workings of the brain or from a subjective psychology of personal experiences. The former sees the mind as an epiphenomenon of the basic physical and physiological processes that determine the working of the brain – the mind as a side effect of neurophysiology. Freud was tempted by this physiological psychology when he began thinking about the unconscious and the discoveries he had been making in the 1890s. His posthumously published 'Project for a scientific psychology' (Freud, 1895) was an attempt to work out a physiological model for psychical functioning. However, that project was abandoned because 'Freud the neurologist was being overtaken by Freud the psychologist' (Strachey, 1957, p. 163).

Freud was uncomfortable with a physiological view of the relation between mind and body because it went against his clinical experiences with his patients; it also went against the German philosophical tradition of humanism, which according to Bettelheim clearly seeps through in Freud's original German writings (Bettelheim, 1983). Freud never quite found his way out of the physiological psychology with which he started, and the mixture of Freud the neurologist and Freud the psychologist is sufficiently blended for Sulloway (1979) to emphasise the biological Freud while Bettelheim emphasises the humanist Freud; both are equally convinced, and neither is really convincing (Young, 1986). Young (1986) has argued that what Freud lacked, and we still do today, is a language with which we can speak about the mind and the body, in fact 'the person' (Strawson, 1959).

Psychophysical parallelism: Freud's position on the mind–body problem is known in philosophy as psychophysical parallelism. There is a mind and there is a brain. Both work in their own ways. The working of one is not translatable into or reducible to the workings of the other. Brain processes are primary and determining but mental events and structures cannot be reduced to brain processes. Yet they must interrelate and Freud never rejected possible future links. But in order to develop his psychology of the unconscious and of the mind, Freud focused on a mentalist theory of a specific field of study that he called psychical reality and left aside the problem of how it relates to the brain.

Interactionism: It is possible to take a further philosophical position and to say that the mind emerges from the activity of the brain, which in turn may be manipulated by the mind. Both Freud and later members of the Kleinian Group, who were considering unconscious phantasy in the late 1930s and early 1940s, pointed out that there is a close interaction between bodily experiences, the source of the instincts and how they become elaborated in activities of the mind called unconscious phantasies, which are close to the bodily experience itself. Thus instinctual stimuli such as hunger can lead to an unconscious phantasy of a relation with a 'bad' object that causes hunger or pain in the stomach. The mind also elaborates unconscious phantasies as a defensive manoeuvre against strong anxieties also experienced in phantasy (Segal, 1964). Such elaborated defensive phantasies, especially in the early phases of infancy, originate in bodily functions. For example, the expulsion of faeces is used to initiate the phantasy of expelling a bad internal object. Later, more symbolic representations such as speaking foul of a person still retain the bodily links. This close interaction between the body and the mind does not mean that psychoanalysis is philosophically interactionist as such but it certainly shows the close links between the body and the development of mind without specifying brain processes as such.

Biology and psychology: Phantasies of expulsion or incorporation create the sense of self and identity, and the specific phantasies put together the particular character of the self. Projective processes also create the perceptions of the social world around which, in turn, through introjective processes, precipitate social forms in the individual. The development of the human infant is a movement out of a world of bodily satisfaction into a world of symbols and symbolic satisfaction. There is a progressive movement out of the body into the symbolic world of the mature mind [see Alpha-function]. Such movement occurs in the generation of thoughts, as well as being the process of psychological development. Such a process is not explained by the Kleinian notion of unconscious phantasy, but it is well described.

Symbols, being inherent in the experience of parts of the body, are therefore an inherent capacity of the human infant from birth. He represents for himself his own sensations as relationships with objects [*see* Unconscious phantasy]. Since the object has a presence for the infant irrespective of the actual objective situation, it is, in a mental world of conceptions, already a symbol. When the infant can come to perceive the objective realities, the meaningfulness of that reality is generated by an investment from the mental representations.

Bettelheim, B. (1983) *Freud and Man's Soul*. London: Hogarth Press.
Freud, S. (1895) 'Project for a scientific psychology'. *S.E. 1*. London: Hogarth Press, pp. 283–397.
Segal, H. (1964) *Introduction to the Work of Melanie Klein*. London: Heinemann.
Strachey, J. (1957) 'Editor's note to "The Unconscious"', *S.E. 14*. London: Hogarth Press, pp. 161–165.
Strawson, P. F. (1959) *Individuals: An Essay in Descriptive Metaphysics*. London: Methuen.
Sulloway, F. (1979) *Freud: Biologist of the Mind*. London: Burnett.
Young, R. (1986) 'Freud: Scientist and/or humanist', *Free Assoc.* 6: 7–35.

Mother

Klein's interest is in the infant's earliest relationship and the way in which this object relationship underpins emotional development and affects all subsequent relationships. The mother is taken by Klein to be the first one who feeds and cares for the infant and Klein uses the words mother and breast interchangeably [*see* Breast]. The mother is also the person with whom the infant at first believes himself to have an exclusive relationship [*see* Oedipus complex]. Klein's theories about the psychic reality of the infant are based on her observations of children, from whom she extrapolates backwards. Klein was concerned to understand the earliest relationship to the mother/breast and what sorts of distortions affect the infant's perception of her. In the early weeks of life the infant knows of mother through sensations arising from the body. Klein believes that the infant's bodily sensations are experienced as objects that have motivations towards him [*see* Internal objects]. There are at the outset different 'mothers', relating to the infant's different experiences of the primary object. Thus there is a 'good' (gratifying) mother and a 'bad' (depriving or absent) mother. These 'mothers' correspond to separate 'infants' – that is, separately experienced states of the infant split from each other and kept separate for defensive purposes [*see* Paranoid-schizoid position; Splitting].

Mourning

For Klein, mourning involves psychic work that is a fundamental and necessary part of development. Klein suggests that mourning at any stage of life involves re-experiencing the infantile depressive position, including loss of the internal good objects of childhood, followed by painful work to renew and reinstate them.

Freud sees the melancholic as burdened internally with an object that cannot be relinquished, whereas the mourner manages to let the object go and is thus able to form new attachments. Klein's more complex conception of the inner world allows a view of the mourner as able to reinstate the lost loved object internally, in a more real and separate form, strengthening rather than depleting the ego in its task of forming new attachments:

> Thus while grief is experienced to the full and despair is at its height, the love for the object wells up and the mourner feels more strongly that life inside and outside will go on after all, and that the lost loved object can be preserved within. At this stage in mourning suffering can become productive. We know that painful experiences of all kinds sometimes stimulate sublimations, or even bring out quite new gifts in some people. . . . Others become . . . more capable of appreciating people and things, more tolerant in their relation to others – they become wiser. . . . It seems that every advance in the process of mourning results in a deepening in the individual's relation to his inner objects.
>
> (Klein, 1940, p. 360)

See Depressive position; Loss

Klein, M. (1940) 'Mourning and its relation to manic-depressive states', in *The Writings of Melanie Klein*, Vol. 1. London: Hogarth Press, pp. 344–369.

Nameless dread

This is a term first used by Karin Stephen (1941) to describe the extreme extent of anxiety in infancy: 'a dread of powerlessness in the face of instinct tension in childhood' (p. 181). 'Nameless dread' was later given a fuller and specific meaning by Bion to describe a state of meaningless fear that comes about in the context of an infant with a mother incapable of 'reverie' [*see* Reverie], a concept that derives from Bion's theory of containing [*see* Container/contained]. When the mother fails to contain the infant's terrors and make them meaningful, this 'projective identification-rejecting-object' [*see* Thinking and knowledge] is felt to strip the meaning from the experience and the baby: he 'therefore reintrojects, not a fear of dying made tolerable, but a nameless dread' (Bion, 1962a, p. 116). With repeated recurrence of this projective failure, an internal object is formed through introjection on the same lines; this object destroys meaning and leaves the subject in a mysterious meaningless world:

> In practice it means that the patient feels surrounded not so much by real objects, things-in-themselves, but by bizarre objects that are real only in that they are the residue of thoughts and conceptions that have been stripped of their meaning and ejected.
>
> (Bion, 1962b, p. 99)

An internal object that strips meaning gives rise to a superego that issues hateful and meaningless injunctions about behaviour.

Bion, W. R. (1962a) 'A theory of thinking', *Int. J. Psycho-Anal.* 43: 306–310; republished in *Second Thoughts*. London: Heinemann (1967), pp. 110–119.
—— (1962b) *Learning from Experience*. London: Heinemann.
Stephen, K. (1941) 'Aggression in early childhood', *Br. J. Med. Psychol.* 18: 178–190.

Narcissism

Klein departs significantly from Freud over the nature of narcissism. Freud (1914) outlines several aspects of narcissism:

- *Primary narcissism* is a stage in which the infant's own ego, as a new unity, is taken as the first object of libidinal love. This stage follows that of auto-erotism and precedes that of object-love: it allows for a unification of the auto-erotic instincts. It is from this basic position, one that is never totally overcome, that libido is extended to objects. Primary narcissism is conceived as objectless and precedes the recognition by the infant of a separate object (Freud, 1914). Freud is not unequivocal about this assertion, as Klein herself (1952a) and other authors (Laplanche and Pontalis, 1973; Segal and Bell, 1991) point out. However he establishes the idea further in his late work, as when he suggests intra-uterine existence as a model of this objectless state (Freud, 1921).
- *Secondary narcissism* refers to a withdrawal of love (libido) from an object that has disappointed through either the threat of loss or some kind of slight, back to a narcissistic love of the ego. A drastic withdrawal of libido from the object onto the ego was thought to be operative in psychoses and equivalent to a withdrawal from external reality (Abraham, 1908; Freud, 1915).
- *Narcissistic object-choice* refers to relations in which the ego loves an object in so far as the object resembles the ego (Freud, 1910, 1914).

In her early work Klein occasionally writes as if she agrees with Freud's notion of a phase of objectless primary narcissism, in spite of the glaring contradiction in what she asserts, for example: 'The phase in which the onset of the Oedipus conflict and its accompanying sadistic masturbation phantasies arise is the phase of narcissism' (Klein, 1932, p. 171). By contrast, in her 1925 paper on tics, she has already disagreed openly with Ferenczi's views of tics as unanalysable, primary narcissistic symptoms. She instead asserts that the tic can be analysed provided 'the object-relations on which it is based' (1925, p. 121) are uncovered. She uncovers the multiple sadistic phantasies of her patient towards his internal parents in intercourse. Klein's implicit non-adherence to the notion of an objectless, primary narcissistic stage becomes explicit after she has conceptualised the paranoid-schizoid position and narcissistic part-object relations. In 'The origins of transference' she writes:

> For many years I have held the view that auto-erotism and narcissism are in the young infant contemporaneous with the first relation to objects – external and internalised. . . . This hypothesis contradicts Freud's concept of auto-erotic and narcissistic *stages* which preclude an object-relation.
>
> (1952a, p. 51)

This is perhaps Klein's most fundamental theoretical difference from classical psychoanalysis and ego psychology [*see* American psychoanalysis in relation to Klein]. In 1952 Klein writes:

> The analysis of very young children has taught me that there is no instinctual urge, no anxiety situation, no mental process which does not involve objects, external and internal; in other words, object-relations are at the centre of emotional life.
>
> (1952a, p. 53)

Klein's views on narcissism

Narcissistic states and withdrawal: Klein states that auto-erotism and narcissism imply 'a love for and relation with the internalised good object which in phantasy forms part of the loved body and self' (1952a, p. 51). She further asserts that in both auto-erotic gratification and narcissistic states there is a withdrawal to the internalised object. She illustrates this withdrawal by referring to Paula Heimann's detailed observation of an infant who could only take her mother's breast again after having sucked her fingers first in auto-erotic gratification. Klein writes:

> '. . . the narcissistic withdrawal was caused by the disturbance in the relation to the mother. . . . By sucking them [her fingers] she re-

established the relation to the internal breast and thus regained enough
security to renew the good relation to the external breast and mother.
(1952b, p. 103)

In contradistinction to Freud the withdrawal from external to internal is
not away from the object and onto the ego but more precisely from the
external object to the internalised object in the ego, that is, to a narcissistic
state. Paula Heimann points out the complexity of this situation. Having
incorporated the good breast the infant can now identify his finger with the
incorporated breast. He can independently produce his own gratification by
sucking his fingers and in so doing turns to his internalised good breast
(Heimann, 1952, p. 146).

Narcissistic object-relations: In 'Notes on some schizoid mechanisms' (1946)
Klein differentiates between narcissistic states and narcissistic object relations and structure (Segal, 1983). A narcissistic state is a withdrawal to an
introjected object. Klein relates narcissistic object relations more directly to
the role of *projective identification* in the split structure of the paranoid-
schizoid position. She asserts that schizoid part-object relations are narcissistic in nature. Klein writes of the projection of both good and bad
parts. Good parts like the ego-ideal are projected, as a result of which the
other person is loved and admired because he contains the good part of the
self. Similarly bad parts are projected so that the object is identified with
this bad part of the self. Narcissistic object relations have a strong element
of control because the projected parts of the self are now controlled by
controlling the other person (Klein, 1946, p. 13).

The emphasis that Klein gives to projective identification in the paranoid-
schizoid position as a means of dealing with persecutory anxiety and the
death instinct links narcissistic object relations to anxiety, aggression and
the death instinct.

Narcissism and envy: Segal (1983) points out that Klein herself does not link
narcissism directly to envy. However, in 'Envy and gratitude' Klein (1957)
describes fully how projective identification is deployed both as an imple-
mentation of envious aims and also as a defence against envy, as in the case
of getting into an object and appropriating its good qualities. Segal spells
out what seems implicit in Klein's own work:

The way primary envy is described by Klein is as a spoiling hostility at
the realisation that the source of life and goodness lies outside. To me
envy and narcissism are like two sides of the same coin.
(1983, p. 270)

Pathological narcissism: The link between envy, destructiveness and pathological narcissism receives its fullest conceptual development in Herbert Rosenfeld's seminal contribution on 'libidinal' and 'destructive' narcissism (1964). It is important to distinguish between 'normal projective identification' and 'pathological projective identification' [*see* Projective identification]. Bion (1957, 1959) and Rosenfeld (1964) distinguish between normal and violent projective identification on the basis of the degree of omnipotence in the phantasy. When the phantasy is omnipotent the identification of a part of the self with the object results in the boundary between them dissolving so that one is the other [*see* Omnipotence]. Rosenfeld distinguishes between two aspects of pathological narcissism, *libidinal* and *destructive*:

- *Libidinal narcissism*: Dependence engenders frustrations that lead to aggression, paranoid anxiety and pain. It also stimulates envy, which is particularly unbearable to the infant because envy increases the difficulty in admitting dependence and frustrations (Rosenfeld, 1964, p. 171). The self deals with the awareness of both situations by omnipotent introjective and projective identification simultaneously. The self appropriates the object's desired qualities either by omnipotent introjective identification or by forceful projective identification (Rosenfeld, 1964, p. 171). Both processes contribute to the creation of an omnipotent or *mad* self-idealisation whereby the awareness of separateness itself, and of envy and frustration, is denied. Narcissistic object relations also entail the projection of undesirable qualities and feelings into the object: the analyst is often pictured and related to as a 'lavatory' mother (Rosenfeld, 1964, p. 171). Narcissistic states are experienced by the patient as ideal: everything unpleasant is evacuated into the analyst and every satisfactory or valuable experience, such as the analyst's capacity to bring relief, is omnipotently appropriated by the patient, who feels he possesses all the goodness. As a result, awareness of psychic reality is dramatically stunted. Libidinal narcissism is achieved predominantly at the expense of the object.
- *Destructive narcissism* is achieved primarily at the expense of the dependent or libidinal self. It is based on an omnipotent idealisation of the destructive or 'bad' parts of the self, which are directed against any positive libidinal object relationship or against any libidinal part of the self that needs an object to depend on it (Rosenfeld, 1971, p. 246). Libidinal and destructive narcissism operate side by side. Rosenfeld links the predominance of destructive narcissism to a more violent envy that appears both as an overwhelming wish to destroy the analyst, who represents the source of life in the transference, and also as extremely violent self-destructive impulses (1971, p. 247). In some patients destructive narcissism is so dominant that they try to get rid of their concern and their love for their objects by killing their loving dependent self.

Leaning on Meltzer's (1968) ideas on the power of the destructive narcissistic organisation and its seductive tyranny over the trapped dependent self, Rosenfeld shows how the destructive parts of the self can become highly organised and represented as a *gang*, like the *mafia*. The members, loyal to each other and to the leader, make the destructive work more effective and powerful and idealised as superior. To change and to receive help is experienced as weakness and failure. Often a *perverse erotisation* of this destructive organisation increases its seductiveness and domination over the rest of the personality (1971, p. 249). The destructiveness manifests as a determined chronic resistance to analysis and the libidinal self feels too weak to oppose the destructive process. Clinically it is essential to find access to the libidinal self and to analyse the infantile nature of the omnipotent processes.

In his seminal papers Rosenfeld (1964, 1971) sees envy as the main motivating factor behind the highly omnipotent identifications and the development of both libidinal and destructive narcissism. In his later work Rosenfeld (1987) makes more explicit references to the contribution of environmental factors such as trauma and failure in containment in the development of pathological narcissism (1987, p. 87).

In *Impasse and Interpretation* (1987) Rosenfeld introduces a distinction between the '*thin-skinned*' and the '*thick-skinned*' narcissist. The latter is insensitive to human feelings and appears dominated by destructive narcissism. Rosenfeld argues that the envy of such patients has to be confronted firmly in order to avoid impasse in analytic treatment. By contrast the thin-skinned narcissist is hypersensitive and easily hurt and is not dominated by destructive narcissism. Rosenfeld thinks that in such patients their narcissism is primarily a compensation for the repeated traumas to their self-regard in early childhood and secondarily a way of triumphing over the parents and the analyst. However, to treat them as if they are identified with the destructive parts of their narcissism leads to re-traumatisation of the patient and to impasse in analytic treatment.

Contemporary Kleinian perspectives: John Steiner voices a view held by a number of contemporary Kleinians that Rosenfeld's important emphasis on the role of trauma and parental intrusion in a patient's pathological narcissism leads him to lose some of his earlier objectivity and sense of balance about the overdetermined nature of the reasons for impasse in an analysis. Steiner feels that Rosenfeld went too far in making the analyst's interpretive stance mostly responsible for impasses with narcissistic patients who had been traumatised (Steiner, 2008).

Another contemporary Kleinian controversy is about the validity of Rosenfeld's distinction between libidinal and destructive narcissism. His theory of destructive narcissism is widely accepted as a seminal contribution. Hanna Segal, however, questions his notion of libidinal narcissism. In her view narcissism and envy are the two sides of the same coin. This entails that narcissism is always destructive because it is hostile to the object as separate and to any life-giving relationship (Segal, 2007). Ronald Britton in contrast finds it useful in the clinical situation at any one moment to distinguish between a narcissism that is primarily libidinal/defensive and one that is hostile/destructive. In his view:

> The formation of a narcissistic object relationship can be motivated by the wish to preserve the capacity for love by making the love-object seem like the self, or it can be aimed at annihilating the object as the representative of otherness.
>
> (Britton, 2003, p. 157)

Narcissistic character structure: Joan Riviere (1936) was the first to offer an original Kleinian formulation of a narcissistic character organisation, highly resistant to change, by using Klein's (1935) newly formulated notion of manic omnipotence and denial of dependency. The structuring of the personality between an omnipotent 'mad' and 'bad' self and an entrapped 'sane' self was later described by Meltzer (1968) and Money-Kyrle (1969). Rosenfeld shows the stability and complexity of this organisation and its relevance in understanding patients on the borderline spectrum. Rosenfeld utilises Klein's later formulations of pathological factors in the paranoid-schizoid position itself (1946, 1957), such as excessive envy and violent projective identification, to develop his theory.

In the 1970s and 1980s a variety of Kleinian authors, many influenced by Rosenfeld, have formulated pathological personality organisations that develop in an attempt to bind the catastrophic consequences of early destructive tendencies (Segal, 1972; O'Shaughnessy, 1981; Steiner, 1981; Joseph, 1982; Brenman, 1985; Sohn, 1985). John Steiner's overarching concept of *pathological organisations*, and later that of *psychic retreats* (Steiner, 1993), integrates the various aspects of these contributions and absorbs fully Rosenfeld's theory of pathological narcissism in its very formulation [*see* Pathological organisations].

Abraham, K. (1908) 'The psycho-sexual differences between hysteria and dementia-praecox', in *Selected Papers of Karl Abraham*. London: Hogarth Press (1927), pp. 73–75.

Bion, W. (1957) 'Differentiation of the psychotic from the non-psychotic personalities', *Int. J. Psycho-Anal.* 38: 266–275.

—— (1959) 'Attacks on linking', *Int. J. Psycho-Anal.* 40: 308–315.

Brenman, E. (1985) 'Cruelty and narrow-mindedness', *Int. J. Psycho-Anal.* 66: 273–281.

Britton, R. (2003) 'Narcissism and narcissistic disorders', in *Sex, Death. and the Superego*. London: Karnac, pp. 151–164.

Freud, S. (1910) 'Leonardo da Vinci and a memory of his childhood', *S.E. 11*. London: Hogarth Press, pp. 59–137.

—— (1914) 'On narcissism', *S.E. 14*. London: Hogarth Press, pp. 67–102.

—— (1917) 'Mourning and melancholia', *S.E. 14*. London: Hogarth Press, pp. 237–258.

—— (1921) 'Group psychology and the analysis of the ego', *S.E. 18*. London: Hogarth Press, pp. 67–134.

Heimann, P. (1952) 'Certain functions of introjection and projection in early infancy', in M. Klein, P. Heimann, S. Isaacs and J. Riviere (eds) *Developments in Psycho-Analysis*. London: Hogarth Press (1952), pp. 122–168.

Joseph, B. (1982) 'Addiction to near death', *Int. J. Psycho-Anal.* 63: 449–456.

Klein, M. (1925) 'A contribution to the psychogenesis of tics', in *The Writings of Melanie Klein*, Vol. 1. London: Hogarth Press, pp. 106–127.

—— (1932) *The Psychoanalysis of Children. The Writings of Melanie Klein*, Vol. 2. London: Hogarth Press.

—— (1935) 'A contribution to the psychogenesis of manic-depressive states', *Int. J. Psycho-Anal.* 16: 145–174.

—— (1946) 'Notes on some schizoid mechanisms', in *The Writings of Melanie Klein*, Vol. 3. London: Hogarth Press, pp. 1–24.

—— (1952a) 'The origins of transference', in *The Writings of Melanie Klein*, Vol. 3. London: Hogarth Press, pp. 48–56.

—— (1952b) 'On observing the behaviour of young infants', in *The Writings of Melanie Klein*, Vol. 3. London: Hogarth Press, pp. 94–121.

—— (1957) 'Envy and gratitude', in *The Writings of Melanie Klein*, Vol. 3. London: Hogarth Press, pp. 176–235.

Laplanche, J. and Pontalis, J.-B. (1973) *The Language of Psycho-Analysis*. London: Hogarth Press.

Meltzer, D. (1968) 'Terror, persecution, dread', *Int. J. Psycho-Anal.* 49: 396–400.

Money-Kyrle, R. (1969) 'On the fear of insanity', in *The Collected Papers of Roger Money-Kyrle*. Strath Tay: Clunie Press (1978), pp. 434–441.

O'Shaughnessy, E. (1981) 'A clinical study of a defensive organisation', *Int. J. Psycho-Anal.* 62: 359–369.

Riviere, J. (1936) 'A contribution to the analysis of the negative therapeutic reaction', *Int. J. Psycho-Anal.* 17: 304–320.

Rosenfeld, H. (1964) 'On the psychopathology of narcissism', *Int. J. Psycho-Anal.* 45: 332–337; republished in *Psychotic States*. London: Hogarth Press (1965), pp. 169–179.

—— (1971) 'A clinical approach to the psycho-analytical theory of the life and death instincts: An investigation into the aggressive aspects of narcissism', *Int. J. Psycho-Anal.* 52: 169–178; reprinted in E. B. Spillius (ed.) *Melanie Klein Today*, Vol. 1. London: Routledge (1988), pp. 239–255.

—— (1987) *Impasse and Interpretation*. London: Tavistock.

Segal, H. (1972) 'A delusional system as a defence against the re-emergence of a catastrophic situation', *Int. J. Psycho-Anal.* 53: 393–401.

—— (1983) 'Some clinical implications of Melanie Klein's work', *Int. J. Psycho-Anal.* 64: 269–276.

Segal, H. and Bell, D. (1991) 'The theory of narcissism in the work of Freud and

Klein', in J. Sandler (ed.) *Freud's: 'On Narcissism: an Introduction'*. London: Yale University Press, pp. 149–174.

—— (2007) 'Narcissism: Comments on Ronald Britton's paper', in *Yesterday, Today and Tomorrow*. London: Routledge, pp. 230–234.

Sohn, L. (1985) 'Narcissistic organization, projective identification and the formation of the identificate', *Int. J. Psycho-Anal*. 66: 201–213.

Steiner, J. (1981) 'Perverse relationships between parts of the self', *Int. J. Psycho-Anal*. 63: 15–22.

—— (1993) *Psychic Retreats: Pathological Organizations in Psychotic, Neurotic and Borderline Patients*. London: Routledge.

—— (2008) 'A personal review of Rosenfeld's contributions to clinical psychoanalysis', in *Rosenfeld in Retrospect: Essays on his Clinical Influence*. London: Routledge, pp. 58–84.

Negative therapeutic reaction

Freud became aware, to his consternation, that there were some patients who reacted badly to analytic interpretations; they got worse with good interpretations, rather than better. He was affronted by the Wolf Man's '. . . habit of producing transitory "negative reactions"; every time something had been conclusively cleared up, he attempted to contradict the effect' (Freud, 1917, p. 69). This sort of negative response could be understood as defiant superiority to the physician, but a little later Freud found this explanation inadequate:

> There are certain people who behave in a quite peculiar fashion during the work of analysis. When one speaks hopefully to them or expresses satisfaction with the progress of the treatment, they show signs of discontent and their condition invariably becomes worse. One begins by regarding this as defiance and as an attempt to prove their superiority to the physician, but later one comes to take a deeper and juster view. One becomes convinced, not only that such people cannot endure any praise or appreciation, but that they react inversely to the progress of the treatment. Every partial solution that ought to result, and in other people does result, in an improvement or a temporary suspension of symptoms produces in them for the time being an exacerbation of their illness; they get worse during the treatment instead of getting better. They exhibit what is known as a 'negative therapeutic reaction'.
> (Freud, 1923, p. 49)

Since 1923 there has been a prolonged effort to understand this problem. Basically there have been two explanations of the negative therapeutic reaction, the two that Freud had already described: it has been explained either as an expression of unconscious guilt or as an attack on the analyst.

Explanations involving the patient's unconscious guilt: The main paper here is Riviere's 'A contribution to the analysis of the negative therapeutic reaction' in 1936. Riviere stressed the importance in the negative therapeutic reaction of object relations involving unconscious guilt – a fear of being responsible for the damage or death of the good object, especially the internalised good object [*see* Depressive position]. She particularly warned against analytic overinterpretation of aggressive impulses, which she thought was likely to lead to more negative therapeutic reactions, and she thought that the guilty and depressed patient's obligation to care for his damaged internal objects took precedence over his receiving any help for himself.

Explanations involving attacks on the analyst: The motive for such attacks is usually attributed to envy of the analyst for his capacity to understand and to help the patient. Abraham, Horney, Klein and Rosenfeld have been the main proponents of envious attack as an explanation of the negative therapeutic reaction.

Abraham (1919), like Freud, found that patients who expressed negative therapeutic reactions begrudged the analyst any positive statements about the progress of the treatment, which he attributed to their need to be superior and to stop the analyst from doing anything clever. Abraham attributed the negative therapeutic reaction largely to the patient's envy, which he regarded as an anal characteristic.

Karen Horney (1936), after a careful review of her patients' behaviour, attributed the negative therapeutic reaction largely to an envious attack on the analyst.

Klein attributes the negative therapeutic reaction to envy of the analyst (1957, pp. 217, 220, 222), saying not only that it is a reaction to a helpful interpretation but also describing how the negative therapeutic reaction may be dealt with therapeutically by the analyst. She says that the analyst may be able slowly and gradually to make his way with the patient towards an integration of the patient's envious and loving feelings:

> Therefore the split-off aspects [envy and destructiveness] become more acceptable and the patient is increasingly able to repress destructive impulses towards loved objects instead of splitting the self. This implies that the projection on the analyst, which turns him into a dangerous and retaliating figure, also diminishes, and that the analyst in turn finds it easier to help the patient towards further integration. That is to say, the negative therapeutic reaction is losing in strength.
>
> (Klein, 1957, p. 225)

Rosenfeld (1964, 1971, 1975, 1987) is particularly concerned with the role of the narcissistic, destructive aspects of the patient, which are involved in his feelings of envy for the analyst and in his negative therapeutic reactions.

This led to his idea of destructive narcissism, involving Freud's concept of the death instinct, which he thought was 'particularly pertinent to the negative therapeutic reaction' (Rosenfeld, 1971). In 1975 and 1987 he expressed the view that to the destructive, narcissistic part of the patient:

> . . . this omnipotent way of existing is experienced and even personified as a good friend or guru who uses powerful suggestions and propaganda to maintain the status quo, a process which is generally silent and often creates confusion.
>
> (Rosenfeld, 1987, p. 87)

Efforts to show the patient that he is actually being dominated and imprisoned by his omnipotence soon make the analyst aware that he is dealing with a very primitive superego, which attacks the analyst and belittles the patient's capacities and his wish to have a constructive relationship with the analyst. Analysis becomes, one might say, a struggle between the analyst and the patient's very primitive superego for the soul of the patient. 'The most confusing element in this process', Rosenfeld says, 'is the successful disguise of the omnipotent structure of relating and the envious, destructive super-ego as benevolent figures' (Rosenfeld, 1987, p. 88).

Rosenfeld (1975) and also Etchegoyen et al. (1987), however, also point out the need to distinguish the negative therapeutic reaction deriving from the envious impulse to spoil the analyst's best efforts and the reaction (perhaps equally negative) to the analyst whose interpretations are just wrong because they are defensive on the analyst's part. Rosenfeld's analysis of destructive narcissism and the very primitive superego has been carried on in much work by Steiner and others on pathological organisations of the personality (Steiner, 1987, 1993) [*see* Pathological organisations].

Abraham, K. (1919) 'A particular form of neurotic resistance against the psychoanalytic method', in *Selected Papers on Psycho-Analysis*. London: Hogarth Press (1927), pp. 303–311.

Etchegoyen, H., Lopez, B. and Rabih, M. (1987) 'Envy and how to interpret it', *Int. J. Psycho-Anal.* 68: 49–61.

Freud, S. (1917) 'From the history of an infantile neurosis', *S.E. 17*. London: Hogarth Press, pp. 3–123.

—— (1923) 'The ego and the id', *S.E. 19*. London: Hogarth Press, pp. 3–66.

Horney, K. (1936) 'The problem of the negative therapeutic reaction', *Psycho-Anal. Q.* 5: 29–44.

Klein, M. (1957) 'Envy and gratitude', in *The Writings of Melanie Klein*, Vol. 3. London: Hogarth Press, pp. 176–235.

Riviere, J. (1936) 'A contribution to the analysis of the negative therapeutic reaction', *Int. J. Psycho-Anal.* 17: 304–320.

Rosenfeld, H. (1964) 'On the psychopathology of narcissism: A clinical approach', *Int. J. Psycho-Anal.* 45: 332–337.

—— (1971) 'A clinical approach to the psycho-analytical theory of the life and death instincts: An investigation into the aggressive aspects of narcissism', *Int. J. Psycho-Anal.* 52: 169–178.

—— (1975) 'Negative therapeutic reaction', in P. Giovacchini (ed.) *Tactics and Techniques in Psycho-Analytic Therapy*, Vol. 2. New York: Jason Aronson, pp. 217–228.

—— (1987) *Impasse and Interpretation*. London: Tavistock.

Steiner, J. (1987) 'Interplay between pathological organizations and the paranoid-schizoid and depressive positions', *Int. J. Psycho-Anal.* 68: 69–80.

—— (1993) *Psychic Retreats: Pathological Organizations in Psychotic, Neurotic and Borderline Patients*. London: Routledge.

Object-Relations School

The term 'object relations' surreptitiously creeps up on the reader of Klein. It eventually gave rise to a whole strand of psychoanalytic theory, centred especially within the British Psychoanalytical Society. The lack of precise definition has been important because it has given free licence for multiple uses of the term. It is variously used, depending on speaker and context, but the dominant usage refers particularly to the theories of Fairbairn, Winnicott and Balint, and more generally to those of the Independent Group. Kleinian and many Contemporary Freudian analysts, however, would also maintain that they deal with object relations in their respective approaches.

The Object-Relations School thus includes a number of different theoretical points of view, and generally indicates those British analysts who focus primarily on the state and character of the objects. It is to be contrasted with the Classical or Ego Psychology School, which focuses more on the instinctual impulses that make up the 'energy' of the interest [*see* American psychoanalysis in relation to Klein].

The Object-Relations School includes Fairbairn, Winnicott and Balint particularly, and in general the so-called Independent Psychoanalysts (Kohon, 1986) of the British Psychoanalytical Society. What they have in common is a tendency to ignore the 'economic' aspects of instinctual energy, this tendency being what distinguishes them from the ego psychologists. Klein is marked out as different by her acceptance of the death instinct. There are two strands in the British Psychoanalytical Society: the Fairbairnian framework, which categorically states that man is not pleasure-seeking at all, but object-seeking; and various intermediate positions – two-factor theories (Eagle, 1984) combining an emphasis on objects with an instinct theory. All these derive part of their inspiration from Klein.

There are many British psychoanalysts who would claim that Klein is not truly part of the Object-Relations School (e.g. Kohon, 1986). They reserve the term for Fairbairn, Balint and Winnicott. Guntrip (1961), for instance, in promoting Fairbairn, drew a particular map of progress in psycho-analytic theory in the last 50 years. It reaches out along a dimension starting with Freud's scientific neurology and progresses towards a psycho-logical theory, whole and uncontaminated by biology. However much exaggerated, the dimension that Guntrip emphasises is a prominent feature of the map. It was also described by Greenberg and Mitchell (1983) as the contrast between a 'drive/structure model' and a 'relational/structure model'.

Both the scientific 'biologism' with which Freud started and the pure 'psychologism' of Fairbairn (and Guntrip) are extreme points. Human beings are both biological and psychological at the same time, and both the tightly biological interpretation of Freud and the instinct-rejecting psy-chology of Fairbairn end up suffering from the same fallacy, both trying to reduce the whole dimension (biology–psychology) to a single, and simple, area of study. Unfortunately, the human mind is poised tantalisingly right across that dimension [*see* Mind–body problem] and psychoanalytic theory needs to reflect this dialectic. Klein, of course, was equally divided in this dilemma as she constantly attempted to balance her loyalty to her patients' experience with a loyalty to Freud's scientific purpose. She remained uncomfortably stretched between biology and psychology.

The beginnings of object-relations theory: As Freud was forced more and more to give importance to transference [*see* Transference], so the patient's relationships gained more and more prominence. The transference rela-tionship is the cornerstone of the practice of psychoanalysis, and theory based on actual practice (seemingly a special characteristic of British psy-choanalysis) inevitably moved the transference relationship increasingly towards the centre of theory as well as practice; this entailed moving the ego's relationships with its objects into the foreground.

Enacted transference: The Dora case threw up a difficult problem for Freud, since he had intended it as an exemplary case for future publication. Since Dora dropped out of her treatment very prematurely after 3 months, he had to think hard about what had gone wrong. He realised that he had not been alive to the negative transference, nor to how intensely relations are felt as actually real in their *enactment* with the analyst (Freud, 1905).

However, it was his problem with another kind of patient that put him more firmly on the road that would lead (others) eventually to the object-relations approach. These patients were the psychotic ones who, he found, did not make a proper transference with him. From the Dora case onwards, he might have been wary that he was missing elements of the transference, but he actually thought it was in the nature of schizophrenia that these patients failed to invest the analyst with instinctual energy. This could not then be used to engage the patient to overcome his resistances. He 'analysed' Judge Schreber from the published memoirs the judge left behind, since he thought this was the only way to understand the mind of a schizophrenic (Freud, 1911). He found that the patient had suffered a 'world disaster', by which he meant that the world as a whole had completely lost its interest for him – that is, no instinctual energy was invested (cathected) in the world. Instead, the schizophrenic reconstructs an imaginary world of delusions and hallucinations to fill in, as it were, the place where the actual world had once been. This separation of two worlds, actual and personal, is of importance as a forerunner of an object-relations point of view [*see* Psychic reality].

Narcissism: At this point (about 1913) Freud brought together certain ideas of an entirely new kind. He was spurred on by his wish to confront and demolish Jung's assertions of non-libidinal experiences. Jung had been a psychiatrist with experience of psychotic patients, while Freud had not. Freud had worked in a neurological sanatorium with hysterical (neurotic) patients and so, as Jung began to pull away from the psychoanalytic movement, Freud was determined to keep his end up in understanding schizophrenics and laying down a libidinal theory of their disorders. As a result of all this Freud really began to see that in some sense the person himself, or some part of his self or his own ideas, could become the object of his own instinctual energies. Thus was born the concept of narcissism (Freud, 1914), and out of this would eventually come an interest in the object itself (self or other) that is invested with libidinal interest.

Introjection of objects: The second great and innovatory step took place in 1917 with Freud's paper 'Mourning and melancholia'. For some time, Freud had been working with Abraham in trying to understand the psychoses. In fact Abraham (1911) had also written a paper on the topic at about the same time as Freud's paper on the schizophrenic judge Schreber. However, Abraham's paper was on manic-depressive psychosis, and he was at some advantage over Freud. The interesting thing about manic-depressive psychosis is that it is intermittent. The patient goes through phases when the condition remits and he comes to appear approximately normal. Abraham then set out to try analysing these patients during the periods of remission. Could he work then as he would with a neurotic patient? The answer, he found, was that he could (Abraham, 1924). This created an interest in manic-depressive illness rather than schizophrenia, and Freud's paper on mourning and melancholia constituted his own reflections upon this disorder. It is a paper with some beautiful descriptions of the conditions of mourning and of melancholia (manic-depressive psychosis), and in it he also produced an extraordinary development in his conceptual thinking. He showed that the work of mourning is a slow, step-like giving up of the cathexis of a loved object that has been lost. He showed too that the condition of melancholia is clinically similar in many respects to mourning and that it entails a similar giving up of a lost loved object. The difference, he argued, was that the melancholic does not give up the object but does something quite different with it. He re-establishes the object inside his own ego and goes on relating to it there. Freud argued that the reason for doing this is a particularly strong element of hate and fury towards the loved object, and that the outcome is a strong hatred and fury focused on the ego as if it were the object. 'The shadow', he said, 'of the object falls upon the ego' (Freud, 1917, p. 249). He called this 'identification' [*see* Identification; Introjection].

At this point Freud was describing a phenomenology of the object and had left aside the economics of the instinctual drives. Having discovered this highly interesting process of identification, which actually causes an 'alteration of the ego', he showed 4 years later (Freud, 1921) that group psychology is based on identification. He had by this time performed the familiar trick that has been the fate of so many psychoanalytic concepts – having been discovered as pathological phenomena in patients, they come to be seen everywhere as an essential ingredient of normal psychology.

Freud's way forward was to show that the development of the superego was based on this process of identification, which entailed the setting up internally of the oedipal loved objects that had to be given up by the young child (Freud, 1923). The boundary of the ego was now seen as permeable not only to directed instinctual energy but also to objects.

Abraham, in the short time that was allowed him before his premature death in 1925, developed Freud's understanding of the internalising process, especially in pointing to its connection with pregenital impulses. He followed up Freud's hints that introjection had something to do with 'cannibalism' and the oral and sadistic impulses and that there was a mirror process in 'projection' or expulsion that was related to the anal impulses. The confluence of some basic defence mechanisms with component instincts and their corresponding erogenous zones must have seemed very elegant and suggestive of a theory rounding out into completion. He was drawn into the realisation that introjection and projection primarily concern the fate of the objects, their location inside or outside the ego and the movement between the two sites. He began filling in this theory with meticulous and detailed examples vividly expressed in the psychopathology of his manic-depressive patients.

Child analysis: After Abraham's death the impetus really passed to Klein, whom he had encouraged to analyse children and to develop her play technique, which by a happy chance gave her a wonderfully clear window into the whole arena of object relations. She gave her children a collection of objects (toys) and watched them arrange the toys in all sorts of relationships to each other. She could then see the instinctual wishes played out visually in front of her as relationships between objects in the most natural way possible – as the play of children [*see* Child analysis; Technique].

Kleinian object-relations theory: What Klein found straight away with her play technique was that her patients played with objects – their toys – and also enacted dramas with the person of the analyst. Very young children seem to have feelings for the object itself, however imaginary [*see* Love]. Thus Klein noticed that from the child's point of view, his objects appeared alive, lovable and loving, menacing, pitiable, and so on – quite different from the objects in Freud's descriptions. In short, in the child's mind there is a full and intense relation with the object conceived in the most animistic and anthropomorphic way. The objects, even toys, lived and felt and died. Anyone can make these simple observations on children's play, and they stand in contrast to the descriptions of instinctual discharges upon passive objects.

Objects and instincts: Her loyalty to Freud's theory of instincts always gave Klein a sense of being firmly and securely embedded within Freudian psychoanalysis, but she set out to describe the patient's experience of his objects and the psychological content of the anxieties about them. She found she could keep both the concepts 'object' and 'instinct' when she saw that the relations with objects were exactly defined by the impulses from libidinal sources (oral, anal, genital). She found that the child believed the object to be suffused with intents and motivations aligned with the child's own particular libidinal impulses active at the moment. The oral infant could believe that the object was another who might itself bite the infant in frustration or retaliation. The child's relation to the object is a phantasy with participant actors and a narrative. Objects, therefore, were the stuff of a child's phantasy life, rather than merely a means to instinctual satisfactions. Yet they are also the latter.

The theoretical links between object relations and instincts seemed difficult to attain, and in 1939 a study group was set up in the British Psychoanalytical Society, known as the Internal Objects Group, which met intermittently during the war years to try to understand and find ways of making these views on objects credible. Several papers resulted from this work (contributions to the Controversial Discussions) [*see* Controversial Discussions]. The most important paper was by Susan Isaacs (1948), in which she described how the instincts find a mental expression as a phantasy in the unconscious mind (unconscious phantasy) – *a phantasy of a relation with an object* [*see* Unconscious phantasy]. This is a tie-up of biological, psychological and ultimately social dimensions in the object-relations stance of Klein.

Abraham, K. (1911) 'Notes on the psycho-analytic investigation and treatment of manic-depressive insanity and allied conditions', in *Selected Papers on Psycho-analysis*. London: Hogarth Press (1927), pp. 137–156.

—— (1924) 'A short study of the development of the libido', in *Selected Papers on Psycho-Analysis*. London: Hogarth Press (1927), pp. 418–501.

Eagle, M. (1984) *Recent Developments in Psychoanalysis*. New York: McGraw-Hill.

Freud, S. (1905) 'Fragment of an analysis of a case of hysteria', *S.E. 7*. London: Hogarth Press, pp. 3–122.

—— (1911) 'Psycho-analytic notes on an autobiographical account of a case of paranoia', *S.E. 12*. London: Hogarth Press, pp. 3–82.

—— (1914) 'On narcissism', *S.E. 14*. London: Hogarth Press, pp. 67–102.

—— (1917) 'Mourning and melancholia', *S.E. 14*. London: Hogarth Press, pp. 237–258.

—— (1921) 'Group psychology and analysis of the ego', *S.E. 18*. London: Hogarth Press, pp. 67–143.

—— (1923) 'The ego and the id', *S.E. 19*. London: Hogarth Press, pp. 3–66.

Greenberg, J. and Mitchell, S. (1983) *Object Relations in Psycho-Analytic Theory*. Cambridge, MA: Harvard University Press.

Guntrip, H. (1961) *Personality Structure and Human Interaction*. London: Hogarth Press.

Isaacs, S. (1948) 'The nature and function of phantasy', *Int. J. Psycho-Anal.* 29: 73–97.

Kohon, G. (1986) *The British School of Psychoanalysis: The Independent Tradition*. London: Free Association Books.

Objects

The term 'object' is a technical one, used originally in psychoanalysis by Freud in his drive theory to denote the object of an instinctual impulse, the person or thing upon which impulses of energy are discharged, an impersonal object that is recognised only for the purposes of the subject's pleasure-seeking, satisfaction and relief. In 1914 in 'On narcissism' Freud describes how the individual may become the object of his own instinctual drives. Increasingly in Freud's work it is not only instinctual drives that are of interest but also the psychological aspects of the relationship to the object. In his important paper, 'Mourning and melancholia' (1917), Freud explores the significance of the feelings of love and hate in managing the loss of a significant person (object). Lost objects are introjected into the ego, which may divide into a part that is identified with the object and a part that has a relationship to the lost object. These ideas develop into Freud's (1923) idea of the superego, a part of the ego that is based on the internalisation of the original objects and is separated off. Abraham (1924) focuses on the projection and introjection of the objects and their movement between being inside and outside the ego [*see* Karl Abraham; Internal objects; Superego].

Klein: As Klein develops her technique with children she observes how they play out their instinctual wishes by ascribing different characteristics to the toys and using them to enact relationships. The relationships between the toys themselves and between the toys and the child are full of feeling, and these objects are experienced by the child as living feeling beings [*see* Child analysis]. Although both Freud's and Klein's theories concern object relationships, their theories are also theories about instincts – in Klein's framework, the object is a component in the mental representation of an instinct – and for this reason neither Freud nor Klein are considered to be members of the so-called 'Object-Relations School' [*see* Internal objects; Object-Relations School].

Objects, phantasy and drives: Klein believes that from the outset the infant exists in relation to objects that are primitively distinguished from the ego – there are object relations from birth. What is experienced by the infant and represented in unconscious phantasy, which at this stage is a concrete experience, is a relationship between the self and an object in which the object is motivated with certain impulses, good or bad. This results from the infant's omnipotent projection of his life and death instincts, including his oral, anal and genital drives into the object and subsequent omnipotent introjection of the object. The phantasied object is felt really to exist inside or outside the subject, and is related to on the basis of its supposed impulses towards the ego. Typically, these very primitive ways of managing, experiencing and interpreting the instinctual sensations lead to intense love and gratitude or hatred and envy. Alongside this omnipotent activity, non-omnipotent projection and introjection are taking place [*see* Internal objects; Unconscious phantasy].

Objects: Klein's developmental theory and theory of how the mind works is concerned with the relationship between the internal and external objects and that between the internal objects and parts of the self in the internal world. The most important internal objects are those derived from the parents. At first both the ego and the object are separated into 'good' and 'bad' 'part-objects' in the 'paranoid-schizoid position' and are gradually integrated into 'whole objects' and a whole ego in the 'depressive position', a fluctuation between these two positions and ways of object relating continues throughout life.

See Bad object; Depressive position; External object; Good object; Ideal object; Internal objects; Internal reality; Paranoid-schizoid position; Part-object; Whole object

Abraham, K. (1924) 'A short study of the development of the libido, viewed in the light of mental disorders', in *The Selected Papers of Karl Abraham*. London: Hogarth Press (1927), pp. 418–501.

Freud, S. (1914) 'On narcissism: An introduction', *S.E. 14*. London: Hogarth Press, pp. 67–102.

—— (1917) 'Mourning and melancholia', *S.E. 14*. London: Hogarth Press, pp. 237–258.

—— (1923) 'The ego and the id', *S.E. 19*. London: Hogarth Press, pp. 3–66.

Obsessional defences

Klein's writings on obsessional neurosis (1932a) and on obsessional mechanisms (1932b) appear in her early work but are not further developed. In her middle period (1935–1946) she uses the generic term 'obsessional defences' to refer to the group of obsessional mechanisms mapped out earlier. In her two papers on the depressive position (1935, 1940) Klein emphasises the separate status of the obsessional defence as an alternative to the manic defence. In 'Notes on some schizoid mechanisms' (1946) she makes a specific link between projective identification and the mechanism of obsessional coercion of others. In the late phase of her work, Klein makes two references to the obsessional defence (1952, 1957). Clearly Klein never lost sight of the importance of the obsessional defence in early development and also as an adjunct to the more primitive, schizoid and manic defences.

Early period: In the early period Klein conceptualises the primitive anxiety situation in terms of a phase of maximal sadism during which the combined parents and the inside of mother's body and its contents are attacked. Obsessional symptoms and mechanisms become active in the second year of life as the early anal stage gives way to the later anal stage (1932b, p. 162). Klein relies on Karl Abraham's formulation (1924) that this transition entails a diminution in the dominance of the anal-sadistic impulses of destroying and expelling and the emergence of the anal tendencies to conserve by retention and control. The wish to retain is accompanied by the feelings of pity and concern for the object (1932b, p. 165). This change means that the superego is not only experienced as talionic and terrifying in character but as a sense of guilt as well (1932b, p. 164). The emergence of obsessional mechanisms is linked to the emergence of guilt and avails the developing child of a new way of combating both primitive anxiety and also guilt stemming from the early superego. Five interrelated obsessional mechanisms can be distinguished from Klein's early writings:

1   *The reaction formations of orderliness, cleanliness and disgust*: For Freud (1908, 1917) the defence of symbolic doing and undoing is at the

base of the reaction formations of cleanliness and orderliness. For Klein the child's acquiring of clean habits, as in toilet training, is fraught with deep anxieties related to phantasies of sadistic attacks on mother's body with destructive excreta. Retaliatory attacks by internal and external objects can lead to the child's terror of excreta and dirt in general. If the child pleases his objects by becoming clean and orderly, his 'good' faeces can serve as evidence against his phantastic fears of their destructive and sadistic quality. When the reaction formations of cleanliness and orderliness are excessive in young children they are a sign that excessive anxiety and guilt are active.

2 *Compulsive accumulations and giving*: Freud (1908, 1917) understood the obsessional character trait of parsimony as a sublimation of the original pleasure in anal retention. Klein's alternative view is that both compulsive accumulation and giving are ways of warding off the terrifying fear of the maternal imago who demands what has been stolen from inside her body. They are also felt to restore the damage done in phantasy and thereby alleviate guilt. Klein points out that in children these defensive compulsions are fraught with uncertainty and doubt because: 'They feel they cannot give back out of their own small body what they have taken out of their mother's body which is so huge in comparison' (1932b, p. 168). The child cannot know for certain whether he has enough to put right the theft and damage he has done inside mother's body. This uncertainty is one of the motivating factors behind the obsessional desire for knowledge with its pedantic, meticulous and overprecise character.

3 *The obsessional desire for knowledge*: The desire to know what is inside mother's body accompanies the child's sadistic urges to take possession of her body and its contents and to attack them with various sadistic aims (1932b, p. 174). The terror of the retaliatory mother combined with the child's uncertainty and inability to know may lead to an obsessional desire to know, with emphasis on knowing every detail, which leads to an inhibition in learning. Erna's inhibition in learning illustrates how her tremendous terror of knowing everything about the destruction she had done to her mother's body in phantasy set up a radical disturbance in her desire for knowledge as a whole [*see* Epistemophilia]:

> The child's original and intensely strong and unsatisfied desire to get information about the shape, size and number of its father's penises, excrements and children inside its mother had turned into a compulsion to measure, add up and count things, and so on.
>
> (Klein, 1932b, p. 175)

4 *Obsessional form of making restitution (reparation)*: For early Klein the omnipotent urges to make restitution or to restore the damage done to

the object are an important way of modifying both anxiety and guilt. In her early work, Klein rarely uses the term reparation, whose full logic emerges in her middle period [*see* Reparation]. Klein, however, hints in the direction of a distinction between a more omnipotent form of making restitution that is based on a denial of omnipotent destructive urges and on 'megalomanic phantasies of exceptional magnitude' and the obsessional form of making restitution (p. 173). The latter has two distinct characteristics: that of the displacement onto trifles and of the compulsion to repeat. She writes:

> By virtue of the mechanism of displacement on to something very small the obsessional patient can seek in very slight achievements a proof of his constructive omnipotence and his capacity to make complete restitution.
>
> (Klein, 1932b, p. 173)

However, the inevitable doubt in his constructive omnipotence becomes an incentive to repeat his actions compulsively.

5   *The obsessional coercion of others*: Obsessionals exercise an often intolerable coercion on people in their surroundings, which they achieve as a result of a manifold projection that Klein describes as follows:

> In the first place he is trying to throw off the intolerable compulsion under which he is suffering by treating his object as though it were his id or his super-ego and by displacing the coercion outside. In doing this he is, incidentally, satisfying his primary sadism by tormenting or subjugating his object.
>
> (Klein, 1932b, p. 166)

The fear of being destroyed or attacked by his introjected objects arouses in the obsessional a compulsion to control his imagos, and since he cannot achieve this he tries to tyrannise over his external object by projection.

When Klein uses the shorthand 'obsessional defences' in her later writings she has in mind any combination of these five mechanisms above.

Middle period: In her two papers on the depressive position (1935, 1940) Klein consistently distinguishes obsessional and manic defences, which she sees as important alternatives for the developing child:

> When the defences of a manic nature fail (defences in which dangers from various sources are omnipotently denied or minimized) the ego is

driven alternatively or simultaneously to combat the fears of deterioration or disintegration by attempted reparations carried out in
obsessional ways.

(Klein, 1940, p. 351)

Freud's notion of symbolic doing and undoing provided the inspiration for
Klein's postulation of a more general process of reparation, which comes to
the fore with the depressive position. But Klein did not abandon her early
work on obsessional ways of making restitution; quite the contrary, she
stresses that omnipotent reparation takes either a manic or an obsessional
form and that the latter cannot be collapsed into the former. She leaves us
with important markers as to what distinguishes and differentiates them.

From a *chronological* point of view, manic defences according to Klein
emerge in the second quarter of the first year of life at a time when
phantasy activity far outstrips motor activity in the child. By contrast the
obsessional defences emerge in the second year of life when control over the
body and motor movement are more advanced. Manic defences are *more
omnipotent* in character than obsessional defences (Klein, 1932b). In manic
reparation the radical denial of persecutory anxiety and damage and guilt is
central, so that reparation proper is impossible. Its phantastic character is
wholly impractical and unrealisable. Everything is conceived on a large
scale or in large numbers in accordance with the grandeur of manic omnipotence, and there is contempt for detail and minor matters (1940, p. 353).
Obsessional reparation is also omnipotent, but less so than the manic form.
It is accompanied by a change from pure phantasy and illusion to motor
actions or their mental equivalents, as in compulsive magical formulas.
These are characterised by attention to detail and a conscientious concen-
tration on minutiae. Each obsessional act is an attempt to undo the persecutory anxiety and guilt. However, because it is omnipotent and concrete, it
leads to uncertainty and doubt and to the compulsion to repeat.

Klein alludes to an important distinction between the manic and obsessional form of exerting omnipotent control over the internalised *parental
couple and their coitus*. She writes that when obsessional features dominate
a clinical presentation '. . . such mastery betokened a forcible separation of
two (or more) objects' and when the manic was in the ascendant 'the
patient had recourse to methods more violent' (1935, p. 278). In the same
text Klein refers more explicitly to the oral cannibalistic aspects of mania
and to the killing of the objects. Klein is hinting that mastery in obsessional
reparation involves keeping the parents separate or preventing them from
touching, whereas in manic reparation the parental coitus is omnipotently
cannibalised or robbed but any concern is radically denied. For Freud
(1926), the taboo on touching underlies the major obsessional defence of
isolation. Klein can be seen to suggest an obsessional mode of controlling
the parental coitus: by preventing them from touching.

These distinctions suggest that although Klein did not develop much further her early ideas on obsessional mechanisms, she maintained a view that the obsessional defence is different from and also an important alternative to the manic defence in working through the conflicts of the depressive position.

Klein's early notion of the obsessional coercion of others contains an implicit description of projective identification. In 'Notes on some schizoid mechanisms' (1946) she makes the connection between projective identification and this particular obsessional mechanism more explicit. She writes: 'One root of obsessional mechanisms may thus be found in the particular identification which results from infantile projective processes' (1946, p. 13). The obsessional need to control others is narcissistic in character. It is a result of excessive projections of parts of the self into another person. The tendency for reparation is not only directed towards objects but also towards parts of self in need of reparation or restoration (p. 13). This particular obsessional form of reparation relies on the schizoid mechanism of projective identification whereby the attempt to gain control over parts of the self takes the form of the coercive control of others.

Later period: In 'Some theoretical conclusions regarding the emotional life of the infant' Klein (1952) stresses again the importance of the obsessional defence as it emerges in the second year of life. She sees it as a progress in the ego's capacity to work through primitive anxieties. She contrasts it to the schizoid and manic defences, which also suggests that for Klein these were the three major groups of defences active in infantile development, thereby retaining the importance of her early writings on the obsessional mechanisms.

Finally, in 'Envy and gratitude' (1957, p. 221) Klein, in a footnote, reiterates the importance of obsessional mechanisms in the second year as there is a decrease in the dominance of projective identification, a greater clarification of internal reality and a more realistic perception of the external world.

Contemporary Kleinian contributions: Three more recent papers explore links between obsessional and schizoid defences, whereas on the whole in Klein's writings the obsessional defences are contrasted more predominantly with the manic defences. Betty Joseph (1966) reiterates Klein's view that severe obsessional states are often based on paranoid states that have preceded it (Klein, 1932b, p. 167). In her paper on the analysis of a 4-year-old child, Joseph shows how, as the acute paranoid anxieties of the child were analysed, an obsessional organisation with rigid and controlling ruminations and rituals took over (Joseph, 1966, p. 184).

In 'Obsessional certainty versus obsessional doubt: From two to three' Ignês Sodré (1991) amalgamates Bion's concepts on thinking [*see* Wilfred

Bion] with those of Ronald Britton on the Oedipus complex [*see* Oedipus complex] to conceptualise two modes of obsessional thinking. Some severe obsessional states show a schizoid adherence to rigidity, certainty and inflexibility, as if a tyrannical thought is constantly keeping out all the other points of view and doubt is strictly forbidden. By contrast, in the more typical obsessional state of doubt thinking is dominated by a constant oscillation between opposing thoughts and no certainty can be achieved. Sodré links the first state to an exclusion of triangularity because the oedipal situation is experienced as a major threat. In the second state the oedipal situation is omnipresent and it is impossible to establish any peaceful, undisturbed coupling of any sort. Obsessional doubt belongs to a different developmental stage when oedipal conflicts are entered into but are extremely intense and seemingly irresolvable.

Couve (2001) explores the role of obsessional organisations in dealing with a fragmented emotional universe, resulting from the effects of extreme schizoid mechanisms. He suggests that the anal symbolic register of expulsion and retention and its copro-symbols gives a more advanced symbolic shape to this underlying psychic landscape of fragmentation and of bizarre objects. The operation of underlying violent projective identification and fragmentary splitting means that symbolisation has been drastically affected. One problem is that work with the more accessible obsessional organisation leaves out the fundamental disturbance, which remains more elusive and difficult to attend to analytically.

Abraham, K. (1924) 'A short study of the development of the libido', in *Selected Papers of Karl Abraham*. London: Hogarth Press (1927), pp. 418–501.

Couve, C. (2001) 'Obsessional dread of the dead: The relations between obsessional and schizoid organisations', *Bull. Br. Psychoanal. Soc.* 37: 1–14.

Freud, S. (1908) 'Character and anal erotism', *S.E. 9*. London: Hogarth Press, pp. 167–175.

—— (1917) 'On transformations of instinct as exemplified in anal erotism', *S.E. 17*. London: Hogarth Press, pp. 125–133.

—— (1926) 'Inhibitions, symptoms and anxiety', *S.E. 20*. London: Hogarth Press, pp. 75–176.

Joseph, B. (1966) 'Persecutory anxiety in a four year-old boy', *Int. J. Psycho-Anal.* 47: 184–189.

Klein, M. (1932a) 'An obsessional neurosis in a six-year-old girl', in *The Writings of Melanie Klein*, Vol. 2. London: Hogarth Press, pp. 35–57.

—— (1932b) 'The relations between obsessional neurosis and the early stages of the super-ego', in *The Writings of Melanie Klein*, Vol. 2. London: Hogarth Press, pp. 149–175.

—— (1935) 'A contribution to the psychogenesis of manic-depressive states', *Int. J. Psycho-Anal.* 16: 145–174; republished in *The Writings of Melanie Klein*, Vol. 1. London: Hogarth Press (1975), pp. 262–289.

—— (1940) 'Mourning and its relation to manic-depressive states', in *The Writings of Melanie Klein*, Vol. 1. London: Hogarth Press, pp. 344–369.

—— (1946) 'Notes on some schizoid mechanisms', *Int. J. Psycho-Anal.* 27: 99–110; republished in *The Writings of Melanie Klein*, Vol. 3. London: Hogarth Press (1975), pp. 1–24.

—— (1952) 'Some theoretical conclusions regarding the emotional life of the infant', in *The Writings of Melanie Klein*, Vol. 3. London: Hogarth Press, pp. 61–93.

—— (1957) 'Envy and gratitude', in *The Writings of Melanie Klein*, Vol. 3. London: Hogarth Press, pp. 176–235.

Sodré, I. (1991) 'Obsessional certainty versus doubt: From 2 to 3', in R. Schafer (ed.) *The Contemporary Kleinians of London*. Madison, CT: International Universities Press, pp. 262–278.

Omnipotence

Klein observed in her clinical work with small children that much of their thinking was omnipotent, in that it did not conform to accepted views of reality. Much of this thinking Klein regards as normal: the introjection of good objects, for example, and the child's consequent belief that such objects are supporting him, and, equally important, the belief that he might be taking in bad objects that were attacking him internally. Klein regards such thinking as part of normal development and does not usually describe it as omnipotent.

Together with splitting, denial and sometimes idealisation, Klein regarded omnipotence as one of the defences defending the personality from the anxieties of the paranoid-schizoid position, and to some extent from the anxieties of the depressive position as well (Klein, 1935 p. 277; 1946, p. 7; 1952a, 1952b). She also pointed out that omnipotent phantasies of destructive attack tended to be stronger and more persistent than omnipotent phantasies of reparation and restitution (Klein, 1932, pp. 172–173; Klein, 1955, p. 158).

Klein, M. (1932) *The Psychoanalysis of Children. The Writings of Melanie Klein*, Vol. 2. London: Hogarth Press.

—— (1935) 'A contribution to the psychogenesis of manic-depressive states', in *The Writings of Melanie Klein*, Vol. 1. London: Hogarth Press, pp. 262–289.

—— (1946) 'Notes on some schizoid mechanisms', in *The Writings of Melanie Klein*, Vol. 3. London: Hogarth Press, pp. 1–24.

—— (1952a) 'The origins of transference', in *The Writings of Melanie Klein*, Vol. 3. London: Hogarth Press, pp. 48–56.

—— (1952b) 'Some theoretical conclusions regarding the emotional life of the infant', in *The Writings of Melanie Klein*, Vol. 3. London: Hogarth Press, pp. 61–93.

—— (1955) 'On identification', in *The Writings of Melanie Klein*, Vol. 3. London: Hogarth Press, pp. 141–175.

Paranoia

From the outset of her work Klein is impressed by the violent quality of children's play and human phantasy life. She soon concludes that inhibitions and neurotic problems in children arise out of their intense fear of their own actual and phantasised aggression and the phantasised retaliation it provokes. She describes the way that children can be trapped in a vicious circle leading to panic and *pavor nocturnus* (night terrors) and wonders about the relation between these states and paranoid psychosis in adults. She treats a severely inhibited child in whom these paranoid fears are so intense that they inhibit all activity, including the ability to create symbols, and she concludes that these fears are the basis for the psychoses (Klein, 1930) [*see* Psychosis].

In 1932, Klein adopts Freud's concept of the death instinct and its deflection and argues that it is this projected destructiveness that forms the basis of the 'bad' object from whom the child anticipates destructive and retaliatory attacks. Klein describes a '. . . vicious circle dominated by the death instinct, in which aggression gives rise to anxiety and anxiety reinforces aggression' (Klein, 1932, p. 150). The prevalence of these paranoid feelings and object relations led Klein in 1935 to contrast the 'depressive position' with a prior '*paranoid*' position, a term that she drops in 1946 when she introduces the term 'paranoid-schizoid position' [*see* Death instinct; Envy; Paranoid-schizoid position; Persecution; Superego].

Klein, M. (1930) 'The importance of symbol formation in the development of the ego', in *The Writings of Melanie Klein*, Vol. 1. London: Hogarth Press, pp. 219–232.
—— (1932) *The Psychoanalysis of Children. The Writings of Melanie Klein*, Vol. 2. London: Hogarth Press.
—— (1946) 'Notes on some schizoid-mechanisms', in *The Writings of Melanie Klein*, Vol. 3. London: Hogarth Press, pp. 1–24.

Paranoid defence against depressive anxiety

Klein first describes the depressive position, then observes that there are a number of important defences against depressive guilt, which she comes to incorporate into her concept of the paranoid-schizoid position [*see* Depressive position; Paranoid-schizoid position]. Klein observes how, repeatedly, there is a retreat from the depressive position when depressive anxieties, particularly guilt, become too strong. For example '. . . paranoid fears and suspicions were reinforced as a defence against the depressive position' (Klein, 1935, p. 274). Klein is said to have regarded the paranoid defence against guilt as her most important discovery. The idea of constant movements between depressive and paranoid-schizoid positions, both defensively and in the service of development, has been taken up extensively in contemporary Kleinian thinking [*see* Ps↔D].

Klein, Melanie (1935) 'A contribution to the psychogenesis of manic-depressive states', in *The Writings of Melanie Klein*, Vol. 1. London: Hogarth Press, pp. 262–289.

Part-objects

The notion of part-objects originates in Abraham's ideas about incorporation. Speaking of manic-depressive patients, he reports:

> . . . one of the patients used very often to have the phantasy of biting off the nose or the lobe of the ear or the breast, of a young girl who he was very fond of. At other times he used to play with the idea of biting off his father's finger . . . We may thus speak of partial incorporation of the object.
>
> (Abraham, 1924, p. 487)

Abraham sees the biting and incorporation of a part of the object as one of the early forms of loving relationship with an object, an ambivalent relationship that contains both loving and biting. In his theory, stages of ambivalent relating to part-objects precede the stage of post-ambivalent true object-love relating towards whole objects.

Using her analysis of children, Klein develops a different model in which ambivalence occurs towards whole objects and is an achievement in the 'depressive position'. Part-object relating, in Klein's theory, is developmentally earlier (possibly similar to Abraham's first pre-ambivalent stage) and is a way to avoid ambivalence in the 'paranoid-schizoid position' [*see* Depressive position; Paranoid-schizoid position].

Part-object relating and the paranoid-schizoid position: Klein thinks of the infantile ego and its experiences as unintegrated and the infant therefore as experiencing or perceiving only a part of the object or mother at any one time. In her view the infant conceptualises experience in terms of bodily parts.

> . . . the object of all these phantasies is, to begin with, the breast of the mother. It may seem curious that the tiny child's interest should be limited to a part of a person rather than to the whole but one must bear in mind first of all that the child has an extremely underdeveloped capacity for perception, physical and mental, and then . . . the tiny child is only concerned with his immediate gratifications.
>
> (Klein, 1936, p. 290)

Klein's view is that the first sensations, for example of satisfaction or pain and hunger, are felt by the infant as being deliberately caused by concrete beings or objects in his body – 'good' or 'bad' objects or part-objects [*see* Internal objects; Unconscious phantasy]. Over time these experiences, for example of being held and fed, will become linked together and a whole picture of the mother will begin to emerge. However, running counter to integration is the binary splitting of the paranoid-schizoid position in which the infant's first task is to split its experience – its experiencing ego and its objects – into 'good' and 'bad'. The infant or individual projects the 'bad' parts of itself and the 'good' parts of itself, respectively, into the 'bad' and 'good' (part-)objects. The objects or part-objects are therefore narcissistic objects in that they contain part of the projector's self. The objects, containing parts of the self that have been projected into them, are then introjected. Particularly in her early writing, Klein thinks of the infant or small child as containing objects that have been introjected at different stages of development (Klein, 1929). The activity of binary splitting separates the 'good' from the 'bad', provides order and enables the infant to securely introject a good object around which to develop. Objects are therefore partial in the bodily, moral and temporal senses [*see* Bad object; Good object; Ideal object].

Part-object as anatomical structure or as function: In his 1959 paper 'Attacks on linking' Bion argues that the part-object relationship is to do with the object's function as well as its physiology, for example the patient's relationship is to the feeding, poisoning, loving or hating breast.

Whole-object relating and the depressive position: As the infant realises that the mother who provides a good experience is also the one who causes bad experiences and that the loved mother is also the hated mother, she becomes perceived to be a whole separate object and the infant begins to recognise which qualities come from her and which from within himself. In 1935 with her theory of the 'depressive position', Klein outlines the ways in which attaining a whole-object relationship results in the loss of an omnipotent view of the world, the loss of a feeling of possessing all the mother's good qualities, a recognition of the self's own bad qualities, and guilt about damage that has been inflicted on her in hatred. All this will cause the infant or individual to recoil and retreat back to a greater or lesser extent into the part-object functioning of the paranoid-schizoid position. A repeated to and fro between part-object and whole-object relating occurs on the threshold of the depressive position.

Abraham, K. (1924) 'A short history of the development of the libido', in *Selected Papers on Psychoanalysis*. London: Hogarth Press (1927), pp. 418–501.
Bion, W. (1959) 'Attacks on linking', *Int. J. Psycho-Anal.* 40: 308–315.

Klein, M. (1927) 'Criminal tendencies in normal children', in *The Writings of Melanie Klein*, Vol. 1. London: Hogarth Press, pp. 170–185.

——— (1929) 'Personification in the play of children', in *The Writings of Melanie Klein*, Vol. 1. London: Hogarth Press, pp. 199–209.

——— (1935) 'A contribution to the psychogenesis of manic-depressive states', in *The Writings of Melanie Klein*, Vol. 1. London: Hogarth Press, pp. 262–289.

——— (1936) 'Weaning', in *The Writings of Melanie Klein*, Vol. 1. London: Hogarth Press, pp. 290–305.

Penis and phallus

In Klein's theory the 'penis' to begin with is a part-object, initially conceived in unconscious phantasy as a part of the combined parent figure. It is believed by the infant to reside inside the mother's body (abdomen or breast) together with all the sexual processes [*see* Combined parent figure]. The phantasy is a very primitive version of the parents in part-object form in an orgy of mutual gratification at the child's expense. The combined nature of the objects increases the child's sense of exclusion from all his objects. It is the earliest and most primitive phantasy that structures the oedipal situation [*see* Oedipus complex].

The desire to know what is inside the mother's body becomes subverted by the envy and jealousy that are stirred up. Thus there are aggressive and sadistic phantasies of forcefully entering the mother's body, and of robbing and destroying by oral, urethral and anal sadistic means the riches that are inside. This includes the relationship with father's penis that is itself attacked. The attack on the combined parents sets the scene for the conflicts and anxieties of the depressive position and the psychic work that will be achieved with the help of the oedipal positions. The relationship that both boy and girl develop with the father's penis plays a crucial role in determining both their masculinity and femininity. In the course of oedipal development the penis becomes more differentiated and linked more directly with the father.

In normal oedipal development (Klein, 1945) the boy deals with his encounter with the combined couple and what is stirred up by turning his desires away from the breast to the father's penis. This homosexual position also lays the foundation for his positive later oedipal position. If the boy has already developed a sufficiently loving relation with the breast this will colour his relation with the paternal penis. The good penis, which he now internalises orally as part of his feminine Oedipus complex, also lays the foundation for a future creative organ. If the fear of the castrating father is mitigated by trust of the good father, the boy can live with his oedipal hatred and rivalry through the recurring switches and oscillations between his two oedipal positions [*see* Oedipus complex]. This good-enough development is, however, easily impeded by many factors such as the

internalisation of a very sadistic parental couple or that of a very destructive paternal penis experienced as overwhelmingly vengeful and castrating.
Such conditions can lead to excessive repression and fears of the boy's
genital desires and an inability to experience the paternal penis and his own
penis as creative and loving.

The girl also begins by turning away from her mother to her father, with
her oral and genital desires to take in the paternal penis as a source of
babies and gifts (Klein, 1945). A good relation with the breast enhances a
good relation with the penis, but the girl's early feminine oedipal position
also sets her in conflict with her mother, whom she has robbed of her
partner. The girl now fears that the vengeful mother will rob her of her
insides, a fear that, if excessive, will affect her later femininity. The girl can
turn to a masculine position by usurping father's penis as her own in order
to placate her vengeful and persecutory mother. The oscillation between
these two oedipal positions will be marred if it is not helped by the early
internalisation of a good breast to begin with, and if the internal parental
couple is very sadistic or if the rival mother is felt to be overwhelmingly
persecutory.

In a normal working-through of the depressive position the combined
parent figure gives way gradually to the idea of whole object: separate
parents who come together independently. The more realistic version of a
good-enough parental intercourse forms an internal loved parental couple
that is the basis of personal well-being and creativity: sexual, intellectual
and aesthetic. This couple can be temporarily disturbed in situations of loss
and mourning but can also be reinstated [*see* Introjection].

Penis-as-link and phallus: Britton (1989) has articulated the profound
'cognitive' implications of a satisfactory working-through of the Oedipus
complex and of the depressive position, which go hand in hand. It is the
achievement of what he calls a *triangular space*, which is vital for the
capacity to think about experience:

> If the link between the parents perceived in love and hate can be
> tolerated in the child's mind, it provides him with a prototype for an
> object relation of a third kind in which he is a witness and not a
> participant. A third position then comes into existence from which
> object relation can be observed. Given this, we can also envisage being
> observed.
>
> (Britton, 1989, p. 87)

In the absence of this internal, triangular mental structure, both emotional
development and analysis are very difficult.

Birksted-Breen (1996) uses her understanding of major trends in French
psychoanalysis to make a very important distinction between the *penis-as-*

link and *the phallus*. The former refers to the mental function of linking and structuring in the manner described by Britton in his notion of triangular space. The phallus, by contrast, refers to a mental space of illusory whole-ness, a state of completeness and of being without need. The phallus is the possession of neither sex but the boy can believe more easily that his penis gives him access to it. By the same token penis envy in women is often not an envy of the penis-as-link but rather an envy of the phallus. The phallus denies lack, denies sexual difference, denies the difference between the generations and also incompleteness, need and dependency and the conflicts that these inevitably engender. The phallus bears a relation to what Henri Rey (1994) calls the 'manic penis': an omnipotent object of erectile grandi-osity linked to the radical denial of psychic reality. Such a mental structure is very different to the penis-as-link, which is a mental area of true sym-bolisation [*see* Symbol formation].

Birksted-Breen, D. (1996) 'Phallus, penis and mental space', *Int. J. Psycho-Anal.* 77: 649–657.

Britton, R. (1989) 'The missing link: Parental sexuality in the Oedipus Complex', in J. Steiner (ed.) *The Oedipus Complex Today.* London: Karnac, pp. 83–101.

Klein, M. (1945) 'The Oedipus complex in the light of early anxieties', in *The Writings of Melanie Klein*, Vol. 1. London: Hogarth Press, pp. 370–419.

Rey, H. (1994) *Universals of Psychoanalysis in the Treatment of Psychotic and Borderline States.* London: Free Association Books.

Persecution

Klein is struck at the outset of her work at the level of violence in children's play and soon concludes that the states of anxiety she finds in children, for example *pavor nocturnus*, are connected with a fear of their own violence. The child feels persecuted by the fear of retaliation. Klein considers this state to be similar to the paranoia of psychotic patients. In her view persecution underlies inhibition in children and she describes (Klein, 1930) an extreme case in which a boy is so persecuted by the fear of his own violence and of his parents' retaliation that he is unable to develop the capacity to symbolise [*see* Child analysis; Paranoia; Psychosis; Sadism; Symbol formation].

Persecution in the paranoid-schizoid position: Once Klein adopts Freud's theory of the life and death instincts she begins to construct a theory in which persecution within or anxiety of annihilation from within is caused by the presence of the death instinct. In her theory of the 'paranoid-schizoid' position (Klein, 1946) the death instinct is projected out by the infant into the object or mother who, as the embodiment of the destructive impulses, is now felt to be a dangerous persecutor. This persecutor when introjected forms the basis of a persecutory superego [*see* Bad object; Paranoid-schizoid position; Projective identification; Superego]. At the same time good libidinal feelings and aspects of the self are projected out into a 'good' object/mother and so the relationship to the mother is to two mothers: a good relationship with a 'good' mother and a bad or persecutory relationship with a 'bad' mother.

Persecution in the depressive position: Over time, if things go well, the two versions of the mother are brought together and persecutory anxieties reduce and good experiences with the real mother allow projections to be taken back. This is the move to the 'depressive position' (Klein, 1940). However, the realisation that the 'good' and 'bad' mother are actually one, and that the 'good' mother is also the mother that has been hated and attacked, arouses guilt. This guilt about damage done may become overwhelming and persecutory. Persecutory guilt may drive the individual back to the defensive splitting into good and bad of the paranoid-schizoid position where the fear of persecution is less anguished than the onset of guilt. Gradually in the working-through of the depressive position persecutory guilt reduces and depressive guilt comes to the fore, accompanied by the pain of mourning and the task of reparation. A to-and-fro process between persecutory and depressive anxieties continues throughout life [*see* Depressive anxiety; Depressive position; Paranoid defence against depressive anxiety].

Klein, M. (1930) 'The importance of symbol formation in the development of the ego', in *The Writings of Melanie Klein*, Vol. 1. London: Hogarth Press, pp. 219–232.
—— (1940) 'Mourning and its relation to manic-depressive states', in *The Writings of Melanie Klein*, Vol. 1. London: Hogarth Press, pp. 344–369.
—— (1946) 'Notes on some schizoid mechanisms', in *The Writings of Melanie Klein*, Vol. 3. London: Hogarth Press, pp. 1–24.

Personification

Klein showed that in their play children turned their toys into persons, imaginary or real, who were of importance in their actual life [*see* Technique], and they worried about the relations between those personified objects.

Personification, ubiquitous in all play, led Klein to the view that all mental activity is conceived as relationships between personified objects. She was impressed with the fluidity and ease with which relations, affects and conflicts could be transferred to new objects [*see* Symbol formation].

Klein's belief in the capacity of children to represent persons, to symbolise and to make a transference was in contrast with Anna Freud's view [*see* Technique].

See Play

Perversion

The existence of sexual perversions led Freud (1905) to posit a view of human sexuality as a complex unity, built on the basis of component instincts in childhood. These gradually become fused across the libidinal organisations or stages and culminate in the Oedipus complex. The outcome of the Oedipus complex is crucial in determining the final shape that adult sexuality takes. The component instincts operate independently to start with and are defined in terms of source (oral, anal, genital) or in terms of aim (voyeurism/exhibitionism, mastery/submission). Infantile sexuality is polymorphously perverse in that it contains the seeds of both later perversions and also of what is considered to be normal sexuality: heterosexual genitality. In spite of the contemporary controversy about the notion of a sexual norm, in formal psychoanalytic terms a sexual perversion is still defined as when sexual pleasure is reached with other objects, as in paedophilia, bestiality, homosexuality, or when the sexual act is taken up exclusively with other regions of the body (oral, anal) or when extrinsic conditions (transvestism, fetishism, voyeurism, sado-masochism) are necessary or sufficient to bring about pleasure. The analytic understanding of the various sexual perversions is dominated by the Freudian tradition and extensions of it. Klein herself and Kleinians in general have not contributed a great deal on the topic of specific adult sexual perversions.

In her early work, when Klein adhered to major tenets of Freud's and Abraham's views on libidinal development (Klein, 1932) she highlighted the ubiquity of sadism, one of the component instincts, in the emotional life of the young infant, especially during the phase of maximal sadism [*see* Libido; Sadism]. In 'Criminal tendencies in normal children' (1927) Klein illustrates clinically the extreme violence of her young patient's oral-cannibalistic and anal-sadistic phantasies against the inside of the mother's body and other early oedipal objects – she even ventures a link with Jack the Ripper. These attacks lead in turn to terrifying internal objects (imagos) as part of the archaic superego. It is this internal terror that leads the child to re-enact these phantasies in various forms of play so as to externalise and personalise them as a defence. Klein's main aim in her paper is to lend support to Freud's hypothesis that criminals are motivated by the unconscious sense of guilt (Freud, 1916). But she also asserts the importance that such violent phantasies are bound to have on sexuality in later life. She goes further: 'Here we find the basis of all the perversions which Freud has discovered to have their origins in the early development of the child' (1927, p. 176). But Klein herself does not pursue her intuition to explore the field of sexual perversions or adult forms of sexual criminality. She leaves her ubiquitous findings of sadism in children curiously unconnected to adult sexual perversions.

Actual adult sexual perversions: It can be said that subsequently Kleinians have tended to regard sexual perversions as a manifestation of early sadistic impulses that distort sexuality. The early notion of sadism later became subsumed under the broader notion of the death instinct and of envy (Klein, 1957) as its primal representative [*see* Death instinct; Sadism]. Excessive envy causes dread and endangers the primal relation with the good object. It interferes with adequate oral gratification and can act as a stimulus towards the intensification of genital desires. Klein uses the notion of *flight into genitality* to refer to such a sexual distortion whereby 'the oral relation becomes genitalised and the genital trends become too much coloured by oral grievances and anxieties' (1957, p. 195). She links this early distortion to later disturbance in the genital sphere, such as obsessional masturbation and promiscuity. Although she does not refer to specific sexual perversions the elements of compulsion and indiscriminate sexual activity are often present in sexual perversions. These various forms of distorted genitality can become equivalent to excited states of destructiveness.

Both Meltzer (1968) and Rosenfeld (1971) establish a specific connection between the destructive narcissistic organisations of their patients [*see* Narcissism; Pathological organisations] and the development of actual sexual perversions. Rosenfeld points out that Freud's notion of the supposed *fusion* of sexuality and destructiveness in perversion does not lessen the destructiveness but instead increases its power over the personality. He sees the erotisation of the destructive in perversions as a case of *pathological fusion* of libidinal and destructive impulses akin to what happens in confusional states (Rosenfeld, 1950, 1952). Unmanageable envious attacks on the good object overwhelm the weaker libidinal impulses, break down the crucial dichotomy between 'good' and 'bad' and lead to confusion. The erotisation of the destructive is an attempt to deal with confusion but also entrenches it.

Meltzer (1968) shows in a clinical example the conjunction of his patient's destructive narcissistic organisation and a sado-masochistic, anal and genital masturbatory perversion. This pleasure sustains the patient from suicide but also propped up his narcissistic aloofness. Analysis reveals the patient's underlying dreaded fantasy attacks and destruction of his mother's body and her babies, and their transference equivalents, which had become erotised in his elaborate masturbatory practices. As his narcissistic organisation weakens and his capacity for psychic pain increases, he relinquishes his sexual perversion.

Meltzer (1973) describes the wide variety of phantasy contents of the envious and sadistic impulses involved in sexual perversions. He distinguishes infantile polymorphous perversity from adult perverse sexuality. He regards the former as an exploration, in so far as the child is capable, of the mystery of his own sexuality, his parents' sexuality and the possibilities of identifying with them. In contrast, adult perversion is driven by destructive impulses to damage sexuality, especially that of the parents and their coitus.

Hunter (1954) and Joseph (1971) analyse cases of fetishism. Joseph's patient reveals a narcissistic organisation of superior aloofness based on appropriative identifications, as described by Rosenfeld (1964), whereby he possesses all the valuable attributes of his objects (e.g. his wife). This leads to claustrophobic anxieties. The dependent and also very sadistic and envious parts of his self are split off and projected in various external objects at first. These cruel parts become subtly and powerfully enacted in the transference, with the analyst left to contain the needy parts of the patient: excited one moment and then left tormented by the patient who is gratified by his cruelty whilst withdrawing into silence. Joseph's detailed work in the transference throws light on the function of the rubber fetish as an envelope in which the patient can withdraw from emotional contact that he fears could be highly destructive and too dangerous.

The Kleinian emphasis on the role of early destructive impulses in shaping adult sexuality also appears in Rosenfeld's re-evaluation of Freud's original hypothesis of the connection between homosexuality and paranoia in his Schreber case (1911). Freud put forward that conscious homosexual feelings felt as unbearable are transformed into their opposite: I (a man) love him (a man) becomes I hate him and, by projection, becomes he hates me, which justifies hating him. Rosenfeld (1949) relies on Klein's 1946 paper to show that in both latent and manifest male homosexuals their homosexuality entails a hostile turning away from mother to an idealisation of father to deny the fear of a more persecutory figure. The homosexuality of his patients can be understood as a defence against early paranoid anxieties from the oral phase. In this way Rosenfeld reverses Freud's original hypothesis.

Character perversion and perversion of the transference: Rosenfeld's theory of *pathological narcissism* (1964, 1971) illustrates in its very fabric the grave dilemma that excessive destructiveness in the form of envy poses for the infantile psyche. Instead of allowing a crucial structuring to begin, whereby what is life-giving and 'good' can be distinguished from what is deadly and 'bad' – a foundation stone for all later development – this healthy split is attacked and dismantled. The good breast/mother felt as separate is enviously attacked, which engenders dread and confusion. This basic disorder has catastrophic consequences because it leads to desperate, omnipotent forms of seeking protection, such as the wanton psychic robbery of the object's attributes (libidinal narcissism) or the idealisation of tightly organised, envious parts of the self into a gang that emboldens its superiority (negative narcissism) by denigrating need, desire and dependency for object relations as humiliating, weak and contemptible.

Leslie Sohn (1985) prefers the term *identificate* rather than identification to describe the hollowness of the narcissist's identity, based as it is on the chameleonic satisfaction and the bland arrogance of being a new object. These desperate strategies set up a *perversion of character* based on confusion, falseness and misrecognition that entrenches a drastic avoidance of psychic reality, object relations and psychic pain and stultifies the potential for development. Actual sexual perversions may be recruited to bolster the narcissistic organisation.

John Steiner's concept of *pathological organisations* incorporates Rosenfeld's notion of pathological narcissism but is also a broader conception [*see* Pathological organisations]. However, it depicts a similar *perversion of character*, albeit with a shift of emphasis on what is perverse. Pathological organisations are complexly assembled so that good parts of self are recruited by the destructive organisation (e.g. the gang) to give it a more healthy appearance. It is misleading to describe the split within the self as being one between a sane self that is an innocent victim kept in prison by a malevolent organisation. Instead, good parts of self can be in a *collusive liaison* with bad parts of self. Steiner points out that a perverse relationship exists so that a healthy part of self may allow itself to be taken *knowingly* by a destructive organisation and this collusion, when externalised, gives rise to a perverse flavour in the analytic relationship (Steiner, 1981). Later Steiner (1985) links this perverse element of collusive liaison to the process of 'turning a blind eye', which he sees as a pervasive and specific defensive process that provides a kind of 'glue' in pathological organisations. He uses specifically Freud's understanding of fetishism, in which the reality of castration is both acknowledged and simultaneously disavowed to explain the notion of turning a blind eye as a *psychic perversion*. In this way Steiner gives a central place in his theory to the attention that Betty Joseph had begun to pay to what can be called the perversion of the transference.

Joseph (1971, 1975) had already focused in great detail on the way in which patients, with a split in the ego as described by Rosenfeld, behave in the analytic relationship and on the technical issues that are raised. She draws attention to the subtle and tenacious ways in which the analyst is seductively or coercively pulled to enact a split-off part of the patient with which he has become identified. She stresses the importance of locating 'the splitting in the ego and clarifying the activities of the different parts' (1975, p. 79). She also shows the way in which patients engage only partially, and get perverse enjoyment from keeping the more lively parts of their personality at an unreachable distance from the analyst [*see* Technique]. Joseph's focus on the *perversion of the transference relationship* bears directly on the question of the negative therapeutic reaction and of chronic resistance to analysis [*see* Negative therapeutic reaction].

Joseph's 1982 paper is a probing clinical illustration of the way in which a destructive organisation is perversely erotised to strengthen its domination over the rest of the personality, a theme advanced by Meltzer (1968) and Rosenfeld (1971). Joseph describes a patient's absorption into despair and hopelessness as a malignant form of self-destructive organisation, which manifests as an addiction to near-death. The patient tries to recruit the analyst to collude by feeling desperate and hopeless, and to react by punishing the patient. This loss of balance then feeds a masochistic triumph over the analysis. The drive towards life and sanity is split off and projected into the analyst. Such analyses can drag on for years if the analyst is not aware of this massive projection and does not interpret it.

Freud, S. (1905) *Three Essays on the Theory of Sexuality*, *S.E. 7*. London: Hogarth Press, pp. 125–245.

—— (1911) 'Psycho-analytic notes on an autobiographical account of a case of paranoia', *S.E. 12*. London: Hogarth Press, pp. 3–82.

—— (1916) 'Some character-types met with in psycho-analytic work', *S.E. 14*. London: Hogarth Press, pp. 309–333.

Hunter, D. (1954) 'Object relation changes in the analysis of fetishism', *Int. J. Psycho-Anal.* 35: 302–312.

Joseph, B. (1971) 'A clinical contribution to the analysis of a perversion', *Int. J. Psycho-Anal.* 52: 441–449.

—— (1975) 'The patient who is difficult to reach', in M. Feldman and E. Bott Spillius (eds) *Psychic Equilibrium and Psychic Change*. London: Routledge, pp. 75–87.

—— (1982) 'On addiction to near death', *Int. J. Psycho-Anal.* 63: 449–456.

Klein, M. (1927) Criminal tendencies in normal children', in *The Writings of Melanie Klein*, Vol. 1. London: Hogarth Press, pp. 170–185.

—— (1932) *The Psychoanalysis of Children. The Writings of Melanie Klein*, Vol. 2. London: Hogarth Press.

—— (1946) 'Notes on some schizoid mechanisms', in *The Writings of Melanie Klein*, Vol. 3. London: Hogarth Press, pp. 1–24.

—— (1957) 'Envy and gratitude', in *The Writings of Melanie Klein*, Vol. 3. London: Hogarth Press, pp. 176–235.

Meltzer, D. (1968) 'Terror, persecution, dread', *Int. J. Psycho-Anal.* 49: 396–400.

—— (1973) *Sexual States of Mind*. Strath Tay: Clunie Press.

Rosenfeld, H. (1949) 'Remarks on the relation of male homosexuality to paranoia, paranoid anxiety and narcissism', *Int. J. Psycho-Anal.* 30: 36–47.

—— (1950) 'Notes on the psychopathology of confusional states in chronic schizophrenia', *Int. J. Psycho-Anal.* 31: 132–137.

—— (1952) 'Notes on the psycho-analysis of the superego conflict in an acute schizophrenic patient', *Int. J. Psycho-Anal.* 33: 111–131.

—— (1964) 'On the psychopathology of narcissism: A clinical approach' in *Psychotic States*. London: Hogarth Press, pp. 34–51.

—— (1971) 'A clinical approach to the psycho-analytical theory of the life and death instincts', *Int. J. Psycho-Anal.* 52: 169–178.

Sohn, L. (1985) 'Narcissistic organisation, projective identification and the formation of the identificate', *Int. J. Psycho-Anal.* 66: 201–213.

Steiner, J. (1981) 'Perverse relationships between parts of the self: A clinical illustration', *Int. J. Psycho-Anal.* 63: 241–252.

—— (1985) 'Turning a blind eye: the cover-up for Oedipus', *Int. Rev. Psycho-Anal.* 12: 161–172.

Phobia

In her early work Klein (1932) makes a link between phobias and early feeding inhibitions on the one hand and obsessional mechanisms on the other. She sees phobias as containing anxieties that arise in the early stages of the formation of the superego. Symptoms in childhood in general, as part of the infantile neurosis, are attempts to modify the terrifying anxieties linked to the phase of maximal sadism in the early oedipal situation and the frightening objects that make up the early superego.

Klein links early eating difficulties to their paranoid origins. She writes:

> In the cannibalistic phase children equate every kind of food with their objects, as represented by their organs, so that it takes on the significance of their father's penis and their mother's breast and is loved, hated and feared like these.
>
> (1932, p. 157)

Foods identified with terrifying internal objects give rise to fears of being poisoned or being destroyed inside. Klein refers to animal phobias that appear in the earlier anal stage, in the second year, as an expression of similar paranoid anxieties to those active in early eating inhibitions. Animal phobias represent a process made up of several moves: first the ejection of the superego and the id, so that by projection they become equated with a real object. Klein mentions the fact that the very early superego is often equated with wild and dangerous animals (oral cannibalism and anal sadism). The second move is to replace a wild animal by a less ferocious animal so that the fear of the father, for example, can be displaced onto this external anxiety-object. She sees animal phobias as 'a far-reaching modification of the fear of the superego' (1932, p. 157).

Klein in the main agrees with Freud's understanding of phobias as being based on projection and displacement (Freud, 1926). But whereas Freud (1918) saw the Wolf Man's phobia as a substitute for oedipal castration anxiety, Klein sees his wolf phobia as an expression of more primitive paranoid anxieties deriving from the devouring introjects of the early superego, with their oral cannibalistic and anal-sadistic elements. The fear of the wolf is primarily a symbolic representation, displaced onto an animal, of the persecutory fear of the devouring part-object penis that the patient's father remained identified with, thereby affecting the Wolf Man's later masculinity in the way Freud described it (Klein, 1932, pp. 158–160). The horse phobia of little Hans, by contrast, reveals none of these early primitive anxieties. The fear instead stems from the more advanced oedipal situation described by Freud (1905).

Klein further asserts that the process of modifying phobias is linked with the obsessional mechanisms that emerge in the later anal stage [*see* Obsessional defences]. She implies that obsessional mechanisms are attempts to deal not only with paranoid anxiety, as phobias are, but also with guilt. This is a new feature in the superego linked with the later anal stage when concern and pity for the damaged object lead to reaction formations. Phobias by contrast are more directly linked with paranoid anxieties. This early work on phobias was not elaborated significantly in Klein's later work but the general idea of phobias as resulting from projection and displacement of persecutory anxiety and objects remained valid.

Contemporary Kleinian contributions: Hanna Segal (1954) describes the way in which her patient developed a phobic solution in her attempts to bind together her fragmented experience owing to excessive fragmentary splitting. Her patient developed a crowd phobia in an attempt to organise her projected experience of fragmentation.

Henri Rey (1994) has developed his influential notion of the *claustro-agoraphobic dilemma* as a basic feature of schizoid states. Schizoid states – a basic disorder in the organisation of the personality – result from pathological schizoid mechanisms such as excessive projective identification and fragmentary splitting [*see* Paranoid-schizoid position]. They create the feeling of living inside the object because different parts of the self are in phantasy within the object. This dependency on the object creates a need for never leaving the object out of one's control. Being inside leads to *claustrophobic* terrors of being trapped forever by a powerful object. However, separation from the object creates an *agoraphobic* sense of impending doom and fragmentation since patients are so dependent on being inside their objects for their identity. This promotes the wish to get back into the object as a place of safety.

Claustro-agoraphobic anxieties are also a result of feeling in the presence of highly persecutory objects, which have been projected and displaced in the space inside the object or in the space away from the object. As Rey points out, there is nowhere safe for the claustro-agoraphobic. The claustro-agoraphobic dilemma captures the meaning that Rey gives to the term borderline. In schizoid states patients end up caught between two alternatives with respect to issues of identity. They are neither male nor female, homo- nor heterosexual, big nor small, but always *on the border*. Rey's conception is broader than the actual anxiety syndrome of claustro-agoraphobia: it is a mental structure whereby the self attempts to deal with excessive paranoid anxieties with a spatial organisation of the self and its objects that affects identity development and object relations. The concepts of pathological organisations and psychic retreats (Steiner, 1993) incor-porate Rey's notion of claustro-agoraphobia in their very fabric [*see* Pathological organisations].

Freud, S. (1905) 'Analysis of a phobia in five-year-old boy', *S.E. 10*. London: Hogarth Press, pp. 5–148.
—— (1918) 'From the history of an infantile neurosis', *S.E. 17*. London: Hogarth Press, pp. 7–104.
—— (1926) 'Inhibitions, symptoms and anxiety', *S.E. 20*. London: Hogarth Press, pp. 77–175.
Klein, M. (1932) *The Psychoanalysis of Children. The Writings of Melanie Klein*, Vol. 2. London: Hogarth Press.
Rey, H. (1994) 'The schizoid mode of being and the space-time continuum (before metaphor)', in J. Magagna (ed.) *Universals of Psychoanalysis in the Treatment of Psychotic and Borderline States*. London: Free Association Books, pp. 8–30.
Segal, H. (1954) 'Schizoid mechanisms underlying phobia formation', *Int. J. Psycho-Anal.* 35: 238–241.
Steiner, J. (1993) *Psychic Retreats: Pathological Organizations in Psychotic, Neurotic and Borderline Patients*. London: Routledge.

Play

Klein developed a method of analysing children based on observing their play, which she analysed as if it were comparable to the free associations of adults and to dreams [*see* Child analysis; Technique]. Anna Freud criticised her for this on the grounds that the child has a different purpose behind his play from the adult's purpose in free association. The latter, Anna Freud contended, resulted from a cooperation with the analyst in the psycho-analytic venture, whereas the child cannot understand the purpose of psychoanalysis. Klein responded to this by showing firstly that both play and free associations are comparable symbolic expressions of the content of the mind, and secondly that the child, from the first interpretation, has an understanding (an unconscious understanding) of the nature of psycho-analysis. At the outset Klein modelled her views on Freud's interest in children's play:

> In their play children repeat everything that has made a great impression on them in real life, and in doing so they abreact the strength of the impression and, as one might put it, make themselves masters of the situation. But on the other hand it is obvious that all their play is influenced by a wish that dominates them the whole of the

time – the wish to be grown up and to be able to do what grown-up people do. It can also be observed that the unpleasurable nature of an experience does not always unsuit it for play. If a doctor looks down a child's throat or carries out some small operation on him, we may be quite sure that these frightening experiences will be the subject of the next game; but we must not in that connection overlook the fact that there is a yield of pleasure from another source. As the child passes over from the passivity of the experience to the **activity of the** game, he hands on the disagreeable experience to one of his playmates and in this way revenges himself on a substitute.

(Freud, 1920, p. 17)

The emphasis here is upon the importance of play in mastering the internal world of the child. The aspect of Freud's descriptions that recognised the turning of a passive experience into an active one was taken up by Waelder (1933) and Anna Freud (1936).

Under the stimulus of the controversy with Anna Freud, Klein (1926, 1929) was at pains to elucidate the processes involved in children's play. She regarded the urge to play as composed of a number of ingredients, most of which are indicated or hinted at in the passage from Freud above. These ingredients were as follows:

- The human mind thinks from the outset in terms of objects in relation to each other and to the subject.
- The child seeks relief from the disasters of his internal world through externalising the worst persecuting situations into the external world.
- Part of the child's natural development is to seek new objects as substitutes for earlier ones, and toys and playmates are one of the forms of practising symbolisation of this kind.
- Turning to new objects is also driven by the conflicts with the early object, so that respite is gained by finding a new object (a symbol).

All these processes are unconscious and represent the mind of the child struggling with the difficulties posed by its impulses and its objects. Play, in Klein's view, was a serious business for the child and not merely a trivial enjoyment, nor just an exercise in mastering the physical environment.

See Creativity; Externalisation; Personification

Freud, A. (1936) *The Ego and the Mechanisms of Defence*. London: Hogarth Press.
Freud, S. (1920) 'Beyond the pleasure principle', *S.E. 18*. London: Hogarth Press, pp. 7–64.
Klein, M. (1926) 'The psychological principles of early analysis', in *The Writings of Melanie Klein*, Vol. 1. London: Hogarth Press, pp. 128–138.

—— (1929) 'Personification in the play of children', in *The Writings of Melanie Klein*, Vol. 1. London: Hogarth Press, pp. 199–209.
Waelder, R. (1933) 'The psycho-analytic theory of play', *Psychoanal. Q.* 2: 208–224.

Play technique

See Child analysis; Technique

Poisoning

One of the innate unconscious phantasies at the oral level is of poisoning mother's milk (or creativity) by attacking and invading her . It is also then feared that the object will put poison into the subject in retaliation. In her early (1921) paper 'The development of a child' Klein describes Fritz's fears of being poisoned by witches and by a soldier and she connects these anxieties to his curiosity and confusion about feeding, urination, defaecation and sex. Fritz equates urine with milk, takes great interest in what his father puts into his mother, is disgusted at what his parents get up to, at times wishes them dead and fears their retaliation. In later papers, Klein outlines the phantasies that she believes exist in the mind of the infant during the late stage of oral-sadism and writes 'these violent modes of attack give place to hidden assaults by the most refined methods which sadism can devise, and the excreta are equated with poisonous substances' (Klein, 1930, p. 220). Later Klein links these attacks to envy and describes the aim of envy as being 'to put badness, primarily bad excrements and bad parts of the self into the mother, and first of all into the breast, to spoil and destroy her' (Klein, 1957, p. 181).

See Child analysis; Envy; Paranoia; Projective identification; Sadism; Unconscious phantasy

Klein, M. (1921) 'The development of a child', in *The Writings of Melanie Klein*, Vol. 1. London: Hogarth Press, pp. 1–53.
—— (1930) 'The importance of symbol formation in the development of the ego', in *The Writings of Melanie Klein*, Vol. 1. London: Hogarth Press, pp. 219–232.
—— (1957) 'Envy and gratitude', in *The Writings of Melanie Klein*, Vol. 3. London: Hogarth Press, pp. 176–235.

Position

The term 'position' gets away from the idea of stages or phases of development and emphasises a model of development in which anxieties, defences, impulses and object relations are grouped together in constellations (ultimately in two 'positions': the 'paranoid-schizoid' and 'depressive') that are both overlapping and fluctuating. The idea of position conveys a much more flexible to-and-fro process than the idea of regression to fixation points in the developmental phases [*see* Ps↔D]. The term 'position' also places an emphasis on relationships. The two 'positions' are the central structures of Klein's theory [*see* Depressive position; Paranoid-schizoid position].

In 'A contribution to the psychogenesis of manic depressive states' (1935) Klein drops the framework of psychosexual stages and in outlining the 'depressive position' places the state of the ego and its relationships within the framework of positions. Later in 'Notes on some schizoid mechanisms' (1946) Klein introduces the concept of the 'paranoid-schizoid' position. In 1948 Klein describes why she has chosen the term 'position' rather than 'phase':

> . . . position was chosen because – though the phenomena involved occur in the first place during the early stages of development – they are not confined to these stages but represent specific groupings of anxieties and defences which appear and re-appear during the first years of childhood.
>
> (Klein, 1948, p. xiii)

Position, libidinal stages and object relations: Previously Klein had used the term to refer to libidinal positions [*see* Libido] — homosexual, heterosexual, etc. (see Klein, 1928, p. 186). Although Klein continues to use the terms 'oral', 'anal', 'phallic', etc., these refer increasingly to kinds of instinctual impulses and to typical unconscious phantasies rather than to stages or strict periods of development [*see* Unconscious phantasy].

Position or defensive structure: At first Klein uses the term 'position' freely and, as well as the 'depressive position', describes a 'paranoid position', a 'manic position' and an 'obsessional position'. Later the 'paranoid', 'manic' and 'obsessional' positions are dropped because they refer simply to typical structures of defences against anxieties, or pathological configurations (Meltzer, 1978). Klein ultimately restricts the term to two fundamental positions of developmental significance – the depressive position with depressive anxiety, and the paranoid-schizoid position with persecutory anxiety.

Psychotic positions: The change of the term from a pathological to a developmental use led to confusions over Klein's meaning. Many read her as suggesting that children are normally psychotic. She was at pains to correct this:

In my former work I have described the psychotic anxieties and mechanisms of the child in terms of phases of development . . . But since in normal development the psychotic anxieties and mechanisms never solely predominate (a fact which, of course, I have emphasized) the term psychotic phases is not really satisfactory. I am now using the term 'position' . . . It seems to me easier to associate with this term . . . the differences between the developmental psychotic anxieties of the child and the psychoses of the adult: e.g. the quick changeover that occurs from a persecution anxiety or depressed feeling to a normal attitude – a changeover that is so characteristic for the child.

(Klein, 1935, p. 276n)

Klein, M. (1928) 'Early stages of the Oedipus complex', in *The Writings of Melanie Klein*, Vol. 1. London: Hogarth Press, pp. 186–198.

—— (1935) 'A contribution to the psychogenesis of manic-depressive states', in *The Writings of Melanie Klein*, Vol. 1. London: Hogarth Press, pp. 262–289.

—— (1946) 'Notes on some schizoid mechanisms', in *The Writings of Melanie Klein*, Vol. 3. London: Hogarth Press, pp. 1–24.

—— (1948) *The Psychoanalysis of Children*, 3rd edition. London: Hogarth Press.

Meltzer, D. (1978) *The Kleinian Development: Part II, Richard Week-by-Week*. Strath Tay: Clunie Press.

Preconception

In Klein's view the infant is born with the capacity to represent physical experience and sensation psychologically [*see* Unconscious phantasy]. When a baby's face is touched, his head turns and he sucks. Assuming that the newborn is capable of experiences, what is the experience of the suckling reflex before it has happened for the first time? Bion introduced the idea of a *preconception*, a psychological entity waiting for a realisation that will 'mate' with it. The preconception is an '*a priori*' knowledge of the breast. Bion also likens it to Kant's concept of an 'empty thought'. The 'unexperienced' preconception mated with a realisation produces a *conception*. A preconception mated with a frustration, however, produces a *thought*, and from this thinking can develop.

See Wilfred Bion; Innate knowledge; Thinking and knowledge

Primal scene

Freud uses the term 'primal scene' to denote the infant or child's experience of the parental couple in intercourse. Typically, he is concerned with the actual witnessing by the child of the parents' copulation. The exhaustive detail in his analysis of the Wolf Man (Freud, 1918) concerns the patient's trauma at sleeping in his parents' bedroom on holiday, the mystifying phantasies that the patient had about it and the wishes to identify with one or the other or both parents.

This case history was published at about the time when Klein was becoming interested in analysis. Klein's earliest work was concerned largely with the child's sexual theories; she soon came to realise the profound distress caused by mystification, frustration and exclusion and the intense aggressive response in even the pleasantest child: '. . . a series of passionate and compulsive questions, which proved to be an expression of curiosity connected with the primal scene . . . was repeatedly followed by outbursts of rage' (Klein, 1925, p. 122). Klein's interest is not on the whole in whether parental intercourse had or had not been witnessed (although see the Erna case: Klein, 1932), but in the child's inevitable preoccupations with phantasy versions of it, often to be observed in their play. For the child's earliest conception of the primal scene in frightening genital and pregenital part-object form she coins her own term, *the combined parent figure* [*see* Combined parent figure; Oedipus complex].

Klein takes up Freud's idea of a 'primal fantasy' or an innate idea of the parental couple, and Bion considers a template for parental intercourse an important 'preconception'. For Bion, only if we can allow the parents to come together in intercourse can we allow mental links generally, and allow thinking itself (e.g. Bion, 1959). Money-Kyrle observes that we strive to know the true nature of the primal scene, but because we cannot bear it we often misrepresent it: 'Indeed every conceivable representation of [the parents' intercourse] seems to proliferate in the unconscious *except the right one*' (Money-Kyrle, 1968, p. 417).

Britton (1989, 1998, 2003) writes extensively about the primal scene and its vicissitudes in the oedipal situation. He discusses (Britton, 1989) the primitive and violent versions of the primal scene in individuals who have not internalised a secure version of the primary relationship with mother. He considers that 'the other room', in which phantasied parental intercourse takes place, can either become the space in the mind for imagination and creativity (Britton, 1998, pp. 120–127), or can become inhabited by sterile daydream.

Sodré (1994) describes how the obsessional person in phantasy invades and controls the primal couple. The sufferer from tormenting obsessional doubt cannot let go of the couple and allow them freely to come together – the Oedipus complex remains unresolved.

Bion, W. (1959) 'Attacks on linking', *Int. J. Psycho-Anal.* 40: 308–315.
Britton, R. (1989) 'The missing link: Parental sexuality in the Oedipus complex', in J. Steiner (ed.) *The Oedipus Complex Today*. London: Karnac, pp. 83–101.
—— (1998) 'The other room and poetic space', in *Belief and Imagination*. London: Routledge, pp. 83–101.

—— (2003) *Sex, Death, and the Superego*. London: Karnac.

Freud, S. (1918) 'From the history of an infantile neurosis', *S.E. 17*. London: Hogarth Press, pp. 3–13.

Klein, M. (1925) 'A contribution to the psychogenesis of tics', in *The Writings of Melanie Klein*, Vol. 1. London: Hogarth Press, pp. 106–127.

—— (1932) 'An obsessional neurosis in a six-year-old girl', in *The Writings of Melanie Klein*, Vol. 2. London: Hogarth Press, pp. 35–57.

Money-Kyrle, R. (1968) 'Cognitive development', in D. Meltzer (ed.) *The Collected Papers of Roger Money-Kyrle*. Strath Tay: Clunie Press, pp. 416–433.

Sodré, I. (1994) 'Obsessional certainty versus obsessional doubt: From two to three', *Psychoanal. Inq.* 14: 379–392.

Projection

Projection was first described by Freud in 1895 and there has been a long history to its meaning since then. The term first came from optics and the new science of map-making in the sixteenth century, arriving in the nineteenth century in the psychology of perception, whence Freud introduced it into psychoanalysis [*see* Projective identification]. There are various senses in which the term 'projection' is used: perception; projection and expulsion; externalising conflict; projection and identity; and projection of parts of the self.

Perception: In the physiological sense, certain experiences are interpreted as projected out beyond the actual extension of the perceptual organ. Thus although the impact of light rays happens physiologically at the retina, the visual interpretation is attributed to some greater or lesser distance in front of the eyes. Similarly, the blind man walking along with his white stick will encounter an obstacle through the tactile sensations in the palm of the hand that is grasping the stick. Nevertheless, he accurately projects his awareness of an object to the other end of the stick. This is 'projection' as normally used in the psychology of perception. On the basis of bodily sensations, the infant construes in a similar way the idea of an object causing those sensations [*see* Instincts; Internal objects]. Projection is therefore part of a normal process of interpreting the sense data of the perceptual system.

Projection and expulsion: Freud (1895) had already noted the link between projection and paranoia. Abraham (1924), in investigating melancholia and the importance in this condition of the 'lost object' or the fear of losing it, recognised that an important phantasy was the anal one of expelling an object physically from the body. He linked the impulse for anal expulsion with the mechanism of projection.

Externalising conflict: Klein found the mechanism of projection important in the externalisation of internal conflicts in children's play with external objects (Klein, 1927). This form of projection in delinquent acts confirmed Freud's view of criminals who act out of an unconscious sense of guilt (Freud, 1916).

Projection and identity: Projection has a primary role in the existence of the ego: 'Projection . . . originates from the deflection of the death instinct outwards and in my view helps the ego to overcome anxiety by ridding it of danger and badness' (Klein, 1946, p. 6). Projection is one of the elemental phantasy activities that locates objects within or without the ego:

> . . . expressed in the language of the oldest – the oral – instinctual impulses, the judgement is: 'I should like to eat this', or 'I should like to spit it out'; and put more generally, 'I should like to take this into myself and to keep that out'. That is to say: 'It shall be inside me' or 'it shall be outside me'. As I have shown elsewhere, the original pleasure-ego wants to introject into itself everything that is good and to eject from itself everything that is bad.
>
> (Freud, 1925, p. 237)

Projection of parts of the self: Another sense in which the term 'projection' was used by both Freud (1895) and Klein (1946) was to attribute certain states of mind to someone else. Something of the ego is thus perceived as occurring in someone else. This is characteristic of the way in which homosexual feelings are avoided. They are typically attributed to someone else, and Freud constructed a complex chain of 'vicissitudes': 'I love him' becomes 'I hate him', which in turn becomes 'he hates me'. Hatred is thus attributed to the other person. Freud (1914) began a study of the phe-nomenology of this kind of relating in his paper on narcissism when he described narcissistic object-choice, in contrast to anaclitic object-choice. However, because Freud had not clearly delineated the object as a field of study in its own right, the use of the term 'projection' became confused, and Klein's usage embodied this confusion.

Klein's usage of 'projection': Klein uses the term 'projection' with many of the above meanings: projection of the internal object; deflection of the death instinct; externalisation of internal conflict; and projection of parts of the self.

Projection of the internal object: This use of the term was taken over from Abraham (1924); for example, an infant crying with hunger experiences the absent mother/breast/bottle as an active presence of a hostile bad object causing the hunger in his tummy [*see* Unconscious phantasy]. Through screaming and crying (and often defaecating), the object comes to be experienced as expelled outside the infant's body, where it is slightly less terrifying.

Projection/deflection of the death instinct: Klein's view of the death instinct projected (or deflected) outwards means that there is a primary inwardly directed aggression that is turned outward against some outside object. The projection of an object (i.e. a relocation of the object) to the outside is a different use of the term 'projection' from the projection outwards of an impulse (redirection of an instinct) towards an external object.

Externalisation of conflict: Klein's original observations were of children acting out a relationship between toys in the external world, in which it is the internal conflict or internal relationship that is projected into the external world. Prurient interest in criminal behaviour and its legal prosecution may be a common case of externalising internal conflicts over certain impulses [*see* Social defence systems].

Projective identification: This is the more traditional Kleinian view of projection in which part of the self is attributed to an object. Thus part of the ego – a mental state, for instance, such as unwelcome anger, hatred or other bad feeling – is seen in another person and quite disowned (denied) in oneself. Klein also thinks that good feelings and attributes of the self are attributed to another person and she includes the attribution of both 'good' and 'bad' qualities in her definition of the term 'projective identification' [*see* Projective identification].

In current usage by British Kleinian analysts the term 'projection' is not sharply distinguished from the term 'projective identification'. 'Projection' tends to be used to mean the general mental mechanism of transferring something from the self to another. 'Projective identification' involves a more detailed consideration of what is projected by whom, to whom and with what effect. All the many forms and contents of projection – of impulse, feeling, thought, part of the self, internal object – are now thought to involve unconscious identification by the projector with the projected attribute. Indeed, in current British Kleinian usage 'projective identification' is really an unpacking of the concept of projection, and it hardly makes sense to give the terms different definitions (Spillius, 1992).

Pathological and normal projective identification: Bion (1959) distinguished two forms of projective identification on this basis: a pathological form conducted with omnipotence and violence, and a 'normal' form without violence and with a consequent maintenance of a sense of internal and external reality. The pathological form of projective identification, in which there is confusion of self with an object, is to be contrasted with empathy, in which the projector remains aware of his own separate identity [*see* Empathy; Projective identification].

Abraham, K. (1924) 'A short study of the development of the libido', in *Selected Papers on Psychoanalysis*. London: Hogarth Press (1927), pp. 418–501.
Bion, W. (1959) 'Attacks on linking', *Int. J. Psycho-Anal.* 40: 308–315.
Freud, S. (1895) 'Draft 1 – paranoia', *S.E. 1*. London: Hogarth Press, pp. 206–212.
—— (1914) 'On narcissism', *S.E. 14*. London: Hogarth Press, pp. 67–102.
—— (1916) 'Some character-types met with in analytic work: III Criminals from a sense of guilt', *S.E. 14*. London: Hogarth Press, pp. 332–333.
—— (1925) 'Negation', *S.E. 19*. London: Hogarth Press, pp. 235–239.
Klein, M. (1927) 'Criminal tendencies in normal children', in *The Writings of Melanie Klein*, Vol. 1. London: Hogarth Press, pp. 170–185.
—— (1946) 'Notes on some schizoid mechanisms', in *The Writings of Melanie Klein*, Vol. 3. London: Hogarth Press, pp. 1–24.
Spillius, E. (1992) 'Clinical experiences of projective identification', in R. Anderson (ed.) *Clinical Lectures on Klein and Bion*. London: Routledge, pp. 81–86.

Ps↔D

Klein had described the movements from the depressive position to the paranoid-schizoid position as a paranoid defence against depressive anxiety [*see* Paranoid defence against depressive anxiety]. In *Elements of Psycho-Analysis* (1963) Bion describes the process of change between the two categories of Ps and D as 'disintegration' and 'reintegration'. He makes a clear statement that the quality of the change 'benignity or otherwise' (1963, p. 35), depends on whether the process is dominated by love, hate or knowledge (L, H or K). Bion suggests that there are similarities between the processes occurring in 'Ps↔D' and in those of container and contained. However, these are neither clear-cut nor straightforward. D, for example, may be an instance of integration but it may also be an agglomeration and as such would provide containment that is 'suggestive' of D but is not equivalent. Also, armed with his view that projective identification may be normal as well as pathological, Bion conceives of a non-pathological move towards the paranoid-schizoid position.

In following Klein's (1923, 1931) view that intellectual development is greatly dependent upon emotional development, Bion (1963) established a theory of thinking [*see* Thinking and knowledge] based on the linking of thoughts, which has the significance for the subject of the linking of parents and their organs in the primal scene [*see* Combined parent figure; Linking]. He developed the model of a container [*see* Container/contained]. The conjunction of mental contents forms a network that serves as a container. In the creative process, thinking involves the dismantling of previous views and theories. In changing one's way of thinking, the container has to be dissolved before it is reformed. Bion regards this dissolution as having the quality of a small psychic catastrophe, a going to pieces and therefore a movement into the paranoid-schizoid position (Ps). The re-forming of a new set of views and theories is a synthesising move reminiscent of the depressive position (D). Bion cites Poincaré's personal account of scientific creativity, with its search for a *selected fact* around which a cloud of as yet unorganised facts could be organised, as an excellent analogy for the movement into the depressive position with the internalisation of the breast (nipple) around which the personality of the infant can become organised.

Creative effort can therefore be viewed as a process, on a small scale, of movements to and fro between the paranoid-schizoid and depressive positions. Bion represented this *to-and-fro* process by the symbol 'Ps↔D'. Later, in *Attention and Interpretation* (1970, p. 124), Bion brings in the terms 'patience' and 'security' instead of Ps and D to differentiate the suffering, persecution and frustration necessary in the course of analytic work from feelings of the paranoid-schizoid position [*see* Wilfred Bion]. Also stressing the need for the capacity to tolerate disintegration, Britton, in 'Before and after the depressive position: Ps(n)→D(n)→Ps(n+1)', (1998) introduces the concept of Dpath, a pathological depressive position state that is a kind of pathological organisation. Britton's ideas build on those in Steiner's 1987 paper 'The interplay between pathological organisations and the paranoid-schizoid and depressive positions' [*see* Pathological organisations].

Prior to this a number of Kleinian analysts working with severe border-line personality disorders had investigated the fluctuations between the paranoid-schizoid and depressive positions: see in particular Joseph (1978, 1989) [*see* Betty Joseph; Psychic change; Psychic equilibrium]. An equilibrium exists between these two positions, around which fluctuations constantly reverberate; they are not to be conceived as stages of development through which the personality progresses to maturity or through which it regresses towards fixation points. Instead there is a constant fluctuation between the two positions all through development, and at each stage of development Ps↔D fluctuations occur. Development and maturation, therefore, exist in another dimension in which the relinquishing of omnipotence and an acknowledgement of external and internal reality are the significant factors. Although these developmental steps are commonly associated with the depressive position, there are moments of paranoid-schizoid functioning in which omnipotence does not play a large part and normal projective identification (empathy), for instance, replaces the pathological form [*see* Projective identification]. All through life there may be realistic anxieties about the survival of the self (the persecutory anxiety typical of the paranoid-schizoid position) and these may be tackled without omnipotence, an aspect of the personality that is known as *normal narcissism*. Equally, situations occur in which the depressive position may revert to omnipotent functioning, such as in pathological states of mourning [*see* Depressive anxiety]. One can conceive of the whole Ps↔D fluctuation moving forward developmentally as a whole, or at times backwards towards omnipotence and an unrealistic loss of separateness.

Bion, W. (1963) *Elements of Psycho-Analysis.* London: Heinemann.
—— (1970) *Attention and Interpretation.* London: Tavistock.
Britton, R. (1998) 'Before and after the depressive position: Ps(n)→D(n)→Ps(n+1)', in *Belief and Imagination.* London: Routledge, pp. 69–81.
Joseph, B. (1978) 'Different types of anxiety and their handling in the analytic situation', *Int. J. Psycho-Anal.* 59: 223–228.
—— (1989) *Psychic Equilibrium and Psychic Change.* London: Routledge.
Klein, M. (1923) 'The role of the school in the libidinal development of the child', in *The Writings of Melanie Klein*, Vol. 1. London: Hogarth Press, pp. 59–76.
—— (1931) 'A contribution to the theory of intellectual development', in *The Writings of Melanie Klein*, Vol. 1. London: Hogarth Press, pp. 236–247.
Steiner, J. (1987) 'The interplay between pathological organisations and the paranoid-schizoid and depressive positions', *Int. J. Psycho-Anal.* 68: 69–80.

Psychic change

This is a basic concept in all schools of psychoanalysis but in Kleinian analysis it has been a topic of special interest to Wilfred Bion and Betty Joseph.

Bion's (1967) thinking about avoiding preoccupation with 'memory and desire' [*see* Memory and desire] has helped Kleinian analysts to focus on the immediate expression of feeling and thought in the present situation of each session. Joseph (1989) suggests that there are two current definitions of psychic change, the first involving short-term change in a patient's mental state or functioning, and the second involving a more long-term and more fundamental change.

Joseph emphasises that the first sort of change is always going on in analysis – it is not static a process, and if the analyst keeps looking for the patient's progress or regression he is likely to disturb his own capacity to observe and to follow the patient and is also likely to make the patient feel pressurised or misunderstood.

Long-term psychic change is what patients come to analysis to achieve, but unconsciously it is also what they dread, for fear of losing their equilibrium and their sense of safety. This type of change involves change in the patient's pattern of projecting feelings and thoughts into his objects, including the analyst; it leads the patient into struggles over separateness, and attempts to reach a more realistic view of his own psychic reality. But to achieve these aims the analyst needs to avoid putting pressure on the patient to conform in some way, and he needs to be able to resist the patient's inevitable efforts to put pressure on the analyst to conform to the patient's expectations and desires. Long-term change is not achieved quickly, and it requires the analyst to have an imaginative and tolerant understanding of the patient's 'total situation' in analysis.

Bion, W. R. (1967) 'Notes on memory and desire', *Psychoanal. Forum* 2: 272–280; reprinted in E. B. Spillius (ed.) *Melanie Klein Today*, Vol. 2. London: Routledge (1988), pp. 17–21.

Joseph, B. (1989) 'Psychic change and the psychoanalytic process', in M. Feldman and E. Spillius (eds) *Psychic Equilibrium and Psychic Change*. London: Routledge, pp. 192–202.

Psychic development

Klein's evolving ideas of psychic development will be outlined:

- *1921 ('The development of a child'), 1923a ('The role of the school in the libidinal development of the child') and 1923b ('Early analysis')*: In these three papers the idea of libido is central in Klein's view of development, and she focuses particularly on anxiety about libido and its resolution. At this time she thought the Oedipus complex developed when the child was between the ages of 2 and 3 years.
- *1926 ('The psychological principles of early analysis')*: The early super-ego and the Oedipus complex begin at the start of the second year. The early superego is cruel and punitive.
- *1927a ('Symposium on child analysis')*: Aggression is stressed for the first time. Oedipus complex and superego begin at weaning. The severity of the superego is caused by the child's own sadistic phantasies.
- *1927b ('Criminal tendencies in normal children')*: Conflict between love and hate is stressed. 'Crimes' are enactments of early sadistic phantasies.
- *1928 ('Early stages of the Oedipus conflict')*: Projection of sadism into parents makes them and their intercourse cruel and frightening to the child – hence the idea of the threatening 'combined parent'. The boy fears castration, the girl fears attack by hostile mother. Young girls are aware of their vagina. At this time Klein still focuses mainly on the problems created by hate.
- *1929 ('Personification in the play of children')*: The id and aspects of the superego are attributed to real or phantasised external objects. Creativity is connected with early anxieties and expresses an impulse to restore damaged objects.
- *1930 ('The importance of symbol formation in the development of the ego')*: In extreme cases (like this one) the ego defends itself against anxiety by expelling sadism, both to rid the self of it and to attack the object.

- *1931 ('A contribution to the theory of intellectual inhibition')*: Sadism is a cause of intellectual inhibition, but sadism is also a basis of curiosity and exploration of the external world. A massive defence against sadism causes intellectual inhibition. Fear of dangers in the self inhibits self-exploration as well.

- *1932 (The Psychoanalysis of Children)*: A major work involving adoption of Freud's theory of the life and death instincts; love is emphasised more than in the earlier papers, leading to study of love and hate in interaction as the basis of mental functioning. First mention of the child's concept of parents as 'combined object' in continual intercourse (Ch. 8, especially p. 132).

- *1933 ('The early development of conscience in the child')*: Early superego is necessarily more cruel than actual parents because of the child's projection of sadism into his 'imagos' of his parents. Formation of superego begins when the child makes its earliest oral introjections. Oedipal tendencies also occur at this early stage. As the child's genital impulses develop, his superego becomes less tyrannical and is gradually developed into 'conscience'.

(In the last four works cited above, genital and positive drives, love and sadism are recognised as influencing development.)

- *1935 ('A contribution to the psychogenesis of manic-depressive states')*: [*see* Depressive position] *and 1940 ('Mourning and its relation to manic-depressive states')*: These two papers mark Klein's introduction of a new theory, the theory of the depressive position, in which she believes that at roughly 4–5 months of age the infant changes from relating to part-objects to being able to relate to whole objects. This means that whereas formerly he was concerned only for himself, he can now identify with his object and he becomes concerned about his object as well as himself. He becomes afraid of losing his loved good object, experiences guilt and even despair and tries to repair the damage he feels he has done. In this way Klein distinguishes between 'paranoic' anxiety (later called 'persecutory') and 'depressive' anxiety. From this time onwards Klein no longer places as much emphasis on libidinal 'phases' of development as she had in her earlier papers. The groupings of anxieties and defences she describes as the depressive position 'occur', she says, 'and recur during the first years of childhood and under certain circumstances in later life' (Klein, 1952, p. 93). The second aspect of the new theory is Klein's view that the normal outcome of the depressive position is the secure internalisation of the good object; if this fails, depressive illness is likely to occur, meaning that the suffering of manic-depressive illness repeats the struggles of the infantile depressive position.

- *1946 ('Notes on some schizoid mechanisms')*: This is another major paper concerned with the delineation of the paranoid-schizoid position, which Klein thinks precedes the depressive position [*see* Paranoid-schizoid position]. She emphasises the defence of splitting of both the emotions of love and hate and of objects into good and bad; and the 'expulsion' (projection) of sadism to relieve the ego and to attack objects; she introduces the concept of projective identification as a main defence in the paranoid-schizoid position [*see* Projective identification]. She says the ego, when fearful of annihilation, splits itself into minute parts (fragmentation), resulting in a split ego, as in schizophrenia, and she emphasises that the ego cannot split the object without itself being split.

- *1948 ('On the theory of anxiety and guilt') and 1960 ('A note on depression in the schizophrenic')*: Klein adds that there can be early forms of depression and guilt that occur in the paranoid-schizoid position.

- *1952 ('Some theoretical conclusions regarding the emotional life of the infant')*: This paper gives a general summary description of early development from birth to latency in terms of her new theory, complete except for the inclusion of her slightly later idea of primary envy in 1957. Klein also makes an explicit reference here to the idea of the parents coming to be happily related to each other, in contrast to parents as the 'combined object' in 'Early stages of the Oedipus conflict' (1928) and *The Psychoanalysis of Children* (1932, especially Ch. 8, p. 132).

- *1957 ('Envy and gratitude')*: Klein adds the importance of the struggle over envy, which she thinks of as having a constitutional basis, as a last and very crucial feature of psychic development.

- *1958 ('On the development of mental functioning')*: Klein states her view that the superego develops with the two instincts of love and hate predominantly in a state of fusion, and that the terrifying internal figures that result from intense destructiveness are not part of the normally developing superego, but exist in a separate area of the mind in the 'deep unconscious'.

Klein, M. (1921) 'The development of a child', in *The Writings of Melanie Klein*, Vol. 1. London: Hogarth Press, pp. 1–53.

—— (1923a) 'The role of the school in the libidinal development of the child', in *The Writings of Melanie Klein*, Vol. 1. London: Hogarth Press, pp. 59–76.

—— (1923b) 'Early analysis', in *The Writings of Melanie Klein*, Vol. 1. London: Hogarth Press, pp. 77–105.

—— (1926) 'The psychological principles of early analysis', in *The Writings of Melanie Klein*, Vol. 1. London: Hogarth Press, pp. 128–138.

—— (1927a) 'Symposium on child analysis', in *The Writings of Melanie Klein*, Vol. 1. London: Hogarth Press, pp. 139–169.

—— (1927b) 'Criminal tendencies in normal children', in *The Writings of Melanie Klein*, Vol. 1. London: Hogarth Press, pp. 170–185.

—— (1928) 'Early stages of the Oedipus conflict', in *The Writings of Melanie Klein*, Vol. 1. London: Hogarth Press, pp. 186–198.

—— (1929) 'Personification in the play of children', in *The Writings of Melanie Klein*, Vol. 1. London: Hogarth Press, pp. 199–209.

—— (1930) 'The importance of symbol formation in the development of the ego', in *The Writings of Melanie Klein*, Vol. 1. London: Hogarth Press, pp. 219–232.

—— (1931) 'A contribution to the theory of intellectual inhibition', in *The Writings of Melanie Klein*, Vol. 1. London: Hogarth Press, pp. 236–247.

—— (1932) *The Psychoanalysis of Children. The Writings of Melanie Klein*, Vol. 2. London: Hogarth Press.

—— (1933) 'The early development of conscience in the child', in *The Writings of Melanie Klein*, Vol. 1. London: Hogarth Press, pp. 248–257.

—— (1935) 'A contribution to the psychogenesis of manic-depressive states', in *The Writings of Melanie Klein*, Vol. 1. London: Hogarth Press, pp. 262–289.

—— (1940) 'Mourning and its relation to manic-depressive states', *The Writings of Melanie Klein*, Vol. 1. London: Hogarth Press, pp. 344–369.

—— (1946) 'Notes on some schizoid mechanisms', in *The Writings of Melanie Klein*, Vol. 3. London: Hogarth Press, pp. 1–24.

—— (1948) 'On the theory of anxiety and guilt', in *The Writings of Melanie Klein*, Vol. 3. London: Hogarth Press, pp. 25–42.

—— (1952) 'Some theoretical conclusions regarding the emotional life of the infant', in *The Writings of Melanie Klein*, Vol. 3. London: Hogarth Press, pp. 61–93.

—— (1957) 'Envy and gratitude', in *The Writings of Melanie Klein*, Vol. 3. London: Hogarth Press, pp. 176–235.

—— (1958) 'On the development of mental functioning', *The Writings of Melanie Klein*, Vol. 3. London: Hogarth Press, 236–246.

—— (1960) 'A note on depression in the schizophrenic', *The Writings of Melanie Klein*, Vol. 3. London: Hogarth Press, pp. 264–267.

Psychic equilibrium

Arising from her work with both normal and more disturbed patients, Betty Joseph has concluded that all patients try to maintain a balance, an equilibrium, between their persecutory and depressive anxieties and a complex system of defences that they have developed in order to try to keep their anxieties under control.

Patients often come to analysis because of a desire for psychic change, but soon find themselves trying to protect and defend their traditional equilibrium. As Joseph puts it:

> Patients come into analysis because they are dissatisfied with the way things are and they want to alter, or want things to alter. There is a

desire for change and pressure towards greater integration; without it analysis would fail. And yet there is a dread of change. Unconsciously they know that the change that they ask for involves an internal shifting of forces, a disturbance of an established mental and emotional equilibrium, a balance unconsciously established of feelings, impulses, defences, and internal figures, which is mirrored in their behaviour in the external world. This balance is maintained by very tightly and finely interlocked elements, and a disturbance in one part must reverberate throughout the personality. Our patients unconsciously sense this and tend therefore to feel the whole process of analysis as potentially threatening.

(Joseph, 1986, p. 193)

Patients come to analysis, in other words, wanting the analyst to help them to understand themselves better, but soon, as Joseph puts it, they are likely to want the analyst to 'stand' their anxiety rather than to help them 'understand' it (Joseph, 1978, p. 108).

Joseph, B. (1978) 'Different types of anxiety and their handling in the analytic situation', in M. Feldman and E. Spillius (eds) *Psychic Equilibrium and Psychic Change*. London: Routledge (1989), pp. 106–115.
—— (1986) 'Psychic change and the psychoanalytic process', in M. Feldman and E. Spillius (eds) *Psychic Equilibrium and Psychic Change*. London: Routledge (1989), pp. 192–202.

Psychic pain

Klein herself does not use the phrase 'psychic pain' but she refers (Klein, 1940) to the pain of grief, which can be very productive. The concept of psychic pain is, however, commonly in use in contemporary Kleinian writing. It is a general term that can apply at one end of the spectrum to depressive pain – the pain of guilt and concern – or at the other end to very persecuting mental experiences. At the primitive end of the spectrum psychic pain may be barely psychic, but felt more as bodily pain. The work of analysis helps the patient to move towards a more depressive experience of psychic pain, which can then lead to reparation and to sublimations. Bion (1970) writes:

People exist who are so intolerant of pain or frustration (or in whom pain or frustration is so intolerable) that they feel the pain but will not suffer it and so cannot be said to discover it . . . the patient who will not suffer pain fails to 'suffer' pleasure.

(Bion, 1970, p. 9)

Elsewhere Bion describes the need for 'the analytic experience to increase the patient's capacity for suffering, even though the patient and analyst may hope to decrease pain itself' (Bion, 1963, p. 62).

Joseph (1981) in her paper 'Towards the experiencing of psychic pain' writes of an indefinable type of psychic pain, on the border between physical and mental, felt by patients when there is an important shift in the balance maintained by the personality. It is a pain that in Joseph's view indicates an emergence from schizoid states of mind, and may usefully lead the patient to seek help.

Abel-Hirsch (2006) develops some ideas of both Bion and Joseph. She distinguishes between experiences, both painful and pleasurable, that are owned and thus experienced meaningfully from within, and a more imposed or constructed quality to pain or pleasure typical of perverse states of mind.

Abel-Hirsch, N. (2006) 'The perversion of pain, pleasure and thought: on the difference between "suffering" an experience and the "construction" of a thing to be used', in D. Nobus and L. Downing (eds) *Psychoanalytic Perspectives/ Perspectives on Psychoanalysis*. London: Karnac, pp. 127–146.
Bion, W. (1963) *Elements of Psychoanalysis*. London: Heinemann.
—— (1970) *Attention and Interpretation*. London: Tavistock.
Joseph, B. (1981) 'Toward the experiencing of psychic pain', in J. Grotstein (ed.) *Do I Dare Disturb the Universe?* Beverly Hills, CA: Caesura, pp. 93–102.
Klein, M. (1940) 'Mourning and its relation to manic-depressive states', in *The Writings of Melanie Klein*, Vol. 1. London: Hogarth Press, pp. 344–369.

Psychic reality

Internal or psychic reality is the psychic world that exists unconsciously and consciously inside the person. Freud's momentous starting point was to realise the power of unconscious forces, to take seriously what neurotic and psychotic patients said to him and to assume that they were conveying something comprehensible that was real to them. Klein elaborated this with the theory of internal objects; she:

> . . . made a discovery that created a revolutionary addition to the model of the mind, namely that we do not live in one world, but in two – that we live in an internal world which is as real a place to live as the outside world . . . Psychic reality could be treated in a concrete way.
>
> (Meltzer, 1981, p. 178)

The internal world: Klein pictures the internal world as filled with objects and parts of self in relationship to each other [*see* Internal objects]. Internal objects can be more or less unconscious and more or less primitive. Early infantile internal objects are experienced concretely within the body and mind – an experience of inside the body [*see* Skin]. The concept of internal objects is complex and cannot be separated from Klein's ideas about unconscious phantasy and the life and death instincts [*see* Unconscious phantasy]. The omnipotent use of the mechanisms of introjection and projection, in which parts of the self are projected out into an object that is then introjected, has a real effect on the internal reality of the individual. For example, aggression that is projected out leaves the individual with the sense of having a weakened ego. The structure of the individual's internal world and the relationships between the internal objects and the parts of the self are affected by, and in turn influence, the predominant defensive constellation operating in the mind of the individual [*see* Depressive position; Paranoid-schizoid position].

Structure of the internal world: The internal world of the individual is conceptualised as having structure and in Kleinian theory the structure and the contents affect each other. For example, both Freud and Klein include the idea of an ego divided into an ego and superego. In Klein's view this division is connected to the early defensive splitting and projection of the death instinct and the ensuing introjection of severe and idealised objects. The strength of the death instinct and the state of and the relationship to the external objects will affect the nature of the introjects into the ego and the superego, and these in turn will affect the degree to which integrative or splitting processes predominate, whether aspects of the objects in the internal world are rigidly separated from each other and whether or not the internal world is fragmented or integrated.

Whereas Freud's model of the mind is a conceptual tool for psychoanalysts to use in their work, the Kleinian approach is that the patient has an unconscious phantasy of his psychic reality, its structure, its contents and the relationships that are taking place. This can often be represented in dreams; a good example comes from Segal (1964), whose patient reported the dream of a naval officer that was of:

> . . . a pyramid. At the bottom of this pyramid there was a rough crowd of sailors bearing a heavy gold book on their heads. On this book stood a naval officer of the same rank as himself, and on his shoulders an admiral. The admiral, he said, seemed in his own way to exercise as great a pressure from above and to be as awe inspiring as the crowd of sailors who formed the base of the pyramid and pressed up from below.
> (Segal, 1964, p. 21)

The patient went on to describe how his dream represented himself, his instincts from below and his conscience from above.

Klein has been criticised for having reified phantasy phenomena and for confusing the level of description with that of theory. However, the internal reality of the patient is reified because it is the patient who reifies it and functions as if psychic reality is equivalent to material reality.

See Internal objects; Unconscious phantasy

Meltzer, D. (1981) 'The Kleinian expansion of Freudian metapsychology', *Int. J. Psycho-Anal.* 62: 177–185.
Segal, H. (1964) *Introduction to the Work of Melanie Klein.* London: Karnac.

Psychosis

The topic of psychosis, especially schizophrenia but also paranoia and manic-depressive psychosis, was of interest to Klein from the beginning of her work. She thought that childhood psychosis was more widespread and serious than was generally recognised (Klein, 1930a, 1930b). Of the twenty children who are mentioned in Klein's writings or listed as having been treated by her at the Berlin Polyklinik, Klein considered four to be schizophrenic and another three to be paranoid (Frank, 2009, Ch. 2). Klein's work on psychosis in children was particularly emphasised in her analysis of 'Erna', a child of 6 years who presented with symptoms of obsessional neurosis masking, Klein came to think, a severe paranoia (Klein, 1932, Ch. 3; see also Frank, 2009, Chs. 6 and 11).

Klein's understanding of schizophrenia was based on many patients, but particularly on the case of 'Dick', a 4-year-old child whom she describes at length in 'The importance of symbol formation in the development of the ego' (Klein 1930a). In the first part of this paper Klein describes a theory of how the ego grows. She says that the child (and of course his/her ego) not only has a libidinal relationship with his parents (including his ideas about their sexual organs) but also has a destructive relationship based on sadism. Because of his phantasies of attacking his parents and their organs, the child has phantasies of his parents attacking him in retaliation. In order to avoid the parents' anticipated attacks, the child, once again in phantasy, displaces his attack from his actual parents to something else that symbolically stands for them, so that a new 'equation' is created. If that symbolic equation becomes too obvious, he can then develop another substitute, a second symbolic equation, and so the sphere of symbolism widens and the ego grows. As Klein puts it:

> A sufficient quantity of anxiety is the necessary basis for an abundance of symbol formation and of phantasy; an adequate capacity on the part of the ego to tolerate anxiety is essential if anxiety is to be satisfactorily worked over, if this basic phase is to have a favourable issue and if the development of the ego is to be successful.
>
> (Klein, 1930a, p. 221)

It was here, however, that her patient Dick had trouble. Klein thinks that he was so frightened by the thought of his own and his parents' destructiveness that he had to stop all phantasies and thoughts that had anything to do with destructiveness. This meant that he lived in a restricted, almost closed world in which nothing much happened. He could hardly talk, only a very few things interested him and no one could understand him. He appeared to be without affect or anxiety – like many schizophrenics, as Klein points out. As Klein puts it: 'The ego's excessive and premature defence against sadism checks the establishment of a relation to reality and the development of phantasy life' (Klein, 1930a, p. 232). This idea, that the early ego needs both to be capable of a certain amount of destructiveness but also to be able to bear some awareness of it, is one of the antecedents to Klein's later formulation of the 'positions', both manic-depressive in 1935 and 1940 and paranoid-schizoid in 1946. In both positions destructive impulses are defended against by splitting, denial, idealisation, introjection, projection and various forms of identification [*see* Depressive position; Paranoid-schizoid position]. Klein thinks that the paranoid-schizoid position of infancy was the fixation point for schizophrenia, and that the depressive position of infancy is the fixation point for manic-depressive psychosis, and this assertion led some critics to assume that Klein thought infants were psychotic. Klein's view, however, is that normal infants might temporarily use modes of thought that bore some resemblance to thinking of psychotics, but that such usage is a temporary and customary aspect of normal development.

Klein's colleagues, particularly Rosenfeld, Bion and Segal, took up her ideas about the growth of the ego and about the positions, and began to work with adult psychotics Many papers were written, and quite rapidly, especially in the 1950s (see Rosenfeld, 1947, 1949, 1950, 1952a, 1952b, 1954, 1963; Segal, 1950, 1954, 1956, 1975; Bion, 1954, 1956, 1957, 1959). All three authors stressed that their technique was as close as possible to the technique used with neurotic patients, the major difference being that many psychotic patients found it difficult to lie on the couch so they either sat up or walked about. All three analysts used and developed Klein's ideas. It does not seem that they secured spectacular cures, but all their papers convey that they felt their understanding of psychosis was greatly enriched by their experiences, and that some understanding by their patients was achieved as well.

It is notable that the number of Kleinian papers on individual psychotic patients diminished after the 1950s. This is probably because of the arrival and increased use of psychotropic drugs in the late 1950s, which probably meant that fewer psychotic patients were encouraged by their GPs or relatives to undertake psychoanalysis. It is perhaps because of this trend that the interest of many psychoanalysts appears to have shifted from psychosis to borderline states (Steiner, 1993; Britton, 1998, 2003). Henri

Rey, Leslie Sohn and David Bell, however, continued to work psycho-analytically with psychotic patients, something they were able to do because they worked within or in association with psychiatric institutions (Rey, 1994; Sohn, 1995; Bell, 2007). Spillius, Hinshelwood, Skogstad and their colleagues have worked with psychotic patients in psychiatric settings, with a particular focus on the effects on patients of the social and cultural setting (Spillius, 1976, 1990; Hinshelwood and Skogstad, 2000).

Bell, D. (2007) 'Einige Betrachtungen zum Realitätsbezug und der Funktion des Glaubens in der Schizophrenie in Britische Konzepte der Psychosentherapie' ('Some observations on the relation to reality and the function of belief in schizophrenic states'), in S. Mentzos and A. Münch (eds) *Britische Konzepte der Psychosentherapie*. Göttingen: Vandenhoeck & Ruprecht.

Bion, W. (1954) 'Notes on the theory of schizophrenia', *Int. J. Psycho-Anal.* 35: 113–118.

—— (1956) 'Development of schizophrenic thought', *Int. J. Psycho-Anal.* 37: 344–346.

—— (1957) 'Differentiation of the psychotic from the non-psychotic personalities', *Int. J. Psycho-Anal.* 38: 266–275.

—— (1959) 'Attacks on linking', *Int. J. Psycho-Anal.* 40: 308–315.

Britton, R. (1998) *Belief and Imagination*. London: Routledge.

—— (2003) *Sex, Death, and the Superego*. London: Karnac.

Frank, C. (2009) *Melanie Klein in Berlin: Her First Psychoanalyses of Children*. London: Routledge.

Hinshelwood, R. D. and Skogstad, W. (2000) *Observing Organisations: Anxiety, Defence and Culture in Health Care*. London: Routledge.

Klein, M. (1930a) 'The importance of symbol formation in the development of the ego', *Int. J. Psycho-Anal.* 11: 24–39; reprinted in *The Writings of Melanie Klein*, Vol. 1. London: Hogarth Press, pp. 219–232.

—— (1930b) 'The psychotherapy of the psychoses', *Br. J. Med. Psychol.* 10: 242–244.

—— (1932) The *Psychoanalysis of Children. The Writings of Melanie Klein*, Vol. 2. London: Hogarth Press.

—— (1935) 'A contribution to the psychogenesis of manic-depressive states', *Int. J. Psycho-Anal.* 16: 145–174.

—— (1940) 'Mourning and its relation to manic-depressive states', *Int. J. Psycho-Anal.* 21: 125–153.

—— (1946) 'Notes on some schizoid mechanisms', *Int. J. Psycho-Anal.* 27: 99–110.

Rey, H. (1994) *Universals of Psychoanalysis in the Treatment of Psychotic and Borderline States*. London: Free Association Books.

Rosenfeld, H. R. (1947) 'Analysis of a schizophrenic state with depersonalization', *Int. J. Psycho-Anal.* 28: 130–139.

—— (1949) 'Remarks on the relation of male homosexuality to paranoia, paranoid anxiety, and narcissism', *Int. J. Psycho-Anal.* 30: 36–47.

—— (1950) 'Notes on the psychopathology of confusional states in chronic schizo-phrenias', *Int. J. Psycho-Anal.* 32: 132–137.

—— (1952a) 'Notes on the psycho-analysis of the super-ego conflict in an acute schizophrenic patient', *Int. J. Psycho-Anal.* 33: 111–131.

—— (1952b) 'Transference-phenomena and transference-analysis in an acute catatonic schizophrenic patient', *Int. J. Psycho-Anal.* 33: 457–464.

—— (1954) 'Considerations regarding the psycho-analytical approach to acute and chronic schizophrenia', *Int. J. Psycho-Anal.* 35: 135–140.

—— (1963) 'Notes on the psychopathology and psycho-analytic treatment of schizophrenia', in *Psychotic States: A Psycho-Analytical Approach.* London: Hogarth Press (1965), pp. 155–168.

Segal, H. (1950) 'Some aspects of the analysis of a schizophrenic', *Int. J. Psycho-Anal.* 3: 268–278.

—— (1954) 'A note on schizoid mechanisms underlying phobia formation', *Int. J. Psycho-Anal.* 35: 238–241.

—— (1956) 'Depression in the schizophrenic', *Int. J. Psycho-Anal.* 37: 339–343.

—— (1975) 'A psychoanalytic approach to the treatment of psychoses', in *The Work of Hanna Segal: A Kleinian Approach to Clinical Practice.* New York: Jason Aronson (1981), pp. 131–136.

Sohn, L. (1995) 'Unprovoked assaults: Making sense of apparently random violence', *Int. J. Psycho-Anal.* 76: 565–575.

Spillius, E. (1976) 'Hospital and society', *Br. J. Med. Psychiatr.* 49: 97–140.

—— (1990) 'Asylum and society', in E. Trist and H. Murray (eds) *The Social Engagement of Social Science*, Vol. 1. London: Free Association Books, pp. 586–612.

Steiner, J. (1993) *Psychic Retreats: Pathological Organizations in Psychotic, Neurotic and Borderline Patients.* London: Routledge.

Realisation

A term used by Bion to describe an action that brings an idea or expectation into concrete existence. In his example a baby has a preconception of a breast, which is realised when the baby encounters an actual breast, which gives rise to a conception (Bion, 1962, p. 179). In Bion's view the concept of realisation is also involved when the preconception of a breast does *not* meet with an experience of an actual breast. In this case it is a negative realisation, a 'no-breast', a frustration that, if tolerated, may give rise to a 'thought' (Bion, 1962) [*see* Thinking and knowledge].

In Bion's view the idea of realisation also plays a role in the conversion of 'O', the 'thing-in-itself', into the world of phenomena ('O' becomes 'K'), which will allow the construction of interpretations and the possible realisation of the patient's unconscious meanings during the analytic session (see Bion, 1965, Ch. 10; Bion, 1970, under 'O').

Joseph Sandler (1976a, 1976b) has used the term actualisation in much the same sense as Bion's use of realisation, except that Sandler's examples concern the experience of adults rather than the imagined experience of infants.

Bion, W. R. (1962) 'A theory of thinking', *Int. J. Psycho-Anal.* 43: 306–310; reprinted in E. Spillius (ed.) *Melanie Klein Today*, Vol. 1. London: Routledge, pp. 178–186.
—— (1965) *Transformations*. London: Heinemann.
—— (1970) *Attention and Interpretation*. London: Tavistock.
Sandler, J. (1976a) 'Dreams, unconscious fantasies and identity of perception', *Int. Rev. Psycho-Anal.* 3: 33–42.
—— (1976b) 'Counter-transference and role-responsiveness', *Int. Rev. Psycho-Anal.* 3: 43–47.

Reparation

Klein recognised early on, in her very youngest patients, that there was a lot of feeling for the people, toys, objects with which they played, particularly following episodes of violence and cruelty:

> . . . we might see the mother cooked and eaten and the two brothers dividing the meal between them . . . But such a manifestation of primitive tendencies is invariably followed by anxiety, and by performances which show how the child now tries to make good and to atone for that which he has done. Sometimes he tries to mend the very same men, trains and so on he has just broken. Sometimes drawing, building and so on express the same reactive tendencies.
>
> (Klein, 1927, p. 175)

> The impression I get of the way in which even the quite small child fights his unsocial tendencies is rather touching . . . One moment after we have seen the most sadistic impulses, we meet with performances showing the greatest capacity for love and the wish to make all possible sacrifices to be loved.
>
> (Klein, 1927, p. 176)

Klein first uses the actual word reparation in relation to phantasied attacks on the object in 1929 in 'Infantile anxiety-situations reflected in a work of art and in the creative impulse'. She sometimes also uses 'restitution' and 'restoration' interchangeably with the word 'reparation'. True reparation is, for Klein, integral to the depressive position. It is grounded in love and respect for the separate other, and involves facing loss and damage and making efforts to repair and restore one's objects. Effective reparation involves a type and degree of guilt that is not so overwhelming as to induce despair, but can engender concern and hope. Reparation itself provides a way out of despair, by promoting virtuous rather than vicious cycles in states of depression. Klein came to think of it as a significant root in all creative activity and indeed as a central part of development: 'The course of libidinal development is thus at every step stimulated and reinforced by the drive for reparation, and ultimately by the sense of guilt' (Klein, 1945, p. 410). As the internal good object is repaired and strengthened by reparative means, so too is the ego with which it is closely identified [*see* Depressive position].

Reparation may be able to be expressed in concrete acts in the external world but this is often wholly or partly impossible; the child has limited control over his environment, and the adult may regret past misdeeds that can no longer be put right. Much reparation must thus take an internal form, including the sad recognition of damage that cannot be repaired, and in fact the core of it occurs at the psychic level. Reparation is distinct from *sublimation*, which involves constructive re-channelling of libidinal and aggressive impulses into more symbolic activities. Reparation is certainly concerned with the impulses but consists of the phantasy of putting right the effects of the aggressive components.

Manic and obsessional reparation: In 'Mourning and its relation to manic-depressive states' (1940) Klein shows that reparation is more or less omnipotent, depending on the capacities of the individual. *Manic reparation* carries a note of triumph, as it is based on a reversal of the child–parent relation, and a denial of dependency, which instead becomes the humiliating lot of the object. Where manic defences against the depressive anxieties are operating forcefully, reparation will therefore be conceived with comparable omnipotence. *Obsessional reparation* consists of compulsive, often magical repetition of actions of the undoing kind without a real creative element. With this, goes forceful control and attempted mastery of the object.

Manic and obsessional repair provide partial solutions, but inevitably involve some degree of triumph and sadism. The object will be felt to suffer further damage, risking further guilt and/or fears of retaliation. In both manic and obsessional reparation the internal mother–father couple are in phantasy prevented from coming together, whereas in reparation proper they are released and allowed to come together.

See Manic defences; Manic reparation; Obsessional defences; Depressive position

Klein, M. (1920) 'Inhibitions and difficulties at puberty', in *The Writings of Melanie Klein*, Vol. 1. London: Hogarth Press, pp. 54–58.

—— (1927) 'Criminal tendencies in normal children', in *The Writings of Melanie Klein*, Vol. 1. London: Hogarth Press, pp. 170–185.

—— (1929) 'Infantile anxiety-situations reflected in a work of art and in the creative impulse', in *The Writings of Melanie Klein*, Vol. 1. London: Hogarth Press, pp. 210–218.

—— (1940) 'Mourning and its relation to manic-depressive states', in *The Writings of Melanie Klein*, Vol. 1. London: Hogarth Press, pp. 344–369.

—— (1945) 'The Oedipus complex in the light of early anxieties', in *The Writings of Melanie Klein*, Vol. 1. London: Hogarth Press, pp. 370–419.

Repression

Originally repression was *the* defence mechanism that Freud described. However he later (Freud, 1926, pp. 163–164, 173–174) began to distinguish others, and so did Anna Freud: 'The significance of repression is reduced to that of "a special method of defence". This new conception of the role of repression suggests an enquiry into the other specific modes of defence' (Anna Freud, 1936, p. 46). A range of defence mechanisms operated by the ego became a major field of study in psychoanalysis (A. Freud, 1936; Fenichel, 1945).

   Klein's clinical material also draws attention to the operation of other mechanisms, but she was confronted particularly with defence mechanisms that were concerned with the contents of the child's ego and body and the kinds of objects in the world around him. She began to think of these as the primitive defence mechanisms and distinguished them from repression. By 1930, she claims specifically:

> It is only in the later stages of the Oedipus conflict that the defence against libidinal impulses makes its appearance; in the earlier stages it is against the accompanying destructive impulses that the defence is directed . . . This defence is of a violent character, different from the mechanism of repression.
>
> (Klein, 1930, p. 220)

When, in the course of the next couple of years, Klein adopts the distinction between the death instinct and libido, she marks out a comparable distinction between primitive defence mechanisms (ranged against anxiety deriving from the death instinct) and repression (dealing with libidinal conflicts and anxieties).

Violence of defences: Primitive defence mechanisms differ from 'neurotic' ones in the degree of violence involved in the obliteration of part of the conscious mind. Klein's emphasis is on the repression (or splitting or denial) of parts of the personality, while in classical psychoanalysis repression tends more to affect the *contents* – affective or cognitive – of the mind rather than its structure. The primitive defence mechanisms severely distort or impoverish the ego. Because they are omnipotent phantasies, there is an actual 'alteration of the ego' when they operate. In repression, which is much less violent, the awareness of internal and external reality is much better maintained. However, the primitive defences may affect the eventual quality of repression:

> The early methods of splitting fundamentally influence the ways in which, at a somewhat later stage, repression is carried out and this in turn determines the degree of interaction between conscious and unconscious. In other words the extent to which the various parts of the mind are 'porous' in relation to one another is determined largely by the strength or weakness of the early schizoid mechanisms.
>
> (Klein, 1952, p. 66)

In her most explicit passage on repression, Klein states:

> The mechanism of splitting underlies repression (as is implied in Freud's concept); but in contrast to the earliest forms of splitting which lead to states of disintegration, repression does not normally result in a disintegration of the self. Since at this stage there is greater integration, within both the conscious and the unconscious parts of the mind, and since in repression the splitting predominantly effects a division between conscious and unconscious, neither part of the self is exposed to the degree of disintegration which may arise in previous stages. However, the extent to which splitting processes are resorted to in the first few months of life vitally influences the use of repression at a later stage. For if early schizoid mechanisms and anxieties have not been sufficiently overcome, the result may be that instead of a fluid boundary between the conscious and unconscious, a rigid barrier between them arises.
>
> (Klein, 1952, pp. 86–87)

The relation between repression and splitting may be illuminated by the idea of vertical and horizontal division. The more severe defence – splitting – divides the mind into two minds, as it were (object relationship and self in each part), with each separate relationship co-existing side by side (horizontally), whereas repression consigns part of the mind, now more integrated, to an unconscious realm without destroying the integrity (vertical division).

The severity of the splitting lessens as the depressive position takes over, with the consequent greater acceptance of external and internal reality: '. . . as the adaptation to the external world increases, the splitting is carried out on planes which gradually become increasingly nearer and nearer to reality' (Klein, 1935, p. 288). Repression gradually emerges with the greater impact of reality and the nature of the actual external objects.

Alpha- and beta-elements: Bion's (1962) distinction between alpha- and beta-elements [*see* Alpha-function; Beta-elements] is an alternative theoretical framework for examining the distinction between repression and the primitive defence mechanisms, in this case projective identification. Alpha-function is the psychological process that generates meaning from raw sense data. It gives rise to mental contents that can be used for thinking and dreaming, and are dealt with by repression. However, if alpha-function fails to operate, the mind accumulates quantities of beta-elements, unthinkable mental contents suitable only for discharge by means of projective identification (pathological), and the mind develops as an apparatus for discharging such accumulations [*see* Thinking and knowledge].

Bion, W. (1962) *Learning from Experience*. London: Heinemann.
Fenichel, O. (1945) *The Psycho-Analytic Theory of the Neurosis*. London: Routledge & Kegan Paul.
Freud, A. (1936) *The Ego and the Mechanisms of Defence*. London: Hogarth Press.
Freud, S. (1926) 'Inhibitions, symptoms and anxiety', *S.E. 20*. London: Hogarth Press, pp. 75–175.
Klein, M. (1930) 'The importance of symbol formation in the development of the ego', in *The Writings of Melanie Klein*, Vol. 1. London: Hogarth Press, pp. 219–232.
—— (1935) 'A contribution to the psychogenesis of manic-depressive states', in *The Writings of Melanie Klein*, Vol. 1. London: Hogarth Press, pp. 262–289.
—— (1952) 'Some theoretical conclusions regarding the emotional life of the infant', in *The Writings of Melanie Klein*, Vol. 3. London: Hogarth Press, pp. 61–93.

Resistance

Klein does not define resistance but she uses the term quite frequently in its general sense as a patient's opposition to the process of making the unconscious conscious. Thus she describes Felix's whistling as an expression of resistance to analysis (Klein, 1925, p. 122n), Fritz's resistance to sexual enlightenment as his wish to stay in the anal phase in order to avoid knowing about his parents' relationship (Klein, 1923, p. 99) and Richard's sudden expression of a resistance in the form of an interruption in his play because he had to repress an awareness of sexual desire for his mother (Klein, 1945, p. 375). She gives many similar examples in 'The technique of early analysis' (1932, pp. 16–34). Klein also describes an adult patient who accepted an interpretation in one part of her mind but resisted all knowledge of it in another part (Klein, 1946, p. 17).

Klein thinks of resistance as an expression of anxiety and negative transference. Speaking of small children's reaction of dislike for strangers, she says:

My experience has confirmed my belief that if I construe the dislike at once as anxiety and negative transference feeling and interpret it as such in connection with the material which the child at the same time produces and then trace it back to its original object, the mother, I can at once observe that the anxiety diminishes. This manifests itself in the beginning of a more positive transference and, with it, of more vigorous play . . . By resolving some part of the negative transference we shall then obtain, just as with adults, an increase in the positive transference and this, in accordance with the ambivalence of childhood, will soon in its turn be succeeded by a re-emerging of the negative.

(Klein, 1927, pp. 145–146)

Klein, M. (1923) 'Early analysis', in *The Writings of Melanie Klein*, Vol. 1. London: Hogarth Press, pp. 72–105.
—— (1925) 'A contribution to the psychogenesis of tics', in *The Writings of Melanie Klein*, Vol. 1. London: Hogarth Press, pp. 106–127.
—— (1927) 'Symposium on child analysis', in *The Writings of Melanie Klein*, Vol. 1. London: Hogarth Press, pp. 139–169.
—— (1932) 'The technique of early analysis;, in *The Writings of Melanie Klein*, Vol. 2. London: Hogarth Press, pp. 16–34.
—— (1945) 'The Oedipus complex in the light of early anxieties', in *The Writings of Melanie Klein*, Vol. 1. London: Hogarth Press, pp. 370–419.
—— (1946) 'Notes on some schizoid mechanisms', in *The Writings of Melanie Klein*, Vol. 3. London: Hogarth Press, pp. 1–20.

Restitution/restoration

These terms were used by Klein in her earlier work, and followed Abraham's (1924) descriptions of the impulse to make good after aggression. Later she used the term 'reparation'.

See Depressive position; Reparation

Abraham, K. (1924) 'A short study of the development of the libido viewed in the light of mental disorders', in *Collected Papers of Karl Abraham*. London: Hogarth Press (1927), pp. 418–501.

Reverie

This term was adopted by Bion (1962a) to refer to a state of mind that the infant requires of the mother. Mother's mind needs to be in a state of calm receptiveness to take in the infant's own feelings and give them meaning [*see* Container/contained]. The idea is that the infant will, through projective identification, induce in the mother states of anxiety and terror that he is unable to make sense of and are felt to be intolerable (especially the fear of death). Mother's reverie is a process of making some sense of it for the infant, a function known as 'alpha-function' [*see* Alpha-function]. Through first of all receiving back his inchoate feelings in more meaningful form, and ultimately through introjection of a receptive, understanding mother – the 'container' itself – the infant can begin to develop his own capacity for reflection on his own states of mind.

When, for some reason, mother is incapable of this reverie for reflective meaning, the infant is unable to receive a sense of meaning from her; instead, he experiences a sense of meaning having been stripped away, resulting in a terrifying sense of the ghastly unknown [*see* Nameless dread]. The reason for an inadequate state of reverie may exist more in the mother or more in the infant. Mother may be too fragile or preoccupied to be in a state of reverie for her infant, or reverie 'is not associated with love for the child or its father' (Bion, 1962b). Alternatively the infant may enviously attack the containing function upon which he depends [*see* Envy].

Winnicott's (1960) concept of holding has some relationship to Bion's concept of reverie (and of containment) but the two come from different theoretical frameworks. Holding is a more global concept, including within it a whole range of environmental provision by the mother. Reverie is a more limited and specific term referring to a mental function.

Bion, W. (1962a) 'A theory of thinking', *Int. J. Psycho-Anal.* 43: 306–310.
—— (1962b) *Learning from Experience.* London: Heinemann
Winnicott, D. W. (1960) 'The theory of the parent–infant relationship', in D. W. Winnicott (1965) *The Maturational Processes and the Facilitating Environment.* London: Hogarth Press (1965), pp. 37–55.

Herbert Rosenfeld

Herbert Rosenfeld was a pioneer and innovator in a number of vital clinical and theoretical areas. Together with Segal (1950) and Bion (1956), he began to treat schizophrenic patients without abandoning the basic technique of psychoanalysis, and he wrote extensively about psychosis and psychotic mechanisms (1952, 1954, 1987). However his work was not limited to psychosis. For example, his clarifications of Klein's concept of projective identification, his work on narcissism and his understanding of transference psychosis extended our understanding of neurotic and borderline patients (1971b).

Rosenfeld was born in Nuremberg in 1910 into a middle-class Jewish family, and came to England to escape Nazi persecution in 1935 (Segal and Steiner, 1987; Grosskurth, 1989). After observing psychotic patients in several mental hospitals he trained as a psychotherapist at the Tavistock Clinic and then started his analysis with Klein as a candidate at the Institute of Psychoanalysis, where he qualified in 1945. He was a tall friendly man with a warm smile and a unique capacity to put himself imaginatively into his patients' position to see things from their point of view.

Schizoid mechanisms: With his first training case, 'Mildred' (1947), Rosenfeld opened up new ground when he described the ego fragmentation that lay behind the patient's depersonalisation. Projective identification was, of course, a central theme and accounted for some of the patient's paranoid fears, especially her fear of being intruded on by the analyst. Later he was to write a classic paper on projective identification in which various types and motives were described (1971b), a paper that remains a standard reference today.

Confusional states: In another early paper (1950) Rosenfeld described confusional states, which can arise when normal splitting between good and bad breaks down. If envy predominates, destructive attacks are mounted against good objects rather than bad ones in a kind of crossover of the split, and a confusion results in which the patient may not be able to distinguish good from bad. These states are particularly unbearable and often lead to the development of a narcissistic omnipotence to create a spurious kind of order.

Narcissistic object relations: Rosenfeld's most original and significant contribution was his work on narcissism, recorded in his two classic papers (1964, 1971a). He was clear that Freud was wrong to suggest that narcissistic patients do not establish a transference. He showed on the contrary that their object relations are intense, being based on omnipotent identifications through which desirable aspects of the object are possessed and undesirable ones are disowned. These projections and identifications function as a defence against separateness and hence enable the patient to avoid destructive and aggressive feelings aroused by frustration, envy and humiliation.

In his second paper on narcissism (1971a) Rosenfeld shows that, in addition to the idealisation of good elements in the self and in the object, the narcissistic patient can idealise destructive elements that are turned to as a source of strength and superiority. These elements are organised into complex structures, often represented as a gang or mafia, which offer protection to the patient but only as long as he adheres to the destructive principles of the organisation. The gang is particularly threatening against any move by the patient to develop a dependent relationship with his good objects.

The final phase of Rosenfeld's analytic approach, 1978–1987: In the final years of his life Rosenfeld became concerned that patients who had been deprived or traumatised in their childhood were likely to be re-traumatised in their analyses unless the analyst took special care to avoid this. In particular he believed that envy should not be too frequently interpreted and that the patient's idealisation of his analyst should not be prematurely interfered with by interpretation. He shifted his attention to focus on the analyst's errors and difficulties and some analysts felt that this attention was unbalanced and led him to overlook the contribution from the patient. It seemed to represent a shift from the fine balance of his classic period in which both the analyst's and the patient's contribution to the analytic relationship was impartially examined and the subtle interactions between them were explored (Steiner, 2008). Others felt that these late views gave new and constructive weight to the effect of the patient's environment and to the harm that analysts may do by repeating (or appearing to repeat) elements of that environment. Everyone agrees, however, that Rosenfeld's late work is a reminder for all analysts to listen carefully to the patient's responses to their interventions, which can help the analyst to monitor errors and attitudes that may otherwise remain unrecognised.

Impasse and Interpretation (1987): Rosenfeld's last work is his book *Impasse and Interpretation*, in which he reviews and revises his thinking on important topics. It contains some vivid clinical descriptions that mostly represent his late and somewhat altered views. The clinical material includes examples of psychotic transferences, which Rosenfeld considered to be a major cause of an impasse developing in the treatment. He recognised that, at times of stress, psychotic mechanisms are deployed and transient psychotic transferences are common. At these times interpretations are heard concretely as facts rather than as ideas. Rosenfeld's close attention to the details of such transference–countertransference interactions is a highlight of his work at its best.

Bion, W. R. (1956) 'Development of schizophrenic thought', *Int. J. Psycho-Anal.* 37: 344–346.

Grosskurth, P. (1989) 'An interview with Herbert Rosenfeld', *Free Assoc.* 10: 23–31.

Rosenfeld H. A. (1947) 'Analysis of a schizophrenic state with depersonalization', *Int. J. Psycho-Anal.* 28: 130–139.

—— (1950) 'Notes on the psychopathology of confusional states in chronic schizophrenias', *Int. J. Psycho-Anal.* 31: 132–137.

—— (1952) 'Notes on the psycho-analysis of the super-ego conflict of an acute schizophrenic patient', *Int. J. Psycho-Anal.* 33: 111–131.

—— (1954) 'Considerations regarding the psycho-analytic approach to acute and chronic schizophrenia', *Int. J. Psycho-Anal.* 35: 135–140.

—— (1964) 'On the psychopathology of narcissism: A clinical approach', *Int. J. Psycho-Anal.* 45: 332–337.

—— (1971a) 'A clinical approach to the psychoanalytic theory of the life and death instincts: An investigation into the aggressive aspects of narcissism', *Int. J. Psycho-Anal.* 52: 169–178.

—— (1971b) 'Contribution to the psychopathology of psychotic states: The importance of projective identification in the ego structure and the object relations of the psychotic patient', in E. Spillius (ed.) *Melanie Klein Today*, Vol. 1. London: Routledge (1988), pp. 117–137.

—— (1987) *Impasse and Interpretation*. London: Tavistock.

Segal, H. (1950) 'Some aspects of the analysis of a schizophrenic', *Int. J. Psycho-Anal*. 30: 268–278

—— and Steiner, R. (1987) 'Obituary. H. A. Rosenfeld (1910–1986)', *Int. J. Psycho-Anal*. 68: 415–419.

Steiner, J. (2008) 'A personal review of Rosenfeld's contribution to clinical psychoanalysis', in *Rosenfeld in Retrospect: Some Essays on his Clinical Influence*. London: Routledge, pp. 58–84.

Sadism

In her early work (1922, 1923) Klein was surprised by the amount of aggression she observed in children's play. Both Freud and Abraham were investigating the prevalence of aggression in manic-depressive psychosis (Abraham, 1911; Freud, 1917), which they described as sadism, and Klein adopted their term. In 1936 she defined sadism as a fusion of aggressive and erotic phantasies and feelings (Klein, 1936, p. 293). Excessive sadism may inhibit the epistemophilic instinct [*see* Component instincts].

The term sadism, however, implies severe pathology and the erotic element in the term has gradually been dropped. In 1932 Klein adopted Freud's idea of the death instinct and the idea of sex as a component of aggression diminished further. Nowadays the tendency is to speak of 'aggression' rather than sadism, and if the term sadism is used, it tends to imply a stronger than usual element of cruelty in the aggression with the implication of gratification in causing suffering (whether the aggression is turned outwards or inwards in the form of masochism). This is different from the sexualisation or libidinalisation of aggression, as in perversion, which involves a fusion of the life and death instincts.

Abraham, K. (1911) 'Notes on the psycho-analytic treatment of manic depressive insanity and allied conditions', in *Selected Papers of Karl Abraham*. London: Hogarth Press (1927), pp. 137–156.

Freud, S. (1917) 'Mourning and melancholia', *S.E. 14*. London: Hogarth Press, pp. 237–258.

Klein, M. (1922) 'Inhibitions and difficulties at puberty', in *The Writings of Melanie Klein*, Vol. 1. London: Hogarth Press, pp. 54–58.

—— (1923) 'The role of the school in the libidinal development of the child', in *The Writings of Melanie Klein*, Vol. 1. London: Hogarth Press, pp. 59–76.

—— (1932) *The Psychoanalysis of Children. The Writings of Melanie Klein*, Vol. 2. London: Hogarth Press.

—— (1936) 'Weaning', in J. Rickman (ed.) *On the Bringing up of Children*. London: Kegan Paul, pp. 31–36.

Hanna Segal

Biography: Born in Poland, Hanna Segal trained as a doctor in Britain and then as a psychoanalyst, becoming a leading member of the Kleinian Group. Her training analyst was Melanie Klein. Segal was the first to analyse a hospitalised schizophrenic patient using a largely unmodified psychoanalytic technique. After Klein's death, she was the leading force in the establishment of the Kleinian Group, and has been extremely active in the elucidation of central Kleinian concepts and making them known more generally. She has written the definitive summaries of Klein's own ideas (Segal, 1964, 1979b).

Segal has made major contributions to psychoanalytic theory and technique and also to literature, socio-political theory and aesthetics. Of all the major Kleinian thinkers Segal is the most well known outside the psychoanalytic world, for example among academics.

Scientific contributions: Segal, together with Scott, Rosenfeld and Bion, contributed to the pioneering of the psychoanalysis of schizophrenics in the 1940s and 1950s. Her work with a schizophrenic patient (Segal, 1950) led her to the understanding of the disturbance in symbol formation in schizophrenia, which formed the basis for one of her foremost contributions to psychoanalysis. This work received its main theoretical exposition in the famous paper of 1957 on symbol formation. Here she showed that symbolic functioning rested upon a tripartite relationship between the symbol, the thing symbolised and the person for which the former can stand for the latter. In true symbolic function the thing symbolised is distinct from the symbol. However in more disturbed states of mind, although symbolisation still functions, the thing symbolised is *equated* with the symbol itself, forming what she termed a *symbolic equation* [*see* Symbol formation; Symbolic equation]. This provided an important clarification of the nature of the psychological disturbance that underlies concrete thinking. The disturbance in the relation to reality that derives from this disordered symbolic functioning causes major difficulties with thought and behaviour and seriously undermines the capacity for psychological development.

In a subsequent (1979a) postscript to her classic (1957) paper on symbol formation, and then in a further (1991) paper, Segal shows how the disturbance in symbolic functioning is derived from the use of pathological projective identification, which confuses objects with parts of the self. The phenomena of disturbed symbol formation, pathological projective identification and a damaged sense of reality are of course closely bound up with states of mind characteristic of the paranoid-schizoid position and this work develops Klein's original working hypothesis that the fixation points for the psychoses lie in this primitive stage of development.

Segal has an abiding interest in the nature of creativity. Her paper 'A psycho-analytic approach to aesthetics' given in 1947 and subsequently published (Segal, 1952) breaks new ground. This paper makes, at one and the same time, a major clinical contribution to the understanding of disturbance in creative functioning, and a key theoretical contribution to aesthetics. She noted that artists blocked in their work had major difficulties in mourning loss.

For Segal the artist is confronted with painful inner situations and his struggle to face this truthfully and to bear this disturbance is intimately related to the artistic work. The work thus expresses his efforts to repair these damaged internal objects. Segal shows how the artistic work is compromised by failure to face these inner situations – some artists become blocked, others take manic flight leading to superficial work. A further advantage of her theory is that it ties the inner work of artistic expression to an understanding of the audience's appreciation – that is, the observer is moved by the work as he identifies unconsciously with the artist's struggle to face the inner situation and to overcome it in the act of making his work. This understanding, of course, does not just apply to creative artists but to creativity in general.

It is clear that, for Segal, artistic creation requires a relatively stable attainment of the depressive position, from which the drive for reparation is mobilised into constructive activity. This view was elaborated by the art critic Adrian Stokes (Stokes, 1963). Segal subsequently wrote a series of papers on aspects of creativity (Segal, 1974, 1981a, 1981b, 1984).

Segal's central concerns (the nature of symbolic function, the elaboration and reconstruction of unconscious phantasy and explorations of the roots of creativity and destructiveness), which have characterised her contributions to both theory and technique in psychoanalysis, are all prefigured in her earliest papers. The understanding of the vicissitudes of the death drive and the elaboration of manic mechanisms feature prominently in her work.

Socio-political contributions: Segal is unique amongst the leading Kleinian thinkers in her demonstration of the relevance of psychoanalysis to socio-political issues. She co-founded 'Psychoanalysts for the Prevention of Nuclear War' (PPNW) and her paper 'Silence is the real crime' (Segal, 1987), read at the inauguration of that organisation, has remained a classic exposition of the psychoanalytic understanding of man's destructiveness and the terrible consequences of its denial. Segal's later papers on the dangers of manic triumphalism following the end of the cold war and on the (first) Iraq war have been further major contributions (see Segal, 1997).

Segal's work on applied analysis should not, however, be thought of as distinct from her mainstream psychoanalytic contributions. These two areas of her work inform and interpenetrate each other throughout her oeuvre. Bell (1997) explores Segal's contribution to both psychoanalysis and culture in the introductory essay of his book *Reason and Passion*, which features a collection of papers inspired by her work. Segal's most recent collection of her own papers, *Yesterday, Today and Tomorrow*, was published in 2007.

The transcript of an interview with Hanna Segal discussing her memories of Melanie Klein and some of her own ideas can be found on the website of the Melanie Klein Trust (http://www.melanie-klein-trust.org.uk/segalinterview 2001.htm).

Bell, D. (1997) *Reason and Passion. A Celebration of the Work of Hanna Segal.* London: Duckworth.

Segal, H. (1950) 'Some aspects of the analysis of a schizophrenic', *Int. J. Psycho-Anal.* 31: 268–278.

—— (1952) 'A psycho-analytic approach to aesthetics', *Int. J. Psycho-Anal.* 33: 196–207.

—— (1957) 'Notes on symbol formation', *Int. J. Psycho-Anal.* 38: 391–397.

—— (1964) *Introduction to the Work of Melanie Klein.* London: Heinemann.

—— (1974) 'Delusion and artistic creativity', *Int. J. Psycho-Anal.* 1: 135–141.

—— (1979a) Postcript to 'Notes on symbol formation', in *The Work of Hanna Segal.* New York: Jason Aronson (1981), p. 60–65.

—— (1979b) *Klein.* London: Fontana.

—— (1981a) 'Psycho-analysis and freedom of thought', in *The Work of Hanna Segal.* New York: Jason Aronson, pp. 217–227.

—— (1981b) 'Manic reparation', in *The Work of Hanna Segal.* New York: Jason Aronson, pp. 147–158.

—— (1984) 'Joseph Conrad and the mid-life crisis', *Int. Rev. Psycho-Anal.* 11: 3–9.

—— (1987) 'Silence is the real crime', *Int. Rev. Psycho-Anal.* 14: 3–12.

—— (1991) 'On symbolism', in *Psychoanalysis, Literature and War.* London: Routledge, pp. 41–48.

—— (1997) 'From Hiroshima to the Gulf War and after: Socio-political expressions of ambivalence', in *Psychoanalysis, Literature and War.* London: Routledge, pp. 157–168.

—— (2007) *Yesterday, Today and Tomorrow.* London: Routledge.

Stokes, A. (1963) *Painting and the Inner World.* London: Tavistock.

Self

Following Freud's description of the structural model (id, ego and super-ego) there was a major move towards a study of the ego rather than the id, and the ways in which the ego relates to and uses its objects. Klein's emphasis was on the importance of relationships with objects. She tended to use the terms 'self', 'ego' and 'subject' interchangeably. The term 'ego', and also 'subject', is used as the complement of 'object'. Later she stated her understanding of Freud's usage, which she herself followed: 'The self is used to cover the whole of the personality, which includes not only the ego but the instinctual life which Freud called the *id*' whereas the ego is '. . . the organized part of the self' which carries out a variety of functions like primitive and more evolved defences against anxiety and mediation between the internal and the external world (Klein, 1959, p. 249).

Ego psychology, by contrast, has taken an interest in the ego's role in the structure, and less in the instinctual life from which the objects stem [*see* Unconscious phantasy]. The difference between 'ego' and 'self' was sharply made by Hartmann (1950) when he distinguished between the ego as a mental organisation objectively described and self as the representation that is cathected in narcissism. The term 'ego' is a technical term thought up by the pragmatic English translators of Freud to enhance the objectivity of psychoanalytic science; it can be seen as a distortion of the German 'ich' (I or me) used by Freud, which gives a more personal or subjective connotation (Bettelheim, 1983).

See Ego

Bettelheim, B. (1983) *Freud and Man's Soul*. London: Hogarth Press.
Hartmann, H. (1950) 'Comments on the psycho-analytic theory of the ego', *Psychoanal. Study Child* 5: 74–96.
Klein, M. (1959) 'Our adult world and its roots in infancy', in *The Writings of Melanie Klein*, Vol. 3. London: Hogarth Press, pp. 247–263.

Skin

Bick (1964) introduced infant observation as part of the training for student child psychotherapists and psychoanalysts [*see* Infant observation]. In the course of doing so she began to notice specific phenomena in the mother–infant interaction that concerned skin stimulation. She developed the idea that skin contact was the most prominent element in the earliest relationship and in the earliest introjections of the ego.

The first object is the one who gives to the infant the feeling of being in existence – having an identity, we might say, at a later stage of development. Observations of the interaction of the mother–infant pair led Bick to understand two opposite states of mind for the infant – either a feeling of being in existence with some coherence or, the opposite, a feeling of dissolution, uncoordination, annihilation. In the very early days and weeks after birth certain events can be seen to be associated with uncoordinated, restless movements of the limbs accompanied by grunting or crying and screaming. These behaviours occur typically when the baby is undressed, his face is washed, he is held precariously or when feeding is interrupted. Other events reduce the apparent uncoordination and distress: when he is carried, dressed after a bath, while feeding or when wrapped in blankets in the cot. These fairly clearly distinguished states are held to correspond to later states of mind that Bick identified as the feeling of going to pieces (annihilation) or containment [*see* Container/contained].

For Klein the infant at birth has an ego that can distinguish objects separate from itself, but Bick was much less certain of that as an endowed cognitive ability – she thought that the whole ego could collapse, and frequently did in the early days and weeks. Although Klein (1946) did describe the falling to bits of the ego, she did not explain how such an extremely fragile ego could introject and project; these are functions that would seem to require a firm degree of ego stability and boundary. After Klein had described the fear of annihilation as a primary experience of the infant, in 1946 she described the intricate details of the projections and introjections that she thought were engaged in by the infant in the process of sustaining the ego, developing a sense of identity and protecting himself from the fear of annihilation [*see* Paranoid-schizoid position]. Bick, how-ever, described this in another framework.

The first object: Keeping the personality together and saving it from falling apart in fragments is experienced *passively* as a function performed initially from outside:

> . . . in its most primitive form the parts of the personality are felt to have no binding force amongst themselves and must therefore be held together in a way that is experienced by them passively, by the skin functioning as a boundary.
>
> (Bick, 1968, p. 484)

In fact, Bick drew attention to and expanded an idea of the very earliest moment of the ego's existence. Klein had described the earliest moment and function of the ego in at least three ways: as a projection of the death instinct (Klein, 1932); as an introjection of the good object to form the core of the ego (Klein, 1935, 1946) [*see* Paranoid-schizoid position]; and as a primary splitting of the ego to prevent undue envy (Klein, 1957). Bick suggested that the baby has to struggle for the capacity to introject and that this capacity is an achievement of both infant and mother: 'The stage of primal splitting and idealization of self and object can now be seen to rest on this earlier process of containment of self and object by their respective "skins"' (Bick, 1968, p. 484).

The internal good object, described by Klein as the core of the ego in the paranoid-schizoid and depressive positions, thus has a preceding condition – the capacity to introject at all:

> . . . this internal function of containing the parts of the self is dependent initially on the introjection of an external object experienced as capable of fulfilling this function . . . Until the containing functions have been introjected, a concept of a space within the self cannot arise. Introjection, the construction of an object in an internal space, is therefore impaired.
>
> (Bick, 1968, p. 484)

The first achievement is to win the concept of a space that holds things. This concept is gained in the form of the experience of an object that holds the personality together.

The skin: The infant, in gaining the nipple in his mouth, has an experience of acquiring such an object – an object that closes the hole in the boundary that the mouth seems to represent. Bick assumed that with this first introjection comes the sense of a space into which objects can be introjected. Through her observations of infants, it seemed to Bick that once an infant has introjected such a primary containing object, he identifies it with his skin – or, to put it another way, skin contact stimulates the experience (unconscious phantasy) of an object containing the parts of his personality as much as the nipple in the mouth does. The skin is an extremely important receptor organ in the young infant: '. . . sometimes we think of our skin as our most intimate possession, while sometimes it is merely the envelope of our true self and of what is inside us' (Schilder and Wechsler, 1935, p. 360). In addition, there are nipple 'substitutes':

> The need for a containing object would seem in the infantile unintegrated state to produce a frantic search for an object – a light, a voice, a smell, or other sensual object – which can hold the attention and thereby be experienced, momentarily at least, as holding the parts of the personality together.
>
> (Bick, 1968, p. 484)

Leaking: Bick described occasions in which this first achievement of the ego goes wrong, and she gave to Meltzer and his co-workers with autistic children (Meltzer et al., 1975) a theory of the lack of internal space that is characteristic of autism.

Without an internal object capable of holding the personality together, the infant cannot project *into* an external object to act as a container. Then the personality simply leaks uncontainedly out into a limitless space. The infant experiences a dissolution or annihilation, which Bick specifically related to the horrors of outer space:

> When the baby is born he is in the position of an astronaut who has been shot out into outer space without a space suit . . . The predominant terror of the baby is of falling to pieces or liquefying. One can see this in the infant trembling when the nipple is taken out of his mouth, but also when his clothes are taken off.
>
> (Bick, 1986, p. 296)

Schmideberg, in the first fully reported case of a child analysis, had also noted the important '. . . role of clothing in overcoming paranoid anxiety' (Schmideberg, 1934, p. 259).

Leaking and pathological projective identification: There is a contrast with Bion's hypothesis in which the first object is one that receives primitive communications from the infant, brought about by projective identification [*see* Container/contained; Linking]. Bick described a prior situation in which the capacity to generate phantasies of a containing space is itself acquired from an object. So the communicative form of projective identification would, in Bick's view, depend on the experience of an object that holds the personality together, derived from skin and mouth sensations. Where Bion described the later experiences of an infant attempting to project into a mother who resisted the projections, Bick described not a crescendo of ever more violent projections to force the object to open up and contain, but instead a situation where there is no object to give the idea of a container, and projective identification of all kinds is disabled. There is then a phantasy of complete, formless, total dissolution of identity and existence.

There is not an absolute distinction to be drawn between the two states described by Bion and by Bick, and it seems that Bick regarded the one problem as running into the next, depending on how securely the internal containing object has been established; conversely it may be felt by the infant as a partial skin, one that tends to develop 'holes'.

The second skin: Bick thought there was a specific reaction to which the infant resorted when the containing object was particularly uncertainly established. To develop a method of holding himself together the infant generates omnipotent phantasies that avoid the need for the passive experience of the object:

> Disturbance of the primal skin function can lead to development of a 'second-skin' formation through which dependence on the object is replaced by a pseudo-independence, by the inappropriate use of certain

mental functions, or perhaps innate talents, for the purpose of creating a substitute for this skin container.

(Bick, 1968, p. 484)

Precocious development of speech – providing the sound of his own voice – and a muscular development so that the body is held palpably rigid and 'together' are typical examples. Symington (1983) and Dale (1983), for instance, have shown how important these concepts have become in modern child psychotherapy, and Symington (1985) has described some of these manifestations in an adult patient. Work with severely disturbed children (Bick, 1986) and with autistic children (Meltzer, 1975; Meltzer et al., 1975) has led to the discovery of a peculiar phenomenon of 'sticking to' objects in the absence of spaces to project into. This was called *adhesion* or *adhesive identification* [*see* Adhesive identification].

There is a similarity between the second-skin phenomenon described by Bick and the phenomenon of the 'false self' described by Winnicott (1960). The false self is a set of personality characteristics, often rather rigid, that are experienced by the individual as not really true to himself but are developed to conceal his own lack of sense of a true being. This underlying lack of identity is related to the experience of annihilation [*see* Annihilation]. In Winnicott's view that experience comes from a premature experiencing of an external object as separate. In Bick's view the same experience of annihilation comes from a deficient experience of an external object that can help the infant by holding his personality together. The terms 'second skin' and 'false self' come from quite different theoretical backgrounds and therefore point to different implications for clinical practice.

Bick, E. (1964) 'Notes on infant observation in psycho-analytic training', *Int. J. Psycho-Anal.* 45: 558–566.

—— (1968) 'The experience of the skin in early object relations', *Int. J. Psycho-Anal.* 49: 484–486.

—— (1986) 'Further considerations of the function of the skin in early object relations', *Br. J. Psychother.* 2: 292–299.

Dale, F. (1983) 'The body as bondage', *J. Child Psychother.* 9: 33–44.

Klein, M. (1932) *The Psychoanalysis of Children. The Writings of Melanie Klein*, Vol. 2. London: Hogarth Press.

—— (1935) 'A contribution to the psychogenesis of manic-depressive states', in *The Writings of Melanie Klein*, Vol. 1. London: Hogarth Press, pp. 262–289.

—— (1946) 'Notes on some schizoid mechanisms', in *The Writings of Melanie Klein*, Vol. 3. London: Hogarth Press, pp. 1–24.

—— (1957) 'Envy and gratitude', in *The Writings of Melanie Klein*, Vol. 3. London: Hogarth Press, pp. 176–235.

Meltzer, D. (1975) 'Adhesive identification', *Contemp. Psycho-Anal.* 11: 289–310.

Meltzer, D., Bremner, J., Hoxter, S., Weddell, D. and Wittenberg, I. (1975) *Explorations in Autism*. Strath Tay: Clunie Press.

Schilder, P. and Wechsler, D. (1935) 'What do children know about the interior of the body?', *Int. J. Psycho-Anal.* 16: 355–360.

Schmideberg, M. (1934) 'The play analysis of a three-year-old girl', *Int. J. Psycho-Anal.* 15: 245–264.

Symington, J. (1983) 'Crisis and survival in infancy', *J. Child Psychother.* 9: 25–32.

—— (1985) 'The survival function of primitive omnipotence', *Int. J. Psycho-Anal.* 66: 481–487.

Winnicott, D. W. (1960) 'Ego distortion in terms of true and false self', in *The Maturational Processes and the Facilitating Environment*. London: Hogarth Press, pp. 140–152.

Social defence systems

In the 1940s during the social mobilisation of the British nation for war – and later for peace – there was considerable interest in social psychology and in the possible relevance of psychoanalysis to problems such as officer selection, treatment of war neuroses and resettlement of prisoners of war. A number of analysts became interested in the way in which the discoveries of psychoanalysis manifested themselves in the phenomena of social psychology. These analysts included Wilfred Bion, Harold Bridger, Siegmund Foulkes, Thomas Main, John Rickman and, a little later, Elliott Jaques and Isabel Menzies.

After the war these ideas moved in various directions to create *group analysis* (Pines, 1983, 1985), the *therapeutic community* (Main, 1946, 1977) and a school of *organisational* studies based at the Tavistock Clinic, which in 1948 became the Tavistock Institute of Human Relations (Rice, 1963, 1965; Trist and Emery, 1997; Trist and Murray, 1990, 1993).

The problem of a social psychology based on the concepts of individual psychology is normally that the social group is conceived as if it were an individual. For instance, Freud's early attempt to understand society (Freud, 1913) was as an aggregate of individuals, a sort of super-individual engaged with the phantasies typical of individuals; but he later (Freud, 1921) laid the foundations for understanding the aggregating bonds in individual psychology with social phenomena growing out of them (Gabriel, 1983). Jaques (1953) took up Freud's ideas of the aggregating bonds: '. . . one of the primary cohesive elements binding individuals into institutionalised human association is defence against psychotic anxiety' (Jaques, 1953, p. 4); and he showed how this may be regarded as resulting from identifications based on introjection and projection.

The work of Bion on basic assumptions in groups [*see* Basic assumptions], Elliott Jaques on the Glacier Metal Company, Isabel Menzies on hospital nurses and several studies of group processes in coal mining and other industries were central in the development of the Tavistock Institute. These studies used both the ideas of social psychology and Klein's (1946) views on the defence mechanisms of projection and introjection in conjunction with identification.

Collective defences: Jaques (1953) described the way in which individuals may use social institutions in order to support their own psychic defences, so that these institutional methods are collective forms of defence, which Jaques called *the social defence system.*

Menzies-Lyth (1960) used the idea of the social defence system in describing how certain procedures had been installed in the nursing routines of a hospital that each new recruit had to learn. These procedures defended individuals against the anxieties inherent in the work, but they also frequently undermined the therapeutic goals of the institution – in this case, care of patients.

The idea of unconscious defences against the anxieties aroused in social and work situations has proved to be a fertile application of Kleinian thought (Rice, 1963; Miller and Gwynne, 1973; de Board, 1979; Hinshelwood, 1987; Menzies-Lyth, 1988, 1989). The 'social defence system' is an important notion that demonstrates the insertion of the individual's unconscious phantasies and defence mechanisms into social processes without reducing the latter to individual psychology.

These ideas have continued to develop, for example in reflections on the emotional pressures brought to bear on professional workers in public service settings. This work has been undertaken in settings such as those of organisational consultancy and in applied psychoanalytic studies in departments of several universities. (e.g. Obholzer and Roberts, 1994; Hoggett, 2000; Hinshelwood and Chiesa, 2002; Huffington et al., 2004; Armstrong, 2005; Cooper and Lousada, 2005; Clarke, Hoggett and Thompson, 2006).

What has happened, however, is that the Tavistock Institute has now basically phased itself out of the application of a psychoanalytic emphasis to the understanding of work situations. The psychoanalytic emphasis has been continued more by the Tavistock Clinic Consultancy Service (e.g. by Anton Obholzer and David Armstrong), by other breakaways from the Tavistock Institute, by university departments such as that of Essex, the University of the West of England, The University of East London and University College London.

Armstrong, D. (2005) *Organisations in the Mind: Psychoanalysis, Group Relations and Organisational Consultancy.* London: Tavistock/Karnac.

Clarke, S., Hoggett, P. and Thompson, S. (2006) *Emotion, Politics and Society.* London: Palgrave Macmillan.

Cooper, A. and Lousada, J. (2005) *Borderline Welfare, Feeling and Fear of Feeling in Modern Welfare.* London: Tavistock/Karnac.

de Board, R. (1979) *The Psycho-Analysis of Organizations.* London: Tavistock.

Freud, S. (1913) *Totem and Taboo, S.E. 13.* London: Hogarth Press, pp. 1–162.

—— (1921) 'Group psychology and the analysis of the ego', *S.E. 18.* London: Hogarth Press, pp. 67–143.

Gabriel, Y. (1983) *Freud and Society.* London: Routledge & Kegan Paul.

Hinshelwood, R. D. (1987) *What Happens in Groups.* London: Free Association Books.

—— and Chiesa, M. (2002) *Organisations, Anxieties and Defences.* London: Whurr.

Hoggett, P. (2000) *Emotional Life and the Politics of Welfare.* Basingstoke: Macmillan.

Huffington, C., Halton, W., Armstrong, D. and Pooley, J. (2004) *Working Beneath the Surface. The Emotional Life of Contemporary Organisations.* London: Tavistock/Karnac.

Jaques, E. (1953) 'On the dynamics of social structure', *Hum. Relat.* 6: 3–23.

Main, T. (1946) 'The hospital as a therapeutic institution', *Bull. Menninger Clin.* 19: 66–70.

—— (1977) 'The concept of the therapeutic community: Variations and vicissitudes', in M. Pines (ed.) *The Evolution of Group-Analysis.* London: Routledge & Kegan Paul (1983), pp. 197–217.

Menzies-Lyth, I. (1960) 'The functioning of a social system as a defence against anxiety', *Hum. Relat.* 13: 95–121.

—— (1988) *Containing Anxiety in Institutions.* London: Free Association Books.

—— (1989) *The Dynamics of the Social.* London: Free Association Books.

Miller, E. and Gwynne, G. V. (1973) A *Life Apart.* London: Tavistock.

Obholzer, A. and Roberts, V. (1994) *The Unconscious at Work: Individual and Organisational Stress in the Human Services.* London: Routledge.

Pines, M. (1983) *The Evaluation of Group-Analysis.* London: Routledge & Kegan Paul.

—— (1985) *Bion and Group Psychotherapy.* London: Routledge & Kegan Paul.

Rice, A. K. (1963) *The Enterprise and its Environment.* London: Tavistock.

—— (1965) *Learning for Leadership.* London: Tavistock.

Trist, E. and Emery, H. (1997) *The Social Engagement of Social Science. Vol. 3. The Socio-Ecological Perspective.* Philadelphia: University of Pennsylvania Press.

Trist, E. and Murray H. (1990) *The Social Engagement of Social Science. Vol. 1. The Social-Psychological Perspective.* Philadelphia: University of Pennsylvania Press.

Trist, E. and Murray H. (1993) *The Social Engagement of Social Science. Vol. 2. The Socio-Technical Perspective.* Philadelphia: University of Pennsylvania Press.

Society

Although Kleinian psychoanalysis has been particularly rigorous about focusing on the intrapsychic world and has often been criticised for a neglect of the external world [*see* External world/environment], it has also given rise to two theories about the external world and society, both of which use the concept of projective identification. The first is Elliott Jaques' (1953) theory of social defence systems [*see* Social defence systems] and the second is Bion's (1962a, 1962b) theory of containing [*see* Container/

contained]. In addition, Bion's theory of basic assumption groups [*see* Basic assumptions] has strong leanings towards a Kleinian perspective (Bion, 1961). He wrote his papers on basic assumptions before becoming a trained Kleinian psychoanalyst and he did not pursue the ideas in that form.

Hanna Segal has not developed a particular Kleinian theory about psychoanalysis and society, although her concern about society and her left-wing political views are well known (Segal, 2007a, 2007b) and she founded, together with Moses Laufer, 'Psychoanalysts for the Prevention of Nuclear War'.

Bion, W. (1961) *Experiences in Groups.* London: Tavistock.
—— (1962a) 'A theory of thinking', *Int J. Psycho-Anal.* 43: 306–310.
—— (1962b) *Learning from Experience.* London: Heinemann.
Jaques, E. (1953) 'On the dynamics of social structure', *Hum. Relat.* 6: 3–23.
Segal, H. (2007a) *Yesterday, Today and Tomorrow.* London: Routledge.
—— (2007b) 'Interview with Jacqueline Rose', in *Yesterday, Today and Tomorrow.* London: Routledge, pp. 237–257.

Splitting

'I attribute to the ego from the beginning of life a need and capacity not only to split but also to integrate itself' (Klein, 1958, p. 245). The concept of splitting is central to Klein's theory in which the individual begins life with the developmentally essential task of achieving a binary split between the 'good' and 'bad' aspects of himself and his object in the 'paranoid-schizoid' position; the individual also splits himself in other ways and then moves painfully on to the process of integration in the 'depressive position'.

Background and Freud's use of the idea: Originating in ideas of dissociation in eighteenth-century philosophy, in which the mind was considered to exist in separate parts, Bleuler (1911) uses the term to explain schizophrenia. In *Studies on Hysteria* (Freud and Breuer, 1895), he and Freud refer to what they call 'the splitting of consciousness' (p. 12). However, with the development of his theories of impulse and defence, Freud's main focus becomes repression. He nonetheless retains the idea of a cleavage or split in the personality to which he frequently returns, in particular in his exploration of conflicts in the ego between its different identifications, for example in his papers 'On narcissism: An introduction' (1914) and 'Mourning and melancholia' (1917), both of which precede the introduction of the term 'superego' in 'The ego and the id' (1923). In 1926 Freud suggests an earlier defensive alteration of the ego:

> It may well be that before its sharp cleavage into an ego and an id, and before the formation of a super-ego, the mental apparatus makes use of

different methods of defence from those which it employs after it has reached these stages of organization.

(Freud, 1926d, p. 164)

In 1927, Freud describes a split in the ego between a part of the ego that is aware of, or at least reacting to reality, and another part that disavows reality – the patient both knows and does not know something at the same time. Freud continues to write about splitting:

> The view which postulates that in all psychoses there is a splitting of the ego could not call for so much notice if it did not turn out to apply to other states more like the neuroses and, finally, to the neuroses themselves.
>
> (Freud, 1940a, p. 202)

Freud's final paper on the subject is 'Splitting of the ego in the process of defence' (1940b). This paper and the ideas arising from it form the basis of a book edited by Bokanowski and Lewkowicz (2009). An earlier book by Grotstein (1985) reviews the history of the concept.

Klein's ideas about splitting

Binary splitting into good and bad: This idea, which becomes the essential developmental task of Klein's 1946 'paranoid-schizoid' position, is built up from two overlapping elements:

* *Protective splitting of the object*: Klein's interest in splitting begins right at the start of her career in her first paper in 1921 in which she suggests that the child splits off an unwanted part of his mother into a witch figure in order to preserve the mother that he loves.
* *Binary splitting of self and object*: Klein notes the extreme characteristics in children and in the figures that they imagine, and she describes Erna, a child in treatment, as showing herself as a 'devil and angel' and 'good and wicked princess' (1927, p. 160). In her 1932 book *The Psychoanalysis of Children* Klein spells out the way in which both the object and the self are divided into 'good' and 'bad' and how this serves to protect and preserve the object:

> In dividing its mother into a 'good' mother and a 'bad' one and its father into a 'good' father and a 'bad' one, it attaches the hatred it feels for its object to the 'bad' one or turns away from it while it directs its restorative trends to its 'good' mother and 'good' father and, in phantasy, makes good towards the damage it has done its parent-imagos in its sadistic phantasies.
>
> (Klein, 1932, p. 222)

Splitting as part of an expulsive and destructive activity: In her early work (1926) Klein views the child as filled with sadistic phantasies of attacking his mother, with the result that she is feared as retaliatory. In a precursor to her ideas about the projecting out of the death instinct, Klein considers the phantasied attack to be an expulsion of sadism as well as an attack:

> This defence, in conformity with the degree of sadism, is of a violent character and differs fundamentally from the later mechanism of repression. In relation to the subject's own sadism the defence implies expulsion, whereas in relation to the object it implies destruction.
>
> (Klein, 1930 p. 220)

Splitting and projection as a constructive activity: The idea of expulsion had come up the year before (1929) when Klein had suggested that containing different 'good' and 'bad' versions of the mother causes the child an unbearable tension that can be relieved by his splitting up and projecting out the different aspects of the mother and the id, thereby displacing the conflict into the outside world where it can be worked on.

Splitting and projective identification: Klein finally combines the strands of her thinking about splitting and gives it a central role in the splitting and projective identification of the 'paranoid-schizoid position' (1946). The concept of splitting is now inextricably linked to the fate of the split-off parts and their effect on the object, the ego, the superego and the internal and external object relationships. Klein's view is that the first act of the ego is to split off and project out into the object its destructive impulses and its loving libidinal impulses; the object is correspondingly split into a 'bad' and a 'good' part:

> The vital need to deal with anxiety forces the early ego to develop fundamental mechanisms and defences. The destructive impulse is partly projected outwards (deflection of the death instinct) and, I think, attaches itself to the first external object, the mother's breast.
>
> (Klein, 1946, p. 4)

> It is, however, not only the bad parts of the self which are expelled and projected, but also good parts of the self.
>
> (Klein, 1946, p. 9)

These part-objects, which are now felt to contain or to be the 'good' and 'bad' parts of the self, are introjected into the ego and superego, both of which are correspondingly split and a cycle of projection and introjection ensues. In this paper Klein states with clarity that the object cannot be split without a corresponding split in the ego:

> I believe that the ego is incapable of splitting the object – internal and external – without a corresponding splitting taking place within the ego. Therefore the phantasies and feelings about the state of the internal object vitally influence the structure of the ego.
>
> (Klein, 1946, p. 6)

Klein considers this binary splitting to be essential for development, as without it the infant cannot introject and protect a 'good' object around which its ego can begin to cohere:

> To return to the splitting process which I take to be a precondition for the young infant's relative stability; during the first few months he predominantly keeps the good object apart from the bad one and thus in a fundamental way preserves it – which also means that the security of the ego is enhanced . . . a certain amount of splitting is essential for integration; for it preserves the good object and later on enables the ego to synthesize the two aspects of it.
>
> (Klein, 1957, pp. 191–192)

All of this happens in phantasy with omnipotence, idealisation and denial. The individual believes in the power of his phantasy and when splitting into 'good' and 'bad' he idealises the 'good' object and denies the existence of the 'bad' aspect of the object and the 'bad' experience.

Pathological outcomes of binary splitting: If splitting is extreme or rigidly held, later integration may be hard to achieve. If it is excessive, the ego is weakened and introjection is impaired.

Other varieties of splitting: The ego can be divided along other lines, for example in her 1946 paper Klein writes about a patient who has split off her emotions. In an exploration of this, Bion describes 'destructive attacks on the link between the patient and the environment or between different aspects of the patient's personality' (Bion, 1959, p. 106).

Splitting into small pieces/fragmentation: Building on an earlier idea of oral sadism leading to the fear of a multitude of bad objects, Klein distinguishes binary splitting, which divides the 'good' from the 'bad', from splitting that fragments:

> However, co-existing with this division, there appear to be various processes of splitting . . . concurrently with the greedy and devouring

internalization of the object – first of all the breast – the ego in varying degrees fragments itself and its objects, and in this way achieves a dispersal of the destructive impulses and of internal persecutory anxieties.

(Klein, 1957, p. 191)

The experience of the ego going to pieces in this way is often seen as a manifestation of the death instinct and a significant number of authors describe the presence in their patients of an extreme, unintegrated and unmodified 'bad' internal object, often considered to be a destructive superego, that attacks and fragments the ego and devastates development [*see* Death instinct; Fragmentation; Internal objects; Superego]. Bion draws attention to the effects of fragmentation of the ego [*see* Wilfred Bion; Bizarre objects].

Splitting occurring on different planes or levels: In 1958 Klein makes an addition to her theory and states that not only are objects taken into the ego and the superego but that extreme objects are located in what she calls 'the deep unconscious' where they remain unmodified [*see* Internal objects; Superego]. Early in her work Klein had suggested that objects or part-objects are taken into the ego at different levels or planes according to the stage of development at which they had been introjected. She was not entirely clear about how this works but she seems to picture an internal world that contains a variety of versions of objects that may be more or less extreme or more or less integrated, depending on the level of consciousness and the degree to which they have been modified by experience. Modification seems to depend on the rigidity or fluidity of the borders between the different levels. These ideas are in part continued by Feldman (2009), who gives a clear account of how he sees the versions of object relationships working in practice.

Splitting on the border of the depressive position and when under stress: Klein's theory is that as the individual (infant or patient) develops and strengthens he becomes increasingly able to integrate 'bad' aspects of himself and his objects and gains the capacity of realistic perception. All of this involves experiencing painful feelings of loss and guilt and, if extreme, may drive the individual to retreat back to the defensive binary splitting or fragmentation of the earlier paranoid-schizoid position. Much has been written about the to-and-fro between integration and renewed splitting [*see* Depressive position].

See Bad object; Denial; Good object; Ideal object; Idealisation; Internal objects; Omnipotence; Paranoid-schizoid position; Projective identification

Other later developments

Split between the psychotic and non-psychotic part of the self: In a continuation of Freud's ideas Bion (1957) writes about a split between the psychotic and non-psychotic parts of the self.

Pathological organisations and pathological introjection: Many writers describe stable defensive systems used by patients in order to keep emotionally vulnerable parts of themselves split off and out of contact with the analyst. In some individuals the central defensive manoeuvre involves identification with an extremely powerful (split) part of the object [*see* Pathological organisations; Projective identification; Herbert Rosenfeld].

Bion, W. (1957) 'Differentiation of the psychotic from the non-psychotic personalities', *Int. J. Psycho-Anal.* 38: 266–275.
—— (1959) 'Attacks on linking', *Int. J. Psycho-Anal.* 40: 308–315.
Bleuler, E. (1911) 'Dementia praecox oder die Gruppe der Schizoprenien', in G. Aschaffenburg (ed.) *Handbuch der Psychiatrie*. Leipzig: Breithep & Hartel.
Bokanowski, T. and Lewkowicz, S. (2009) *On Freud's 'Splitting of the Ego In the Process of Defence'*. London: Karnac.
Feldman, M. (2009) *Doubt, Conviction and the Analytic Process*. London: Routledge.
Grotstein, J. (1985) *Splitting and Projective Identification*. New York: Jason Aronson.
Freud, S. (1914) 'On narcissism: An introduction', *S.E. 14*. London: Hogarth Press, pp. 67–102.
—— (1917) 'Mourning and melancholia', *S.E. 14*. London: Hogarth Press, pp. 237–258.
—— (1923) 'The ego and the id', *S.E. 19*. London: Hogarth Press, pp. 3–66.
—— (1926) 'Inhibitions, symptoms and anxiety', *S.E. 20*. London: Hogarth Press, pp. 75–174.
—— (1927) 'Fetishism', *S.E. 21*. London: Hogarth Press, pp. 149–157.
—— (1940a) 'An outline of psycho-analysis', *S.E. 23*. London: Hogarth Press, pp. 139–207.
—— (1940b) 'Splitting of the ego in the process of defence', *S.E. 23*. London: Hogarth Press, pp. 271–278.
—— and Breuer, J. (1895) *Studies on Hysteria. S.E. 2*. London: Hogarth Press.
Klein, M. (1921) 'The development of the child', in *The Writings of Melanie Klein*, Vol. 1. London: Hogarth Press, pp. 1–53.
—— (1926) 'The psychological principles of early analysis', in *The Writings of Melanie Klein*, Vol. 1. London: Hogarth Press, pp. 128–138.
—— (1927) 'Symposium on child analysis', in *The Writings of Melanie Klein*, Vol. 1. London: Hogarth Press, pp. 139–169.
—— (1929) 'Personification in the play of children', in *The Writings of Melanie Klein*, Vol. 1. London: Hogarth Press, pp. 199–209.
—— (1930) 'The importance of symbol formation in the development of the ego', in *The Writings of Melanie Klein*, Vol. 1. London: Hogarth Press, pp. 219–232.

—— (1932) *The Psychoanalysis of Children. The Writings of Melanie Klein*, Vol. 2. London: Hogarth Press.

—— (1946) 'Notes on some schizoid mechanisms', in *The Writings of Melanie Klein*, Vol. 3. London: Hogarth Press, pp. 1–24.

—— (1957) 'Envy and Gratitude', in *The Writings of Melanie Klein*, Vol. 3. London: Hogarth Press, pp. 176–235.

—— (1958) 'On the development of mental functioning', in *The Writings of Melanie Klein*, Vol. 3. London: Hogarth Press, pp. 236–246.

Structure

Freud's models of the mind as a complex structure made up of various parts, each with their own characteristics and in dynamic conflict with each other, were a considerable advance over the undifferentiated notions of the mind as a rational and unitary consciousness. He produced two models of the structure of the mind: first the topographical model of unconscious, preconscious and conscious (Freud, 1915) and later (Freud, 1923) the structural model of id, ego and superego. There is an overlap between the two models and also a new element that reflects Freud's increasing preoccupation with the strength of the unconscious sense of guilt and with the importance of identification in the formation of the self. He introduced the new element of a superego that is separate from and watches over the ego. He linked the superego to the identification by introjection with parental figures, particularly the father. These figures were themselves the repository of id impulses by projection. Following the introduction of the structural model, ego psychology concentrated on the structure of the ego's mechanisms of defence (A. Freud, 1936) and of adaptation (Hartmann, 1939). Klein made a more selective use of aspects of the structural model without any ambition to develop the model as such any further. Her work led her eventually to offer her own views of mental structure in her theory of the two positions.

Klein and Freud's structural model: In her early work Klein (1932) writes with the structural model in mind. She is one of the first analytic theoreticians readily to accept Freud's second drive dualism between the life and death instincts/drives. She later conceptualises the death drive in the way it is experienced by the infant: as a paranoid anxiety of annihilation in relation to a persecuting object. The life instincts fuel the defences sought by the ego for protection. This conceptualisation allows her to give the dualism between the life and death instincts in the id a very direct clinical relevance. But Klein's view of the structure of the personality is more concerned with the way instinctual conflict and the protection sought against primitive anxieties lead to the formation of objects and object relations, which become internalised. These internal objects and object relations populate the internal world as it develops through different structures. Klein's concept of the internal world can be said to be a particular development of the novelty that Freud introduced in his structural theory: the division between the ego and the superego and the importance of identification in the formation of both.

Klein's concept of the internal world incorporates the features of Freud's (1915) systems: hallucinatory wish-fulfilment, primary process thinking and the predominance of psychic reality and phantasy activity. Klein refers to the very concrete nature of objects and object relations in the deeper and inaccessible layers of the unconscious and to the more representational objects in the upper layers [*see* Internal objects; Introjection]. However, it can be said that Klein assumes rather than formally adheres to a topographical conception as such. Hanna Segal (2007, p. 85) suggests that Klein's model of the internal world does not include the id as a topographical structure. Klein's overarching notion of the self includes perceptions, instincts, desires and defences, which are all expressed in object relations. Her notion of self implies a topographical element but Klein does not have a topographical model as such.

The severe superego is an important therapeutic concern. Klein from her early period was preoccupied with the sadistic character of the early superego in children and its effect on ego development. Her notion of the internal world can be described as a conception that places centre-stage the structure of the ego and its internal objects. It is not that Klein does not think in terms of the superego, but she is more interested in exploring the forces that shape the objects that are internalised and their effects on the ego. Thus some introjected objects remain separate from the ego and the relation the ego has with them promotes or inhibits ego development. Other internal objects are more available for the ego to identify with: they can be assimilated and contribute to the growth and integration of the ego. Heimann (1942, 1952) begins to elaborate the structuring of this internal world in terms of the degree of assimilation – or lack of assimilation – of objects into the ego [*see* Assimilation].

Structure in the paranoid-schizoid and depressive positions: Klein provides her model of two structures of the ego and its internal objects. In the paranoid-schizoid position the internal world of ego and objects is split into an idealised and a persecutory world owing, to the dominance of splitting and projective identification. The omnipotently idealised good breast is the root of the later ego-ideal. The internal persecutory breast is the root of the persecutory superego [*see* Superego]. In normal development, omnipotent projections are sufficiently modified so that a less idealised 'good' breast is set up inside the self as a source of reassurance against the internal and external persecutory breast. The 'good' breast becomes part of a benevolent superego and also forms a focal point in the ego that promotes integration (Klein, 1946). Under the fear of annihilation the ego can fragment itself and the object further into minute parts. Excessive fragmentary splitting can lead to very disintegrated psychotic states. In more normal development fragmentation does not dominate and the withdrawal of projections and the identification with the 'good' breast allow the ego to reach a position of whole-object relating.

Entry into the depressive position entails a considerable enlargement of psychic reality and of its complexity. Paranoid anxiety needs to have decreased sufficiently. The ego needs to be sufficiently integrated for there to be a more successfully established internal object that is both loved and hated. The introjected combined parental couple is an oedipal object: the maternal body contains all the sexual processes, fantasised siblings and the father's penis. It is this combined object that is loved and hated, hence the depressive anxiety that the ego cannot protect its loved internal objects. Projective processes have decreased and introjective identification is resorted to as a defence against depressive anxiety. The identification with the good internalised mother who is felt to be injured reinforces the drive to make reparation and to inhibit destructive impulses. The ego cannot develop love for its good objects and an identification with them without having to negotiate a crushing feeling of guilt and despair in relation to them. This central drama in the depressive position is worked through with the help of the manic and obsessional defences and the oedipal positions [*see* Depressive position; Introjection; Oedipus complex].

The process of working-through, which continues throughout life, allows the ego to establish more stable and realistic identifications with the loved parents and other objects inside the self. It becomes possible to experience both their separate existence and their own union as sources of security that mitigate tolerable forms of rivalry and jealousy. As a rule in the course of normal development the superego objects tend to become more fused and integrated. The gap between the ego and superego also diminishes, and so does the gap between these internal objects and external ones, which gives a sense of mental stability [*see* Internal objects; Superego].

For Klein, the mind has two structures of the self and its objects that are never transcended. If the evolution from the paranoid-schizoid (Ps) to the depressive (D) structure is crucial for mental stability, this evolution is never complete. The depressive structure is the more mature one but it is regularly threatened by the paranoid-schizoid structure and functioning. Bion (1963) has suggested that these structures are in a dynamic equilibrium with each other on the model of a chemical equilibrium. A continuous movement between Ps and D takes place so that neither dominates with any degree of completeness or permanence. In Bion's framework regression to Ps functioning involves dispersal and disintegration, whereas

D functioning is more integrative. Bion draws attention to the positive aspects of experiencing and tolerating paranoid-schizoid chaos and disintegration without breaking down (Spillius, 2007). Britton (2001) develops and elaborates further Bion's model of development and regression as a continuous process through life and in any analysis. He also distinguishes regressions to Ps, which are in the service of development, as compared to more pathological regressions, which are versions of both Ps and D that in fact constitute a form of psychic retreat (Steiner, 1993). Developmental gains accrue from more fluid movements from Ps to D over time (Britton, 2001, p. 70).

Klein (1940) had herself pointed out how the ubiquitous situation of loss and mourning in life threatens psychic equilibrium. At the centre of the pain of mourning is the loss of cohesion and harmony between the ego and the internal parents – the internal relation with the loved objects is in peril and chaos prevails. The vengeful and damaged internal parents cause both persecutory and depressive anxieties. Manic triumph is a means of gaining mastery over them. When mania abates, pining and sorrow for the loved internal objects come back and allow for the reinstatement of the loved parents – the re-establishment of cohesive and harmonious relations between the ego and its internal objects. This continuous working-through strengthens the process of introjective identification with loved objects and the ego's integration and stability [*see* Depressive position].

Klein does not think of the two mental structures of the positions with a topographical model in mind. However, Segal (2001, 2007) points out that they are not unrelated to Freud's first and second topographies. She reiterates what Klein had pointed out: In the developmental shift from the paranoid-schizoid to the depressive position, repression takes over from splitting as the leading mechanism of defence. A horizontal splitting of the self into different parts leads to the topographical division between the conscious and the unconscious. Segal also suggests that Bion's model of the container and contained is relevant in this context. Bion (1962) uses the concept of projective identification to build a model in which the infant's inchoate, unorganised beta-elements of experience are projected into the emotionally receptive mother, who transforms them into alpha-elements. The internalisation of the container/contained becomes part of the mental apparatus, which coincides with the shift from paranoid-schizoid to depressive functioning.

Segal emphasises further that Bion saw repression as a contact barrier, a part of the mind in which there is a constant transformation between beta- and alpha-elements. This is where symbolisation happens, so that primitive contents, which Freud called thing-presentations, are transformed into word-presentations to be used by the ego. This allows the person 'continuous contact with his or her unconscious in a way necessary to be in contact with external reality as well' (Segal, 2007, p. 87).

Pathological structures of self and objects: Klein (1946) makes a distinction between the normal paranoid-schizoid structure and processes and the more pathological ones that occur when envy is excessive (Klein, 1957). Klein, aided by Rosenfeld, Segal and Bion in their work with psychotic patients, maps out the severe disturbances caused by envy in the paranoid-schizoid position itself, such as:

- Envious attacks on the goodness of the separate breast/mother, such as robbing and spoiling by violent projective identification, lead to a failure in dichotomous splitting – to confusion between 'good' and 'bad' and also between self and object (Rosenfeld, 1952; Klein, 1957).
- The psychotic part of the personality, driven by excessive envy, develops a hatred of internal and external reality and of all that makes for an awareness of it (Bion, 1957). Excessive fragmentary splitting and violent projective identification mutilate infantile mental functions, imprison the capacity for contact with reality and lead to a hatred of emotional life.
- Envy leads to dread of having destroyed the source of life itself. Klein (1957) spells out in detail the various defences deployed to avoid the unbearable experience of envy. These defences are highly resistant to change and undermine analytic progress.

Pathological narcissism: In his theory Rosenfeld depicts an omnipotent character structure made up of a mad self-idealisation, whereby all the good attributes are possessed by the deluded self, and an idealisation of the organised destructive parts of self assembled into a gang. The gang thrives on a negative superiority achieved through a hatred of object relations and of the dependent self, which seeks and values such relations. These two components of the pathological narcissistic character, built on excessive forms of appropriative and expulsive projective identification, are attempts to defend against the dread caused by envious attacks on the source of life itself. But these defences embody and express the malignant destructiveness they attempt to protect against and have the paradoxical and tragic effect of stunting and imprisoning the sane libidinal self. This fundamental disturbance in the paranoid- schizoid position affects the working-through of both positions and creates the severe distortions in the structure of the self and of its objects seen in psychotic patients and those on the borderline spectrum [*see* Narcissism; Pathological organisations].

Pathological organisations: John Steiner's overarching concept of pathological organisations (1981, 1993) allows for the integration of many important contributions by contemporary Kleinians that emerged in the 1970s and 1980s [*see* Pathological organisations]. These organisations stem from a basic disorder in the paranoid-schizoid position: the collapse of dichotomous splitting owing to excessive destructive tendencies linked to envy and/or trauma, and also excessive fragmentary splitting and projective identification. These organisations are attempts to reorganise this collapse and to manage the psychotic anxieties that ensue (confusion, fragmentation, disintegration) by re-creating a split between bad and protective objects. They do so by assembling the fragmented bits of self and objects into narcissistic organisations, such as the gang or the mafia as described by Rosenfeld. Such organisations masquerade as protective ones by promising shelter from pain and anxiety, but they do so at the cost of keeping a more libidinal part of the self imprisoned and undeveloped. There is often a collusive liaison with a sado-masochistic character between the two parts of the self. The libidinal self is not innocent and it also allows itself to be seduced by the destructive organisation.

The concept of pathological organisations also embodies Henri Rey's notion of the claustro-agoraphobic organisation of the self and objects in the schizoid state (Rey, 1994). There is no safe place for the patient in a schizoid state: he feels claustrophobic inside the object and agoraphobic outside, and ends up in a borderline position. Pathological organisations are conceptualised by Steiner as situated on the border of both the paranoid-schizoid and the depressive positions. They show none of the reversibility and fluidity characteristic of the normal schizoid defences and later of the normal manic and obsessional defences. The patient experiences them as psychic retreats that are ideal and free from pain but also as prisons (Steiner, 1993). However, attempts by the patient to move out of the retreat and to face paranoid-schizoid or depressive anxieties are felt as overwhelmingly threatening (disintegrative panic and unbearable guilt) and the protection of the retreat is sought again. A rigid equilibrium is thereby maintained and proves to be extremely tenacious and resistant to change. Pathological organisations are an attempt to bind an excess of early destructiveness but are themselves extremely destructive. In their severe forms they seriously undermine any emotional development. They help to understand character disorders of various severity across the borderline spectrum in that they reveal the defective structure of a split ego and of pathologically assembled objects that provide a masquerade of identity and integration rather than promote real ego development.

The ego-destructive superego: Bion introduced the term ego-destructive superego (1962) and linked it with failure in containment (1959). Such a development stems from early failure in the container/contained relationship. This is due to the mother being in a state of mind that prevents reverie and the containment of her infant's projections, to the infant's inability to tolerate the mother's capacity, which provokes excessive envy, or to a combination of both. Such failure leads to increasingly forceful and violent projective identification and the re-introjection is effected with similar violence and forcefulness. The object is felt to be incapable of accepting projections and as stripping the infant of all the goodness he brings. The object is experienced as a wilfully misunderstanding object that causes nameless dread. This object is internalised as a pathological superego with severe ego-destructive consequences. It is a superego that systematically denudes and strips, finds fault with everything and enviously asserts 'moral superiority without any morals' (Bion, 1962).

Brenman (1985) has described such an envious, omnipotent and cruel superego, which drove his patient to justify cruelty and avoid guilt by severely narrowing his perception and thinking and by restricting dependency on the object. O'Shaughnessy (1999) also describes such a destructive superego that has the dangerous aim of dissociating the patient, of attacking the link with the object and of producing a guilt that is peculiar because it makes everything worse in contradistinction with conscience or a more integrated superego that leads to constructive and reparative activity. The ego-destructive superego entrenches deep splits in the self and has the pathological effect of stunting the capacity for development [*see* Internal objects; Superego].

Split-off psychosis: Bick (1968) describes the preservation, in the very young infant, of an external rigid 'façade' to the personality. She describes 'second-skin phenomena' [*see* Skin], the purpose of which is to protect the infant from the experience of a catastrophic going-to-pieces or dissolving (Symington, 1983) [*see* Annihilation]. In order to protect himself from the lack of a holding object to which the infant can adequately relate, various methods of muscular or verbal activity provide a form of focusing his attention into an integrated state, whereas this would normally be achieved by the mother's nipple and breast.

Sidney Klein (1980) describes evidence in dreams of hard encapsulated objects that contain split-off psychotic parts of the personality, which may occur even in neurotic patients. The idea of a restricted domain of psychosis, as a separate enclave of omnipotent phantasy in keeping with the subject's wishes to deny a disagreeable reality, had been mentioned early on by Freud (1924, p. 187).

Bick, E. (1968) 'The experience of the skin in early object relations', *Int. J. Psycho-Anal.* 49: 484–486.

Bion, W. (1957) 'Differentiation of the psychotic from the non-psychotic personalities', *Int. J. Psycho-Anal.* 38: 266–275.

—— (1959) 'Attacks on linking', *Int. J. Psycho-Anal.* 40: 308–315.

—— (1962) *Learning from Experience*. London: Heinemann.

—— (1963) *Elements of Psychoanalysis*. London: Heinemann.

Brenman, E. (1985) 'Cruelty and narrow-mindedness', *Int. J. Psycho-Anal.* 66: 273–281.

Britton, R. (2001) 'Beyond the depressive position: Ps (n+1)', in C. Bronstein (ed.)
Kleinian Theory: A Contemporary Perspective. London: Whurr, pp. 63–76.

Freud, A. (1936) *The Ego and the Mechanisms of Defence*. London: Hogarth Press.

Freud, S. (1915) 'The unconscious', *S.E. 14*. London: Hogarth Press, pp. 159–209.

—— (1923) 'The ego and the id', *S.E. 19*. London: Hogarth Press, pp. 3–66.

—— (1924) 'The loss of reality in neurosis and psychosis', *S.E. 19*. London:
Hogarth Press, pp. 183–187.

Hartmann, H. (1939) *Ego Psychology and the Problem of Adaptation* (English
translation, 1958). London: Imago.

Heimann, P. (1942) 'A contribution to the problem of sublimation and its relation
to the process of internalization', *Int. J. Psycho-Anal.* 23: 8–17.

—— (1952) 'Preliminary notes on some defence mechanisms in paranoid states', *Int.
J. Psycho-Anal.* 33: 208–213.

Klein, M. (1932) *The Psychoanalysis of Children. The Writings of Melanie Klein*,
Vol. 2. London: Hogarth Press.

—— (1940) 'Mourning and its relation to manic-depressive states', in *The Writings
of Melanie Klein*, Vol. 1. London: Hogarth Press, pp. 344–369.

—— (1946) 'Notes on some schizoid mechanisms', in *The Writings of Melanie Klein*,
Vol. 3. London: Hogarth Press, pp. 1–24.

—— (1957) 'Envy and gratitude', in *The Writings of Melanie Klein*, Vol. 3. London:
Hogarth Press, pp. 176–235.

Klein, S. (1980) 'Autistic phenomena in neurotic patients', *Int. J. Psycho-Anal.* 61:
395–402.

O'Shaughnessy, E. (1999) 'Relating to the super-ego', *Int. J. Psycho-Anal.* 80:
861–870.

Rey, H. (1994) *Universals of Psychotherapy in the Treatment of Psychotic and
Borderline States*. London: Free Association Books.

Rosenfeld, H. (1952) 'Notes on the psycho-analysis of the super-ego conflict in an
acute schizophrenic patient', *Int. J. Psycho-Anal.* 33: 111–131.

Segal, H. (2001) 'Changing models of the mind', in C. Bronstein (ed.) *Kleinian
Theory: A Contemporary Perspective*. London: Whurr, pp. 157–164.

—— (2007) *Yesterday, Today and Tomorrow*. London: Routledge.

Spillius, E. (2007) 'Kleinian thought: Overview and personal view', in *Encounters
with Melanie Klein: Selected Papers of Elizabeth Spillius*. London: Routledge, pp.
25–64.

Steiner, J. (1981) 'Perverse relationships between parts of the self: A clinical
illustration', *Int. J. Psycho-Anal.* 63: 241–253.

—— (1993) *Psychic Retreats: Pathological Organisations in Psychotic, Neurotic and
Borderline Patients*. London: Routledge.

Symington, J. (1983) 'Crisis and survival in infancy', *J. Child Psychother.* 9: 25–32.

Symbolic equation

In Klein's accounts of her child patients' play, sometimes the child is able to play symbolically without too much anxiety but at other times the symbolic representatives of the archaic objects attract the same anxiety as if the child were relating to the archaic objects directly. This makes sense in the context of Hanna Segal's work on the distinction between 'symbol proper' and 'symbolic equation' [*see* Symbol formation]. In her work with a schizophrenic patient Segal observes:

> . . . there was no distinction between the symbol and the thing symbolized . . . He blushed, stammered, giggled and apologized after bringing a canvas stool. He behaved as if he had offered me an actual faecal stool. It was not merely a symbolic expression of his wish to bring me his stool. He felt that he had actually offered it to me.
>
> (Segal, 1950, p. 104)

In her 1957 paper 'Notes on symbol formation' Segal gives a further example and makes an important distinction:

> Patient A . . . was once asked by his doctor why he had stopped playing the violin since his illness. He replied with some violence, 'Why? Do you expect me to masturbate in public?' Another patient, B, dreamed one night that he and a young girl were playing a violin duet. He had associations to fiddling, masturbating, etc., from which it emerged clearly that the violin represented his genital and playing the violin represented a masturbatory phantasy of a relation with the girl. Here then are two patients who apparently use the same symbols in the same situation: a violin representing the male genital, and playing the violin representing masturbation. The way in which the symbols function, however, is very different. For A the violin had become so completely equated with his genital that to touch it in public became impossible.
>
> (Segal, 1957, pp. 49–50)

Patient A's equation of the object with the thing symbolised was part of a habitual disturbance to his reality that resulted from the use of the concrete, pathological form of projective identification [*see* Projective identification]. The result was that the symbol lost its distinction from the original and attracted the same conflicts and inhibitions as the original. When there is a failure to distinguish between the thing symbolised and the symbol there is:

> . . . a disturbance in the relation between the ego and the object. Parts of the ego and internal objects are projected into an [external] object and identified with it. The differentiation between the self and object is obscured. Since a part of the ego is then confused with the object, the symbol – which is a creation and a function of the ego – becomes, in turn, confused with the object which is symbolized.
>
> (Segal, 1957, p. 53)

The true symbol is recognised as having its own characteristics separate from that which it symbolises, but in the symbolic equation the degree of projection into the new symbolic object means that it remains too close to the original, attracting the same conflicts and inhibitions.

With progress towards the depressive position [*see* Depressive position] whole objects are recognised, internal and external worlds are better distinguished and objects are experienced as separate from the self, having their own qualities rather than being largely coloured by the subject's projections. Symbolic objects can thus be used freely and creatively, without the anxiety associated with their archaic precursors. Omnipotent phantasy possession of the external object is given up and mourned:

> In the symbolic equation the symbol-substitute is felt to *be* the original object . . . is used to deny the absence of the ideal object. . . . The . . . symbol proper . . . is felt to *represent* the object; its own characteristics are recognised, respected and used. It arises . . . when separation from the object, ambivalence, guilt and loss can be experienced and tolerated. The symbol is used not to deny but to overcome loss.
>
> (Segal 1957 p. 395)

Segal, H. (1950) 'Some aspects of the analysis of a schizophrenic', *Int. J. Psycho-Anal.* 31: 268–278; republished in *The Work of Hanna Segal*. New York: Jason Aronson, pp. 101–120.

—— (1957) 'Notes on symbol formation', *Int. J. Psycho-Anal.* 38: 391–397; republished in *The Work of Hanna Segal*. New York: Jason Aronson, pp. 49–65.

Symptom

Klein's main interest is in anxiety and in the object relations behind it; in particular she is interested in the anxiety caused by destructive impulses and wishes. All symptoms for Klein are linked to an underlying object relationship. In 1925, contradicting both Ferenczi (1921) and Abraham (1921), who had regarded the symptom of a tic as a primary narcissistic phenomenon, Klein asserts that its basis is in an object relationship. In her early work she thinks of children as being filled with oedipal jealousy and rage and she reasons that this is the cause of the various symptoms that she observes: for example, inhibited learning and obsessional behaviour are seen as attempts by the child to minimise the damage that he might cause to his objects, and night terrors are thought to be due to fears that the attacked object will retaliate. After adopting Freud's idea of the death instinct in 1932, Klein now thinks of the death instinct as the primary cause of anxiety: the death instinct that is projected out can be experienced as the presence of a 'bad' frightening external object (persecution and paranoia) and the death instinct that remains within or that is introjected in the form of a 'bad' internal object may lead at worst to psychosis and fragmentation of the ego. Obsessional and manic activities are seen by Klein as unsuccessful attempts to deny damage or to repair damage done [*see* Child analysis; Depressive position; Internal objects; Obsessional defences; Paranoia; Persecution; Projective identification; Psychosis; Symbol formation].

Conversion symptoms, hypochondria and psychosomatic illness: Riviere (1952) and Heimann (1952) discuss certain bodily symptoms in the context of narcissism. The relationship with an internal object can reach delusional proportions in which the individual develops bizarre conscious beliefs about his body based on the unconscious phantasies of a malignant object inside. Such a development is based on identifying a part of the body with a 'bad' persecuting object that has been introjected. Meltzer (1987) notes the difference between psychosomatic illness, in which there is actual pathological change in the body itself, and hypochondria and conversion symptoms. Using Bion's ideas, he hypothesises a link between the accumulation of unprocessed sense data and bodily pathology, and suggests that psychosomatic illness occurs at the level of the translation from bodily instinct to mental representation when alpha-function fails [*see* Alpha-function; Hysteria].

Abraham, K. (1921) 'Contribution to a discussion on tic', in *Selected Papers on Psycho-Analysis*. London: Hogarth Press (1927), pp. 323–325.
Ferenczi, S. (1921) 'Psycho-analytic observations on tic', in *Further Contributions to the Theory and Technique of Psycho-Analysis*. London: Hogarth Press, pp. 142–174.
Heimann, P. (1952) 'Certain functions of introjection and projection in early infancy', in M. Klein, P. Heimann, S. Isaacs and J. Riviere (eds) *Developments in Psycho-Analysis*. London: Hogarth Press, pp. 128–168.
Klein, M. (1925) 'A contribution to the psychogenesis of tics', in *The Writings of Melanie Klein*, Vol. 1. London: Hogarth Press, pp. 106–127.
—— (1932) *The Psychoanalysis of Children. The Writings of Melanie Klein*, Vol. 2. London: Hogarth Press.
Meltzer, D. (1987) *Studies in Extended Metapsychology*. Strath Tay: Clunie Press.
Riviere, J. (1952) 'General introduction', in M. Klein, P. Heimann, S. Isaacs and J. Riviere (eds) *Developments in Psycho-Analysis*. London: Hogarth Press, pp. 1–36.

Teeth

The teeth represent the organs of oral sadism [*see* Sadism]. Growing the teeth produces pain in the mouth, which gives rise to the *unconscious phantasy* of persecutors in the mouth biting the infant, who fears retaliatory aggression. The tooth is a terrifying realisation for the infant of a hostile internal (part-) object.

See Internal objects

Thinking and knowledge

Kleinian psychoanalysis has made important contributions concerning thinking, learning, knowledge and the nature of belief.

The epistemophilic instinct: The epistemophilic instinct is for Freud a part-instinct, a part of the libido concerned with voyeurism and exhibitionism, but becomes in Klein's early work a central instinct in its own right. Klein in 'Early stages of the Oedipus conflict' (1928) and 'The importance of symbol formation in the development of the ego' (1930) sees the epistemophilic instinct as exploratory and necessary but also inevitably aggressive, involving phantasies of getting inside the mother to find and often to take over or destroy the riches within – notably mother's babies and father's penis. The inevitable fear of retaliation can then inhibit curiosity and the capacity to learn. In her later work, where love and hate appear in a more balanced way and persecutory and depressive guilt become distinguished, Klein does not mention the epistemophilic instinct as such again. However, ideas about curiosity and exploration implicitly become more complex, with scope for reparative as well as destructive motives. Although Klein does not make thinking and disorders of thought a central theme of her later work, two of her ideas are important starting points of later work on thinking: her work on symbols (Klein, 1930) and her idea about projective identification (Klein, 1946).

Phantasy as hypothesis testing: Segal (1974) in her paper 'Phantasy and other mental processes' describes the process that uses unconscious phantasies as hypotheses to be tested against reality. This leads to discrimination between internal and external reality and lays the foundation for thinking and the use of symbols proper.

Bion's theory of thinking: Bion, in a series of papers and books, extends and uses the idea of projective identification as a central concept in developing a theory of thinking that has had a profound effect on Kleinian psychoanalysis (Bion 1959, 1962a, 1962b, 1963, 1965, 1967, 1970). He frequently acknowledges his debt to Freud's (1911) 'Formulations of the two principles of mental functioning'. In this body of work Bion uses a model for understanding the process of thinking that has proved very influential. One of Bion's starting points is his study of the fractured thinking of psychotic patients. The abnormal way in which they use their mental apparatus leads him to an understanding of normal thinking.

The first part of the model is similar to Segal's idea of phantasy being used as a hypothesis for testing against reality. Bion talks of *'preconceptions'*: pre-existing dispositions in the infant's mind to discover certain things, such as a satisfying breast. Bion also hypothesises an innate grasp of the linking of two objects and the relationship between them, based on the innate expectation of the relationship between mouth and nipple, and between penis and vagina. When the infant encounters a *'realisation'* – something that approximates sufficiently to an inborn expectation, for example of a breast – a *'conception'* is produced. Under good internal and external conditions the temporary absence of the breast can be tolerated and a preconception can mate with a *'negative realisation'* (i.e. an absent breast, a frustration) to become a *'thought'* of a breast:

> Is a 'thought' the same as an absence of a thing? If there is no 'thing', is 'no thing' a thought and is it by virtue of the fact that there is 'no thing' that one recognises that 'it' must be a thought?
>
> (Bion, 1962b, p. 35)

Klein had pointed out that in the paranoid-schizoid position an absent, frustrating object is felt to be a bad object. In Bion's schema, if the infant's capacity for enduring frustration is sufficient, the 'no breast' experience is transformed into a thought, which helps to sustain the infant until the external breast arrives again. This is thus another angle on the depressive position. This development of an ability to think bridges the gap between need and satisfaction and thus makes frustration more tolerable; a benign cycle begins to take shape in the infantile psyche. Gradually, the capacity evolves to think that the bad feeling is occurring because the good object is absent, and may return.

When little or no frustration can be tolerated, however, the 'absent breast' remains a paranoid-schizoid phenomenon – a bad experience fit only for evacuation. Bion writes thus:

> Incapacity for tolerating frustration tips the scale in the direction of evasion of frustration. The result is a significant departure from the events that Freud describes as characteristic of thought in the phase of dominance of the reality principle. What should be a thought, a product of the juxtaposition of preconception and negative realisation, becomes a bad object, indistinguishable from a thing-in-itself, fit only for evacuation. Consequently the development of an apparatus for thinking is disturbed and instead there takes place a hypertrophic development of the apparatus of projective identification. The model I propose for this development is a psyche that operates on the principle that evacuation of a bad breast is synonymous with obtaining sustenance from a good breast.
>
> (Bion, 1962a, pp. 113–114)

There is in addition a 'half way house' where omnipotence and omniscience are substituted for thinking and for learning from experience:

If intolerance of frustration is not so great as to activate the mechanisms of evasion and yet is too great to bear the dominance of the reality principle, the personality develops omnipotence as a substitute for the mating of the preconception, or conception, with the negative realisation. This involves the assumption of omniscience as a substitute for learning from experience by aid of thoughts and thinking. There is therefore no psychic activity to discriminate between true and false. Omniscience substitutes for the discrimination between true and false a dictatorial affirmation that one thing is morally right and the other wrong.

(Bion, 1962a, p. 114)

The other part of Bion's model has come to be called the theory of the *container and contained*. O'Shaughnessy (1981) gives a good concise description of this model in her paper 'W.R Bion's theory of thinking and new techniques in child analysis'. In 'A theory of thinking', Bion (1962a) talks of a 'realistic' or communicative type of projective identification that has an actual affect on the recipient:

As a realistic activity [projective identification] shows itself as behaviour calculated to arouse in the mother feelings of which the infant wishes to be rid. If the infant feels it is dying it can arouse fears that it is dying in the mother. A well-balanced mother can accept these and respond therapeutically: that is to say in a manner that makes the infant feel it is receiving its frightened personality back again but in a form that it can tolerate.

(Bion, 1962a, pp. 114–115)

A mother capable of what Bion calls *reverie* can accept and transform the projected feeling into a tolerable form, which the infant can reintroject. This process of transformation Bion calls *alpha-function* [*see* Alpha-function]. If all goes well the infant re-introjects not only the particular bad thing transformed into something tolerable, but eventually introjects the containing/alpha-function itself, and thus has the beginning of a means within his own mind of tolerating frustration and for thinking. Symbolisation, a 'contact barrier' between conscious and unconscious, dream thoughts and a concept of space and time can all develop. *Beta-function* on the other hand is a means of ridding the mind of stimuli, of abolishing experience rather than transforming it. *Beta-elements* [*see* Beta-elements] are fit only for expulsion from the mind, whereas *alpha-elements* are the raw material for dreaming and thinking.

Problems in this progression may occur on the environmental (maternal) side, when the mother cannot contain the infant's unbearable experiences. The infant will then experience what meaning there is being stripped away by a wilfully misunderstanding object, giving rise to a particular quality of terror known as *nameless dread*. On the other side, in Bion's view, the infant may have such a high degree of innate envy that he cannot tolerate and use the mother's alpha-function. In these circumstances there is a reversal of alpha-function with a retreat from the depressive position to the paranoid-schizoid position and a reversal from verbal representation to more concrete representation and finally bodily states.

Spillius (1988) points out in her introduction to the section on Thinking in *Melanie Klein Today* that the container/contained model of the development of thinking has lessened the divide between emotion and cognition, for it is as much concerned with describing how emotions become meaningful as with describing a model of how the capacity to think develops. Importantly, the external object is an integral part of the system. Bion's formulation shows that the environment is important, and in what way. Spillius comments that:

> Bion did not do as much as he might have to link his three models. It is surely repeated experiences of alternations between positive and negative realisations that encourage the development of thoughts and thinking. And the return of an absent mother gives rise to an important instance, repeated many times in childhood (and in an analysis), of a mother taking in and transforming, or failing to transform, the bad-breast-present experience.
>
> (Spillius, 1988, p. 156)

K and minus K: In *Learning from Experience* Bion (1962b) further elaborates the model of container/contained and thinking as an emotional experience of getting to know oneself or another person, which he designates as 'K', in distinction from the more usual psychoanalytic preoccupations with love (L) and hate (H). He says that K is as essential for psychic health as is food for physical well-being. In other words, K can be seen as a more elaborated form of Klein's epistemophilic instinct. He also describes the evasion of knowing and of truth, which he calls 'minus K'. For Bion (1957) there is a dynamic conflict between two aspects of the mind. On the one hand, 'the psychotic part of the personality', to the fore in psychotics but present to some extent in us all, seeks to evade reality by evacuative projection of any painful or disturbing mental content. The non-pychotic part of the personality can bear and seeks truth. Bion sees truth and an accurate perception of internal and external reality as essential nourishment for the mind.

Bion and the grid: Bion (1965) in *Transformations* develops the idea of the 'grid', an instrument for use after sessions to examine and catalogue the patient's type and level of mental functioning. The horizontal axis of the grid represents the uses to which thoughts may be put; the vertical axis represents growth in sophistication and abstractness.

Roger Money-Kyrle: Money-Kyrle (1968) in 'Cognitive development' expresses Bion's work on the formation of thoughts and symbols in his own particular systematic way:

> The theory of conceptual development has to be extended to include, not only growth in the number and scope of concepts, but also the growth of each single concept through at least three stages: a stage of concrete representation, which strictly speaking is not representational at all, since no distinction is made between the representation and the object or situation represented; a stage of ideographic representation as in dreams; and a final stage of conscious, and predominantly verbal thought.
>
> (Money-Kyrle, 1968, p. 422)

'Concrete representations' are at the level of concrete unconscious phantasies. 'Ideographs' are equivalent to alpha-elements, usable mental contents. The progression through these stages can be linked to movement towards the depressive position. Money-Kyrle is concerned also with the individual's capacity to develop proper orientation in space and time, which he sees at base as an ability to become aware of one's separateness in space and time from the feeding breast coupled with one's dependence on it.

Money-Kyrle (1968, 1971) points out how patients' difficulties are often rooted in unconscious misconceptions and delusions. Our innate propensity to discover the truth meets emotional blocks. Our misconceptions about the primal scene, in particular, are linked to our difficulty in bearing a basic 'fact of life': that we are the product of our parents' intercourse. Other basic facts that are hard to know are our dependence on another to nourish us, and the fact that life is finite.

Henri Rey: Henri Rey (1979, 1994) synthesises ideas of Klein, Bion and Piaget in order to conceptualise the development of the concepts of space and time. Like Bion, Rey approaches his subject through the analysis of psychotic and borderline patients, where space and time are perceived abnormally.

Donald Meltzer: Meltzer, in his own innovative and imaginative thinking, has been greatly influenced by Bion. In 1986 he published a collection of papers (*Studies in Extended Metapsychology*) that extends Bion's work by demonstrating its clinical applications.

Symbolisation, belief and knowledge: Thinking is closely linked to symbol formation. Klein shows, for example in 'Dick' (Klein, 1930), how grossly impaired symbol formation limits intellectual development. Some early work (Klein 1923) also illustrates well the way in which symbolisation, which still functions at a very concrete level, leads to fears about schoolwork and inhibitions in learning. This is easier to make sense of once we have Segal's (1957) distinction between the symbol proper and the symbolic equation [*see* Symbol formation]. Ernest Jones (1916, 1948) points out:

> No knowledge is recognised to be mythological by the person who believes in it . . . this is also true of symbolism. It is only when we disbelieve in their literal and objective reality that we recognise them to be symbols.
>
> (Jones, 1948, p. 132)

Segal (1981) draws attention to the apparent paradox that the freedom to think may be experienced as a limitation of our freedom. She says:

> Freedom of thought – and at best, I think we still have a very limited freedom in that respect – means the freedom to know our own thoughts and that means knowing the unwelcome as well as the welcome, anxious thoughts, those felt as 'bad' or 'mad', as well as constructive thoughts and those felt as 'good' or 'sane'. . . . The freer we are to think . . . the richer our experience. But like all freedoms, it is also felt as a bind in that it makes us feel responsible for our thoughts.
>
> (Segal, 1981, p. 227)

Britton (2008), in an appreciation of Segal's work, comments that he learnt from Hanna Segal that the increase of freedom that psychoanalysis can give comes from knowing what we believe. Until then we are imprisoned by what we believe. He says:

> From Hanna Segal I learnt that we could add to the aphorism that those who do not learn from history are condemned to repeat it, that those who do not recognise that their symbols are symbolic are imprisoned by them. . . . Unless we infuse the world with symbolic significance we find it a meaningless place and unless we invest our acts with symbolic purpose we have no sense of satisfaction or meaning in our lives. . . . If we live unknowingly in a symbolic world we are prisoners of our own minds mistaking our wishes and fears for doom and destiny, our dreams for events, our symbolic objects for the articles of the physical universe and our phantasies for facts. Thus we can only act or react, we cannot think, we are not free to think.
>
> (Britton, 2008)

Britton (1998) in his own paper 'Belief and psychic reality' describes how, when belief is attached to a phantasy or an idea (whether conscious or unconscious), the idea is treated as a fact that then has emotional and behavioural consequences. The realisation that something is belief rather than knowledge is a secondary process that depends on viewing the belief from outside the system of the belief itself. This depends on internal objectivity, an internal third position, which depends in turn upon the internalisation and tolerance of the early Oedipus situation. When a belief fails the test of reality it has to be relinquished and mourned – an important part of working-through in analysis.

Bion, W. (1957) 'Differentiation of the psychotic from the non-psychotic personalities', *Int. J. Psycho-Anal.* 38: 266–275.
—— (1959) 'Attacks on linking', *Int. J. Psycho-Anal.* 40: 308–315.
—— (1962a) 'A theory of thinking', *Int. J. Psycho-Anal.* 43: 306–310; reprinted in *Second Thoughts*. London: Heinemann (1967), pp. 110–119.
—— (1962b) *Learning from Experience*. London: Heinemann.
—— (1963) *Elements of Psychoanalysis*. London: Heinemann.
—— (1965) *Transformations*. London: Heinemann.
—— (1967) 'Notes on memory and desire', *Psychoanal. Forum* 2: 272–280.
—— (1970) *Attention and Interpretation*. London: Heinemann.
Britton, R. (1998) 'Belief and psychic reality', in *Belief and Imagination*. London: Routledge, pp. 8–18.
—— (2008) 'Reflections on some contributions of Hanna Segal to psychoanalytic theory', Lecture given at University College London.
Freud, S. (1911) 'Formulations on the two principles of mental functioning', *S. E.* 12. London: Hogarth Press, pp. 215–226.
Jones, E. (1916) 'The theory of symbolism', *Br. J. Psychol.* 9: 181–229.
—— (1948) 'The theory of symbolism', in *Papers on Psychoanalysis*. London: Maresfield Reprints, pp. 87–144.
Klein, M. (1923) 'The role of the school in the libidinal development of the child', in *The Writings of Melanie Klein*, Vol. 1. London: Hogarth Press, pp. 59–76.
—— (1928) 'Early stages of the Oedipus conflict', in *The Writings of Melanie Klein*, Vol. 1. London: Hogarth Press, pp. 186–198.
—— (1930) 'The importance of symbol formation in the development of the ego', in *The Writings of Melanie Klein*, Vol. 1. London: Hogarth Press, pp. 219–232.
—— (1946) 'Notes on some schizoid mechanisms', in *The Writings of Melanie Klein*, Vol. 3. London: Hogarth Press, pp. 1–24.
Meltzer, D. (1986) *Studies in Extended Metapsychology*. Strath Tay: Clunie Press.
Money-Kyrle, R. (1968) 'Cognitive development', *Int. J. Psycho-Anal.* 49: 691–698; republished in *The Collected Papers of Roger Money-Kyrle*. Strath Tay: Clunie Press (1978), pp. 416–433.
—— (1971) 'The aim of psychoanalysis', *Int. J. Psycho-Anal.* 52: 103–106.
O'Shaughnessy, E. (1981) 'W.R. Bion's theory of thinking and new techniques in child analysis', in E. Spillius (ed.) *Melanie Klein Today*, Vol. 2. London: Routledge (1988), pp. 177–190.
Rey, H. (1979) 'Schizoid phenomena in the borderline', in J. LeBoit and A. Capponi

(eds) *Advances in the Psychotherapy of the Borderline Patient*. New York: Jason Aronson, pp. 449–484.

—— (1994) *Universals of Psychoanalysis in the Treatment of Psychotic and Borderline States*. London: Free Association Books.

Segal, H. (1957) 'Notes on symbol formation', *Int. J. Psycho-Anal.* 38: 391–397.

—— (1974) 'Phantasy and other mental processes', in *The Work of Hanna Segal*. London: Free Association Books, pp. 41–48.

—— (1981) *Delusion and Artistic Creativity and other Psychoanalytic Essays*. New York: Jason Aronson.

Spillius, E. (1988) *Melanie Klein Today* Vol. 1. London: Routledge.

Transference

Transference has been known from the very beginning of psychoanalysis but the way it is understood and its impact on theoretical development have constantly changed. The concept of transference has taken several forms that have unfolded over the course of more than a century: At first it was an untoward event; and then it was the psychoanalyst's ally in overcoming resistances, when hypnotic methods showed themselves to be limited and only transiently beneficial. It could present a form of resistance to analysis by making the working relationship into an emotional one; then it came to be seen as the re-enactment of the past, giving a new clarity to the psychoanalytic reconstruction of the details of childhood experiences, especially traumas. Alternatively, the enactment in the consulting room could be seen as the externalisation of current unconscious phantasy; and, finally, transference can be seen as a complex and sometimes multiply-split set of relationships of the patient with the analyst.

Transference as 'an untoward event': When Breuer first reported to Freud what was termed by them 'an untoward event' (Jones, 1953), it was in fact the realisation that Anna O. had fallen in love with Breuer. Breuer then decided straight away that his method was unethical for a medical practitioner, and he left the field for Freud to struggle on alone. Freud was more circumspect. He looked around the edges of the ethical problem and, being a well-brought-up natural scientist, he adopted the characteristic neutrality to ethical questions. He decided to look at Anna O.'s love as a phenomenon for study. This meant abstaining from any personal satisfaction in the relationship. The love was to be held as a phenomenon that was entirely remote from the actual person of the analyst, and when he found the anxious affections of his other female patients turning towards him in the same way, he refused to accept that it was due to his own personal charms. Thus, transference was looked at anew – from being an untoward and unethical happening it became a phenomenon for study.

Transference as a means of overcoming resistances: At the time when Freud began to relinquish the hypnotic method for gaining access to the patient's unconscious, he had ready to hand the transference as an alternative means for overcoming the resistances to psychoanalytic exploration. Transference at that stage (in the 1890s) was thought of as the positive affection of the patient for the analyst, which the analyst used as if it were a charge of energy [*see* Libido] to set against the resistance to recalling memories from the past. Freud relied on the positive feelings and loyalty of the patient to press him or her to relax the repressive forces.

Transference resistance: Transference was abruptly brought to Freud's attention again by the Dora case. In a general sense, Freud had already realised that the patient could harbour unnaturally hostile feelings towards the analyst, as well as unnaturally positive feelings. However, he delayed acknowledging their importance until Dora broke off her analysis very prematurely and with a good deal of unkindness. Freud was especially affected because he had intended to use the Dora analysis in order to describe an exemplary case that would be a model for future practice. Dora made him swallow his pride and recognise that this had been a model of how *not* to practise – at least a model of how not to deal with transference. Freud's overcoming of his disappointment was only part of the adjustment he had to make.

The importance of the negative transference meant a revision of both his practice of psychoanalysis and of his theories. Freud tended to take two views of this occurrence in the case of Dora. First he regarded the transference, in which the whole analysis was broken off, as a form of resistance against the work of analysis and the recovery of memories and phantasies from the past (Freud, 1912). By engaging in an intensity of feeling towards the analyst the patient was attempting, through seduction or hostility, to thwart the process of understanding the past. Secondly, Freud also thought of the relationship between Dora and himself as an enactment of a specific relationship: it was revenge for her desired lover's lack of interest in her, the desired lover being 'Herr K' and ultimately Dora's father. Unintentionally Freud had discovered the importance of *repetition in the transference* (Freud, 1915), it was no longer a matter of retrieving hazy memories confused by a patient's efforts to keep them repressed.

In spite of this painful lesson in transference, Freud remained, as always, reluctant to give up completely his earlier views. Even today, descriptions of transference sometimes imply that it can be not only a force for therapeutic development but also an expression of forceful and unproductive resistance to analysis.

Enacting unconscious phantasy: Over the years since Freud's work a new meaning has developed concerning the idea of a re-enactment of the past.

This further development has resulted from the work of Klein. Perhaps one of the important factors in her view of transference was the fact that she was working with children, at least one of whom (Rita) was as young as 2 years and 9 months, and therefore at a time when the traumatising events were assumed to be taking place. Thus the re-enactments of children were not from the far-distant past but from their immediate present. The whole of their play was a series of enactments of all kinds of events and relationships. The vivacity and vigour of the re-enactment were astonishing to Klein. What, then, were the children enacting in their play? Clearly children enact not only their actual experiences but also their phantasy life. Klein took this seriously. Play, she thought, was in earnest; it was not just for amusement. It was the child's own way of relating to himself his own worst fears and anxieties as well as his deepest desires. The relationships enacted in the consulting room were expressions of the child's efforts to encompass the experiences and phantasies of his daily life – sometimes rewarding, sometimes traumatic.

Returning to the practice of adult psychoanalysis, this new realisation had a profound effect on both theory and practice. Transference, already regarded as an enactment in the consulting room, was now regarded as a re-enactment of current phantasy experiences. This view of transference as coming out of the here-and-now experiences during the session has been bolstered by the development of, and emphasis upon, the notion of unconscious phantasy [*see* Unconscious phantasy]. The transference is, however, moulded upon the infantile mechanisms with which the patient managed his experiences long ago:

> . . . the patient is bound to deal with his conflicts and anxieties re-experienced towards the analyst by the same methods he used in the past. That is to say, he turns away from the analyst as he attempted to turn away from his primal objects.
>
> (Klein, 1952, p. 55)

The distant 'past' is not the only factor, however, for an individual's methods of managing his anxieties and conflicts may have been influenced by other experiences that have occurred in between the distant 'past' and the current 'present'.

What Klein started was a particular emphasis in looking at the material that patients produced. She focused on the patient's anxieties and on his relationships to his objects in the past and in the present, which she called his 'total situation'. All aspects of a patient's experiences and phantasies should be explored. From the 1940s onwards Klein introduced a further development. Abraham (1919) and subsequently many other analysts pointed to hidden aspects of the patient's relationship to the analyst: usually it is negative aspects that are concealed. Klein could embrace this with her developing theory in the 1940s when she began to understand the importance of splitting. She could show that all material given in the course of free association in an analytic session may show aspects of the immediate transference to the analyst now, even when the material does not refer explicitly to the analyst or even when it apparently consists of childhood memories [*see* Technique]:

> For instance reports of patients about their daily life, relations, and activities not only give an insight into the functioning of the ego, but also reveal – if we explore the unconscious content – the defences against the anxieties stirred up in the transference situation . . . he tries to split the relations to him [the analyst], keeping him either as a good or as a bad figure: he deflects some of the feelings and attitudes experienced towards the analyst on to other people in his current life, and this is part of 'acting out'.
>
> (Klein, 1952, pp. 55–56)

The sequence of associations in the material is really an account of the (unconsciously) splintered set of remnants of the relationship with the analyst, often very immature aspects of that relationship. The task of the analyst is to understand how he is represented in this myriad of conflicting ways, and that they may be brought back together in what Donald Meltzer has described as a 'gathering of the transference' (Meltzer, 1968).

Acting-out in the transference: In Kleinian thinking the term transference has thus gradually come to encompass all aspects of the patient's relationship with the analyst. This emphasis has been particularly important in the work of Betty Joseph [*see* Psychic change; Psychic equilibrium], who has demonstrated that patients use the transference not just for the gaining of satisfaction of their impulses but also for the support of their defensive positions [*see* Acting-out/acting-in]. The patient attempts to 'use us – analysts – to help them with anxiety' (Joseph, 1978, p. 223). Joseph describes the ways, sometimes extremely subtle ways, in which patients attempt 'to draw us into their defensive systems' (Joseph, 1985). Joseph uses Klein's term, 'the total situation' (Joseph, 1985) to characterise the way patients express their conscious and unconscious thoughts and experiences in the transference relationship.

Countertransference: In the course of the historical journey of the concept of 'transference', a somewhat similar journey was traversed by the concept of 'countertransference'. This too started as an interference and something offputting of which the analyst was very wary. Psychoanalysts sheltered behind the idea that they could present a blank screen to their patients because they may actually have been frightened of how much they were stirred by their patients (Fenichel, 1941). However, from about 1950 onwards the idea of the analyst as a blank and mechanical operator fairly quickly fell into disrepute, for two reasons: an analyst cannot, in practice, keep his personality to himself; and the feelings that an analyst discovers in himself in the course his sessions have, if carefully processed, considerable importance in understanding the state of mind of the patient [*see* Counter-transference].

Abraham, K. (1919) 'A particular form of neurotic resistance against the psycho-analytic method', in *Selected Papers on Psychoanalysis*. London: Hogarth Press (1927), pp. 303–311.

Fenichel, O. (1941) *Problems in Psycho-Analytic Practice*. New York: The Psycho-Analytic Quarterly Inc.

Freud, S. (1912) 'The dynamics of transference', *S.E. 12*. London: Hogarth Press, pp. 97–108.

—— (1915) 'Remembering, repeating and working through', *S.E. 14*. London: Hogarth Press, pp. 121–145.

Jones, E. (1953) *The Life and Work of Sigmund Freud*, Vol. 1. London: Hogarth Press.

Joseph, B. (1978) 'Different types of anxiety and their handling in the analytic situation', *Int. J. Psycho-Anal.* 59: 223–228.

—— (1985) 'Transference – the total situation', *Int. J. Psycho-Anal.* 66: 447–454.

Klein, M. (1952) 'The origins of transference'. in *The Writings of Melanie Klein*, Vol. 3. London: Hogarth Press, pp. 48–56.

Meltzer, D. (1968) *The Psycho-Analytic Process*. Strath Tay: Clunie Press.

Treatment alliance

The idea of the treatment alliance, also sometimes called 'therapeutic alli-ance' or 'working alliance', is an important concept in ego psychology and, in England, in the thinking of many Contemporary Freudian analysts. It is rarely used by Kleinians.

The treatment alliance is thought to be anchored in the 'real' or 'non-transference' relationship of patient and analyst, and is concerned with the patient's ability to recognise his need for treatment and his willingness to work constructively with the analyst to achieve self-understanding. The idea of the treatment alliance is not synonymous with the positive transference, which can often include idealisation and denial and may lead to an erotic transference in which the patient evades the work of self-understanding (Freud, 1915). In spite of difficulty in defining the concept of the treatment alliance, the analysts who use the concept find it clinically useful. Joseph Sandler describes the need for the psychoanalyst to attempt to determine at the outset of a patient's analysis whether the patient has the capacity to form an alliance, and whether he can develop sufficient appropriate motivation to build an alliance during the course of analysis to enable him to weather the stresses and strain of treatment. (Sandler, Dare and Holder, 1973).

Betty Joseph has a different view. She says:

> . . . the achieving and developing of such abilities are part of the work of analysis: the fluctuations towards and away from potentially more mature object relations and capacity for curiosity are elements that we are working with all the time and are therefore elements that emerge in the transference as we work, rather than being prerequisites for undertaking or continuing treatment.
>
> (Joseph, 1990)

Freud, S. (1915) 'Observations on transference-love', *SE 12*. London: Hogarth Press, pp. 157–171.

Joseph, B. (1990) 'The treatment alliance and the transference – in children and adults'. Paper given at *The Weekend Conference for English-Speaking Members of European Societies*, 12–14 October.

Sandler, J., Dare, C. and Holder, A. (1973) 'The treatment alliance', in *The Patient and the Analyst*. London: Karnac, pp. 27–36.

The unconscious

Freud's original notion of the unconscious system is one of the few concepts that have remained relatively unchanged in the course of the development of all the schools of psychoanalysis. The unconscious system is a more primitive part of the mind and is active from the beginning of infantile life. It is inaccessible directly to consciousness but becomes manifest in the form of derivatives. Although unknown, it exerts a dominating influence on the life of the person. It is a fact in psychoanalysis that most of mental life is not accessible to the conscious mind (Freud, 1915).

Freud's notion of the unconscious is unique in that, as a system, it has different mental contents, different properties and different modes of functioning than those of the preconscious and conscious systems (Freud, 1915). The dominant mental activity is the hallucinatory fulfilment of repressed instinctual wishes by phantasy or psychic reality. Wishes are fulfilled by primary process, namely condensation and displacement, which Freud explains by using his economic model of the free mobility of unbound cathexes. In the upper systems the energy is bound to mental contents. Freud also refers to another conceptualisation: the unconscious is not ruled by language or by thought identity but instead by perceptual identity. The categories of time and space are disregarded so that mental representations can be substituted for each other on the basis of their perceptual identity (Freud, 1915; Laplanche and Pontalis, 1973). Dreams, symptoms, parapraxes and transference phenomena are distorted enough expressions of the unconscious mind that can make their way to consciousness. The bedrock of the unconscious is primal phantasies, which send out more symbolic derivatives into consciousness (Laplanche and Pontalis, 1973).

Klein and her followers have fully accepted Freud's concept of the unconscious but they have developed the notion of unconscious phantasy in their own way [see Unconscious phantasy]. Another important elaboration and difference lies in Klein's assertion that the infantile mind functions by projection and introjection from the beginning. Whilst these basic processes follow the logic of omnipotent wishful hallucinations, they lead to Klein's central notion of the internal world, which overlaps with Freud's concept of the unconscious but is broader as a concept. It also allows for a greater degree of interaction with the world of external objects through repeated cycles of projection–introjection.

The internal world, largely unconscious, is populated by objects that in the deep unconscious are very concrete and become more representational closer to consciousness [see Internal world]. These objects are in a set of organised and structured relationships with each other according to the logic of the two positions. An unconscious phantasy is a state of activity of one or more of these 'internal' object relations. Isaacs writes that instincts, when active physiologically, become mentally represented as relationships with objects. Thus a somatic sensation becomes elaborated as a mental experience of a relationship with an object that causes the sensation. The object is felt in phantasy to be motivated to cause that sensation and is loved or hated by the ego according to whether the sensation is pleasant or unpleasant. In this way a sensation that hurts becomes a mental representation of a relationship with a 'bad' object that is intending to hurt and damage the ego.

The unconscious is constructed from basic bodily and affective experiences that are elaborated as relationships with objects. The Kleinian concept of the internal world rests on the primacy of phantasy, which is fundamental in setting up internal object relations. Klein eschews Freud's economic model in her metapsychology and instead an object-relations, dynamic model of anxiety and conflict occupies centre stage [see Economic model].

Freud, S. (1915) 'The unconscious', *S.E. 14*. London: Hogarth Press, pp. 159–215.
Laplanche, J. and Pontalis, J.-B. (1973) *The Language of Psycho-Analysis*. London: Hogarth Press.

Unconscious guilt

Freud (1916) drew attention to the strength of the unconscious sense of guilt in characters who commit a crime in order to get punished, and in those whose longed-for success is wrecked once it is achieved. The severity of conscience in more regressed psychopathologies such as obsessional neurosis and melancholia led him to postulate the concept of the superego (1923) as the guilt-provoking agency that plays a central role in character development.

The change to the structural theory led to widespread psychoanalytic interest in guilt and in the need for punishment. After he had formulated the second dualism between the life and death instincts (1919) Freud took a fresh look at masochism (1924) and other analysts soon began examining the issue, for example Glover (1926) and Fenichel (1928). In 'The economic problem of masochism' (1924) Freud refers to moral masochism and to feminine masochism in men, which reveal a masochistic erotic satisfaction in being punished by the sadistic superego. He suggests that primary masochism is present from the beginning of life and the pleasure in being alive is to be constantly re-established against the masochistic tendency towards self-destruction.

Klein makes use of rich material from child analyses to contribute significantly to the theory of unconscious guilt. Child analysis material shows the early occurrence of remorse, regret and guilt and their origins in aggressive and sadistic object relations [*see* Aggression; Superego]. In her 1927 paper Klein confirms Freud's view that criminal *behaviour* is dealt with by an externalisation of the guilt that is felt unconsciously. The external situation reflects the form of the sadistic *internal* attacks on the ego by a harsh superego, represented as hostile internal objects. She confirms that the mechanism behind this is the substitution of an external punishment to alleviate the sadistic and terrifying internal states that provoke complete helplessness. A harsh, external substitute punishment is felt to be less terrifying. It is concrete rather than phantastic and uncontrollable; it can also be evaded by concealment or by discrediting the accuser [*see* Criminality].

This use of Freud's theory of externalising the internal state also becomes important for Klein in understanding the process of play [*see* Technique] and of symbol formation [*see* Symbol formation]. The externalisation is a defence against terrifying internal imagos (unconscious guilt) and at the same time creates the possibility of using symbols (Klein, 1929, 1930). The movement from one object to another, which in this case is from internal objects to external ones, also becomes a cornerstone of her theories of child development (Klein, 1932). When the relationship with one object becomes too hostile, new objects are sought to externalise and to disperse the anxiety: for instance, the movement from mother, who disappoints the infant at weaning and creates a crisis of sadism and persecution, towards a search for a new object, father.

Fenichel, O. (1928) 'The clinical aspect of the need for punishment', *Int. J. Psycho-Anal.* 9: 47–70.

Freud, S. (1916) 'Some character-types met with in psycho-analytic work: III Criminals from a sense of guilt', *S.E. 14*. London: Hogarth Press, pp. 332–333.

—— (1923) 'The ego and the id', *S.E. 19*. London: Hogarth Press, pp. 3–66.

—— (1924) 'The economic problem of masochism', *S.E. 19*. London: Hogarth Press, pp. 157–170.

Glover, E. (1926) 'The neurotic character', *Int. J. Psycho-Anal.* 7: 11–29.

Klein, M. (1927) 'Criminal tendencies in normal children', in *The Writings of Melanie Klein*, Vol. 1. London: Hogarth Press, pp. 170–185.

—— (1929) 'Personification in the play of children', in *The Writings of Melanie Klein*, Vol. 1. London: Hogarth Press, pp. 199–209.

—— (1930) 'The importance of symbol formation in the development of the ego', in *The Writings of Melanie Klein*, Vol. 1. London: Hogarth Press, pp. 219–232.

—— (1932) *The Psychoanalysis of Children. The Writings of Melanie Klein*, Vol. 2. London: Hogarth Press.

Whole object

This is a term implied in Abraham's work on the vicissitudes of the object and its relation to the development of the libido (Abraham, 1924). Abraham's theory of partial objects and 'partial love' is given a radically new meaning by Klein [*see* Part-objects].

The depressive position: The capacity to perceive a person 'as he really is' is an achievement that demands more than the maturing of the perceptual apparatus. The 'good' object that satisfies the infant's needs and the 'bad' object that keeps him waiting come to be recognised as one and the same person, a *whole object* (Klein, 1935) [*see* Depressive position]. It is not just the physical presence but the *emotional reality* of the other that comes to be recognised. The whole object has its own very mixed set of feelings and motives, and in addition the object is recognised as *being able to suffer*, like the subject. Objects are no longer defined by the subject's own feelings and needs.

Love and concern: Abraham describes part-objects as merely those giving gratification to the subject, by satisfying his needs or being treated as a possession, as in the later anal stage; 'true object-love' arises only when the object is appreciated as a whole, with its own objective qualities. Klein, however, thinks that love and gratitude occur from the start. Any object that gratifies enhances gratitude and love, and one that frustrates provokes hate and paranoia. In the case of part-objects there is an abrupt switch between love and hate according to the infant's state of need or satisfaction, but in the depressive position feelings for the object acquire a stability and the new dimension of concern for the object. It is an achievement to reach a capacity for concern because it is painful to the subject – the object's pain is the subject's pain.

See Depressive position; Love; Part-objects

Abraham, K. (1924) 'A short study of the development of the libido', in *Selected Papers in Psycho-Analysis*. London: Hogarth Press (1927), pp. 418–501.
Klein, M. (1935) 'A contribution to the psychogenesis of manic-depressive states', *The Writings of Melanie Klein*, Vol. 1. London: Hogarth Press, pp. 262–289.

Bibliography of Kleinian publications 1920–1989

The place of publication is London unless otherwise indicated.

1920

Klein, M. 'Der Familienroman in Statu Nascendi', *Int. Z. Psychoanal.* 6: 151–155.
Riviere, J. 'Three notes', *Int. J. Psycho-Anal.* 1: 200–203.

1921

Klein, M. 'Eine Kinderentwicklung', *Imago* 7: 251–309; (1923) 'The development of a child', *Int. J. Psycho-Anal.* 4: 419–474.
Rickman, J. 'An unanalysed case: Anal erotism, occupation and illness', *Int. J. Psycho-Anal.* 2: 424–426.

1922

Klein, M. 'Hemmungen und Schwierigkeiten im Pubertätsalter', *Die Neue Erziehung*, Vol. 4; (1975) 'Inhibitions and difficulties at puberty', in *The Writings of Melanie Klein*, Vol. 1. Hogarth Press, pp. 54–58.

1923

Isaacs, S. 'A note on sex differences from a psycho-analytic point of view', *Br. J. Med. Psychol.* 3: 288–308.
Klein, M. 'Die Rolle der Schule für die libidinöse Entwicklung des Kindes', *Int. Z. Psychoanal.* 9: 323–344; (1924) 'The role of the school in the libidinal development of the child', *Int. J. Psycho-Anal.* 5: 312–331.
—— 'Zur Frühanalyse', *Imago* 9: 222–259; (1926) 'Infant analysis', *Int. J. Psycho-Anal.* 7: 31–63.

1924

Riviere, J. 'A castration symbol', *Int. J. Psycho-Anal.* 5: 85.

1925

Klein, M. 'Zur Genese des Tics', *Int. Z. Psychoanal.* 11: 332–349; (1948) 'A contribution to the psychogenesis of tics', in *Contributions to Psycho-Analysis.* Hogarth Press, pp. 117–139.

1926

Klein, M. 'Die Psychologischen Grundlagen der Frühanalyse', *Imago* 12: 365–376; (1926) 'The psychological principles of early analysis', *Int. J. Psycho-Anal.* 8: 25–37.

Rickman, J. 'A psychological factor in the aetiology of descensus uteri, laceration of the perineum and vaginismus', *Int. J. Psycho-Anal.* 7: 363–365; (1926) *Int. Z. Psychoanal.* 12: 513–516.

—— (1926–1927) 'A survey: The development of the psycho-analytical theory of the psychoses', *Br. J. Med. Psychol.* 6: 270–294; 7: 321–374.

1927

Klein, M. 'Criminal tendencies in normal children', *Br. J. Med. Psychol.* 7: 177–192.

—— 'Symposium on child analysis', *Int. J. Psycho-Anal.* 7: 339–370.

Riviere, J. 'Symposium on lay analysis', *Int. J. Psycho-Anal.* 8: 370–377.

Searl, N. M. 'Symposium on lay analysis', *Int. J. Psycho-Anal.* 8: 377–380.

1928

Isaacs, S. 'The mental hygiene of pre-school children', *Br. J. Med. Psychol.* 8: 186–193; republished in *Childhood and After.* Routledge & Kegan Paul (1948), pp. 1–9.

Klein, M. 'Fruhstadien des Odipuskonfliktes', *Int. Z. Psychoanal.* 14: 65–77; (1928) 'Early stages of the Oedipus conflict', *Int. J. Psycho-Anal.* 9: 167–180.

—— 'Notes on "A dream of forensic interest" by D. Bryan', *Int. J. Psycho-Anal.* 9: 255–258.

Money-Kyrle, R. 'The psycho-physical apparatus', *Br. J. Med. Psychol.* 8: 132–142; republished in *The Collected Papers of Roger Money-Kyrle.* Strath Tay: Clunie Press (1978), pp. 16–27.

—— 'Morals and super-men', *Br. J. Med. Psychol.* 8: 277–284; republished in *The Collected Papers of Roger Money-Kyrle.* Strath Tay: Clunie Press (1978), pp. 28–37.

Rickman, J. *Index Psycho-Analyticus 1893–1926.* Hogarth Press.

—— *The Development of the Psycho-Analytical Theory of the Psychoses 1893–1926.* Baillière, Tindall & Cox.

1929

Isaacs, S. 'Privation and guilt', *Int. J. Psycho-Anal.* 10: 335–347; republished in *Childhood and After.* Routledge & Kegan Paul (1948), pp. 10–22.

Klein, M. 'Personification in the play of children', *Int. J. Psycho-Anal.* 19: 193–204; (1929) *Int. Z. Psychoanal.* 15: 171–182.

—— 'Infantile anxiety-situations reflected in a work of art and in the creative impulse', *Int. J. Psycho-Anal.* 10: 436–443; (1931) 'Fruhe Angstsituationen im Spiegel künstlerischer Darstellungen', *Int. Z. Psychoanal.* 17: 497–506.

Riviere, J. 'Womanliness as a masquerade', *Int. J. Psycho-Anal.* 10: 303–313.

Searl, N. M. 'The flight to reality', *Int. J. Psycho-Anal.* 10: 280–291.

—— 'Danger situations of the immature ego', *Int. J. Psycho-Anal.* 10: 423–435.

1930

Klein, M. 'The importance of symbol formation in the development of the ego', *Int. J. Psycho-Anal.* 11: 24–39; (1930) 'Die Bedeutung der Symbolbildung für die Ichentwicklung', *Int. Z. Psychoanal.* 16: 56–72.

—— 'The psychotherapy of the psychoses', *Br. J. Med. Psychol.* 10: 242–244.

Riviere, J. 'Magical regeneration by dancing', *Int. J. Psycho-Anal.* 10: 340.

Schmideberg, M. 'The role of psychotic mechanisms in cultural development', *Int. J. Psycho-Anal.* 11: 387–418.

Searl, N. M. 'The role of ego and libido in development', *Int. J. Psycho-Anal.* 11: 125–149.

Sharpe, E. F. 'Certain aspects of sublimation and delusion', *Int. J. Psycho-Anal.* 11: 12–23.

—— 'The technique of psycho-analysis', *Int. J. Psycho-Anal.* 11: 251–277, 361–386; republished in *Collected Papers in Psycho-Analysis.* Hogarth Press (1950), pp. 9–106.

Strachey, J. 'Some unconscious factors in reading', *Int. J. Psycho-Anal.* 11: 322–331.

1931

Klein, M. 'A contribution to the theory of intellectual inhibition', *Int. J. Psycho-Anal.* 12: 206–218.

Money-Kyrle, R. 'The remote consequences of psycho-analysis on individual, social and instinctive behaviour', *Br. J. Med. Psychol.* 11: 173–193; republished in *The Collected Papers of Roger Money-Kyrle.* Strath Tay: Clunie Press (1978), pp. 57–81.

Schmideberg, M. 'A contribution to the psychology of persecutory ideas and delusions', *Int. J. Psycho-Anal.* 12: 331–367.

1932

Isaacs, S. 'Some notes on the incidence of neurotic difficulties in young children', *Br. J. Educ. Psychol* 2: 71–91, 184–195.

Klein, M. *The Psychoanalysis of Children.* Hogarth Press; (1930) *Die Psychoanalyse des Kindes.* Vienna: Internationaler Psychoanalytischer Verlag.

Rickman, J. 'The psychology of crime', *Br. J. Med. Psychol.* 12: 264–269.

Riviere, J. 'Jealousy as a mechanism of defence', *Int. J. Psycho-Anal.* 13: 414–424.
Searl, N. M. 'A note on depersonalization', *Int. J. Psycho-Anal.* 13: 329–347.

1933

Isaacs, S. *Social Development in Young Children.* Routledge & Kegan Paul.
Klein, M. 'The early development of conscience in the child', in S. Lorand (ed.) *Psychoanalysis Today.* New York: Covici-Friede, pp. 149–162.
Money-Kyrle, R. 'A psycho-analytic study of the voices of Joan of Arc', *Br. J. Med. Psychol.* 13: 63–81; republished in *The Collected Papers of Roger Money-Kyrle.* Strath Tay: Clunie Press (1978), pp. 109–130.
Schmideberg, M. 'Some unconscious mechanisms in pathological sexuality and their relation to normal sexuality', *Int. J. Psycho-Anal.* 14: 225–260.
Searl, N. M. 'The psychology of screaming', *Int. J. Psycho-Anal.* 14: 193–205.
—— 'Play, reality and aggression', *Int. J. Psycho-Anal.* 14: 310–320.
—— 'A note on symbols and early intellectual development', *Int. J. Psycho-Anal.* 14: 391–397.

1934

Isaacs, S. 'Rebellious and defiant children', in *Childhood and After.* Routledge & Kegan Paul (1948), pp. 23–35.
Klein, M. 'On criminality', *Br. J. Med. Psychol.* 14: 312–315.
Middlemore, M. 'The treatment of bewitchment in a puritan community', *Int. J. Psycho-Anal.* 15: 41–58.
Money-Kyrle, R. 'A psychological analysis of the causes of war', *The Listener*; republished in *The Collected Papers of Roger Money-Kyrle.* Strath Tay: Clunie Press (1978), pp. 131–137.
Schmideberg, M. 'The play analysis of a three-year-old girl', *Int J. Psycho-Anal.* 15: 245–264.
Stephen, K. 'Introjection and projection: guilt and rage', *Br. J. Med. Psychol.* 14: 316–331.
Strachey, J. 'The nature of the therapeutic action of psycho-analysis', *Int. J. Psycho-Anal.* 15: 127–159; (1969) *Int. J. Psycho-Anal.* 50: 275–292.

1935

Isaacs, S. 'Bad habits', *Int. J. Psycho-Anal.* 16: 446–454.
—— *The Psychological Aspects of Child Development.* Evans Bros.
—— 'Property and possessiveness', *Br. J. Med Psychol.* 15: 69–78; republished in *Childhood and After.* Routledge & Kegal Paul (1948), pp. 36–46.
Klein, M. 'A contribution to the psychogenesis of manic-depressive states', *Int. J. Psycho-Anal.* 16: 145–174.
Schmideberg, M. 'The psycho-analysis of asocial children', *Int. J. Psycho-Anal.* 16: 22–48; (1932) *Int. Z. Psychoanal.* 18: 474–527.
—— 'Zum Verständnis massenpsychologischer Erscheinungen', *Imago* 21: 445–457.
—— 'The psychological care of the baby', *Mother and Child* 6: 304–308.

Sharpe, E. F. 'Similar and divergent unconscious determinants underlying the sublimation of pure art and pure science', *Int. J. Psycho-Anal.* 16: 186–202; republished in *Collected Papers on Psycho-Analysis*, Hogarth Press (1950), pp. 137–154.

1936

Isaacs, S. 'Personal freedom and family life', *New Era* 17: 238–243.

Isaacs, S., Klein, M., Middlemore, M., Searl, M. and Sharpe, E. *On the Bringing Up of Children* (ed. J. Rickman). Kegan Paul.

Klein, M. 'Weaning', in J. Rickman (ed.) *On the Bringing Up of Children*. Kegan Paul, pp. 31–36.

Rickman, J. (ed.) *On the Bringing Up of Children*. Kegan Paul.

Riviere, J. 'On the genesis of psychical conflict in earliest infancy', *Int. J. Psycho-Anal.* 17: 395–422; republished in M. Klein, P. Heimann, S. Isaacs and J. Riviere (eds) *Developments in Psycho-Analysis*. Hogarth Press (1952), pp. 37–66.

—— 'A contribution to the analysis of the negative therapeutic reaction', *Int. J. Psycho-Anal.* 17: 304–320.

1937

Isaacs, S. *The Educational Value of the Nursery School*. The Nursery School Association; republished in *Childhood and After*. Routledge & Kegan Paul (1948), pp. 47–73.

Klein, M. 'Love, guilt and reparation', in M. Klein and J. Riviere (eds) *Love, Hate and Reparation*. Hogarth Press, pp. 57–91.

Money-Kyrle, R. 'The development of war', *Br. J. Med. Psychol.* 17: 219–236; republished in *The Collected Papers of Roger Money-Kyrle*. Strath Tay: Clunie Press (1978), pp. 138–159.

Rickman, J. 'On "unbearable" ideas and impulses', *Am. J. Psychol.* 50: 248–253.

Riviere, J. 'Hate, greed and aggression', in M. Klein and J. Riviere (eds) *Love, Hate and Reparation*. Hogarth Press, pp. 3–56.

Strachey, J. 'Contribution to a symposium on the theory of the therapeutic results of psycho-analysis', *Int. J. Psycho-Anal.* 18: 139–145.

1938

Isaacs, S. 'Psychology and the school', *New Era* 19: 18–20.

Schmideberg, M. 'Intellectual inhibition and disturbances in eating', *Int. J. Psycho-Anal.* 19: 17–22.

Thorner, H. A. 'The mode of suicide as a manifestation of phantasy', *Br. J. Med. Psychol.* 17: 197–200.

1939

Isaacs, S. 'Modifications of the ego through the work of analysis', in *Childhood and After*. Routledge & Kegan Paul (1948), pp. 89–108.
—— 'Criteria for interpretation', *Int. J. Psycho-Anal.* 20: 148–160; republished in *Childhood and After*. Routledge & Kegan Paul (1948), pp. 109–121.
—— 'A special mechanism in a schizoid boy', *Int. J. Psycho-Anal.* 20: 333–339; republished in *Childhood and After*. Routledge & Kegan Paul (1948), pp. 122–128.
Money-Kyrle, R. *Superstition and Society*. Hogarth Press.
Strachey, J. 'Preliminary notes upon the problem of Akhnaton', *Int. J. Psycho-Anal.* 20: 33–42.

1940

Isaacs, S. 'Temper tantrums in early childhood in their relation to internal objects', *Int. J. Psycho-Anal.* 21: 280–293; republished in *Childhood and After*. Routledge & Kegan Paul (1948), pp. 129–142.
Klein, M. 'Mourning and its relation to manic-depressive states', *Int. J. Psycho-Anal.* 21: 125–153.
Rickman, J. 'On the nature of ugliness and the creative impulse', *Int. J. Psycho-Anal.* 21: 294–313.

1941

Middlemore, M. *The Nursing Couple*. Hamish Hamilton.
Strachey, A. 'A note on the use of the word "internal"', *Int. J. Psycho-Anal.* 22: 37–43.
Winnicott, D. W. 'The observation of infants in a set situation', *Int. J. Psycho-Anal.* 22: 229–249.

1942

Heimann, P. 'A contribution to the problem of sublimation and its relation to processes of internalization', *Int. J. Psycho-Anal.* 23: 8–17.
Klein, M. 'Some psychological considerations', in Waddington et al. (eds) *Science and Ethics*. Allen & Unwin.
Money-Kyrle, R. 'The psychology of propaganda', *Br. J. Med. Psychol.* 42: 82–94; republished in *The Collected Papers of Roger Money-Kyrle*. Strath Tay: Clunie Press (1978), pp. 160–175.

1943

Bion, W. and Rickman, J. 'Intra-group tensions in therapy: Their study as a task of the group', *Lancet* ii, 678–681; republished in *Experiences in Groups*. Tavistock (1961), pp. 11–26.

Isaacs, S. 'An acute psychotic anxiety occurring in a boy of four years', *Int. J. Psycho-Anal.* 24: 13–32; republished in *Childhood and After.* Routledge & Kegan Paul (1948), pp. 143–185.

1944

Milner, M. 'A suicidal symptom in a child of three', *Int. J. Psycho-Anal.* 25: 53–61.

Money-Kyrle, R. 'Towards a common aim: A psycho-analytical contribution to ethics', *Br. J. Med. Psychol.* 20: 105–117; republished in *The Collected Papers of Roger Money-Kyrle.* Strath Tay: Clunie Press (1978), pp. 176–197.

—— 'Some aspects of political ethics from the psycho-analytic point of view', *Int. J. Psycho-Anal.* 25: 166–171.

1945

Isaacs, S. 'Notes on metapsychology as process theory', *Int. J. Psycho-Anal.* 26: 58–62.

—— 'Fatherless children', in P Volkov (ed.) *Fatherless Children.* NEF Monograph No. 2; republished in *Childhood and After.* Routledge & Kegan Paul (1948), pp. 186–207.

—— 'Children in institutions', in *Childhood and After.* Routledge & Kegan Paul (1948), pp. 208–236.

Klein, M. 'The Oedipus complex in the light of early anxieties', *Int. J. Psycho-Anal.* 26: 11–33.

Milner, M. 'Some aspects of phantasy in relation to general psychology', *Int. J. Psycho-Anal.* 26: 143–152.

Riviere, J. 'The bereaved wife', in P. Volkov (ed.) *Fatherless Children.* NEF Monograph No. 2.

Winnicott, D. W. 'Primitive emotional development', *Int. J. Psycho-Anal.* 26: 137–142.

1946

Bion, W. 'The leaderless group project', *Bull. Menninger Clin.* 10: 77–81.

Klein, M. 'Notes on some schizoid mechanisms', *Int. J. Psycho-Anal.* 27: 99–110; republished in M. Klein, P. Heimann, S. Isaacs and J. Riviere (eds) *Developments in Psycho-Analysis.* Hogarth Press (1952), pp. 292–320.

Scott, W. C. M. 'A note on the psychopathology of convulsive phenomena in manic-depressive states', *Int. J. Psycho-Anal.* 27: 152–155.

1947

Money-Kyrle, R. 'Social conflict and the challenge to psychology', *Br. J. Med. Psychol.* 27: 215–221; republished in *The Collected Papers of Roger Money-Kyrle.* Strath Tay: Clunie Press (1978), pp. 198–209.

Rosenfeld, H. 'Analysis of a schizophrenic state with depersonalization', *Int. J. Psycho-Anal.* 28: 130–139; republished in *Psychotic States*. Hogarth Press (1965), pp. 13–33.

Scott, W. C. M. 'On the intense affects encountered in treating a severe manic-depressive disorder', *Int. J. Psycho-Anal.* 28: 139–145.

Stephen, A. 'The superego and other internal objects', *Int. J. Psycho-Anal.* 28: 114–117.

Thorner, H. A. 'The treatment of psychoneurosis in the British Army', *Int. J. Psycho-Anal.* 27: 52–59.

1948

Bion, W. 'Psychiatry in a time of crisis', *Br. J. Med. Psychol.* 21: 81–89.

Isaacs, S. 'On the nature and function of phantasy', *Int. J. Psycho-Anal.* 29: 73–97; republished in M. Klein, P. Heimann, S. Isaacs and J. Riviere (eds) *Developments in Psycho-Analysis*. Hogarth Press (1952), pp. 67–121.

—— *Childhood and After*. Routledge & Kegan Paul.

Joseph, B. 'A technical problem in the treatment of the infant patient', *Int. J. Psycho-Anal.* 29: 58–59.

Klein, M. *Contributions to Psycho-Analysis*. Hogarth Press.

—— 'A contribution to the theory of anxiety and guilt', *Int. J. Psycho-Anal.* 29: 114–123.

Munro, L. 'Analysis of a cartoon in a case of hypochondria', *Int. J. Psycho-Anal.* 29: 53–57.

Scott, W. C. M. 'Some embryological, neurological, psychiatric and psycho-analytic implications of the body schema', *Int. J. Psycho-Anal.* 29: 141–155.

—— 'Notes on the psychopathology of anorexia nervosa', *Br. J. Med. Psychol.* 21: 241–247.

—— 'Some psychodynamic aspects of disturbed perception of time', *Br. J. Med. Psychol.* 21: 111–120.

—— 'A psycho-analytic concept of the origin of depression', *Br. Med. J.* 1: 538–540; republished in M. Klein, P. Heimann and R. Money-Kyrle (eds) *New Directions in Psycho-Analysis*. Tavistock (1955), pp. 39–47.

1949

Heimann, P. 'Some notes on the psycho-analytic concept of introjected objects', *Int. J. Psycho-Anal.* 22: 8–17.

Rosenfeld, H. 'Remarks on the relation of male homosexuality to paranoia, paranoid anxiety and narcissism', *Int. J. Psycho-Anal.* 30: 36–47; republished in *Psychotic States*. Hogarth Press (1965), pp. 34–51.

Scott, W. C. M. 'The "body scheme" in psycho-therapy', *Br. J. Med. Psychol.* 22: 139–150.

Thorner, H. A. 'Notes on a case of male homosexuality', *Int. J. Psycho-Anal.* 30: 31–35.

1950

Bion, W. 'The imaginary twin', in *Second Thoughts*. Heinemann (1967), pp. 3–22.

Heimann, P. 'On counter-transference', *Int. J. Psycho-Anal.* 31: 81–84.

Klein, M. 'On the criteria for the termination of a psycho-analysis', *Int. J. Psycho-Anal.* 31: 78–80, 204.

Money-Kyrle, R. 'Varieties of group formation', *Psychoanal. Social Sci.* 2: 313–330; republished in *The Collected Papers of Roger Money-Kyrle*. Strath Tay: Clunie Press (1978), pp. 210–228.

Rosenfeld, H. 'Note on the psychopathology of confusional states in chronic schizophrenia', *Int. J. Psycho-Anal.* 31: 132–137; republished in *Psychotic States*. Hogarth Press (1965), pp. 52–62.

Segal, H. 'Some aspects of the analysis of a schizophrenic', *Int. J. Psycho-Anal.* 31: 268–278; republished in *The Work of Hanna Segal*. New York: Jason Aronson (1981), pp. 101–120; and in E. Spillius (ed.) *Melanie Klein Today*, Vol. 2. Routledge (1988), pp. 96–114.

Sharpe, E. F. *Collected Papers in Psycho-Analysis*. Hogarth Press.

Winnicott, D. W. 'Hate in the counter-transference', *Int. J. Psycho-Anal.* 30: 69–74.

1951

Jaques, E. *The Changing Culture of a Factory*. Routledge & Kegan Paul.

Klein, S. 'Contribution to a symposium on group therapy', *Br. J. Med. Psychol.* 24: 223–228.

Langer, M. *Maternidad y Sexo*. Buenos Aires: Editorial Nova.

Money-Kyrle, R. *Psycho-Analysis and Politics*. Duckworth.

—— 'Some aspects of state and character in Germany', in G. Wilbur and W. Munsterberger (eds) *Psycho-Analysis and Culture*. New York: International Universities Press, pp. 280–292; republished in *The Collected Papers of Roger Money-Kyrle*. Strath Tay: Clunie Press (1978), pp. 229–244.

1952

Bion, W. 'Group dynamics: a review', *Int. J. Psycho-Anal.* 33: 235–247; republished in M. Klein, P. Heimann and R. Money-Kyrle (eds) *New Directions in Psycho-Analysis*. Tavistock (1955), pp. 440–477; and in *Experiences in Groups*. Tavistock (1961), pp. 141–191.

Evans, G. 'Early anxiety situations in the analysis of a boy in the latency period', *Int. J. Psycho-Anal.* 33: 93–110; republished in M. Klein, P. Heimann and R. Money-Kyrle (eds) *New Directions in Psycho-Analysis*. Tavistock (1955), pp. 48–81.

Heimann, P. 'Certain functions of projection and introjection in early infancy', in M. Klein, P. Heimann, S. Isaacs and J. Riviere (eds) *Developments in Psycho-Analysis*. Hogarth Press, pp. 122–168.

—— 'Notes on the theory of the life and death instincts', in M. Klein, P. Heimann, S. Isaacs and J. Riviere (eds) *Developments in Psycho-Analysis*. Hogarth Press, pp. 321–337.

—— 'A contribution to the re-evaluation of the Oedipus complex – the early stages', *Int. J. Psycho-Anal.* 33: 84–93; republished in M. Klein, P. Heimann and R. Money-Kyrle (eds) *New Directions in Psycho-Analysis.* Tavistock (1955), pp. 23–38.

—— 'Preliminary notes on some defence mechanisms in paranoid states', *Int. J. Psycho-Anal.* 33: 208–213; republished as 'A combination of defence mechanisms in paranoid states', in M. Klein, P. Heimann and R. Money-Kyrle (eds) *New Directions in Psycho-Analysis.* Tavistock (1955), pp. 240–265.

—— and Isaacs, S. 'Regression', in M. Klein, P. Heimann, S. Isaacs and J. Riviere (eds) *Developments in Psycho-Analysis.* Hogarth Press, pp. 169–197.

Klein, M. 'Some theoretical conclusions regarding the emotional life of the infant', in M. Klein, P. Heimann, S. Isaacs and J. Riviere (eds) *Developments in Psycho-Analysis.* Hogarth Press, pp. 198–236.

—— 'On observing the behaviour of young infants', in M. Klein, P. Heimann, S. Isaacs and J. Riviere (eds) *Developments in Psycho-Analysis.* Hogarth Press, pp. 237–270.

—— 'The origins of transference', *Int. J. Psycho-Anal.* 33: 433–438.

—— 'The mutual influences in the development of the ego and the id', *Psychoanal. Study Child* 7: 51–53.

—— Heimann, P., Isaacs, S. and Riviere, J. *Developments in Psycho-Analysis.* Hogarth Press.

Milner, M. 'Aspects of symbolism in comprehension of the not-self', *Int. J. Psycho-Anal.* 34: 181–195; republished as 'The role of illusion in symbol formation', in M. Klein, P. Heimann and R. Money-Kyrle (eds) *New Directions in Psycho-Analysis.* Tavistock (1955), pp. 82–108.

Money-Kyrle, R. 'Psycho-analysis and ethics', *Int. J. Psycho-Anal.* 33: 225–234; republished in M. Klein, P. Heimann and R. Money-Kyrle (eds) *New Directions in Psycho-Analysis.* Tavistock (1955), pp. 421–440; and in *The Collected Papers of Roger Money-Kyrle.* Strath Tay: Clunie Press (1978), pp. 264–284.

Munro, L. 'Clinical notes on internalization and identification', *Int. J. Psycho-Anal.* 33: 132–143.

Riviere, J. 'General introduction', in M. Klein, P. Heimann, S. Isaacs and J. Riviere (eds) *Developments in Psycho-Analysis.* Hogarth Press, pp. 1–36.

—— 'The unconscious phantasy of an inner world reflected in examples from English literature', *Int. J. Psycho-Anal.* 33: 160–172; republished in M. Klein, P. Heimann and R. Money-Kyrle (eds) *New Directions in Psycho-Analysis.* Tavistock (1955), pp. 346–369.

—— 'The inner world in Ibsen's *Master-Builder*', *Int. J. Psycho-Anal.* 33: 173–180; republished in M. Klein, P. Heimann and R. Money-Kyrle (eds) *New Directions in Psycho-Analysis.* Tavistock (1955), pp. 370–383.

Rosenfeld, H. 'Notes on the psycho-analysis of the superego conflict in an acute catatonic patient', *Int. J. Psycho-Anal.* 33: 111–131; republished in M. Klein, P. Heimann and R. Money-Kyrle (eds) *New Directions in Psycho-Analysis.* Tavistock (1955), pp. 180–219; and in *Psychotic States.* Hogarth Press (1965), pp. 63–103; and in E. Spillius (ed.) *Melanie Klein Today*, Vol. 1. Routledge, pp. 14–51.

—— 'Transference-phenomena and transference-analysis in an acute catatonic schizophrenic patient', *Int. J. Psycho-Anal.* 33: 457–464; republished in *Psychotic States.* Hogarth Press (1965), pp. 104–116.

Sandford, B. 'An obsessional man's need to be kept', *Int. J. Psycho-Anal.* 33: 144–152; republished in M. Klein, P. Heimann and R. Money-Kyrle (eds) *New Directions in Psycho-Analysis.* Tavistock (1955), pp. 266–281.

—— 'Some psychotherapeutic work in maternity and child welfare clinics', *Br. J. Med. Psychol.* 25: 2–15.

Segal, H. 'A psycho-analytic approach to aesthetics', *Int. J. Psycho-Anal.* 33: 196–207; republished in M. Klein, P. Heimann and R. Money-Kyrle (eds) *New Directions in Psycho-Analysis.* Tavistock (1955), pp. 384–407; and in *The Work of Hanna Segal.* New York: Jason Aronson (1981), pp. 185–206.

Thorner, H. A. 'Examination anxiety without examination', *Int. J. Psycho-Anal.* 33: 153–159; republished as 'Three defences against inner persecution', in M. Klein, P. Heimann and R. Money-Kyrle (eds) *New Directions in Psycho-Analysis.* Tavistock (1955), pp. 384–407.

—— 'The criteria for progress in a patient during analysis', *Int. J. Psycho-Anal.* 33: 479–484.

1953

Davidson, A. and Fay, J. *Phantasy in Childhood.* Routledge & Kegan Paul.

Garma, A. 'The internalized mother as harmful food in peptic ulcer patients', *Int. J. Psycho-Anal.* 34: 102–110.

Jaques, E. 'On the dynamics of social structure', *Hum. Relat.* 6: 10–23; republished as 'The social system as a defence against persecutory and depressive anxiety', in M. Klein, P. Heimann and R. Money-Kyrle (eds) *New Directions in Psycho-Analysis.* Tavistock (1955), pp. 478–498.

Money-Kyrle, R. *Toward a Rational Attitude to Crime.* The Howard League; republished in *The Collected Papers of Roger Money-Kyrle.* Strath Tay: Clunie Press (1978), pp. 245–252.

Racker, H. 'A contribution to the problem of counter-transference', *Int. J. Psycho-Anal.* 34: 313–324; republished as 'The countertransference neurosis', in H. Racker (ed.) *Transference and Counter-Transference.* Hogarth Press (1968), pp. 105–126.

Segal, H. 'A necrophilic phantasy', *Int. J. Psycho-Anal.* 34: 98–101; republished in *The Work of Hanna Segal.* New York: Jason Aronson (1981), pp. 165–171.

1954

Bion, W. 'Notes on the theory of schizophrenia', *Int. J. Psycho-Anal.* 35: 113–118; expanded as 'Language and the schizophrenic', in M. Klein, P. Heimann and R. Money-Kyrle (eds) *New Directions in Psycho-Analysis.* Tavistock (1955), pp. 220–239; and republished in *Second Thoughts.* Heinemann (1967), pp. 23–35.

Heimann, P. 'Problems of the training analysis', *Int. J. Psycho-Anal.* 35: 163–168.

Hunter, D. 'Object relation changes in the analysis of fetishism', *Int. J. Psycho-Anal.* 35: 302–312.

Munro, L. 'Steps in ego-integration observed in play analysis', *Int. J. Psycho-Anal.*

35: 202–205; republished in M. Klein, P. Heimann and R. Money-Kyrle (eds) *New Directions in Psycho-Analysis*. Tavistock (1955), pp. 109–139.

Racker, H. 'Notes. on the theory of transference', *Psychoanal. Q.* 23: 78–86; republished in *Transference and Counter-Transference*. Hogarth Press (1968), pp. 71–78.

—— 'On the confusion between mania and health', *Samiska* 8: 42–46; republished as 'Psycho-analytic technique and the analyst's unconscious mania', in H. Racker (ed.) *Transference and Counter-Transference*. Hogarth Press (1968), pp. 181–185.

Rosenfeld, H. 'Considerations regarding the psycho-analytic approach to acute and chronic schizophrenia', *Int. J. Psycho-Anal.* 35: 138–140; republished in *Psychotic States*. Hogarth Press (1965), pp. 117–127.

Segal, H. 'A note on schizoid mechanisms underlying phobia formation', *Int. J. Psycho-Anal.* 35: 238–241; republished in *The Work of Hanna Segal*. New York: Jason Aronson (1981), pp. 137–144.

1955

Bion, W. 'Language and the schizophrenic', in M. Klein, P. Heimann and R. Money-Kyrle (eds) *New Directions in Psycho-Analysis*. Tavistock, pp. 220–239.

Klein, M. 'The psycho-analytic play technique: Its history and significance', in M. Klein, P. Heimann and R. Money-Kyrle (eds) *New Directions in Psycho-Analysis*. Tavistock, pp. 3–22.

—— 'On identification', in M. Klein, P. Heimann and R. Money-Kyrle (eds) *New Directions in Psycho-Analysis*. Tavistock, pp. 309–345.

——, Heimann, P. and Money-Kyrle, R. *New Directions in Psycho-Analysis*. Tavistock.

Money-Kyrle, R. 'An inconclusive contribution to the theory of the death instinct', in M. Klein, P. Heimann and R. Money-Kyrle (eds) *New Directions in Psycho-Analysis*. Tavistock, pp. 499–509.

Rodrigue, E. 'The analysis of a three-year-old mute schizophrenic', in M. Klein, P. Heimann and R. Money-Kyrle (eds) *New Directions in Psycho-Analysis*. Tavistock, pp. 140–179.

—— 'Notes on menstruation', *Int. J. Psycho-Anal.* 36: 328–334.

Stokes, A. 'Form in art', in M. Klein, P. Heimann and R. Money-Kyrle (eds) *New Directions in Psycho-Analysis*. Tavistock, pp. 406–420.

1956

Bion, W. 'Development of schizophrenic thought', *Int. J. Psycho-Anal.* 37: 344–346; republished in *Second Thoughts*. Heinemann (1967), pp. 36–43.

Heimann, P. 'Dynamics of transference interpretations', *Int. J. Psycho-Anal.* 37: 303–310.

Jaques, E. *Measurement of Responsibility*. Tavistock.

Money-Kyrle, R. 'The world of the unconscious and the world of common sense', *Br. J. Philos. Sci.* 7: 86–96; republished in *The Collected Papers of Roger Money-Kyrle*. Strath Tay: Clunie Press (1978), pp. 318–329; and in E. Spillius (ed.) *Melanie Klein Today*, Vol. 2. Routledge (1988), pp. 22–33.

—— 'Normal counter-transference and some of its deviations', *Int. J. Psycho-Anal.* 37: 360–366; republished in *The Collected Papers of Roger Money-Kyrle*. Strath Tay: Clunie Press (1978), pp. 330–342.

Rodrigue, E. 'Notes on symbolism', *Int. J. Psycho-Anal.* 37: 147–158.

Segal, H. 'Depression in the schizophrenic', *Int. J. Psycho-Anal.* 37: 339–343; republished in *The Work of Hanna Segal*. New York: Jason Aronson (1981), pp. 121–130; and in E. Spillius (ed.) *Melanie Klein Today*, Vol. 1. Routledge (1988), pp. 52–60.

1957

Bion, W. 'Differentiation of the psychotic from the non-psychotic personalities', *Int. J. Psycho-Anal.* 38: 266–275; republished in *Second Thoughts*. Heinemann (1967), pp. 43–64; and in E. Spillius (ed.) *Melanie Klein Today*, Vol. 1. Routledge (1988), pp. 61–78.

Klein, M. *Envy and Gratitude*. Tavistock.

Racker, H. 'A contribution to the problem of psychopathological stratification', *Int. J. Psycho-Anal.* 38: 223–239; republished as 'The meanings and uses of counter-transference' in *Transference and Counter-Transference*. Hogarth Press (1968), pp. 127–173.

—— 'Analysis of transference through the patient's relations with the interpretation', in *Transference and Counter-Transference*. Hogarth Press (1968), pp. 79–104.

Segal, H. 'Notes on symbol formation', *Int. J. Psycho-Anal.* 38: 391–397; republished in *The Work of Hanna Segal*. New York: Jason Aronson (1981), pp. 49–64; and in E. Spillius (ed.) *Melanie Klein Today*, Vol. 1. Routledge (1988), pp. 87–101.

Strachey, A. *The Unconscious Motives of War*. George Allen & Unwin.

1958

Bion, W. 'On hallucination', *Int. J. Psycho-Anal.* 39: 144–146; republished in *Second Thoughts*. Heinemann (1967), pp. 65–85.

—— 'On arrogance', *Int. J. Psycho-Anal.* 39: 341–349; republished in *Second Thoughts*. Heinemann (1967), pp. 86–93.

Garma, A. 'Peptic ulcer and pseudo-peptic ulcer', *Int. J. Psycho-Anal.* 39: 104–107.

Jaques, E. 'Psycho-analysis and the current economic crisis', in J. Sutherland (ed.) *Psycho-Analysis and Contemporary Thought*. Hogarth Press, pp. 125–144.

Klein, M. 'On the development of mental functioning', *Int. J. Psycho-Anal.* 39: 84–90.

Langer, M. 'Sterility and envy', *Int. J. Psycho-Anal.* 39: 139–143.

Money-Kyrle, R. 'Psycho-analysis and philosophy', in J. Sutherland (ed.) *Psycho-Analysis and Contemporary Thought*. Hogarth Press, pp. 102–124; republished in *The Collected Papers of Roger Money-Kyrle*. Strath Tay: Clunie Press (1978), pp. 297–317.

—— 'On the process of psycho-analytical inference', *Int. J. Psycho-Anal.* 59: 129–133; republished in *The Collected Papers of Roger Money-Kyrle*. Strath Tay: Clunie Press (1978), pp. 343–352.

Pichon-Riviere, A. 'Dentition, walking and speech in relation to the depressive position', *Int. J. Psycho-Anal.* 39: 167–171.

Racker, H. 'Psycho-analytic technique', in *Transference and Counter-Transference*. Hogarth Press (1968), pp. 6–22.

—— 'Classical and present techniques in psycho-analysis', in *Transference and Counter-Transference*. Hogarth Press (1968), pp. 23–70.

—— 'Psycho-analytic technique and the analyst's unconscious masochism', *Psychoanal. Q.* 27: 555–562; republished in *Transference and Counter-Transference*. Hogarth Press (1968), pp. 174–180.

—— 'Counterresistance and interpretation', *J. Am. Psychoanal. Assoc.* 6: 215–221; republished in *Transference and Counter-Transference*. Hogarth Press (1968), pp. 186–192.

Riviere, J. 'A character trait of Freud's', in J. Sutherland (ed.) *Psycho-Analysis and Contemporary Thought*. Hogarth Press, pp. 145–149; reprinted in A. Hughes (ed.) *The Inner World and Joan Riviere*. Karnac (1991), pp. 350–354.

Rosenfeld, H. 'Some observations on the psychopathology of hypochondriacal states', *Int. J. Psycho-Anal.* 39: 121–128.

—— 'Contribution to the discussion on variations in classical technique', *Int. J. Psycho-Anal.* 39: 238–239.

—— 'Discussion on ego distortion', *Int. J. Psycho-Anal.* 39: 274–275.

Segal, H. 'Fear of death: Notes on the analysis of an old man', *Int. J. Psycho-Anal.* 39: 187–191; republished in *The Work of Hanna Segal*. New York: Jason Aronson (1981), pp. 173–182.

1959

Bion, W. 'Attacks on linking', *Int. J. Psycho-Anal.* 40: 308–315; republished in *Second Thoughts*. Heinemann (1967), pp. 93–109; and in E. Spillius (ed.) *Melanie Klein Today*, Vol. 1. Routledge (1988), pp. 87–101.

Heimann, P. 'Bemerkungen zur Sublimierung', *Psyche* 13: 397–414.

Joseph, B. 'An aspect of the repetition compulsion', *Int. J. Psycho-Anal.* 40: 213–222; republished in *Psychic Equilibrium and Psychic Change*. Routledge (1989), pp. 16–33.

Klein, M. 'Our adult world and its roots in infancy', *Hum. Relat.* 12: 291–303; republished in 'Envy and gratitude', in *The Writings of Menalie Klein*, Vol. 3. Hogarth Press, pp. 247–263.

Rosenfeld, H. 'An investigation into the psycho-analytic theory of depression', *Int. J. Psycho-Anal.* 40: 105–129.

Taylor, J. N. 'A note on the splitting of interpretations', *Int. J. Psycho-Anal.* 40: 295–296.

1960

Jaques, E. 'Disturbances in the capacity to work', *Int. J. Psycho-Anal.* 41: 357–367.

Joseph, B. 'Some characteristics of the psychopathic personality', *Int. J. Psycho-Anal.* 41: 526–531; republished in *Psychic Equilibrium and Psychic Change.* Routledge (1989), pp. 34–43.

Klein, M. 'On mental health', *Br. J. Med. Psychol.* 40: 237–241.

—— *Narrative of a Child Analysis.* Hogarth Press (1961).

—— *Our Adult World and Other Essays.* Heinemann (1963).

—— 'Some reflections on the Oresteia', in *Our Adult World and Other Essays.* Heinemann (1963), pp. 23–54.

—— 'On the sense of loneliness', in *Our Adult World and Other Essays.* Heinemann (1963), pp. 99–116.

Menzies-Lyth, I. 'The functioning of a social system as a defence against anxiety', *Hum. Relat.* 11: 95–121; republished as Tavistock Pamphlet No. 3. Tavistock Institute of Human Relations (1970); and in *Containing Anxiety in Institutions: Selected Essays*, Vol. 1. Free Association Books (1988), pp. 43–85.

Money-Kyrle, R. 'On prejudice – a psycho-analytical approach', *Br. J. Med. Psychol.* 33: 205–209; republished in *The Collected Papers of Roger Money-Kyrle.* Strath Tay: Clunie Press (1978), pp. 353–360.

Racker, H. 'A study of some early conflicts through their return in the patient's relation with the interpretation', *Int. J. Psycho-Anal.* 41: 47–58.

Rosenfeld, H. 'A note on the precipitating factor in depressive illness', *Int. J. Psycho-Anal.* 41: 512–513.

—— 'On drug addiction', *Int. J. Psycho-Anal.* 41: 467–475.

Soares de Souza, D. 'Annihilation and reconstruction of object-relationships in a schizophrenic girl', *Int. J. Psycho-Anal.* 41: 554–558.

Stokes, A. 'A game that must be lost', *Int. J. Psycho-Anal.* 41: 70–76.

Williams, H. W. 'A psycho-analytic approach to the treatment of the murderer', *Int. J. Psycho-Anal.* 41: 532–539.

1961

Bion, W. *Experiences in Groups.* Tavistock.

——, Segal, H. and Rosenfeld, H. 'Melanie Klein', *Int. J. Psycho-Anal.* 42: 4–8.

Klein, M. *Narrative of a Child Analysis.* Hogarth Press.

Money-Kyrle, R. *Man's Picture of his World.* Duckworth.

1962

Bick, E. 'Child analysis today', *Int. J. Psycho-Anal.* 43: 328–332; republished in M. Harris and E. Bick (eds) *The Collected Papers of Martha Harris and Esther Bick.* Strath Tay: Clunie Press (1987), pp. 104–113; and in E. Spillius (ed.) *Melanie Klein Today*, Vol. 2. Routledge (1988), pp. 168–176.

Bion, W. *Learning from Experience.* Heinemann.

—— 'A theory of thinking', *Int. J. Psycho-Anal.* 43: 306–310; republished in *Second Thoughts.* Heinemann (1967), pp. 110–119; and in E. Spillius (ed.) *Melanie Klein Today*, Vol. 1. Routledge (1988), pp. 178–186.

Grinberg, L. 'On a specific aspect of countertransference due to the patient's projective identification', *Int. J. Psycho-Anal.* 43: 436–440.

Langer, M. 'Selection criteria for the training of psycho-analytic students', *Int. J. Psycho-Anal.* 43: 272–276.

Rosenfeld, H. 'The superego and the ego-ideal', *Int. J. Psycho-Anal.* 43: 258–263.

Segal, H. 'The curative factors in psycho-analysis', *Int. J. Psycho-Anal.* 43: 212–217; republished in *The Work of Hanna Segal*. New York: Jason Aronson (1981), pp. 69–80.

Stokes, A. 'On resignation', *Int. J. Psycho-Anal.* 43: 175–181.

1963

Bion, W. *Elements of Psycho-Analysis*. Heinemann.

Grinberg, L. 'Relations between psycho-analysts', *Int. J. Psycho-Anal.* 44: 363–367.

Meltzer, D. 'A contribution to the metapsychology of cyclothymic states', *Int. J. Psycho-Anal.* 44: 83–97.

—— 'Concerning the social basis of art', in A. Stokes (ed.) *Painting and the Inner World*. Tavistock, pp. 19–45.

Money-Kyrle, R. 'A note on migraine', *Int. J. Psycho-Anal.* 44: 490–492; republished in *The Collected Papers of Roger Money-Kyrle*. Strath Tay: Clunie Press (1978), pp. 361–365.

Rosenfeld, H. 'Notes on the psychopathology and psycho-analytic treatment of depressive and manic-depressive patients', in *Psychiatric Research Report No. 17*. Washington: American Psychiatric Association, pp. 73–83.

—— 'Notes on the psychopathology and psycho-analytic treatment of schizophrenia', in *Psychiatric Research Report No. 17*. Washington: American Psychiatric Association, pp. 61–72.

Segal, H. and Meltzer, D. 'Narrative of a child analysis', *Int. J. Psycho-Anal.* 44: 507–513.

1964

Bick, E. 'Notes on infant observation in psycho-analytic training', *Int. J. Psycho-Anal.* 45: 558–566; republished in M. Harris and E. Bick (eds) *The Collected Papers of Martha Harris and Esther Bick*. Strath Tay: Clunie Press (1987), pp. 240–256.

Bicudo, V. L. 'Persecuting guilt and ego restriction', *Int. J. Psycho-Anal.* 45: 358–363.

Grinberg, L. 'On two kinds of guilt: their relation with normal and pathological aspects of mourning', *Int. J. Psycho-Anal.* 45: 366–371.

Hoxter, S. 'The experience of puberty', *J. Child Psychother.* 1(2): 13–26.

Langer, M., Puget, J. and Teper, E. 'A methodological approach to the teaching of psycho-analysis', *Int. J. Psycho-Anal.* 45: 567–574.

Meltzer, D. 'The differentiation of somatic delusions from hypochondria', *Int. J. Psycho-Anal.* 45: 246–250.

O'Shaughnessy, E. 'The absent object', *J. Child Psychother.* 1(2): 134–143.

Rosenfeld, H. 'On the psychopathology of narcissism: A clinical approach', *Int. J. Psycho-Anal.* 45: 332–337; republished in *Psychotic States*. Hogarth Press (1965), pp. 169–179.

—— 'The psychopathology of hypochondriasis', in *Psychotic States*. Hogarth Press (1965), pp. 180–199.

—— 'An investigation into the need of neurotic and psychotic patients to act out during analysis', in *Psychotic States*. Hogarth Press (1965), pp. 200–216.

—— 'The psychopathology of drug addiction and alcoholism', in *Psychotic States*. Hogarth Press (1965), pp. 217–242.

—— 'Object relations of the acute schizophrenic patient in the transference situation', in P. Solomon and B. C. Glueck (eds) *Recent Research on Schizophrenia*. Washington: American Psychiatric Association, pp. 59–68.

Segal, H. *Introduction to the Work of Melanie Klein*. Heinemann; republished by Hogarth Press (1973).

—— 'Phantasy and other mental processes', *Int. J. Psycho-Anal.* 45: 191–194; republished in *The Work of Hanna Segal*. New York: Jason Aronson (1981), pp. 41–48.

Williams, A. H. 'The psychopathology and treatment of sexual murderers', in I. Rosen (ed.) *The Pathology and Treatment of Sexual Deviation*. Oxford: Oxford University Press, pp. 351–377.

1965

Bion, W. *Transformations*. Heinemann.

Harris, M. 'Depression and the depressive position in an adolescent boy', *J. Child Psychother.* 1: 33–40; republished in M. Harris and E. Bick (eds) *The Collected Papers of Martha Harris and Esther Bick*. Strath Tay: Clunie Press (1987), pp. 53–63; and in E. Spillius (ed.) *Melanie Klein Today*, Vol. 2. Routledge (1988), pp. 158–167.

Jaques, E. 'Death and the mid-life crisis', *Int. J. Psycho-Anal.* 46: 502–514; republished in E. Spillius (ed.) *Melanie Klein Today*, Vol. 2. Routledge (1988), pp. 226–248.

Klein, S. 'Notes on a case of ulcerative colitis', *Int. J. Psycho-Anal.* 46: 342–351.

Lush, D. 'Treatment of depression in an adolescent', *J. Child Psychother.* 1(3): 26–32.

Money-Kyrle, R. 'Success and failure in mental maturations', in *The Collected Papers of Roger Money-Kyrle*. Strath Tay: Clunie Press (1978), pp. 397–406.

Rosenbluth, D. 'The Kleinian theory of depression', *J. Child Psychother.* 1: 20–25.

Rosenfeld, H. *Psychotic States*. Hogarth Press.

Stokes, A. *The Invitiation to Art*. Tavistock.

1966

Grinberg, L. 'The relation between obsessive mechanisms and states of self-disturbance: Depersonalization', *Int. J. Psycho-Anal.* 46: 177–183.

Harris, M. and Carr, H. 'Therapeutic consultations', *J. Child Psychother.* 1(4): 13–31; republished in M. Harris and E. Bick (eds) *The Collected Papers of Martha Harris and Esther Bick*. Strath Tay: Clunie Press (1987), pp. 38–52.

Joseph, B. 'Persecutory anxiety in a four-year-old boy', *Int. J. Psycho-Anal.* 47: 184–188.

Malin, A. S. and Grotstein, J. S. 'Projective identification in the therapeutic process', *Int. J. Psycho-Anal.* 47: 26–31.

Meltzer, D. 'The relation of anal masturbation to projective identification', *Int. J. Psycho-Anal.* 47: 335–342; republished in E. Spillius (ed.) *Melanie Klein Today*, Vol. 1. Routledge (1988), pp. 102–116.

Money-Kyrle, R. 'A note on the three caskets', in *The Collected Papers of Roger Money-Kyrle*. Strath Tay: Clunie Press (1978), p. 407.

—— 'British schools of psycho-analysis', in S. Arieti (ed.) *American Handbook of Psychiatry*. New York: Basic Books, pp. 225–229; republished in *The Collected Papers of Roger Money-Kyrle*. Strath Tay: Clunie Press (1978), pp. 408–425.

Racker, H. 'Ethics and psycho-analysis and the psycho-analysis of ethics', *Int. J. Psycho-Anal.* 47: 63–80.

Rodrigue, E. 'Transference and a-transference phenomena', *Int. J. Psycho-Anal.* 47: 342–348.

Stokes, A. 'On being taken out of one's self, *Int. J. Psycho-Anal.* 47: 523–530.

1967

Bion, W. 'Notes on memory and desire', *Psycho-Anal. Forum* 2: 272–273, 279–280; republished in E. Spillius (ed.) *Melanie Klein Today*, Vol. 2. Routledge (1988), pp. 17–21.

—— *Second Thoughts*. Heinemann.

Bleger, J. 'Psycho-analysis of the psycho-analytic frame', *Int. J. Psycho-Anal.* 48: 511–519.

—— *Simbiosis y Ambiguedad*. Buenos Aires: Paidos.

Boston, M. 'Some effects of external circumstances on the inner experience of two child patients', *J. Child Psychother.* 2(1): 20–32.

Grinberg, L., Langer, M., Liberman, D., de Rodrigue, E. and de Rodrigue, G. 'The psycho-analytic process', *Int. J. Psycho-Anal.* 48: 496–503.

Meltzer, D. *The Psycho-Analytic Process*. Heinemann.

Pick, I. 'On stealing', *J. Child Psychother.* 2(1): 67–79.

Rodrigue, E. 'Severe bodily illness in childhood', *Int. J. Psycho-Anal.* 48: 290–293.

Segal, H. 'Melanie Klein's technique', in B. Wolman (ed.) *Psycho-Analytic Techniques*. New York: Basic Books, pp. 188–190; republished in *The Work of Hanna Segal*. New York: Jason Aronson (1981), pp. 3–24.

1968

Bick, E. 'The experience of the skin in early object relations', *Int. J. Psycho-Anal.* 49: 484–486; republished in M. Harris and E. Bick (eds) *The Collected Papers of Martha Harris and Esther Bick*. Strath Tay: Clunie Press (1987), pp. 114–118; and in E. Spillius (ed.) *Melanie Klein Today*, Vol. 1. Routledge (1988), pp. 187–191.

Gosling, R. 'What is transference?', in J. Sutherland (ed.) *The Psycho-Analytic Approach*. Baillière, Tindall & Cassell, pp. 1–10.

Grinberg, L. 'On acting-out and its role in the psycho-analytic process', *Int. J. Psycho-Anal.* 49: 171–178.

Harris, M. 'The child psychotherapist and the patient's family', *J. Child Psychother.* 2(2): 50–63; republished in M. Harris and E. Bick (eds) *The Collected Papers of Martha Harris and Esther Bick.* Strath Tay: Clunie Press (1987), pp. 18–37.

Jaques, E. 'Guilt, conscience and social behaviour', in J. Sutherland (ed.) *The Psycho-Analytic Approach.* Baillière, Tindall & Cassell, pp. 31–43.

Meltzer, D. 'Terror, persecution, dread', *Int. J. Psycho-Anal.* 49: 396–400; republished in *Sexual States of Mind.* Strath Tay: Clunie Press (1973), pp. 99–106; and in E. Spillius (ed.) *Melanie Klein Today,* Vol. 1. Routledge (1988), pp. 230–238.

Money-Kyrle, R. 'Cognitive development', *Int. J. Psycho-Anal.* 49: 691–698; republished in *The Collected Papers of Roger Money-Kyrle.* Strath Tay: Clunie Press (1978), pp. 416–433; and in J. Grotstein (ed.) *Do I Dare Disturb the Universe?* Beverly Hills, CA: Caesura (1981), pp. 537–550.

Munro, L. 'Comment on the paper by Alexander and Isaacs on the psychology of the fool', *Int. J. Psycho-Anal.* 49: 424–425.

Racker, H. *Transference and Counter-Transference.* Hogarth Press.

Rodrigue, E. 'The fifty thousand hour patient', *Int. J. Psycho-Anal.* 50: 603–613.

Rosenbluth, D. '"Insight" as an aim of treatment', *J. Child Psychother.* 2(2): 5–19.

Spillius, E. B. 'Psycho-analysis and ceremony', in J. Sutherland (ed.) *The Psycho-Analytic Approach.* Baillière, Tindall & Cassell, pp. 52–77; republished in E. Spillius (ed.) *Melanie Klein Today,* Vol. 2. Routledge (1988), pp. 259–283.

1969

Brenman, E. 'The psycho-analytic point of view', in S. Klein (ed.) *Sexuality and Aggression in Maturation: New Facets.* Baillière, Tindall & Cassell, pp. 1–13.

Grinberg, L. 'New ideas: conflict and evolution', *Int. J. Psycho-Anal.* 50: 517–528.

Meltzer, D. 'The relation of aims to methodology in the treatment of children', *J. Child Psychother.* 2(3): 57–61.

Menzies-Lyth, I. 'The motor-cycle: growing up on two wheels', in S. Klein (ed.) *Sexuality and Aggression in Maturation: New Facets.* Baillière, Tindall & Cassell, pp. 37–49; republished in I. Menzies-Lyth (ed.) *The Dynamics of the Social: Selected Essays,* Vol. 2. Free Association Books (1989), pp. 142–157.

—— 'Some methodological notes on a hospital study', in S. H. Foulkes and G. Stewart-Price (eds) *Psychiatry in a Changing Society.* Tavistock, pp. 99–112; republished in I. Menzies-Lyth (ed.) *Containing Anxiety in Institutions: Selected Essays,* Vol. 1. Free Association Books (1988), pp. 115–129.

Money-Kyrle, R. 'On the fear of insanity', in *The Collected Papers of Roger Money-Kyrle.* Strath Tay: Clunie Press (1978), pp. 434–441.

Rosenfeld, H. 'On the treatment of psychotic states by psycho-analysis: An historical approach', *Int. J. Psycho-Anal.* 50: 615–631.

Williams, A. H. 'Murderousness', in L. Blom-Cooper (ed.) *The Hanging Question.* Duckworth.

1970

Bion, W. *Attention and Interpretation.* Tavistock.

Brenner, J. 'Some factors affecting the placement of a child in treatment', *J. Child Psychother.* 2(4): 63–67.

Grinberg, L. 'The problem of supervision in psycho-analytic education', *Int. J. Psycho-Anal.* 51: 371–383.

Jackson, J. 'Child psychotherapy in a day school for maladjusted children', *J. Child Psychother.* 2(4): 54–62.

Jaques, E. *Work, Creativity and Social Justice.* Heinemann.

Menzies-Lyth, I. 'Psychosocial aspects of eating', *J. Psychosom. Res.* 14: 223–227; republished in *The Dynamics of the Social: Selected Essays*, Vol. 2. Free Association Books (1989), pp. 142–157.

Riesenberg-Malcolm, R. 'El espejo: Una fantasia sexual perversa en una mujer, vista como defensa contra un derrume psicotico', *Rev. Psicoanal.* 27: 793–826; republished as 'The mirror: A perverse sexual phantasy in a woman seen as a defence against psychotic breakdown', in E. Spillius (ed.) *Melanie Klein Today*, Vol. 2. Routledge (1988), pp. 115–137.

Rioch, M. J. 'The work of Wilfred Bion on groups', *Psychiatry* 33: 56–66.

Rosenbluth, D. 'Transference in child psychotherapy', *J. Child Psychother.* 2(4): 72–87.

Szur, R. 'Acting-out', *J. Child Psychother.* 2(4): 23–38.

Thorner, H. A. 'On compulsive eating', *J. Psychosom. Res.* 14: 321–325.

Wittenberg, I. *Psycho-Analytic Insight and Relationships: A Kleinian Approach.* Routledge & Kegan Paul.

1971

Harris, M. 'The place of once weekly treatment in the work of an analytically trained child psychotherapist', *J. Child Psychother.* 3(1): 31–39.

Joseph, B. 'A clinical contribution to the analysis of a perversion', *Int. J. Psycho-Anal.* 52: 441–449; republished in *Psychic Equilibrium and Psychic Change.* Routledge (1989), pp. 51–56.

Money-Kyrle, R. 'The aim of psycho-analysis', *Int. J. Psycho-Anal.* 52: 103–106; republished in *The Collected Papers of Roger Money-Kyrle.* Strath Tay: Clunie Press (1978), pp. 442–449.

Rosenfeld, H. 'A clinical approach to the psycho-analytical theory of the life and death instincts: an investigation into the aggressive aspects of narcissism', *Int. J. Psycho-Anal.* 52: 169–178; republished (1988) in E. Spillius (ed.) *Melanie Klein Today*, Vol. 1. Routledge (1988), pp. 235–255.

—— 'Contribution to the psychopathology of psychotic states: The importance of projective identification in the ego structure and the object relations of the psychotic patient', in P. Doucet and C. Laurin (eds) *Problems of Psychosis.* Amsterdam: Excerpta Medica, pp. 115–128; republished in E. Spillius (ed.) *Melanie Klein Today*, Vol. 1. Routledge (1988), pp. 117–137.

Rustin, M. 'Once-weekly work with a rebellious adolescent girl', *J. Child Psychother.* 3(1): 40–48.

Wittenberg, I. 'Extending fields of work', *J. Child Psychother.* 3(1): 22–30.

1972

Boston, M. 'Psychotherapy with a boy from a children's home', *J. Child Psychother.* 3(2): 53–67.

Hoxter, S. 'A study of a residual autistic condition and its effects upon learning', *J. Child Psychother.* 3(2): 21–39.

Rosenfeld, H. 'A critical appreciation of James Strachey's paper on the nature of the therapeutic action of psycho-analysis', *Int. J. Psycho-Anal.* 53: 455–461.

Segal, H. 'The role of child analysis in the general psycho-analytic training', *Int. J. Psycho-Anal.* 53: 147–161.

—— 'A delusional system as a defence against re-emergence of a catastrophic situation', *Int J. Psycho-Anal.* 53: 393–403.

—— 'Melanie Klein's technique of child analysis', in B. Wolman (ed.) *Handbook of Child Psycho-Analysis.* New York: Van Nostrand Rheinhold, pp. 401–414; republished in *The Work of Hanna Segal.* New York: Jason Aronson (1981), pp. 25–37.

—— 'A propos des objets internes' (A note on internal objects), *Nouv. Rev. Psychanal.* 10: 153–157.

1973

Etchegoyen, R. H. 'A note on ideology and technique', *Int. J. Psycho-Anal.* 54: 485–486.

Harris, M. 'The complexity of mental pain seen in a six-year-old child following sudden bereavement', *J. Child Psychother.* 3(3): 35–45; republished in M. Harris and E. Bick (eds) *The Collected Papers of Martha Harris and Esther Bick.* Strath Tay: Clunie Press (1987), pp. 89–103.

Meltzer, D. *Sexual States of Mind.* Strath Tay: Clunie Press.

1974

Bion, W. *Bion's Brazilian Lectures 1.* Rio de Janeiro: Imago Editora.

Grinberg, L. and Grinberg, R. 'The problem of identity and the psychoanalytic process', *Int. Rev. Psycho-Anal.* 1: 499–507.

Henry, G. 'Doubly deprived', *J. Child Psychother.* 3(4): 15–28.

Hughes, A. 'Contributions of Melanie Klein to psycho-analytic technique', in V. J. Varma (ed.) *Psychotherapy Today.* Constable, pp. 106–123.

Klein, S. 'Transference and defence in manic states', *Int. J. Psycho-Anal.* 55: 261–268.

Meltzer, D. 'Mutism in infantile autism, schizophrenia and manic depressive states: The correlation of clinical psychopathology and linguistics', *Int. J. Psycho-Anal.* 55: 397–404.

Rosenfeld, H. 'Discussion on the paper by Greenson on transference: Freud or Klein?', *Int. J. Psycho-Anal.* 55: 49–51.

Segal, H. 'Delusion and artistic creativity', *Int. Rev. Psycho-Anal.* 1: 135–141; republished in *The Work of Hanna Segal.* New York: Jason Aronson (1981), pp.

207–216; and in E. Spillius (ed.) *Melanie Klein Today*, Vol. 2. Routledge (1988), pp. 249–258.

1975

Bion, W. *Bion's Brazilian Lectures 2*. Rio de Janeiro: Imago Editora.

—— *A Memoir of the Future: 1. The Dream*. Rio de Janeiro: Imago Editora.

Grinberg, L., Sor, D. and Tabak de Bianchedi, E. *Introduction to the Work of Bion*. Strath Tay: Clunie Press.

Harris, M. 'Some notes on maternal containment in "good enough" mothering', *J. Child Psychother*. 4: 35–51; republished in M. Harris and E. Bick (eds) *The Collected Papers of Martha Harris and Esther Bick*. Strath Tay: Clunie Press (1987), pp. 141–163.

Joseph, B. 'The patient who is difficult to reach', in P. Giovacchini (ed.) *Tactics and Techniques in Psycho-Analytic Therapy*, Vol. 2. New York: Jason Aronson, pp. 205–216; republished in E. Spillius (ed.) *Melanie Klein Today*, Vol. 2. Routledge (1988), pp. 48–60; and in B. Joseph (ed.) *Psychic Equilibrium and Psychic Change*. Routledge (1989), pp. 75–87.

Meltzer, D. 'Adhesive identification', *Contemp. Psycho-Anal*. 11: 289–310.

——, Bremner, J., Hoxter, S., Weddell, D. and Wittenberg, I. *Explorations in Autism*. Strath Tay: Clunie Press.

Menzies-Lyth, I. 'Thoughts on the maternal role in contemporary society', *J. Child Psychother*. 4: 5–14; republished in *Containing Anxiety in Institutions: Selected Essays*, Vol. 1. Free Association Books (1988), pp. 208–221.

Rey, H. 'Intra-psychic object-relations: The individual and the group', in L. Wolberg and M. Aronson (eds) *Group Therapy: An Overview*. New York: Stratton, pp. 84–101.

Rosenfeld, H. 'The negative therapeutic reaction', in P. Giovacchini (ed.) *Tactics and Techniques in Psycho-Analytic Therapy*, Vol. 2. New York: Jason Aronson, pp. 217–228.

Segal, H. 'A psycho-analytic approach to the treatment of schizophrenia', in M. Lader (ed.) *Studies of Schizophrenia*. Ashford: Headley Bros, pp. 94–97.

Turquet, P. 'Threats to identity in the large group', in L. Kreeger (ed.) *The Large Group*. Constable, pp. 87–144.

1976

Bion, W. 'Emotional turbulence', 'On a quotation from Freud', and 'Evidence', in *Clinical Seminars and Four Papers*. Abingdon: Fleetwood Press (1987).

Grinberg, L., Gear, M. C. and Liendo, E. C. 'Group dynamics according to a semiotic model based on projective identification and counteridentification', in L. R. Wolberg et al. (eds) *Group Therapy*, New York: Stratton, pp. 167–179.

Harris, M. 'Infantile elements and adult strivings in adolescent sexuality', *J. Child Psychother*. 4(2): 29–44; republished in M. Harris and E. Bick (eds) *The Collected Papers of Martha Harris and Esther Bick*. Strath Tay: Clunie Press (1987), pp. 121–140.

Jaques, E. *A General Theory of Bureaucracy*. Heinemann.

Meltzer, D. 'The delusion of clarity of insight', *Int. J. Psycho-Anal.* 57: 141–146.

Orford, E. 'Some effects of the absence of his father on an eight-year-old boy', *J. Child Psychother.* 4(2): 53–74.

1977

Alvarez, A. 'Problems of dependence and development in an excessively passive autistic boy', *J. Child Psychother.* 4(3): 25–46.

Bion, W. *A Memoir of the Future: 2. The Past Presented.* Rio de Janeiro: Imago Editora.

—— *Seven Servants.* New York: Jason Aronson.

—— 'Emotional disturbance', in P. Hartocollis (ed.) *Borderline Personality Disorders.* New York: International Universities Press, pp. 3–13; republished in *Two Papers: The Grid and Caesura.* Rio de Janeiro: Imago Editora, pp. 1–34.

—— 'On a quotation from Freud', in P. Hartocollis (ed.) *Borderline Personality Disorders.* New York: International Universities Press, pp. 511–517; republished in *Two Papers: The Grid and Caesura.* Rio de Janeiro: Imago Editora, pp. 35–56.

Grinberg, L. 'An approach to the understanding of borderline patients', in P. Hartocollis (ed.) *Borderline Personality Disorders.* New York: International Universities Press, pp. 123–141.

Grotstein, J. S. 'The psycho-analytic concept of schizophrenia', *Int. J. Psycho-Anal.* 58: 403–452.

Harris, M. 'The Tavistock training and philosophy', in D. Daws and M. Boston (eds) *The Child Psychotherapist.* Aldershot: Wildwood, pp. 291–314; republished in M. Harris and E. Bick (eds) *The Collected Papers of Martha Harris and Esther Bick.* Strath Tay: Clunie Press, pp. 259–282.

Segal, H. 'Counter-transference', *Int. J. Psycho-Anal. Psychother.* 6: 31–37; republished in *The Work of Hanna Segal.* New York: Jason Aronson (1981), pp. 81–88.

—— 'Psycho-analysis and freedom of thought' [Inaugural Lecture, Freud Memorial Professor, University College, London, H. K. Lewis]; republished in *The Work of Hanna Segal.* New York: Jason Aronson (1981), pp. 217–227; and in J. Sandler (ed.) *Dimensions of Psychoanalysis.* Karnac (1989), pp. 51–63.

—— and Furer, M. 'Psycho-analytic dialogue: Kleinian theory today', *J. Am. Psychoanal. Assoc.* 25: 363–385.

1978

Bion, W. *Four Discussions with W.R. Bion.* Strath Tay: Clunie Press.

Elmhurst, S. I. 'Time and the pre-verbal transference', *Int. J. Psycho-Anal.* 59: 173–180.

Etchegoyen, R. H. 'Some thoughts on transference perversion', *Int. J. Psycho-Anal.* 59: 45–53.

Grinberg, L. 'The "razor's edge" in depression and mourning', *Int. J. Psycho-Anal.* 59: 245–254.

Grotstein, J. S. 'Inner space: Its dimensions and its co-ordinates', *Int. J. Psycho-Anal.* 59: 55–61.

Jaques, E. *Health Services.* Heinemann.

Joseph, B. 'Different types of anxiety and their handling in the analytic situation', *Int. J. Psycho-Anal.* 59: 223–228; republished in *Psychic Equilibrium and Psychic Change*. Routledge (1989), pp. 106–115.

Meltzer, D. *The Kleinian Development*. Strath Tay: Clunie Press.

—— 'A note on Bion's concept "reversal of alpha-function"', in *The Kleinian Development*. Strath Tay: Clunie Press, pp. 119–126; republished in J. Grotstein (ed.) *Do I Dare Disturb the Universe?* Beverly Hills, CA: Caesura (1981), pp. 529–535.

—— 'Routine and inspired interpretations', *Contemp. Psycho-Anal.* 14: 210–225.

Money-Kyrle, R. *The Collected Papers of Roger Money-Kyrle*. Strath Tay: Clunie Press.

—— 'On being a psycho-analyst', in *The Collected Papers of Roger Money-Kyrle*. Strath Tay: Clunie Press, pp. 457–465.

Rosenfeld, H. 'Notes on the psychopathology and psycho-analytic treatment of some borderline states', *Int. J. Psycho-Anal.* 59: 215–221.

Saunders, K. 'Shakespeare's "The Winter's Tale", and some notes on the analysis of a present-day Leontes', *Int. Rev. Psycho-Anal.* 5: 175–178.

Segal, H. 'On symbolism', *Int. J. Psycho-Anal.* 55: 315–319.

Tustin, F. 'Psychotic elements in the neurotic disorders of children', *J. Child Psychother.* 4(4): 5–17.

Williams, A. H. 'Depression, deviation and acting-out', *J. Adolesc.* 1: 309–317.

Wittenberg, I. S. 'The use of "here and now" experiences in a teaching conference on psychotherapy', *J. Child Psychother.* 4(4): 33–50.

1979

Bion, W. *A Memoir of the Future: 3. The Dawn of Oblivion*. Strath Tay: Clunie Press.

—— 'Making the best of a bad job', in *Clinical Seminars and Four Papers*. Abingdon: Fleetwood Press (1987), pp. 247–257.

Gallwey, P. L. G. 'Symbolic dysfunction in the perversions: Some related clinical problems', *Int. Rev. Psycho-Anal.* 6: 155–161.

Grinberg, L. 'Counter-transference and projective counter-identification', *Contemp. Psycho-Anal.* 15: 226–247.

Grotstein, J. S. 'Who is the dreamer who dreams the dream and who is the dreamer who understands it?', *Contemp. Psycho-Anal.* 15: 110–169; republished in *Do I Dare Disturb the Universe?*. Beverly Hills, CA: Caesura (1981), pp. 357–416.

Harris, M. 'L'apport de l'observation de l'interaction mère-enfant', *Nouv. Rev. Psychanal.* 19: 99–112; republished in M. Harris and E. Bick (eds) *The Collected Papers of Martha Harris and Esther Bick*. Strath Tay: Clunie Press (1987), pp. 225–239.

Hinshelwood, R. D. 'The community as analyst', in R. D. Hinshelwood and N. Manning (eds) *Therapeutic Communities: Reflections and Progress*. Routledge & Kegan Paul, pp. 103–112.

Menzies-Lyth, I. 'Staff support systems: task and anti-task in adolescent institutions', in R. D. Hinshelwood and N. Manning (eds) *Therapeutic Communities: Reflections and Progress*. Routledge & Kegan Paul, pp. 197–207;

republished in I. Menzies-Lyth (ed.) *Containing Anxiety in Institutions: Selected Essays*, Vol. 1. Free Association Books (1988), pp. 222–235.

Money-Kyrle, R. 'Looking backwards – and forwards', *Int. Rev. Psycho-Anal.* 60: 265–272.

Rey, H. 'Schizoid phenomena in the borderline', in J. LeBoit and A. Capponi (eds) *Advances in Psychotherapy of the Borderline Patient.* New York: Jason Aronson, pp. 449–484; republished in E. Spillius (ed.) *Melanie Klein Today*, Vol. 1. Routledge (1988), pp. 203–229.

Rhode, M. 'One life between two people', *J. Child Psychother.* 5: 57–68.

Rosenfeld, H. 'Difficulties in the psycho-analytic treatment of the borderline patient', in J. LeBoit and A. Capponi (eds) *Advances in Psychotherapy of the Borderline Patient.* New York: Jason Aronson, pp. 187–206.

—— 'Transference psychosis in the borderline patient', in J. LeBoit and A. Capponi (eds) *Advances in Psychotherapy of the Borderline Patient.* New York: Jason Aronson, pp. 485–510.

Segal, H. *Klein.* Fontana.

Steiner, J. 'The border between the paranoid-schizoid and the depressive positions in the borderline patient', *Br. J. Med. Psychol.* 52: 385–391.

1980

Alvarez, A. 'Two regenerative situations in autism: reclamation and becoming vertebrate', *J. Child Psychother.* 6: 69–80.

Bion, W. *Bion in São Paulo and New York.* Strath Tay: Clunie Press.

—— *Bion's Brazilian Lectures 3.* Rio de Janeiro: Imago Editora; republished in *Clinical Seminars and Four Papers.* Abingdon: Fleetwood Press (1987), pp. 1–220.

Brenman, E. 'The value of reconstruction in adult psycho-analysis', *Int. J. Psycho-Anal.* 61: 53–60.

Elmhirst, S. I. 'Bion and babies', *Annu. Psycho-Anal.* 8: 155–167; republished in J. Grotstein (ed.) *Do I Dare Disturb the Universe?* Beverly Hills, CA: Caesura (1981), pp. 83–91.

—— 'Transitional objects and transition', *Int. J. Psycho-Anal.* 61: 367–373.

Gammil, J. 'Some reflections on analytic listening and the dream screen', *Int. J. Psycho-Anal.* 61: 375–381.

Grinberg, L. 'The closing phase of the psycho-analytic treatment of adults and the goals of psycho-analysis', *Int. J. Psycho-Anal.* 61: 25–37.

Grotstein, J. S. 'A proposed revision of the psycho-analytic concept of primitive mental states', *Contemp. Psycho-Anal.* 16: 479–546.

—— 'The significance of the Kleinian contribution to psycho-analysis', *Int. J. Psycho-Anal. Psychother.* 8: 375–498.

Klein, S. 'Autistic phenomena in neurotic patients', *Int. J. Psycho-Anal.* 61: 395–402; republished in J. Grotstein (ed.) *Do I Dare Disturb the Universe?* Beverly Hills, CA: Caesura (1981), pp. 103–114.

Wilson, S. 'Hans Andersen's nightingale', *Int. Rev. Psycho-Anal.* 7: 483–486.

1981

Etchegoyen R. H. 'Instances and alternatives of the interpretative work', *Int. Rev. Psycho-Anal.* 8: 401–421.

Gosling, R. 'A study of very small groups', in J. Grotstein (ed.) *Do I Dare Disturb the Universe?* Beverly Hills, CA: Caesura, pp. 633–645.

Grinberg, L. 'The "Oedipus" as a resistance against the "Oedipus" in psycho-analytic practice', in J. Grotstein (ed.) *Do I Dare Disturb the Universe?* Beverly Hills, CA: Caesura, pp. 341–355.

Grotstein, J. S. *Do I Dare Disturb the Universe?* Beverly Hills, CA: Caesura.

—— *Splitting and Projective Identification.* New York: Jason Aronson.

—— 'Wilfred R. Bion: The man, the psycho-analyst, the mystic', in *Do I Dare Disturb the Universe?* Beverly Hills, CA: Caesura, pp. 1–35.

Harris, M. 'The individual in the group: on learning to work with the psycho-analytic method', in J. Grotstein (ed.) *Do I Dare Disturb the Universe?* Beverly Hills, CA: Caesura, pp. 647–660; republished in M. Harris and E. Bick (eds) *The Collected Papers of Martha Harris and Esther Bick.* Strath Tay: Clunie Press (1987), pp. 332–339.

Jaques, E. 'The aims of psycho-analytic treatment', in J. Grotstein (ed.) *Do I Dare Disturb the Universe?* Beverly Hills, CA: Caesura, pp. 417–425.

Joseph, B. 'Toward the experiencing of psychic pain', in J. Grotstein (ed.) *Do I Dare Disturb the Universe?* Beverly Hills, CA: Caesura, pp. 93–102; republished in *Psychic Equilibrium and Psychic Change.* Routledge (1989), pp. 88–99.

—— 'Defence mechanisms and phantasy in the psychological process', *Bull. Eur. Psycho-Anal. Fed.* 17: 11–24; republished in *Psychic Equilibrium and Psychic Change.* Routledge (1989), pp. 116–126.

Mancia, M. 'On the beginning of mental life in the foetus', *Int. J. Psycho-Anal.* 62: 351–357.

—— and Meltzer, D. 'Ego-ideal functions and the psychoanalytic process', *Int. J. Psycho-Anal.* 62: 243–249.

Mason, A. 'The suffocating superego: psychotic break and claustrophobia', in J. Grotstein (ed.) *Do I Dare Disturb the Universe?* Beverly Hills, CA: Caesura, pp. 139–166.

Meltzer, D. 'The relation of splitting of attention to splitting of self and objects', *Contemp. Psycho-Anal.* 17: 232–238.

—— 'The Kleinian expansion of Freudian metapsychology', *Int. J. Psycho-Anal.* 62: 177–185.

Menzies-Lyth, I. 'Bion's contribution to thinking about groups', in J. Grotstein (ed.) *Do I Dare Disturb the Universe?* Beverly Hills, CA: Caesura, pp. 661–666; republished in *The Dynamics of the Social: Selected Essays*, Vol. 2. Free Association Books (1989), pp. 19–25.

O'Shaughnessy, E. 'A clinical study of a defensive organization', *Int. J. Psycho-Anal.* 62: 359–369; republished in E. Spillius (ed.) *Melanie Klein Today*, Vol. 1. Routledge (1988), pp. 292–310.

—— 'A commemorative essay on W.R. Bion's theory of thinking', *J. Child Psychother.* 7: 181–192; republished in E. Spillius (ed.) *Melanie Klein Today*, Vol. 2. Routledge (1988), pp. 177–190.

Riesenberg-Malcolm, R. 'Expiation as a defence', *Int. J. Psycho-Anal. Psychother.* 8: 549–570.

—— 'Melanie Klein: Achievements and problems', *Rev. Psicoanal.* 3: 52–63; republished in English in R. Langs (ed.) *The Yearbook of Psychoanalysis and Psychotherapy*, Vol. 2. Emerson, NJ: Newconcept Press (1986), pp. 306–321.

—— 'Technical problems in the analysis of a pseudo-compliant patient', *Int. J. Psycho-Anal.* 62: 477–484.

Rosenfeld, H. 'On the psychopathology and treatment of psychotic patients', in J. Grotstein (ed.) *Do I Dare Disturb the Universe?* Beverly Hills, CA: Caesura, pp. 167–179.

Segal, H. *The Work of Hanna Segal.* New York: Jason Aronson.

—— 'The function of dreams', in J. Grotstein (ed.) *Do I Dare Disturb the Universe?* Beverly Hills, CA: Caesura, pp. 579–587; republished in *The Work of Hanna Segal.* New York: Jason Aronson, pp. 89–97.

—— 'Manic reparation', in *The Work of Hanna Segal.* New York: Jason Aronson, pp. 147–158.

Thorner, H. A. 'Notes on the desire for knowledge', in J. Grotstein (ed.) *Do I Dare Disturb the Universe?* Beverly Hills, CA: Caesura, pp. 589–599.

—— 'Either/or: A contribution to the problem of symbolization and sublimation', *Int. J. Psycho-Anal.* 62: 455–464.

Tustin, F. *Autistic States in Children.* Routledge & Kegan Paul.

—— 'Psychological birth and psychological catastrophe', in J. Grotstein (ed.) *Do I Dare Disturb the Universe?* Beverly Hills, CA: Caesura, pp. 181–196.

1982

Bion, W. *The Long Weekend, 1897–1919.* Abingdon: Fleetwood.

Brenman, E. 'Separation: A clinical problem', *Int. J. Psycho-Anal.* 63: 303–310.

Etchegoyen, R. H. 'The relevance of the "here and now" transference interpretation for the reconstruction of early development', *Int. J. Psycho-Anal.* 63: 65–75.

Harris, M. 'Growing points in psycho-analysis inspired by the work of Melanie Klein', *J. Child Psychother.* 8: 165–184.

Jaques, E. *The Form of Time.* Heinemann.

Joseph, B. 'On addiction to near death', *Int. J. Psycho-Anal.* 63: 449–456; republished in E. Spillius (ed.) *Melanie Klein Today*, Vol. 1. Routledge (1988), pp. 293–310; and in *Psychic Equilibrium and Psychic Change.* Routledge (1989), pp. 127–138.

Meltzer, D., Milana, G., Maiello, S. and Petrelli, D. 'The conceptual distinction between projective identification (Klein) and container-contained (Bion)', *J. Child Psychother.* 8: 185–202.

Rustin, M. 'Finding a way to the child', *J. Child Psychother.* 8: 145–150.

Segal, H. 'Early infantile development as reflected in the psycho-analytical process: Steps in integration', *Int. J. Psycho-Anal.* 63: 15–22.

Steiner, J. 'Perverse relationships between parts of the self: A clinical illustration', *Int. J. Psycho-Anal.* 63: 241–252.

Williams, A. H. 'Adolescence, violence and crime', *J. Adolesc.* 5: 125–134.

Wittenberg, I. 'On assessment', *J. Child Psychother.* 8: 131–144.

1983

Alvarez, A. 'Problems in the use of the counter-transference: Getting it across', *J. Child Psychother.* 9: 7–23.

Boston, M. and Szur, R. *Psychotherapy with Severely Deprived Children.* Routledge & Kegan Paul.

Cornwall, J. (Symington) 'Crisis and survival in infancy', *J. Child Psychother.* 9: 25–32.

Dale, F. 'The body as bondage', *J. Child Psychother.* 9: 33–45.

Etchegoyen, R. H. 'Fifty years after the mutative interpretation', *Int. J. Psycho-Anal.* 64: 445–459.

Folch, T. E. de 'We – versus I and you', *Int. J. Psycho-Anal.* 64: 309–320.

Hinshelwood, R. D. 'Projective identification and Marx's concept of man', *Int. Rev. Psycho-Anal.* 10: 221–226.

Joseph, B. 'On understanding and not understanding: Some technical issues', *Int. J. Psycho-Anal.* 64: 291–298; republished in *Psychic Equilibrium and Psychic Change.* Routledge (1989), pp. 139–150.

Mancia, M. 'Archaeology of Freudian thought and the history of neurophysiology', *Int. Rev. Psycho-Anal.* 10: 185–192.

O'Shaughnessy, E. 'On words and working through', *Int. J. Psycho-Anal.* 64: 281–289; republished in E. Spillius (ed.) *Melanie Klein Today*, Vol. 2. Routledge (1988), pp. 138–151.

Rosenfeld, H. 'Primitive object relations and mechanisms', *Int. J. Psycho-Anal.* 64: 261–267.

Segal, H. 'Some clinical implications of Melanie Klein's work', *Int. J. Psycho-Anal.* 64: 269–276.

Sohn, L. 'Nostalgia', *Int. J. Psycho-Anal.* 64: 203–211.

Spillius, E. B. 'Some developments from the work of Melanie Klein', *Int. J. Psycho-Anal.* 64: 321–332.

Taylor, D. 'Some observations on hallucinations: Clinical applications of some developments of Melanie Klein's work', *Int. J. Psycho-Anal.* 64: 299–308.

Williams, M. H. '"Underlying pattern" in Bion's *Memoir of the Future*', *Int. Rev. Psycho-Anal.* 10: 75–86.

Wilson, S. 'Experiences in groups: Bion's debt to Freud', *Group Anal.* 16: 152–157.

Wittenberg, I., Henri, G. and Osbourne, E. *The Emotional Experience of Learning and Teaching.* Routledge & Kegan Paul.

1984

Barrows, K. 'A child's difficulties in using his gifts and imagination', *J. Child Psychother.* 10: 15–26.

Bianchedi, E., Antar, R., Fernandez Bravo de Podetti, M. R., Grassano de Piccolo, E., Miravent, I., Pistiner de Cortinas, L., Scalozub de Boschan, L. and Waserman, M. 'Beyond Freudian metapsychology: The metapsychological points of view of the Kleinian School', *Int. J. Psycho-Anal.* 65: 389–398.

Grinberg, L. and Rodriguez, J. F. 'The influence of Cervantes on the future creator of psycho-analysis', *Int. J. Psycho-Anal.* 65: 155–168.

Klein, S. 'Delinquent perversion: Problems in assimilation: A clinical study', *Int. J. Psycho-Anal.* 64: 307–314.

Meltzer, D. *Dream Life.* Strath Tay: Clunie Press.

—— 'A one-year-old goes to nursery', *J. Child Psychother.* 19: 89–104.

Segal, H. 'Joseph Conrad and the mid-life crisis', *Int. Rev. Psycho-Anal.* 11: 3–9.

Tustin, F. 'Autistic shapes', *Int. Rev. Psycho-Anal.* 11: 279–290.

Waddell, M. 'The long weekend', *Free Assoc.* Pilot Issue: 72–84.

Wilson, S. 'Character development in *Daniel Deronda*: A psycho-analytic view', *Int. Rev. Psycho-Anal.* 11: 199–206.

1985

Alvarez, A. 'The problem of neutrality: Some reflections on the psychoanalytic attitude in the treatment of borderline and psychotic children', *J. Child Psychother.* 11: 87–103.

Bion, W. *All My Sins Remembered* and *The Other Side of Genius.* Abingdon: Fleetwood.

Brenman, E. 'Cruelty and narrow-mindedness', *Int. J. Psycho-Anal.* 66: 273–281; republished in E. Spillius (ed.) *Melanie Klein Today*, Vol. 1. Routledge (1988), pp. 256–270.

—— 'Hysteria', *Int. J. Psycho-Anal.* 66: 423–432.

Brenman Pick, I. 'Working through in the counter-transference', *Int. J. Psycho-Anal.* 66: 157–166; republished in E. Spillius (ed.) *Melanie Klein Today*, Vol. 2. Routledge (1988), pp. 34–47.

—— 'Development of the concepts of transference and counter-transference', *Psychoanal. Psychother.* 1: 13–23.

—— 'Breakdown in communication: On finding the child in the analysis of an adult', *Psychoanal. Psychother.* 1: 57–62.

—— 'Male sexuality: A clinical study of forces that impede development', *Int. J. Psycho-Anal.* 66: 415–422.

Dresser, I. 'The use of transference and counter-transference in assessing emotional disturbance in children', *Psychoanal. Psychother.* 1: 95–106.

Etchegoyen, R. H. 'Identification and its vicissitudes', *Int. J. Psycho-Anal.* 66: 3–18.

——, Barutta, R., Bonfanti, L., Gazzaro, A., de Santa Colan, F., Suguier, G. and de Berenstein, S. 'On the existence of two working levels in the process of working through', *J. Melanie Klein Soc.* 12(1): 58–81.

—— and Ribah, M. 'The psycho-analytic theory of envy', *J. Melanie Klein Soc.* 13(1): 50–80.

Gallwey, P. 'The psychodynamics of borderline personality', in D. E. Farrington and J. Gunn (eds) *Aggression and Dangerousness.* Chichester: Wiley, pp. 127–152.

Goldie, L. 'Psycho-analysis in the National Health Service general hospital', *Psychoanal. Psychother.* 1: 23–34.

Grinberg, L. 'Bion's contribution to the understanding of the individual and the group', in M. Pines (ed.) *Bion and Group Psychotherapy.* Routledge & Kegan Paul, pp 176–191.

Herman, N. *My Kleinian Home.* Quartet.

Hinshelwood, R. D. 'Questions of training', *Free Assoc.* 2: 7–18.

Hughes, A., Furgiuele, P. and Bianco, M. 'Aspects of anorexia nervosa in the therapy of two adolescents', *J. Child Psychother.* 11(1): 17–33.

Jackson, J. 'An adolescent's difficulties in using his mind: Some technical problems', *J. Child Psychother.* 11(1): 105–119.

Jackson, M. 'A psycho-analytical approach to the assessment of a psychotic patient', *Psychoanal. Psychother.* 1: 11–22.

Joseph, B. 'Transference: The total situation', *Int. J. Psycho-Anal.* 66: 447–454; republished in E. Spillius (ed.) *Melanie Klein Today*, Vol. 2. Routledge (1988), pp. 61–72; and in *Psychic Equilibrium and Psychic Change*. Routledge (1989), pp. 156–167.

Klein, S. 'The self in childhood: A Kleinian point of view', *J. Child Psychother.* 11(2): 31–47.

Lucas, R. 'On the contribution of psycho-analysis to the management of psychotic patients in the National Health Service', *Psychoanal. Psychother.* 1: 2–17.

Menzies-Lyth, I. 'The development of the self in children in institutions', *J. Child Psychother.* 11: 49–64; republished in *Containing Anxiety in Institutions: Selected Essays*, Vol. 1. Free Association Books (1989), pp. 236–258.

Segal, H. 'The Klein–Bion model', in A. Rotherstein (ed.) *Models of the Mind*. New York: International Universities Press, pp. 35-47.

Segal, J. *Phantasy in Everyday Life*. Penguin.

Sohn, L. 'Narcissistic organization, projective identification and the formation of the identificate', *Int. J. Psycho-Anal.* 66: 201–213; republished in E. Spillius (ed.) *Melanie Klein Today*, Vol. 1. Routledge (1988), pp. 271–292.

—— 'Anorexic and bulimic states of mind in the psycho-analytic treatment of anorexic/bulimic patients and psychotic patients', *Psychoanal. Psychother.* 1: 49–55.

Steiner, J. 'Turning a blind eye: The cover-up for Oedipus', *Int. Rev. Psycho-Anal.* 12: 161–172.

—— 'The training of psychotherapists', *Psychoanal. Psychother.* 1: 56–63.

Steiner, R. 'Some thoughts about tradition and change arising from an examination of the British Psycho-Analytical Society's Controversial Discussions 1943–1944', *Int. Rev. Psycho-Anal.* 12: 27–71.

Symington, J. (Cornwall) 'The establishment of female genital sexuality', *Free Assoc.* 1: 57–75.

—— 'The survival function of primitive omnipotence', *Int. J. Psycho-Anal.* 66: 481–487.

Thorner, H. A. 'On repetition: Its relationship to the depressive position', *Int. J. Psycho-Anal.* 66: 231–236.

Williams, M. H. 'The tiger and "O": A reading of Bion's *Memoir* and auto-biography', *Free Assoc.* 1: 33–56.

1986

Bick, E. 'Further considerations of the function of the skin in early object relations: Findings from infant observation integrated into child and adult analysis', *Br. J. Psychother.* 2: 292–299.

Britton, R. 'The infant in the adult', *Psychoanal. Psychother.* 2: 31–44.

Grosskurth, P. *Melanie Klein*. Hodder & Stoughton.

Hinshelwood, R. D. 'A "dual" materialism', *Free Assoc.* 4: 36–50.

—— 'Electicism: The impossible project', *Free Assoc.* 5: 23–27.

Joseph, B. 'Envy in everyday life', *Psychoanal. Psychother.* 2: 23–30; republished in *Psychic Equilibrium and Psychic Change*. Routledge (1989), pp. 181–191.

Meltzer, D. *Studies in Extended Metapsychology*. Strath Tay: Clunie Press.

—— 'On first impressions', *Contemp. Psycho-Anal.* 22: 467–470.

Menzies-Lyth, I. 'Psycho-analysis in non-clinical contexts: On the art of captaincy', *Free Assoc.* 5: 65–78.

O'Shaughnessy, E. 'A three-and-a-half-year-old boy's melancholic identification with an original object', *Int. J. Psycho-Anal.* 67: 173–179.

Piontelli, A. *Backwards in Time*. Strath Tay: Clunie Press.

Rey, J. H. 'Reparation', *J. Melanie Klein Soc.* 4(1): 5–11.

—— 'The schizoid mode of being and the space-time continuum', *J. Melanie Klein Soc.* 4(2): 12–52.

—— 'Psycholinguistics, object relations theory and the therapeutic process', *J. Melanie Klein Soc.* 4(2): 53–72.

—— 'The psychodynamics of psycho-analytic and psycholinguistic structures', *J. Melanie Klein Soc.* 4(2): 73–92.

—— 'Psychodynamics of depression', *J. Melanie Klein Soc.* 4(2): 93–116.

Riesenberg-Malcolm, R. 'Interpretation: The past in the present', *Int. Rev. Psycho-Anal.* 13: 433–443; republished in E. Spillius (ed.) *Melanie Klein Today*, Vol. 2. Routledge (1988), pp. 73–89.

Steiner, R. 'Responsibility as a way of hope in the nuclear era: Some notes on F. Fornari's *Psycho-Analysis of War*', *Psychoanal. Psychother.* 2: 75–82.

Tustin, F. *Autistic Barriers in Neurotic Patients*. Karnac.

Waddell, M. 'Concept of the inner world in George Eliot's work', *J. Child Psychother.* 12: 109–124.

Williams, A. H. 'The ancient mariner: Opium, the saboteur of self-therapy', *Free Assoc.* 6: 123–144.

1987

Bion, W. *Clinical Seminars and Four Papers*. Abingdon: Fleetwood Press.

Etchegoyen, R. H., Lopez, B. and Rabih, M. 'Envy and how to interpret it', *Int. J. Psycho-Anal.* 68: 49–61.

Harris, M. 'Depressive paranoid and narcissistic features in the analysis of a woman following the birth of her first child and the death of her own mother', in M. Harris and E. Bick (eds) *The Collected Papers of Martha Harris and Esther Bick*. Strath Tay: Clunie Press, pp. 53–63.

—— 'Towards learning from experience in infancy and childhood', in M. Harris and E. Bick (eds) *The Collected Papers of Martha Harris and Esther Bick*. Strath Tay: Clunie Press, pp. 164–178.

—— 'The early basis of adult female sexuality and motherliness', in M. Harris and E. Bick (eds) *The Collected Papers of Martha Harris and Esther Bick*. Strath Tay: Clunie Press, pp. 185–200.

—— 'A baby observation: The absent mother', in M. Harris and E. Bick (eds) *The Collected Papers of Martha Harris and Esther Bick*. Strath Tay: Clunie Press, pp. 219–224.

—— 'Bion's conception of a psycho-analytic attitude', in M. Harris and E. Bick (eds) *The Collected Papers of Martha Harris and Esther Bick*. Strath Tay: Clunie Press, pp. 340–344.

Herman, N. *Why Psychotherapy?* Free Association Books.

Hinshelwood, R. D. 'The psychotherapist's role in a large psychiatric institution', *Psychoanal. Psychother.* 2: 207–215.

—— *What Happens in Groups*. Free Association Books.

Mason, A. 'A Kleinian perspective on clinical material presented by Martin Silverman', *Psycho-Anal. Inq.* 7: 189–197.

Meltzer, D. 'On aesthetic reciprocity', *J. Child Psychother.* 13(2): 3–14.

Obholzer, A. 'Institutional dynamics and resistance to change', *Psychoanal. Psychother.* 2: 201–206.

Pasquali, G. 'Some notes on humour in psycho-analysis', *Int. Rev. Psycho-Anal.* 14: 231–236.

Piontelli, A. 'Infant observation from before birth', *Int. J. Psycho-Anal.* 68: 453–463.

Rhode, E. *On Birth and Madness*. Duckworth.

Rosenfeld, H. *Impasse and Interpretation*. Tavistock.

Segal, H. 'Silence is the real crime', *Int. Rev. Psycho-Anal.* 14: 3–12; republished in *J. Melanie Klein Soc.* 5(1): 3–17.

Steiner, J. 'The interplay between pathological organization and the paranoid-schizoid and depressive positions', *Int. J. Psycho-Anal.* 68: 69–80; republished in E. Spillius (ed.) *Melanie Klein Today*, Vol. 1. Routledge (1988), pp. 324–342.

Steiner, R. 'A world wide trade mark of genuineness', *Int. Rev. Psycho-Anal.* 14: 33–102.

Tognoli Pasquali, L. 'Reflections on Oedipus in Sophocles' tragedy and in clinical practice', *Int. Rev. Psycho-Anal.* 14: 475–482.

1988

de Bianchedi, E., Scalozub de Boschan, L., Pistiner de Cortinas, L. and Grassano de Piccolo, E. 'Theories on anxiety in Freud and Melanie Klein: Their metapsychological status', *Int. J. Psycho-Anal.* 69: 359–368.

Brenman Pick, I. 'Adolescence: Its impact on patient and analyst', *Int. Rev. Psycho-Anal.* 15: 187–194.

Dresser, I. 'An adopted child in analysis', *Psychoanal. Psychother.* 3: 235–246.

Elmhirst, S. I. 'The Kleinian setting for child analysis', *Int. Rev. Psycho-Anal.* 15: 5–12.

Etchegoyen, R. H. 'The analysis of Little Hans and the theory of sexuality', *Int. Rev. Psycho-Anal.* 15: 37–43.

Folch, T. E. de 'Communication and containing in child analysis: Towards terminability', *Int. J. Psycho-Anal*, 69: 105–112; republished in E. Spillius (ed.) *Melanie Klein Today*, Vol. 1. Routledge, pp. 206–217.

—— 'Guilt bearable and unbearable: A problem for the child in analysis', *Int. Rev. Psycho-Anal.* 15: 13–24.

Hughes, A. 'The use of manic defence in the psycho-analysis of a ten-year-old girl', *Int. Rev. Psycho-Anal.* 15: 157–164.

Joseph, B. 'Projection and projective identification: Clinical aspects', in E. Spillius (ed.) *Melanie Klein Today*, Vol. 1. Routledge, pp. 138–150; republished in J. Sandler (ed.) *Projection, Identification, Projective Identification*. Karnac, pp. 65–76; and in *Psychic Equilibrium and Psychic Change*. Routledge (1989), pp. 168–180.

—— 'Object relations and clinical practice', *Psycho-Anal. Q.* 57: 626–642; republished in *Psychic Equilibrium and Psychic Change*. Routledge (1989), pp. 203–215.

Mancia, M. 'The dream as religion of the mind', *Int. J. Psycho-Anal.* 69: 419–426.

Meltzer, D. and Williams, M. H. *The Apprehension of Beauty*. Strath Tay: Clunie Press.

Menzies-Lyth, I. *Containing Anxiety in Institutions: Selected Essays*, Vol. 1. Free Association Books.

—— 'A psychoanalytic perspective on social institutions', in E. Spillius (ed.) *Melanie Klein Today*, Vol. 2. Routledge, pp. 284–299.

Piontelli, A. 'Pre-natal life and birth as reflected in the analysis of a two-year-old psychotic girl', *Int. Rev. Psycho-Anal.* 15: 73–81.

Rey, H. 'That which patients bring to analysis', *Int. J. Psycho-Anal.* 69: 457–470.

Riesenberg-Malcolm, R. 'The constitution and operation of the super-ego', *Psychoanal. Psychother.* 3: 149–159.

—— 'Construction as reliving history', *Bull. Eur. Psycho-Anal. Fed.* 31: 3–12.

Rustin, M. 'Encountering primitive anxieties: Some aspects of infant observation as a preparation for clinical work with children and families', *J. Child Psychother.* 14(2): 15–28.

Sanders, K. *A Matter of Interest*. Strath Tay: Clunie Press.

Spillius, E. B. *Melanie Klein Today: Developments in Theory and Practice*, Vols 1 and 2. Routledge.

Steiner, R. '"Paths to Xanadu . . ." Some notes on the development of dream displacement and condensation in Sigmund Freud's *Interpretation of Dreams*', *Int. Rev. Psycho-Anal.* 15: 415–454.

Symington, J. (Cornwall) 'The analysis of a mentally handicapped youth', *Int. Rev. Psycho-Anal.* 15: 243–250.

Tustin, F. 'The "black hole" – a significant element in autism', *Free Assoc.* 11: 35–50.

—— 'Psychotherapy with children who cannot play', *Int. Rev. Psycho-Anal.* 15: 93–106.

Waddell, M. 'Infantile development: Kleinian and post-Kleinian theory, infant observation practice', *Br. J. Psychother.* 4: 313–328.

1989

Berke, J. *The Tyranny of Malice*. New York: Simon & Schuster.

Britton, R. 'The missing link: Parental sexuality and the Oedipus complex', in J. Steiner (ed.) *The Oedipus Complex Today: Clinical Implications*. Karnac, pp. 83–101.

——, Feldman, M. and O'Shaughnessy, E. *The Oedipus Complex Today: Clinical Implications*. Karnac.

Feldman, M. 'The Oedipus complex: Manifestations in the inner world and the therapeutic situation', in R. Britton, M. Feldman and E. O'Shaughnessy (eds) *The Oedipus Complex Today: Clinical Implications*. Karnac, pp. 103–128.

Herman, N. *Too Long a Child*. Free Association Books.

Hinshelwood, R. D. 'Little Hans's transference', *J. Child Psychother*. 15(1): 63–78.

—— 'Social possession of identity', in B. Richards (ed.) *Crises of the Self*. Free Association Books, pp. 75–83.

Jackson, M. 'Treatment of the hospitalized borderline patient: A Kleinian perspective', *Psycho-Anal. Inq*. 9: 554–569.

—— and Tarnopolsky, A. 'The borderline personality', in R. Bluglass and P. Bowden (eds) *The Principles and Practice of Forensic Psychiatry*. Churchill Livingston.

Joseph, B. *Psychic Equilibrium and Psychic Change*. Routledge.

—— 'Psychic change and the psycho-analytic process', in *Psychic Equilibrium and Psychic Change*. Routledge, pp. 192–202.

—— 'On passivity and aggression: their interrelationship', in *Psychic Equilibrium and Psychic Change*. Routledge, pp. 67–74.

Meltzer, D. 'Concerning the stupidity of evil', *Melanie Klein and Object Relat*. 7(1): 19–21.

Menzies-Lyth, I. *The Dynamics of the Social: Selected Essays*, Vol. 2. Free Association Books.

Obholzer, A. 'Psycho-analysis and the political process', *Psychoanal. Psychother*. 4: 55–66.

O'Shaughnessy, E. 'The invisible Oedipus complex', in R. Britton, M. Feldman and E. O'Shaughnessy (eds) *The Oedipus Complex Today: Clinical Implications*. Karnac, pp. 129–150

—— 'Seeing with meaning and emotion', *J. Child Psychother*. 15(2): 27–31.

Piontelli, A. 'A study on twins before birth', *Int. Rev. Psycho-Anal*. 16: 413–426.

Sandler, J. *Dimensions of Psychoanalysis*. Karnac.

Sayers, J. 'Melanie Klein and mothering', *Int. Rev. Psycho-Anal*. 16: 363–376.

Steiner, D. 'The internal family and the facts of life', *Psychoanal. Psychother*. 4: 31–42.

Steiner, J. 'The psycho-analytic contribution of Herbert Rosenfeld', *Int. J. Psycho-Anal*. 70: 611–617.

Steiner, R. '"It's a new kind of diaspora . . ."' *Int. Rev. Psycho-Anal*. 16: 35–78.

Temperley, J. 'Psychoanalysis and the threat of nuclear war', in B. Richards (ed.) *Crises of the Self*. Free Association Books, pp. 259–267.

Waddell, M. 'Living in two worlds: Psychodynamic theory and social work practice', *Free Assoc*. 15: 11–35.

—— 'Experience and identification in George Eliot's novels', *Free Assoc*. 17: 7–27.

—— 'Growing up', *Free Assoc*. 17: 90–105.